CRIMINAL PROCEDURE

THIRD EDITION

Other Books in the *Essentials of Canadian Law* Series

CRIMINAL PROCEDURE

THIRD EDITION

STEVE COUGHLAN
Professor of Law
Dalhousie University

Criminal Procedure, third edition
© Irwin Law Inc., 2016

Published in 2016 by

Irwin Law Inc.
14 Duncan Street
Suite 206
Toronto, ON
M5H 3G8

www.irwinlaw.com

ISBN: 978-1-55221-418-3
e-book ISBN: 978-1-55221-419-0

Cataloguing in Publication available from Library and Archives Canada

Ontario Media Development
Corporation
Société de développement
de l'industrie des médias
de l'Ontario

Printed and bound in Canada.

1 2 3 4 5   19 18 17 16 15

SUMMARY
TABLE OF CONTENTS

DETAILED
TABLE OF CONTENTS

FOREWORD

When writing the foreword to the second edition of this book, I confidently predicted that there would be a third. And here it is already — small wonder. The jurisprudence has developed in important and varied respects even in the short time since the second edition appeared in 2012. While no further evidence of Professor Coughlan's talent or industry is needed, this third edition demonstrates that neither is on the wane. In keeping the book so current, Professor Coughlan has ensured that it will continue to serve the profession well, both as a mature overview of the underlying principles and as an up-to-date resource of the leading jurisprudence and scholarly commentary.

That a sophisticated overview is much needed cannot be in doubt. In criminal procedure, as Professor Coughlan astutely observes, important questions of legal principle and societal values underlie almost every question. The complex technicality of the subject must be mastered, but not to the neglect of the underlying fundamental principles and deeply held values that are in play. Each edition of this book has succeeded in striking this balance: the rules are there, but they are always placed in the broader context of the underlying principles and values.

As have previous editions, this latest one offers a quickly accessible and sure-footed guide over tricky terrain. But that is not all. For those with more experience, it provides a concise yet sophisticated review of the underlying principles of the law — quick access to the "big picture" — which can be so helpful in coming to terms with new problems and formulating or responding to new arguments. While this is a short book, it is not one just for beginners.

One of life's most satisfying experiences is to watch a gifted student thrive through sustained hard work. Steve Coughlan has provided all of his former teachers at the Dalhousie Law School, including this one, with that experience. I can even forgive him his occasional missteps in his criticisms of the Supreme Court of Canada, although he has been remarkably gentle in relation to some of my more controversial efforts. To welcome this third edition, I say simply bravo and encore.

Thomas A. Cromwell
Supreme Court of Canada
November, 2015

PREFACE

One of my colleagues argues that an advantage of teaching in this field is that one can use the same exam problem from year to year, because the correct answer keeps changing. The developments in the three years since the second edition of this book appear give support to his claim. No chapter is unaffected.

These effects include significant new decisions with regard to arbitrary detention, search and seizure (particularly in relation to reasonable expectation of privacy and to searches relating to electronic devices), general warrants, bail, jury selection, and other areas. Some of these developments have brought welcome clarity to areas of law that have long needed it, while others seem to have injected ambiguity where it did not seem to exist before. Consideration in this third edition of changes to the caselaw and to the *Criminal Code* is current to December 2015.

Steve Coughlan
Halifax

ACKNOWLEDGEMENTS

FOR THE FIRST EDITION

No book is ever exclusively the product of the author, and that mould has not been broken with this one, so many "thank yous" are in order, though it is a delicate task not to ignore important people while at the same time not thanking the entire academy. Many people have contributed to whatever merits this book has, though its demerits remain my own.

A central pleasure of returning to teach where one has been a student is the opportunity to work, as a colleague, with those who have formerly been one's instructors—though that implies a more stark division between the roles than exists in practice. In particular, it was a pleasure to work in a variety of capacities with Tom Cromwell, now Justice Cromwell of the Supreme Court of Canada, whose ongoing patience with me has extended to reading this manuscript and kindly agreeing to write the foreword. In addition, my law school professors in Criminal Procedure and Criminal Law—Bruce Archibald and Dick Evans, respectively—have been valued colleagues for many years, from whom I have continued to learn. I should also single out former dean Dawn Russell, without whose many years of support I would never have been in a position to pursue an academic career.

My understanding of the subject matter of this book is enhanced greatly by Don Stuart and Tim Quigley—not only because of their own authoritative texts in these areas, but also through my work with the two of them on other projects. Both are unselfish scholars whose advice and assistance have helped not only me but many others across the country interested in criminal law.

This particular book owes its genesis to Patrick Healy, now the Honourable Judge Patrick Healy of the Cour du Québec, who was its original architect, and much of its current structure and content are still owed to his initial idea or to discussions with him about it. I am also grateful to Jeff Miller at Irwin Law for his commitment to this project, and to Dan Wiley for his invaluable technical assistance.

Finally, let me thank my partner in so many things, my wife, Dale Darling, for her ongoing encouragement and support.

FOR THE THIRD EDITION

In addition to those thanked in the first edition, I would like to add my appreciation to the Schulich School of Law for research funding to help with this third edition, to Mitch Huberman and Joanna Schoepp for their assistance, and to Kate Revington, Mary McLean, Gillian Buckley, Alisa Posesorski, and Heather Raven of Irwin Law for editorial and technical assistance.

CHAPTER 1

INTRODUCTION

In this book, *criminal procedure* will be taken to mean the body of rules and principles that govern the investigation, prosecution, and adjudication of any offence enacted by Parliament for which an accused person would have a criminal record if found guilty by a court exercising jurisdiction under the *Criminal Code*.[1] In other words, criminal procedure governs the procedural aspects relating to indictable and summary conviction offences enacted by Parliament pursuant to its legislative authority in matters of criminal law.

This definition of the subject excludes many procedural aspects of penal law. For example, it does not include law that is enacted for

---

1 Unless otherwise indicated, all statutory references in this book are to the *Criminal Code* of Canada, RSC 1985, c C-46 [*Code*]. All references to sections of the *Canadian Charter of Rights and Freedoms*, Part I of the *Constitution Act, 1982*, being Schedule B to the *Canada Act 1982* (UK), 1982, c 11 [*Charter*] will be preceded by "*Charter.*" See *Criminal Records Act*, RSC 1985, c C-47, s 3, which refers to a conviction of an offence under an Act of Parliament or a regulation made under an Act of Parliament. The procedure prescribed in the *Code* applies to all indictable offences and all offences punishable on summary conviction that have been enacted by Parliament. Notwithstanding the broad definition of this book's scope, the criminal jurisdiction of the Canadian military is excluded from consideration here, but it should be noted that this includes a distinctive body of procedural and evidentiary law. Also excluded from consideration is criminal procedure as it applies to young persons under the *Youth Criminal Justice Act*, SC 2002, c 1. For discussion of the latter issue, see Nicholas Bala & Sanjeev Anand, *Youth Criminal Justice Law*, 3d ed (Toronto: Irwin Law, 2012).

the enforcement of offences that are created by provincial or territorial legislatures and within their constitutional competence.[2] Nor does
criminal procedure govern all offences enacted by Parliament. The
Contraventions Act[3] was created to provide a non-criminal mechanism for the enforcement of some regulatory offences. Further, there
are many penal matters that are largely administrative, such as disciplinary offences within the Canadian Armed Forces or the Royal Canadian Mounted Police, and procedural law for the enforcement of those
offences is properly considered part of administrative law.[4] Similarly,
although correctional law is related to the administration of criminal
justice, its substantive content has more to do with administrative law
than with criminal procedure.[5]

This is a formal and conventional statement of the subject of this
book, but something more is desirable to introduce the themes that ani-
mate this area of the law. Criminal procedure comprises an enormous
array of rules and principles in the administration of criminal justice.
Many are highly technical and have narrow application. Others, such
as "due process," raise fundamental issues of principle and influence
virtually all aspects of procedural law. It would be foolhardy to suggest
that all of these rules and principles have resulted in a clear and rational system that expresses agreed-upon values.[6] But it would be foolish
not to recognize that both the most picayune rules and the grandest
principles are important. For instance, what do we mean by "justice"?
Hundreds of years of history attempt to offer an answer of one sort, but
section 2 of the *Criminal Code* offers an answer of an entirely different
kind. Taken together, these fiddly details and these fundamental values
express the standard of justice in Canadian criminal procedure.

What, then, is criminal procedure about? Martin Friedland opened
his study of double jeopardy with this claim: "The history of the rule

---

2   See, for example, *Provincial Offences Act*, RSO 1990, c P.33; *Code of Penal Proce-
      dure*, CQLR c C-25.1. In every province or territory, there is analogous legisla-
      tion.
3   SC 1992, c 47. Among other features, liability for a contravention does not entail
      a criminal record: s 63.
4   *National Defence Act*, RSC 1985, c N-5, Part III; *Royal Canadian Mounted Police
      Act*, RSC 1985, c R-10, Part IV.
5   *Corrections and Conditional Release Act*, SC 1992, c 20.
6   For a sustained critique of the lack of clarity and the complexity in the law, see
      Tim Quigley, *Procedure in Canadian Criminal Law*, 2d ed (Toronto: Thomson
      Carswell, 2005). This point was often made in working papers and reports
      of the Law Reform Commission of Canada. See, for example, *Our Criminal
      Procedure* (Ottawa: Law Reform Commission of Canada, 1988), and *Recodifying
      Criminal Procedure* (Ottawa: Law Reform Commission of Canada, 1991).

against double jeopardy is the history of criminal procedure. No other doctrine is more fundamental or all-pervasive."[7] The same claim could likely be made, in the same terms, for many other principles of the criminal law, such as *habeas corpus*, the presumption of innocence, or protection against self-incrimination. It matters little whether such a claim could be made for any one principle because what connects them all, as well as all of the technical rules, is another idea. The history of criminal procedure is the history of rules and principles that constrain or affirm the state's power to place a person in jeopardy of investigation, prosecution, and punishment for the commission of a criminal offence. No concept is more fundamental or pervasive in criminal procedure than jeopardy in this broad sense.

The interests of individuals can come into conflict with those of the state in many ways. Restricting discussion solely to the criminal realm, there are issues around the circumstances of a person who is suspected, accused, or found guilty of criminal wrongdoing. A person is in jeopardy of prosecution if an investigation produces reasonable grounds to believe that an offence has been committed and the evidence is sufficient to proceed. A person on trial is in jeopardy of conviction and a criminal record if found guilty. A person found guilty is in jeopardy of a sentence, and that sentence might involve not only a criminal record, but also a loss of liberty. In this sense, jeopardy exists whenever the state invokes the power of the criminal law against a person suspected or accused of wrongdoing, and it describes the risk of lawful intrusion or deprivation that such a person faces.

It is not possible to think about jeopardy in the manner just described without also thinking of broader principles of legality, legitimacy, and fairness. If the state is entitled to use its power to enforce the criminal law, and if an individual person might be subject to the intrusion implied by investigation, prosecution, and conviction, a fuller notion of jeopardy requires attention to rules and principles that define the legitimate use of the state's power and, at the same time, the value of individual liberty and security of the person. These concerns are not exclusive to the criminal law, obviously, but they are the central concerns of criminal procedure. Indeed, the negotiation and renegotiation of due process are constant themes of criminal procedure. There is a constant tension between the interest of the state to ensure the collective security of its subjects and the interest of those subjects in liberty and privacy.

Jeopardy and due process are not subjects of general agreement. The law governing criminal procedure, to borrow a phrase from the late

---

7   Martin Friedland, *Double Jeopardy* (Oxford: Clarendon Press, 1969) at 3.

Justice Brian Dickson, as he then was, not only lies in "a field of conflict-ing values"[8] it *is* a field of conflicting values. In the years preceding the *Charter*, it was argued by many that the law did not accord sufficient protection to persons in jeopardy.[9] Certainly, the *Charter* has forced everyone involved in the administration of criminal justice to recon-sider the relation between the power of the state to enforce the law and the protection of persons who might be put in jeopardy.[10] Since 1982 there has been no more powerful engine of law reform than the *Charter* and, as a result, there have been profound changes in the law relating to criminal procedure. This development has occurred as the courts have given meaning to specific provisions of the *Charter*. The guaran-tee against unreasonable search and seizure in section 8, the right to counsel in section 10(b), and the right to trial within a reasonable time in section 11(b) have significantly altered the manner in which the po-lice conduct their work and the manner in which prosecutors present their case in court. The right of the accused to make full answer and defence to the prosecution case has also led to important changes in the handling of criminal cases, not least of which is the right of the accused generally to have disclosure of the prosecution case before trial.

Interpretation of the *Charter* is not the sole or direct cause of all re-cent developments in criminal procedure. Important developments have been influenced by the *Charter* in a somewhat more indirect manner. For some time before 1982, and for some time thereafter, notions of jeopardy and due process were typically thought to concern a conflict between the interests of the state and the interests of the accused. Comparatively little attention was given to the notion that third parties, who might not share the interests of the state or those of the accused, deserved recogni-tion and enforcement of their interests within the law on criminal pro-cedure. Most notable among these are the victims and alleged victims of crime.[11] Their interests in privacy and equality have been specifically

---

8   *R v Sault Ste Marie*, [1978] 2 SCR 1299 at 1310.

9   See, for example, Stanley A Cohen, *Due Process of Law* (Toronto: Carswell, 1977); Ed Ratushny, *Self-Incrimination in the Canadian Criminal Process* (Toronto: Car-swell, 1979); Walter Tarnopolsky, *The Canadian Bill of Rights*, 2d ed (Toronto: Mc-Clelland & Stewart, 1975). Since its creation in 1964, the Canadian Civil Liberties Association has been a vigilant advocate of such protection.

10   The literature is vast, but see, for example, David Paciocco, *Getting Away with Murder* (Toronto: Irwin Law, 1999); Kent Roach, *Due Process and Victims' Rights* (Toronto: University of Toronto Press, 1999); Kent Roach, *The Supreme Court on Trial* (Toronto: Irwin Law, 2001); and Don Stuart, *Charter Justice in Canadian Criminal Law*, 6th ed (Toronto: Thomson Carswell, 2014).

11   See, for example, *R v Seaboyer*, [1991] 2 SCR 577; *R v O'Connor*, [1995] 4 SCR 411; and *R v Darrach*, [2000] 2 SCR 443.

invoked as the courts and Parliament have redefined important areas of procedure, such as disclosure by the prosecution or the production of evidence. Other parties, including the public, have also intervened to ensure that the administration of criminal justice is conducted in a manner that respects interests such as the freedom of expression.[12]

If it is accurate to state that the rules and principles of criminal procedure are a field of conflicting values, then it is also accurate that there is no dominant set of values within it. Kent Roach has argued that, in addition to concerns for effective crime control and for due process, there may be seen in recent Canadian law a more pronounced concern for the alleged victims of crime and for other third parties than was previously the case.[13] He has argued that this increased concern for victims is sometimes expressed in a manner that favours the values of efficient crime control and, on some occasions, in a manner that favours other values.

In the field of conflicting values that is criminal procedure there are broad areas for both consensus and conflict. In the development of constitutional principles, the adjudication of cases, and the formulation of measures for law reform, there is also frequent reference to the metaphorical idea that the resolution of conflict may be found in "balance." Balance, in the sense of a mathematical equipoise of weights resting upon a fulcrum, rarely exists in a state of nature. In the law, and most conspicuously the criminal law, if there is balance, it is always artificial and always delicate. The state of the law at any given point should reflect deliberate and authoritative choices by people about the appropriate distribution of weight to be made among recognized values. A claim to balance is only a claim that a given distribution is acceptable for the moment: there is no claim to balance that can eliminate the conflict of values and the eventual need for redistribution among them.

The purpose of this book is to provide an introduction to the principal features of Canadian criminal procedure. Some topics are treated in elaborate detail and some, such as the amendments dealing with terrorism, are not addressed in any detail. This book should provide a survey of the structure and the architecture of criminal procedure. Within these formal categories and, indeed, in almost every aspect of the subject, the reader will be reminded that there are important questions of principle and value that suffuse the law. These questions invite debate, even though debate and argument are not the main themes of the text.

---

12   See, for example, *Dagenais v Canadian Broadcasting Corporation*, [1994] 3 SCR 835; and *R v Mentuck*, [2001] 3 SCR 442.

13   See Roach, *Due Process and Victims' Rights*, above note 10.

Nevertheless, reconsider the quotation from Professor Friedland above. Double jeopardy refers generally to the idea that a person may not be prosecuted or convicted *twice* for the same offence. Jeopardy on its own, then, refers to the proposition that no person should be investigated, prosecuted, convicted, or sentenced even *once* by the state, except in accordance with rules and principles that express values of legality, legitimacy, and fairness. Those values have changed profoundly between the time when modern criminal procedure began to take shape and today. And, of course, those values continue to evolve today with changes both small and great. This book endeavours, in a modest way, to show the past, the present, and the possible future.

FURTHER READINGS

BALA, NICHOLAS, & SANJEEV ANAND. *Youth Criminal Justice Law*, 3d ed (Toronto: Irwin Law, 2012).

COHEN, STANLEY A. *Due Process of Law* (Toronto: Carswell, 1977).

FRIEDLAND, MARTIN. *Double Jeopardy* (Oxford: Clarendon Press, 1969).

LAW REFORM COMMISSION OF CANADA. *Our Criminal Procedure* (Ottawa: Law Reform Commission of Canada, 1988).

———. *Recodifying Criminal Procedure*, Report 33 (Ottawa: Law Reform Commission of Canada, 1991).

PACIOCCO, DAVID. *Getting Away with Murder* (Toronto: Irwin Law, 1999).

QUIGLEY, TIM. *Procedure in Canadian Criminal Law*, 2d ed (Toronto: Thomson Carswell, 2005).

RATUSHNY, ED. *Self-Incrimination in the Canadian Criminal Process* (Toronto: Carswell, 1979).

ROACH, KENT. *Due Process and Victims' Rights* (Toronto: University of Toronto Press, 1999).

———. *The Supreme Court on Trial* (Toronto: Irwin Law, 2001).

STUART, DON. *Charter Justice in Canadian Criminal Law*, 6th ed (Toronto: Thomson Carswell, 2014).

TARNOPOLSKY, WALTER. *The Canadian Bill of Rights*, 2d ed (Toronto: McClelland & Stewart, 1978).

SOURCES OF CRIMINAL PROCEDURE

Broadly speaking, the sources for criminal procedure, as for criminal law more generally, are derived from the constitution, statutes, and common law. However, it is useful to discuss each of those areas in more depth, and to do so it is convenient to distinguish between the sources of police investigative powers on the one hand and the sources of the rules of pre-trial and trial procedure on the other.

A. SOURCES OF POLICE POWER

Deciding the amount of power to be granted to police in a society is a difficult challenge. Police power is one of the most obvious and potentially most intrusive means by which government interferes with the lives of individuals. A society in which police have excessive power risks suppression. However, a society in which police have insufficient ability to investigate and prevent crime risks lawlessness. Both extremes are to be avoided, but there is a broad range between them, with scope for reasonable disagreement over exactly where the right balance lies.

Police powers derive from two main sources: statute and common law. In addition, it is necessary to discuss the extent to which police effectively have powers based on the consent of a person being investigated.

1) Constitution

Any discussion of constitutional law in Canada must consider the question of division of powers under the *Constitution Act, 1867*[1] as well as the impact of the *Canadian Charter of Rights and Freedoms*, introduced as part of the *Constitution Act 1982*.[2] The former issue has relatively little direct impact on the question of police powers. Both Parliament and the provincial legislatures have the jurisdiction to create police forces, and both levels of government have done so. In addition, though, many provinces have contracted with the Royal Canadian Mounted Police (RCMP), the federal police force, to provide policing services within the province. Even in such cases, however, the RCMP remains under federal legislative jurisdiction, so that, for example, a complaint would have to be brought to the appropriate federal body rather than a provincial police complaints board.[3]

Whatever the constitutional basis for their existence, however, the police will rely primarily on rules of criminal procedure set out in the *Criminal Code* in enforcing the criminal law. That matter lies squarely within Parliament's jurisdiction, thanks to section 91(27) of the *Constitution Act, 1867*, which assigns authority over "the Procedure in Criminal Matters," to the federal government. Police in various provinces can have additional powers conferred by provincial statutes. Further, the duties assigned to police by their governing legislation, whether federal or provincial, can sometimes be relevant.[4] Nonetheless, in the vast majority of occasions, section 91(27) means that it is federal legislation that will determine the extent of police investigative powers.

A much more relevant constitutional law question in this context is the role of the *Charter*. Its importance is twofold. First, any law concerning criminal procedure that is inconsistent with the *Charter* can be struck down unless it can be justified as a reasonable limitation upon guaranteed rights by reference to section 1.[5] Second, the investigation and prosecution of crime in each case must be conducted in a manner

---

1   (UK), 30 & 31 Vict, c 3, reprinted in RSC 1985, App II, No 5.

2   Being Schedule B to the *Canada Act 1982* (UK), 1982, c 11. Sections 1–44 of the *Constitution Act, 1982* are referred to as the *Canadian Charter of Rights and Freedoms* or, more commonly, as the *Charter*.

3   See, for example, *Alberta (Attorney General) v Putnam*, [1981] 2 SCR 267.

4   See, for example, *R v Godoy*, [1999] 1 SCR 311 [*Godoy*], where the Court looked to the duties of police as set out in s 42 of the *Police Services Act*, RSO 1990, c P.15, in order to help determine whether the *Waterfield* test was met. The *Waterfield* test is discussed in greater detail at Section A(3)(b), below in this chapter.

5   *Constitution Act, 1982*, above note 2, s 52.

that is consistent with rights guaranteed by the *Charter*. Failure to do so will give rise to a remedy under section 24.

The *Charter*, especially the rights in sections 7 to 14 under the heading "Legal Rights," affects all aspects of criminal procedure from police conduct through to bail, trial procedure, and sentencing. Sections 8 to 10, dealing with search, detention, and arrest, are all directly concerned with investigative powers, and they will be discussed at much greater length below. Further, in the absence of more precise guarantees, section 7 may be invoked as a source of "principles of fundamental justice." Although this section has had a greater impact on issues of substantive criminal law than on investigative powers, it has been held to guarantee the right to remain silent and is a source of constitutional protection against abuse of process.[6]

The *Charter* has enhanced the protection of civil liberties in Canada, and the extent of these effects will be reviewed in subsequent chapters. Paradoxically, the *Charter* has also been a direct and indirect cause of the expansion of police powers. It has been a direct cause of this expansion when judicial interpretation of a right in the *Charter* has created a power that did not previously exist in law. This has occurred in the interpretation of section 8, which protects against unreasonable search and seizure, and in the interpretation of section 9, which protects against arbitrary detention.[7] In essence, what has happened is that *Charter* analysis has dictated that a lawful search will not be unreasonable, and a lawful detention will not be arbitrary. In some situations in which an accused has been searched or detained in the absence of any statutory authority, courts have been faced with a choice between finding a *Charter* violation or finding a new common law power authorizing the police action. As will be discussed below, courts have increasingly been inclined towards the latter course of action.[8]

The *Charter* has also been an indirect cause of the expansion of police powers when courts have found particular police action objectionable, but have suggested powers that would still be consistent with guaranteed rights. This type of judicial interpretation has sometimes given Parliament guidance for legislative expansion of police powers. This would appear to be most evident in relation to matters of search and seizure.[9]

---

6   See, for example, *R v O'Connor*, [1995] 4 SCR 411 [*O'Connor*], or *R v Babos*, 2014 SCC 16.

7   See the discussion in Chapters 4 and 5.

8   See Section A(3)(b), below in this chapter.

9   See, for example, *R v Wong*, [1990] 3 SCR 36; *R v Wise*, [1992] 1 SCR 527. See also the discussion in Michal Fairburn, "Twenty-Five Years in Search of a Reasonable Approach" in Jamie Cameron & James Stribopoulos, eds, *The Charter and Criminal Justice: Twenty-Five Years Later* (Toronto: LexisNexis Butterworths, 2008).

2) Statute

The primary source of police powers is the *Criminal Code*. It creates powers for police to directly enforce the law, as well as a great number of powers aimed at investigating crime, such as search warrants and wiretap provisions.

Sections 494 to 528 of the *Code*, for example, create a statutory scheme allowing police officers (and others) to arrest an accused or compel an accused's appearance in court via a summons or appearance notice.[10] Police arrest powers are quite broad, creating a power of arrest in almost every situation a peace officer might encounter; virtually the only circumstance in which there is no arrest power is where the police officer does not find the accused committing the offence and the offence is only a summary conviction one. Sections 25 to 33 create related powers, allowing the use of force to execute powers authorized by law, to prevent the commission of some offences, or to prevent a breach of the peace. In some circumstances, even the use of deadly force is authorized.

Other provisions in the *Code* create extensive powers for police to search.[11] Section 487 creates the general search warrant provision in the *Code*, allowing a justice to issue a warrant authorizing the search of a "building, receptacle or place" and the seizure of evidence found there. Warrants under section 487 are typically issued when a justice is satisfied that the search will produce evidence with respect to the commission of an offence. However, the provision also allows a warrant to be issued where there are reasonable grounds to believe that the search will find (1) something in respect of which an offence has been committed; (2) the whereabouts of a person believed to have committed an offence; (3) property intended to be used to commit an offence; or (4) property relating to a criminal organization. *Code* provisions also authorize the seizure of the material searched for, as well as material in addition to that specified in the warrant.[12] Further, the *Code* contains a general power to seize without a warrant anything that an officer reasonably believes was obtained by the commission of an offence, has been used in the commission of an offence, or will afford evidence in respect of an offence, provided the officer was lawfully present.[13]

---

10   See the discussion in Chapters 6 and 7.
11   See the discussion in Chapter 4.
12   Section 489(1).
13   The *Code* also creates a few isolated powers to search and seize without warrant; among them are s 199(2), which deals with common gaming houses (which also creates what amounts to a power of arrest of those found in the common gaming house), and s 462(2), which deals with counterfeit money.

In addition to the general search warrant provision, a great number of individual police investigative powers have been incorporated into the *Code*. These include authorizations to

1) use a tracking device to monitor the location of a person or object;[14]
2) obtain transmission data concerning electronic communications;[15]
3) perform video surveillance on a location;[16]
4) install a wiretap device to monitor telecommunications or private communications;[17]
5) obtain blood samples;[18]
6) obtain handprints, fingerprints, footprints, or impressions of teeth or other parts of the body;[19] and
7) obtain DNA samples.[20]

Some of these provisions, such as the wiretap and DNA sample items, are part of comprehensive schemes set out within the *Code*, while other powers are defined in a single section.

Beyond these specific warrant provisions, the *Code* also includes section 487.01, which allows a peace officer to apply for a warrant to "use any device or investigative technique or procedure or do anything" that would be an unreasonable search and seizure if it were not done under a warrant.[21] Further, section 487.11 of the *Code* provides that a peace officer may "exercise any of the powers described in subsection 487(1) [search warrants] or 492.1(1) [tracking devices] without a warrant if the conditions for obtaining a warrant exist but by reason of exigent circumstances it would be impracticable to obtain a warrant."

Supporting these various warrant provisions is section 487.1, which allows officers to apply for a warrant to obtain a blood sample or a search warrant by telephone. That provision has been made applicable in other circumstances outside the *Criminal Code*, to obtain a search warrant under the *Controlled Drugs and Substances Act*.[22] Other investigative techniques are also authorized by statute, such as breathalyzer demands and approved screening device tests to investigate impaired drivers.[23]

---

14   Sections 492.1(1) & (2).
15   Section 492.2.
16   Section 487.01(4).
17   See Part VI of the *Code*.
18   Section 256.
19   Section 487.091. See also the *Identification of Criminals Act*, RSC 1985, c I-1.
20   Section 487.05.
21   See the discussion in Chapter 5, Section B.
22   SC 1996, c 19, s 11(2).
23   Section 254.

Sometimes, statutes other than the *Code* also create investigative techniques. Provincial legislation has authorized random stops of vehicles, which are used to check for both mechanical fitness and impaired drivers.[24] Other legislation, both federal and provincial, creates other investigative techniques. Legislation in British Columbia, for example, creates an obligation for a motorist involved in an accident to report the accident to the police.[25] The Ontario *Coroners Act*[26] authorizes taking samples of bodily fluids in the investigation of deaths.[27] The *Customs Act*[28] authorizes searches of people crossing the border to enter Canada.[29] The *Firearms Act*[30] authorizes inspectors without a warrant to enter premises, including dwelling houses, to search for prohibited firearms on reasonable grounds. Although not strictly a police power, various administrative schemes create a power to compel a person to testify, potentially giving self-incriminatory evidence.[31] There are limits placed on the extent to which evidence gained in these administrative manners can be later obtained by the police via a search warrant.[32]

A very broad police power is contained in section 25.1 of the *Criminal Code*. It permits police officers, under various circumstances, to perform acts that would, for any other person, constitute a crime; in other words, it permits the police to sometimes break the law in the course of their investigations.

Considering the broad nature of powers given to police statutorily, it is not surprising that, on more than one occasion, the Supreme Court has sounded a note of caution about allowing police to have nonstatutory powers too readily. In *R v Kokesch*, for example, it was stated that "this Court consistently has held that the common law rights of the property holder to be free of police intrusion can be restricted only

---

24 See *R v Ladouceur*, [1990] 1 SCR 1257, considering the application of the *Highway Traffic Act*, RSO 1980, c 198, s 189(a)(1).

25 See *R v White*, [1999] 2 SCR 417, considering the application of the *Motor Vehicle Act*, RSBC 1979, c 288, s 61.

26 RSO 1990, c C.37.

27 *R v Colarusso*, [1994] 1 SCR 20.

28 RSC 1985 (2d Supp), c 1, s 1.

29 *R v Simmons*, [1988] 2 SCR 495; *R v Monney*, [1999] 1 SCR 652.

30 SC 1995, c 39, ss 102 and 104. There is an obligation to give reasonable notice in the case of a dwelling house.

31 See, for example, *Thomson Newspapers Ltd v Canada (Director of Investigation and Research, Restrictive Trade Practices Commission)*, [1990] 1 SCR 425, dealing with s 17 of the former *Combines Investigation Act*, RSC 1970, c C-23.

32 See the discussion in *R v Jarvis*, [2002] 3 SCR 757; *R v Ling*, 2002 SCC 74; and *Re Application under s 83.28 of the Criminal Code (Re)*, 2004 SCC 42. Complicating matters, however, see *R v Nolet*, 2010 SCC 24.

by powers granted in clear statutory language."[33] Choosing the balance between protection of individual liberty and the need for public security, and the appropriate power to be given to the police in order to satisfy the latter concern without unduly sacrificing the former, is a process best undertaken in the legislative realm, where there is at least the potential for public debate. Despite expressing this concern on a number of occasions, however, the Supreme Court has not, in fact, consistently shown restraint in extending common law police powers. To that topic we now turn.

3) Common Law

There are three senses in which police may be said to have common law powers. First, there are some powers that were historically given to police, and which have continued to exist despite the codification of most police powers. Second, the ancillary powers doctrine allows courts to create and authorize new common law police powers. Finally, there is a sense in which the police have the common law power to do anything that has no negative consequences for the officer concerned and which results in evidence being admitted at a trial. Although this latter "default" sense is not usually spoken of as a common law power, it is a phenomenon that needs to be acknowledged.

a) Historical Common Law Powers

Historical common law powers include the power of the police to search incident to an arrest or to enter a private dwelling in "hot pursuit" of a person fleeing arrest. Both powers are interesting illustrations of common law powers, in particular because of the flexibility of such powers. This feature can be both an advantage and a disadvantage in a system where predictability is a virtue.

The power to search incident to arrest was confirmed in Canadian law by the Supreme Court in *Cloutier v Langlois*.[34] Relying on British cases dating to 1829, American cases back to 1848, and Canadian cases from as early as 1895, the Court decided that there already existed in Canada, through the common law, a power for police officers to search a person who had been arrested. This power, the Court said,

> holds that the police have a power to search a lawfully arrested person and to seize anything in his or her possession or immediate

---

33   [1990] 3 SCR 3 at 17. See also *R v Colet*, [1981] 1 SCR 2.
34   *Cloutier v Langlois*, [1990] 1 SCR 158 [*Cloutier*].

surroundings to guarantee the safety of the police and the accused, prevent the prisoner's escape or provide evidence against him.[35]

Therefore, even though the *Criminal Code* did not specify such a search power, the police nonetheless had the power to search an arrested person for one of these three purposes.

A feature of the common law, however, is its ability to evolve — sometimes in desirable directions, sometimes not. In the case of search incident to arrest, the scope of the power has gradually shifted without the kind of public debate that would characterize an equivalent change to a statutory power. The original rationale for allowing the police to search for evidence incident to arrest was to prevent the destruction of any evidence that might be in the immediate control of the accused. However, the actual wording of *Cloutier* does not preclude wider searches for evidence, and within a short time other courts were interpreting the search power to allow recovery, without a warrant, of any evidence relevant to the guilt or innocence of the accused, whether at risk of destruction or not. In *R v Speid*, for example, the Ontario Court of Appeal held that a search of a vehicle that was still in the vicinity of the arrest was validly incidental to the arrest, even though it did not take place at the time of the arrest, and despite the fact that a warrant had been refused.[36]

In *R v Stillman*, the Supreme Court noted that two lines of authority had developed, suggesting that a broader search incident to arrest applied in the case of searching a vehicle.[37] In the context of searches of the person, the Court said that search incident to arrest did not extend beyond discovering evidence that might go out of existence.[38] However, by the time they decided *R v Caslake*, the Court had rewritten the allowed purposes for search incident to arrest to "ensur[e] the safety of the police and public, the protection of evidence from destruction at the hands of the arrestee or others, and the discovery of evidence which can be used at the arrestee's trial."[39] In *Caslake*, the Court did not acknowledge that this greater emphasis on gathering evidence was a change to the underlying purposes that were said to authorize the power in *Cloutier*.[40]

---

35   *Ibid* at para 49.
36   [1991] OJ No 1558.
37   [1997] 1 SCR 607 [*Stillman*].
38   *Ibid* at para 41.
39   [1998] 1 SCR 51 at para 19 [*Caslake*].
40   *Ibid*.

Subsequently, the Court returned to the power to search incident to arrest to determine whether the power includes the authority to conduct strip searches. In *R v Golden*,[41] the Court acknowledged that the scope of search incident to arrest had not been fully delineated and, in particular, that whether it contained the power to conduct strip searches had never been settled. In that context, the Court decided further restrictions needed to be imposed. Reasonable and probable grounds are not generally a requirement of search incident to arrest; that is precisely why the separate "incidental" power has arisen, to allow a search flowing from nothing more than the fact of an arrest. However, to do more than conduct a "frisk" search, the Court held, police must have reasonable and probable grounds to believe that a strip search is necessary in the particular circumstances of the arrest.[42] Further, the Court held, such searches must be conducted at a police station unless the police have reasonable and probable grounds to believe that the search cannot be postponed. These additional requirements were imposed by the Court to reflect the greater intrusiveness of strip searches and to attempt to maintain the appropriate balance between individual privacy rights and the needs of law enforcement. They are an explicit effort to have the common law develop in accordance with *Charter* principles.[43] In a similar way, the Court later articulated special rules governing search incident to arrest in regard to cell phones because of the enhanced privacy interest involved.[44]

Performing an arrest within a private dwelling house provides another illustration of the common law's ability to evolve, but it also illuminates the difficulty of determining exactly what common law powers the police have. In *Eccles v Bourque*,[45] for example, the Court confirmed that the police have the power at common law to arrest within a private dwelling and laid down rules for entering the dwelling without the permission of the owner. As noted in *R v Landry* "the Court was simply reaffirming common law principles of some considerable antiquity."[46] That case dealt with a situation in which a warrant did exist but was technically invalid, and so it was felt for a time that the rules created might cover only that situation. In *Landry*, however, the Court held that the rules applied to any warrantless arrest, not just to the civil context of

---

41   2001 SCC 83 [*Golden*].
42   *Ibid* at para 98.
43   *Ibid* at para 86.
44   *R v Fearon*, 2014 SCC 77. See the further discussion of search incident to arrest in Chapter 4.
45   [1975] 2 SCR 739.
46   [1986] 1 SCR 145 at para 19 [*Landry*].

Eccles v Bourque.[47] Subsequently in *R v Macooh*[48] the Court also held that, at least in cases of hot pursuit, this right extended beyond indictable offences to cover provincial offences, as well.

In *R v Feeney*,[49] however, the Court further decided that the common law rules that had developed in a pre-*Charter* context[50] needed to be re-examined. Although the common law had held that a dwelling house was entitled to particular protection since *Semayne's Case*,[51] those privacy interests had become even more important with the passage of the *Charter*. Warrantless entry into a dwelling, the Court held, should, like a warrantless search, be *prima facie* unreasonable. An exception was allowed for hot pursuit, and the issue of whether an exception should be allowed for exigent circumstances was discussed but not settled. Otherwise, warrantless entries to arrest would *prima facie* violate the *Charter*. To deal with the situation, the Court read a warrant provision into the *Code*, a step that has since been undertaken more formally by Parliament.[52]

b) New Common Law Powers — the "Ancillary Powers" Doctrine

A further feature of common law powers is that the boundaries are never closed: it is always possible for new common law police powers to be created. Sometimes, this issue arises in the context of a charge against an accused for assaulting or obstructing an officer in the execution of duty when that officer has not been acting under statutory authority. The question therefore becomes whether the officer had any power at common law. The question can also arise when an accused claims a violation of a *Charter* right, such as that in section 9, the right not to be arbitrarily detained. An accused who has been legally detained has not been arbitrarily detained, case law has held, and so, in the absence of any statutory authority, the question becomes whether the detention was lawful due to a common law power.

Canadian caselaw has adopted a test from the British decision in *R v Waterfield* to determine this question. The *Waterfield* test asks two questions: "first, does the conduct fall within the general scope of any duty imposed by statute or recognized at common law; and second,

---

47   *Ibid.*
48   [1993] 2 SCR 802.
49   [1997] 2 SCR 13.
50   Although *Landry*, above note 46, was decided in 1986, the facts predate the *Charter*.
51   (1604), 5 Co Rep 91a, 77 ER 194 (KB).
52   Sections 529.1–529.5.

does the conduct, albeit within the general scope of such a duty, involve an unjustifiable use of powers associated with the duty."[53]

The Supreme Court has relied on this test to support police powers to protect foreign dignitaries,[54] to enter premises without a warrant or reasonable grounds to investigate a shooting,[55] to stop cars randomly to check for impaired drivers,[56] to set up roadblocks,[57] to forcibly enter an apartment to investigate a disconnected 911 call,[58] to detain individuals for investigative purposes, and, in some circumstances, to conduct searches of those individuals.[59]

Many authors have argued that great caution ought to be shown before relying on the common law in this way.[60] First, *Waterfield* itself was not intended to allow the creation of new common law powers; rather, it was intended as a way of understanding the limits on existing police powers. In *Waterfield*, the police had attempted to prevent the accused from driving away in a car they wished to examine. The accused drove the car at a constable who was physically blocking his path and was therefore charged with assaulting an officer in the execution of duty. He was found not guilty as the court reasoned that, although an officer's duty might include preserving evidence, the constable was not *authorized* to prevent removal of the car. After setting out what has become known as the "*Waterfield* test," Ashworth J immediately distinguishes between police duties and police powers, pointing to the limits on the latter. He refers approvingly to *Davis v Lisle*, noting that

> even if a police officer had a right to enter a garage to make inquiries, he became a trespasser after the appellant had told him to leave the premises, and that he was not, therefore, acting thenceforward in the execution of his duty, with the result that the appellant could not be convicted of assaulting or obstructing him in the execution of his duty.[61]

---

53 [1963] 3 All ER 659 (CA) [*Waterfield*].
54 *R v Knowlton*, [1974] SCR 443.
55 *R v Stenning*, [1970] SCR 631 [*Stenning*].
56 *R v Dedman*, [1985] 2 SCR 2 [*Dedman*].
57 *R v Clayton*, 2007 SCC 32 [*Clayton*].
58 *Godoy*, above note 4.
59 *R v Mann*, [2004] 3 SCR 59 [*Mann*].
60 See, for example, Steve Coughlan, "Police Detention for Questioning: A Proposal—Part I" (1985) 28 *Criminal Law Quarterly* 64; Patrick Healy, "Investigative Detention in Canada" (2005) *Criminal Law Review* 98; James Stribopoulos, "In Search of Dialogue: The Supreme Court, Police Powers and the *Charter*" (2005) 31 *Queen's Law Journal* 1; and Steve Coughlan, "Common Law Police Powers and the Rule of Law" (2007) 47 *Criminal Reports* (6th) 266.
61 *Waterfield*, above note 53 at 662.

That Canadian law has not been consistent with the original intent of *Waterfield* is most clear from *R v Stenning*.[62] The facts of *Stenning* are very similar to *Davis v Lisle*: an officer entered premises without any statutory authority to do so and was assaulted by a person inside. The *Waterfield* test was applied in *Stenning*, finding that, although the officer might have been a trespasser, he, nonetheless, was in the execution of duty because he was investigating, and therefore the accused *was* guilty of assaulting an officer in the execution of duty.

Further, the actual terms of the *Waterfield* test are broad enough to potentially justify, *post facto*, a broad range of police behaviour, therefore injecting undesirable uncertainty into the law. The Court noted in *R v Dedman* that the common law duties of the police include the "preservation of the peace, the prevention of crime, and the protection of life and property."[63] In other words, the police have very broad duties, so it is unlikely that the first branch of the *Waterfield* test will fail to be met in any given case. The second branch of the test, the Court observed in *Godoy*,

> depends on a number of factors including the duty being performed, the extent to which some interference with individual liberty is necessitated in order to perform that duty, the importance of the performance of that duty to the public good, the liberty interfered with, and the nature and extent of the interference.[64]

While these factors could, in some cases, fail to be satisfied, as interpreted, *Waterfield* nonetheless creates a test with the ability to authorize at common law an extremely wide range of police behaviour that has not been statutorily authorized. In the detention context, for example, the *Waterfield* test has been taken to allow police to make any detention which is reasonably necessary in the totality of the circumstances.[65] That test is so broadly framed as to provide virtually no advance guidance, something that is particularly troublesome when one considers the after-the-fact nature of common law powers. When arising in the context of a charge of resisting an officer in the execution of duty, the recognition of a new common law power has the effect of making the accused criminally liable for behaviour that he could not have known in advance to be illegal.[66]

---

62 *Stenning*, above note 55.

63 *Dedman*, above note 56 at para 14.

64 *Godoy*, above note 4 at para 18, quoting from *R v Simpson* (1993), 79 CCC (3d) 482 (Ont CA).

65 *R v Aucoin*, 2012 SCC 66, describing the decision in *Clayton*, above note 57.

66 Further on this issue, see the range of opinions on the Court's approach in *Godoy*, above note 4, in Graeme G Mitchell, "R. v. Godoy: Constitutional Accommo-

Further, common law powers will be articulated over the course of one or more judicial decisions, as opposed to being set out in a single provision of a statute. In consequence, the exact nature of any given power is less knowable and less certain.[67]

Given the wide range of powers pre-authorized by statute or available to police by warrant provisions in the *Code*, the ability to apply for a telewarrant, and the proliferation of communications technology in society, the need for broad common law powers is quite small. Although the Court seems to feel some conflict over these powers, *Waterfield* has been used frequently in recent years. Members of the Supreme Court have acknowledged that "*Waterfield* is an odd godfather for common law police powers" but nonetheless have favoured using it on the basis that "[b]uilding a composite picture of police common law powers by way of narrow precedents is not a quick fix but in the absence of Parliamentary action it is the least worst solution."[68] On the other hand, other members of the Court have argued that this developing practice of relying on *Waterfield* does not mean that "the Court should always expand common law rules, in order to address perceived gaps in police powers or apprehended inaction by Parliament."[69]

c) "Default" Common Law Powers

Courts do not talk about police officers having the power to do anything that will not result in some remedy being granted to an accused, but, nonetheless, a proper understanding of the ability of the police to interfere with the liberty of individuals requires recognition of this phenomenon. It results from a combination of *Charter* and pre-*Charter* law.[70]

---

dation of Public Service Programs" (1999) 21 *Criminal Reports* (5th) 217; Don Stuart, "*Godoy*: The Supreme Court Reverts to the Ancillary Powers Doctrine to Fill a Gap in Police Power" (1999) 21 *Criminal Reports* (5th) 225; and Heather Pringle, "The Smoke and Mirrors of *Godoy*: Creating Common Law Authority while Making *Feeney* Disappear" (1999) 21 *Criminal Reports* (5th) 227.

67 *R v MacDonald*, 2014 SCC 3, illustrates this point nicely. The Supreme Court there splits 4:3 over whether their own earlier decision in *Mann*, above note 59, had created a safety search power based on reasonable grounds to believe or on reasonable suspicion.

68 *Clayton*, above note 57 at paras 75 & 76, Binnie J concurring in the result.

69 *R v Kang-Brown*, 2008 SCC 18 at para 6. This statement was made by LeBel J on behalf of four judges. Justice Binnie, in response, held that it was too late to hold back from expanding common law powers, saying "[w]e have crossed the Rubicon," at para 22.

70 On this issue generally, see Steve Coughlan, "*Charter* Protection against Unlawful Police Action: Less Black and White Than It Seems" in Benjamin L Berger & James Stribopoulos, *Unsettled Legacy: Thirty Years of Criminal Justice under the Charter* (Markham, ON: LexisNexis, 2012).

Prior to the *Charter*, there was effectively no basis to exclude relevant evidence in Canada. As long as evidence was reliable, the means by which it had been obtained virtually did not matter.[71] Since the *Charter*, section 24(2) allows, in some cases, for the exclusion of evidence. However, section 24(2) depends upon the accused establishing the breach of a *Charter* right: where no *Charter* violation is found, the pre-*Charter* position on evidence still applies. In such circumstances, the evidence will be admitted.

This means that, as it delimits various *Charter* rights and establishes that certain activities by the police will not constitute a *Charter* breach, the Court is effectively authorizing the police to engage in those activities despite the absence of any statutory power. The clearest example concerns the section 8 right to be secure against unreasonable search and seizure. The Court has held that an accused has a section 8 right only if she has a reasonable expectation of privacy. The Court has also defined various circumstances in which an accused does *not* have such an expectation. There is no reasonable expectation of privacy in electricity consumption records, for example.[72] In most cases, a warrantless search is *prima facie* illegal and will violate section 8 of the *Charter* if not justified in some way. But obtaining an accused's electricity consumption records does not bring into play any reasonable expectation of privacy, and so section 8 is not invoked. Therefore, there are no consequences for police acting without statutory or common law authority: no stay will be issued and no evidence will be excluded, since no *Charter* breach occurred. Although the Court does not describe this as "giving the police the power to obtain electricity consumption records without a warrant," this is a distinction without a difference.

Other cases have found that a guest in an apartment generally has no reasonable expectation of privacy engaged by a search of that apartment,[73] and passengers do not normally have an expectation of privacy in a motor vehicle.[74] These decisions effectively reflect that the police have the power to search apartments and vehicles as long as they are seeking evidence to incriminate a guest or passenger, rather than the tenant or driver. Although no explicit statutory power exists, and

---

71   *R v Wray*, [1971] SCR 272. A small residual power to exclude extremely prejudicial evidence of little probative value was articulated in that case. Subsequently, the Court has begun to speak about this non-*Charter* exclusionary power in a way that suggests it might have greater vigour than it had seemed at the time: see, for example, *R v Buhay*, 2003 SCC 30 at para 40.

72   *R v Plant*, [1993] 3 SCR 281.

73   *R v Edwards*, [1996] 1 SCR 128.

74   *R v Belnavis*, [1997] 3 SCR 341.

no pre-existing or ancillary common law power will be invoked, the evidence will be admitted just as though the police were acting with authority.

A similar phenomenon has developed with regard to the issue of detention. The Court concluded in *R v Suberu* that a person subject to an investigative detention has the right to counsel.[75] As a result, in ambiguous cases where no right to counsel has been given, trial judges are "forced to choose between finding that there was a detention and associated violations of ss. 9 and 10(b) and finding that there was no detention and no *Charter* violation."[76] In *Suberu* itself, a police officer engaged the accused in questioning for a short time, but the Court concluded that this was merely exploratory and did not result in the accused being detained. Since there will be no arbitrary detention and no right to counsel if there is no detention, this decision has, in effect, created a power of "exploratory questioning" for police.[77]

What are being referred to here as "default common law powers" mean that, on a *de facto* basis, police *can* engage in particular types of behaviour without the possibility of anyone objecting. However, it is important to distinguish that situation from real statutory or common law powers. The question of whether police were authorized by law to act as they did can arise in many contexts: for example, a search without lawful authority will violate section 8 of the *Charter*, while a detention without lawful authority will violate section 9. In this context a default power should not be regarded as "lawful authority."

This point was made by the Court in *R v Spencer*, where the police obtained the accused's IP address from his Internet service provider without a warrant, something that would normally be an unreasonable search.[78] Some provincial courts of appeal had found that this was lawful due to the combined effect of two provisions: a section in the *Personal Information Protection and Electronic Documents Act*, which permitted businesses to disclose information to a government agency which identified its "lawful authority,"[79] and a provision in the *Criminal Code*, which stated, in essence, that police could ask someone to voluntarily provide

---

75   2009 SCC 33 [*Suberu*].

76   Hamish Stewart, "The *Grant* Trilogy and the Right against Self-Incrimination" (2009) 66 *Criminal Reports* (6th) 97 at 100. On this issue, see also Steve Coughlan, "Great Strides in Section 9 Jurisprudence" (2009) 66 *Criminal Reports* (6th) 75.

77   See the discussion of this issue in Chapter 5, Section C(1).

78   2014 SCC 43 [*Spencer*].

79   SC 2000, c 5, s 7(3).

information.[80] The Court held that the combination of these two provisions could not combine to create a search power. The *Code* provision was "a declaratory provision that confirms the existing common law powers of police officers to make enquiries," but "lawful authority" had to mean something more than just the ability to make a bare request.[81]

4) Consent

Cooperation by a suspect is effectively another source of police powers. As Martin J noted:

> Although a police officer is entitled to question any person in order to obtain information with respect to a suspected offence, he, as a general rule, has no power to compel the person questioned to answer . . . . If, however, the suspect chooses to answer questions put to him by the police, his answers are admissible if the prosecution establishes that his statements were voluntary.[82]

This principle, that police need no statutory or common law authority to obtain evidence by making a request of a suspect, can arise in many contexts. It arises, for example, in considering whether an accused has voluntarily chosen to speak to police, to appear in a lineup, to provide DNA samples, or to stop a vehicle.

Police conduct lineups quite frequently, but there is no statutory or common law authority allowing them to require an accused to participate.[83] Equally, however, the Court has never decided whether an accused has a positive right to refuse to participate in a lineup.[84] As a result, although a suspect need not agree, evidence that the accused refused to appear in a lineup can be introduced at trial. Further, if the suspect does not participate in a lineup, the police are permitted to obtain identification evidence in other ways: by simply showing only the accused to a witness, for example.[85] Since this procedure is typically

---

80   At the time *Spencer* was decided, section 487.014 of the *Code* read:

> For greater certainty, no production order is necessary for a peace officer or public officer enforcing or administering this or any other Act of Parliament to ask a person to voluntarily provide to the officer documents, data or information that the person is not prohibited by law from disclosing.

81   *Spencer*, above note 78 at paras 71–73.

82   *R v Esposito* (1985), 49 CR (3d) 193 (Ont CA), quoted in *R v Hicks* (1988), 64 CR (3d) 68 (Ont CA), aff'd [1990] 1 SCR 120.

83   *R v Ross*, [1989] 1 SCR 3.

84   *R v Marcoux (No 2)*, [1973] 3 OR 861 (CA).

85   *Ibid.*

even less attractive than a lineup for a suspect, most of those asked to appear in a lineup agree to do so. Thus, although there is no power to compel lineups, consent of a suspect is a perfectly adequate source of authority from the police perspective.

As a result, it is important to be able to determine whether there truly has been consent to whatever activity the police have carried out. Mere compliance does not constitute consent: it is simply a failure to object. Consent requires actual agreement and cooperation.[86] Most people are not aware of the limits of police power, the Court has noted, and are frequently unaware that they could refuse to comply with a request. Therefore, in those circumstances, it cannot be said that the accused has really consented. Thus, pulling a car over to the side of the road when directed to,[87] emptying the contents of a sports bag,[88] or complying with a breathalyzer demand without first calling counsel,[89] for example, cannot automatically be considered a consensual action. A person will not be held to have consented in the absence of sufficient information about the right she is giving up: choosing requires not just preferring one option over another, but also having sufficient available information to make that preference meaningful.[90] It has been held that, in addition to the requirement that any consent be voluntary, the giver of the consent must be aware of the nature of the police conduct to which he was being asked to give consent, that he was aware of his right to refuse, and that he was aware of the potential consequences of giving the consent.[91]

Issues also arise around the limits of an accused's consent. For example, the Supreme Court has held that to take a DNA sample provided for the investigation of one offence and use it for purposes other than those consented to violates the guarantee against unreasonable search and seizure, specifically in the investigation of another offence.[92] On the other hand, they have also held that, if an accused does consensually provide DNA samples without attaching limits to their potential use, then the accused no longer has a reasonable expectation of privacy in the sample and the police are free to use it in any way they wish.[93]

Finally, it is worth noting that consent, even if given initially, can be revoked. In *R v Thomas*, for example, police entered a house where

86   *R v Knox*, [1996] 3 SCR 199 at para 10.
87   *Dedman*, above note 56.
88   *R v Mellenthin*, [1992] 3 SCR 615.
89   *R v Therens*, [1985] 1 SCR 613.
90   *R v Borden*, [1994] 3 SCR 145 at para 34 [*Borden*].
91   *R v Wills* (1992), 12 CR (4th) 58 (Ont CA).
92   *Borden*, above note 90.
93   *R v Arp*, [1998] 3 SCR 339. See the discussion below in Chapter 4.

a noisy party was taking place, eventually leading to a confrontation in which they arrested the owner of the house for assaulting a peace officer in the execution of duty. The Court held that the only basis on which the police were in the house was by the consent of the owner, and that consent had been withdrawn before the confrontation arose. Accordingly, the police were not acting in the execution of duty and the accused was acquitted.[94]

B. SOURCES OF PRE-TRIAL AND TRIAL PROCEDURE

1) Constitution

a) Division of Powers

As noted above, section 91(27) of the *Constitution Act, 1867* reserves the power to make laws in relation to "the Criminal Law, except the Constitution of Courts of Criminal Jurisdiction, but including the Procedure in Criminal Matters," to the exclusive legislative jurisdiction of Parliament. Although the effect of this division of power is to make decisions of Parliament by far the most important to criminal procedure, provincial jurisdiction also has a significant impact. For example, the provinces are competent to create superior and provincial courts with jurisdiction within their territorial limits.[95] Judges of the former are appointed by the Governor General, pursuant to section 96 of the *Constitution Act, 1867*, while judges of the latter are appointed by the appropriate Lieutenant Governor. Both of these federally or provincially appointed judges can hear criminal matters, even though the subject matter of criminal law is in federal jurisdiction. Further, while Parliament has exclusive authority to establish penitentiaries,[96] in which sentences of two years or more are served, the provinces maintain jails for shorter terms of imprisonment.[97] And while Parliament has the au-

---

94   *R v Thomas*, [1993] 1 SCR 835.

95   *Constitution Act, 1867*, above note 1, s 92(14). See also *R v Ritcey*, [1980] 1 SCR 1077.

96   *Constitution Act, 1867*, above note 1, s 91(28).

97   *Ibid*, s 92(6). On the division of penal institutions between federal and provincial authority and, in particular, the division at sentences of two years, see Mary Campbell, "*A Most Vexatious Burden*": *Jurisdiction in Canadian Correctional Law* (LLM thesis, McGill University, 1997) [unpublished]. See also Martin Friedland, *A Century of Criminal Justice* (Toronto: Carswell, 1984) at 61–62; and HG Needham, "Historical Perspectives on the Federal–Provincial Split in Jurisdiction in Corrections" (1980) 22 *Canadian Journal of Criminology* 298.

thority to make laws that define police powers in criminal matters, including powers of arrest and search, the provision of police services is a matter that forms part of the administration of justice within a province or territory.[98]

The allocation of jurisdiction over criminal procedure to Parliament reflects a deliberate policy at Confederation that the criminal law should be national in scope.[99] This objective is more easily achieved in statutory law than in judicial decisions, which leave open the possibility of inconsistency among provinces and even within provinces. It might be noted, however, that statutory law relating to criminal procedure is not uniform in all parts of Canada. For example, the structure of the courts is not the same in all jurisdictions, nor is the allocation of jurisdiction to those courts.[100] The courts have also held that some aspects of criminal procedure may be applied differentially across Canadian jurisdictions. That is, the constitution of Canada does not require uniform application of the law in all parts of the country.[101]

There have been challenges to the validity of provincial legislation on the grounds that it trespasses upon Parliament's exclusive jurisdiction over matters of criminal law.[102] There have also been challenges to federal legislation that created criminal offences on the basis that the particular law reached into the provincial sphere, rather than being a proper exercise of power under section 91(27) of the *Constitution Act, 1867*.[103] In addition, there have been challenges suggesting that some aspects of criminal procedure were not within Parliament's legislative competence according to the division of powers.[104]

---

98   Section 92(14). See Peter Hogg, *Constitutional Law of Canada*, 5th ed (Toronto: Carswell, 2007) (loose-leaf) ch 19.

99   See Friedland, above note 97 at 47–49. See also the opening words of s 8 of the *Criminal Code*.

100 Québec and Nunavut, in particular, have different structures than most provinces and territories. In Nunavut, because of the great distances and scattered population, a unified criminal court has been created rather than maintaining separate inferior and superior courts.

101 See, for example, *R v Turpin*, [1989] 1 SCR 1296; *R v S(S)*, [1990] 2 SCR 254; and *R v Furtney*, [1991] 3 SCR 89.

102 See, for example, *Johnson v Alberta (Attorney General)*, [1954] SCR 127; *R v West-endorp*, [1983] 1 SCR 43; and *R v Morgentaler*, [1993] 3 SCR 463.

103 See, for example, *Canada (AG) v PHS Community Services Society*, 2011 SCC 44; *Reference re Firearms Act (Canada)*, [2000] 1 SCR 783; *Reference re Validity of Section 5(a) of the Dairy Industry Act*, [1949] SCR 1; and *Proprietary Articles Trade Association v Attorney-General for Canada*, [1931] AC 310 (JCPC).

104 See *MacMillan Bloedel Ltd v Simpson Inc*, [1995] 4 SCR 725; *R v Romanowicz* (1999), 138 CCC (3d) 225 (Ont CA).

One particular division-of-powers issue that, in the words of the Court, "seems to have 'boiled up' rather late in our constitutional jurisprudence" was the question of whether the constitutional authority to prosecute criminal offences rests with the federal or the provincial government.[105] As a matter of fact, prosecutions were, at the time of Confederation and for a considerable period thereafter, conducted exclusively by the provinces (other than private prosecutions, discussed below). About 100 years after Confederation, Parliament created federal legislation, some of it constitutionally justified as criminal law under section 91(27), which was to be prosecuted by federally appointed prosecutors. For the most part, these consisted then, as they do today, of narcotics offences, now found in the *Controlled Drugs and Substances Act*.[106] This development led to a series of constitutional challenges to determine whether appointing prosecutors was constitutionally a matter of criminal procedure under section 91(27) (and therefore federal) or a matter of administration of justice in the province under section 92(14) (and therefore provincial).

Incrementally, the cases worked their way to a conclusion and eventually reached the final decision that the authority to decide who will prosecute criminal offences has always rested with the federal government and that the fact that provinces had conducted virtually all prosecutions was simply a practical accommodation resting on the abstention of the federal government from appointing prosecutors.[107] As a result, federal legislation that appointed federal prosecutors in the case of some offences did not violate the division of powers.

It is important to recognize, though, that these decisions did not purport to remove any ability for the provinces to appoint prosecutors. Parliament had created a few exceptions to the practice of provincially appointed prosecutors, and those exceptions were constitutional. Parliament had not opted to take over the task of criminal prosecutions generally (though seemingly the decisions mean that it could), with the result that, as a matter of practice, the great bulk of criminal law offences are prosecuted by provincial authorities. This reality is reflected in the definition of "Attorney General" in section 2 of the *Code*, which generally defines the term to mean the attorney general of the province where the proceedings are taken. This approach is subject to a few ex-

---

105 *Canada (Attorney General) v Canadian National Transportation Ltd; Canada (Attorney General) v Canadian Pacific Transport Co*, [1983] 2 SCR 206 at 235 [*AG (Canada)*].

106 Above note 22.

107 See *AG (Canada)*, above note 105. See also *R v Hauser*, [1979] 1 SCR 984; and *R v Wetmore (County Court Judge)*, [1983] 2 SCR 284.

ceptions, such as terrorism offences, where the federal attorney general is also included. Similarly, there are a few provisions, such as section 579.1, which give the federal attorney general a power to intervene in some prosecutions, which is roughly parallel to the power to intervene given to provincial attorneys general in section 579.

A similar issue arises around the establishment of courts. Many aspects of criminal procedure are assigned to "superior courts," which have authority pursuant to section 96 of the *Constitution Act, 1867*. As a matter of constitutional law, exclusive jurisdiction over powers that are integral to the operation of a superior court and, therefore, part of their core functions cannot be assigned to some other court or body, whether that body is federally or provincially created.[108]

b) The *Canadian Charter of Rights and Freedoms*

The impact of the *Charter* on investigative powers was noted above. In fact, it has also had considerable significance on rules of pre-trial and trial procedure. Some of the *Charter's* "Legal Rights" provisions are aimed directly at such issues: for example, section 14 guarantees the right to an interpreter and section 13 protects against having self-incriminating testimony used. Other rights, though somewhat less specific, also have a direct bearing on these types of procedural issues: the section 11(b) right to a trial within a reasonable time or the section 11(e) right not to be denied reasonable bail without just cause, for example. Further, the guarantee in section 7 of procedures that are in accordance with the principles of fundamental justice has been held to guarantee the right to make full answer and defence[109] and the right to silence.[110] It is also the basis upon which the Supreme Court developed principles relating to pre-trial disclosure by the prosecution.[111]

---

108 *R v Ahmad*, 2011 SCC 6 [*Ahmad*]. In *Ahmad*, the issue was that, under the *Canada Evidence Act*, RSC 1985, c C-5, the Federal Court is given authority to decide whether a claim of national security privilege exists, which would therefore prevent disclosure of certain information to an accused in a criminal trial. The Court found that there was no constitutional problem. What was essential was that the superior court retained the ability to ensure that an accused would receive a fair trial. Since the superior court retained the ability to decide what remedy the accused would receive in light of any non-disclosure, which might include a stay of proceedings, the constitutional requirements were met.

109 See, for example, *R v Chambers*, [1990] 2 SCR 1293; *R v Rose*, [1998] 3 SCR 262; *R v Mills*, [1999] 3 SCR 668 [*Mills*]; and *R v McClure*, 2001 SCC 14.

110 See *R v Hebert*, [1990] 2 SCR 151; and *R v Liew*, [1999] 3 SCR 227. See also the Court's discussion of this right in *R v Singh*, 2007 SCC 48.

111 See, for example, *R v Stinchcombe*, [1991] 3 SCR 326; and *R v Dixon*, [1998] 1 SCR 244. See also the discussion in Chapter 8.

Another effect of the *Charter* has been a reconsideration of the personal and public interests involved in criminal procedure. Until comparatively recently, criminal procedure was typically conceived as a matter involving the interests of the state and the accused. Civil liberties were understood to refer to the rights of the persons suspected or accused of wrongdoing. Interpretation of the *Charter* has brought an important change to these views. The courts have recognized that complainants, witnesses, and other third parties might have constitutional rights under the *Charter* that could be invoked and enforced in the course of criminal proceedings. Thus, for example, the right to a reasonable expectation of privacy has been identified as a reason not to disclose the personal records of complainants in the prosecution of sexual offences.[112] Similarly, freedom of expression has been invoked as a reason to allow a broadcaster the right to publish an account of some proceedings.[113] Further, in interpreting the right to a trial within a reasonable time, the Court's analysis has taken into account the societal interest in trials occurring promptly.[114]

The extent to which a person other than the accused may claim and enforce a right under the *Charter* during proceedings against the accused remains to be developed. It is of great significance, however, that this focus has already become an important part of the constitutional aspects of criminal procedure. This is not only apparent in decisions that would give third parties standing to assert their rights in court; concern for the rights and interests of third parties has also had a powerful influence on the development of legislation in criminal procedure.[115]

2) Statute

The essential elements of criminal procedure are found in the *Criminal Code*. The *Code* is not the sole statutory source of rules and principles of criminal procedure, however, because there are many additional elements scattered throughout federal legislation.[116] Specific police

---

112 *O'Connor*, above note 6, and *Mills*, above note 109.

113 See, for example, *Dagenais v Canadian Broadcasting Corp*, [1994] 3 SCR 835; *Canadian Broadcasting Corp v New Brunswick (Attorney General)*, [1996] 3 SCR 480; *R v Mentuck*, [2001] 3 SCR 442; and *Re Vancouver Sun*, [2004] 2 SCR 332.

114 See *R v Morin*, [1992] 1 SCR 771.

115 See the discussion of this issue in Kent Roach, *Due Process and Victims' Rights* (Toronto: University of Toronto Press, 1999).

116 See, for example, *Controlled Drugs and Substances Act*, above note 22; *Customs Act*, above note 28; *Firearms Act*, above note 30; *Fisheries Act*, RSC 1985, c F-14;

powers, for example, can be found in dozens of statutes dealing with different matters within federal jurisdiction. These are especially clear in relation to search and seizure. Many statutes also contain specific provisions that affect procedural aspects of the enforcement of criminal offences. There are also statutes that stand apart from the *Code* but contain important elements of criminal procedure, for example, the *Identification of Criminals Act*[117] and the *Criminal Records Act*.[118]

The presentation of the rules and principles of criminal procedure in the *Code* has become increasingly complex with successive amendments. There are important features in the introductory part, including some definitions applicable throughout (though other definitions are also found within particular parts) and provisions concerning the liability of persons who exercise powers under the *Code*. There are also important aspects of procedure that are found among parts of the *Code* that comprise substantive offences. Illustrations of this include the provisions on electronic surveillance,[119] the application for disclosure of personal records,[120] and the procedure for taking breath or blood samples in suspected cases of impaired driving.[121]

The *Criminal Code* contains twenty-eight parts, and most of the provisions concerning procedure are found beginning in Part XIV. The general organizing principle is the chronological sequence of a criminal prosecution. This organizing principle is more approximate than rigorous, but it remains the only discernible principle for the order of these parts of the *Code*. Each individual part comprises clusters of provisions that are thematically linked, although the thematic coherence of some parts is less apparent than in others. The major procedural themes in Part XIV and the following are jurisdiction, search and seizure, compelling appearance, preliminary inquiry, trial procedure for summary conviction offences, and for indictable offences tried with or without a jury, sentencing, judicial review, and appeal.

It should also be noted that there are many cross-references among the various parts, with the result that the rules governing one set of

---

Competition Act, RSC 1985, c C-34; *Food and Drugs Act*, RSC 1985, c F-27; *Income Tax Act*, RSC 1985 (5th Supp), c 1; *Proceeds of Crime (Money Laundering) and Terrorist Financing Act*, SC 2000, c 17; *Security of Information Act*, RSC 1985, c O-5; *Crimes Against Humanity and War Crimes Act*, SC 2000, c 24; *Youth Criminal Justice Act*, SC 2002, c 1; *Excise Act*, RSC 1985, c E-14; *Bankruptcy and Insolvency Act*, RSC 1985, c B-3.

117 Above note 19.
118 RSC 1985, c C-47.
119 Section 184.
120 Section 278.1ff.
121 Section 254ff.

procedures are found in whole or in part in an entirely different place. Somewhat oddly, much of Canadian criminal trial procedure derives from procedure in jury trials, the rules for which are found in Part XX of the *Code*. As a matter of fact, few criminal trials are conducted with a jury, and, indeed, most occur in provincial courts that cannot have juries. However, the rules in Part XX are incorporated by reference in other parts, and they therefore have general application.[122]

3) Common Law

The *Criminal Code* is not, strictly speaking, a code. It is not a single, comprehensive statement of Canadian criminal law because, as already noted, there are many other statutes that deal with aspects of criminal law in Canada. The *Code* prohibits the prosecution of common law offences, with the exception of criminal contempt, but it expressly preserves the power of the courts to develop new common law defences. It contains no complete general part.[123] Hence, the *Code* is more accurately defined as a consolidation of the principal elements of Canadian criminal law.[124]

This description is particularly apt as regards procedure. The *Code* establishes the architectural elements of criminal procedure and provides, in addition, many of the details, but it is not a comprehensive statement of positive rules. To fill in the gaps, two sources may be called in aid. The first, which is not properly described as the common law, is the judicial interpretation of statutory provisions; it is not the common law at work because it is no more than interpretation of what the legislature has said. Nevertheless, the common law is often useful in this exercise because it is an important historical source of analogies and other guidance.

The second source is the common law itself. In some instances, where the *Code* is incomplete, the common law might provide a source for the resolution of ambiguity. Indeed, the *Code* occasionally makes reference to principles of the common law without any further develop-

---

122 Sections 572 and 795.

123 A general part would specify the blameworthy states of mind for each offence. Its absence has been identified as a shortcoming for which "[l]egislative intervention is sorely needed": *R v Tatton*, 2015 SCC 33 at para 25.

124 For further discussion, see Alan Mewett, "The Criminal Law, 1867–1967" (1967) 45 *Canadian Bar Review* 726; Josiah Wood & Richard Peck, eds, *One Hundred Years of the Criminal Code in Canada* (Ottawa: Canadian Bar Association, 1993). See also Gerry Ferguson, "From Jeremy Bentham to Anne McLellan: Lessons on Criminal Law Codification" in Don Stuart, Ronald J Delisle, & Allan Manson, *Towards a Clear and Just Criminal Law* (Toronto: Carswell, 1999) 192.

ment or elaboration. For example, the *Code* expressly recognizes the power of the courts to punish for contempt (this is, substantively, the only common law crime that still exists in Canada, preserved in section 9). However, because it is a common law crime, there is no definition of the offence and no procedure for such cases. In effect, therefore, the *Code* incorporates the common law by reference, as it relates to contempt for a substantive definition and for procedure.[125]

Similarly, in instances where the *Code* is silent, the common law might afford a solution of its own. Many illustrations might be given, but two will suffice. The doctrine of abuse of process leading to a stay of proceedings is a creation of the courts in Canada and, accordingly, until it was partly merged with the principles of fundamental justice in section 7 of the *Charter*, it was a creature of the common law.[126] The rule against multiple convictions is also a development of the courts at common law that extends the principle of protection against double jeopardy.[127]

4) Rules of Court

Section 482 of the *Criminal Code* allows for the creation of rules of court by the various courts of criminal jurisdiction. These rules and practice directions are administrative in nature, and their purpose is the effective and efficient administration of the criminal law within the jurisdiction to which they apply. Rules of court cannot alter the rights and liabilities of any party as they stand within the Constitution, statute, or common law: that is, they cannot be inconsistent with the law.[128] Nonetheless, rules of court can have a major impact: bans on broadcasting judicial proceedings are established by rules of court, for example. Such a ban violates the section 2(b) *Charter* guarantee of freedom of expression, but can be saved under section 1.[129]

Of growing importance in the administration of the courts, especially in large urban areas where, consequently, the courts have a large volume of cases, are procedures for the management of cases. Section 482.1 provides that trial and appellate courts may make rules for this purpose. The courts have discretion to determine whether there should

---

125 See *United Nurses of Alberta v Alberta (Attorney General)*, [1992] 1 SCR 901; and *R v Arradi*, 2003 SCC 23.

126 See, for example, *R v Jewitt*, [1985] 2 SCR 128; and *O'Connor*, above note 6.

127 See *R v Kienapple*, [1975] 1 SCR 729; and *R v Prince*, [1986] 2 SCR 480.

128 See, for example, *R v Purdy*, 2010 BCCA 413, holding that the court cannot rely on the power to make rules of court as a means of creating appeal rights not already set out in the *Code*.

129 *Canadian Broadcasting Corp v Canada (Attorney General)*, 2011 SCC 2.

be such rules and, if so, what the purpose and content should be. Once made, however, they are mandatory.

Further, section 551.1 allows for the appointment of a case management judge on the application of the prosecutor, the accused, or a supervising judge.[130] A case management judge can be appointed where that is necessary for the proper administration of justice, which, in practical terms, seems to mean that it is reserved for complex cases: the legislation was intended to respond to the problems that arise in so-called "mega-trials." That judge (who might or might not be the trial judge) is empowered to take steps aimed at making the process more efficient, such as assisting the parties to identify the witnesses to be heard, encouraging the parties to make admissions and reach agreements, or adjudicating matters before trial, such as questions of disclosure, the admissibility of evidence, *Charter* motions, and so on.[131] In addition, the case management judge can adjudicate issues during trial referred by the trial judge, potentially in a joint hearing which will affect more than one related trial.[132]

5) Judicial Independence

Although judicial independence is not strictly a separate source of criminal procedure, the Supreme Court has described it as the "the lifeblood of constitutionalism in democratic societies."[133] This principle is referred to in sections 96 to 100 of the *Constitution Act, 1867* and in section 11(d) of the *Charter*, but it also extends beyond the limited situations covered by those provisions.

Judicial independence requires both individual independence (that of individual judges) and institutional independence (that of the court of which the judge is a member). It depends on objective guarantees of the judiciary's freedom from influence or any interference by others in security of tenure, financial security, and administrative independence. The historic rationale for judicial independence was to ensure that judges were able to decide individual cases without governmental interference. More recently, it has also come to be seen as important to the courts'

---

130 Section 551.1 allows the Chief Justice, the Chief Judge of the court before which the trial will be held, or some judge designated to make the decision or order a case management judge on her own motion.

131 Section 551.3.

132 Sections 551.6 & 551.7. See the discussion of case management judges and other issues related to "mega-trials" in Christine Mainville, "Report on the CIAJ's Complex Criminal Trials Roundtable" (2015) 62 *Criminal Law Quarterly* 339.

133 *R v Beauregard*, [1986] 2 SCR 56 at 70.

role of ensuring protection of the rule of law and of acting as a shield against unwarranted deprivations by the state of the rights and freedoms of individuals. It includes a core administrative component extending to administrative decisions that bear on the exercise of the judicial function such as assignment of judges, sittings of the court, and direction of the administrative staff engaged in carrying out these functions.[134]

Concerns about judicial independence led provinces to amend their processes for appointing justices of the peace to ensure that these officials will be capable of acting in a proper judicial manner when dealing with applications by police to obtain warrants, lay charges, and so on.[135]

FURTHER READINGS

CAMPBELL, MARY. *"A Most Vexatious Burden": Jurisdiction in Canadian Correctional Law* (LLM thesis, McGill University, 1997) [unpublished].

COUGHLAN, STEVE. "Police Detention for Questioning: A Proposal—Part I" (1985) 28 *Criminal Law Quarterly* 64.

———. "Common Law Police Powers and the Rule of Law" (2007) 47 *Criminal Reports* (6th) 266.

———. "Great Strides in Section 9 Jurisprudence" (2009) 66 *Criminal Reports* (6th) 75.

FAIRBURN, MICHAL. "Twenty-Five Years in Search of a Reasonable Approach" in Jamie Cameron & James Stribopoulos, eds, *The Charter and Criminal Justice: Twenty-Five Years Later* (Toronto: LexisNexis Butterworths, 2008).

FERGUSON, GERRY. "From Jeremy Bentham to Anne McLellan: Lessons on Criminal Law Codification" in Don Stuart, Ronald J Delisle, & Allan Manson, *Towards a Clear and Just Criminal Law* (Toronto: Carswell, 1999) 192–218.

FRIEDLAND, MARTIN. *A Century of Criminal Justice* (Toronto: Carswell, 1984).

HEALY, PATRICK. "Investigative Detention in Canada" (2005) *Criminal Law Review* 98.

---

134 *Ontario v Criminal Lawyers' Association of Ontario*, 2013 SCC 43.
135 *Ell v Alberta*, [2003] 1 SCR 857.

Hogg, Peter. *Constitutional Law of Canada*, 5th ed (Toronto: Carswell, 2007) (loose-leaf) ch 19.

Mainville, Christine. "Report on the CIAJ's Complex Criminal Trials Roundtable" (2015) 62 *Criminal Law Quarterly* 339.

Mewett, Alan. "The Criminal Law, 1867–1967" (1967) 45 *Canadian Bar Review* 726.

Mitchell, Graeme G. "*R v Godoy*: Constitutional Accommodation of Public Service Programs" (1999) 21 *Criminal Reports* (5th) 217.

Needham, HG. "Historical Perspectives on the Federal–Provincial Split in Jurisdiction in Corrections" (1980) 22 *Canadian Journal of Criminology* 298.

Pringle, Heather. "The Smoke and Mirrors of *Godoy*: Creating Common Law Authority while Making *Feeney* Disappear" (1999) 21 *Criminal Reports* (5th) 227.

Roach, Kent. *Due Process and Victims' Rights* (Toronto: University of Toronto Press, 1999).

Stewart, Hamish. "The *Grant* Trilogy and the Right against Self-Incrimination" (2009) 66 *Criminal Reports* (6th) 97.

Stribopoulos, James. "In Search of Dialogue: The Supreme Court, Police Powers and the *Charter*" (2005) 31 *Queen's Law Journal* 1.

Stuart, Don. "*Godoy*: The Supreme Court Reverts to the Ancillary Powers Doctrine to Fill a Gap in Police Power" (1999) 21 *Criminal Reports* (5th) 225.

Wood, Josiah, & Richard Peck, eds. *One Hundred Years of the Criminal Code in Canada* (Ottawa: Canadian Bar Association, 1993).

ELEMENTS OF CRIMINAL PROCEDURE

A. CLASSIFICATION OF OFFENCES AND MODE OF TRIAL

1) Introduction

Over a number of years, and with increasing amendments to the *Criminal Code*, the procedures for deciding the mode of trial have become needlessly complex. The current scheme is "based more on the accidents of history than on any rational plan."[1] As a practical matter, it is easiest to understand the current system first by imagining the very simple system that, at least conceptually, underlies it and then by looking at the variety of exceptions that serve to effectively conceal that model.

Imagine a system of prosecuting crimes that has only two types of offences and two methods of prosecution: less serious offences that are prosecuted in lower courts, and more serious offences that are prosecuted in superior courts. That seems to be the underlying theory of our classification and mode of trial system, but it is subject to amendments, exceptions, and sub-exceptions relating to the number of types of offences, the number of modes of trial, and the provision to the accused of a choice of mode of trial in some cases and then the removal of

---

1   Law Reform Commission of Canada, *Classification of Offences* (Ottawa: Law Reform Commission of Canada, 1986) at 1 [*Classification of Offences*].

that choice in others. We shall pursue each of these issues in more detail below, but an overview of how these exceptions overlay the simple model will be a useful starting point.

First, in one sense, our system has only two types of offences: summary conviction offences and indictable offences. However, the model is made more complex because the *Code* provides for a great number of offences that can be prosecuted in either fashion: these are referred to as "hybrid offences."

Second, there are not really only two modes of trial, but three. One mode of trial is in front of the "court of criminal jurisdiction," and the other mode of trial is in front of the "superior court of criminal jurisdiction." However, the superior court can hear matters in two ways: either without a jury (a judge-alone trial) or with a jury.

Third, we do not automatically send all less serious offences to the lower court and all more serious matters to the superior court. For summary conviction offences that equation does hold, and the only mode of trial for them is in the court of criminal jurisdiction. In the case of indictable offences, however, the accused is not forced to choose the top-of-the-line mode of trial and can instead choose whether to have a trial by superior court judge and jury, by superior court judge alone, or by provincial court judge. This choice is referred to as an "election."

Fourth, having given that election to the accused, the *Code* then takes it away again in a number of situations. For example, section 469 lists a series of offences that must be tried by a judge and jury, so the accused is given no election. Further, section 553 lists a number of offences that will be tried in provincial court, and so again the accused is given no election. In principle, the rationale for these two lists is that since section 469 contains such serious offences—for example, murder—the public interest demands a jury trial. In contrast, section 553 lists offences that are less serious than most indictable offences (though not so much less serious as to be summary conviction offences, it seems), and so there is no justification to offer the accused any choice beyond provincial court.

Fifth, if the trial will eventually take place in a superior court (either a judge alone, or a judge and jury), the matter does not go immediately to trial, but can first be referred to a preliminary inquiry in front of the provincial court. Only if this proceeding concludes that there is sufficient evidence will a trial actually take place.

Finally, there are various other exceptions to exceptions, such as the ability of the Crown, in some cases, to compel a jury trial, regardless of the accused's election, or the ability of the accused to re-elect having made one election, and so on.

One might also note that the way in which the *Code* is drafted does not contribute to an easy understanding of this structure. Section 471, for example, states that trial by jury is compulsory for all indictable offences, unless some other *Code* provision creates an exception to that requirement. Other *Code* provisions then create exceptions for literally *every* offence. One could easily gain the impression that trial by jury is the norm when, in fact, it is a rarity.

2) Types of Offences

Criminal offences are classified as indictable or offences punishable on summary conviction. These are the only two classifications in Canadian criminal procedure. In every statutory provision that creates an offence, Parliament designates the offence by one classification or the other.[2] However, for many offences, Parliament has applied a hybrid classification to allow the prosecutor discretion as to whether to proceed by indictable-offence procedure or summary conviction procedure. That is, the offence is designated to fall into either category. Offences thus designated are typically called hybrid, or "dual procedure," offences. These are not a third category of offence, however: they are offences where the Crown has a choice whether to proceed summarily or indictably.[3] Once that election is made, the procedure for that type of offence will be followed.

---

2   The *Contraventions Act*, SC 1992, c 47, creates another category of offence called a "contravention," which means, according to s 2, "an offence that is created by an enactment and is designated as a contravention by regulation." Section 8 prohibits the designation of an indictable offence. Section 4 states that the purposes of the Act are to provide a procedure for the prosecution that distinguishes between criminal and regulatory offences and to abolish the legal consequences of conviction. Section 63 specifically provides that there shall be no criminal record upon conviction. In sum, a contravention is not properly classified as a criminal offence, even though Parliament might have originally enacted the offence under the authority of s 91(27) of the *Constitution Act, 1867* (UK), 30 & 31 Vict, c 3.

3   If the Crown fails to elect a mode of procedure and the accused then enters a plea before a summary conviction court, the Crown will generally be deemed to have elected to proceed summarily (*R v RVF*, 2011 NSCA 71 at para 15; *R v Robert* (1973), 13 CCC (2d) 43 (Ont CA)). However, the *Interpretation Act*, RSC 1985, c I-21, s 34, provides that an offence which can be prosecuted by indictment is an indictable offence, which is usually taken to govern the decision with regard to mode of trial in circumstances other than a simple entry of a plea and trial in summary conviction court (*R v Paul-Marr*, 2005 NSCA 73; *R v Mitchell* (1997), 121 CCC (3d) 139 (Ont CA)). For that same reason, hybrid offences are treated as indictable offences for the exercise of police powers: see, for example, *Collins v Brantford Police Services Board* (2001), 158 CCC (3d) 405 (Ont CA).

In broad terms, indictable offences are more serious than summary conviction offences but, unfortunately, the classification of the offence is not always a reliable indication of its relative seriousness. It is certainly true that indictable offences carry a higher maximum penalty than summary conviction offences but this, by itself, is not a sound or sophisticated gauge of the seriousness of crimes. Some serious offences of violence may be prosecuted by way of summary conviction procedure while many nonviolent, property offences must be prosecuted by indictable procedure. Neither the severity of the maximum penalty nor the perceived seriousness of violence provides a sound basis to explain why offences have been designated as they have. Indeed, the existence of hybrid offences, and the growing numbers of them, seems only to provide acknowledgment that the classification of offences is not something that can easily be rationalized by reference to their seriousness.

Nevertheless, the classification of offences is one of the most important organizing principles in the law of criminal procedure. The most obvious is perhaps the jurisdiction of the courts over offences, but some other ramifications of the classification might be noted briefly. The scope of police powers is affected by the classification of offences. The power of the police to arrest, for example, is defined differently for summary conviction and indictable offences.[4] Procedures for compelling appearance and interim release, whether by authority of the police or a judge, are also affected by the classification of the offence with which the accused will be charged or already has been charged.[5]

The classification of offences, of course, has a profound effect on the manner in which proceedings are conducted in court. Another major difference between summary conviction and indictable offences is that there is no "statute of limitations" for the latter, but there is for the former. Summary conviction offences are usually time-barred six months after the completion of the offence.[6] In a case where the only available charge is a summary conviction offence, the classification might therefore determine whether there can be any proceedings at all. If a hybrid offence could be charged in relation to conduct that was completed more than six months previously, the prosecutor is not generally time-barred against proceeding by way of indictment.[7] However,

---

4   Section 495.

5   See Part XVI.

6   Section 786(2). Note that the provision allows summary proceedings outside this time limit if both the Crown and the accused consent.

7   *R v Phelps* (1993), 79 CCC (3d) 550 (Ont CA).

doing so might be an abuse of process if the Crown had initially elected to proceed summarily and re-elects only to avoid the limitation period.[8]

The classification of offences has important consequences with regard to the mode of procedure and the jurisdiction of the courts. Virtually all prosecutions begin with a charge document that is called an "information."[9] In all summary conviction matters, and some indictable matters, the information remains the document of charge throughout the proceedings. In such cases the proceedings at trial are conducted in the provincial court.[10] For most other indictable offences, however, the usual procedure is to begin with a preliminary inquiry on the information before a provincial court judge (preliminary inquiries will be the subject of Chapter 9). The inquiry provides an opportunity for the parties to test the evidence of selected witnesses on specific issues. If the accused is committed for trial upon completion of the inquiry, the prosecutor may file a new document of charge, called the "indictment," in the court where the accused will be tried. In most provinces the trial court will be the superior court: the exceptions are Québec, where the provincial court has jurisdiction to try all offences except those in which there is trial by judge and jury, and Nunavut, which has a unified federal–provincial criminal court.[11] Thus, the classification of the offence as a summary conviction matter or as an indictable matter has a controlling effect on most elementary matters of jurisdiction.

Another important aspect of whether an offence is classified as summary conviction or indictable concerns sentencing. Indictable offences are typically defined to allow a maximum term of imprisonment that exceeds two years. This definition does not mean, of course, that all indictable offences are punished with imprisonment exceeding two years. Nonetheless, the point is significant because summary conviction offences allow a maximum of six months or a fine of two thousand dollars, or both, unless Parliament prescribes a higher maximum. In other words, a convicted accused is likely to receive a lighter sentence if the Crown has elected to proceed summarily rather than indictably on a hybrid offence. However, the Court has made clear that a sentence should not be "scaled down" or "scaled up" simply by reason of the Crown's election: the issue is always whether the sentence is a fit one.[12]

---

8   *R c Quinn* (1989), 54 CCC (3d) 157 (Que CA).
9   Part XXVIII, Form 2.
10   By virtue of s 553 of the *Code*, offences within the absolute jurisdiction of the provincial court are classified as indictable, but they are tried on an information.
11   Section 552.
12   *R v Solowan*, 2008 SCC 62.

There are a few provisions where Parliament has attached penalties greater than six months to a summary conviction offence, but Parliament has never attached a maximum of more than eighteen months.[13] As previously noted, offenders sentenced to terms of less than two years are incarcerated in provincial jails, whereas offenders sentenced to more than two years are incarcerated in federal penitentiaries. Provincial jails, therefore, house offenders serving sentences for offences that might be summary conviction or indictable, provided that the actual term in the warrant of committal is less than two years. Inmates in federal penitentiaries are necessarily there to serve sentences for indictable offences. These factors are relevant in important ways, including the prosecutor's exercise of discretion with regard to hybrid offences and plea discussions.

Finally, the *Criminal Code* provides different arrangements for appeal in summary conviction and indictable matters.[14] The former are heard by the superior court of the province and the latter are heard in the court of appeal. There are also provisions in the *Code*[15] and the *Supreme Court Act*[16] dealing with appeals to the highest court in criminal matters. These matters are further discussed in Chapter 12.

Much criticism has been made of the current classification of offences.[17] Some form of classification is obviously necessary, but the thrust of most critiques has been that the system of classification in current Canadian law is irrationally complex and no longer has any prescriptive coherence. Dividing offences into the approximate categories of "more serious" and "less serious" through the distinction between indictable and summary conviction offences has some intuitive attraction, but we now have the oddities that some indictable offences are treated as summary for all purposes but sentencing, while some summary conviction offences are treated as much closer to indictable solely for the purpose of sentencing. The distinctions are becoming so porous that it is difficult to see principle operating at a very strong level. Instead, the system reflects the anomalous accretion of particular rules and practices as Canadian law emerged from its origins in English law and was progressively adapted to accommodate Canadian needs. The

---

13   Offences punishable by eighteen months summary conviction have been called "super summaries": see, for example, ss 264.1 and 271.

14   Sections 675 and 813.

15   See, in particular, s 677 and ss 691–96.

16   RSC 1985, c S-26.

17   See, for example, Tim Quigley, *Procedure in Canadian Criminal Law*, 2d ed (Toronto: Thomson Carswell, 2005) (loose-leaf) ch 3. See also *Classification of Offences*, above note 1.

Law Reform Commission of Canada and others have argued that the current classification of offences is a profound impediment to needed reform of Canadian criminal procedure in all areas, but especially as regards the jurisdiction of the courts over offences.[18]

3) Mode of Trial

The *Constitution Act, 1867* gives provinces the authority to establish courts within their territorial jurisdiction.[19] In the *Criminal Code*, Parliament allocates jurisdiction over offences to the courts thus created by the provinces.[20] This section looks at some of the devices Parliament uses in defining the jurisdiction of the courts for trial, appeal, and other purposes.

For trial, the *Code* allocates jurisdiction over summary conviction offences to the provincial court. Indictable offences, on the other hand, may be tried either in a "superior court of criminal jurisdiction" or a "court of criminal jurisdiction." According to section 468, the superior court of the province is competent to try any indictable offence, but, in practice, the allocation of jurisdiction is more complex. Section 468 is broad, but it must be seen in the light of section 469, which provides that a court of criminal jurisdiction is also competent to try all indictable offences except for fourteen listed offences. For practical purposes, then, it is the "court of criminal jurisdiction" that has general competence to try indictable offences other than those offences that are specifically enumerated as being within the "exclusive jurisdiction" of the superior court. For further complexity, however, section 553 of the *Code* reserves to the provincial court the "absolute jurisdiction" to try a variety of offences listed there, almost all of them property offences. The "exclusive" jurisdiction of a court means that an offence can be prosecuted in that court alone and that no other court, even in principle, will have jurisdiction. Thus, any offence listed in section 469 can be tried only in the superior court. By virtue of section 468, jurisdiction over all other indictable offences is concurrent between the provincial and superior court, subject only to the definition of a "court of criminal jurisdiction" in section 552. Offences listed in section 553 are in the "absolute jurisdiction" of the provincial court in the sense that

---

18 Law Reform Commission of Canada, *Our Criminal Procedure* (Ottawa: Law Reform Commission of Canada, 1988).

19 Above note 2, s 92(15).

20 See Patrick Healy, "Constitutional Limits on the Allocation of Trial Jurisdiction to the Superior or Provincial Court in Criminal Matters" (2003) 48 *Criminal Law Quarterly* 31.

their jurisdiction does not depend upon the election of the accused.[21] In other words, the provincial court is the only court that *will* exercise jurisdiction with regard to the offences listed in that section, not that the superior court has no jurisdiction.[22]

There is little difficulty in identifying the superior court of criminal jurisdiction or the provincial court. What is the "court of criminal jurisdiction" that has general competence to try indictable offences not reserved to either the superior court of criminal jurisdiction or the provincial court judge? A partial definition is provided in section 2 of the *Code*, but a more useful guide to practice is the definition of "judge" in section 552. When read with others, this provision states that in all provinces, except Quebec, a judge of the superior court has jurisdiction to try any indictable offence except those reserved to the exclusive jurisdiction of the superior court or those reserved to the provincial court by section 553. The Cour du Québec has jurisdiction to try all indictable cases except those reserved to the superior court of criminal jurisdiction.[23]

The terms "superior court of criminal jurisdiction" and "court of criminal jurisdiction" are neither clear nor essential. To minimize the difficulty it is advisable to bear two points in mind with regard to indictable offences. The exclusive jurisdiction of the superior court is defined in section 469. The absolute jurisdiction of the provincial court is defined in section 553. For the rest, the court of criminal jurisdiction as defined in section 2 is (at least in theory) the court of trial, and for practical purposes, the court is identified in section 552.

As noted above, however, there is yet another qualification. For all indictable offences, except those in the exclusive jurisdiction of the superior court or the absolute jurisdiction of the provincial court, the accused has a right of election as to the mode of trial, that is, a right to choose among trial by jury, trial by judge alone, or trial by a judge

---

21   *R v Tucker* (2006), 213 CCC (3d) 89 (Ont CA).

22   In some circumstances, an absolute jurisdiction offence might end up in a superior court, for example, because upon hearing the evidence at trial in superior court, it becomes apparent that the value involved was low enough that the offence fell within section 553. In such a case, the superior court has jurisdiction to continue the trial nonetheless: *R v Holliday* (1973), 26 CRNS 279 (Alta SCAD). Similarly, section 555(1) permits a trial judge in some circumstances to convert a trial into a preliminary inquiry and send the trial to the superior court: this power could be used in the case of an absolute jurisdiction offence: *R v Turton* (1988), 44 CCC (3d) 49 (Alta CA).

23   That is, the Cour du Québec will not hear trials of offences listed in s 469 or of any offence where the accused elects trial by jury.

of the provincial court.[24] Thus, although the *Code* stipulates that all of these offences may be tried by a court of criminal jurisdiction, the right of election allows the accused a choice of jurisdictions. Many factors influence this election, and most conspicuous among them is that by electing trial before the provincial court, an accused waives the right to request a preliminary inquiry.

In addition to the right of election, the accused may be entitled to a re-election under certain conditions.[25] In some circumstances the accused can re-elect as of right, but in other cases the consent of the prosecutor is needed. In broad terms, it is easier to re-elect "down" from trial in superior court to trial by provincial court. It is also easier to re-elect the earlier the decision is made. For example, an accused who elects trial by provincial court judge can re-elect "up" as of right until fourteen days before trial, but only with the prosecutor's consent thereafter.[26]

The right to re-elect is by no means absolute, however, and is considerably narrowed if the prosecutor refuses consent. The election of the accused may also be pre-empted by the prosecution if the attorney general prefers a direct indictment (which can require the matter to go to trial without a preliminary inquiry[27]) or requires trial by judge and jury for an offence punishable by more than five years.[28]

Apart from appeal and trial, the allocation of jurisdiction is important for a wide variety of functions, including the issuance of forms of process and the conduct of hearings, such as bail applications and preliminary inquiries. Many of these functions are identified and discussed throughout this text. Here, it is important to note a broader point. Only superior courts have general and inherent jurisdiction, which means, among other things, that the superior court is the court of first instance for any justiciable issue not otherwise allocated by statute.[29] Provincial courts only have the powers that are expressly given to them by legislation. This means, in principle, that they are subject to review by way of a prerogative writ unless such relief is specifically excluded by law. The most common among these is the writ of *certiorari*, which may be issued by a superior court to quash a decision of a judge in a lower court who has acted without jurisdiction.

---

24   Section 536.
25   Section 561ff.
26   Section 561(2).
27   Section 577.
28   Section 568.
29   *MacMillan Bloedel Ltd v Simpson*, [1995] 4 SCR 725.

B. JURISDICTION

"Jurisdiction" is a word used variously to mean power, authority, competence, or geographical space. It is used to describe the functions of police officers, judges, courts, legislative bodies, and others. It is also used to describe limitations upon them. In criminal procedure, all of these various meanings are used in different contexts and, given the importance attached to several, this chapter introduces elementary notions of jurisdiction in criminal procedure.

1) Jurisdiction to Prosecute

Almost all criminal cases in Canada are public prosecutions conducted by agents of the attorney general. In principle, however, anyone may commence a prosecution by laying an information. If the information is sworn, a private prosecution may proceed unless the case is taken over by the attorney general.

a) Public Prosecutions

The attorney general is the principal law officer of the Crown, which means that she is the chief barrister and solicitor for the government.[30] There is an attorney general in the federal government and in each of the provincial governments.

Prosecutions are almost never conducted personally by the attorney general, but by persons who are legally authorized to act in his name.[31] Section 2 of the *Code* specifies that the attorney general may be represented by her deputy.[32] With regard to public prosecutions, the definition of "prosecutor" in section 2 includes counsel appearing for the attorney general with regard to indictable offences. Some provinces have adopted a model in which routine responsibility for the conduct of criminal prosecutions is confided to a senior person called the "director of public prosecutions." This model does not change the constitutional position of the attorney general as chief law officer of the Crown, but it does ensure a measure of professional independence for purposes of prosecution. It also helps guarantee greater openness and account-

---

30   See John Edwards, *The Law Officers of the Crown* (London: Sweet & Maxwell, 1964); and John Edwards, *The Attorney General, Politics and the Public Interest* (London: Sweet & Maxwell, 1984).

31   *R v Harrison*, [1977] 1 SCR 238. Unless the personal intervention of the attorney general is required by law, the agent may exercise the powers of the attorney general: see, for example, *R v Light* (1993), 78 CCC (3d) 221 at 253 (BCCA).

32   Section 2. See also *Interpretation Act*, above note 3, s 24.

ability around decisions to lay or withdraw charges, at least where the attorney general is directly involved. Counsel may include not only professional prosecutors but also private counsel who are appointed *ad hoc* to act on behalf of the attorney general.[33] With regard to summary conviction matters, the definition of "prosecutor" in section 785 allows prosecution by the attorney general, counsel appearing for her, or an "agent." In some instances, a summary conviction prosecution may also be conducted by a peace officer.[34]

Apart from general principles governing the authority to prosecute, Parliament occasionally imposes a requirement that a prosecution cannot proceed without the consent of the attorney general. This requirement is found in section 7 of the *Code* in the case of some offences over which Canada exerts extraterritorial jurisdiction or in the provision that creates the offence in other cases.[35] In most instances where consent is required, it refers to the attorney general of the province, but there are numerous exceptions where the consent of the attorney general of Canada is required.[36] There are also instances where either attorney general can provide the necessary consent.[37] In most cases, proof of consent need not be established unless the issue of jurisdiction to prosecute on this ground is raised by the accused; some exceptions apply, however.[38] Where this requirement exists, it virtually guarantees that a private prosecution could not be commenced because the likelihood that the attorney general would give consent in such a case is theoretically real but practically nil.

The requirement for the consent of the attorney general is presumably intended to ensure a critical examination of cases before charges are laid. It arguably exists in relation to offences that are likely to be highly sensitive to the public or that otherwise require rigorous consideration

---

33 *R v Moscuzza* (2003), 63 OR (3d) 636 (CA).

34 See the definition of "prosecutor" in s 785, which includes an agent. However, an agent may not prosecute an indictable offence, even if the trial is in provincial court: see *R v Edmunds*, [1981] 1 SCR 233.

35 See, for example, s 136 (giving contradictory evidence), s 319(6) (wilful promotion of hatred), s 174 (public nudity), or s 251(3) (unseaworthy vessel).

36 Sections 7(4.3), 83.24, 136, 166, 172, 318, 319, 754, and 803 for the former, and ss 7(2.33), 7(7), 54, 119, and 477.2 for the latter.

37 See the offences listed under (f) and (g) of the definition of "Attorney General" in s 2.

38 See *Minot v Canada (Attorney General)*, 2011 NLCA 7 [*Minot*], or *R v Sunila* (1987), 35 CCC (3d) 289 (NSSCAD), for the former point. Section 477.2(4) of the *Code* specifically requires that the consent of the attorney general must be filed with the clerk of the court: most provisions requiring consent do not contain a provision parallel to this.

of the public interest in prosecution. However, the Law Reform Commission of Canada suggests that there is no obvious unifying factor among offences where consent is required.[39] The Commission was also critical of the non-public nature of the decision and the fact that an attorney general was not required to give reasons for either granting or refusing consent to a prosecution: in their view no offences should have a consent requirement.[40]

There are several ways in which the requirement for consent is expressed in the *Criminal Code* and other statutes.[41] Despite these variations, the essential distinction to retain is between cases in which the personal consent of the attorney general is required[42] and the majority of instances in which the statute demands only the "consent of the attorney general." In the latter case, there is some scope for ambiguity as to precisely what is required. Something less than the personal consent of the attorney general would be sufficient, but anything less than the consent of prosecuting counsel in the particular case might be inadequate. Accordingly, such authorization might be sought from senior prosecuting counsel within the territorial jurisdiction in which the case arises: broadly speaking, the consent should be given by someone senior enough to be commensurate with the seriousness of the prosecution.[43] This person might be senior counsel responsible for the direction of prosecutions in a province or region. In any case, where some form of consent is required, it should be given in writing and placed before the court.

The attorney general and her agents have a large measure of discretion in the conduct of prosecutions beyond the requirement of consent to some offences. The prosecutor exercises various statutory powers, such as deciding whether an accused must have a jury trial, whether to proceed by direct indictment, or whether to enter a stay of proceedings.[44] In addition, what is termed "prosecutorial discretion" covers a wide range of prosecutorial decision-making. It includes whether to pursue a charge laid by police, stay proceedings, accept a guilty plea to a lesser charge, withdraw from criminal proceedings altogether, or take control

---

39   Law Reform Commission of Canada, *Controlling Criminal Prosecutions: The Attorney General and the Crown Prosecutor* (Ottawa: Law Reform Commission of Canada, 1990) at 67 [*Controlling Criminal Prosecutions*].

40   *Controlling Criminal Prosecutions, ibid* at 68.

41   See, for example, ss 7, 54, 119, 174, and 385.

42   For example, s 485.1.

43   *Minot*, note 38 at paras 31–37.

44   Sections 568, 577, and 579.

of a private prosecution.[45] It also includes the decision to repudiate a plea agreement, pursue a dangerous offender application, charge multiple offences, negotiate a plea, proceed summarily or by indictment, or initiate an appeal.[46] In some provinces, the prosecution has input into whether to charge an offence and, if so, what charges.[47]

Prosecutorial discretion is seen as a necessary part of a properly functioning criminal justice system, which advances the public interest by enabling prosecutors to make discretionary decisions without fear of judicial or political interference, thus fulfilling their *quasi*-judicial role as "ministers of justice."[48] As a result, courts will not review exercises of prosecutorial discretion unless it is shown that there has been an abuse of process.[49] However, decisions that simply form part of a Crown prosecutor's tactics or conduct before the court, not part of the core prosecutorial functions, are not insulated from review in the same way and instead are governed by the inherent jurisdiction of a court to control its own processes.[50]

b) Private Prosecutions

As previously noted, any person may commence a criminal prosecution by swearing an information before a competent judicial authority. The concept of a private prosecution is ancient in the common law, and it reflects the right of every person subject to the sovereign to invoke the protection of the law by making a complaint of a breach of the King's Peace. In modern terms, a private prosecutor is any prosecutor under the *Code* who is not an agent of the attorney general. It should not be thought, however, that a private prosecution of alleged crime is in any way a private action between the parties. The private prosecutor is not a plaintiff but is allowed under the criminal law to prosecute in the place of the attorney general.

Although the right to commence a private prosecution is ancient, the growth and development of the role of the attorney general as the public prosecutor has diminished the frequency and the significance of

---

45   *Krieger v Law Society of Alberta*, 2002 SCC 65 at para 46 [*Krieger*].

46   *R v Anderson*, 2014 SCC 41 [*Anderson*].

47   *R v Lafrance*, [1975] 2 SCR 201. See the discussion in *R v Regan*, 2002 SCC 12, of the ways in which the institutional arrangements between police and the Crown differ from province to province with regard to authority over charging decisions.

48   *Anderson*, above note 46 at para 37; *Miazga v Kvello Estate*, 2009 SCC 51.

49   *Anderson*, above note 46; *Krieger*, above note 45; *R v Nixon*, 2011 SCC 34.

50   *Krieger*, above note 45, para 47. See also the further discussion of this issue in Chapter 10, Section B(2)(c)(ii).

private prosecutions. Indeed, virtually the only reason that motivates people today to commence a private prosecution is that a public prosecutor has decided not to proceed, either because there is insufficient evidence to sustain the case or because prosecution of the alleged offence is otherwise not in the public interest. Thus, private prosecutions now tend to occur only when the attorney general or his agent has refused to lay charges.

The formal procedure for the commencement of a private prosecution is the same whether the offence alleged is indictable or summary, but the position is not the same for purposes of trial. Assuming that a judge receives and endorses the information, the informant becomes the prosecutor. The prosecutor has carriage of the case from that point and must conform to all of the obligations that prosecutors are obliged to fulfil. A private prosecutor, for example, would be no less bound by the obligation to make full disclosure to the defence than an agent of the attorney general.

A private prosecutor can appear personally or be represented by counsel.[51] If the offence is indictable and the accused is entitled to a preliminary inquiry, a private prosecution may proceed to the conclusion of the preliminary inquiry. At this point, however, the *Criminal Code* erects barriers to the continuation of the prosecution at trial. If the accused is ordered to stand trial after a preliminary inquiry, a private prosecutor may not prefer an indictment against that person without the written authorization of a judge in the court of trial. Similarly, in the event that there was no preliminary inquiry or there was a preliminary inquiry at which the accused was discharged, the private prosecutor may not prefer a direct indictment without the written order of a judge.[52]

In all cases, indictable or summary, the attorney general may intervene in a private prosecution for the purpose of assuming the carriage of the prosecution or for the purpose of entering a stay of proceedings. With respect to indictable offences, this power is recognized expressly in section 579 of the *Code*. A similar power is given in section 579.1 to the attorney general of Canada with respect to private prosecutions concerning federal offences outside the *Code* in which no provincial attorney general has intervened. With respect to summary conviction offences, the definition of "prosecutor" refers to instances in which the attorney general has not intervened, but there is no express provision

---

51   Section 785.
52   Section 577. See also *Johnson v Inglis* (1980), 52 CCC (2d) 385 (Ont HCJ); *Garton v Whelan* (1984), 14 CCC (3d) 449 (Ont HCJ), discussing the circumstances in which a judge should consent.

in Part XXVII of the *Code* that is comparable to section 579 or 579.1. It is arguable that express provision is not necessary because the power of an attorney general to intervene is well established at common law.

The *Criminal Code* includes procedural steps that must be observed at the commencement of a private prosecution. These were enacted to simplify and expedite proceedings. Section 507.1 requires that any information laid under section 504 by a private informant must be referred to a judge of the provincial court or, in Québec, a judge of the Cour du Québec. It is also possible to refer the matter to a justice designated specifically for this purpose if there is one in the jurisdiction. This judicial officer will decide whether a charge will be laid and whether to compel the appearance of the accused to answer that charge by summons or by arrest warrant. No such decision can be made unless the judge or designated justice has heard and considered the allegations of the informant and the evidence of any witnesses. Further, he must be satisfied that the attorney general has already received a copy of the information, with reasonable notice of the date for hearing the informant and witnesses, and been given the opportunity to appear at the hearing to cross-examine witnesses and call any other relevant evidence.

If neither a summons nor a warrant is issued at the conclusion of the hearing, the presiding judge or designated justice will endorse the information to that effect. If the informant does not seek to compel the issuance of process within six months of this endorsement, the matter is closed. If such proceedings are taken but no process is issued, the information is deemed never to have been laid.

Finally, there are several provisions of the *Code* that allow for a privately laid information to be received and, if endorsed, to lead to the issuance of an order for the respondent to be bound over. Such an order is usually referred to as a "peace bond" because the central condition will be a promise to "keep the peace and be of good behaviour" for a period of time up to one year. The model is found in section 810: any person who has reason to believe that an indictable offence will be committed upon her or upon a third party may swear an information to this effect and, if it is received, seek an order for the respondent to be bound over upon conditions. There are also several similar orders that nominally can be sought by any person, though in practice they are sought by the state. These include applications based on the fear that the respondent will commit a criminal organization, terrorism, sexual, or serious personal injury offence.[53] A peace bond is meant to

---

53   Sections 810.01, 810.1, & 810.2.

be preventive rather than punitive, and an application for one does not amount to charging an offence, but a failure to abide by the conditions of a peace bond is an offence.[54] These forms of procedure have become increasingly important in daily practice.

2) Territorial Jurisdiction

a) Extraterritoriality

Two separate issues need to be discussed with regard to extraterritoriality: prescriptive jurisdiction, which deals with the issue of whether offences in the *Criminal Code* apply outside Canadian territory; and enforcement jurisdiction, which deals with the extent to which Canadian officials can act outside Canada.

As a general rule, prescriptive jurisdiction matches up with the territory of Canada: that is, a person can be held liable under Canadian criminal law only for an offence that he commits within Canadian territorial limits. This principle of limitation is based upon the historical rationale that a violation of the criminal law is a violation of the sovereign's peace. Accordingly, the scope of the criminal law is normally co-extensive with the territorial sovereignty of the state. This principle is expressed in section 6(2) of the *Criminal Code*.

Similar to almost every rule of criminal procedure, this general principle is subject to exceptions. First, in a variety of provisions, the *Code* and other statutes explicitly create exceptions giving Canadian courts jurisdiction over offences committed outside Canadian territorial limits.[55] Generally speaking, these provisions reflect obligations or agreements contracted by Canada in treaties with other states. However, the extraterritorial jurisdiction created in the *Code* does not, in every case, map onto pre-existing international agreements. Some, though few, reflect a deliberate decision in policy to extend the reach of Canadian jurisdiction.[56] Second, the Supreme Court of Canada has held that, if an offence is committed abroad but has a "real and substantial" connection to Canada, it falls within the class of offences committed in

---

54   Section 811. See the discussion in *R v Budreo* (2000), 32 CR (5th) 127 (Ont CA).

55   See, for example, ss 7, 57, 58, 74, 75, and 465.

56   See, for example, ss 7(3.74) & 7(3.75), which give extraterritorial jurisdiction over terrorism offences other than those covered by treaties. For a review of the underlying theory behind extraterritoriality in criminal law, see Robert J Currie & Steve Coughlan, "Extraterritorial Criminal Jurisdiction: Bigger Picture or Smaller Frame?" (2007) 11 *Canadian Criminal Law Review* 141; and Steve Coughlan et al, *Law Beyond Borders: Extraterritorial Jurisdiction in an Age of Globalization* (Toronto: Irwin Law, 2014).

Canada.[57] This is not truly an exercise of extraterritorial jurisdiction, but rather extended territoriality taking into account that the offence can be partly located in Canada. Based on this rule, it has been found, for example, that courts have jurisdiction over an accused for behaviour that occurred outside of Canada's boundaries, if that behaviour was in violation of a court order issued in Canada.[58]

With regard to enforcement jurisdiction, the issue that has attracted the most judicial attention is the extent to which *Charter* rights apply abroad. For example, suspects are sometimes interrogated while outside Canada, most often by foreign police but sometimes by Canadians. Canadian police might also be involved in searches conducted in other countries. A question has arisen, therefore, as to the extent to which an accused can complain of a failure to comply with *Charter* standards when the alleged failure occurred outside Canada.

As a generalization, it is safe to say that the *Charter* is unlikely to have much influence on investigative techniques employed abroad. Foreign officials cannot be expected to comply with *Charter* standards and their failure to do so will not give rise to a *Charter* violation. The fact that US police do not give a warning in accordance with section 10(b) requirements, for example, cannot give rise to a section 10(b) claim. However, if the conditions in which a statement was obtained are particularly egregious, it is possible that attempting to introduce that evidence at a trial in Canada might constitute a section 7 violation.[59] The *Charter* was found to apply in *R v Cook*, where two Canadian police officers went to the United States and interrogated an accused after having given him a section 10(b) warning that was clearly deficient.[60] However, *Cook*'s authority is overshadowed by the Supreme Court's later decision in *R v Hape*, which (while not calling *Cook* wrong on its own facts) concluded that the approach to extraterritorial application of the *Charter* in *Cook* was wrong.[61]

In *Hape*, Canadian police participated in several warrantless searches in the Turks and Caicos Islands that, if conducted in Canada, would have violated section 8. There was no evidence in the case as to whether the

---

57 *Libman v The Queen*, [1985] 2 SCR 178.
58 See, for example, *R v Greco* (2001), 159 CCC (3d) 146 (Ont CA) (where an assault committed by the accused in Cuba was found to be a breach of his probation order), or *R v Rattray*, 2008 ONCA 74 (where the accused was proven to be in possession of a firearm in Michigan, which constituted a breach of court orders issued in Canada prohibiting him from possessing firearms).
59 See the discussion in *R v Harrer*, [1995] 3 SCR 562; *R v Terry*, [1996] 2 SCR 207.
60 [1998] 2 SCR 597.
61 2007 SCC 26 [*Hape*].

searches complied with Turks and Caicos law. The Court held, though, that the accused could not claim a *Charter* violation. The general approach laid out in that case requires courts to answer two questions. The first, for the *Charter* to have any prospect of applying, is whether section 32 is met: under this section, the *Charter* is applicable only to Canadian state actors. However, even if a Canadian state actor is involved, consideration of comity between nations will normally mean that the *Charter* does not apply to that person's activities abroad. The *Charter* will apply only if there is an exception to sovereignty, such as evidence that the foreign state consented to the application of *Charter* standards: the Court observed that "[i]n most cases, there will be no such exception and the *Charter* will not apply."[62] In that event, the second question is whether admitting evidence obtained through the foreign investigation renders the trial unfair, thus giving rise to a section 7 violation. In most cases, however, neither part of the test will be met. Thus, the *Charter* has a minimal impact on investigations conducted outside Canada.

Nonetheless, the possibility does still exist. In *Hape* the Court had held that comity did not justify Canadian participation in activities of a foreign state or its agents that were contrary to Canada's international obligations: there would be no deference where the actions complained of violated international law and fundamental human rights. In *Canada (Justice) v Khadr* the Court relied on that exception to find that the *Charter* did apply to the actions of Canadian officials who had interviewed a Canadian citizen being detained by the US government at Guantanamo Bay. The Court noted that various aspects of US government officials' behaviour at Guantanamo Bay had already been found by the US Supreme Court to violate international law. In that event comity concerns did not justify deference to the foreign state and so the *Charter* was applicable extraterritorially.[63]

b) Territorial Jurisdiction within Canada

Proof that a Canadian court has jurisdiction over an offence committed within or without Canada is a necessary condition of criminal liability, but it is not the end of the analysis. The court must be satisfied that it has jurisdiction over the offence, whether that offence was allegedly committed outside Canada or within its territorial limits. Having jurisdiction requires more than the offence occurring in Canada, however. In keeping with the adage that all crime is local, a criminal prosecu-

---

62   *Ibid* at para 113.
63   2008 SCC 28.

tion will typically be conducted in the judicial district within which an offence is alleged to have been committed.[64] Precisely where this is will depend upon the manner in which a province or territory has organized its courts. Further, the *Code* provides that if the offence is alleged to have occurred in an unorganized area within a province, it may be prosecuted in the nearest judicial district.[65] Offences occurring in parts of Canada that are not in any province and not in the internal waters or territorial seas of Canada can be prosecuted in any province.[66]

Not all offences are committed in a single place, of course. As a result, there can be jurisdiction in more than one country, more than one province or territory, or more than one judicial district within a province or territory.[67] While no province or territory may assert jurisdiction over an offence wholly committed in another, a prosecution may be conducted in any province or territory in which an element of the alleged offence occurred. This principle therefore allows for concurrent jurisdiction. Territorial jurisdiction in a province will be found when there is a link between the judicial district of the court and the offence in the sense that some part of the *actus reus* of the offence occurred in that district.

In *R v Bigelow*,[68] for example, the accused was charged with detaining a child with the intent to deprive the mother of lawful custody. He had picked up the child for an access visit in Ontario and then flown to Alberta before the scheduled time to return the child. His argument was that the offence of "detaining" had not occurred in Ontario but in Alberta, and, therefore, that the Ontario trial court lacked jurisdiction.

The Ontario Court of Appeal acknowledged that section 478 would prevent an Ontario court from trying an offence "committed entirely in another province." However, the Court noted that offences could have elements that signify they were committed in more than one province, and identified three such grounds: (1) continuity of operation, (2) commission of an overt act, and (3) the generation of effects. These three grounds are not entirely distinct and can overlap with each other. This would be the case, for example, where a telemarketing scheme that originates in one province causes the victim to make a decision to her detriment in another province and leads to the deposit of funds to the offender's credit in a third province. In such a case, all three of the grounds

---

64   Where the offence occurred extraterritorially this is not possible, of course. In such cases, the *Code* typically provides that the offence can be prosecuted anywhere in Canada: see, for example, s 83.25.

65   Section 480.

66   Sections 481 & 481.1.

67   *R v L(DA)* (1996), 107 CCC (3d) 178 (BCCA).

68   (1982), 69 CCC (2d) 204 (Ont CA) [*Bigelow*].

identified in *Bigelow* would operate. In *Bigelow* itself the commission of the overt act of boarding a plane with the child in Ontario as well as the facts that this act was part of a preplanned scheme and that the mother was deprived of her custody rights in Ontario because of this act, was sufficient to give Ontario courts jurisdiction.[69]

People alleged to have committed an offence do not always stay in the judicial district that would have territorial jurisdiction. The *Code* provides that such persons may be transferred to the judicial district in which the offence is alleged to have been committed.[70] Following arrest, a judge may issue a warrant that, in effect, authorizes the forced removal of the accused to the jurisdiction in which the prosecution will take place.[71] Further, although a court cannot *try* an offence committed wholly in another jurisdiction, it is permitted to accept a guilty plea from an accused and impose sentence, provided the attorney general consents.[72] The *Code* does not allow the accused to be tried on the merits in the place where he is found because the evidence is not there. The consent of the attorney general ensures that a disposition of the case upon a guilty plea is consistent with the public interest.

A trial that is scheduled within the judicial district of the alleged offence may be moved to another district within the same province. Section 599 provides that a change of venue may be ordered if it is "expedient to the ends of justice."[73] This would appear to confer a broad discretion upon the court, but, in practice, a change of venue has always been exceptional. It may be sought by the prosecutor or the accused, and the applicant must show cause as to why a change of venue is necessary. Clearly, the application will be granted if there are grounds to believe that a jury in that venue could not try the accused impartially, but applications for a change of venue are not restricted to a lack of impartiality in a jury trial. Further, questions of jury partiality in a particular location, at least where they arise out of extensive pre-trial publicity, might be better resolved through the challenge for cause procedures in the *Code* rather than through a change of venue. Whether the trial is by jury or judge alone, a change of venue may be ordered if the applicant can identify a cogent reason to suggest that the

---

69   See also *R v Trudel, ex p Horbas & Myhaluk*, [1969] 3 CCC 95 (Man CA).

70   See, for example, s 543, permitting a justice conducting a preliminary inquiry to have the inquiry and the accused transferred to the jurisdiction where the offence is alleged to have occurred.

71   Sections 503(3) and 528.

72   Section 478(3).

73   In addition, s 599(1)(b) permits a change of venue to be ordered if there is no jury panel in the district where the prosecution has begun.

trial would be unfair or prejudicial to either party if it continued where it began.[74] The potential unfairness must relate to the location of the trial: where it relates to the evidence to be heard, moving the trial to a different location will not solve matters.[75]

3) Jurisdiction over the Accused

Apart from jurisdiction over the subject-matter of an offence, no court can adjudicate in respect of a particular person unless it also has jurisdiction over the accused, often also referred to as "jurisdiction over the person." The central question is whether the accused is properly before the court. Initially, a court has jurisdiction over an accused if he is arrested or in custody within its territorial jurisdiction, or was lawfully ordered to stand trial in that court.[76] However, courts can lose jurisdiction over an accused through various irregularities.

For practical purposes the question has arisen chiefly in relation to the exercise of jurisdiction by provincial courts. As their authority to adjudicate is statutory, courts can lose their jurisdiction over the accused by an error or omission relating to the process by which the accused is required to appear in court, such as appearances, adjournments, or the conduct of proceedings in the absence of the accused.[77] The primary effect of a loss of jurisdiction over the person is relatively minor: an accused who failed to appear in court following some flawed process could not be charged with the separate offence of failure to appear, but nothing is likely to prevent the Crown from regaining jurisdiction over the accused and continuing the proceedings on the original charge. At one point these issues caused some concern,[78] but there are fewer such difficulties today. First, some of the rules that potentially caused a loss of jurisdiction over the person have been removed from

---

74   *R v Charest* (1990), 57 CCC (3d) 312 (Que CA).

75   *R v Suzack* (2000), 30 CR (5th) 346 (Ont CA).

76   Section 470. See also s 798 with regard to summary conviction offences.

77   For example, ss 505 and 508 of the *Code* lay out two steps in the process of compelling an accused person to appear in front of a court: s 505 deals with laying an information before a justice after an appearance notice has been issued, and s 508 deals with the justice deciding whether to act on that information (see the discussion in Chapter 6, Section C(1)). A defect in the process at either stage would mean that the court has lost jurisdiction over the person; however, the defect would not affect the underlying information, and so jurisdiction over the offence would not be lost: see *R v Markovic* (2005), 200 CCC (3d) 449 (Ont CA); and *R v Ladouceur*, 2013 ONCA 328.

78   See the discussion of the history of some such problems in *R v Millar*, 2012 ONSC 1809.

the *Code*. Second, section 485 now excuses most errors relating to the appearance of the accused. Because of that section, jurisdiction over an offence is not lost simply because a judge fails to exercise jurisdiction at any particular time or fails to comply with any of the *Code* provisions respecting adjournments or remands. Generally speaking, jurisdiction over an accused is not lost because of non-appearance.[79] Finally, the courts have broad authority to issue process, such as a bench warrant for arrest, which allows jurisdiction over the person to be regained in the event that it is lost.[80] Indeed, some authorities suggest that a court obtains jurisdiction over the person so long as the person is present in court, no matter what process has brought that person there.[81]

Perhaps the most common situation today in which there is a loss of jurisdiction over the accused occurs in the case of non-compliance with section 650, which gives the accused the right to be present at the whole of his trial. Occasionally, accused are, because no one adverts to the impact of that rule, absent for small portions of trial such as a chambers meeting or discussion carried on in the absence of a jury. At one time such errors caused difficulty because, even if the impact on the accused's interests was minimal, the error would necessarily result in a successful appeal: section 686(1)(b)(iii) allows an appeal to be dismissed where an error of law is harmless, but this was found not to apply to jurisdictional errors.[82] Subsequently, section 686(1)(b)(iv) was added to the appeal provisions, allowing appeals to be dismissed despite a jurisdictional error as long as the trial court had jurisdiction over the class of the offence and the accused suffered no prejudice.[83]

Apart from the possibility of losing jurisdiction, there are some persons over whom the courts have no jurisdiction. These include persons under the age of twelve, who are presumed by section 13 of the *Code* to be incapable of crime and persons who are immune from prosecution for reasons of policy. The most obvious example of immunity is that extended to diplomats, but there was also an ancient principle that the Crown is immune from liability, based on the fiction that the sovereign can do no wrong.[84] It is noteworthy, though, that various amendments

---

79   Section 485(1.1).

80   Section 485(2).

81   *R v Lindsay* (2006), 207 CCC (3d) 296 (BCCA).

82   *R v Meunier*, [1966] SCR 399.

83   Section 686(1)(b)(iv). This provision covers loss of jurisdiction due to a failure to comply with s 650: see *R v Khan*, 2001 SCC 86, adopting the reasoning from *R v Cloutier* (1988), 43 CCC (3d) 35 (Ont CA).

84   See *Interpretation Act*, above note 3, s 17; and *R v Eldorado Nuclear Ltd; Uranium Canada Ltd*, [1983] 2 SCR 551.

to the *Code*, intended to expand the circumstances in which organizations can be held criminally liable, include "public body" in the definition of "organization."[85] This could have the effect, in some cases, of extending the liability of the Crown.

4) Jurisdiction in Time

Indictable offences are generally not barred by a period of limitation or prescription. In other words, offences committed many years previously might still be prosecuted, subject, of course, to considerations about the quality of evidence.[86] Summary conviction matters, however, are barred six months following the completion of the offence.[87] These matters will influence the decision of prosecutors as to whether to proceed by indictment in the prosecution of hybrid offences.[88] Some difficulty can arise in determining when the time limit for prosecuting an alleged summary conviction offence has passed.[89]

Where the Crown elects to proceed summarily, a hybrid offence is treated in all respects as a summary conviction offence. Equally, where the Crown has not expressly elected but the trial has proceeded before a summary conviction court, it will be presumed that the Crown elected to proceed summarily. If it subsequently transpires that the proceedings were time-barred because they were instituted more than six months after the offence was alleged to have been committed, there are several possibilities. The first is that the proceedings might still take place because the Crown and the accused agree.[90] If there is no such agreement and the trial has not been completed, a mistrial should be declared. If the trial has been completed and the accused was convicted, an appeal on the ground that the proceedings were statute-barred should be granted. If that is the only basis upon which the appeal is granted, or if a mistrial was declared, the Crown is entitled to start new proceedings by way of indictment, unless in the circumstances, to do so would be an abuse of process. However, if the accused was acquitted at trial, the

---

85   Section 2, and *An Act to Amend the Criminal Code (Criminal Liability of Organizations)*, SC 2003, c 21.

86   The most common instances of this are the prosecutions of what are known widely as "historical sexual offences."

87   Section 786(2).

88   *R v Belair* (1988), 41 CCC (3d) 329 (Ont CA); *R v Kalkhorany* (1994), 89 CCC (3d) 184 (Ont CA).

89   *R v Belgal Holdings Ltd*, [1967] 3 CCC 34 (Ont HCJ).

90   Section 786(2), allows for this possibility. The accused might be motivated to agree to what would otherwise be a time-barred proceeding in order to avoid the higher range of penalties available in the case of indictable offences.

Crown is not entitled to appeal on the basis that the proceedings were statute-barred: "Having elected to proceed by way of summary conviction before the right court, the Crown should not be heard to complain *after an adverse adjudication on the merits* that it neglected to obtain the consent of the accused before the accused was acquitted!"[91]

It is an elementary feature of the principle of legality that criminal offences do not have retrospective application, from which it follows that a court has no jurisdiction to try a charge of conduct that was not an offence when it occurred. This principle is confirmed in the *Criminal Code* and in section 11(g) of the *Charter*. In *R v Finta*, the Supreme Court stated that there is a partial exception to this principle for war crimes allegedly committed in Europe during the Second World War. The Court qualified the retroactive application of provisions of the *Code* concerning such crimes as a partial exception to the principle because the alleged crimes took place before they were declared offences in Canada. Nonetheless, the Court was satisfied that such offences were recognized as crimes in international law at the time of their commission, which meant the prosecution did not violate section 11(g).[92]

Note that the rule against retrospective application applies to substantive criminal law whereas procedural rules are ordinarily presumed to have immediate effect and, therefore, will apply retrospectively. However, it will not always be straightforward to decide whether a provision is substantive or procedural. In general, a law will be classified as procedural in this analysis only if it is exclusively so and will be classified as substantive if it creates or impinges on vested rights.[93]

The right to trial within a reasonable time, guaranteed by section 11(b) of the *Charter*, is not typically seen as an aspect of jurisdiction. Nevertheless, it should be mentioned because unreasonable delay can cause a *Charter* violation and the remedy for it is a stay of proceedings. When granted, the net effect is that the state has run out of the time within which it can prosecute the accused. Technically, this does not mean that there is a loss of jurisdiction arising from unreasonable delay. But the effect of the stay is a judicial order that there is no jurisdiction to proceed.

Obviously, trial within a reasonable time is a principle of procedural fairness, and for that reason it finds a place in the Constitution, among the principles of fundamental justice. Unreasonable delay has two possible causes, essentially. First, it may be attributed to one of the parties, or conceivably the court, but if the responsible party is the accused

---

91   *R v Dudley*, 2009 SCC 58 at para 6 [emphasis in original].
92   [1994] 1 SCR 701.
93   *Re Application under Section 83.28 of the Criminal Code*, 2004 SCC 42.

there will be no remedy under section 24 of the *Charter*. The second is institutional delay that is attributable to the absence of adequate resources for the administration of justice in a timely manner. Delay of this nature is most likely to be found in large urban jurisdictions that have a high volume of cases. Such a delay was the case in *R v Askov*,[94] and, as a result, measures were taken to rectify the systemic difficulties identified by the Supreme Court in that instance. The Court's subsequent decision in *R v Morin*[95] placed a much greater emphasis on the need for the accused to demonstrate that actual prejudice arose from the delay, which dramatically reduced the number of applications brought under this section. After that, in *R v Godin*, the Court encouraged lower courts "not to lose sight of the forest for the trees" and seemed to place renewed emphasis on the presumption of prejudice.[96] No settled position has been reached on how the right is now dealt with: see the discussion in Chapter 10, Section B(2)(c)(i).

5) Jurisdiction under the *Charter*

Section 24 of the *Charter* allows a court of competent jurisdiction to grant an appropriate and just remedy for the breach of rights guaranteed by that part of Constitution.[97] But what is a court of competent jurisdiction? Could the accused argue at a bail hearing that he had been arbitrarily detained or that his right to counsel had been breached? Could he argue that he did not have adequate disclosure from the prosecution? Could he seek the exclusion of evidence obtained in violation of a guaranteed right? Could he seek a remedy at the preliminary inquiry?

In *R v Mills*[98] the Supreme Court decided that a court of competent jurisdiction means, for most practical purposes in criminal matters, the trial court. The majority observed that the *Charter* itself included no express allocation of jurisdiction. On this basis, then, it was appropriate to determine if a judge at a preliminary inquiry was a court of

---

94   [1990] 2 SCR 1199 [*Askov*].

95   [1992] 1 SCR 771.

96   2009 SCC 26 at para 18 [*Godin*].

97   The issue for purposes of this section is the meaning of "court of competent jurisdiction." An "appropriate and just" remedy can include orders related to the trial process, such as adjournments or orders for disclosure, but also other remedies such as a stay of proceedings, damages, or a sentence reduction. On the range of remedies available generally, see, for example, *Doucet-Boudreau v Nova Scotia (Minister of Education)*, 2003 SCC 62; *R v Bjelland*, 2009 SCC 38; *Vancouver (City) v Ward*, 2010 SCC 27; and *Henry v British Columbia (AG)*, 2015 SCC 24.

98   [1986] 1 SCR 863 [*Mills*].

competent jurisdiction by reference to the ordinary principles of juris-diction in criminal matters. In this regard, the *Criminal Code* did not expressly attribute jurisdiction over constitutional issues to provincial courts presiding over preliminary inquiries.

The Court's decision that a judge conducting a preliminary inquiry is not a court of competent jurisdiction to decide issues under the *Charter* was affirmed in *R v Hynes*.[99] While the proposition concerning a lack of statutory jurisdiction is weak in principle, it has been reinforced by other considerations. One such consideration is that this position avoids the possibility of contradictory decisions at the preliminary inquiry and trial. Another is that it avoids the likelihood of interlocutory appeals that would arise if constitutional remedies were granted at the preliminary inquiry. In short, there are arguments based upon the efficient administration of cases that support the decisions in *Mills* and *Hynes*. However, there is some awkwardness about this position, too. It effectively requires a judge to ignore a possible *Charter* breach, no matter how glaring it might be. In any event, amendments have radically trimmed the scope of preliminary inquiries, and so the significance of these issues is diminished.

For procedural purposes, however, there remains a question about which court a *Charter* application can be addressed to when there is no pending trial. In these instances, the court of competent jurisdiction is the superior court. This assessment is undoubtedly consistent with orthodox principles of jurisdiction, the most basic of which is that the superior court is a court of general and inherent jurisdiction that can hear any justiciable issue not otherwise expressly assigned to another court.

However, it is also possible that the "court" of competent jurisdic-tion will be an administrative tribunal rather than a traditional court. Some decisions within the criminal process (such as how to deal with persons found not criminally responsible by reason of mental disorder) are given to administrative bodies. The Court has concluded that such tribunals will be courts of competent jurisdiction for *Charter* purposes if they have been given the ability to decide questions of law and the ability to decide *Charter* issues has not been removed by statute. If those conditions are met, the tribunal has the ability to grant any remedy which is otherwise available to it as a *Charter* remedy. In other words, once a tribunal is found to be a court of competent jurisdiction it is presumed to have jurisdiction over any remedies not removed from it.[100]

---

99   [2001] 3 SCR 623 [*Hynes*].

100   *R v Conway*, 2010 SCC 22. See the discussion in Steve Coughlan, "Tribunal Jurisdiction over *Charter* Remedies: Now You See It, Now You Don't" (2010) 75 *Criminal Reports* (6th) 238.

C. STATUTORY OVERVIEW OF PROCEDURE FROM CHARGING DECISION TO TRIAL

One major obstacle to getting a real sense of how criminal procedure works at the trial stage is the fact that the relevant sections are found in widely disparate parts of the *Code*. As noted above, the *Code* is arranged in a roughly chronological fashion, but there are exceptions to this rule. For example, the procedures for summary conviction offences are set out nearly at the end, in Part XXVII, but nonetheless incorporate many earlier provisions by reference. Liberal use of the *Code*'s index is necessary simply to find where to look for the right rules. Therefore, it might be useful to lay out a brief road map showing the various routes that might be followed, from the commencement of proceedings to an eventual trial, and the relevant *Code* sections.

Under section 504, anyone can lay an information alleging the commission of an offence in front of a justice of the peace. This information will, according to section 506, be in Form 2, which is found in section 849. Under section 788, this is the document under which a summary conviction trial will take place.

The justice of the peace decides, under section 507, whether to issue a summons or a warrant, where "a case for doing so is made out,"[101] to require the accused to attend court. Note that these are two distinct steps: whether to do anything, and if so, whether to proceed by warrant or summons. Under section 507(3), the evidence is taken on oath.

Alternatively, rather than initially seeking process under section 504, a peace officer might have arrested a person without a warrant. That person may still be in custody or may have already been released at some stage on an appearance notice.[102] In that event, section 505 creates an obligation to present whatever process was issued to a justice of the peace. Section 508 then imposes an obligation on the justice to perform a screening process similar to that in section 507.

Presuming the matter goes further, the accused will be arrested or will receive the summons that was issued. If the accused was arrested, she will (under section 503) be taken in front of a justice of the peace who will decide whether to hold or release her. This bail hearing will be conducted in accordance with the procedures in section 515. Frequently, as a practical matter, bail hearings are by a judge rather than a justice of the peace.

Following any issues concerning the release of the accused will be the "arraignment"—the accused's initial appearance in court to an-

---

101 Section 507(1)(b).
102 See the discussion in Chapter 6.

swer the charge. If the offence is hybrid, the Crown should elect whether to proceed by indictment or summary conviction at this stage. If the matter is a summary conviction offence, automatically or by election, the accused enters a plea and will be tried on the information in Form 2. However, it is possible at this stage for that information to be withdrawn and a different information laid. The procedures in Part XXVII apply to summary conviction trials, and under section 798, a summary conviction court judge has jurisdiction. If the matter is indictable, section 471 says the trial must be by judge and jury unless some other part of the *Code* specifies otherwise. In fact, exceptions of some sort are then made for every offence, and the vast majority of criminal trials occur without a jury. Most indictable offences can be tried in any court.

Section 469 gives a superior court of criminal jurisdiction (defined in section 2 for each province) the ability to try any offence. Section 468 gives a court of criminal jurisdiction (also defined in section 2 for each province) the ability to try any offence other than those listed in section 469. Section 554 gives a provincial court the ability to try any offence other than those listed in section 469. "Provincial court" is also defined in this section of the *Code*, and in some provinces that definition overlaps with the definition of "court of criminal jurisdiction."

Although section 471 mandates jury trials as the putative norm, section 558 says that an accused can elect not to have a jury, except for the offences listed in section 469. Further, section 473 states that an accused can elect not to have a jury, even for the offences listed in section 469, with the attorney general's consent.

Normally, therefore, a choice of mode of trial exists and, under section 536(2), the accused is asked to elect a mode of trial. However, if the offence is listed as in the absolute jurisdiction of a magistrate, then the accused does not elect and is tried in provincial court.[103] Similarly, if the offence is listed in section 469, the accused does not elect and is sent to a trial by judge and jury (subject to the attorney general's consent to dispense with the jury, as in section 473).

If the accused refuses to elect, then according to section 565(1)(c), the trial will be by judge and jury. The same is also true, under section 567, if there is more than one co-accused and they elect differently from one another. Further, even if the accused does not want a jury, the attorney general can compel a jury trial if the offence is punishable by more than five years, under section 568.

If the accused elects trial by a provincial court judge, the accused can then enter a plea and the trial can take place at any point.

---

103 Section 553.

If the accused elects trial by judge alone or trial by judge and jury, then under section 535, there might be a preliminary inquiry if the accused or the Crown request one. Preliminary inquiries are governed by the procedures in Part XVII of the *Code* (see Chapter 9). Note that an accused does not enter a plea at the preliminary inquiry stage: that is done in front of the court where the trial will take place.

A provincial court judge has the ability to convert a trial for an indictable offence into a preliminary inquiry under section 555(1) where this seems appropriate "for any reason." Similarly, under section 555(2), where the value of a stolen item turns out to be high enough that the offence was not one of absolute jurisdiction, the accused is offered an election, and the trial might become a preliminary inquiry. Conversely, where, under section 561(1)(a), an accused re-elects "down" to trial by provincial court judge during the preliminary inquiry, that preliminary can be turned into a trial under section 562.

The accused has various rights of re-election set out in section 561. Depending on whether the accused is re-electing up or down, and the point to which the proceedings have advanced, re-election is either as of right or requires consent from the prosecutor.

If an accused elects trial by judge and jury but then fails to appear, then, under section 598, the later trial will not be in front of a judge and jury unless the accused shows a legitimate excuse.

Following the preliminary inquiry, the judge will either discharge the accused or order the accused to stand trial on some offence in respect of the transaction charged. These powers are set out in section 548(1), but neither result is quite what it sounds like. First, "ordering the accused to stand trial" has no independent effect. It is simply a precondition to further action, normally by the Crown. For an indictable offence trial to take place, a new document, an "indictment" (hence "indictable offence") must be "preferred" (that is, laid in front of the trial court to commence trial). According to section 566, the indictment may be in Form 4 (also found in section 849). Section 576 dictates that an indictment can be preferred only on a basis set out in the *Criminal Code*. Some of those bases are set out in section 574, which permits an indictment to be preferred (1) on a charge for which the preliminary inquiry judge ordered the person to stand trial, or (2) on any charge founded on the facts disclosed at the preliminary inquiry. This latter provision means that the indictment may charge a different offence than the one charged in the information.

Where no preliminary inquiry is requested, section 574(1.1) permits an indictment to be preferred on any charge set out in an information after the accused has made an election on it.

Normally, these powers to prefer an indictment would be relied upon by a Crown prosecutor, but section 574(3) permits a private prosecutor to prefer an indictment with leave of the intended trial court.

Note that discharging the accused does not guarantee that the accused will not stand trial. Under section 577, an indictment can also be preferred where no preliminary inquiry was held, a preliminary inquiry was commenced but not concluded or, most notably, a preliminary inquiry was held and *the accused was discharged*. An indictment under these circumstances, usually referred to as a "direct indictment," requires the written consent of the attorney general, or, in the case of a private prosecution, an order of a judge of the court where the information is preferred.

The various discretionary powers of the Crown prosecutor mentioned above do not violate the *Charter*, provided they are not used abusively. The Crown also has other powers, including staying the proceedings with the ability to recommence them within one year, under section 579, and intervening to take over a private prosecution, under sections 579.01 and 579.1.

FURTHER READINGS

COUGHLAN, STEVE. "Tribunal Jurisdiction over *Charter* Remedies: Now You See It, Now You Don't" (2010) 75 *Criminal Reports* (6th) 238.

———— ET AL. *Law Beyond Borders: Extraterritorial Jurisdiction in an Age of Globalization* (Toronto: Irwin Law, 2014).

CURRIE, ROBERT J, & STEVE COUGHLAN. "Extraterritorial Criminal Jurisdiction: Bigger Picture or Smaller Frame?" (2007) 11 *Canadian Criminal Law Review* 141.

EDWARDS, JOHN. *The Law Officers of the Crown* (London: Sweet & Maxwell, 1964).

————. *The Attorney General, Politics and the Public Interest* (London: Sweet & Maxwell, 1984).

HEALY, PATRICK. "Constitutional Limits on the Allocation of Trial Jurisdiction to the Superior or Provincial Court in Criminal Matters" (2003) 48 *Criminal Law Quarterly* 31.

LAW REFORM COMMISSION OF CANADA. *Classification of Offences* (Ottawa: Law Reform Commission of Canada, 1986).

————. *Our Criminal Procedure* (Ottawa: Law Reform Commission of Canada, 1988).

————. *Controlling Criminal Prosecutions: The Attorney General and the Crown Prosecutor* (Ottawa: Law Reform Commission of Canada, 1990).

QUIGLEY, TIM. *Procedure in Canadian Criminal Law*, 2d ed (Toronto: Thomson Carswell, 2005) ch 3.

CHAPTER 4

SEARCH AND SEIZURE

A. INTRODUCTION

Other than in powers of arrest, the ability of police to interfere with the liberty of individuals is most evident in powers of search and seizure. Powers to search exist within the *Criminal Code* and other statutes and are also found at common law. Powers to seize are typically associated with search powers, though there are occasional exceptions to that rule.

The study of the law of search and seizure is made simpler by early decisions concerning section 8 of the *Canadian Charter of Rights and Freedoms*, which protects against "unreasonable search and seizure." The Court decided that, for purposes of section 8, a search which was not authorized by law was unreasonable.[1] The effect of that decision is to make the law of search and seizure and the *Charter* rules around search and seizure essentially co-extensive: broadly speaking, what is not authorized by law violates the *Charter*, but what is authorized by law does not. Accordingly, to understand the law of search and seizure, one needs to focus on the section 8 right.

One immediate consequence of this fact is that for section 8 to apply, as with any other *Charter* right, there must be state action involved.[2]

---

1   *R v Collins*, [1987] 1 SCR 265 [*Collins*].
2   In *Schreiber v Canada (Attorney General)*, [1998] 1 SCR 841, for example, the applicant objected to the gathering of information about his financial records in Switzerland. The Court held that the only action to which the applicant could

Typically, this will be the case, such as when a search is conducted by police or other investigative arms of the state. In some circumstances, other people, such as school officials, can constitute state actors.[3] Further, an individual can become an agent of the state in certain circumstances, if she conducts herself differently in an interaction because of her relationship to police or other state officials.[4] Without that sort of relationship, however, a private individual such as a security guard is not a state actor, and so *Charter* rights do not arise.[5]

Considering whether there has been an unreasonable search requires looking at two questions: was what occurred a search? And, if so, was the search unreasonable? All section 8 cases, no matter what the context, follow the same basic structure. First, it is necessary to decide whether the police investigative technique constituted a "search": that question is answered by determining whether the person had a "reasonable expectation of privacy."[6] If the answer is no, then whatever occurred was not a "search," and section 8 could not have been violated. On the other hand, if the answer is yes, then there was a search, and the second question must be asked: Was the search unreasonable? That second question is answered by applying the three-part *Collins* test: (1) was the search authorized by law; (2) was the law itself reasonable; and (3) was the manner in which the search was carried out reasonable?[7]

This chapter will follow that structure, looking first at reasonable expectation of privacy and then at the *Collins* test. However, there are additional foundational rules and principles that need to be recognized at the start.

---

object under the *Charter* was that taken by Canadian state officials, which was limited to sending a letter of request to Swiss officials. Sending that letter of request did not by itself violate his *Charter* rights.

3   *R v M(MR)*, [1998] 3 SCR 393 [*M(MR)*].

4   *R v Broyles*, [1991] 3 SCR 595; *R v Buhay*, 2003 SCC 30 [*Buhay*].

5   *Buhay*, *ibid*; *R v Jacobs*, 2014 ABCA 172. See also the discussion in Chapter 3, Section B(5).

6   In *Hunter v Southam Inc*, [1984] 2 SCR 145 [*Hunter*], the Supreme Court specifically rejected the notion that the intent of s 8 was to protect property rights and, instead, said that the important issue was privacy. The Court also observed that the s 8 right "might protect interests beyond the right of privacy" (*ibid* at 159). David Stratas, "*R v B(SA)* and the Right against Self-Incrimination: A Confusing Change of Direction" (2003) 14 *Criminal Reports* (6th) 227 [*Stratas*], observes that "while the Court opened the door to s 8 covering interests other than privacy back in *Hunter v Southam* in 1984, it has never gone through that door in any later case." In *R v SAB*, 2003 SCC 60 [*SAB*], the Court considered the extent to which s 8 protected an accused against self-incrimination, and that is to date still the only case that has considered anything other than privacy concerns when dealing with s 8.

7   *Collins*, above note 1 at para 23.

An important rule was established in one of the earliest *Charter* decisions, *Hunter v Southam Inc*: a warrantless search is *prima facie* unreasonable. That particular rule is a consequence of the more general principle that the purpose of section 8 is "*preventing* unjustified searches before they happen, not simply of determining, after the fact, whether they ought to have occurred in the first place."[8] The effect of this rule is to create a practical distinction between warrantless searches and searches with a warrant. In the former case, the burden shifts to the Crown to demonstrate that, despite the absence of a warrant, the search was nonetheless authorized by law.[9] There are, in fact, warrantless search powers, for the most part created at common law, and therefore typically less well defined than statutory powers. As a result, section 8 cases concerning warrantless searches tend to focus on the first step in the *Collins* test: Was the search authorized by law? On the other hand, in cases where a warrant provision exists and a warrant has been issued, that first step tends not to be controversial: instead, argument is more likely to focus on the second and third steps, whether the law itself is reasonable, and whether the manner of search was reasonable. Similarly, discussion of whether there was a reasonable expectation of privacy tends not to arise in cases of searches with a warrant: the fact that a warrant was required makes it obvious that there *was* such an expectation. Thus, although the same test applies in both situations, there are practical differences in application between searches with a warrant and searches without a warrant. Accordingly, this chapter will discuss those two situations separately.

One final overarching governing principle about searches must be noted. Rules relating to search and seizure (like all rules of criminal procedure) try to balance two competing interests: "that of the individual to be free of intrusions of the state and that of the state to intrude on the privacy of the individual for the purpose of law enforcement."[10] *Hunter* noted that the question was "whether in a particular situation the public's interest in being left alone by government must give way to the government's interest in intruding on the individual's privacy in order to advance its goals, notably those of law enforcement."[11] In

---

8 *Hunter*, above note 6 at 160 [emphasis in original].

9 *Ibid* at 161: s 8 "require[s] the party seeking to justify a warrantless search to rebut this presumption of unreasonableness."

10 *Baron v Canada*, [1993] 1 SCR 416 at para 24 [*Baron*]. See also *SAB*, above note 6 at para 43, where the Court noted that the issue in considering search powers is the balance between "the truth-seeking interests of law enforcement and the equally essential respect for individual rights."

11 *Hunter*, above note 6 at 159.

general, "[t]he state's interest in detecting and preventing crime begins to prevail over the individual's interest in being left alone at the point where credibly-based probability replaces suspicion."[12]

That standard creates a kind of benchmark against which all search powers can be measured. In essence, *Hunter* establishes that, where there is the "normal" expectation of privacy and the "normal" state interest, a search cannot be justified based on anything less than reasonable grounds. Sometimes, however, a person will have a reduced expectation of privacy, while in other circumstances, it will be enhanced: a search of a vehicle is usually regarded as relatively unintrusive, for example, while a body cavity search is a significant intrusion.[13] This change in the nature of the individual interest can shift the balance. Equally, the nature of the state interest can shift the balance. Search incident to arrest, for example,[14] is justified not because a person arrested has a lesser expectation of privacy, but because the immediate interest of the state in protecting the security of the arresting officer and others increases at the point of arrest.[15] Similarly, the state's interest in DNA evidence is significant, since it is a particularly powerful tool either to show an accused's guilt or prevent wrongful convictions.[16] The result of changing the nature of the competing interests in this way means that sometimes it is appropriate either to allow searches more readily or make them more difficult to authorize.

These considerations can be true of both warrantless searches and searches with a warrant, and we will see departures from the *Hunter* benchmark both upward and downward.[17] In some cases, searches will be allowed based on mere "reasonable suspicion" that an offence has been committed, as opposed to "reasonable grounds to believe."[18] In other

---

12 *Hunter, ibid* at 167.

13 On the reduced expectation of privacy in a vehicle generally, see *R v Wise*, [1992] 1 SCR 527 [*Wise*]; *R v Belnavis*, [1997] 3 SCR 341 [*Belnavis*]; and *R v Fliss*, [2002] 1 SCR 535 [*Fliss*]. On the intrusive nature of body cavity searches, see *R v Simmons*, [1988] 2 SCR 495 [*Simmons*].

14 See discussion at Section C(1)(a)(ii)(b), below in this chapter.

15 *R v Caslake*, [1998] 1 SCR 51 at para 17 [*Caslake*].

16 *SAB*, above note 6 at para 51.

17 Departures from the norm can also be justified based on a change in the state interest being protected. For example, searches are more readily permitted at border crossings, due as much to the enhanced state interest in preventing the entry of undesirable persons and prohibited goods as to the reduced expectation of privacy: *Simmons*, above note 13.

18 As will be noted below, a warrantless search using a sniffer dog is permitted based on reasonable suspicion, and a warrant to attach a device which will track the location of a vehicle (but not of a person) is allowed on reasonable suspicion.

cases, "reasonable grounds to believe" alone will not be enough, and it will also be necessary for the Crown to prove other factors, such as that issuing a particular warrant is in the best interests of the administration of justice.[19]

The Supreme Court has summarized these points:

> If, in the first instance, a reasonable expectation of privacy is determined to exist, a search intruding upon that interest will engage s 8 of the *Charter*. Because the *Charter* protects only against unreasonable searches, the next step after a reasonable expectation of privacy has been established is to inquire whether the search is reasonable. A search involving a *Charter*-protected privacy interest will be reasonable if the police are authorized by law to conduct the search, if the law authorizing the search is reasonable, and if the search is conducted in a reasonable manner (*R v Collins*, [1987] 1 SCR 265, at p 278). In most cases, this requires obtention of a search warrant requiring police to satisfy a judicial authority that there are reasonable and probable grounds to believe that a search will reveal evidence of an offence (see, e.g., *Criminal Code*, RSC 1985, c C-46, s 487). In certain situations where only a lowered expectation of privacy is recognized, police must instead have a reasonable suspicion that a search will uncover evidence of an offence before they may undertake it (see, e.g., *Kang-Brown*). Where no reasonable expectation of privacy is established, no threshold justification is required because the search does not trigger *Charter* protection (see, e.g., *Patrick*).[20]

With this overview established, we turn to the first question, that of reasonable expectation of privacy.

---

19   As will be noted below, electronic surveillance of communications without the consent of the parties requires showing not only reasonable grounds but also "investigative necessity," which amounts to showing that other evidence-gathering methods are unlikely to succeed. The common law power of conducting a strip search incident to arrest, as opposed to a pat-down search, requires not only reasonable grounds to think that an offence has been committed, but also reasonable grounds to believe that the person searched has a weapon and is a danger to the police or others: *R v Golden*, 2001 SCC 83 [*Golden*].

20   *R v Gomboc*, 2010 SCC 55 at para 20 [*Gomboc*]. There is no single majority opinion in *Gomboc*, but this passage from the judgment of Deschamps J (subscribed to directly by four of the nine judges) is not controversial.

B. REASONABLE EXPECTATION OF PRIVACY

It is important to note from the very start that a reasonable expectation of privacy plays two distinct roles in a search and seizure analysis. As already noted, it is what defines whether the police investigative technique is or is not a search: if the technique does not infringe a reasonable expectation of privacy, then it is not a search. Second, it helps define whether a particular search power is or is not "reasonable": simply put, if a person has a reduced expectation of privacy, then a lesser justification is needed before infringing on it, and if that person has an enhanced expectation of privacy, then a greater justification is needed.[21]

Courts tend only to engage in a single reasonable expectation of privacy analysis, but it is important to keep clearly in mind the difference between these two roles. At the first stage, the analysis is asking a purely binary question: Is there or is there not a reasonable expectation of privacy? As the Court has observed, "[a] reasonable though diminished expectation of privacy is nonetheless a reasonable expectation of privacy."[22] If there is, then the investigation constituted a search. It is not actually necessary, in determining this threshold question, to ask *where* on a scale of privacy expectations the accused's interest falls. At the second stage, however, of deciding whether the search that occurred was reasonable, a sliding scale is used.[23]

---

21 It is also frequently relevant in a third way: to help determine whether, if a person's s 8 right has been violated, the person is likely to receive a remedy; that is, the Court has established a test for exclusion of evidence, one consideration in which is the impact on the accused's *Charter*-protected interests: *R v Grant*, 2009 SCC 32 [*Grant*]. In that analysis, therefore, evidence is more likely to be excluded if the accused had a high expectation of privacy and less likely to be excluded in the case of a reduced expectation. An illegal search of a vehicle in which there is said to be a reduced expectation of privacy is a less serious violation, for example, than an unlawful body cavity search: see, for example, *Belnavis*, above note 13; *Fliss*, above note 13; and *Wise*, above note 13. More generally, the Court held in *Grant*, above in this note at para 78 that "[a]n unreasonable search that intrudes on an area in which the individual reasonably enjoys a high expectation of privacy, or that demeans his or her dignity, is more serious than one that does not."

22 *R v Cole*, 2012 SCC 53 at para 9 [*Cole*].

23 *R v Plant*, [1993] 3 SCR 281 [*Plant*], illustrates the wisdom of keeping a clear distinction between these two possible approaches. Police relied on the accused's electricity consumption records to seek a warrant to search his residence for marijuana, but they initially obtained those records without a warrant. The Court suggests at times that Plant had "no reasonable expectation of privacy with respect to the computerized electricity records" (at 295), at other times that he "cannot be said to have held a reasonable expectation of privacy in relation to

At the first stage, many things have been found to cross the threshold and therefore to be classified as a search. Frisking suspects, having them turn out their pockets, and so on are searches, but so is the passive technique of conducting a "bedpan vigil."[24] Both the physical act of installing a tracking device in a car and the subsequent electronic monitoring of that car's movements constitute searches.[25] An inspection of a workplace is a search.[26] A wiretap is a search,[27] as is video surveillance and all existing or future technology allowing the state to intrude electronically on privacy.[28] Executing a search warrant on the interior of a building is, of course, a search, but so is inspecting the perimeter of the building.[29] Using a drug-sniffer dog to smell a person's belongings or vehicle is a search.[30] Indeed, since it intrudes on a person's reasonable expectation of privacy, it is also a search when the police knock on a door to see whether they will be able to smell marijuana when it is opened.[31]

The same approach applies to deciding whether a "seizure" has occurred. The issue is not whether some measure of compulsion or deprivation was involved, but whether the accused's reasonable expectation of privacy was infringed. Thus, for example, making copies of a company's documents constitutes a seizure.[32] Further, even if a doctor willingly hands over a blood sample to the police, this will still be considered a seizure if the doctor was authorized to have the blood sample

---

the computerized electricity records *which outweighs* the state interest in enforcing the laws relating to narcotics offences" (at 296) [emphasis added]. If the latter characterization is the correct one, the Court really ought to have engaged in more analysis concerning the reasonableness of the search, not just Plant's expectation of privacy.

See also Lisa M Austin, "Is Consent the Foundation of Fair Information Practices? Canada's Experience under *PIPEDA*" (2006) 56 *University of Toronto Law Journal* 181, noting that "[a]lthough the threshold question and the balancing question are distinct, the jurisprudence is replete with examples where the two have been conflated." She suggests that this results in a kind of "double counting" against individual privacy interests, which inappropriately minimizes otherwise reasonable expectations of privacy.

24 *R v Monney*, [1999] 1 SCR 652.
25 *Wise*, above note 13.
26 *Amax Potash Ltd v Saskatchewan*, [1977] 2 SCR 576 [*Potash*].
27 *R v Duarte*, [1990] 1 SCR 30 [*Duarte*].
28 *R v Wong*, [1990] 3 SCR 36 at 43–44 [*Wong*].
29 *R v Kokesch*, [1990] 3 SCR 3 [*Kokesch*].
30 *R v Kang-Brown*, 2008 SCC 18 [*Kang-Brown*]; *R v AM*, 2008 SCC 19 [*AM*]; *R v Chehil*, 2013 SCC 49 [*Chehil*]; *R v MacKenzie*, 2013 SCC 50 [*MacKenzie*].
31 *R v Evans*, [1996] 1 SCR 8 [*Evans*]. The Court reaffirmed in *R v Patrick*, 2009 SCC 17 at para 52 [*Patrick*], the correctness of the rulings in *Kokesch*, above note 29 and *Evans*.
32 *Potash*, above note 26.

only for limited purposes.[33] Nonetheless, there is a distinction to be drawn between evidence that is "seized" and evidence that is merely "found." Thus, if the police take a sample of blood from a car seat at the scene of an accident, such action will not infringe the accused's reasonable expectation of privacy and will not be a seizure.[34]

Because it does not matter *to what extent* a reasonable expectation of privacy exists at the threshold stage, this test ought to be easy to meet: as noted earlier, this is a purely binary yes/no question. At a policy level, that also ought to be the case. To say that there is no reasonable expectation of privacy is to remove the police conduct from any possible scrutiny under section 8: if there was no reasonable expectation of privacy, then what occurred was not a search, and so no court will ever be entitled to assess whether what the state did was "unreasonable" or not.[35] The whole point of section 8 is to balance competing interests,[36] but to find no reasonable expectation of privacy is to remove any possibility of balancing. Put starkly, if some police investigative technique is found not to infringe a reasonable expectation of privacy, it amounts to saying that the police can use the technique any time, against anyone, anywhere, without the possibility of advance oversight or after-the-fact review. In contrast, to say that a person *does* have a reasonable expectation of privacy is not to say that she should be immune from search: merely that the search power must be a reasonable one.

In this context, it is worth noting that "reasonable expectation of privacy" is not an all-or-nothing issue. It is possible to give up the interest for some purposes while retaining it in other ways. For example, the reasonable expectation of privacy in one's home might be given up to the extent that visitors are given an implied licence to knock on the door to communicate with the resident: however, that implied licence does not give police the right to knock on the door if their real purpose is to conduct a warrantless "olfactory search."[37] Implied consent allowing a doctor to take a blood sample for medical purposes does not eliminate the reasonable expectation that the sample will not be used for other purposes.[38] A person speaking in the presence of others has accepted the risk of being seen and heard by those present, but that

---

33   *R v Dyment*, [1988] 2 SCR 417 [*Dyment*].
34   *R v Leblanc* (1981), 64 CCC (2d) 31 (NBCA), cited in *Dyment*, above note 33.
35   See, for example, *M(MR)*, above note 3 at para 31: "[I]f there is no reasonable expectation of privacy held by an accused with respect to the relevant place, there *can be no* violation of s 8" [emphasis added].
36   *Baron*, above note 10.
37   *Evans*, above note 31.
38   *Dyment*, above note 33.

does not imply any agreement to a permanent electronic record of the remarks being made.[39]

For the most part, the threshold stage has not been used as a barrier to section 8 protection, but that is not universally the case. Part of the difficulty arises from the *post facto* nature of the determination and from the unintended consequence of the combination of two rules: "if there is no reasonable expectation of privacy there was no search" and "a warrantless search is *prima facie* unreasonable." If one were building a set of search powers from the ground up, one might look at a situation and conclude "the accused has a much reduced expectation of privacy, but it is not non-existent, so the police should be required to obtain a warrant, but it should be relatively easy to obtain." In fact, though, courts typically are confronted with such situations after the fact, not beforehand, and the police have not, in fact, obtained a warrant or there would be no *Charter* claim. In such cases, a finding that there was a search will inevitably result in the finding that it was unreasonable because of the absence of a warrant. In close cases, therefore, it cannot be surprising that the option of concluding that the accused had no reasonable expectation of privacy (and therefore that what the police did was not a "search," after all) is sometimes an attractive way to avoid the conclusion that there was a *Charter* violation.[40]

As a final point about the threshold stage, note the potentially harmful long-term consequence to finding that a person had no reasonable expectation of privacy in close cases: it encourages police to push the envelope. If police are faced with a situation in which they know that they have no search power, they have a choice between not searching or searching on the chance that a judge will later decide that the accused had no reasonable expectation of privacy. From a principled constitutional perspective, we would like police to adopt the first choice: the purpose of section 8 is, after all, "*preventing* unjustified searches before they happen."[41] It is therefore unfortunate if courts adopt an approach which encourages police to adopt the second.

At the second stage of determining whether the search conducted was reasonable or not, calibrating the exact nature of the accused's rea-

---

39   *Wong*, above note 28 at para 22; *Duarte*, above note 27; and *Fliss*, above note 13.

40   Although courts do sometimes seem to feel this pressure, it is an unnecessary one because another option exists. A violation of s 8 does not automatically lead to the exclusion of the evidence. Evidence would be excluded under s 24(2) only following an analysis based on the factors set out in *Grant*, above note 21. One of those factors takes into account the accused's *Charter*-protected interests, and so if there was only a minimal reasonable expectation of privacy, it is much less likely that the evidence would be excluded.

41   *Hunter*, above note 6 at 160 [emphasis in original].

sonable expectation of privacy becomes more important. In fact, there is a test for determining that issue, but one general observation should be made first.

It is crucial to recognize that "reasonable" in this context is intended to be an assessment of *entitlement* to privacy, not a measure of whether a person, as a matter of fact, *has* privacy. Reasonable expectation of privacy "is not a purely factual inquiry. The reasonable expectation of privacy standard is normative rather than simply descriptive."[42] The assessment is "laden with value judgments which are made from the independent perspective of the reasonable and informed person who is concerned about the long-term consequences of government action for the protection of privacy."[43] In particular, reasonable expectation of privacy should *not* be judged based on a risk analysis. Speaking in the particular context of video surveillance, the Court noted that "we can only be sure of being free from surveillance today if we retire to our basements, cloak our windows, turn out the lights and remain absolutely quiet."[44] The correct question is to ask about "the standards of privacy that persons can *expect* to enjoy in a free and democratic society."[45] Thus, for example, a person whose property is stolen still has a reasonable expectation of privacy in that property, despite the obvious fact that the thief has, at least temporarily, rendered that interest ineffective in any practical sense.[46]

That a risk analysis is not the proper approach is unambiguous. Unfortunately, there is still sometimes a tendency for courts to slip into looking at the ease with which things *can* be searched and taking that to determine the reasonable expectation of privacy analysis. In part, this might be the case because, although there is a structured test for analyzing privacy, asking about the normative entitlement to privacy is not explicitly one of the steps: that principle is meant to govern the overarching approach rather than be inquired into independently. Beyond that, of course, it is easier to go about assessing whether privacy *can* be intruded on in a particular situation and harder to assess whether it *should* be intruded upon, and so there can be a tendency to fall into the easier but incorrect approach.[47]

---

42   *R v Spencer*, 2014 SCC 43 at para 18 [*Spencer*].
43   *Patrick*, above note 31. See also *R v Tessling*, [2004] 3 SCR 432 at para 42 [*Tessling*].
44   *Wong*, above note 28 at para 11.
45   *Ibid* at para 46 [emphasis added].
46   *R v Law*, [2002] 1 SCR 227.
47   See, for example, *R v Boersma*, [1994] 2 SCR 488, aff'g [1993] BCJ No 2748 at para 11 (CA), where the Court upheld a British Columbia Court of Appeal decision that an accused growing marijuana on Crown land had no reasonable expectation of privacy based on the question of "whether they were susceptible

That said, let us turn to the actual test for determining whether a person has a reasonable expectation of privacy, usually referred to as the "totality of the circumstances" test.[48] Over a number of years, the Court has identified various factors to be taken into account, gradually adapting the test as different relevant considerations have come to light. As it is applied now, these factors are considered under four headings: (1) the subject matter of the alleged search; (2) the claimant's interest in the subject matter; (3) the claimant's subjective expectation of privacy in the subject matter; and (4) whether this subjective expectation of privacy was objectively reasonable, having regard to the totality of the circumstances.[49] Many different considerations can arise under each heading, and exactly what factors will be taken into account in any given case depends on which are most relevant. No single factor is controlling; it is a matter of weighing the considerations and coming to a conclusion.

The "subject matter of the alleged search" is sometimes obvious, but not necessarily. The real subject matter needs to be identified precisely because, for example, a person with no privacy interest in a place might nonetheless have a reasonable expectation of privacy with regard to an item found in that place.[50] Similarly, other factors in the test might apply differently depending on how the subject matter is identified: garbage bags might be in public view although their contents are not, for example.[51]

This subject matter of the search is to be assessed not "narrowly in terms of the physical acts involved or the physical space invaded, but

---

to being seen by other people." See the discussion of this issue in James Stribopoulos, "Reasonable Expectation of Privacy and 'Open Fields'—Taking the American 'Risk Analysis' Head On" (1999) 25 *Criminal Reports* (5th) 351. In *R v Kwiatkowski*, 2010 BCCA 124, it was found that an accused had no reasonable expectation of privacy in the contents of greenhouses located in a wooded and difficult-to-access portion of a remote rural property, on the basis that a police officer flying over neighbouring property 1000 feet away and using a telephoto lens on one occasion saw a plant he thought was marijuana through an open door. See also the discussion in Steve Coughlan, "*Kwiatkowski*: Privacy Protection and Risk Analysis: Losing the Forest in the Telephoto Shots of the Trees" (2010) 73 *Criminal Reports* (6th) 260. See also Austin, above note 23.

48   *R v Edwards*, [1996] 1 SCR 128 at para 31 [*Edwards*].

49   *Spencer*, above note 42 at para 18. See also *Tessling*, above note 43 at para 42, or *Patrick*, above note 31 at para 27.

50   *Edwards*, above note 48; *Belnavis*, above note 13, and *Plant*, above note 23, all raise this possibility, though, in fact, none of the accused succeeded with the claim. In *Belnavis*, for example, the Court allowed the possibility that a passenger who had no reasonable expectation of privacy in the vehicle in which she was found might, nonetheless, have had a reasonable expectation of privacy in the bags next to her, making a search of those bags unreasonable.

51   *Patrick*, above note 31 at para 53.

rather by reference to the nature of the privacy interests potentially compromised by the state action."[52] So, for example, in *R v Patrick* the police took a garbage bag from the accused's property, and the Crown argued that the subject matter of the search should be considered only that: garbage. The Court held that that argument "assumes away" the point in issue and that the subject matter of the search should be considered in light of the reason the police seized the bag: because it was "a bag of 'information' whose contents, viewed in their entirety, paint a fairly accurate and complete picture of the householder's activities and lifestyle."[53] In *R v Kang-Brown* the police used a sniffer dog on the accused's luggage, and the Court rejected the position that the subject matter of the search was the air around the bag: rather, the subject matter was the contents of the bag, an inference about which could be made from the dog's reactions.[54] In *R v Spencer* the police knew that a particular IP address had downloaded child pornography and obtained the accused's name and address from the service provider. The Court held there that the subject matter of the search was not merely the accused's name and address, which would not attract much privacy protection, but instead "the identity of a subscriber whose Internet connection is linked to particular, monitored Internet activity."[55]

The second factor, the claimant's interest in the subject matter, is not normally an obstacle to a privacy claim. Where a person's house, vehicle, pocket, or body cavity is searched, it is obvious that she has a direct interest. The accused's interest need not be proprietary or even necessarily a possessory to attract privacy protection.[56] In *Spencer*, for example, the fact that the accused used an Internet connection with permission of the subscriber was sufficient to give him an interest capable of attracting privacy protection in that Internet activity.

A noteworthy point about the accused's interest is that whether the activity is illegal or not should not be taken into account. In *R v Wong*, for example, the police had placed a hidden camera in a hotel room. The Ontario Court of Appeal had concluded that a person who rents a hotel room in order to conduct illegal gambling has no reasonable expectation of privacy, but the Supreme Court held that this was the wrong way to frame the issue. The question that had to be asked was whether someone renting a hotel room had a reasonable expectation of privacy—the nature of the activity carried on within it was

---

52   *Spencer*, above note 42 at para 31, quoting *R v Ward*, 2012 ONCA 660 at para 65.
53   *Patrick*, above note 31 at para 30.
54   *Kang-Brown*, above note 30.
55   *Spencer*, above note 42 at para 33.
56   See, for example, *Plant*, above note 23 at 291.

not relevant.[57] Similarly, in *Patrick* the Alberta Court of Appeal had reasoned that the accused had no privacy interest in evidence (found in garbage bags) that he was involved in manufacturing drugs because that information was not part of the core biographical details to which privacy protection ought to be extended. The Supreme Court rejected that approach, holding: "The issue is not whether the appellant had a legitimate privacy interest in the concealment of drug paraphernalia, but whether people generally have a privacy interest in the concealed contents of an opaque and sealed 'bag of information.'"[58] Equally in *Spencer* the issue was whether people generally have a privacy interest in their Internet activity: that the accused's particular activity was to download child pornography did not change the question.[59]

Although many types of interests are sufficient to satisfy this consideration, it is possible for a claim to fail based largely on this factor. For example, in *R v Edwards*, police conducted a warrantless search of an apartment rented by the accused's girlfriend, which meant that it was, if it was a search, an unreasonable one. However, the accused could object under the *Charter* only if it was a violation of *his* section 8 right, rather than a violation of someone else's rights. That is, unless the accused personally had a reasonable expectation of privacy in his girlfriend's apartment, *he* did not have a reasonable expectation of privacy in that location and so he had no section 8 claim. In fact, the Court found that, based on the totality of the circumstances, he was only a "privileged guest" in the apartment, rather than a person who had a reasonable expectation of privacy in it.[60] In *R v Belnavis*, this same reasoning led to the conclusion that a passenger in a vehicle—at

---

57   *Wong*, above note 28 at para 19.

58   *Patrick*, above note 31 at para 32. There, the Court also said: "The issue ought to be framed in terms of the privacy of the area or thing being searched and the potential impact of the search on the person being searched, not the nature or identity of the concealed items."

59   *Spencer*, above note 42 at para 36: "the issue is not whether Mr. Spencer had a legitimate privacy interest in concealing his use of the Internet for the purpose of accessing child pornography, but whether people generally have a privacy interest in subscriber information with respect to computers which they use in their home for private purposes."

60   The Court reached this conclusion based on a number of considerations most of which have subsequently come to be included in other portions of the reasonable expectation of privacy test as articulated in *Patrick*, above note 31, or *Spencer*, above note 42; see *Edwards*, above note 48 at para 31. It is therefore arguable that this consideration does not purely fall under "the nature of the accused's interest." However, the Court has regularly restructured the totality of the circumstances test and the way factors are to be considered, and in its current formulation, this seems to be the most appropriate place to include it.

least on the facts of that case—had no reasonable expectation of privacy.[61] Once again, that meant that the accused had no section 8 claim, despite a warrantless search that the trial judge found to have taken place without reasonable and probable grounds.

One can envision these cases as ruling that because the accused had no reasonable expectation of privacy, she was not searched at all and therefore could not have been unreasonably searched. However, the result is also sometimes presented as a question of standing: that an accused does not have standing to object to the violation of someone else's section 8 right. *Belnavis* adopts the former description, while *Edwards* uses the latter. Both *Edwards* and *Belnavis* saw vigorous dissenting judgments from LaForest J, decrying the dilution of section 8 protection that was inherent in the decisions. They have also been criticized, for example, for giving police an improper motive to conduct searches they know to be unreasonable.[62] Nonetheless, they remain a part of the reasonable expectation of privacy test.

---

61 *Belnavis*, above note 13. *Belnavis* is not meant to establish that a passenger *never* has a reasonable expectation of privacy in a vehicle; the decision is always to be made based on the totality of the circumstances. See, for example, *R v Dreyer*, 2008 BCCA 89, where the Court of Appeal concluded that the passenger in a vehicle who was being driven, as he often was, by his sister "had the same expectation of privacy of his property in the car as would a passenger with a shopping bag in a taxi" (para 13). In contrast, see *R v Plummer*, 2011 ONCA 350 [*Plummer*], which does deny standing to raise s 8 to a person sitting in a car, but which has been criticized for being too formulaic in its reasoning: see Paul Calarco, "*R v Plummer*: Standing to Challenge Searches" (2011) 85 *Criminal Reports* (6th) 62.

62 Steven Penney, "Unreasonable Search and Seizure and Section 8 of the *Charter*: Cost-Benefit Analysis in Constitutional Interpretation" (2013) 62 *Supreme Court Law Review* (2d) 101 at para 44, observes:

Consider the following scenario: police suspect (without objective grounds) that a group of young Aboriginal or African-Canadian men are drug traffickers and collectively use a particular car or apartment for their business. If police search either place without grounds or a warrant, they will undoubtedly violate the section 8 rights of the owner or driver of the car as well as the residents of the apartment. Any evidence obtained would likely be excluded in any prosecution of these individuals. But it is unlikely that any other person found in the car or apartment could make a section 8 claim. Knowing this, police have an incentive to search illegally, since not searching will uncover no evidence, but searching could reveal evidence admissible against those without sufficient possessory interests.

In contrast to *Edwards*, above note 48, and *Belnavis*, above note 13, see *R v Pelucco*, 2015 BCCA 370 [*Pelucco*]. The accused had been exchanging text messages with a person to whom he was trying to sell cocaine. Unbeknownst to the accused, the other person had been arrested (unlawfully) in the midst of

The third general heading for reasonable expectation of privacy claims is the claimant's subjective expectation of privacy in the subject matter. The Court has observed that the subjective expectation portion of the analysis is "not a high hurdle," that testimony from the accused about her subjective expectation is not a necessary requirement, and that a subjective expectation of privacy in activities associated with the home is to be presumed.[63] In R v Cole the accused's subjective expectation of privacy in the informational content of his laptop was inferred simply from the facts that he used it to browse the Internet and stored personal information on the hard drive.[64]

Further, the Court has warned against allowing the subjective issue to settle matters:

> The *subjective* expectation of privacy is important but its absence should not be used too quickly to undermine the protection afforded by s 8 to the values of a free and democratic society. In an age of expanding means for snooping readily available on the retail market, ordinary people may come to fear (with or without justification) that their telephones are wiretapped or their private correspondence is being read . . . . Suggestions that a diminished *subjective* expectation of privacy should automatically result in a lowering of constitutional protection should therefore be opposed. It is one thing to say that a person who puts out the garbage has no reasonable expectation of privacy in it. It is quite another to say that someone who fears their telephone is bugged no longer has a subjective expectation of privacy and thereby forfeits the protection of s 8. Expectation of privacy is a normative rather than a descriptive standard.[65]

Despite this clear statement that a subjective expectation of privacy is not a *sine qua non*, there is a lurking ambiguity over the point. In describing the privacy analysis in *Patrick* the Court asked whether the accused subjectively had a reasonable expectation of privacy and "if so"

---

the conversation and the police began sending replies that led to the accused being arrested and charged. Pelucco successfully argued that the police violated *his* reasonable expectation of privacy in reading his text messages on the other person's cell phone, seized as a result of the unlawful arrest.

63 *Patrick*, above note 31 at para 37.
64 *Cole*, above note 22 at para 43.
65 *Tessling*, above note 43 at para 42 [emphasis in original]. See also *Patrick*, above note 31 at para 14: "A government that increases its snooping on the lives of citizens, and thereby makes them suspicious and reduces their expectation of privacy, will not thereby succeed in unilaterally reducing their constitutional entitlement to privacy protection."

whether that expectation was reasonable.[66] The phrase "if so" could indicate that a failure at the subjective stage relieves the judge of the need to go any further.[67] The subsequent formulation of the test in *Spencer* does not use the words "if so," but it does describe the fourth heading in the test as "whether this subjective expectation of privacy was objectively reasonable":[68] that *could* be read as stating that there must be a subjective expectation of privacy. It seems unlikely that the Court intended to signal a reverse of its previous unambiguous position that a subjective expectation of privacy is not essential in such an oblique and stealthy fashion. It would also not make sense for a single factor to be determinative in what is always referred to as the "*totality* of the circumstances" test. Nonetheless, it is not an impossible reading. This assessment matters especially because accused persons often choose not to testify, even on a *voir dire*, and so there might be no direct evidence about that person's subjective expectation. One hopes this point will be clarified at some near opportunity.

The fourth heading is whether an expectation of privacy would be objectively reasonable. This heading is subject to the most variation in application from case to case, and, indeed, the Court has noted that "there is no definitive list of factors that must be considered in answering this question."[69] For example, in *Edwards*, a number of factors were said to be relevant: presence at the time of the search; possession or control of the property or place searched; ownership of the property or place; historical use of the property or item; and the ability to regulate access, including the right to admit or exclude others from the place.[70] In *Patrick*, a long and different list of considerations was used: the place where the alleged "search" occurred and whether the police trespassed; whether the informational content of the subject matter was in public view; whether the informational content of the subject matter had been abandoned; whether the information was already in the hands of third parties and if so whether it was subject to an obligation of confidentiality; whether the police technique was intrusive in relation to the privacy interest; whether the use of the evidence-gathering technique was itself objectively unreasonable; and whether the informational content exposed any intimate details of the appellant's lifestyle or information

66   *Patrick, ibid* at para 27.
67   *R v Grunwald*, 2010 BCCA 288. See also *R v Chehil*, 2009 NSCA 111 [*Chehil* NSCA], noting this ambiguity.
68   *Spencer*, above note 42 at para 18.
69   *Cole*, above note 22 at para 45.
70   *Edwards*, above note 48 at para 45.

of a biographical nature.[71] In *Spencer*, in contrast, the objective reasonableness question was determined almost exclusively by considering the contractual and statutory framework governing the accused's Internet usage.[72]

There is a good reason for this wide variation from case to case, which relates to a growing understanding of the nature of "privacy." A reasonable expectation of privacy includes at least three separate types of interest that ought to be distinguished: (1) personal privacy, (2) territorial privacy, and (3) informational privacy.[73] Personal privacy relates essentially to the body, though it covers a range of situations: whether one can be frisked, strip-searched, or subject to a body cavity search, for example. Territorial privacy relates to searches of places and is contingent on the particular place being searched (a person typically has the greatest degree of privacy in a home, less in a motor vehicle, and less still in a prison, for example). Informational privacy protects "a biographical core of personal information which individuals in a free and democratic society would wish to maintain and control from dissemination to the state" as well as "information which tends to reveal intimate details of the lifestyle and personal choices of the individual."[74]

It is largely because "privacy" does not have a single meaning that the list of relevant factors in the objective assessment can vary so widely. In listing relevant factors in *Edwards*, the Court had territorial privacy in mind, and so the considerations are relevant to that issue. Whether the accused was present or not at the time of the search could affect how reasonable the search of an apartment might be, for example, and so is a useful territorial privacy consideration. However, it is a factor which could not fail to be satisfied in the context of a body cavity search but which will never be satisfied when police obtain information from an Internet service provider, and so it is difficult to see how it is even relevant to either personal or informational privacy. Therefore, depending on the type of privacy claim at issue, different factors will be taken into account.

Cases need not be rigidly fitted into one of the three types of privacy: those are merely analytical guides, and a claim can assert overlapping

---

71 *Patrick*, above note 31 at para 27.

72 *Spencer*, above note 42 at para 52ff.

73 *Tessling*, above note 43 at para 20. See also *SAB*, above note 6 at para 40, relying on *Dyment*, above note 33: "privacy may include territorial or spacial aspects, aspects related to the person, and aspects that arise in the informational context."

74 *Tessling*, above note 43 at para 25 [emphasis omitted], quoting *Plant*, above note 23.

interests.[75] In *Tessling*, for example, police trained a Forward Looking Infrared camera (FLIR) on the accused's home following a tip that he was conducting a marijuana grow operation, in order to determine the pattern and amount of heat being emitted: that was found to be a partly territorial claim, since the police were interested in what was going on inside the house, but primarily an informational privacy interest.[76]

At one point there appeared to be some danger of informational privacy becoming the "weak sister" of privacy claims. Personal privacy, raising issues of body cavity or strip searches and the autonomy of the person, has been seen as particularly important.[77] Similarly, territorial privacy has long been recognized as very important: in the maxim that a home is a person's castle, for example.[78] In *Plant*, *Tessling*, and *Patrick*, in contrast, claims that might have been seen as being about the home were cast as informational privacy claims, and in each case the accused was found to have no reasonable expectation.[79] For a time, lower courts held that observations such as how an accused behaved while in an ambulance, or the undetectable-by-humans odours coming from belongings, to be mere information.[80] In particular, it was often observed that

---

75   *Patrick*, above note 31 at para 26.

76   *Tessling*, above note 43 at para 24. Similarly in *Gomboc*, above note 20 at para 22, police attached a Digital Readout Ammeter (DRA) to power lines entering the accused's home, in order to detect the pattern of electrical usage. This was treated as straddling informational and territorial privacy.

77   See also *Golden*, above note 19, or *Dyment*, above note 33.

78   Among other cases referring to the notion, see *Tessling*, above note 43, *R v Silveira*, [1995] 2 SCR 297 [*Silveira*], or *R v Feeney*, [1997] 2 SCR 13 [*Feeney*].

79   *Plant*, above note 23, permitted police to obtain electrical consumption records about the accused's home from a power company without a warrant. *Tessling*, above note 43, as noted, concerned the use of a FLIR to detect heat patterns in the home, and *Patrick*, above note 31, involved reaching across the accused's property line to take garbage bags.

       In *Tessling* the Court held that the FLIR information did not attract informational privacy because on its own it was "meaningless." Stuart criticized this reasoning, pointing out that if the records reveal no personal information, the Court should not have concluded that they helped give reasonable grounds for issuing a search warrant: Don Stuart, *Charter Justice in Canadian Criminal Law*, 5th ed (Toronto: Thomson Carswell, 2010) at 268. See also Renée Pomerance, "Shedding Light on the Nature of Heat: Defining Privacy in the Wake of *R v Tessling*" (2005) 23 *Criminal Reports* (6th) 229; James A Stringham, "Reasonable Expectations Reconsidered: A Return to the Search for a Normative Core for Section 8?" (2005) 23 *Criminal Reports* (6th) 245; and Steve Coughlan & Marc S Gorbet, "Nothing Plus Nothing Equals . . . Something?: A Proposal for FLIR Warrants on Reasonable Suspicion" (2005) 23 *Criminal Reports* (6th) 239.

80   See, for example, *R v LaChappelle*, 2007 ONCA 655; *R v Taylor*, 2006 NLCA 41; *R v Brown*, 2006 ABCA 199 [*Brown* 2006]. *Brown* 2006 has since been reversed

the information in question was not part of the accused's "biographical core of personal information" and so was not protected by the *Charter*. In each case the result was that the Court found the accused to have no reasonable expectation of privacy, and therefore no search in the meaning of section 8 had occurred: consequently, there was no section 8 violation. These cases were the subject of critical comment.[81]

Fortunately, informational privacy seems ultimately to have come into its own. In *R v Morelli*, for example, where the accused was subject to a search warrant which resulted in his home computer being searched, it was held that it was difficult to imagine a search which could be more intrusive, extensive, or invasive of privacy.[82] Similarly, in *Spencer* the Court re-emphasized that informational privacy protects not *just* "biographical core" material, but also "information which tends to reveal intimate details of the lifestyle and personal choices of the individual."[83]

Indeed, *Spencer* goes further, elaborating and expanding on the meaning of "informational privacy." That concept includes at least three conceptually distinct but overlapping concepts: privacy as secrecy, priva-

---

by the Supreme Court of Canada: *Kang-Brown*, above note 30. The decision is complex because there are four opinions and no clear majority on any single approach. However, all nine judges agreed that there was a reasonable expectation of privacy and that the dog sniff was a search. Indeed, only one judgment even discusses that question, with the other seven judges taking it as simply unquestioned that the dog sniff was a search. In the companion case, *AM*, above note 30, Binnie J did suggest that a dog sniff was "through the wall" technology, and that, unlike a FLIR, it permitted precise inferences about the concealed interior.

81   See Don Stuart, "Police Use of Sniffer Dogs Ought to Be Subject to *Charter* Standards: Dangers of *Tessling* Come to Roost" (2005) 31 *Criminal Reports* (6th) 255; Steve Coughlan, "Privacy Goes to the Dogs" (2006) 40 *Criminal Reports* (6th) 31; Jonathan Shapiro, "Narcotics Dogs and the Search for Illegality: American Law in Canadian Courts" (2007) 43 *Criminal Reports* (6th) 299.

82   2010 SCC 8 at para 2 [*Morelli*]. The Court also held at para 105:

As I mentioned at the outset, it is difficult to imagine a more intrusive invasion of privacy than the search of one's home and personal computer. Computers often contain our most intimate correspondence. They contain the details of our financial, medical, and personal situations. They even reveal our specific interests, likes, and propensities, recording in the browsing history and cache files the information we seek out and read, watch, or listen to on the Internet.

See also *Cole*, above note 22, finding a teacher to have a reasonable expectation of privacy in the contents of a laptop which was issued to him by the school board for which he worked.

83   *Spencer*, above note 42 at para 27. See also the discussion of "biographical core" information in Penney, above note 62.

cy as control, and privacy as anonymity.[84] Privacy as secrecy is reflected in many areas of the law and is primarily concerned with confidentiality. This is related to privacy as control, which is the claim to determine for oneself when, how, and to what extent personal information is communicated to others. Privacy as anonymity matters when pieces of information are already known, but are not yet connected to any individual: for example, when an accused knows that there is a police informant but does not know who that informant is. In such cases, the privacy "is not simply the individual's name, but the link between the identified individual and the personal information provided anonymously."[85]

Privacy as anonymity is particularly important in the context of Internet usage. People can reasonably wish, for example, to present ideas publicly without being associated with them. Further, the Internet gathers a great deal of information about individuals without their knowledge or control, but guarding the link between the information and the identity of the person to whom it relates assures the user that the activity remains private. Accordingly, the identity of a person linked to his or her use of the Internet gives rise to a privacy interest beyond that inherent in the person's name, address, and telephone number found in the subscriber information. In *Spencer* itself, this meant that the police request to the Internet service provider for subscriber information corresponding to specifically observed, anonymous Internet activity engaged a high level of informational privacy.[86]

There are at least two particular considerations about the objective reasonableness portion of the totality of the circumstances test that remain something of a problem point: the role of abandonment and the impact of private contracts or public regulatory schemes.

Abandonment was the central issue in *Patrick*. The police reached across the accused's back fence to take garbage bags that he had left for collection adjacent to his property line in an open container where they were within easy reach of anyone walking by. The accused's privacy claim failed because he was found to have abandoned the bags. This was so not because it was physically possible for others to reach the garbage bags, but rather because the accused "had done everything required of him to commit his rubbish to the municipal collection system."[87]

Abandonment is a powerful doctrine capable of defeating an otherwise strong privacy claim. All other factors favoured Patrick's privacy

---

84   *Spencer*, above note 42 at para 38.
85   *Ibid* at para 42.
86   *Ibid* at para 51.
87   *Patrick*, above note 31 at para 55.

claim, but it failed because he had abandoned the bags.[88] It is therefore important that some careful limits be set on the concept. In *Patrick*, for example, although the Court was not concerned that the police violated the accused's airspace by reaching across the fence to take the garbage bags, they stressed that that did not mean that police could take garbage bags left on a porch, in a garage, or within the immediate vicinity of the dwelling house: in those cases, the accused would not unequivocally have abandoned them.[89] Similarly, the police could not rent a cherry picker to take items from parts of the property not within reach on the basis that they would not be able to without setting foot on it.[90]

Further, *R v Stillman* held: "where an accused who is not in custody discards a kleenex or cigarette butt, the police may ordinarily collect and test these items without any concern about consent. A different situation is presented when an accused in custody discards items containing bodily fluids."[91] In that case, the accused was found not to have abandoned a tissue which he threw in a garbage can, since he was in custody for many days and could not possibly avoid creating bodily samples at some point. Similarly, in *R v Nguyen*, the Ontario Court of Appeal found a seizure, and a section 8 violation, when police officers offered an accused a piece of gum while transporting him from detention to court, knowing that he would need to discard the gum before he entered the courtroom.[92]

That said, there is a tendency for the Crown to argue abandonment any time an accused has parted company in some way with an object or information, sometimes successfully. It has been suggested that when an accused who is being pursued or otherwise interacting with the police throws away a backpack, tosses a gun out a window, pulls the battery from a BlackBerry and throws it to the ground, runs away leaving behind a jacket, jumps out of a vehicle in order to flee, or even hands over a document on request, he should be found to have abandoned any privacy interest in the item.[93] The same argument has been

---

88 *Ibid* at para 40.
89 *Ibid* at para 62.
90 *Ibid* at paras 62 and 44.
91 [1997] 1 SCR 607 at para 62 [*Stillman*].
92 (2002), 48 CR (5th) 338 (Ont CA) [*Nguyen*].
93 See, respectively, *R v Nesbeth*, 2008 ONCA 579 [*Nesbeth*]; *R v Stevens*, 2012 ONCA 307 [*Stevens*], leave to appeal to SCC refused, [2012] SCCA No 23; *R v Tsekouras*, 2014 ONSC 2420 [*Tsekouras*]; *R v Reddy*, 2010 BCCA 11; *R v Gambilla*, 2015 ABQB 40 [*Gambilla*]; *R v Leong*, 2014 BCPC 99. See also *Plummer*, above note 61, where the accused was found both to have no reasonable expectation of privacy in a handgun he had left behind when fleeing the scene, but also to

made around the deletion of computer files[94] or the failure to password-protect a cell phone.[95] Sometimes, these claims have succeeded.[96] An equally plausible claim in most of these situations is that the accused is *asserting*, rather than renouncing, a privacy interest by taking such action, but is faced with limited options as to how to make such an assertion.[97] In fact, such situations will often be tailor-made for the "privacy as anonymity" argument from *Spencer*: what the person is trying to keep private is the link between her and the information.

More work remains to be done in this area.

The other continuing problem point is the impact of private contracts or public regulatory schemes. There have been many cases where police have obtained information from an Internet service provider, electrical company, or other business without a warrant. A question which has arisen on such occasions is whether the accused had a reasonable expectation of privacy in the information.[98] In such cases, a controlling factor has frequently been either the terms of the contract between the company and the customer, or the terms of the *Personal*

---

have sufficient control over it to be guilty of possession. Criticizing that decision, see Calarco, above note 61.

94 *R v McNeice*, 2013 BCCA 98 [*McNeice*].

95 In *R v Fearon*, 2014 SCC 77 at para 53 [*Fearon*], the Court held that "[a]n individual's decision not to password protect his or her cell phone does not indicate any sort of abandonment of the significant privacy interests one generally will have in the contents of the phone."

96 *Nesbeth*, above note 93, *Stevens*, above note 93, and *Gambilla*, above note 93, were all cases where the accused was found to have no remaining privacy interest. See also *R v LB*, 2007 ONCA 596, where the accused was asked who owned a satchel sitting near him and replied "I don't know," when as a matter of fact it was his: he was found to be precluded from putting forward a s 8 claim because he had renounced his privacy interest.

97 This is essentially the conclusion in some cases. *McNeice*, above note 94, for example, observes at para 52 that "deletion of the files is more consistent with an intention on the part of the user to destroy the information, or at least to conceal it from view by anyone else, including himself." See also *Tsekouras*, above note 93. For further discussion of abandonment, see the discussion in Penney, above note 62, and Steve Coughlan, "On Abandonment and Flight" (2014) 10 *Criminal Reports* (7th) 322.

98 See *Chehil* NSCA, above note 67, dealing with an airline passenger manifest. For pre-*Spencer* cases considering whether a person has a privacy interest in the name and address associated with a particular IP address, see *R v Ward*, 2008 ONCJ 355; *R v Friers*, 2008 ONCJ 740; *R v Trapp*, 2009 SKPC 5; and *R v Wilson*, [2009] OJ No 1067 (SCJ), for decisions where an accused was found not to have a reasonable expectation of privacy, and *R v Kwok*, [2008] OJ No 2414 (Ct J), and *R v Cuttell*, 2009 ONCJ 471, for cases reaching the opposite conclusion. *Spencer*, above note 42, concluded that a reasonable expectation of privacy did exist.

Information Protection and Electronic Documents Act, often known as *PIPEDA*.[99]

In *R v Godbout*, for example, a clause in a contract with a courier company said "governmental authorities . . . may also open and inspect any shipment and its contents at any time." The British Columbia Court of Appeal found "that that clause negated any objectively reasonable expectation of privacy."[100] In other cases, some courts have reasoned roughly along the lines that since *PIPEDA* or the individual contract envisions the possibility of information being provided to the police in *some* circumstances, the accused cannot reasonably expect privacy: in that event, obtaining the information is not a "search" and so no warrant is necessary. Ironically, this approach results in the protection of privacy act diminishing privacy protection.

This issue was directly before the Court in *Spencer*, where the question was whether the accused had a reasonable expectation of privacy in the ISP records linking him to the IP address that had downloaded child pornography. The Crown argued the accused had no such expectation, relying both on the terms of the contract and on *PIPEDA*. The Court concluded that Spencer was, in fact, entitled to section 8 protection and that "the contractual and statutory framework may be relevant to, but not necessarily determinative of, whether there is a reasonable expectation of privacy."[101] In that case, the contract was confusing and equivocal, but supported the existence of a reasonable expectation of privacy since it narrowly circumscribed the Internet service provider's right to disclose the personal information of subscribers. Similarly, the existence of some possibility of disclosure of information under *PIPEDA* did not have the consequence that no reasonable expectation of privacy existed.[102]

Spencer is a very positive development with regard to the issue of private contracts. It stresses a normative approach, which is the important issue. In principle, nothing prevents all Internet service providers from including a clause in their privacy policies which says "we will hand over any information about you to anyone we want any time we

---

99 SC 2000, c 5 [*PIPEDA*].

100 *R v Godbout*, 2014 BCCA 319 at para 27. Note that this decision adopts a risk analysis rather than a normative-based approach to privacy: see Steve Coughlan, "Signing Away Rights: Should Private Contracts Trump the *Charter*?" (2014) 13 *Criminal Reports* (7th) 124.

101 *Spencer*, above note 42 at para 54.

102 *Ibid* at para 62: "*PIPEDA* thus cannot be used as a factor to weigh against the existence of a reasonable expectation of privacy since the proper interpretation of the relevant provision itself depends on whether such a reasonable expectation of privacy exists."

want," which would mean that as *a matter of fact* contractual schemes would remove all privacy protection from everyone. But it would not be reasonable as a matter of the kind of privacy we are entitled to *expect*—that is, on a normative analysis—for Internet service providers to adopt such a policy and ought not to lead to the normative conclusion that a reasonable expectation of privacy had disappeared. Subscriber agreements are private arrangements and typically are contracts of adhesion negotiated between parties without equal bargaining power: access to the Internet or, indeed, to anything else should not be made to depend upon contracting away one's constitutional rights. *Spencer* is a strong step in that direction.

However, *Spencer* did not go so far as to say that private contracts or public regulatory schemes could not be relevant to the privacy analysis. They can still affect the balance in some fashion, and so it seems likely further issues will need to be decided in this area.

C. WAS THE SEARCH UNREASONABLE? THE *COLLINS* TEST

As noted in the introduction to this chapter, whether a search is reasonable is in all cases governed by the three-part *Collins* test: Was the search authorized by law? Was the law itself reasonable? And was the manner of search reasonable? A failure at any stage will mean that the search is unreasonable and, therefore, violates section 8.

We will consider those three steps in turn, within the first two steps dealing separately with warrantless searches and searches with a warrant. Although in principle the same questions are being asked in each situation, different considerations tend to arise.

1) Was the Search Authorized by Law?

a) Warrantless Searches

It was noted previously that the police derive authority from three sources: statute, common law, and consent.[103] All three sources are relevant to determining whether a warrantless search is reasonable. First, various statutory provisions, some of which are contained in the *Code* but most in other statutes, allow warrantless searches in certain circumstances. Second, some existing common law rules allow for warrantless searches, such as search incident to arrest and search incident

---

103 See Chapter 2.

to investigative detention. In principle, the ancillary power doctrine would allow the creation of new, common law, warrantless search powers. But, also in principle, that ought to be unlikely. *Hunter* points out that the role of the *Charter* is to determine the limits on police power, not to create new search powers.[104] On a number of occasions, the Court has observed that it is Parliament's role, not that of the Court, to determine whether new search powers are necessary:

> it does not sit well for the courts, as the protectors of our fundamental rights, to widen the possibility of encroachments on these personal liberties. It falls to Parliament to make incursions on fundamental rights if it is of the view that they are needed for the protection of the public in a properly balanced system of criminal justice.[105]

Indeed, the Court has held that the common law should not be interpreted to allow searches in situations where there is a statutory scheme that applies to determine whether searches are permitted.[106] However, the possibility of creating new common law search powers remains open, and it seems as though the Court might be more inclined to opt for this approach than it once was: see, for example, the discussion below of the new category of "safety searches."[107] Finally, there are also circumstances in which warrantless searches have been permitted because the accused were taken to have consented to them.

i)   Authorization by Statute

Warrantless searches are provided for in the criminal law context and in various administrative schemes. In the criminal law context, warrantless powers to search can be found in both the *Code* and the *Controlled Drugs and Substances Act*.[108] Each of these powers has been amended

---

104 *Hunter*, above note 6 at 156: the *Charter* "is intended to constrain governmental action inconsistent with those rights and freedoms; it is not in itself an authorization for governmental action."

105 *Wong*, above note 28 at para 35. See also *R v Landry*, [1986] 1 SCR 145 at 187, and *R v Bernard*, [1988] 2 SCR 833 at 891.

106 *Evans*, above note 31 at para 24. Note, as well, that only existing common law powers and the ancillary doctrine are relevant sources of authority in this context. It was noted in Chapter 2 that police effectively have the power to adopt any practice that will not result in the exclusion of evidence. Although that point remains true, it is clear that it is not what the Court has in mind when speaking of a search being "authorized by law." Although many violations do not lead to the exclusion of evidence, they may still be s 8 violations.

107 *R v MacDonald*, 2014 SCC 3 [*MacDonald*], discussed at Section C(1)(a)(ii)(d), below in this chapter.

108 SC 1996, c 19 [*CDSA*].

to conform to *Charter* decisions concerning predecessor sections. The need for this step was not surprising, since warrantless searches are *prima facie* unreasonable. Therefore, these statutory powers depend on the existence of some fact that creates an out-of-the-ordinary situation. In each case, there is an attempt to limit the warrantless power to circumstances where it can be said that the state interest takes priority over individual privacy interests.

Section 11 of the *CDSA* allows a peace officer to obtain a warrant to search a place for a controlled substance, for anything in which a controlled substance is concealed, for offence-related property, or for evidence in respect of an offence under the *CDSA*. While executing that search warrant, however, under section 11(5), a peace officer is entitled to search any person found in the place, if the officer has reasonable grounds to believe that the person has the controlled substance or thing set out in the warrant. This power is broader than the normal search warrant provision in section 487 of the *Code*, which does not permit searches of the person; it is, however, more limited than the predecessor provision in the *Narcotic Control Act*.[109] That provision permitted police officers to search any person found in a place being searched for narcotics, based on nothing more than their presence in the location. In *R v Debot*, the Ontario Court of Appeal held that a similar provision in the *Food and Drugs Act*[110] would not be reasonable and read it down to situations where the officer also had reasonable grounds to search the person.[111] Section 11(5) involves a slight broadening of police power, since the *NCA* search power was limited to a search for narcotics, while the *CDSA* warrant allows a search for other things, such as evidence of an offence, as well. This difference is unlikely to lead any court to conclude that the appropriate balance found in *Debot* has been upset.[112]

---

109 RSC 1985, c N-1, repealed 1996, c 19, s 94 [*NCA*].

110 RSC 1985, c F-27.

111 [1989] 2 SCR 1140, aff'g (1986), 30 CCC (3d) 207 (Ont CA) [*Debot*].

112 This change in wording also resolves another difficulty that had confronted the Crown in *R v Grant*, [1993] 3 SCR 223 [*Grant* 1993]. In that case, police had conducted a warrantless perimeter search of the accused's property, looking for information based upon which they could obtain a search warrant. The Court noted that under the statutory provision in question, police could conduct warrantless searches only when looking for a narcotic. Therefore, the warrantless perimeter search could fall under the power granted by the statute only if the police thought they would find narcotics in the perimeter, which, of course, was not their expectation. By allowing searches for evidence of an offence as well as for controlled substances, s 11(7) of the *CDSA*, above note 108, removes that difficulty.

A superficially similar power, found in s 199(2) of the *Code*, permits an officer to take any person into custody and to seize any evidence found while in a

A further warrantless search power is found in section 11(7) of the *CDSA*, permitting an officer to conduct a warrantless search when the grounds for a warrant exist but exigent circumstances make it impracticable to obtain a warrant. Once again this is in accordance with *Charter* cases on the predecessor section, which had not been limited to exigent circumstances, but was read down in that way.[113] Equivalent provisions allowing warrantless searches in exigent circumstances are found in section 487.11 of the *Criminal Code*, in relation to the search warrant provision in section 487, and in sections 117.02 and 117.04(2). Again, these provisions intend to balance the potentially competing interests of individuals and law enforcement. Courts have held, for example, that warrantless searches of a vehicle may be more readily allowed, since there could be a danger of a vehicle leaving the scene, but have refused to create a blanket exemption for vehicle searches in general.[114] What matters is the impracticability of obtaining a warrant in the particular case: "exigent circumstances will generally be held to exist if there is an imminent danger of the loss, removal, destruction or disappearance of the evidence if the search or seizure is delayed."[115]

In addition, a great variety of individual provisions in various federal and provincial statutes allow for investigative techniques that meet the definition of a search. Various cases have dealt with provisions of the *Food and Drugs Act*,[116] the *Customs Act*,[117] the Nova Scotia *Education Act*,[118] and various administrative schemes.[119] Indeed, the leading case, *Hunter*, is itself based on a provision in the *Combines Investigation Act*.[120] Finally, there are occasional warrantless seizure powers in the *Code*, such as those authorizing the seizure of a weapon from a person

---

common gaming house; however, the provision does not explicitly confer a power to search the persons found and amounts to an arrest power. Although a power to search incident to arrest may thereby arise, it is not a statutory power.

113   *R v Rao* (1984), 40 CR (3d) 1 (Ont CA) [*Rao*]. See also *Grant* 1993, above note 112. Note that in *Grant* 1993, the Crown conceded that the provision as written violated the *Charter*.

114   *Grant* 1993, *ibid*; *R v D(ID)* (1987), 61 CR (3d) 292 (Sask CA) [*D(ID)*].

115   *Grant* 1993, above note 112 at 243.

116   *Debot*, above note 111.

117   *Simmons*, above note 13.

118   *M(MR)*, above note 3.

119   *Rao*, above note 113, for example, attaches an appendix listing twelve statutes outside the criminal law sphere containing warrantless search powers. See the separate discussion of administrative searches at Section C(2)(b)(ii)(a), below in this chapter.

120   *Hunter*, above note 6.

who cannot produce a licence for it,[121] of cocks from a cockpit,[122] or of counterfeit money.[123]

An important instance of a search power *not* being created by law was established by the Court in *Spencer*, dealing with a situation which had arisen in many cases and had been subject to conflicting decisions: obtaining subscriber information from an Internet service provider.[124] Some courts had taken the view that the "lawful authority" for obtaining such information could, in essence, be created through circular reasoning. *PIPEDA*, a federal statute intended to protect privacy rights, allows disclosure to a police officer who has identified her "lawful authority to obtain the information."[125] This was combined with a provision in the *Code* stating that nothing prevents a peace officer "to ask a person to voluntarily provide to the officer documents, data or information that the person is not prohibited by law from disclosing."[126] Combining these two provisions, it was sometimes held that the ability to ask an Internet service provider to voluntarily provide the documents *was* the police officer's "lawful authority" under *PIPEDA* and, therefore, that this was a method by which police could obtain information without needing to seek a warrant.

Spencer authoritatively rejected that position:

> 487.014(1) is a declaratory provision that confirms the existing common law powers of police officers to make enquiries, as indicated by the fact that the section begins with the phrase "[f]or greater certainty": see *Ward*, at para. 49. *PIPEDA* is a statute whose purpose, as set out in s. 3, is to increase the protection of personal information. Since in the circumstances of this case the police do not have the power to conduct a search for subscriber information in the absence of exigent circumstances or a reasonable law, I do not see how they could gain a new search power through the combination of a declaratory provision and a provision enacted to promote the protection of personal information.[127]

---

121 Section 117.03.

122 Section 447(2).

123 Section 462(2).

124 *Spencer*, above note 42.

125 *PIPEDA*, above note 99, s 7(3)(c.1).

126 At the time of *Spencer*, above note 42, this was the wording of s 487.014 of the *Code*. The relevant sections have since been changed, but a similar provision is now found at s 487.0195.

127 *Spencer*, above note 42 at para 73. *R v TELUS Communications Co*, 2015 ONSC 3964 at para 18 [*TELUS* 2015], observes:

> I do note that TELUS has, in the past, willingly provided to the police, without any court order or other authorization, the name and address of its customers,

ii) Authorization by Common Law

a.   General

The goal of search and seizure law is to protect a reasonable expectation of privacy, primarily by preventing unreasonable searches before they take place. Generally, greater privacy should be expected with regard to one's person rather than a place. Therefore, it is ironic that although searches of a place generally require a warrant, searches of the person are most often authorized on a common law and warrantless basis. With few exceptions (such as a warrant to obtain a blood or DNA sample), searches of the person are not authorized by warrant provisions; hence, they are not typically subject to judicial oversight beforehand, but instead are assessed for validity after the fact. The most important of these common law powers to discuss is search incident to arrest, though other issues are also worth consideration.

b.   Search Incident to Arrest

When the police have validly arrested a person they are entitled, within some limits, to search that person. A form of this rule has existed for centuries, and in 1990, with *Cloutier v Langlois*,[128] the Court decided that a properly delimited power was consistent with *Charter* protections. Deciding what counts as proper delimitation has not, however, been so straightforward in the years since this rule with "nebulous parameters"[129] was upheld. Nonetheless, making this evaluation is particularly important. Although, in principle, warrantless searches are intended to be the exception rather than the rule, as a matter of fact, searches incident to arrest are generally taken to constitute the majority of searches conducted by police.[130] Therefore, the limits on this power need to be clear and accepted.[131]

Search incident to arrest does not require that the police have reasonable grounds for the search. It simply flows from the fact that the accused has been arrested.[132] The search is justified not because of a reduced expectation of privacy on the part of the arrested person nor because of exigent circumstances, but rather because the police have

---

on a simple request being made by a police service advising that such information was needed for an ongoing police investigation. TELUS says that it has changed that practice as a result of the decision of the Supreme Court of Canada in *R. v. Spencer*, [2014] 2 S.C.R. 212.

128 [1990] 1 SCR 158 [*Cloutier*].

129 *Golden*, above note 19 at para 23.

130 *Ibid* at para 84; Stanley A Cohen, "Search Incident to Arrest: How Broad an Exception to the Warrant Requirement?" (1988) 63 *Criminal Reports* (3d) 182.

131 *Stillman*, above note 91 at 27.

132 *Debot*, above note 111 at para 3 (SCC); *Caslake*, above note 15 at para 20.

an increased need to gain control of things or information following an arrest, which outweighs the individual's interest in privacy.[133] Accordingly, although the accused has been arrested or detained and so is entitled to be told of the right to counsel, the search does need to wait on the accused exercising that right.[134]

In *Cloutier*, the Court held that the search can extend not only to the accused personally but also to the surrounding area. As a result, a search made incident to arrest may include searching the building or vehicle in which the accused is arrested. However, much depends on the particular circumstances of the case. For example, the police cannot contrive to arrest a person in a particular location as a pretext for performing a warrantless search of that location.[135] Further, searches of vehicles and of homes have tended to be treated differently. Courts have found it relatively easy to approve of vehicle searches, accepting, for example, that removing a loose door panel might be part of a search incident to an arrest.[136] Searches of the home, in contrast, raise greater privacy issues for the accused. The Supreme Court of Canada has yet to pronounce on the issue, but the Ontario Court of Appeal has decided that searches of a home incident to arrest are not allowed, other than in exceptional circumstances. Exceptional circumstances are situations in which a particularly compelling state interest arises. A risk of physical harm to those at the scene, for example, is likely to justify a warrantless entry into an arrestee's home where the simple interest in obtaining evidence would not do so.[137] Thus, the police may be permitted to search an accused's house incident to an arrest if there is reason to suspect that an injured person or an armed accomplice might be there. As with search incident to arrest generally, this power does not depend on the existence of reasonable and probable grounds, but it will be limited to the search that is necessary to fulfill the particular purpose.

The Court has also imposed other limitations on search incident to arrest. For example, the search must be related to the arrest made. In other words, if the search is made for more than safety reasons, there must be some prospect of finding evidence relevant to the arrest made. Where an accused is arrested for traffic violations, therefore, a search incident to the arrest does not justify looking in the trunk of the car

---

133 *Caslake, ibid* at para 17. See also *Fearon*, above note 95 at para 25.

134 *Debot*, above note 111 at para 3 (SCC).

135 *R v Lim (No 2)* (1990), 1 CRR (2d) 136 (Ont HCJ), as cited in *R v Smellie*, [1994] BCJ No 2850 at para 49 (CA) [*Smellie*].

136 *Smellie, ibid.* See also the discussion contrasting searches of vehicles to searches of the person.

137 *R v Golub* (1997), 9 CR (5th) 98 (Ont CA) [*Golub*].

(once the officer's safety has been secured, nothing more is justified).[138] Similarly, an accused that is known to have a history of drug offences cannot be searched for drugs if the actual arrest is for a traffic viola- tion.[139] Although reasonable grounds for the search are not required, the officer must be able to explain the valid purpose for the search related to the reason for the arrest.[140] This approach is intended to be consistent with the goal of preventing unreasonable searches before they happen rather than remedying them after the fact.[141]

The Court has been reluctant to impose strict temporal limits on search incident to arrest. A search can be incidental to an arrest even if it precedes the formal arrest. However, the grounds for the arrest must have already existed — evidence found during the search cannot then help justify the arrest.[142] There is also no strict time limit on how long after the arrest the search can take place. For example, a search of a vehicle six hours later could still be incidental to the arrest depending on the factors affecting the timing. The further in time from the arrest, the less likely the inference that the search is incidental to that arrest; but there is no absolute rule. What matters is the actual purpose moti- vating the search.[143]

Although the Court has phrased the requirements in a variety of ways, the power to search incident to arrest depends essentially on three questions: Was the arrest lawful? Was the search truly incidental to that arrest? Was the search conducted in a reasonable manner?[144] Of these, it is the second factor that is in dispute most frequently and is the most important limit,[145] though each can be an issue.[146]

Whether a search is truly incidental to an arrest depends on the purpose behind that search: the search must be undertaken to achieve

---

138   *Caslake*, above note 15 at para 22.

139   *Golden*, above note 19 at para 92.

140   *Caslake*, above note 15 at para 25.

141   *Hunter*, above note 6.

142   *R v Polashek* (1999), 25 CR (5th) 183 (Ont CA); *Debot*, above note 111 (Ont CA).

143   *Caslake*, above note 15 at para 18. See also *R v Nolet*, 2010 SCC 24 at para 50 [*Nolet*].

144   See, for example, *Stillman*, above note 91 at para 27. In *Cloutier*, above note 128, the three factors listed by the Court were (1) the power did not impose a duty; (2) the search must be for a valid objective; and (3) the search must not be con- ducted in an abusive fashion. The stipulation that the power does not impose a duty is not really a limit (it would be difficult for an accused to object to the fact that the police exercised their discretion to search unless there were also facts showing the search was not for a valid objective), though whether the arrest was lawful can function as a limit.

145   *Caslake*, above note 15 at para 25.

146   See, for example, *R v Klimchuk* (1991), 67 CCC (3d) 385 (BCCA) [*Klimchuk*], where the search was not incident to arrest because the arrest was not lawful.

some valid purpose connected to the arrest. Accordingly, the police officer's motives and purposes for the search are a central issue. If the search was done to intimidate or put pressure on the accused, for example, then it was not incidental.[147] Further, if a search is conducted because of a policy to search everyone arrested, that will not be sufficiently incidental. Rather, the Court has held, the search must be incidental on both objective and subjective criteria.[148] Not only must a valid purpose objectively exist, but subjectively, the officer must have made an individualized decision to conduct the search for that purpose. Thus, in *Cloutier*, for example, although the police force in question maintained a general directive to search everyone arrested, the Court noted that the officers in the case had exercised their discretion in choosing to search the accused.[149] In *R v Caslake*, though, the officer testified that he conducted the search only because of an RCMP (Royal Canadian Mounted Police) policy to inventory the contents of an impounded car.[150] Thus, although objectively a search incident to the accused's arrest would have been justifiable, the actual search conducted was not incidental to the arrest. The Court has adopted this approach to be more consistent with the goal of preventing the occurrence of unjustified searches, rather than remedying them after the fact.[151]

In general, the Court has held that for the search to be an incident of the arrest, the officer must have had one of several particular purposes. The Court has not always been perfectly consistent on what those purposes are, but they are generally taken to include three things: ensuring the safety of the police and the public, protecting evidence from destruction at the hands of the arrestee or others, and discovering evidence that can be used at the arrestee's trial.[152] Although the circumstances that would cause the issue to arise are infrequent, there remains some ambiguity in the caselaw over whether this third purpose relates to *any* evidence or whether it is, in some cases, restricted to evidence that may go out of existence if the search was delayed.

---

147 *Cloutier*, above note 128, and *Caslake*, above note 15.
148 *Caslake*, ibid.
149 *Cloutier*, above note 128.
150 *Caslake*, above note 15.
151 *Ibid* at para 27. See also *Golub*, above note 137, where the Ontario Court of Appeal makes note that the search of the accused's house was not based on a pre-set protocol, but on a decision made at the scene by the officer in charge based on the available information.
152 *Caslake*, above note 15. See the discussion of this issue in Stephen G Coughlan, "Developments in Criminal Procedure: The 1997–98 Term" (1999) 10 *Supreme Court Law Review* 273 at 319.

The original purposes of this search power were related only to short-term goals: to find items that might allow the arrested person to harm the officer or to escape and to prevent evidence under the control of the arrestee from being destroyed. In *Stillman*, the Court noted that after *Cloutier*, some courts of appeal had extended the search power beyond preventing evidence from being destroyed and had added the third broader purpose of finding evidence relevant to the guilt or innocence of the accused.[153] The Court rejected that broader goal on the facts of *Stillman*, which concerned taking various bodily samples from the accused (including scalp and pubic hair, as well as dental impressions) because there was "no likelihood that the appellant's teeth impressions would change, nor that his hair follicles would present a different DNA profile with the passage of time."[154] Therefore, the search could not be justified as an incident of the arrest. Similarly, in *R v Golden*, dealing with the more intrusive issue of strip searches, the Court focused on the risk of disposal of evidence in assessing the reasonableness of the search power.[155]

However, in *Stillman*, the Court left open the question of whether the broader purpose might be acceptable when the search involved a vehicle rather than the accused's person. In *Caslake*, a case actually dealing with a vehicle, it adopted a broader formulation of the type of evidence for which police can search. The Court listed both preventing the destruction of evidence and finding evidence that could be used at the accused's trial as legitimate purposes for the search.[156] Thus, although it did not explicitly acknowledge that it had done so, the Court followed the line of authorities that expanded the search incident to arrest power in the case of vehicles.

In general, cases now routinely cite all three purposes, including "obtaining evidence to use at trial," as the purposes that can make a search be genuinely incidental to the arrest. It might be that the best way to understand the situation is to think of there being a special rule that bodily samples cannot be seized as an incident of an arrest. That rule is based on the heightened expectation of privacy in a person's body and the fact that evidence such as an accused's DNA is not in danger of being destroyed or altered.[157] However, in other contexts evidence can be sought whether it is in danger of going out of existence or not.

---

153   *Stillman*, above note 91.
154   *Ibid* at para 49.
155   *Golden*, above note 19 at para 93.
156   *Caslake*, above note 15 at para 19.
157   *Stillman*, above note 91 at para 42: "the invasive nature of body searches demands higher standards of justification." This rule is consistent generally with

In *R v Fearon* that was the way in which the Court envisioned bodily sample searches: as a modification of the ordinary rules in the case of a particularly invasive search.[158] Two other modifications to the ordinary rules exist.

The first modification deals with strip searches. Most searches incident to arrest are justified because the police have a heightened interest in searching the accused that outweighs the accused's reasonable expectation of privacy. However, the accused's expectation of privacy becomes higher in the case of a strip search. Accordingly, strip searches cannot routinely follow on arrest. A routine strip search conducted in good faith, without violence, will violate section 8 if there are no compelling reasons for the search in the particular circumstances. The police must be able to point to reasonable grounds to believe that a strip search, rather than the more usual pat-down, is required in the particular circumstances.[159] The Court has also identified body cavity searches as a type of search even more intrusive than strip searches. Although the Court has yet to decide the point, the reasoning in *Golden* seems to clearly indicate that a body cavity search could not proceed without, at least, the same level of justification as needed for a strip search. Indeed, given the greater intrusiveness of the search, the Court may well decide that greater justification is required for a warrantless bodily cavity search, or that no such search should be permitted without a warrant.[160]

As for the second modification, the Court has created special rules around the search of cell phones incident to arrest. Cell phones raise particularly acute privacy concerns, because they

> may have immense storage capacity, may generate information about intimate details of the user's interests, habits and identity without the knowledge or intent of the user, may retain information even after the user thinks that it has been destroyed, and may provide access to information that is in no meaningful sense "at" the location of the search.[161]

A cell phone search, however, is less intrusive than either a bodily sample or strip search because those searches "*invariably* and *inherently*"

---

the Court's view, for example, in *Simmons*, above note 13, that the greater the intrusion, the greater the need for justification for the search.

158 *Fearon*, above note 95 at para 44.
159 *Golden*, above note 19.
160 On a related issue, see *R v Saeed*, 2014 ABCA 238, holding that police cannot take a penile swab as part of a search incident to arrest. Judgment from the Supreme Court is pending: 2015 SCCA No 93.
161 *Fearon*, above note 95 at para 51.

constitute very great invasions of privacy, while cell phone searches have only the potential to do so.[162] As a result, the Court rejected the suggestions that there should be a categorical prohibition on search incident to arrest of cell phones, that there should be a reasonable and probable grounds requirement, or that such searches should be limited to exigent circumstances.

Instead, cell phone searches are subject to three additional requirements, which are aimed at limiting their intrusiveness and keeping them within the truly "incidental" range. First, such searches can be undertaken only if the investigation will be significantly hampered without the ability to promptly search the cell phone incident to arrest. This requirement is similar to the question of whether evidence is in danger of going out of existence: cell phone searches are permitted only where there is thought to be another suspect still at large, stolen property that could be immediately recovered, firearms unaccounted for, or something similar. In the absence of such circumstances, "it is hard to see how police could show that the prompt search of a suspect's cell phone could be considered truly incidental to the arrest as it serves no immediate investigative purpose."[163] Second, police cannot engage in an open-ended search of the contents of the cell phone: in general, they will be only able to examine things such as recently sent or drafted emails, texts, photos, and the call log, since those are the only sorts of items likely to have a link to the need for prompt examination. Any search more extensive than that would require the police to obtain a warrant. Finally, police are required to take detailed notes of what they have examined on the device and how it was searched.[164] This requirement is meant both to focus the officers on searching only for those things that are truly incidental and to facilitate after-the-fact review, since prior authorization has not taken place.[165]

c.   Search during an Investigative Detention

In *R v Mann*, the Court created a common law power of search incident to investigative detention.[166] While superficially similar to search incident to arrest, this search power has some noteworthy differences.

---

162   *Ibid* at para 55. Note in this regard that the Court chose not to distinguish, in the rule it created, between "smart" and "dumb" phones, holding that the same rules would apply to all.

163   *Ibid* at para 80.

164   *Ibid* at para 83.

165   *Ibid* at para 82.

166   2004 SCC 52 [*Mann*]. In *Mann*, the Court also first approved the existence of a police power to detain for investigative purposes. See the discussion of that power in Chapter 7.

Specifically, it cannot accurately be described as a search "incident to" investigative detention (although that is the Court's phrasing in *Mann*). When a suspect has been arrested, no independent reasonable grounds for a search need to exist because the arrest itself would have been illegal without such grounds (that is what is meant by describing the search as "incidental to" that arrest). An investigative detention, however, is defined precisely by the absence of reasonable grounds for an arrest. As a result, the Court has held that a search cannot automatically be conducted in such circumstances. Rather, there must be independent reasonable grounds specifically justifying the search.

Further, the scope of a search incident to investigative detention is more limited than a search incident to arrest because it is limited to concerns of officer or public safety. A search incident to arrest can be conducted on those grounds, or to protect evidence from destruction at the hands of the arrestee or others, and to discover evidence to be used at trial.[167]

Further, the Court notes that, in accordance with *R v Collins*, the search must be conducted in a reasonable manner. In this context, that translates into a requirement that the search must be limited to a pat-down of the accused. Only if that pat-down gives rise to reasonable grounds to believe that a more intrusive search is necessary will an officer be enabled to proceed further and, for example, reach into a suspect's pocket. In addition, the search must be both objectively and subjectively justified. Ultimately, the Court concluded:

> where a police officer has reasonable grounds to believe that his or her safety or that of others is at risk, the officer may engage in a protective pat-down search of the detained individual. Both the detention and the pat-down search must be conducted in a reasonable manner.[168]

On the facts of *Mann*, the Court concluded that the initial pat-down search was justified (Mann had been stopped in connection with a break and enter and so may have had tools that could be used as weapons, and was stopped after midnight in an area with no other people

---

167 *Caslake*, above note 15. It has been argued that lower courts have begun to expand the search power relating to investigative detentions: see Scott Latimer, "The Expanded Scope of Search Incident to Investigative Detention" (2007) 48 *Criminal Reports* (6th) 201.

168 *Mann*, above note 166 at para 45. Note that lower courts since have argued that a search during an investigative detention is not (despite this clear language in *Mann*) limited to a pat-down search of the accused: see, for example, *Plummer*, above note 61.

around).[169] However, there was no justification for going beyond the initial pat-down. On the initial pat-down the officer felt something soft in the accused's pocket, but that did not reasonably give rise to safety concerns, and so the officer was not justified in then reaching into the pocket to see what was there. Therefore, the search violated section 8. Indeed, the Court found the violation to be serious enough to justify the exclusion of the evidence under section 24(2).

d. Safety Searches

The Supreme Court's 2014 decision in *R v MacDonald* introduced another common law search power to Canadian law.[170] Both search incident to arrest and search incident to investigative detention had brought along with them the power for police to search a person for safety purposes: that is, to see whether he has a weapon which could be a threat to the officer or others. In the case of an arrest, reasonable grounds to believe that the person had already committed an offence needed to be made out; in the case of a detention, reasonable grounds to believe that the person had a weapon were needed. In *MacDonald*, the Court turned that into a freestanding power which could be exercised in any circumstance where the requirements were made out, without needing to be "incident" to something else.

A police officer had attended at MacDonald's condominium in response to a noise complaint and knocked on the door. MacDonald opened the door only partway and did not answer when the officer asked what he was holding in his hand, hidden behind his leg. Thinking that the object might be a knife, the officer pushed the door open further, saw that the object, in fact, was a gun, and forced her way into the apartment. The Court concluded that the officer was authorized by the common law in acting as she had. Specifically, they applied the *Waterfield* test as it has been developed in Canada to allow for the creation of new common law powers.[171] That test requires first that the officer was acting within the general scope of her duties, which was satisfied because the police have a common law duty to protect life and safety. The second question was whether what the officer did was a justifiable

---

169 *Mann*, above note 166 at para 47. The absence of other people is a curious rationale. The only purpose for which such searches are permitted is to protect the safety of the officer *or others*. That would suggest that the presence of other people would increase the justification for a search, which, in turn, suggests that their absence would reduce the need. The presence of others and their absence cannot both add to the justification for the search.

170 *MacDonald*, above note 107.

171 See the discussion of *R v Waterfield*, [1963] 3 All ER 659 (CA), in Chapter 2, Section A(3)(b).

exercise of powers associated with the duty, or as it has come to be phrased in the jurisprudence on this test, whether the police action was *reasonably necessary* for the carrying out of the particular duty in light of all the circumstances.[172] In considering whether this test is made out in any particular situation, the Court held that three sets of factors must be considered: (1) the importance of the performance of the duty to the public good; (2) the necessity of the interference with individual liberty for the performance of the duty; and (3) the extent of the interference with individual liberty. Where weighing these factors leads to the conclusion that a search should be allowed, that search is authorized by law.[173]

Some structure has been imposed on this otherwise situation-specific test. First, such a search will be authorized by law only if the police officer believes on reasonable grounds that his or her safety or that of the public is at stake and that, as a result, it is necessary to conduct a search. Second, the infringement on individual liberty will be justified only to the extent that it is necessary to search for weapons. In that event, although the way in which a safety search is carried out will vary from case to case, the authority for the search runs out at the point at which the search for weapons is finished.[174]

It is possible that the law in this area is not yet fully developed. In fact, *MacDonald* saw a 4:3 split over the exact standard for the safety search power. The majority held that, as noted, the power existed only when the police had reasonable grounds to believe that a threat to safety was present. The three judge minority, in contrast, would have held that the power should be permitted on the lower standard of "reasonable suspicion" (see the more detailed discussion of reasonable grounds versus reasonable suspicion later in this chapter, in Section C(2)). This had been a question of some disagreement earlier in the Court,[175] and given that there is not yet a decision with a five-judge majority on the point, it is possible that the standard could change.

---

172 See, in particular, for the development of this test in Canada, the discussion in Chapter 5, Section C.

173 *MacDonald*, above note 107 at para 37.

174 *Ibid* at para 39.

175 In *R v Aucoin*, 2012 SCC 66 [*Aucoin*], a search was found to be unreasonable by both the majority and the minority. In *Aucoin*, the minority would have held that all searches for safety purposes required reasonable grounds; the majority held that the particular search in that case required reasonable grounds but refused to commit to the more general proposition. Justice Moldaver wrote the majority decision in *Aucoin* and was the author of the dissent in *MacDonald*, above note 107.

e. Sniffer Dog Searches

Sniffer dog searches—that is, the use of trained dogs to detect the smell of marijuana or other narcotics—can be thought of as having meandered their way into existence in Canadian law. Police began using sniffer dogs on backpacks, at airports or bus stations, or while inspecting vehicles without any kind of authorization. This use was challenged as violating section 8 on the basis that it was a warrantless search. Most of the early caselaw focused on the question of whether the use of a sniffer dog was a search *at all*: that is, the Crown argued with some success that a person had no reasonable expectation of privacy in the smells coming from their belongings, especially smells that were not detectable by human senses. This argument succeeded at times, for example in *Kang-Brown*, where the Alberta Court of Appeal concluded that the accused whose bag was sniffed by a dog at a bus station had not been subject to a search and therefore had no section 8 claim.[176]

The Supreme Court of Canada reversed that particular finding, but in an odd way. Nine judges rendered four separate decisions in *Kang-Brown*, and there is no set of reasoning that can be considered the majority. Somewhat oddly, all nine judges simply take for granted that the accused *did* have a reasonable expectation of privacy (without addressing the reasons for the contrary conclusion below) and therefore that the use of a sniffer dog was a search. Where they disagreed was over whether that search was authorized by law. Four judges—the largest single group of judges but the dissent in the end—would have held that there was no authority for the search and, therefore, there was a section 8 violation. Two different cohorts of two judges each subscribed to decisions saying that police had a common law power to use a sniffer dog where they had reasonable suspicion about the particular accused. Finally, one judge would have held that police had the power to use a sniffer dog based on "generalized suspicion": that is, since there is reason in general to be suspicious of things arriving at airports, police could use sniffer dogs there.[177]

The result left some uncertainty, but police took the decision to amount to an endorsement of a reasonable suspicion common law sniffer dog power, presumably on the theory that four judges had adopted that view and one judge had allowed for an even broader power. That was where the matter stood for four years, until the matter returned

---

176 *Brown* 2006, above note 80.

177 On the same day it decided *Kang-Brown*, above note 30, the Court also handed down *AM*, above note 30, concerning the use of sniffer dogs without reasonable suspicion or reasonable grounds at a school. The judges split in exactly the same 4:2:2:1 fashion in *AM* as in *Kang-Brown*.

to the Supreme Court in *Chehil* and *MacKenzie*, when the existence of a reasonable suspicion sniffer dog search power was authoritatively confirmed: "In *Kang-Brown*, a majority of the Court found that the decision to deploy a sniffer dog meets the *Collins* test where the police have a reasonable suspicion based on objective, ascertainable facts that evidence of an offence will be discovered."[178]

Specifically, in order to deploy a drug-sniffing dog, the police must be able to point to a constellation of facts that reasonably support the suspicion of drug-related activity that the dog deployed is trained to detect. Doing this does not require the police to point to a specific ongoing crime or to identify the precise illegal substance being searched for, but it must be linked to the possession, traffic, or production of drugs or other drug-related contraband.[179] The Court also elaborated in *Chehil* on the meaning of "reasonable suspicion": this aspect of the case will be discussed in Section C(2)(a), below in this chapter, when the reasonableness of warrantless search laws is considered.

f.   Exigent Circumstances

As a general proposition, exigent circumstances can be relevant to whether a warrantless search is permitted not as the justification for the search itself, but rather for conducting the search without a warrant: that is, grounds for the search other than the exigent circumstances themselves must exist independently. The role of exigent circumstances is to justify conducting a search without risking the delay involved in getting judicial pre-authorization. As the Court said in *R v Colarusso*, "absent exigent circumstances, there is a requirement of prior authorization by a judicial officer as a precondition to a valid seizure for the criminal law purposes."[180] For the most part, that is still the approach taken by the law, though as will be discussed at the end of this section, cracks in that approach seem to be developing.

The Court first adopted this approach in interpreting various statutory powers that create warrantless searches. The *NCA*,[181] for example, allowed police officers to search a place other than a dwelling house if they had reasonable grounds to believe narcotics were present. It was held that to comply with section 8, this and similar provisions needed to be read down to allow a warrantless search only where exigent

---

178   *Chehil*, above note 30 at para 19.
179   *Ibid* at paras 36 & 37.
180   [1994] 1 SCR 20 at para 70 [*Colarusso*].
181   Above note 109.

circumstances made it impracticable to obtain a warrant.[182] Subsequent legislative change has enacted this principle uniformly.[183]

"Exigent circumstances" in the search and seizure context[184] has been defined in a manner consistent with its role: "an imminent danger of the loss, removal, destruction or disappearance of the evidence if the search or seizure is delayed."[185] The decision is to be made on a case-by-case basis. It had, for example, been argued that a warrantless search exemption for vehicles should exist, on the basis that they are mobile and can quickly leave the scene.[186] The Court rejected this argument, holding that "[w]hile the fact that the evidence sought is believed to be present on a motor vehicle, water vessel, aircraft or other fast moving vehicle will often create exigent circumstances, no blanket exception exists for such conveyances."[187]

Although the consistent position of the law for some time has been that exigent circumstances do not constitute authority for a search,[188] the Court in 2014 in *MacDonald* created a common law "safety search" power (see the discussion in Section C(1)(a)(ii)(d), above in this chapter). Although *MacDonald* made only brief reference to exigent circumstances in its discussion, some lower courts are possibly treating it as an exigent circumstances warrantless search power.[189] A reaffirmation by the Court that exigent circumstances by themselves are not the source of a search power would be helpful.

---

182 *Grant* 1993, above note 112; *R v Wiley*, [1993] 3 SCR 263 [*Wiley*]; *Rao*, above note 113; *D(ID)*, above note 114.

183 See s 487.11 of the *Code*, and s 11(7) of the *CDSA*, above note 108. To similar effect, see also ss 117.02 and 117.04(2) of the *Code*, dealing with warrantless seizures of weapons.

184 For a criticism of jurisprudence suggesting that "exigent circumstances" has been broadened unacceptably, primarily in the warrantless entry context, see Heather Pringle, "Kicking In the Castle Doors: The Evolution of Exigent Circumstances" (2000) 43 *Criminal Law Quarterly* 86.

185 *Grant* 1993, above note 112.

186 *D(ID)*, above note 114; *Grant* 1993, above note 112; *Klimchuk*, above note 146.

187 *Grant* 1993, above note 112 at para 32.

188 See, for example, *Silveira*, above note 78 at para 50:

> The principle that a search of a dwelling-house without a warrant is unjustifiable is firmly entrenched in the common law. It goes back at least 230 years, when in *Entick v. Carrington, supra*, it was flatly stated that if state authorities enter a house without the express permission of Parliament or the common law, they commit a trespass. No exception to this principle has since been made to permit a search in exigent circumstances or otherwise.

189 See *R v Fountain*, 2015 ONCA 354. The decision focuses on the issue of exigent circumstances, but might ultimately rest on the finding that the *MacDonald* safety search power is met.

In addition to justifying the failure to obtain a warrant for a search, exigent circumstances can be relevant in other ways. In *Golden*, for example, the Court held that strip searches should ordinarily be held at a police station and could take place in the field only in exigent circumstances. In that context, such circumstances would include an urgency to search for weapons that might pose an immediate threat and it would be unsafe to wait and conduct the strip search at the police station.[190] Similarly, exigent circumstances can be relevant to the exclusion of evidence. A court might find that, although a search was illegal, exigent circumstances made the violation less serious, thus affecting the analysis under section 24(2) of the *Charter*.[191]

iii) Authorization by Consent

The final fashion in which a warrantless search can be authorized is if the suspect consents to the search. The central questions to be asked in such cases concern whether the consent was valid and the extent of the consent.

The Court has recognized that an apparent consent must be taken with a grain of salt. In *R v Dedman*, dealing with a random stop by police officers of a vehicle, it observed:

> because of the intimidating nature of police action and uncertainty as to the extent of police powers, compliance in such circumstances cannot be regarded as voluntary in any meaningful sense . . . . A person should not be penalized for compliance with a signal to stop by having it treated as a waiver or renunciation of rights, or as supplying a want of authority for the stop.[192]

As the Ontario Court of Appeal has noted, "acquiescence and compliance signal only a failure to object; they do not constitute consent."[193] Therefore, a certain balance must be struck in considering consent. On the one hand, it is reasonable in some situations for police officers to ask a person, in the absence of reasonable grounds, whether she will consent to a search. On the other hand, such a search will be warrantless and therefore *prima facie* unreasonable. Further, the consent will have acted as a waiver of *Charter* rights, and the standard for finding waiver has appropriately been set high.[194]

---

190 *Golden*, above note 19.
191 *Silveira*, above note 78; *Klimchuk*, above note 146.
192 [1985] 2 SCR 2 at para 59 [*Dedman*].
193 *R v Wills* (1992), 12 CR (4th) 58 at para 44 (Ont CA) [*Wills*].
194 *R v Clarkson*, [1986] 1 SCR 383.

In some circumstances, police with suspicions but without reasonable grounds will try to create a situation in which they can obtain the suspect's consent to a search.[195] Such a search may be permissible, but sometimes a suspect will feel no option but to consent to the search. It is important, therefore, to determine when consent is valid. The Court has noted that a valid waiver requires that the accused have at least "sufficient available information to make the preference meaningful."[196] The Ontario Court of Appeal in R v Wills held that several conditions need to be satisfied:

> In order for consent to operate as a waiver of section 8 rights, the Crown must establish on balance that i) there was a consent, express or implied; ii) the giver of the consent had the authority to give the consent in question; iii) the consent was voluntary and was not the product of police oppression, coercion or other external conduct which negated the freedom to choose whether to not to allow the police to pursue the course of conduct requested; iv) the giver of the consent was aware of the nature of the police conduct to which he or she was being asked to give consent; v) the giver of the consent was aware of his or her right to refuse to permit the police to engage in the conduct requested, and; vi) the giver of the consent was aware of the potential consequences of giving the consent.[197]

Therefore, although there is no constitutional obligation to inform a suspect of the right to refuse a search, failure to do so will likely result in the search being found involuntary.[198]

There is not always an obligation to inform an accused of the right to counsel prior to a consented search.[199] In some circumstances, the accused will have been detained prior to the search and so is entitled to be informed under section 10(b). In that event, the failure to inform the accused of the right to counsel could lead to violations under both section 10(b) and section 8.[200] Further, when the search is nominally conducted with the suspect's consent, the police are required to suspend the search until the suspect has had the opportunity to consult with counsel.[201] However, if there is no *Charter* right to counsel, the

---

195 See, for example, R v Truong, 2002 BCCA 315; and R v Jones, 2002 NSSC 101.
196 R v Borden, [1994] 3 SCR 145 at para 34 [Borden], quoting Wills, above note 193.
197 Wills, ibid.
198 R v Lewis (1998), 38 OR 3d 540 (CA) [Lewis].
199 Wills, above note 193.
200 R v France, 2002 NWTSC 32.
201 Debot, above note 111.

important question is whether the suspect's consent was informed, a standard that may be achieved without access to counsel.

A further issue arises around the actual scope of consent given by a suspect. In some situations, evidence that is obtained from an accused can be used only for limited purposes.[202] Further, an accused can sometimes attach limits to the extent of the consent given.[203] It can be difficult in practice, however, to tell whether this has occurred or what limits apply.

In *Borden*,[204] police were investigating an accused in connection with two sexual assaults. A DNA sample was left at the scene of the first offence, but not the second. The accused was arrested for the second assault, and as part of their investigation the police asked him whether he would supply hair samples and a blood sample. Their primary motive was to see whether the sample would connect Borden to the first offence. They did not specifically disclose that fact to him, though the consent form he signed was deliberately worded to use the plural: "investigations."

The Court held that Borden had not consented to the use of his bodily samples in connection with the first investigation. Since there was also no statutory or common law authority allowing police to use them, the seizure was not authorized by law and his section 8 right was violated. It concluded:

> It was incumbent on the police, at a minimum, to make it clear to the respondent that they were treating his consent as a blanket consent to the use of the sample in relation to other offences in which he might be a suspect . . . it will not be necessary for the accused to have a detailed comprehension of every possible outcome of his or her consent. However, his or her understanding should include the fact that the police are also planning to use the product of the seizure in a different investigation from the one for which he or she is detained.[205]

This broad proposition has been narrowed by the Court's later decision in *R v Arp*.[206] The police must disclose any specific uses they intend at the time they take the sample. However, if further possible uses arise later, there is no bar to using the sample. In *Arp*, the accused

---

202 See *Dyment*, above note 33, where the Court held that blood samples taken by a doctor for medical purposes cannot simply be handed over to the police for use in a criminal investigation.

203 *Colarusso*, above note 180.

204 *Borden*, above note 196.

205 *Ibid* at paras 39–40.

206 [1998] 3 SCR 339 [*Arp*].

had consented to provide hair samples in connection with a murder investigation. He was informed that any evidence arising from the samples would be used against him. In fact, he was discharged at the preliminary inquiry for that offence, but three years after providing the hair samples he was investigated for a second murder. Police used a warrant to obtain the hair samples, and DNA testing linked him to the second murder. Relying on *Borden*, the accused objected to use of the sample provided for one investigation in a different investigation, but the Court dismissed his appeal. The Court re-affirmed that any consent must be an informed one, but also held that

> if neither the police nor the consenting person limit the use which may be made of the evidence then, as a general rule no limitation or restriction should be placed on the use of that evidence . . . the obligation imposed on the police in obtaining a valid consent extends only to the disclosure of those anticipated purposes known to the police at the time the consent was given.[207]

On the facts of *Arp*, the Court held that the original seizure by consent was valid because the police did not know that Arp would later be the suspect in another homicide, and they did inform him that any evidence gathered would be used in court. In the absence of a specific limitation to his consent, the Court held that the accused had given up any expectation of privacy in the hair sample. Accordingly, his section 8 right was not violated.

Even where consent is not valid, it can still have some relevance. In deciding under section 24(2) whether evidence should be excluded, some courts have held that an officer's mistaken belief that the accused had consented to the search made the section 8 breach less serious.[208]

Finally, note that consent can be given only by the person with the privacy interest: that is, there is no doctrine of "third party consent." In *Cole* the police had conducted a warrantless search of a laptop used by a teacher which had been issued to him by a school board. The search was conducted because the school board had turned the laptop over to the police, reporting it to contain nude photographs of a student. The Court rejected the argument that the search had been conducted with the consent of the school board. Although the accused had a diminished reasonable expectation of privacy, it was still *his* expectation, and to say that a third party could waive it would be inconsistent with the rules requiring such a consent to be fully informed and voluntary. The Court

---

207 *Ibid* at paras 87–88. See also *R v Colson*, 2008 ONCA 21.
208 See *Lewis*, above note 198; *R v Daley*, 2001 ABCA 155.

noted that although third party consent was an accepted doctrine in the United States, the privacy analysis there was based on the risk analysis approach which has been rejected in Canada.[209]

b) Searches with a Warrant

One foundational principle of section 8 law is that a warrantless search is *prima facie* unreasonable.[210] The creation of this rule has had an observable effect on the state of the law. Specifically, in a number of early *Charter* cases, police undertook particular forms of investigation and did so without a warrant because no warrant provision that would have authorized the investigation in question existed. The Court found the search, therefore, to violate the *Charter*, and in response Parliament created a new warrant provision.

Wong is a seminal example of this approach. The police wanted to investigate illegal gambling in a hotel room, and to do so installed a hidden camera to visually record the activity. Had they been planning to audiotape, they could have obtained an electronic surveillance authorization under Part VI of the *Code*, but those provisions did not deal with videotaping. The search warrant provisions in section 487 of the *Code*, the only real alternative that existed at the time, was limited to obtaining warrants to search for physical items: the images captured by a video camera would not fall within that category. As a result, no warrant *could* have authorized the police action, and so they proceeded without a warrant. The Crown argued, in essence, that in the absence of a scheme imposing limits on police investigative techniques, it was open to the police to proceed as they had; the Court concluded that this approach "wholly misunderstands" the way section 8 works.[211] Rather, they held, the police were allowed to use an investigative technique only if some law specifically authorized them to do so. In addition, the Court held that any such authorizations should not be created at common law, but instead should come from Parliament:

> it does not sit well for the courts, as the protectors of our fundamental rights, to widen the possibility of encroachments on these personal liberties. It falls to Parliament to make incursions on fundamental

---

209 *Cole*, above note 22 at paras 74–79.
210 *Hunter*, above note 6.
211 *Wong*, above note 28 at para 28.

rights if it is of the view that they are needed for the protection of the public in a properly balanced system of criminal justice.[212]

As a result, many changes have been made to the *Code* in the years since *Wong* either to add powers in situations where a search was found unconstitutional or to avoid any such finding in the first place. Where once the search warrant provision in section 487 of the *Code* was followed immediately by section 488, there are now more than forty other provisions in between.[213] Warrant provisions now not only authorize searches of places for things with search warrants, but also obtaining data from financial organizations,[214] using devices to track the movements of persons or vehicles,[215] obtaining records identifying who has transmitted a particular message,[216] obtaining DNA from a suspect,[217] video surveillance,[218] and more. Indeed, the general warrant provision in section 487.01 of the *Code* literally has the potential to authorize the police to "do any thing." That particular provision is so broad in its impact as to go beyond merely being a search power, and so it is not discussed here, but instead is discussed in Chapter 5.

i)   Searching Places for Things: Section 487[219]

The search warrant provision, found in section 487 of the *Criminal Code*, raises a number of issues worthy of note. Broadly, section 487 is a way to authorize searches of physical locations for physical objects.

---

212 *Ibid* at para 35. They held as well at para 36:

> It is for Parliament, and Parliament alone, to set out the conditions under which law enforcement agencies may employ video surveillance technology in their fight against crime. Moreover, the same holds true for any other technology which the progress of science places at the disposal of the state in the years to come. Until such time as Parliament, in its wisdom, specifically provides for a code of conduct for a particular invasive technology, the courts should forebear from crafting procedures authorizing the deployment of the technology in question.

213 Further on this, see the discussion in Michal Fairburn, "Twenty-Five Years in Search of a Reasonable Approach" (2008) 40 *Supreme Court Law Review* (2d) 55. Note that because of successive amendments to the same powers, the *Code* contains sections with such remarkable numbers as s 487.055(1)(c.1).

214 Section 487.018.

215 Section 487.017. See also s 492.1.

216 Section 487.015. See also s 492.2.

217 Section 487.04ff.

218 Section 487.01(4).

219 Section 11(1) of the *CDSA*, above note 108, though not identical in wording, is closely modelled on s 487 of the *Code*, and any analysis of the latter is likely to apply equally to the former.

That is not absolutely true, since it is, for example, possible to obtain a warrant to get data from a computer, but it is the general thrust of the provision. In fact, that is more limiting than it might appear at first glance, and a good deal of the proliferation of other warrant provisions can be traced to the fact that often the police want to obtain evidence which is not a "thing."

Section 487 allows the issuance of a warrant for the search of a "building, receptacle or place" if satisfied on oath of reasonable grounds that evidence falling into one of four categories will be found. Each element, which reflects various aspects of the need for restraint in the use of investigative powers, is worth considering in turn.

A warrant must be issued by a justice: this requirement of the *Code* means that section 487 complies with one of the minimum constitutional prerequisites laid down in *Hunter*.[220] That justice must be sure that some particular person is charged with responsibility for the search. This does not require that only one officer be named, that no one not named in the warrant can participate in the search, or that everyone named in the warrant must participate; however, "there must be some person responsible for the way the search is carried out."[221] This issue of accountability is a reflection of the need for restraint in the use of state power. In the context of warrants issued under the previous *Narcotic Control Act*,[222] the Court characterized a warrant that did not describe the officer who was to conduct the search, limit the times during which the search could be conducted, or list the items being searched for as "a fishing license, not a search warrant."[223]

In addition, a person executing a search warrant has a duty to have it with her where feasible and produce it on request.[224] Where a team of people execute a warrant it is sufficient for one of them to have a copy, and even in the case of a search by forced entry, the better practice would be for that person to be among the first group of officers in the door. However, the duty will still be complied with so long as the person in charge of the search has a copy and is immediately at hand.[225]

---

220 *Hunter*, above note 6 at 162. See the further discussion of these requirements in Section C(2), below in this chapter.

221 *R v Strachan*, [1988] 2 SCR 980 at para 28. The Court observes at para 30 that "the warrant should make it clear who is in charge of, and responsible for, the search . . . . Listing an entire drug squad by name in a warrant may undermine the effectiveness of the naming requirement just as much as a failure to name anyone at all."

222 Above note 109, s 94.

223 *R v Genest*, [1989] 1 SCR 59 [*Genest*].

224 Section 29.

225 *R v Cornell*, 2010 SCC 31 [*Cornell*].

The power to search is limited to a "building, receptacle or place." This authority does not allow a warrant to be issued to search a person[226] or to take hair samples.[227] This latter finding has become of less importance since the passage of section 487.05 of the *Code*, which allows for warrants to take bodily samples in order to obtain DNA. "Place" includes the area surrounding a building, which has two main consequences. First, it means that a warrant is available to search the exterior of buildings and the surrounding area. This leads to the result that, since it would be possible to obtain a warrant to search the area around a house in principle, a search of that area without a warrant is *prima facie* unreasonable, in accordance with the rule laid down in *Hunter*.[228] Second, when coupled with the need for specificity in warrants, this also means that a warrant to search the area around a house (the curtilage) does not include the ability to seize items found inside the house, while a warrant to search a house might not include the ability to search the area around the house or other buildings on the property.[229]

The justice must be satisfied of more than the possibility that evidence will be found; otherwise, intrusions based only on suspicion would be too readily permitted.[230] Further, the justice must be given facts that show the basis for the reasonable and probable grounds and not simply be satisfied that the police officer has such a belief.[231] The Court has noted that the affidavit supporting a warrant need not be

> as lengthy as *À la recherche du temps perdu*, as lively as the *Kama Sutra*, or as detailed as an automotive repair manual. All that it must do is set out the facts fully and frankly for the authorizing judge in order that he or she can make an assessment of whether these rise to the standard required in the legal test for the authorization. Ideally, an affidavit should be not only full and frank but also clear and concise.[232]

In this context, the Court has discouraged the use of "boiler plate" language in applications, on the basis that it adds little and can imply

---

226   *Laporte v Laganière* (1972), 8 CCC (2d) 343 (Que CA) [*Laporte*].
227   *R v Légère*, [1998] NBJ No 712 (CA).
228   *Debot*, above note 111; *Kokesch*, above note 29; *Plant*, above note 23. However, see *Grant* 1993, above note 112, where the Court held that although the power in s 10 of the *NCA*, above note 109, to conduct warrantless searches of a place other than a dwelling house violated s 8, the section did not need to be struck down completely, but rather could be read down to apply only in exigent circumstances.
229   See, for example, *R v Chuhaniuk*, 2010 BCCA 403.
230   *Hunter*, above note 6 at 167.
231   *R v Pastro* (1988), 42 CCC (3d) 485 at 511 (Sask CA).
232   *R v Araujo*, [2000] 2 SCR 992 at para 46 [*Araujo*].

meaning not there. The Court has also recommended using affidavits directly from those with firsthand knowledge of the facts therein, such as the officers conducting the investigation.[233]

Beyond that, the requirement that the justice be satisfied on oath of reasonable grounds is interesting primarily for the issues of what will constitute reasonable grounds and how they may be obtained. For entirely understandable reasons, warrants are issued on an *ex parte* basis: the need for effective law enforcement certainly justifies not informing a suspect in advance of a search that will take place.[234] However, in accordance with the principle of restraint, it is open to an accused to argue after the fact that, even though the warrant was issued by an independent decision-maker based on sworn information, the warrant ought not to have been issued.[235]

Cases have held that the information justifying the issuing of a warrant can be hearsay and need not be admissible in court. Similarly, the information might be privileged, because the police obtained the information from a confidential informer, for example. The Court has held that the identity of an informer need not be disclosed, either on an application to quash or at trial, unless the accused shows that disclosure of the identity of the informer "is necessary to establish the innocence of the accused" (known as the "innocence at stake" exception).[236] In any other circumstance, the legitimate needs of law enforcement to protect the identity of informers outweigh the interests of the accused to openness and disclosure. This can, however, lead to issues in defending the warrant later: see the discussion in Section C(1)(b)(v), below in this chapter.

There are some limits on the type of information that can justify a warrant. In particular, the information must have been legally gathered; therefore, a warrant based solely on information gained through

---

233 *Ibid* at para 48.
234 See the discussion of this issue in R v SAB, 2001 ABCA 235 [*SAB* CA], holding that *ex parte* applications for warrants generally do not violate the *Charter*, whether the *Code* provision specifies that approach or not. In particular, the Alberta Court of Appeal held in *SAB* CA that *ex parte* applications for DNA warrants are acceptable because, although a suspect's DNA cannot be changed despite notice of the application, the suspect might flee if given notice. The Supreme Court of Canada upheld this result (*SAB*, above note 6) without making specific reference to the possibility of flight. The Court also noted that s 487.05(1) does not prevent a judge from requiring that an application be *inter partes* in particular cases: see para 56.
235 See the discussion at Section C(1)(b)(v), below in this chapter.
236 *R v Leipert*, [1997] 1 SCR 281.

a *Charter* violation will be quashed. In *Kokesch*,[237] for example, the police conducted a search of the exterior of the accused's residence. They found a metal vent covered with plywood, heard machines humming inside, and smelled marijuana from the edge of the plywood. Based on this information, the police obtained a search warrant for the premises that was subsequently quashed. Since the officers had no reasonable grounds to inspect the perimeter of the accused's residence initially, and since that inspection was itself a search, their observations—and therefore the evidence that was the basis for the search warrant—violated the *Charter*.[238] Accordingly, those observations could not be used as a basis for the warrant, and the evidence obtained through use of the warrant itself was excluded.[239]

The Court has also upheld the individual right to privacy in less clear circumstances, such as where police knock on a suspect's door in order to gain reasonable grounds for a search by, for example, smelling marijuana inside.[240] Although homeowners can sometimes be taken to have issued an implied invitation to anyone to knock on the door, that invitation is for limited purposes. When the police approach the residence and knock on the door for other purposes, their behaviour constitutes a warrantless search, which is *prima facie* unreasonable. On the other hand, if the police approach for other legitimate reasons, but then

---

237 *Kokesch*, above note 29.

238 See, in contrast, *Wiley*, above note 182 where, although the police relied on evidence obtained from a perimeter search to obtain a search warrant, there was still enough information to justify the warrant even without those observations, and the warrant was allowed to stand.

239 Of course, it is not the case that evidence obtained in violation of s 8 or any other section of the *Charter* will be immediately excluded. Rather, that is a question that must be decided under s 24(2) of the *Charter*. It had been suggested that, in drug cases, the Court was generally quite reluctant to exclude drugs found as a result of an unconstitutional search: see Don Stuart, "Eight Plus Twenty-Four Two Equals Zero" (1998) 13 *Criminal Reports* (5th) 50. See also Nathan JS Gorham, "Eight Plus Twenty-Four Two Equals Zero-Point-Five" (2003) 6 *Criminal Reports* (6th) 257. However, those analyses were based on the test for exclusion of evidence in *Stillman*, above note 91. In *Grant*, above note 21, the Court created a new analytical scheme for the exclusion of evidence, leading to the formation of new patterns: see Michael Madden, "Empirical Data on Section 24(2) under R. v. Grant" (2010) 78 *Criminal Reports* (6th) 278; Thierry Nadon, "Le paragraphe 24(2) de la Charte au Québec depuis *Grant* : si la tendance se maintient!" (2011) 86 *Criminal Reports* (6th) 33; and Ariane Asselin, "Trends for Exclusion of Evidence in 2012" (2013) 1 *Criminal Reports* (7th) 74.

240 *Evans*, above note 31.

discover evidence giving them reasonable grounds to search, there will be no *Charter* violation.[241]

In addition, the types of things for which search warrants may be issued must be noted. The *Code* sets out four categories: (1) anything on or in respect of which an offence has been committed; (2) anything that will provide evidence regarding an offence or the location of a person suspected of committing an offence; (3) anything reasonably believed to be intended to be used to commit an offence for which the person could be arrested without warrant; or (4) offence related property.[242] "Offence related property" is defined in section 2 of the *Code* to mean, essentially, property that has been or will be used in committing an indictable offence.

These purposes for a search are broad, but they are not unlimited. They allow warrants to search not just for evidence of an offence, but also for evidence allowing the Crown to determine whether an accused will be able to put forward a successful defence, such as due diligence.[243] The Court has noted:

> The words "in respect of" are, in my opinion, words of the widest possible scope. They import such meanings as "in relation to", "with reference to" or "in connection with." The phrase "in respect of" is probably the widest of any expression intended to convey some connection between two related subject matters.[244]

However, although the purpose for the search is broad, there are some limits. In particular, the purposes have been interpreted as limiting the power to a search for physical items and therefore do not allow the seizure of the contents of a bank account.[245]

---

241 See, for example, *R v Duong* (2002), 49 CR (5th) 165 (BCCA), leave to appeal to SCC refused, [2002] SCCA No 112, where the police approached the accused's door while looking for witnesses to a home invasion in the area, but then formed reasonable and probable grounds to believe he was committing a narcotics offence, which authorized an arrest and a search incident to that. See also *R v Roy*, 2010 BCCA 448, where undercover officers purporting to sell marijuana were invited into the accused's home to see marijuana of the quality the accused wished to buy. The Court of Appeal concluded that the police had never acted outside the scope of the express invitation to them, and so they had not infringed the accused's reasonable expectation of privacy.

242 Sections 487(1)(a)–(c.1).

243 See *CanadianOxy Chemicals Ltd v Canada (AG)*, [1999] 1 SCR 743.

244 *Ibid* at para 16, quoting from *Nowegijick v the Queen*, [1983] 1 SCR 29 at 39.

245 See *Re Banque Royale du Canada and the Queen* (1985), 44 CR 3d 387 at 389 (Que CA). The Court quotes with approval the Law Reform Commission of Canada:

> 196. Another anachronism is the restriction of most search and seizure powers to "things", particularly in the case of those powers concerned with

Special limits have been imposed to govern situations where a computer is found in the location for which a search warrant has been obtained. The Court noted in *R v Vu* that "[c]omputers differ in important ways from the receptacles governed by the traditional framework and computer searches give rise to particular privacy concerns."[246] Computers store immense amounts of information in comparison to other receptacles such as filing cabinets, create some information whether the user wants it created or not, and retain information even after the user has tried to delete it. Further, a search of a computer connected to a network or the Internet is no longer really a search of the location for which the warrant was issued. Because these are unusual and special privacy considerations, the Court held, it will not be clear that a justice of the peace issuing a search warrant took them into account—unless, that is, the ability to search such a computer was specifically mentioned in the warrant. Accordingly, that special rule has been created: if police want to be able to search a computer found at the scene, they must satisfy the justice in advance that the type of material they are seeking could reasonably be expected to be on a computer, and the warrant must specifically authorize the search of the computer. If that has not occurred but the police find a computer which might reasonably be thought to obtain the type of material sought, the police are limited to seizing that computer and then seeking a warrant to search it.

Important as a limit on the search warrant power is the need for specificity in advance. It is not sufficient for police simply to show that they believe some sort of evidence will be found if a search occurs. Rather, they must inform the issuing justice, with some reasonable degree of precision, *what* evidence will be found. At a policy level this is a reflection of the difference between warrantless searches and those conducted with a warrant: in the latter case, the power to search rests in the warrant itself, and the officer should simply be seen as carrying out the instructions in it. Thus, for example, an application for a warrant that specified one publication by name but otherwise only indicated that "other obscene materials" would be found was quashed with respect to all but the one named magazine, because it left too much to

---

the recovery of the fruits of crime. The original common law search warrant developed by Hale was for stolen "goods". This focus on tangible objects was carried into subsequent provisions for search and seizure covering crimes of theft, including the present subsection 443(1) [now s 487] of the *Criminal Code*. This focus, however, excludes from coverage forms of property such as funds in financial accounts, or information from computers, which may also represent the fruits of a crime.

246 2013 SCC 60 at para 2.

the discretion of the officers.[247] Nonetheless, the degree of specificity required varies with the type of offence: it will be more difficult for investigators to specify in advance precisely what evidence they will find of tax evasion or fraud, for example, and so more latitude must be shown in such cases.[248] In addition, a further reason for making the warrant specific is so that the person whose property is searched is sufficiently informed of the reason for that search.[249]

Once again what is reflected here is the balancing of the legitimate interests of the individual and the state. The purpose of prior authorization, whether considering the search as a possible *Charter* violation or not, is to prevent a search from occurring unless it is genuinely shown to be necessary. Where the police cannot say, in advance and with some degree of precision, what evidence they think will be found, the warrant begins to look more like "a fishing license."[250]

However, the legitimate interests of law enforcement are not sacrificed. The *Code* also contains section 489, which allows the police who are searching under a warrant to seize items not mentioned in the warrant if they believe on reasonable grounds that they were obtained by, were used in, or afford evidence concerning an offence. In other words, as long as the warrant was validly issued, then the intrusion on the suspect's privacy has been justified. If, in the course of that search, different evidence is found, then new considerations arise, justifying the seizure of that unanticipated material. Provided that the reviewing courts are vigilant not to engage in *post facto* justification of warrants simply because evidence was found, rather than judging them based on the information provided to the issuing justice, this is a workable compromise.

The balance of rights between the state's interests in investigating crime and the interests of individuals is reflected in a slightly different way with regard to the issue of sealing orders. The public can have an interest in seeing the information used by police to obtain search warrants or the search warrants themselves, but the police might see an ongoing need to keep that information confidential. The Court has held that the appropriate balance of interests in this situation favours openness and that "[o]nce a search warrant is executed, the warrant and the information upon which it is issued must be made available to the public unless an applicant seeking a sealing order can demonstrate

---

247 *R v Times Square Book Store* (1985), 48 CR (3d) 132 (Ont CA) [*Times Square*].
248 *R v Church of Scientology* (No 6) (1986), 27 CCC (3d) 193 (Ont HCJ).
249 *Alder v Alberta* (*Attorney General*) (1977), 37 CCC (2d) 234 (Alta SCTD).
250 *Genest*, above note 223.

that public access would subvert the ends of justice."[251] In reaching this conclusion, the Court applied the same standard that it created in the case of publication bans to search warrants.[252]

Finally, note should be taken of section 488 of the *Code*, which requires that a warrant shall be executed by day unless reasonable grounds for executing it by night are provided to the issuing justice, and the warrant itself authorizes its execution by night.

ii) Electronic Surveillance

The provisions in Part VI of the *Criminal Code* are long-standing sections dealing with wiretaps and other forms of intercepting communications, which are referred to as "interceptions."[253] Rather than speaking of a warrant in this context, the provisions refer to "authorizations," though the concept is the same. These provisions are very detailed, and only a general overview will be provided here.[254]

These provisions deal specifically with intercepting private communications by means of devices: that is, they do not deal with every conceivable situation in which one person overhears a conversation of another. Each of those key terms has been defined in section 183 of the *Code*.

A "private communication" means an oral communication or telecommunication "that is made under circumstances in which it is reasonable for the originator to expect that it will not be intercepted by any person other than the person intended by the originator to receive it." To "intercept" means to listen to, record, or acquire the substance of a communication, and the devices in question are "any device or apparatus that is used or is capable of being used to intercept a private communication" other than a hearing aid.

Intercepting private communications engages a particularly strong privacy interest, which is demonstrated by the fact that it is an offence to intercept absent an authorization, by virtue of section 184 of the *Code*. As a result, authorizations are more difficult to obtain than other

---

251 *Toronto Star Newspapers Ltd v Ontario* (2005), 29 CR (6th) 251 (SCC), relying on *Attorney General of Nova Scotia v MacIntyre*, [1982] 1 SCR 175.

252 See *Dagenais v Canadian Broadcasting Corp*, [1994] 3 SCR 835, as well as *Vancouver Sun (Re)*, [2004] 2 SCR 332. See also *Ottawa Citizen Group Inc v Ontario* (2005), 31 CR (6th) 144 (Ont CA), concerning the search warrants in the Maher Arar case. See also the discussion of publication bans in Chapter 11, Section F(2).

253 Sections 183–196.1.

254 For a more complete discussion, see Robert W Hubbard, Peter M Brauti, & Scott K Fenton, *Wiretapping and Other Electronic Surveillance: Law and Procedure* (Toronto: Thomson Carswell, 2000) (loose-leaf), or James G Carr & Patricia L Bellia, *The Law of Electronic Surveillance* (Eagan, MN: West, 2011).

warrants. Many rules are parallel to those for search warrants: authorizations can be issued only by a person acting judicially who has a reasonable belief that an offence has been (or will be, in this case) committed and that information will be obtained through the authorization.[255] However, other additional requirements are imposed as well.

The provisions distinguish between consent and non-consent interceptions: in the former, one party to the conversation has agreed to it being intercepted, while in the latter no one has consented. Non-consent electronic surveillance (whether audio or video)[256] is available only in the case of offences listed in section 183. That is an ever-expanding list, but it is to date still something less than all offences.

Consent and non-consent interceptions both require evidence on oath creating reasonable grounds, but they vary as to who must act judicially in this regard. Consent authorization applications can be made to a provincial court or superior court judge:[257] non-consent applications can be made only to a superior court.[258] In either case, the application cannot be made to a justice of the peace in the way that search warrant applications can be.

Further, interceptions have special provision as to *who* can make the application. In the case of consent interceptions, peace officers and public officers are allowed to apply for the authorization, while in the case of non-consent interceptions, the list of eligible applicants is much smaller: the attorney general, the minister of Public Safety, or a specially designated agent.[259]

Consent interceptions contain the rule that the issuing judge can attach conditions in the public interest.[260] Non-consent applications, however, are subject to stricter requirements: the judge must be satisfied that the authorization would be in the best interests of the administration of justice[261] and that the "investigative necessity" requirement is

---

255 Strictly, this is the language of s 184.2(3)(c), dealing with consent authorizations, while s 185(1)(e), dealing with non-consent authorizations, asks whether there are reasonable grounds to believe that intercepting the communications may assist the investigation of the offence.

256 Provisions for video surveillance were added as an adjunct to the general warrant provisions in s 487.01 and adopt the rules governing audio surveillance.

257 *Ibid*, s 184.2(2).

258 *Ibid*, s 186(2).

259 *Ibid*, s 185(1).

260 *Ibid*, s 184.2(4)(d).

261 There is a slight incongruity here. Consent interceptions are not subject to this requirement if they deal only with audio surveillance. However, all video surveillance, including consent interceptions, must be authorized under the general warrant provisions, and all general warrants are subject to the "best

met. The "best interests" requirement "imports as a minimum requirement that the issuing judge must be satisfied that there are reasonable
and probable grounds to believe that an offence has been, or is being,
committed and that the authorization sought will afford evidence of
that offence."[262] These requirements are not otherwise explicit in the
section and are required to render the section constitutional. "Investigative necessity" encompasses three possibilities: that other methods
have been tried and have failed, that as a practical matter no other
method of investigation is likely to succeed, or that because of the urgency of the matter other methods would be impractical.[263] However,
the investigative necessity requirement does not apply to investigations
for criminal organization or terrorism offences.[264] Non-consent authorizations cannot intercept communications at the office or residence
of a solicitor, unless there are reasonable grounds to believe that that
solicitor has been or is about to become a party to an offence.[265]

An emerging and controversial issue is whether Part VI has a broader application to the interception of electronic communications than
has been understood until now. Resolving this rests on two related
questions. First, can text messages, Facebook posts, and other messages sent electronically or by social media constitute "private communications"? Second, does "interception" have a temporal component:
that is, must the state acquire the substance of the communication as
it occurs for Part VI to be triggered, or is it still an interception if that
occurs after the fact? In *R v TELUS Communications Co*, the police obtained a general warrant requiring TELUS to deliver, each day for the
next two weeks, the text messages sent between two telephone numbers in the previous twenty-four hours. Five of the seven members of
the Court deciding the case found that that was not a valid general warrant.[266] Justice Abella for three deciding judges concluded that what the

---

interests" requirement: s 487.01(1)(b). It is hard not to see this as happenstance
rather than a deliberate policy choice. See also *R v Li*, 2013 ONCA 81, noting
the ambiguity created by the fact that provincial court judges have jurisdiction
to issue general warrants but not non-consent authorizations, and therefore
that it is unclear whether they can issue general warrants for non-consent video
surveillance.

262 *Duarte*, above note 27 at para 24.
263 See section 186(1)(b), and *Araujo*, above note 232. The third branch is referred
to in *Araujo* as dealing with emergency situations.
264 Section 186(1.1). This has been challenged but upheld: *R v Lucas*, 2014 ONCA
561.
265 Section 186(2).
266 2013 SCC 16 [*TELUS*]. See the further discussion of *TELUS* in Chapter 5, Section B.

police were trying to do required them to be authorized under Part VI: the text messages were "private communications," TELUS's computer system was a "device," and obtaining them after the fact constituted "intercepting" them. No majority opinion on the point arose, since the other two judges concurring in the result expressed no view on that point, and the two dissenting judges specifically reject the position. Justice Cromwell for the dissent noted that Abella J's approach would cause Part VI to be applicable to many situations, such as copying emails from a seized BlackBerry, seizing copies of Internet chats from a computer, and so on, where, in the past, ordinary search warrants or production orders have been seen as sufficient.

In the wake of *TELUS*, courts are in the process of determining whether it has caused Part VI to have wider application. Some cases have found, based on Abella J's reasoning in TELUS, that Part VI applies to chats on a Facebook wall, to past (as opposed to prospective) text messages stored by an Internet service provider, or to surveillance camera footage showing an accused's BlackBerry screen.[267] Other cases have rejected the view that Part VI applies to past text messages[268] or to texts read on the accused's cell phone.[269] This matter will require further development by courts.

Time limits are imposed on the length of any interception. Non-consent interceptions can last at most sixty days, though renewals (of up to sixty days each) are available.[270] Consent authorizations are also limited to sixty days.[271] No provision specifically envisions a renewal of a non-consent authorization, but further applications for a new authorization are possible.[272] When the offences being investigated relate to organized crime or terrorism, however, all these time limits increase to one year.[273]

Finally, note that the *Code* also contains some "abbreviated" versions of the powers. In the case of consent authorizations, a temporary

---

267 See, respectively, *R v Mills* (2013), 7 CR (7th) 268 (NLPC); *R v Croft*, 2013 ABQB 640; and *R v Ley*, 2014 BCSC 2108.

268 *R v Belcourt*, 2015 BCCA 126; *R v Carty*, 2014 ONSC 212. See also *Pelucco*, above note 62, which accepts that text messages are private communications but does not accept that Part VI always governs reading them.

269 *R v Thompson*, 2013 ONSC 4624 [*Thompson*].

270 Sections 186(4)(e) and 186(7).

271 Section 184.2(4)(e).

272 Section 184.2(2)(e). The existence and particulars of a previous authorization must be disclosed. It is also possible to seek a new authorization rather than a renewal for a non-consent authorization. This course of action is appropriate if the old authorization has expired, or if the terms are to be changed by adding new parties or new locations: *R v Thompson*, [1990] 2 SCR 1111.

273 Section 186.1.

authorization lasting thirty-six hours is available under section 184.3: these are available only in circumstances of urgency where it would be impracticable for the person seeking the authorization to appear personally. Similarly, section 188 allows a thirty-six-hour authorization for non-consent authorizations if the judge "is satisfied that the urgency of the situation requires that interception of private communications commence before an authorization could, with reasonable diligence, be obtained under section 186." The notion behind these temporary authorizations seems to be that the applicant will use the thirty-six hours in order to bring a proper application under section 184.2 or section 185.

Beyond that, interceptions are sometimes available without an authorization. Section 184.1 permits an agent of the state to intercept a private communication if three conditions are met: (1) one of the parties to the communication consents to the interception; (2) that the stage agent believes on reasonable grounds that there is a risk of bodily harm to the person who consented; and (3) the purpose of the interception is to prevent the bodily harm. These interceptions, however, are limited to protective purposes: that is, any private communications intercepted are not admissible as evidence and must be destroyed as soon as practicable.[274] Similarly, section 184.4 creates an exigent circumstances exception specific to non-consent interceptions. The situation must be so urgent that not even a temporary authorization is available, the interception must be "immediately necessary to prevent an offence that would cause serious harm to any person or to property," and one party to the communication must be either the person who would cause the harm or the intended victim. If those conditions are met, then a police officer (that is, a narrower range than an "agent of the state" under section 184.1) can intercept private communications without any judicial authorization. The Supreme Court has upheld the constitutionality of this section, as long as provision for after-the-fact notice of the interception is incorporated.[275]

iii) Search of the Person: DNA Warrants

It was noted above that statutory search powers have, traditionally, not allowed search of the person. However, amendments to the *Criminal*

---

274 Sections 184.1(2) & (3). The exception is that the evidence is admissible in proceedings relating to actual, attempted, or threatened bodily harm. Evidence based on s 184.1 is generally inadmissible because the conditions triggering it would usually be met in undercover police operations, which would allow interceptions in virtually all of those cases. This would be inconsistent with the "protection of privacy" theory behind interceptions: *R v Riley* (2008), 60 CR (6th) 105 (Ont SCJ).

275 *R v Tse*, 2012 SCC 16. Such provisions are now found in ss 195 and 196.1.

Code have authorized searches that have exactly that effect, allowing the taking of bodily samples for DNA analysis. In particular, warrants that allow the police to obtain hair, buccal swabs, or blood samples from a suspect can be issued. In a general outline, the rules surrounding DNA warrants are similar to those surrounding search warrants. As is appropriate, however, the greater intrusiveness of allowing a search directly affecting bodily integrity is balanced by greater protections for privacy (see the further discussion of this point below in Section C(2)). The Court has held that these provisions do not violate section 8 of the *Charter*.[276]

The basic requirements for a DNA warrant necessitate that a provincial court judge be satisfied by information on oath that a bodily substance connected with an offence[277] has been found, that a person was a party to the offence, and that DNA analysis of the substance will provide evidence about whether the bodily substance was from that person. These conditions more or less parallel the corresponding requirements for a search warrant; although note that the application cannot be made to a justice of the peace. There is also an explicit statement of the rule, implicit for search warrants, that conditions can be imposed to make the taking of the sample reasonable in the circumstances.[278]

Other requirements act to limit the availability of DNA warrants. They are available only in the case of "designated offences," for example, which consist of lists of offences in section 487.04. When the provisions were first introduced, these lists consisted predominantly of sexual offences and offences causing death or bodily harm: they have since grown longer (as did the similar list relating to electronic surveillance). In addition, the judge is required to believe that issuing the warrant is in "the best interests of the administration of justice."[279] Issuing a DNA warrant that is unnecessary will not be in the public interest, though this is not the equivalent of the "investigative necessity" requirement for non-consent authorizations.[280] The Ontario Court of Appeal has held that the presence of a *Charter* violation in the course of obtaining grounds for a DNA warrant is not alone sufficient to prevent the warrant being issued, though the court reserved judgment on whether

---

276 *SAB*, above note 6.
277 The *Code* specifies that the substance could have been found at the place the offence was committed, on or within the body of the victim, on anything worn or carried by the victim, or on or within the body of any person or thing "at any place associated with the commission of the offence": s 487.01(4)(b).
278 Section 487.06(2).
279 Section 487.05(1).
280 *SAB*, above note 6 at para 54.

a "pattern of wilful and flagrant misconduct on the part of the police could lead a judge to deny a DNA warrant on the ground that it would be contrary to the best interests of justice to do so."[281] Section 487.05(2) also requires the judge to have regard to "all relevant matters," which will include the nature of the offence, the circumstances of its commission, and whether a qualified peace officer or other person is available to take the sample.

Other provisions also aim at counterbalancing the intrusiveness of DNA warrants. A peace officer executing the warrant is required to inform the suspect of its contents, the nature of the procedures for taking samples, the purpose for taking them, and the police officer's authorization to use force.[282] In taking the sample, the officer is also required to respect the accused's privacy in a manner that is reasonable under the circumstances. Further, the *Code* requires that the samples taken and the results of analysis should not be used for any other purpose than the investigation of a designated offence meeting the warrant requirements.[283] Failure to comply with this obligation is actually an offence.[284] In addition, in many circumstances there is an obligation to destroy the samples taken and the results obtained. This is the case where the analysis shows that the sample does not come from the person, the person is acquitted, or (unless new proceedings are commenced) one year has passed after a discharge at a preliminary inquiry, a withdrawal of charges, or a stay of proceedings.

In addition to these requirements, additional rules exist when the DNA warrant concerns a young person. In that event, the young person is to be informed of the right to a reasonable opportunity to consult with and have the warrant executed in the presence of counsel, a parent, or other adult.[285] This requirement is similar to the rules concerning statements by young persons.[286]

The Court found the DNA warrant provisions to survive *Charter* scrutiny in *SAB*. In particular, it was argued that the provisions were unconstitutional on the grounds that such searches should be available only as a last resort (similar to investigative necessity for interceptions), that a higher standard than reasonable grounds should be required for such a warrant, and that a DNA warrant should not be issued *ex parte*. The Court rejected these arguments, holding, in essence, that the differ-

---

281 *Nguyen*, above note 92.
282 Section 487.07(1).
283 Sections 487.08(1) & (2).
284 Section 487.08(3).
285 Section 487.07(4).
286 *Youth Criminal Justice Act*, SC 2002, c 1, ss 146(2)(c) & (d).

ences between DNA warrants and search warrants did not justify these particular higher standards. The Court noted that, although DNA warrants are quite intrusive in an informational sense, they are also more focused than wiretaps and would not intrude on the privacy of third parties. The state's interest in the evidence was also quite high, since it could be virtually conclusive either to prove an accused's guilt or to prevent a wrongful conviction. A judge issuing a DNA warrant would consider whether it was necessary in the interests of justice, which might act as a type of "last resort" rule where necessary, and would permit a judge to allow an *inter partes* application where appropriate.[287]

The Court also considered whether the principle against self-incrimination was violated by the provisions, but held that, given the absence of reliability concerns about DNA evidence and the additional safeguards built into the DNA warrant application process, this principle was not violated.[288]

A further aspect of DNA warrants that should be noted is the portion of the *Code* creating a DNA databank. Those provisions allow the gathering of DNA samples at the time of a finding of guilt[289] not for the purpose of investigating a particular crime, but rather to create a bank of information (similar to books of mugshots or collections of fingerprints) to be used in the future. The offences for which DNA warrants are available are divided into "primary designated offences" (nearly all of which involve sexual assault or homicide) and "secondary designated offences." In addition, the scheme divides the primary designated offences into two groups: those in subsection 487.04(a) and (c.02) (primarily sexual or violent offences) and the other primary designated offences (primarily what might be thought of as security-related offences such as hijacking or various terrorism offences, and predecessor versions of the offences in subsection (a)). The scheme operates slightly differently with regard to each of those three categories.

Where an accused is convicted of a primary designated offence in subsection 487.04(a) or (c.02), the court simply "shall make an order" authorizing a DNA sample to be taken for the DNA databank.[290] These offences are primarily current statutory versions of sexual offences. If the accused is convicted of one of the other primary designated offences (a broader range of current offences and historical versions of

---

287 *SAB*, above note 6 at paras 44–56.
288 See the discussion of this aspect of the case, which is more directly relevant to potential s 7 claims, in Stratas, above note 6 and Don Stuart, "*R. v. B. (S.A.)*: Annotation" (2003) 14 *Criminal Reports* (6th) 208.
289 Section 487.051(1).
290 Section 487.051(1).

various sexual offences), the court again shall make an order, but the accused has the opportunity to persuade the court otherwise. Specifically, there is no obligation to make an order if the accused satisfies the court the impact of the order on his privacy would be grossly disproportionate to the public interest in the protection of society and proper administration of justice.[291] It will be rare for such a challenge to succeed.[292] The convicted person will be required to prove that the circumstances depart markedly from the cases Parliament is likely to have had in mind in drafting the provisions[293] and that no terms or conditions could adequately restore the proper balance.

In the case of a conviction for a secondary designated offence, the court may make an order on the application of the prosecutor if satisfied it is in the best interests of the administration of justice to do so. This same standard applies if the accused, rather than being convicted, is found not criminally responsible for *any* designated offence.[294] The "best interests" standard is to be judged taking into account the person's criminal record, whether the person was previously found not criminally responsible on account of mental disorder for a designated offence, the nature of the offence, the circumstances surrounding its commission, and the impact such an order would have on the person's privacy and security of the person. As a practical matter, the convicted person is held to have a minimal privacy interest.[295] On the other hand, the state interest is quite significant and includes deterring potential repeat offenders, promoting the safety of the community, detecting when a serial offender is at work, assisting in the solving of cold crimes, streamlining investigations, and assisting the innocent through early exclusion from suspicion or by exonerating the wrongfully convicted.[296] The result is that such orders are granted in most cases.[297]

It is also possible to make retroactive orders in some cases; that is, beyond making orders for historical offences if the conviction occurs in the present, the scheme also permits some orders to be made with regard to offenders convicted before the DNA databank provisions were

---

291   Section 487.051(2).

292   *R v RC*, 2005 SCC 61 at para 65, citing *R v Jordan*, 2002 NSCA 11 [*Jordan*].

293   *Jordan*, ibid, adopted in *R v May*, 2009 BCCA 161, and *R v BR*, 2011 NLCA 23.

294   Section 487.051(3).

295   *R v Durham*, 2007 BCCA 190 at para 12 [*Durham*].

296   *R v Briggs* (2001), 157 CCC (3d) 38 at para 22 (Ont CA), relied on in many other cases, such as *Durham*, above note 295, or *R v Bacon*, 2013 BCCA 397 [*Bacon*]. See also *R v PRF* (2001), 48 CR (5th) 310 (Ont CA).

297   See *Durham*, above note 295 at para 12, or *R v Awasis*, 2009 BCCA 134 at para 59. Nonetheless, the trial judge does have the discretion to decline to make an order: see, for example, *Bacon*, above note 296.

enacted. These retroactive provisions are limited to a relatively narrow range, including dangerous offenders, those convicted of murder, and those still serving sentences for certain sexual offences at the time of the application.[298]

The DNA databank provisions have been upheld by the Court, though it is worth observing that the scheme has been made applicable to an increased number of offences and offenders since then.[299] In rejecting challenges to the legislation, based on both section 8 and section 11 of the *Charter*, the Court held:

> Society's interest in using this powerful new technology to assist law enforcement agencies in the identification of offenders is beyond dispute. The resulting impact on the physical integrity of the targeted offenders is minimal. The potential invasive impact on the right to privacy has carefully been circumscribed by legislative safeguards that restrict the use of the DNA data bank as an identification tool only. As convicted offenders still under sentence, the persons targeted by s. 487.055 have a much reduced expectation of privacy. Further, by reason of their crimes, they have lost any reasonable expectation that their identity will remain secret from law enforcement authorities. Having regard to the interests at stake and the procedural safeguards afforded by the legislative scheme, I have also concluded that the *ex parte* nature of the proceedings meets the dictates of procedural fairness afforded under s. 7 of the *Charter*. Finally, ss. 11(h) and 11(i) of the *Charter* are inapplicable. The taking of DNA samples does not constitute a punishment within the meaning of s. 11 anymore than the taking of fingerprints or other identification measures.[300]

In addition to DNA warrants, the *Code* also contains a provision creating an "impression warrant" that allows a peace officer to obtain a handprint, footprint, tooth impression, or impression of any part of the body.[301] Seemingly, Parliament's assumption is that such procedures will necessarily be less invasive of a person's bodily integrity and privacy than obtaining DNA samples, since few limitations surround such warrants, other than a requirement that issuing the warrant be in the best interests of the administration of justice. There is room to question this assumption: an impression of "any part of the body" has the potential to invade privacy quite significantly. Further, in *Stillman* the Court described taking dental impressions as "a lengthy and highly intrusive

---

298 Section 487.055.
299 *R v Rodgers*, [2006] 1 SCR 554.
300 *Ibid* at para 5.
301 Section 487.092.

process" that, in the particular context of that case, amounted to "the abusive exercise of raw physical authority by the police."[302]

Impression warrants may be issued by a justice in respect of any offence, based on reasonable grounds to believe that the print will provide information concerning the offence. This wording does not seem to require that the person from whom the impression is taken be a suspect. Conditions that make the search and seizure reasonable in the circumstances can be imposed to ensure that the warrant is in the best interests of the administration of justice.

iv) Other Statutory Search Warrant Provisions

Other warrant provisions allow for the gathering of particular kinds of evidence that could not be obtained under a search warrant, which is restricted to tangible "things." Section 492.1 allows for tracking warrants, which authorize police to attach a device which will track the location of a thing or person. Notably, the section treats these two situations separately: tracking the location of a person requires reasonable grounds to *believe* that an offence has been or will be committed and that tracking the person will assist in the investigation of the offence. Where it is only a thing, such as a vehicle, which is to be tracked, the warrant can be issued on the lower standard of reasonable *suspicion*.[303] Either warrant is limited to a maximum of sixty days or one year in the case of organized crime or terrorism offences.[304]

The *Code* also contains a provision allowing for "transmission data" warrants, which, in 2015, replaced what had been called "number recorder" warrants, which were aimed at telephones. The expanded power is primarily aimed at capturing the same kind of information about communications in addition to those through telephones. These warrants are aimed at tracking information about communications other than the contents of those communications: in essence, anything that will indicate which devices communicated with one another, for how

---

302 *Stillman*, above note 91 at para 46.

303 Sections 492.1(1) & (2). The Court in *Wise*, above note 13, found a *Charter* violation where the police used a tracking device without a warrant. However, they observed that a device which determines only the location of the item to which it is attached is a minimal intrusion on privacy and could be justified based on reasonable suspicion. A predecessor version of s 492.1 was introduced in response to that decision and used the reasonable suspicion standard. The current version of the section was introduced in 2015 as part of the *Protecting Canadians from Online Crime Act*, SC 2014, c 31; it notes the distinction between tracking things and tracking people. See the further discussion of reasonable suspicion in Section C(2), below in this chapter.

304 Sections 492.1(4) & (5).

long, from where, how large a file was exchanged, and so on.[305] The warrants are available on the reasonable suspicion standard and are limited to a maximum of sixty days or one year in the case of organized crime or terrorism offences.[306]

Outside the *Code*, the *CDSA* creates a search warrant provision which is quite similar to section 487: the application is made to a justice, is made on oath, and must satisfy the justice on reasonable grounds.[307] Since the particular offence in question will relate to controlled substances, the requirement that there be evidence of an offence is specific to that context: the justice must be persuaded that drugs, something containing drugs, offence related property, or evidence of a *CDSA* offence will be found. However, there are some unique features of drug warrants. First, only a peace officer (not a public officer) can be empowered to search under the warrant. Second, although section 487 warrants require special authorization to be executed at night,[308] drug warrants are executable at night as a matter of course. Third, the power to search persons differs between the two. Search warrants authorize the search of a location but not of persons found at that location. Drug warrants, on the other hand, do authorize such personal searches, if the executing officer has reasonable grounds to believe that the person has the things set out in the warrant on their person. This difference is accounted for by the nature of the offence and the simplicity with which drugs could be hidden on the person.

In addition to these warrants, other statutory provisions contain more specific search powers. Most notably, a number of sections of the *Code* contain what are known as "production orders." The purpose of a production order, as opposed to a warrant, is to employ it with regard to bodies that are likely to have relevant information but that can

---

305 *TELUS* 2015, above note 127 at para 15:

> The function of a transmission data recorder warrant ("TDRW") is to provide the police with information regarding the activity on a cellular telephone. More specifically, it can be used to reveal communications made to and from the phone, that is, calls made to and from the phone and text messages sent to and from the phone. If so configured, it may permit other communications, such as email messages or social media contacts, to be tracked. Whichever communications are being tracked, however, the TDRW does not reveal the content of any of those communications. In other words, the TDRW reveals the fact of a communication between phones but not the actual communication.

See s 492.2(6), for the precise definition.

306 Sections 492.2(4) & (5).

307 Above note 108, s 11.

308 Section 488.

be expected to cooperate with the police: banks, telephone companies, Internet service providers, and so on. Indeed, the relevant provisions specify that they cannot be served on the person who is under investigation.[309] When cooperation can be expected, it is easier for both the police and the body whose records are sought if the information is assembled by the people who already have control of the records. There are several production orders, paralleling various warrant provisions in the *Code*. The general production order is found in section 487.014. This section allows a judge to order a person other than the target of the investigation to produce or prepare documents or data. The grounds upon which these production orders can issue are functionally equivalent to those for search warrants: reasonable grounds to believe that an offence has been (or will be, in this case) committed and that the person has documents or data that will provide evidence respecting that offence. There will, of course, be costs caused by complying with production orders, but no compensation is necessarily available to the parties required to produce documents.[310] However, it is possible for an entity served with a production order to challenge that order, and a judge can revoke or vary the order if satisfied that it is unreasonable in the circumstances to require the applicant to prepare or produce the document or that production of the document would disclose information that is privileged or otherwise protected from disclosure by law.[311] Where the cost of compliance is unreasonable, an application to vary or revoke the order could be made.[312]

Other specific production orders can be issued with regard to transmission data and tracking data, therefore being equivalent to those warrant provisions. Two separate production orders relating to transmission data exist: one to be used when police know that a communication was made but do not know who has the transmission data (for example, they do not know which carrier handled the cell-phone call) and the other when the police know that a particular entity has the information sought.[313] Like tracking and transmission data warrants, these production orders are available on the lower standard of reasonable suspicion. Further, a production order relating to limited

---

309 See ss 487.014(4), 487.015(5), 487.016(4), 487.017(4), and 487.018(5).

310 *Tele-Mobile Co v Ontario*, 2008 SCC 12 [*Tele-Mobile*].

311 Section 487.0193.

312 In *Tele-Mobile*, above note 310, the Court noted this possibility based on the exemption section in force at the time. There are some differences in wording between the former s 487.015(4)(b) and the current s 487.0193, but they are relatively minor and so it seems this possibility should still exist.

313 Sections 487.015 & 487.016.

financial information—for example, the name of a person associated with a particular account, or the number of the account that goes with a particular name—can also be issued on reasonable suspicion.[314]

In addition to these warrants and production orders, the *Protecting Canadians from Online Crime Act* in 2015 added to the *Code* preservation demands and preservation orders, whose primary purpose is to assist with production orders. Either a preservation demand or order requires a person who is in possession or control of computer data not to destroy it: the goal is to give a peace officer enough time to seek a production order or warrant. A preservation demand can be made by a peace officer personally and expires after twenty-one days; no new demand can be made.[315] A preservation order is issued by a justice or judge and lasts at most ninety days.[316] Both of these powers are based on reasonable suspicion, and like production orders cannot be served on the person under investigation.[317]

Finally, there are a number of other quite specific warrant provisions in the *Code*. Some of these warrant provisions are for purely investigative purposes. For example, section 256 provides for warrants to obtain a blood sample from a person suspected of driving while impaired. Other warrant provisions are in whole or in part motivated by the nature of the item searched for. That is, the goal of the seizure is not simply to obtain evidence concerning a crime, but also has a preventive aspect. This motive seems to help explain the separate warrant provisions dealing with common gaming houses,[318] hate propaganda,[319] valuable minerals,[320] the search power in section 11 of the *Controlled Drugs and Substances Act*,[321] and the power to seize explosives.[322] Although it does not explicitly create a search power, this also appears to be the motive behind section 164, which permits a justice to issue a warrant for the seizure of voyeuristic recordings, intimate images, obscene publications, crime comics, child pornography, or advertisements for sexual

---

314 Section 487.018.
315 Sections 487.012(4) and (6). The demand does not expire for ninety days if it is made in relation to an offence committed under the law of a foreign state.
316 Section 487.013(6).
317 Sections 487.012(3) and 487.013(5).
318 Section 199. That section also authorizes taking into custody anyone found in the common gaming house or common bawdy house.
319 Sections 320 & 320.1.
320 Section 395.
321 Above note 108.
322 Section 492.

services.[323] Indeed, the preventive concern can be dominant over the investigative one. For example, section 117.04 allows the police to seek a warrant to search for and seize a weapon on the grounds that it is not in the interests of safety for the person to have it.[324] Similar forfeiture concerns motivate provisions that allow warrants to search for property that can be forfeited under proceeds of crime legislation.[325] It is worth noting that the Ontario Court of Appeal has struck down section 117.04 for failing to comply with the standards in *Hunter*.[326] Although the section requires the justice to be satisfied that it is not desirable for a named person to possess a firearm or other weapon, it does not require the justice to be satisfied that the person is in possession of such an item. The court found that, without that requirement, the provision permits too sweeping a search power, which could not be saved under section 1 of the *Charter*.

v) Reviewing Warrants
The whole purpose of requiring a warrant for searches is so that there is judicial oversight in advance of the search. However, that does not mean that there is no scope for after-the-fact review as well. To fully understand searches with a warrant, then, it is necessary to consider the rules governing their review.

The *Code* contains no provisions that allow for an appeal from the decision to issue a warrant, and in the absence of such a statutory provision, there is no right of appeal.[327] This is true even if there is an issue as to whether the search violated section 8 of the *Charter*, because the *Charter* does not create new appeal procedures.[328] It is possible to challenge the issuance of a warrant through *certiorari*, but this approach has been called an "idle exercise" since it does not result in either the return

---

323 Some of these provisions are long-standing, while others have been added later. For example, the seizure power dealing with advertisements for sexual services was added in the *Protection of Communities and Exploited Persons Act*, SC 2014, c 25, which made various changes to the law around prostitution, while the seizure power concerning intimate images was added in the *Protecting Canadians from Online Crime Act*, SC 2014, c 31.

324 This section, unlike the others discussed here, does not explicitly require that the information be provided on oath. In *R v Hurrell* (2002), 4 CR (6th) 169 (Ont CA) [*Hurrell*], the Ontario Court of Appeal held that the word "application" in the section should be read as a term of art, requiring that it be under oath.

325 Section 462.32(1).

326 *Hurrell*, above note 324.

327 *Knox Contracting Ltd v Canada*, [1990] 2 SCR 338; *Kourtessis v MNR*, [1993] 2 SCR 53.

328 *R v Meltzer*, [1989] 1 SCR 1764.

of the items seized or their exclusion as evidence.[329] For this reason it will generally be preferable to leave challenges to the warrant to the trial stage. If a warrant is quashed, then the search was warrantless, which means that it was *prima facie* unreasonable and in violation of section 8. However, it will still need to be determined whether the evidence should be excluded under section 24(2), a determination that depends on considerations broader than just those that relate to the warrant. As a result, that decision can be made only at trial, when the overlapping questions of violation and remedy can be dealt with together.[330] A pre-trial challenge to the warrant is possible, but is appropriate only where issues such as preventing a search arise.[331]

The central issue in reviewing a warrant is whether the requirements for its issuance under the *Code* have been met. Thus, for example, if the warrant fails to adequately describe the premises to be searched or the offence under investigation, the warrant can be quashed.[332] More commonly, however, the issue is whether there is a problem with the "Information to Obtain" (ITO) which was presented to the justice in the application for the warrant.

For example, inaccurate information about the suspect, which could contribute to the reasonable grounds for the search, can affect the decision.[333] In addition, the informant must present all material facts, whether favourable or not, and is not permitted to choose those that make it most likely that the warrant will be issued. If relevant facts are omitted or unrelated facts are presented in a way to suggest a connection between them, then the ITO might be misleading: it need not be intentionally misleading for it to be quashed.[334]

The reviewing judge, however, does not decide whether the warrant *should* have been issued. Rather, the question is whether there was evidence upon which the issuing judge *could* have decided to issue the warrant.[335] The actual result of the search is not relevant on review.[336]

One particular issue that arises in this context is when a warrant has been issued based on an ITO containing information from a confidential

---

329 *R v Zevallos* (1987), 59 CR (3d) 153 at 158 (Ont CA) [*Zevallos*].
330 *Ibid*; *R v Tanner* (1989), 46 CCC (3d) 513 (Alta CA); *R v Williams* (1987), 38 CCC (3d) 319 (YTCA).
331 *Zevallos*, above note 329.
332 *Bergeron v Deschamps*, [1978] 1 SCR 243.
333 *R v Sismey* (1990), 55 CCC (3d) 281 (BCCA) [*Sismey*].
334 *Morelli*, above note 82.
335 *R v Garofoli*, [1990] 2 SCR 1421 at 1452 [*Garofoli*]. *Garofoli* concerns a wiretap authorization, but the same standard is applicable to search warrants: see *R v Breton* (1994), 93 CCC (3d) 171 (Ont CA).
336 *Descoteaux v Mierzwinski*, [1982] 1 SCR 860.

informant. Before being disclosed to the accused and filed in court, such an ITO will be edited to remove any information that might identify the informant.[337] The difficulty is that such an ITO, on its redacted face, might no longer contain enough material for the reviewing judge to say that the warrant could have been issued: in that event the warrant will be quashed. In essence, the Crown is faced with the dilemma that they can either preserve the confidentiality promised to the informant or show that the warrant was properly issued, but they cannot do both.

To address this problem, the Supreme Court suggested in *R v Garofoli* a procedure which could be used in such situations—what is usually referred to as "step six in *Garofoli*":

> 6. If, however, the editing renders the authorization insupportable, then the Crown may apply to have the trial judge consider so much of the excised material as is necessary to support the authorization. The trial judge should accede to such a request only if satisfied that the accused is sufficiently aware of the nature of the excised material to challenge it in argument or by evidence. In this regard, a judicial summary of the excised material should be provided if it will fulfill that function. It goes without saying that if the Crown is dissatisfied with the extent of disclosure and is of the view that the public interest will be prejudiced, it can withdraw tender of the wiretap evidence.[338]

Although this option exists, Crown prosecutors seem to be reluctant to use it. There have been suggestions that it ought to be employed more frequently, though not all judges agree that it is a desirable option.[339]

In addition to review of the issuance of a search warrant on the facial basis above, review can also take place on a sub-facial basis: whether it is possible, by going behind the form of the affidavit, to attack the

---

337 See also s 487.3, permitting an order prohibiting access to or disclosure of any information relating to the warrant, for purposes such as protecting the identity of a confidential informant.

338 *Garofoli*, above note 335 at 1461.

339 See *R v Rocha*, 2012 ONCA 707, citing *R v Learning*, 2010 ONSC 3816, and arguing that prosecutors ought to try more frequently to rely on step six, so that jurisprudence can be developed about how to apply it. To some extent this is occurring, at least in Ontario: see, for example, *R v Sahid*, 2011 ONSC 979; *R v Brown*, 2011 ONSC 6223; *R v Farrugia*, 2012 ONCJ 830; *R v Herdsman*, 2012 ONCJ 739; *R v Iyeke*, 2014 ONSC 2208; or *R v Burgher*, 2014 ONSC 4527. See also David Tice, "Into the Black: Litigating Search Warrants and Wiretaps under the Sixth Step of *Garofoli*" (2014) 61 *Criminal Law Quarterly* 102; and Chris De Sa, "*Garofoli* Step 6: Getting Behind the Black" (2014) 61 *Criminal Law Quarterly* 418.

reliability of its content.[340] Nonetheless, cross-examination on the ITO to perform a sub-facial challenge is not automatically available. Some early cases suggested that the applicant must show on a *prima facie* basis that there was deliberate falsehood, omission, or a reckless disregard for the truth by the person swearing the affidavit before cross-examination would be permitted.[341] In *Garofoli*, however, the Court held that, although cross-examination should not be the general rule and that leave of the reviewing judge was required, the standard of a *prima facie* case was too high. Rather, all that is necessary is a basis for the view that "the cross-examination will elicit testimony tending to discredit the existence of one of the preconditions to the authorization, as for example the existence of reasonable and probable grounds."[342] Cross-examination should normally be limited to questions aimed at showing there was no basis for issuing the warrant.[343]

On review, evidence that was used in support of the warrant may be excised from the application. Information that was misleading[344] or that the police should have known was not true[345] may be removed from the material that potentially justified the issuance of the warrant. Equally, if evidence used to justify the warrant was obtained through a *Charter* breach, that evidence will also be excluded.[346] If relevant evidence ought to have been included in the ITO but was omitted, that material can be taken into account on review.[347] The question then becomes whether the remaining evidence could have been sufficient to justify issuing the warrant.

It may be possible for the Crown to amplify the grounds that justified the issuance of the warrant if evidence is excised at the review hearing. However, this possibility exists only where the error leading to the excision occurred despite good faith on the part of the police.[348] The Court has noted that amplification requires a delicate balance. To never permit it would sometimes mean that a warrant was overturned due to some technical error, although the police had valid grounds to obtain that warrant. Conversely, if amplification were too readily allowed, it

---

340 *Araujo*, above note 232 at para 50.
341 *R v Collins* (1989), 69 CR (3d) 235 (Ont CA).
342 *Garofoli*, above note 335 at 1465. The Court has subsequently reaffirmed this standard: *R v Pires*, [2005] 3 SCR 343.
343 *Garofoli*, above note 335 at 1465.
344 *Sismey*, above note 333.
345 *Garofoli*, above note 335.
346 *Evans*, above note 31; *Grant* 1993, above note 112; *Wiley*, above note 182.
347 *Morelli*, above note 82 at para 60.
348 *Araujo*, above note 232 at para 58.

could circumvent the *Charter* requirement of prior authorization for the warrant.[349]

Some earlier cases suggested that the basis upon which evidence was excised was of little importance in the reviewing process. In *R v Bisson*, for example, the Court held that "errors in the information presented to the authorizing judge, whether advertent or even fraudulent, are only factors to be considered in deciding to set aside the authorization and do not by themselves lead to automatic vitiation of the wiretap authorization."[350] The issue, the Court suggested, was whether, after the fraudulent information had been removed, the remaining information was sufficient to justify issuance of the warrant. Subsequently, however, the Court recognized a basis for review beyond whether sufficient evidence remains. Although in agreement that fraud does not automatically lead to quashing a warrant, the Court held that

> [t]his does not mean that errors, particularly deliberate ones, are irrelevant in the review process. While not leading to automatic vitiation of the warrant, there remains the need to protect the prior authorization process. The cases just referred to do not foreclose a reviewing judge, in appropriate circumstances, from concluding on *the totality of the circumstances* that the conduct of the police in seeking prior authorization was so subversive of that process that the resulting warrant must be set aside to protect the process and the preventive function it serves.[351]

Accordingly, it now seems clear that reviewing courts can quash a warrant based either on the inadequacy of the material remaining after some information is excised, or based on behaviour of the police that intentionally misled or otherwise subverted the process of prior authorization.[352]

2) Was the Law Itself Reasonable?

a) Warrantless Searches
As noted earlier, there tends to be little separate discussion of the second step in the *Collins* test in the case of warrantless searches. In the

---

349   *Ibid* at para 59.

350   [1994] 3 SCR 1097 at para 2.

351   *Araujo*, above note 232 at para 54, cited from *R v Morris* (1998), 134 CCC (3d) 539 at para 43 (NSCA) [emphasis added by Supreme Court].

352   See, generally, Robert W Hubbard & Scott K Fenton, "Supreme Court of Canada Wiretap Update — February 2001" (delivered at Search and Seizure Law in Canada, the Professional Development Program, Osgoode Hall Law School, Toronto, 3 November 2001).

case of common law search powers, deciding that the power exists at all requires a court to decide its extent. Since the common law is to be developed in a way that is consistent with the *Charter*, the result will be to settle the question of whether the law is reasonable. Common law powers are created by application of the *Waterfield* test, but that test, like the *Collins* test, asks about reasonableness, and so the two tests overlap.[353] The effect of this approach is to render redundant, for searches based on common law powers, the separate step of asking "is the law itself reasonable?" This is so not because the question is unimportant, but because it will already have been answered. Thus, for example, in *Golden* the Court considered a strip search as an incident to an arrest and articulated the new requirement that a strip search could be conducted only if there were reasonable and probable grounds to believe it was necessary. Then, turning to this second phase of the *Collins* test, they held that "as interpreted above, the common law power to search incident to arrest conforms with the constitutional protection against unreasonable search and seizure."[354]

Much the same is true of statutory warrantless search powers, where courts tend to read down the statute in a way that makes the power coincide with constitutional minimum standards. Thus, for example, in *Grant* the Court found that the search power in section 10 of the *Narcotic Control Act* had to be read down to apply only in exigent circumstances.[355] When the law has been interpreted in this way, there is no real scope to then ask separately whether the law is reasonable.[356]

There is, however, one issue worth discussing here: the distinction between "reasonable suspicion" and "reasonable grounds to believe." This distinction is relevant to both warrantless searches and those conducted with a warrant, but the Court has primarily articulated the

---

353 *Mann*, above note 166 at para 44. The most extreme example of this approach is in *R v Clayton*, 2007 SCC 32, where (as the minority noted) the creation of the common law power is substituted entirely for the *Charter* analysis: see paras 58–63. However, it is a power to detain, not a search power, which is the central issue in that case.

354 *Golden*, above note 19 at para 104. To similar effect, see also *Caslake*, above note 15. In *Stillman*, above note 91 at para 49, the Court paid lip service to the notion of having two steps:

> The common law power of search incidental to arrest cannot be so broad as to encompass the seizure without valid statutory authority of bodily samples in the face of a refusal to provide them. If it is, then the common law rule itself is unreasonable, since it is too broad and fails to properly balance the competing rights involved.

355 *Grant* 1993, above note 112.

356 To similar effect, see *R v Jacques*, [1996] 3 SCR 312; *Garofoli*, above note 335.

distinction in cases involving common law powers. The important policy issue here was adverted to in the Introduction to this chapter and has been implicit in the discussion of specific powers: that although in general the balance between individual and state interests means that searches are allowed only "at the point where credibly-based probability replaces suspicion,"[357] nonetheless, some search powers permit searches more readily, and some less readily.

Reasonable suspicion searches are an example of that: where the impact of a search on a person's privacy interests is seen as relatively minimal, the standard for being allowed to search is lower.[358] This is the rationale behind allowing sniffer dog searches on reasonable suspicion, for example: merely having a dog with the ability to detect one thing—narcotics—smell the air around a piece of luggage is less intrusive than opening that bag and going through all of its contents. As the Court held in *Chehil*:

> In *Hunter*, this Court also recognized that this balancing of interests can justify searches on a lower standard where privacy interests are reduced, or where state objectives of public importance are predominant (p. 168). Thus, the Court has found reasonable suspicion to be a sufficient threshold in certain investigative contexts, and Parliament has employed this standard when authorizing certain searches in legislation.[359]
>
> In the case of sniff searches, the use of the reasonable suspicion standard reflects, in part, the minimal intrusion of a dog sniff. For a physical search of luggage incident to arrest, which will be more intrusive, the more exacting reasonable and probable grounds standard is engaged, as the arrest must be justified.[360]

The Court spent some time in *Chehil* elaborating on the "reasonable suspicion" standard. Because it is lower than "reasonable belief" it deals only with the possibility of crime, not its probability, which "necessarily means that in some cases the police will reasonably suspect that innocent people are involved in crime."[361] But although the standard is lower, it must still be based on objectively reasonable facts and must amount to more than a generalized suspicion that something

---

357 *Hunter*, above note 6 at 167.

358 See criticism of the reasonable suspicion standard in Peter Sankoff & Stéphane Perrault, "Suspicious Searches: What's So Reasonable about Them?" (1999) 24 *Criminal Reports* (5th) 123.

359 *Chehil*, above note 30 at para 23.

360 *Ibid* at paras 23–24 [footnotes omitted].

361 *Ibid* at para 28.

is going on.[362] Reasonable suspicion must be based on a totality of the circumstances, which means that both the inculpatory and exculpatory information must be taken into account. Some individual factors might be incriminating all on their own, but this need not be the case: ambiguous factors that are capable of innocent explanation can, nonetheless, when taken with other considerations, contribute to reasonable suspicion. As the Court says:

> The same is true of factors that may "go both ways", such as an individual's making or failing to make eye contact. On their own, such factors cannot support reasonable suspicion; however, this does not preclude reasonable suspicion arising when the same factor is simply one part of a constellation of factors.[363]

Criminal behaviour need not be the only inference available for a suspicion to be reasonable.[364] Beyond that, police have no duty to investigate further to eliminate possible innocent explanations before conducting a search, and the reasonableness of the search should be assessed based on the circumstances the police were aware of at the time of the execution of the search.[365] Finally, officer training and experience can enter into the objective test for reasonableness, but such claims ought not to be accepted uncritically: "[e]vidence as to the specific nature and extent of such experience and training is required so that the court may make an objective assessment of the probative link between the constellation of factors relied on by the police and criminality."[366]

b) Searches with a Warrant

The point that the amount of protection offered an individual goes up or down in proportion to the strength of her privacy interest and the strength of the state interest is most obviously present in searches with

---

362 *Ibid* at paras 27 and 30.
363 *Ibid* at para 31.
364 *Ibid* at para 32.
365 *Ibid* at para 34.
366 *Ibid* at para 47. See also the companion decision handed down the same day in *MacKenzie*, above note 30. In *Chehil* all nine justices agreed that the reasonable suspicion standard was met. In *MacKenzie* there was a 5:4 split, with the dissent warning against the creation of broad categories of suspicious behaviour into which almost anyone could fall, which would risk transforming the standard of reasonable suspicion into a generalized suspicion standard, which had earlier been rejected by the Court. For discussion of officer training and experience, see Steve Coughlan, "Learning from Experience about Learning from Experience: Modifying the Objective Test for Arrest and Detention" (2013) 4 *Criminal Reports* (7th) 245.

a warrant. The criteria for various warrant provisions have already been set out above, and this section will not repeat all of those individual requirements. However, it will show by way of example how the standard goes up or down. When there is the "normal" state interest in investigating crime and the "normal" privacy interest on the part of the subject of the search, section 487 search warrants set the standard. When there is either a higher state interest or a lower privacy interest, warrants based on less protection to the individual can be justified. Conversely, when either the state interest is lower or the personal interest is higher, a greater degree of protection is required.

The benchmark was set in the very early *Charter* decision of *Hunter*.[367] That case involved search warrants issued to investigators under the *Combines Investigation Act* by the members of the Restrictive Trade Practices Commission, and the question was whether that arrangement violated section 8: it was found that it did. The Court's reasons amounted to setting the standard for a warrant provision being reasonable as the second step in the *Collins* test, though, in fact, *Hunter* predates *Collins*.

There were two particular frailties in the scheme in question. First, the point of pre-authorization is to allow someone impartial: "the decision to grant or withhold the warrant requires the balancing of two interests: that of the individual to be free of intrusions of the state and that of the state to intrude on the privacy of the individual for the purpose of law enforcement."[368] A member of the Restrictive Trade Practices Commission was not independent enough to perform that task appropriately. Second, the search did not require reasonable grounds to believe either that an offence had been committed or that evidence would be found before a warrant could be issued. The Court concluded:

> reasonable and probable grounds, established upon oath, to believe that an offence has been committed and that there is evidence to be found at the place of the search, constitutes the minimum standard, consistent with s 8 of the *Charter,* for authorizing search and seizure.[369]

Hunter found that in the ordinary case the standards for a warrant include four factors. First, the warrant must have been issued by someone who is capable of acting judicially. Second, that person must be satisfied of the necessary factors on a "reasonable grounds to believe" standard. Third, the evidence must have been given on oath, and finally, it must give the person issuing the warrant reasonable grounds

---

367 *Hunter*, above note 6.
368 *Baron*, above note 10 at para 24.
369 *Hunter*, above note 6 at 168.

to believe (as opposed to suspect) that an offence has been committed and that evidence will (rather than might) be found by the search. It has also been found that a warrant provision that does not leave any residual discretion with the issuing judge will violate section 8.[370] In fact, these requirements are satisfied by section 487, which allows search warrants to be seen as representative of the benchmark.[371]

That the standard varies according to how privacy and state interests differ from the norm is reflected in the requirements of the various statutory search powers. Note, for example, that the requirements for the issuance of a general production order, which engages exactly the same individual and state interests as a search warrant but simply provides practical convenience in gathering the evidence, are the same as those for a search warrant. On the other hand, some production orders are seen as gathering less intrusive information: the name of a bank account holder.[372] For the most part, this sort of information will allow the police only to go and seek further authorization, for example, to now seek a search warrant because they have identified the person to investigate. Alternatively, production orders are available to obtain "transmission data," but this is explicitly defined as information that "does not reveal the substance, meaning or purpose of the communication."[373] These production orders and others infringe on privacy less than other searches, and so are available on reasonable suspicion.

Similarly, note that tracking warrants are divided into two categories: those that track the location of items, which can be issued on reasonable suspicion, and those that track the location of people, which require reasonable grounds. This difference reflects that tracking a person's location is more intrusive than tracking property.

Further, the addition of greater protection can also easily be seen in the requirements of other warrant provisions. For example, additional requirements are imposed in the case of electronic surveillance and DNA warrants, both of which engage particularly high privacy interests. First, DNA warrants and authorizations are not available for all offences: in each case, they are available only to investigate particularly serious offences, where a higher state interest is at play.[374] Further, both

---

370 *Baron*, above note 10 at para 24.
371 The Supreme Court has not explicitly approved s 487, though it was found by the Ontario Court of Appeal to be in compliance with the requirements of *Hunter*, above note 6: see *Times Square*, above note 247.
372 Section 487.018.
373 Section 487.011.
374 See the definition of "offence" in s 183 and the lists of designated offences in s 487.04.

of those sets of provisions have the minimum *Hunter* requirements, but in addition impose other conditions before a warrant can be issued. For example, *Hunter* requires only that the warrant be issued by someone capable of acting judicially, and for the most part, warrants are available from a justice of the peace. Consent authorizations and DNA warrants, on the other hand, cannot be obtained from a justice: only a provincial superior court judge has the authority. Non-consent authorizations are even more restricted and can be obtained only from a superior court judge. In addition, even after the minimum *Hunter* standards are met, non-consent authorizations and DNA warrants can be issued only if the judge is also satisfied that issuing the warrant is in the best interests of the administration of justice.[375] Beyond that, non-consent authorizations also require that investigative necessity be met.[376]

Essentially, the thing to be recognized is that for a law to be reasonable, it must properly balance the individual and state interests. *Hunter* and section 487 of the *Code* provide a benchmark against which to measure that balance: a law which permits a search relatively easily cannot be allowed to apply when a more serious privacy interest is at stake. This issue is central to the Court's reasoning in *TELUS*, a case discussed in Chapter 5 when considering general warrants.[377]

The primary way in which the question of the reasonableness of a law arises in the search with a warrant context is by variations in the actual requirements of the provisions. However, it is not the only way in which that consideration is reflected. In addition, there are special cases in which the Court has held that the way in which a particular statutory power is to be interpreted or applied should vary depending on the context. We shall consider four such situations: (1) regulatory searches, (2) searches by school officials, (3) searches of media offices, and (4) searches of lawyers' offices.[378]

---

375 Sections 186(1)(a) and 487.05(1), respectively. This is also true of general warrants: s 487.01(1)(b).

376 Section 186(1)(b).

377 *TELUS*, above note 266. Justice Moldaver in that case observes at para 71, for example, that

> [i]f the police sought a general warrant, they would have to meet the requirements of s. 487.01 which are deliberately stricter than those for a conventional warrant. For example, the requirements that a general warrant can only be issued by a judge, not a justice of the peace, and that issuance must be in the best interests of justice themselves serve to ensure that the general warrant remains a rearguard warrant of limited resort.

378 One might note as well in this context the decision in *Laporte*, above note 226. The police were seeking a search warrant to authorize surgery to remove a bullet from a suspect's shoulder. The Crown argued that the suspect's shoulder fell

c) Special Cases

i) Regulatory Searches

The Court has held on many occasions that *Charter* rights must be interpreted in a way consistent with the context in which they arise. This is equally true in the case of section 8, where the Court has held that the approach to section 8 rights as described in *Hunter* does not apply outside the criminal law context. On some occasions, the state's primary interest in conducting a search will not be to prosecute a criminal offence, but rather to enforce the rules of some regulated activity. In that event, the state may well have an interest in "the restaurateur's compliance with public health regulations, the employer's compliance with employment standards and safety legislation . . . the developer's or homeowner's compliance with building codes or zoning regulations [or] compliance with minimum wage, employment equity and human rights legislation."[379] Effective regulation of these areas may require surprise inspections or the examination of records, and, therefore, the Court has held that people engaged in these activities have a lower expectation of privacy in relation to those activities. Accordingly, searches and seizures that do not comply with the *Hunter* standards may nonetheless be reasonable under section 8.

On this basis, the Court has concluded that compelling a person to testify regarding predatory pricing procedures under the *Combines Investigation Act*,[380] or to produce various documents under the *Income Tax Act*[381] or the British Columbia *Securities Act*[382] does not constitute unreasonable search or seizure. Although possible prosecution could follow from engaging in the behaviour being investigated, the investigations and the offences are not criminal offences. Accordingly, a search can sometimes be reasonable, even if the *Hunter* protections are not in place.

---

within s 487 as a "building, receptacle or place," but the judge refused to read the section in a way which would allow for the warrant. He concluded that the interest of the accused in the physical integrity of his body was a much more important interest than that intended to be covered by s 487 and, therefore, outweighed the state's interest in investigation.

379 *Thomson Newspapers Ltd v Canada (Director of Investigation and Research, Restrictive Trade Practices Commission)*, [1990] 1 SCR 425.

380 *Ibid.*

381 *R v McKinlay Transport Ltd*, [1990] 1 SCR 627; *R v Jarvis*, [2002] 3 SCR 757 [*Jarvis*]; *R v Ling*, 2002 SCC 74.

382 *British Columbia Securities Commission v Branch*, [1995] 2 SCR 3. See also *Comité paritaire de l'industrie de la chemise v Potash; Comité paritaire de l'industrie de la chemise c Sélection Milton*, [1994] 2 SCR 406, regarding inspection of documents relating to work arrangements.

The Court has at times recognized the importance of keeping this exception in its proper, limited place, so that it does not undermine the *Hunter* standards. In *Colarusso*,[383] for example, the coroner seized blood samples after a fatal traffic accident under provisions of the Ontario *Coroners Act*.[384] No judicial pre-authorization was needed for such a seizure. On the facts, it was clear that the seizure was just as much for the purposes of the police investigation into criminal charges as it was for the legitimate purpose of an inquest (the police transported the samples to the analyst, gave up their previous efforts to obtain a sample from the accused, and so on). The Court held that the evidence was not admissible in the criminal proceedings. Although no difficulty would arise in using the evidence in the context of an inquest "once the evidence has been appropriated by the criminal law enforcement arm of the state for use in criminal proceedings, there is no foundation on which to argue that the coroner's seizure continues to be reasonable."[385]

Later, in *R v Jarvis* the Court attempted to distinguish more clearly when the different levels of *Charter* protection apply. In that case the accused was required to produce various pieces of information under the *Income Tax Act*, a statute that the Court notes depends on self-reporting and, therefore, is especially dependent on the honesty of taxpayers. As a result, broad inspection and audit powers are necessary to maintain the integrity of the tax system. At a certain point, however, investigation as to whether a taxpayer has remitted sufficient funds to the government can become an investigation into whether that taxpayer should be prosecuted for an offence. Accordingly, the Court said, differing levels of *Charter* protection might be found within the same statute. As a general guideline, administrative officials must cease to use their broader investigative powers, such as mandatory inspection or production of documents, "where the predominant purpose of a particular inquiry is the determination of penal liability," or, put another way, where there has been a "crystallization of the adversarial relationship."[386] Determining when officials have "crossed the Rubicon," as the Court puts it, depends on consideration of various factors, none of which is conclusive

---

383   *Colarusso*, above note 180.

384   RSO 1990, c C.37.

385   *Colarusso*, above note 180. See the similar point in *R v White*, [1999] 2 SCR 417, where an accused was obliged under the British Columbia *Motor Vehicle Act*, RSBC 1996, c 318, to report an accident to the police. Although that provision did not violate the principle against self-incrimination inherent in s 7 if the statement was confined to the context in which it was taken, it would violate s 7 to let the statement be used in criminal proceedings.

386   *Jarvis*, above note 381 at paras 88 and 102, respectively.

on its own. These include, in the income tax context, whether there are reasonable grounds to lay charges, whether the general conduct of the authorities was consistent with a criminal investigation, whether an auditor's files have been transferred to investigators, whether an auditor effectively acted as an agent for investigators and whether the investigators intended that, whether the evidence concerns liability to taxation or prosecution, and other circumstances.[387]

The general justification for departing from the *Hunter* standards in regulatory contexts is the principle that *Charter* rights must be interpreted in context. That principle is well established, but its application does create a potential slippery slope around section 8 protection. In *Jarvis*, for example, the Court specifically notes that nothing prevents an auditor from passing files to investigators or stops investigators from using that evidence. This stance seems inconsistent with the approach in *Colarusso*.[388] Further, there is surely some irony in the fact that *Hunter*, the case that first delineated the high standards to which searches are generally to be held under section 8, itself concerned a search in a regulatory context. The Court suggests in *Jarvis* that the search in *Hunter* was a greater violation of privacy expectations because it authorized entry onto private premises.[389] Still, it must be said that, despite the steps taken in *Jarvis* to help clarify when different levels of *Charter* protection apply, there remains considerable scope for difference of opinion. Therefore, in many cases, the decision as to whether a search was reasonable will be made only after the fact. That is a departure from the goal of section 8, which is to prevent unreasonable searches from occurring.

The situation is further muddied by the decision in *R v Nolet*. In that case the police stopped a tractor trailer driving through Saskatchewan, relying on regulatory powers to stop and search from provincial motor vehicle legislation. At some point while examining the truck the officer became suspicious of criminal activity, and eventually he found a large sum of cash inside a duffel bag in the cab. A further search turned up drugs in a hidden compartment. The trial judge had found the initial search of the cab to violate section 8: although the officer had tried still to use regulatory powers to conduct the search, his predominant purpose by that time was the investigation of a criminal offence. The Supreme Court of Canada, however, held that that was incorrect reasoning.[390]

---

387 *Ibid* at para 94.
388 *Colarusso*, above note 180. See also David Stratas, "'Crossing the Rubicon': The Supreme Court and Regulatory Investigations" (2003) 6 *Criminal Reports* (6th) 74.
389 *Jarvis*, above note 381 at para 61.
390 *Nolet*, above note 143.

The Court concluded that as long as the officer still had a continuing regulatory purpose upon which to justify the search, it did not matter what the officer's predominant purpose was.[391] Indeed, they held that reliance on *Jarvis* in this context was misplaced. *Jarvis* had concerned using powers relating to a civil dispute for purposes of a penal proceeding, they held: in *Nolet* the context was always penal.[392]

Nonetheless, it is clear that the Court has not intended to abandon the notion that powers created for one context with less severe consequences than a criminal proceeding cannot be used for criminal prosecution purposes. In *Cole*, for example, a teacher was discovered by a school technician to have nude and semi-nude photographs of a student stored on his laptop. The school board was entitled, because of its statutory obligation to maintain a safe environment for students, to examine the teacher's laptop and was authorized to make a CD of the material found. However, when the board then handed that CD to the police without a warrant, the accused's section 8 rights were violated. Although the school board had acquired lawful possession of the laptop for administrative purposes, that did not give the police a power to search: "[w]here a lower constitutional standard is applicable in an administrative context, as in this case, the police cannot invoke that standard to evade the prior judicial authorization that is normally required for searches or seizures in the context of criminal investigations."[393]

Exactly when regulatory search powers can or cannot be used is now less clear than it might have been.

ii)   Searches by School Officials

Most statutory search powers are given to peace officers or at least to public officers such as customs officers.[394] In *R v M(MR)*, however, the Court decided that, in some circumstances, school officials such as a vice-principal can have statutory search powers.[395] Strictly the decision in that case dealt only with the Nova Scotia *Education Act*, but subsequent cases have found the equivalent statutes in other provinces to be similar enough that the same power exists there.[396]

---

391   *Ibid* at para 41.
392   See the discussion in Steve Coughlan, "Stopping Vehicles on a Downhill Slope: *R v Nolet*" (2010) 76 *Criminal Reports* (6th) 24.
393   *Cole*, above note 22 at para 69.
394   See the definition of "public officer" in s 2 of the *Code*.
395   *M(MR)*, above note 3.
396   See, for example, *R v Ermine*, 2014 SKPC 162; *R v JM*, 2012 BCPC 126; or *R v SMZ*, [1998] MJ No 587 (CA).

In *M(MR)* the accused was a student at a junior high school. Based on a tip that the accused would be selling drugs at a school dance, the vice-principal told the accused to come to his office. An RCMP officer who had been requested by the vice-principal arrived at this point and was present in the room as the vice-principal searched the accused, finding a bag of marijuana in his sock. The vice-principal gave the bag to the officer who arrested the accused. The accused argued at trial that he had been subject to an unreasonable search.

The Court agreed that the accused had a reasonable expectation of privacy: a diminished one because of the school environment, but he did have one. They also agreed that the search by the vice-principal constituted state action: *not* because the vice-principal had acted as an agent of the state (he had not, they found) but because school officials themselves for these purposes constituted state actors. In other words, what was at issue was, in essence, a regulatory search rather than a criminal search. Had this been a search by an agent of the police, the ordinary *Hunter* standards and, in particular, the need for a warrant, would have applied. Because it was a search in a non-criminal context, a different standard could apply.

The question therefore became whether the search was authorized by law, as the *Collins* test requires. In this case, there was no explicit statutory search power. Nor could the *Waterfield* test be applied to create a common law power since it was not a police officer who had searched. However, the Nova Scotia *Education Act* and regulations imposed a duty on the school officials to maintain proper order and discipline in the school, and this "by necessary implication authorizes searches of students."[397] Obviously, the exact nature of that power had to be articulated by the Court, though they noted that the reduced expectation of privacy coupled with the need to protect students meant that "a more lenient and flexible approach should be taken to searches conducted by teachers and principals than would apply to searches conducted by the police."[398]

Specifically, they concluded that searches by school officials should not be subject to the presumption of unreasonableness by reason of being warrantless. Instead, a school official can search without a warrant if she has reasonable grounds to believe that there has been a breach of school regulations or discipline and that a search of a student would reveal evidence of that breach. Those reasonable grounds might arise from "information received from one student considered to be credible, information received from more than one student, a teacher's or principal's

---

397 *M(MR)*, above note 3 at para 51.
398 *Ibid* at para 47.

own observations, or any combination of these pieces of information which the relevant authority considers to be credible."[399]

One oddity around M(MR) ought to be noted, namely, that it has sometimes been mischaracterized in later decisions. The decision is unambiguous in stating that the school official "must have reasonable grounds to *believe*" that a rule was broken and evidence will be found.[400] It has been wrongly described, however, as creating a search power based on reasonable *suspicion*.[401] M(MR) did discuss that US caselaw on school searches was based on the reasonable suspicion standard and after that observed that a relaxing of the *Hunter* requirements was also appropriate in Canada. Nonetheless, the relaxation actually adopted was to dispense with the warrant requirement: it is simply wrong to say M(MR) created a search power based on reasonable suspicion.

iii) Searches of Media Offices

Special concerns come into play when warrants are issued for the search of media offices. In that event, the guarantee of freedom of the press in section 2(b) of the *Charter* becomes relevant. However, the Court has consistently held that there are no additional formal requirements.[402]

These special considerations should affect the way in which a justice of the peace decides whether to issue a warrant, but only because they "provide a backdrop against which the reasonableness of the search may be evaluated. It requires that careful consideration be given not only to whether a warrant should issue but also to the conditions which might properly be imposed upon any search of media premises."[403]

It had been argued that search warrants should not be issued in relation to media offices unless it was specifically shown that no reasonable alternative source of obtaining the information was available, or that reasonable steps had been taken to obtain the information from that alternative source. The Court agreed that the media play a vital role in a democracy and that they would generally be innocent third parties in relation to any criminal proceedings. Nonetheless, they refused to impose any absolute preconditions on such warrants. Alternative sources of information are a relevant factor for a justice of the peace to consider in deciding whether to issue a warrant, and the Court noted

---

399   *Ibid* at para 50.

400   *Ibid* [emphasis added].

401   See the decision of Binnie J in *AM*, above note 30 at para 45, or footnote 1 in *Chehil*, above note 30, for the claim that it is based on reasonable suspicion.

402   See *R v National Post*, 2010 SCC 16, in which the applicant unsuccessfully sought a reconsideration of the principles that are set out below.

403   *Canadian Broadcasting Corp v New Brunswick (Attorney General)*, [1991] 3 SCR 459 at para 32.

that information in that regard should normally be disclosed in the warrant application. Other factors would also be relevant to the decision, however, including whether the search would unduly impede the gathering or dissemination of news, or whether the information had already been broadcast or published. Thus, for example, in *Canadian Broadcasting Corp v Lessard*[404] the warrant application did not disclose anything about alternative sources of information. The Court agreed that disclosure of such information would have been preferable. However, the search was conducted reasonably and there was no interference with the operation of the television station. Further, the news in question had already been broadcast, leading the Court to conclude that seizure of the tapes would not have a chilling effect on sources for the media. On balance, despite the omission of information about alternative sources, the Court held that the warrant was properly issued.

iv) Searches of Lawyers' Offices

The issue of searches of lawyers' offices first arose for the Court in *Descôteaux v Mierzwinski*,[405] where police went to a legal aid office with a search warrant, seeking evidence that a suspect had falsely represented his income in order to obtain legal aid. This highlighted the danger that the use of search warrants could on occasion come into conflict with protecting solicitor–client privilege. As a result, Parliament placed section 488.1 in the *Code*, intending that it should govern the situation. In fact, that provision was then found, in *Lavallee, Rackel & Heintz v Canada (Attorney General)*, to insufficiently protect solicitor–client privilege and to violate section 8 as a result.[406] The Court chose to strike down the entire provision in order to give Parliament an opportunity to redraft it, but set out general principles that would govern such searches in the interim. As a matter of fact Parliament has never enacted replacement legislation, and so the Court's general principles

---

404 [1991] 3 SCR 421.

405 [1982] 1 SCR 860.

406 2002 SCC 61 [*Lavallee*]. The Court commented at para 36:

> Since *Hunter*, this Court has striven to strike an appropriate balance between privacy interests on the one hand and the exigencies of law enforcement on the other . . . . Sometimes, however, the traditional balancing of interests involved in a s. 8 analysis is inappropriate. As it was stated in *R. v. Mills*, [1999] 3 S.C.R. 668, at para. 86, "the appropriateness of the balance is assessed according to the nature of the interests at stake in a particular context, and the place of these interests within our legal and political traditions". Where the interest at stake is solicitor–client privilege—a principle of fundamental justice and civil right of supreme importance in Canadian law—the usual balancing exercise referred to above is not particularly helpful.

about how to apply section 487 when lawyers' offices are targeted still set out the governing law.

Those principles are as follows:

1. No search warrant can be issued with regards to documents that are known to be protected by solicitor–client privilege.

2. Before searching a law office, the investigative authorities must satisfy the issuing justice that there exists no other reasonable alternative to the search.

3. When allowing a law office to be searched, the issuing justice must be rigorously demanding so to afford maximum protection of solicitor–client confidentiality.

4. Except when the warrant specifically authorizes the immediate examination, copying and seizure of an identified document, all documents in possession of a lawyer must be sealed before being examined or removed from the lawyer's possession.

5. Every effort must be made to contact the lawyer and the client at the time of the execution of the search warrant. Where the lawyer or the client cannot be contacted, a representative of the Bar should be allowed to oversee the sealing and seizure of documents.

6. The investigative officer executing the warrant should report to the justice of the peace the efforts made to contact all potential privilege holders, who should then be given a reasonable opportunity to assert a claim of privilege and, if that claim is contested, to have the issue judicially decided.

7. If notification of potential privilege holders is not possible, the lawyer who had custody of the documents seized, or another lawyer appointed either by the Law Society or by the court, should examine the documents to determine whether a claim of privilege should be asserted, and should be given a reasonable opportunity to do so.

8. The Attorney General may make submissions on the issue of privilege, but should not be permitted to inspect the documents beforehand. The prosecuting authority can only inspect the documents if and when it is determined by a judge that the documents are not privileged.

9. Where sealed documents are found not to be privileged, they may be used in the normal course of the investigation.

10. Where documents are found to be privileged, they are to be returned immediately to the holder of the privilege, or to a person designated by the court.[407]

---

407 *Ibid* at para 49.

3) Was the Manner of Search Reasonable?

Even if a search power exists and that power is reasonable, the *Collins* test allows a court to find that the actual search in question was unreasonable because of the manner in which it was conducted. In looking at this question, there is no strong reason to distinguish between searches with a warrant and those without.[408]

In *Collins*, the accused was searched for drugs by an officer who grabbed her by the throat at the first moment. The Court agreed that a search power may have existed, but noted that "without very specific information, a seizure by the throat, as in this case, would be unreasonable."[409] In general, the more intrusive the nature of the search, the greater the constraints on the way in which the search can reasonably be performed.[410] Thus, for example, in *Golden*, beyond deciding the circumstances in which strip searches incident to arrest were permitted, the Court went on to suggest guidelines for the manner in which such searches could be conducted. These guidelines raise issues such as the number and gender of the officers conducting the search, the location of the search, how quickly the search is conducted, and so on.[411]

One context in which the question of the reasonableness of the manner of search often arises is in the case of a "hard entry" or "dynamic entry" to execute a search warrant. Most commonly, this occurs in connection with drug searches where the police believe that the inhabitants of the building might be armed or that the evidence might be quickly destroyed. The ordinary rule is that police must obey the "knock and announce" rule, by which they would give notice of their presence, identify themselves as peace officers, and show their warrant.[412] Where the police do not do so, the onus is on the police to explain why: the greater the departure, the heavier the onus.[413] The Court in *R v Cornell* laid out several governing principles for dynamic entries.

---

408 To some extent in the case of common law police powers, there can be overlap between this third stage of the *Collins* test and the *Waterfield* test; that is, the existence of the common law power depends on the officer's actions having been reasonably necessary, and so "[i]f the extent of the infringement is greater than what is required to search for weapons, the search will not be authorized by law." *MacDonald*, above note 107 at para 47.

409 *Collins*, above note 1 at para 24.

410 *Golden*, above note 19 at para 87.

411 *Ibid* at para 101.

412 *Eccles v Bourque*, [1975] 2 SCR 739; *Genest*, above note 223.

413 *Cornell*, above note 225.

First, the dynamic entry must be justified based on the information known to the police at the time: it cannot be justified *post facto*, but equally the discovery that no weapons were in the place searched after all does not automatically invalidate the search. Second, the police must be allowed a certain amount of latitude in the manner in which they choose to enter premises because they cannot be expected in advance to measure precisely the amount of force that will be required. Finally, on review, the trial judge's assessment of the facts in these regards must be accorded substantial deference.[414]

A dynamic entry will be found to have been unreasonably conducted if the police simply follow a blanket policy to use them in all drug raids, for example.[415] The fact that a policy exists, however, is not necessarily fatal to the validity of the manner of search if the facts of the case justified a dynamic entry.[416]

As discussed above, when looking at reasonable expectation of privacy, a *Charter* breach can be asserted only by the person whose *Charter* rights were violated.[417] Nonetheless, the *Charter* rights of others can be relevant to the manner in which a search is conducted. In *R v Thompson*, for example, a wiretap authorization allowed the police to tap not only the accused's telephone, but also other telephones to which he might resort, including pay phones. The Court acknowledged that it was permissible for authorizations to permit tapping of public phones and that, therefore, the search was authorized by law. However, no restrictions had been placed on the wiretap, such as allowing interception only when there were reasonable grounds to believe the accused was using the public telephone in question at the time. In some cases, the police simply installed listening devices and left them activated in case the accused came along, an approach that likely resulted in the interception of hundreds of unrelated private calls. On those facts, "given the extent of the invasion of privacy authorized in this case, a total absence of any protection for the public created a potential for the carrying out of searches and seizures that were unreasonable."[418]

---

414   *Ibid* at paras 22–25. In *Cornell* itself, the Court was divided 4:3 over whether the dynamic entry violated the *Charter*. The majority deferred to the trial judge's conclusions, while a vigorous dissent argued that there was no basis for the police to have concluded that anyone's safety was at risk. See the discussion of the case in H Archibald Kaiser, "*Cornell*: A Divided Court Accords to Much Latitude to the Police — 'Canada Is Not a Police State'" (2010) 76 *Criminal Reports* (6th) 263.

415   *R v Lau*, 2003 BCCA 337; *R v Schedel*, 2003 BCCA 364.

416   *R v DeWolfe*, 2007 NSCA 79.

417   *Edwards*, above note 48 at para 34.

418   *Thompson*, above note 269.

As *R v Thompson* makes clear, there could be some difficulty reconciling the notion that the *Charter* rights of other persons are relevant to the manner of the search when, according to the facts in *Debot*,[419] the accused's own *Charter* rights are not relevant to that determination. In any event, in *Edwards*[420] the Court appears to limit the relevance of third party rights to cases where there is a "potentially massive invasion of . . . privacy."

The so-called "tower dump" warrants, where police seek to obtain information concerning cell-phone calls that have been routed through a particular tower, are one such area of contention of increasing concern. Such warrants can have an impact on many people other than the targets of the investigation.[421] To date, no clear principles for governing the situation have emerged.

FURTHER READINGS

Austin, Lisa M. "Is Consent the Foundation of Fair Information Practices? Canada's Experience under *PIPEDA*" (2006) 56 *University of Toronto Law Journal* 181.

Calarco, Paul. "*R v Plummer*: Standing to Challenge Searches" (2011) 85 *Criminal Reports* (6th) 62.

Cohen, Stanley A. "Search Incident to Arrest: How Broad an Exception to the Warrant Requirement?" (1988) 63 *Criminal Reports* (3d) 182.

―――. "The Paradoxical Nature of Privacy in the Context of Criminal Law and the *Canadian Charter of Rights and Freedoms*" (2002) 7 *Canadian Criminal Law Review* 125.

Coughlan, Steve. "Privacy Goes to the Dogs" (2006) 40 *Criminal Reports* (6th) 31.

---

419 *Debot*, above note 111.
420 *Edwards*, above note 48.
421 See, for example, *R v Rogers Communications Partnership*, 2014 ONSC 3853 at para 11, where the judge noted:

> The existing order will require TELUS to disclose the personal information of at least 9,000 individuals. Rogers estimates that it will be required to conduct 378 separate searches and retrieve approximately 200,000 records related to 34,000 subscribers.

————. "*Kwiatkowski*: Privacy Protection and Risk Analysis: Losing the Forest in the Telephoto Shots of the Trees" (2010) 73 *Criminal Reports* (6th) 260.

————. "Stopping Vehicles on a Downhill Slope: *R v Nolet*" (2010) 76 *Criminal Reports* (6th) 24.

————. "Learning from Experience about Learning from Experience: Modifying the Objective Test for Arrest and Detention" (2013) 4 *Criminal Reports* (7th) 245.

————. "Signing Away Rights: Should Private Contracts Trump the *Charter*?" (2014) 13 *Criminal Reports* (7th) 124.

————, & MARC S GORBET. "Nothing Plus Nothing Equals . . . Something?: A Proposal for FLIR Warrants on Reasonable Suspicion" (2004) 23 *Criminal Reports* (6th) 239.

DE SA, CHRIS. "*Garofoli* Step 6: Getting Behind the Black" (2014) 61 *Criminal Law Quarterly* 418.

FAIRBURN, MICHAL. "Twenty-Five Years in Search of a Reasonable Approach" (2008) 40 *Supreme Court Law Review* (2d) 55.

GORHAM, NATHAN JS. "Eight Plus Twenty-Four Two Equals Zero-Point-Five" (2003) 6 *Criminal Reports* (6th) 257.

HUBBARD, ROBERT W, & SCOTT K FENTON. "Supreme Court of Canada Wiretap Update — February 2001" (delivered at Search and Seizure Law in Canada, the Professional Development Program, Osgoode Hall Law School, Toronto, 3 November 2001).

HUTCHISON, SCOTT C, & JAMES C MORTON. *Search and Seizure Law in Canada* (Toronto: Carswell, 1991) (loose-leaf).

JONES, BROCK. "Reconciling Reasonable Expectation of Privacy and Modern Technologies: US and Canadian Approaches" (2011) 83 *Criminal Reports* (6th) 28.

KAISER, H ARCHIBALD. "*Patrick*: Protecting Canadians' Privacy Interest in Garbage; 'A Step Too Far' for the Supreme Court" (2009) 64 *Criminal Reports* (6th) 30.

————. "*Cornell*: A Divided Court Accords to Much Latitude to the Police — 'Canada Is Not a Police State'" (2010) 76 *Criminal Reports* (6th) 263.

————. "*Gomboc*: The Supreme Court Weakens the Search Warrant Requirement and Facilitates Police Investigations, Again" (2011) 79 *Criminal Reports* (6th) 245.

LATIMER, SCOTT. "The Expanded Scope of Search Incident to Investigative Detention" (2007) 48 *Criminal Reports* (6th) 201.

LAW REFORM COMMISSION OF CANADA. *Search and Seizure* (Ottawa: Law Reform Commission of Canada, 1984).

LUTHER, GLEN. "Consent Search and Reasonable Expectation of Privacy: Twin Barriers to the Reasonable Protection of Privacy in Canada" (2008) 41 *University of British Columbia Law Review* 1.

MACKINNON, WILLIAM. "Discarding Reasonable Expectations of Privacy: A Critique of *R v Patrick*" (2010) 47 *Alberta Law Review* 1037.

———. "Section 8 Meets the iPhone: Searching Cell Phones Incident to Arrest" (2011) 84 *Criminal Reports* (6th) 232.

MCINNES, JOHN S. "Sniffing Out a Theory of Privacy after *Kang-Brown* and *M.(A.)*" (2009) 47 *Supreme Court Law Review* (2d) 53.

PENNEY, STEVEN. "Conceptions of Privacy: A Comment on *R v Kang-Brown* and *R v A.M.*" (2008) 46 *Alberta Law Review* 203.

———. "Unreasonable Search and Seizure and Section 8 of the *Charter*: Cost-Benefit Analysis in Constitutional Interpretation" (2013) 62 *Supreme Court Law Review* (2d) 101.

POMERANCE, RENÉE. "Shedding Light on the Nature of Heat: Defining Privacy in the Wake of *R v Tessling*" (2005) 23 *Criminal Reports* (6th) 229.

PRINGLE, HEATHER. "Kicking In the Castle Doors: The Evolution of Exigent Circumstances" (2000) 43 *Criminal Law Quarterly* 86.

QUIGLEY, TIM. *Procedure in Canadian Criminal Law*, 2d ed (Toronto: Thomson Carswell, 2005) (loose-leaf) ch 8.

———. "The Impact of the *Charter* on the Law of Search and Seizure" (2008) 40 *Supreme Court Law Review* (2d) 117.

SANKOFF, PETER, & STÉPHANE PERRAULT. "Suspicious Searches: What's So Reasonable about Them?" (1999) 24 *Criminal Reports* (5th) 123.

SHAPIRO, JONATHAN. "Narcotics Dogs and the Search for Illegality: American Law in Canadian Courts" (2007) 43 *Criminal Reports* (6th) 299.

STEWART, HAMISH. "Normative Foundations for Reasonable Expectations of Privacy" (2011) 54 *Supreme Court Law Review* (2d) 335.

STRATAS, DAVID. "'Crossing the Rubicon': The Supreme Court and Regulatory Investigations" (2003) 6 *Criminal Reports* (6th) 74.

————. "*R v B(SA)* and the Right against Self-Incrimination: A Confusing Change of Direction" (2003) 14 *Criminal Reports* (6th) 227.

STRIBOPOULOS, JAMES. "Reasonable Expectation of Privacy and 'Open Fields'—Taking the American 'Risk Analysis' Head On" (1999) 25 *Criminal Reports* (5th) 351.

STRINGHAM, JAMES AQ. "Reasonable Expectations Reconsidered: A Return to the Search for a Normative Core for Section 8?" (2005) 23 *CriminalReports* (6th) 245.

STUART, DON. "Eight Plus Twenty-Four Two Equals Zero" (1998) 13 *Criminal Reports* (5th) 50.

————. "Police Use of Sniffer Dogs Ought to Be Subject to *Charter* Standards: Dangers of *Tessling* Come to Roost" (2005) 31 *Criminal Reports* (6th) 255.

————. *Charter Justice in Canadian Criminal Law*, 6th ed (Toronto: Thomson Carswell, 2014) ch 3.

TICE, DAVID. "Into the Black: Litigating Search Warrants and Wiretaps under the Sixth Step of *Garofoli*" 2014 61 *Criminal Law Quarterly* 103.

CHAPTER 5

OTHER INVESTIGATIVE POWERS

A. INTRODUCTION

This chapter deals with police investigative techniques other than searches with and without a warrant, which were discussed in Chapter 4. There are a number of such techniques—indeed, as the discussion below will show, there is, in principle, no necessary limit to their number—but the discussion here will focus on three specific areas. All three areas, this discussion suggests, show a significant expansion in police powers, all postdating, and in some cases ironically due to, the *Charter.*

First, section 487.01 of the *Code,* which creates "general warrants," will be examined. Most of the principles relating to the review of the issuance of search warrants discussed in Chapter 4 apply equally to these warrants, and they also authorize techniques that infringe on a reasonable expectation of privacy. As a result, it would have been possible to discuss them in that chapter. However, general warrants can authorize techniques going well beyond anything that one would traditionally think of as a search—in the terms of the statute, they are available to authorize police to "do any thing"—and so they are worth singling out for particular discussion.

Second, police powers of detention will be considered. There are statutory powers of detention, some of which occur in the investigative process (breathalyzer tests, for example, involve a power to detain). What will be of most interest, however, are post-*Charter* developments in caselaw that expand the powers of detention given to the police at common law and, indeed, expand the notion of "common law powers" themselves.

Finally, section 25.1 of the *Code*, which authorizes designated officers to break the law, will be discussed. It is perhaps obvious without elaboration that this provision might be a cause for concern about the expansion of police powers.

B. GENERAL WARRANTS: SECTION 487.01

Section 487.01 of the *Code* contains what is normally referred to as the "general warrant provision."[1] It was introduced in the wake of a decision by the Supreme Court about warrantless searches, and is intended to provide for warrants to perform investigative techniques not covered by other *Code* provisions. It is sometimes described as filling the gap left by section 487 and other warrant provisions in the *Code*, though it is a question for debate as to whether there could properly have been said to be a gap.

In *R v Wong*, the police had placed a small video camera in a hotel room to record activities within.[2] Had they wanted to audiotape the room, they would have had to comply with the *Code* provisions dealing with wiretaps. However, those provisions make no mention of video cameras, so the police argued that they needed no special permission; that is, in the absence of specific limitations on their powers, they were free to use whatever investigative means they chose. That approach, the Supreme Court decided, "wholly misunderstands *Duarte*. It is the *Charter*, specifically s. 8, that protected the appellant there and it is the *Charter* that protects the present appellant . . . s. 8 was designed to provide continuing protection against unreasonable search and seizure and to keep pace with emerging technological development."[3] In other words, the Court relied on the principle that individuals are to be free

---

1   It is worth being aware of some ambiguity associated with this term. The *Code* contains search warrants in s 487 but also has many much more specific warrant powers (see Chapter 4, Section C(1)(b)). Because there are so many specific warrant provisions, judges sometimes refer to s 487 search warrants as the "general warrant provisions." In addition, one will occasionally see references to the common law principle that there cannot be a "general warrant": that is, a search warrant must be aimed at a particular person and particular evidence: see, for example, *R v Noble*, [1985] OJ No 809 at para 17 (CA).

2   *R v Wong*, [1990] 3 SCR 36 at para 28 [*Wong*].

3   *Ibid*.

from state interference unless such interference is specifically author-ized. The Court noted that, in the absence of authorization, video sur-veillance fell into the general category of warrantless searches, which are *prima facie* unreasonable. The Court also held that it was not their role to create authorization for video surveillance — that was a decision for Parliament to make:

> Until such time as Parliament, in its wisdom, specifically provides for a code of conduct for a particular invasive technology, the courts should forebear from crafting procedures authorizing the deploy-ment of the technology in question. The role of the courts should be limited to assessing the constitutionality of any legislation passed by Parliament which bears on the matter.[4]

One would most naturally read *Wong*, which refers to George Or-well's "classic dystopian novel" *1984*[5] in its reasoning, as a recognition of the right of individuals to be generally free from state interference: "The notion that the agencies of the state should be at liberty to train hidden cameras on members of society wherever and whenever they wish is fundamentally irreconcilable with what we perceive to be ac-ceptable behaviour on the part of government."[6] However, Parliament appears to have read the decision to make precisely the opposite invi-tation. Section 487.01, although it does not quite allow agents of the state to search "wherever and whenever" they wish, verges dangerously close to that direction.[7]

Put broadly, the problem facing the police in *Wong* was that no war-rant was available for placement of a video camera, but without a war-rant, the search was *prima facie* unreasonable. Parliament's response to the decision was to enact section 487.01, which is aimed at avoiding loss of evidence in cases of video surveillance, and in essentially any other case as well. Section 487.01 creates warrants to "use any device or investigative technique or procedure *or do any thing* described in the warrant that would, if not authorized, constitute an unreasonable

---

4   *Ibid* at para 36.
5   *Ibid* at para 15, referring to George Orwell, *1984* (New York: Harcourt, Brace, 1947).
6   *Wong*, above note 2.
7   One would, of course, comply with the letter of the principle, "the police only have the powers explicitly given to them," if one explicitly gave the police the power to do anything, but that would clearly violate the notion of restraint that is the spirit of the principle. A similar approach can be seen in the government's approach to the rule of law reflected in s 25.1 of the *Code*, discussed in Section D, below in this chapter.

search and seizure."[8] In other words, Parliament took a decision that relied on the assumption that there need to be limits to police investigative techniques and used it to justify a provision creating an unlimited range of potential police investigative techniques. It is hard to reconcile this approach with the conclusion in *Hunter v Southam Inc* that "an assessment of the constitutionality of a search and seizure, or of a statute authorizing a search and seizure, must focus on its 'reasonable' or 'unreasonable' impact on the subject of the search or the seizure, and not simply on its rationality in furthering some valid government objective."[9] Section 487.01 seems to be justified only for the purpose of furthering a government objective.

In 2013 the Court handed down its decision on *R v TELUS Communications Co*, which begins to rein in the very broad scope of the provision, suggesting that it should be "used sparingly as a warrant of limited resort."[10] However, that decision runs against the tide of two decades of expansive use of the power, and so attitudes about how it ought to be employed might be difficult to change.[11] We shall first consider what the section states and how it was initially interpreted, then turn to the later limitation of it.

Section 487.01 can be thought of as containing two investigative techniques: (1) the very general power noted above, and (2) the power to engage in video surveillance. As video surveillance must meet all the requirements of general warrants and additional requirements as well, it is sensible to discuss the more general power first.

It is most useful to examine the general warrant in terms of the similarities and differences that arise from a comparison with section 487. Some features are common to the two provisions. A warrant in each depends on reasonable grounds being established by an information provided on oath, for example. A section 487.01 warrant also does not permit interference with bodily integrity, and can be subject to conditions. Both of these requirements are specifically stated in section 487.01, though they were only implicit in section 487.[12]

---

8   Section 487.01(1) [emphasis added].

9   *Hunter v Southam Inc*, [1984] 2 SCR 145 at 160 [*Hunter*].

10 2013 SCC 16 at para 56 [*TELUS*].

11 See also Steve Coughlan, "General Warrants at the Crossroads: Limit or Licence?" (2003) 10 *Criminal Reports* (6th) 269; and Steve Coughlan, "*R. v. Ha*: Upholding General Warrants without Asking the Right Questions" (2009) 65 *Criminal Reports* (6th) 41 [Coughlan, "*R. v. Ha*"].

12 See *Re Laporte and the Queen* (1972), 29 DLR (3d) 651 (Que QB), and *Descôteaux v Mierzwinski*, [1982] 1 SCR 860.

Of the requirements that are unique to section 487.01, some make the provision wider than the standard search warrant provision, while others are intended to attach greater restrictions. This, of course, is as it should be in a provision intended to balance competing interests, though it is questionable whether the balance has been adequately achieved.

The general warrant provision is obviously broader not only because it allows a search for physical evidence, but also because it allows the police to use any device, technique, or procedure, or "do any thing." The Ontario Court of Appeal has held that "do any thing" is to be read literally and broadly and is not limited to practices such as the use of devices.[13] In particular, that means that section 487.01 can be used to issue a warrant to search a location, as section 487 potentially authorizes. This capability is significant primarily because it represents another way in which section 487.01 is broader than section 487. The section allows an application based not just on reasonable grounds to believe that an offence has been committed, but on the basis that an offence "will be committed."[14] In combination, these interpretations mean that the general warrant provision creates an "anticipatory search warrant." In that context, it is worth noting that the general warrant provision is also broader in that such a search is not limited to a building, receptacle, or place, as section 487 is (it cannot, however, interfere with bodily integrity).

An additional requirement in section 487.01(1)(c) is that no other statutory provision can authorize the procedure in question. It is primarily worth noting what this provision does *not* mean.

First, this requirement does not prevent the police from obtaining a general warrant even though a search warrant might already be available: even if they are in a position to conduct a search and seizure, the police are still entitled to use other investigative techniques and to obtain a general warrant to do so.[15]

Further, this section is not the equivalent of the section 186(1)(b) limitation on wiretaps that no other technique is likely to succeed. That provision is intended to act as a limit on the use of wiretaps by showing that they are, if not precisely a last resort, something similar to that.[16]

---

13   *R v Noseworthy* (1997), 33 OR (3d) 641 (CA) [*Noseworthy*].

14   Section 487.01(1)(a). Ordinary search warrants do have a small anticipatory component in s 487(1)(c) that permits the seizure of anything "intended to be used for the purpose of committing any offence against the person for which a person may be arrested without warrant."

15   *R v Ford*, 2008 BCCA 94 [*Ford*].

16   Note that s 186 is incorporated into s 487.01 when a warrant for video surveillance is sought. In *R v Araujo*, [2000] 2 SCR 992 at para 29, the Court held that there was no requirement for all other techniques to have been unsuccessfully

On the face of it, that is not what the "not other provision" requirement does: it can be read not to provide a limit but to show that there are no limits on the techniques that could be authorizable—that approach describes how many cases have interpreted the provision. For example, courts have considered applications under section 487.01: to install a digital recording ammeter for the purpose of recording the cycling pattern of electricity usage in a residence,[17] to make electronic copies of data in a computer system,[18] to perform phallometric testing,[19] to use a forensic fluorescent light to illuminate the inside of a vehicle to look for bloodstains,[20] and to record the sender and addressee information on mail delivered to a post office box.[21] General warrants have also been issued to stop a drug courier's vehicle on the pretext of a traffic stop in order for police to appear to accidentally discover the narcotics in the trunk, and to do damage to a vehicle in the course of seizing narcotics from the trunk in order to make the seizure seem like a theft.[22] In these latter two cases, the purpose of the particular investigative technique was to permit the police to seize a single drug shipment without exposing the fact that the conspiracy was under investigation. Note that the first of the two, the "pretext stop," amounts to the police being given a warrant to violate section 10(a) of the *Charter*, the right to be informed of the reason for one's detention, as well as other *Charter* rights, such as the right to disclosure.

In the first twenty years, courts showed little restraint in the way in which they interpreted this prerequisite, essentially allowing anything police could envision to potentially fall within the provision. In particular, a distinction which *ought* to have been drawn was not recognized: the distinction between those techniques for which no warrant provision existed because they had never been contemplated at the time other warrant provisions were created, and those things for which no warrant provision existed because of a deliberate decision not

---

attempted, but that there should be "practically speaking, no other reasonable alternative method of investigation."

17   *R v Christensen*, 2001 ABPC 227. Note that since the Court's decision in *R v Gomboc*, 2010 SCC 55, in some cases, a person will not have a reasonable expectation of privacy in the information disclosed by a digital recording ammeter, and so no warrant of any type would be needed.

18   *Keating v Nova Scotia (Attorney General)*, 2001 NSSC 85.

19   *R v Rayworth*, [1999] OJ No 5289 (SCJ), aff'd without reference to this issue, [2001] OJ No 4111 (CA).

20   *Criminal Code of Canada (Re)*, 2002 SKPC 11.

21   *Canada Post Corp v Canada (Attorney General)* (1995), 95 CCC (3d) 568 (Ont Ct Gen Div).

22   See *R v HHN*, 2000 ABPC 173, and *R v Knight*, 2008 NLCA 67, respectively.

to authorize them. This is the point referred to earlier: the question of whether general warrants fill a "gap."

In *Wong*, it seems perfectly plausible to suppose that the law had simply not kept up with technology and, therefore, no provisions authorizing video surveillance had yet been put in the *Code*. It is not reasonable to draw that same conclusion with regard to every investigative technique that police can think of. In *R v Ha*, for example, the Ontario Court of Appeal found that this requirement had been met because "there is no provision in the *Code*, the *CDSA* [*Controlled Drugs and Substances Act*], or in any other federal statute that would authorize an unlimited number of covert entries and searches on private property over a two-month period."[23] Surely it would be reasonable to at least ask whether the reason no such provision exists is that such a search power ought not to exist.[24] Similarly, in *R v Noseworthy*[25] the Ontario Court of Appeal found that the general warrant provisions authorized "anticipatory warrants": that is, a warrant to search a place issued at a time when there are not yet reasonable grounds to believe that the item sought is there. It is true that the search warrant provisions would not authorize such a search. One might equally have argued, however, that Parliament had set out in section 487 the minimum requirements for obtaining a search warrant: if those requirements are not met, surely a warrant should not be issued, rather than issued under section 487.01 instead.

TELUS has now addressed this point.[26] In *TELUS* the police wished to obtain text messages between two parties, covering a two-week period in the past and a two-week period in the future. They obtained a production order for the past messages, but for the prospective messages obtained a general warrant which obliged TELUS, on a daily basis, to produce the text messages sent or received within the previous twenty-four hours. The issue was whether that prospective order could be made under the general warrant provisions: the Court held that it could not, though in a divided decision which hinders the case's precedential value to a certain extent. However, on many of the key principles about how to interpret section 487.01, there was some sort of consensus.

Justice Abella, writing for three judges, concluded that what the police were doing was intercepting a private communication within the meaning of Part VI of the *Code* and, therefore, that they were obliged to seek an authorization under that part: in that event, the "no other

---

23   2009 ONCA 340 [*Ha*].
24   See Coughlan, "*R. v. Ha*," above note 11.
25   Above note 13.
26   Above note 10.

provision" requirement for a general warrant was not met. Her decision finds that the general warrant in the case was not properly issued, but says little about how to interpret section 487.01 in general, other than to note that it is "residual" and should not be applied presumptively.[27]

Justice Moldaver, writing for two judges, spends more time on the general warrant requirements. In particular, he concludes that the "no other provision" requirement should include not only situations where the police are doing something that is identical to another provision (*literally* intercepting a private communication) but should also be seen as preventing the police from using a general warrant to do something that is "substantively equivalent" to what another provision would authorize. He reaches this conclusion precisely because the provision is "meant to fill gaps, not create them."[28] Most clearly, his decision demonstrates that a general warrant cannot be used as a means of engaging in an investigative technique which ought to be subject to even more stringent preconditions, such as an interception.[29] However, the decision goes beyond that and extends this same observation to other warrant provisions. Justice Moldaver holds that the purpose of the "no other provision" requirement is to see to it "that the general warrant is used sparingly as a warrant of limited resort."[30] He observes:

> in creating the general warrant, Parliament did not erase every other search authorization from the *Code* and leave it to judges to devise general warrants on an *ad hoc* basis as they deem fit. Courts must therefore be careful to fill a legislative lacuna only where Parliament has actually failed to anticipate a particular search authorization.[31]

Justice Cromwell, writing for two judges, dissents in the result and also specifically disagrees with Moldaver J's view that general warrants are to be used sparingly and that they eliminate techniques that are substantively equivalent to other provisions. At a level of principle, however, he agrees that "this does not mean that the court should authorize anything the police seek to do simply because it is not authorized elsewhere"[32] and also agrees that "[t]he section should not be approached on the assumption that Parliament intended that every investigative technique not authorized elsewhere could be authorized

---

27   *Ibid* at paras 18–19.
28   *Ibid* at para 93.
29   *Ibid* at para 76: a general warrant cannot be used "to avoid the rigours of a more demanding legislative authorization such as Part VI."
30   *Ibid* at para 56.
31   *Ibid* at para 78.
32   *Ibid* at para 170.

under s. 487.01(1)."[33] In Cromwell J's view, however, this should be accomplished not through the "no other provision" requirement, but through the separate requirement in section 487.01 that the warrant must be in the best interests of the administration of justice.

Because Abella J concurs with Moldaver J's "substantively equivalent" approach (without discussing the issue at all), that is the majority result.[34] This approach to the "no other provision" requirement has the ability to rein in the use of section 487.01. In essence, until this point some courts seem to have adopted the approach of saying "the application would not *succeed* under another provision; therefore, no other provision authorizes this technique." That seems to be the basis upon which anticipatory searches were approved under *Noseworthy*, for example. That is precisely the argument that the "substantively equivalent" argument is meant to prevent. Now the proper question is this: "If this application would succeed or fail under another section, is that other section the governing authority?" That is the point of looking for substantive equivalence: to locate those situations where the rules have anticipated investigative techniques such as the one in question and have set out limits for their use.

Although *TELUS* has the potential to limit the use of general warrants, it remains to be seen whether that will be its impact. Justice Moldaver distinguished rather than overturned *Ha* and *Ford*, for example, both cases discussed above as examples where the proper limits were not recognized.[35] There is no obvious difference in the number of cases in which general warrants were in dispute pre- and post-*TELUS*,[36] but whether this is because judges in issuing warrants have not yet begun to think they should be used sparingly or because there are still many cases "in the system" is impossible to tell.

As noted above, some aspects of section 487.01 make it broader in application, and although the "no other provision" requirement was initially taken to broaden its scope as well, *TELUS* indicates that it should have the effect of keeping the power in check. Other aspects of section 487.01 are also intended to make it more restrictive than section 487. First, the warrant can be issued only by a judge or justice, not by a justice

---

33   *Ibid* at para 190.

34   *Ibid* at para 20.

35   *Ibid* at para 69 referring to *Ha*, above note 23, and *Ford*, above note 15. *R v Abdullahi*, 2014 ONSC 6036, relies on *Ha*, citing Moldaver J's approval of *Ha* in *TELUS*.

36   Based on a search of electronic databases of caselaw for the term "general warrant" in the two years prior to and after *TELUS*. See *R v Abzakh*, 2014 ABQB 372, relying on *TELUS* to find the terms of a general warrant too broad.

of the peace.[37] Second, the judge can attach conditions "to ensure that any search or seizure authorized by the warrant is reasonable in the circumstances."[38] Finally, there is a specific requirement that the judge be satisfied that "it is in the best interests of the administration of justice to issue the warrant."[39]

Difficulties have been noted at times with the procedures used by justices of the peace in issuing warrants,[40] so requiring that a general warrant can be issued only by a judge does show a commitment to greater formality. However, *Hunter* had already required that whoever issued a warrant, whether under the *Code* or any other statute, had to be capable of acting judicially. Perhaps the terms of section 487.01 give greater grounds for confidence that this standard will consistently be met, though it is arguable that, inferentially, the heightened requirement suggests that the minimum constitutional standard is not consistently met in the case of other warrants.[41]

The ability to attach conditions has the potential to provide for sufficient balancing of individual freedom against the investigative needs of the state, but it does not guarantee such balancing. Only the conditions that "the judge considers advisable" need to be imposed, and so a great deal will depend upon which judges the police choose to approach when seeking a general warrant.

More work might be done by the separately imposed requirement that issuing the warrant is in the best interests of the administration of justice. This additional requirement holds the greatest hope of providing a reasonable limit on the search power and balancing the greater

---

37   The Court noted in *R v SAB*, 2003 SCC 60 at para 38, that the similar requirement in the case of DNA warrants showed that Parliament was attentive to the seriousness of the interests at stake. In *TELUS* this is said to be a factor showing that general warrants are meant to be "a rearguard warrant of limited resort" (para 71).

38   Section 487.01(3).

39   Section 487.01(1)(b).

40   It was noted, for example, in *Criminal Code of Canada (Re)*, above note 20 at para 11, that the relative lack of formality in having warrants issued by justices of the peace is efficient but

> the J.P. has in many instances become involved in a manner which has raised questions about the requisite judicial neutrality . . . see, for example, *R. v. Gray* (1993), 22 C.R. (4th) 114 (Man. C.A.); *R. v. Hallman* [2001] B.C.J. No. 1966 (B.C.S.C.); *R. v. Howe* [1994] B.C.J. No. 2731 (B.C.C.A.); *R. v. McCluskie* [1995] B.C.J. No. 1075 (B.C.S.C.); *R. v. Clarkson* [1999] B.C.J. No. 559 (B.C.S.C.); *R. v. Kelly* [1995] B.C.J. No. 1369 (B.C.C.A.); *R. v. Baker* [1997] 7 W.W.R. 713 (Sask. Q.B.); and *R. v. Paulson* [1993] B.C.J. No. 1944 (B.C.S.C.).

41   See, generally, the discussion of this issue and protocol for applying for s 487.01 warrants set out in *Criminal Code of Canada (Re)*, above note 20.

intrusiveness of the rest of the section. What do these words mean? *TELUS* holds that the "best interests" requirement is, in the abstract, meant to "ensure that the general warrant remains a rearguard warrant of limited resort," but does not give any real substance to that test.[42] In *Ha* the Ontario Court of Appeal found that the "best interests" requirement meant at least that a general warrant could not be used in circumstances that would amount to a "fishing expedition." In finding the general warrant in that case to meet this prerequisite, the court looked at the nature of the offence being investigated, the need for the investigative technique, the duration of the warrant, and the existence of conditions in the warrant.[43]

The constitutionality of the general warrant provisions was not raised in *TELUS*. In *R v Lucas* the Ontario Court of Appeal acknowledged that there were legitimate concerns about the provisions but that interpreted properly they were constitutional, at least with regard to anticipatory search warrants.[44] They noted that section 487.01 had been taken to allow for anticipatory search warrants, which on the face of it conflicts with the requirement in *Hunter* that the application establish that an offence *has been* committed and that evidence *is* in the place to be searched: anticipatory warrants permit searches when an offence *will be* committed and evidence *will be* in a location. Relying, in part, on the conclusion in *TELUS* that general warrants were to be used sparingly, the Court of Appeal concluded that anticipatory search warrants were constitutional under section 487.01 if two main conditions were met: (1) the particular offences to be committed had to be specified and reasonable grounds established to show that those particular offences will be committed, and (2) conditions should be attached so that the warrant is executed only when there are reasonable grounds to believe that information about that specific offence will be obtained. They suggested as safeguards that

- The conditions in the anticipatory warrant must be explicit, clear, and narrowly drawn so as to avoid misunderstanding or manipulation by government agents.

---

42   *TELUS*, above note 10 at para 71: the requirements of s 487.01 "are deliberately stricter than those for a conventional warrant. For example, the requirements that a general warrant can only be issued by a judge, not a justice of the peace, and that issuance must be in the best interests of justice themselves serve to ensure that the general warrant remains a rearguard warrant of limited resort." The dissent would have relied on the "best interests" criterion as the way to combat "the assumption that Parliament intended that every investigative technique not authorized elsewhere could be authorized under s. 487.01(1)": see para 190.

43   *Ha*, above note 23.

44   2014 ONCA 561.

- The triggering event must be ascertainable and preordained.
- The warrant should restrict the officers' discretion in detecting the occurrence of the event to almost ministerial proportions, similar to a search party's discretion in locating the place to be searched.[45]

These conditions did not need to be in the statute itself, but issuing anticipatory warrants would not violate section 8 of the *Charter* if they were understood to be implicit in the "best interests" requirement.

The last issue to discuss is the video surveillance provisions of section 487.01, which incorporate all of the other general warrant requirements and additional ones as well. Section 487.01(4) imposes the particular obligation that a warrant for video surveillance[46] in circumstances where a suspect has a reasonable expectation of privacy shall contain conditions that respect the privacy of the individual as much as possible. It is not immediately apparent how one should read this section in comparison with section 487.01(3), which simply allowed a judge issuing a general warrant to attach conditions to make the search or seizure "reasonable in the circumstances." Presumably, this should be taken as imposing an enhanced degree of concern for privacy when video surveillance is in issue, to reflect the greater potential for infringing on privacy.

The real limits on video surveillance are not found directly in section 487.01(4), but rather in its incorporation of the rules concerning consent and non-consent electronic surveillance: those rules are considered in Chapter 4, Section C(1)(b)(ii). This has the effect that, unlike other procedures potentially authorized under section 487.01, non-consent videotaping can be used only when other techniques have failed or are doubtful to succeed, due to the incorporation of the "investigative necessity" requirement.[47] The requirement of presenting an annual report concerning authorizations is also incorporated.

Around the video surveillance provisions exists one small anomaly relating to which judge has jurisdiction to issue the warrant. A general warrant can be issued by either a provincial court judge or a superior court judge. However, section 487.01(4) incorporates the provisions in

---

45   *Ibid* at para 116.

46   Strictly speaking, s 487.01(4) refers only to an authorization to "observe" by means of television cameras, although it has been held to include recording by that means as well: *R v McCreery*, [1996] BCJ No 2405 (SC).

47   It has also been suggested that the reference to a suspect's reasonable expectation of privacy in s 487.01(4) is a "limiting feature" on the accused's right which is not present in the case of audiotaping. In other words, in some circumstances, a suspect might be protected against audiotaping but not be protected against videotaping. See *R v Pangman*, 2000 MBQB 85 at para 27.

Part VI which limit jurisdiction to issue authorizations solely to superior court judges. As a result, there is some ambiguity over whether a provincial court judge does or does not have jurisdiction to issue a video surveillance warrant.[48]

C. POWERS OF DETENTION

1) Definition of Detention

Detention can have more than one meaning and so could deal, for example, with long-term interferences with liberty, such as those involved in being placed in a psychiatric facility following a not criminally responsible by reason of mental disorder finding[49] or being declared a dangerous offender.[50] In this context, however, it is detention at the investigative stage that is relevant (those detentions most similar to arrests in their purpose and duration). Essentially, that amounts to considering detentions where rights may arise under section 10 of the *Charter*. Section 10 gives various rights on arrest or detention, including the right to counsel, and the definition of "detention" was initially developed in that context, although the same definitions apply to detention under section 9.[51] Much of the discussion of those issues is contained in Chapter 7 and will also be relevant here, although there can be an issue over precisely when the section 10(b) right "kicks in" where a detention, rather than an arrest, is at issue.

The Court has delineated the types of detentions in which those rights arise with reasonable clarity. In *R v Thomsen*, the Court held:

1. In its use of the word "detention", s. 10 of the *Charter* is directed to a restraint of liberty other than arrest in which a person may reasonably require the assistance of counsel but might be prevented or impeded from retaining and instructing counsel without delay but for the constitutional guarantee.
2. In addition to the case of deprivation of liberty by physical constraint, there is a detention within s. 10 of the *Charter*, when a police officer or other agent of the state assumes control over the movement of a person by a demand or direction which may have

---

48   See *R v Li*, 2013 ONCA 81, referring to but not settling this question.
49   *R v Owen*, 2003 SCC 33.
50   *R v Johnson*, 2003 SCC 46.
51   *R v Hufsky*, [1988] 1 SCR 621 at para 12 [*Hufsky*].

significant legal consequence and which prevents or impedes access to counsel.

3. The necessary element of compulsion or coercion to constitute a detention may arise from criminal liability for refusal to comply with a demand or direction, or from a reasonable belief that one does not have a choice as to whether or not to comply.

4. Section 10 of the *Charter* applies to a great variety of detentions of varying duration and is not confined to those of such duration as to make the effective use of *habeas corpus* possible.[52]

In other words, "detention" can include not only those situations where the police have an actual legal power to compel a person to remain, but also some situations of "psychological detention" in which no such power exists, yet the person complies with the police demand nonetheless.[53] Detentions include not only breathalyzer demands at the side of the road, but also demands for breath samples for a roadside screening device[54] or a breathalyzer demand made at an accused's home after the accused has been initially questioned by consent without being detained.[55]

An accused can be detained despite an absence of a physical restraint and despite the fact that he was not physically prevented from making a telephone call to counsel.[56] Similarly, the fact that a person has complied with a police request to stop is not sufficient to make the stop voluntary and therefore not a detention.[57]

The primary purpose of granting *Charter* rights on detention and, in particular, the right to contact counsel, is to protect the detainee from possible self-incrimination.[58] It is designed to deal with interactions between the individual and the state, normally, though not exclusively, in the context of the investigation of a criminal offence. A demand by a school's vice-principal that a student comes to the office is not a detention in the relevant sense.[59] Similarly, routine questioning

---

52 [1988] 1 SCR 640 at 649 [*Thomsen*].

53 *R v Therens*, [1985] 1 SCR 613 [*Therens*].

54 *Thomsen*, above note 52.

55 *R v Schmautz*, [1990] 1 SCR 398.

56 *Ibid.*

57 *R v Dedman*, [1985] 2 SCR 2 [*Dedman*].

58 *R v Bartle*, [1994] 3 SCR 173.

59 *R v M(MR)*, [1998] 3 SCR 393. For criticism of the Nova Scotia Court of Appeal decision to the same effect, see A Wayne MacKay, "Don't Mind Me, I'm From the R.C.M.P.: *R v M(MR)* — Another Brick in the Wall between Students and Their Rights" (1997) 7 *Criminal Reports* (5th) 1.

of everyone entering the country by customs officials is not a detention, though singling out a particular person for a strip search is.[60]

Although there is a particular focus on the right to obtain legal advice, the Court has been resistant to arguments that the right should be reduced in situations where legal advice would have been of limited value to the accused. That counsel would likely have informed a detainee of the obligation to comply with a breathalyzer demand, for example, does not affect the content of the *Charter* section 10(b) right or the likelihood of the evidence being excluded under section 24(2).[61] Similarly, the fact that there was a statutory power to conduct a search, whether the detainee consented or not, does not mean that the detainee would not have benefited from the advice of counsel.[62]

Although the Court acknowledged the concept of psychological detention very early in *Charter* jurisprudence, it took quite some time before they articulated a definition of "detention" which was useful in that context. Whether a person has been detained by physical constraint is usually easy to determine, as is whether the person has been detained by the exercise of legal authority. Psychological detention, however, is both harder to define and harder to judge. This is especially so in the case of encounters between police and individuals on the street, though it can also be true of more formal questioning that takes place at a police station.[63]

A wide range of potential on-the-street interactions can arise. Police might simply be at the scene of an accident questioning everyone, witnesses and those involved, alike. In other cases, police simply question

---

60 *R v Simmons*, [1988] 2 SCR 495 [*Simmons*]. The same reasoning has been held to apply to those leaving the country through customs: *R v Nagle*, 2012 BCCA 373.

61 *Therens*, above note 53.

62 *Simmons*, above note 60. See also *R v Strachan*, [1988] 2 SCR 980 at para 44, where the Court rejected an approach that "would result in treating violations of s. 10(b) differently depending on the role counsel could have performed and would invite idle speculation on what might have happened if the accused had exercised the right to counsel."

63 For discussion of detention in the context of questioning at a police station, see *R v DEM* (2001), 156 Man R (2d) 231 (CA); *R v Johns* (1998), 14 CR (5th) 302 (Ont CA); *R v Hawkins*, [1993] 2 SCR 157; *R v Moran* (1987), 36 CCC (3d) 225 (Ont CA) [*Moran*]. *Moran* was usually considered by other courts to create the test to be applied in these circumstances. The Supreme Court's decision in *R v Grant*, 2009 SCC 32 [*Grant*], now creates a general test for when an accused has been psychologically detained. *Grant* deals with a street encounter, but there is nothing in the discussion to suggest that the definition of detention there is confined to that context. The majority do not explicitly discuss *Moran* or police station interviews, but nonetheless one should take *Grant* to be the governing authority in that context as well.

persons they meet on the street or whom they drive by, asking the person her name or purpose, or asking to see identification. Sometimes, the questioning might not be entirely random, and police might, for example, question a person who partly meets the description of a person wanted for an offence. In other cases, factors such as the time, location, or race of the person questioned may have factored into an officer's decision to ask questions. Clearly, some of these persons should be considered detained and others should not.

The difficulty in this area arises from the fact that there are competing legitimate interests. Not every conversation between a police officer and an individual should automatically be considered a detention: police interviewing the witnesses to a traffic accident should not be obliged to warn each of them of the right to counsel. The Court has, however, recognized the concept of psychological detention precisely because most people do not know whether they are compelled to comply with police requests or not, and so cooperation cannot always be seen as truly voluntary.[64]

Further, the primary justification for the section 10(b) right is that people interacting with the police are entitled to be protected from potential self-incrimination. In situations where an actual offence is being investigated and the extent of a person's involvement is unclear, there is a benefit for police, and a corresponding detriment to the individual, to be able to characterize the individual as merely a witness, not a suspect, and therefore not advise that person of the right to counsel. The less likely it is that a situation will be classified as a detention, the greater the risk that rights will not be adequately protected. Equally, where the police are nominally "randomly" asking questions on the street, the potential that the detention would be seen as arbitrary is that much greater. If it is not a detention, however, there is no potential for courts to engage in the balancing involved in deciding whether it was arbitrary or not. Among other issues, it becomes more difficult to determine whether the detention was random, or whether it was in reality based, in part, on improper motives, such as the race of the person.[65] The net effect would be a potential expansion of police power: not by design, but in result. This expansion would, based on the caselaw, often arise

---

64   *Therens*, above note 53.

65   On the issue of race as a factor in these decisions, see David Tanovich, "*R. v. Griffiths*: Race and Arbitrary Detention" (2003) 11 *Criminal Reports* (6th) 149, and David Tanovich, "Using the *Charter* to Stop Racial Profiling: The Development of an Equality-Based Conception of Arbitrary Detention" (2002) 40 *Osgoode Hall Law Journal* 145 [Tanovich, "Using the *Charter*"]. See also David Tanovich, *The Colour of Justice* (Toronto: Irwin Law, 2006).

in exactly those situations where the person questioned would have benefited from legal advice. An accused who gives his name, which the police then run through Canadian Police Information Centre (CPIC) while continuing to engage in conversation, may well have wanted to know that there was no obligation to remain or to answer questions, particularly when he is then arrested for violating curfew or on an outstanding warrant.[66]

It was those issues that the Court tried to resolve with the decision in *R v Grant*. They concluded that the question of whether there was a detention should be settled by an objective detainee-centred approach. In other words, the important question is not whether the person felt detained, nor whether the police intended to detain the person; rather, psychological detention was to be determined by "whether the reasonable person in the individual's circumstances would conclude that he or she had been deprived by the state of the liberty of choice" as to whether to stay or go.[67]

The Court also listed various factors that can be taken into account in determining this question. These are as follows:

(a) The circumstances giving rise to the encounter as they would reasonably be perceived by the individual: whether the police were providing general assistance; maintaining general order; making general inquiries regarding a particular occurrence; or, singling out the individual for focussed investigation.

(b) The nature of the police conduct, including the language used; the use of physical contact; the place where the interaction occurred; the presence of others; and the duration of the encounter.

(c) The particular characteristics or circumstances of the individual where relevant, including age; physical stature; minority status; level of sophistication.[68]

In *Grant* itself the Court concluded that the accused had been detained. He had been approached on the street by a police officer who stepped in his path and asked him general questions: at that stage he was not detained. However, he was then told to keep his hands in front of him, two other officers arrived and showed their badges, and pointed questions aimed at determining whether he had anything he should not were asked. The questioning was respectful but inherently intimidating, especially given the accused's age (he was eighteen) and that he

---

66   See, for example, *R v H(CR)*, 2003 MBCA 38 [*H(CR)*]; *R v Tammie*, 2001 BCSC
     366 [*Tammie*]; *R v Powell* (2000), 35 CR (5th) 89 (Ont Ct J).

67   *Grant*, above note 63 at para 44.

68   *Ibid.*

was outnumbered. Accordingly, the accused had become psychologic-ally detained. The Court reached this conclusion even though the accused did not testify, and so did not say that he felt detained. The Court noted that this was not fatal to the claim, precisely because the test is objective.

In a concurring opinion Binnie J argued that a wholly claimant-centred approach was inadequate and that the perceptions of the police ought also to be factored into the analysis.[69] He argued that there is a significant difference between the police saying "stay put" to the witnesses to an accident or to an obvious suspect which ought to be reflected in the analysis. In addition, he argues that leaving the police perspective out of the analysis means that if police can mask their true intentions a person might not be detained.

There is some force to this suggestion. To the contrary, though, it is worth recognizing that the claim by the police that they would have let a person leave if the person had asked to do so, or even had refused to answer questions, had, pre-*Grant*, frequently resulted in a finding that the person was not detained: the person therefore had no claim to have been arbitrarily detained.[70] That amounted to the paradoxical result that the absence of any power authorizing the police to do the thing they were doing made it *less* likely there was a *Charter* violation. The majority's approach in *Grant* avoids that dilemma.[71]

To really understand how the question of whether an accused was psychologically detained is answered, however, it is necessary also to look at the decision in *R v Suberu*, handed down by the Court on the same day as *Grant*.[72] Suberu was in a liquor store where a person he was with was using a stolen gift card: a police officer arrived at the scene as Suberu was leaving, and Suberu said to him, "He did this, not me, so I guess I can go." The officer replied: "Wait a minute. I need to talk to you before you go anywhere." The officer followed Suberu outside, where he posed half a dozen questions and then asked Suberu for his identification and registration. Eventually, the officer received more information by radio, arrested the accused, and advised him of his right to counsel. The issue in *Suberu* was whether the officer had violated the accused's

---

69   See also Tim Quigley, "Was It Worth the Wait? The Supreme Court's New Approaches to Detention and Exclusion of Evidence" (2009) 66 *Criminal Reports* (6th) 88 [Quigley, "Was It Worth the Wait?"] for the same opinion.

70   See, for example, *H(CR)*, above note 66; *R v LB*, 2007 ONCA 596; or *Tammie*, above note 66.

71   See the discussion in Steve Coughlan, "Great Strides in Section 9 Jurisprudence" (2009) 66 *Criminal Reports* (6th) 75 [Coughlan, "Great Strides"].

72   2009 SCC 33 [*Suberu*].

section 10(b) right to counsel by not cautioning him when he was first detained. The Ontario Court of Appeal had concluded there was no section 10(b) violation because a short delay was permissible in the context of an investigative detention. The Supreme Court of Canada rejected that view, holding that the right to counsel arises immediately upon an investigative detention. However, they upheld the result in the courts below on the basis that Suberu had not been detained *at all* until he was arrested: they concluded that the definition of detention "gives the police leeway to engage members of the public in non-coercive, exploratory questioning without necessarily triggering their *Charter* rights relating to detention."[73]

This conclusion was surprising. All the judges at every level below had concluded that there *was* a detention and disagreed over only the legal consequences of that detention. Justice Binnie argued in a dissenting judgment that this application of the test in *Grant* was mistaken and underestimated the coercive power of police commands. On the facts the accused had been leaving and had been told by an officer to wait and answer some questions. Holding that "[g]enerally speaking, the police mean what they say when they direct a citizen to stay put," he would have concluded that the accused was detained.[74]

The effect of the Supreme Court reaching the conclusion it did has been to create a kind of sorting mechanism for assessing detentions. *Suberu* is being taken to have established the notion of an "exploratory investigation" which does not amount to a detention.[75] In essence, police have been given the power to engage in exploratory questioning to orient themselves, even if doing so results in them investigating and eventually arresting an accused.[76]

The Court observed in *Suberu* that "[t]he line between general questioning and focussed interrogation amounting to detention may be difficult to draw in particular cases."[77] Courts certainly do apply the test for psychological detention from *Grant* and try to consider each of those factors. A factor which tends to weigh heavily in the analysis is the nature of the questioning and other things the officer says to the

---

73   *Ibid* at para 45.

74   *Ibid* at para 50. See also the discussion in Quigley, "Was It Worth the Wait?," above note 69, and Coughlan, "Great Strides," above note 71.

75   See, for example, *R v Mihalik*, 2010 ABPC 253; *R v Johnson*, 2010 ONSC 1490; *R v Oulton*, 2011 ABQB 243; *R v Bagnato*, 2011 ONSC 2440; *R v Lyons*, 2011 ABPC 297; *R v Munro*, 2012 ONSC 43; *R v Smith*, 2012 ONCJ 116 [*Smith* 2012]; *R v Goodwin*, 2014 ABPC 170; or *R v Chui*, 2015 ONSC 552.

76   See the discussion of "default" common law powers in Chapter 2, Section A(3)(c).

77   *Suberu*, above note 72 at para 29.

accused.[78] In *R v Koczab* (SCC), for example, the statement of the officer to the accused "I just have to go to my car for a minute" was found to be an implied direction not to leave.[79] This was distinguished from the officer's statement in *Suberu* that "I need to talk to you before you go anywhere," based on timing. As a practical matter, the decision as to whether a particular accused was detained often comes down to whether the facts are seen as more like *Grant* or more like *Suberu*.[80]

2) Common Law Powers of Detention

a) Introduction

Section 9 of the *Charter* guarantees everyone the right to be free from arbitrary detention. As was just discussed, in *Grant* the Court put forward an objective detainee-centric test for whether a person has been detained; in addition, that case sets out a framework for deciding whether such a detention will be "arbitrary" within the meaning of section 9 of the *Charter*.

For some considerable time, the Court had deliberately left unsettled whether a detention could be unlawful (in the sense that the police acted outside of their powers to arrest or detain) but nonetheless not be arbitrary for purposes of section 9.[81] One view was that, for example, an arrest made in circumstances that fell just short of reasonable grounds might not be arbitrary.[82]

Grant makes clear that that is not the case: the Court holds that "for a detention to be non-arbitrary, it must be authorized by a law which is itself non-arbitrary."[83] Indeed, the Court did more than simply settle the point that an unlawful detention was, by definition, arbitrary. Rather, they laid down an analytical framework for section 9.

---

78   See, for example, the discussions of whether there was or was not a focused interrogation in *R v Peterson*, 2013 MBCA 104; *R v Kalturnyk*, 2014 MBPC 24; or *R v Moulton*, 2015 ONSC 1047.

79   See *R v Koczab*, 2014 SCC 9 [*Koczab* SCC], which adopted the reasons of the dissenting judge in *R v Koczab*, 2013 MBCA 43.

80   *R v Peacock*, 2009 ONCJ 479 at para 28:

> At its simplest, answering the question of whether the defendant was detained depends on whether the totality of circumstances renders him closer to the fact pattern presented in *Grant* or that captured by the facts in *Suberu*.

Cases approaching the issue on this basis include *R v Reddy*, 2010 BCCA 11; *R v Sonne*, 2011 ONSC 6700 [*Sonne*]; *R v Simpenzwe*, 2009 ABQB 579; and *Smith* 2012, above note 75.

81   See, for example, *R v Latimer*, [1997] 1 SCR 217.

82   *R v Duguay* (1985), 18 CCC (3d) 289 (Ont CA).

83   *Grant*, above note 63 at para 56.

In essence, the approach to section 9 now mirrors the three-step *Collins* approach to searches under section 8.[84] First, in order to avoid a section 9 violation, the detention must have been authorized by law.[85] Second, the law itself must not be arbitrary, which means that it cannot be random and must be based on criteria that are reasonable and can be clearly expressed.[86] Finally, the manner in which the detention is effected must be reasonable and not arbitrary: for example, no more than is necessary should have been done to effect the detention, and a lawful power must not have been used for an improper purpose such as racial profiling.[87] The rest of the discussion in this section will focus almost exclusively on the first question, whether the detention is authorized by law, and particularly by the common law, since that is where the most challenging issues have arisen.

Some powers of detention exist by statute. The ability to make breathalyzer demands, some random routine traffic stops, and some aspects of customs searches, for example, are legislatively created detentions.[88] Detentions that are created only by common law are more controversial. The Court has increasingly used the *Waterfield* test to create new common law police powers.[89] In *R v Dedman* it authorized a program of random stops of vehicles. Subsequently in the detention context, it relied on *R v Waterfield* to create police powers of investigative detention short of arrest, to permit a police roadblock, and eventually to permit any detention which is reasonably necessary in the circumstances.[90]

---

84 See the discussion in Chapter 4, Section A.

85 *Grant*, above note 63 at para 56.

86 *Ibid*. See also *R v Ladouceur*, [1990] 1 SCR 1257 [*Ladouceur*]; and *R v Wilson*, [1990] 1 SCR 1291 [*Wilson*].

87 See the discussion of *R v Aucoin*, 2012 SCC 66 [*Aucoin*], in Section C(2)(d), below in this chapter, for the need for the application of a detention power to be reasonably necessary. See also, for example, *R v Storrey*, [1990] 1 SCR 241 at para 19: "That is to say, there is no indication that the arrest was made because a police officer was biased towards a person of a different race, nationality or colour, or that there was a personal enmity between a police officer directed towards the person arrested. These factors, if established, might have the effect of rendering invalid an otherwise lawful arrest."

88 See, for example, *Therens*, above note 53; *Ladouceur*, above note 86; *R v Monney*, [1999] 1 SCR 652; *Simmons*, above note 60. Note, in particular, *R v Orbanski*; *R v Elias*, 2005 SCC 37, holding that the power to conduct roadside sobriety tests was implicit in the general power to stop vehicles in s 76.1(1) of Manitoba's *Highway Traffic Act*, SM 1985–86, c 3.

89 See the discussion of the *Waterfield* test in Chapter 2.

90 [1963] 3 All ER 659 [*Waterfield*]. See *R v Mann*, 2004 SCC 52 [*Mann*]; *R v Clayton*, 2007 SCC 32 [*Clayton*]; and *Aucoin*, above note 87.

In *Dedman*, the Court considered the RIDE program of randomly stopping vehicles with the goal of detecting impaired drivers. No statutory authority allowed the stops, so the question became whether they were authorized at common law. The majority of the Court, relying on *Waterfield*, held that they were.

The *Waterfield* test involves asking two questions of the conduct of the police: whether "(a) such conduct falls within the general scope of any duty imposed by statute or recognized at common law and (b) whether such conduct, albeit within the general scope of such a duty, involved an unjustifiable use of powers associated with the duty."[91]

The Court held that the random stops satisfied both aspects of the test. Preventing crime and protecting life and property by controlling traffic, the goals of the RIDE program, were well within the scope of duties of the police. Given the seriousness of the problem of impaired driving, the need to deter it, the fact that driving is a licensed activity, the well-publicized nature of the program, and that the stop would be of a short duration and minimal inconvenience, the interference was deemed not unreasonable. Accordingly, the use of power was not unjustifiable, and the police were authorized to make the stops at common law.

Dedman determined that there was a common law power to randomly stop vehicles, but did not consider whether such random stops violated section 9 of the *Charter*. Two subsequent cases, *R v Hufsky* and *R v Ladouceur*, concluded that random vehicle stops could be upheld under the *Charter*.[92] In both of those cases the power of detention was authorized by law, but the law itself was found to be arbitrary, since the discretion over which vehicle to stop lay in the absolute discretion of a police officer. However, in each case, the section 9 violation was found to be saved under section 1 because of concerns about highway safety.[93]

---

91   *Waterfield*, above note 90, quoted in *Dedman*, above note 57 at para 66. See also *R v Decorte*, [2005] 1 SCR 133, which upheld the ability of First Nations constables to conduct RIDE stops just outside a reserve, though in that case, that ability was based on a statutory power.

92   *Hufsky*, above note 51; *Ladouceur*, above note 86.

93   In *Hufsky*, above note 51, vehicle stops at fixed checkpoints were saved unanimously under s 1, in part, because such anti–drunk driving programs were well publicized. In *Ladouceur*, a "roving random stop" power, unrelated to a program to stop drunk driving, was saved by a 5:4 margin. The majority thought the situation analogous enough to *Hufsky* that the same rationale would apply. The minority at para 8 described the situation as the "last straw," since it meant the Court was approving a power for police to "stop any vehicle at any time, in any place, without having any reason to do so" which was "a total negation of the freedom from arbitrary detention guaranteed by s. 9 of the *Charter*." The result in *Ladouceur* is probably largely responsible for the fact that it took two decades

Those cases held that a law authorizing a detention based on no criteria will be arbitrary: conversely, a detention will not be arbitrary if it is based on criteria that are reasonable and can be clearly expressed.[94]

Some instances of unreasonable criteria for stops can be found. In the Ontario Court of Appeal decision in *R v Calderon*,[95] for example, the court found a section 9 violation when the police had stopped a vehicle based on what they claimed a drug-interdiction course had taught them were indicators that the occupants were drug couriers. The "indicators" that the officers had relied upon were the presence of cell phones, a pager, a road map, some fast food wrappers, and two duffel bags, as well as the notion that the car being driven seemed too expensive "for what the driver and the passenger looked to me."[96] The last criterion was rejected outright as an inappropriate criterion, but so ultimately were the preceding ones. All of those factors, the court held, were neutral and were unsurprising items to find in a car. Each of the officers acknowledged on cross-examination that they had stopped many cars based on these "indicators" and had never before found drugs. The stop based on these neutral and unreliable factors was therefore an arbitrary detention.

There is a developing jurisprudence on stops based on racial profiling and a recognition that it leads to a finding of a section 9 violation. Clear guidelines have yet to be laid down by the Supreme Court of Canada, though lower courts have grappled with the issue. In *R v Brown*, for example, the Ontario Court of Appeal acknowledged the possibility that, in some cases, police stops might be improperly motivated by the race of the accused, leading to a section 9 violation. Such cases, they held, are unlikely to be proven by direct evidence, and so must be inferred from the circumstances:

> where the evidence shows that the circumstances relating to a detention correspond to the phenomenon of racial profiling and provide a basis for the court to infer that the police officer is lying about why he or she singled out the accused person for attention, the record is then capable of supporting a finding that the stop was based on racial profiling.[97]

---

before a real s 9 jurisprudence began to develop: if that violation could be saved under s 1 there would have seemed little reason to try to establish a s 9 violation.

94   *Wilson*, above note 86.

95   (2004), 23 CR (6th) 1 (Ont CA).

96   *Ibid* at para 61.

97   (2003), 173 CCC (3d) 23 at para 45 (Ont CA) [*Brown*].

Although racial profiling has been recognized in principle, successful racial profiling claims at trial have been few.[98] Whether this is because the phenomenon is rare, because prosecutors exercise their discretion not to proceed when it has occurred, or because proving it even when it has occurred is difficult is not clear.

The decision in *Dedman* has been properly criticized for its use of *Waterfield*, which was intended to be a way to understand the limits on existing police powers, not to be a method of creating new powers.[99] Nonetheless, as discussed in Chapter 2, the use of *Waterfield* to expand police powers is well entrenched in Canadian law. We have already seen that it was used in *Dedman* to create a vehicle stop power. More significantly, it has been used to create various powers of detention relating to individuals.

In *R v Mann*, the Court relied on *Waterfield* to decide that police officers who do not have reasonable grounds to arrest a person have the power to stop that person for investigative purposes, nonetheless, if they have "reasonable grounds to detain."[100] The Court also relied on *Waterfield* in *R v Clayton*.[101] On the surface, *Clayton* creates only a police power to set up roadblocks, but as will be seen when that case is discussed, the approach taken to *Waterfield* in *Clayton* is extremely expansive. The later decision in *R v Aucoin* confirms that it created exactly the "general power of detention" that the Court warned against creating in *Mann*.[102]

It is best to begin by discussing the "investigative detention" power created in *Mann*.

b) Investigative Detention

The first suggestion that there was a power of investigative detention in Canada came in the Ontario Court of Appeal decision in *R v Simpson*. That decision suggested that such a power existed on some occasions, though not on the facts of that case itself. There was no general power

---

98   See, for example, *R v Khan* (2004), 24 CR (6th) 48 (Ont SCJ). See David Tanovich, "Operation Pipeline and Racial Profiling" (2002) 1 *Criminal Reports* (6th) 52; and Tanovich, "Using the *Charter*," above note 65. See also *R v Lam*, 2014 ONSC 3538, which does not find that there was racial profiling but adverts at para 207 to the officers' "astounding lack of understanding as to cross-race identification dangers."

99   See, for example, James Stribopoulos, "A Failed Experiment? Investigative Detention: Ten Years Later" (2003) 41 *Alberta Law Review* 335 at 348–52; Don Stuart, "R. v. Dedman: Annotation" (1985) 46 *Criminal Reports* (3d) 194 at 195. See also the discussion of *Waterfield* in Chapter 2, Section A(3)(b).

100   *Mann*, above note 90.

101   Above note 90.

102   *Aucoin*, above note 87.

to detain, the Court noted, but they held that a person could be briefly detained for questioning "if the detaining officer has some 'articulable cause' for the detention."[103] Articulable cause—which is a consciously lower standard than the "reasonable grounds to believe" required for an arrest—was said to be a necessary but not sufficient condition for the detention, and the detention was meant to be brief. This approach was adopted by a number of other courts of appeal, though later courts largely ignored the notion that articulable cause was only the first step and turned that concept into the test for detention.[104] Further, the notion that articulable cause should normally support only a brief detention to ask for identification was largely lost, as many courts added an automatic ability to search the person as an incident to the detention or even to use reasonable force in effecting the detention.[105]

Although investigative detention based on articulable cause proved popular with lower courts, it was unpopular with commentators, who generally saw it as an expansion of police powers and a diminution of individual liberty created with too little attention to principle.[106] However, the issue was settled by the Court's decision in *Mann*.[107] In *Mann*

---

103 (1993), 20 CR (4th) 1 at para 58 (Ont CA) [*Simpson*].

104 A very incomplete list of cases applying the doctrine includes *R v Burke* (1997), 118 CCC (3d) 59 (Nfld CA); *R v Chabot* (1993), 86 CCC (3d) 309 (NSSCAD); *R v Boudreau* (2001), 196 DLR (4th) 53 (NBCA); *R v Lewis*, (1998), 38 OR (3d) 540 (CA); *R v Lake*, (1997), 113 CCC (3d) 208 (Sask CA) [*Lake*]; *R v Dupuis* (1994), 162 AR 197 (CA); *R v Yum*, 2001 ABCA 80 [*Yum*]; *R v TAV* (2001), 48 CR (5th) 366 (Alta CA); and *R v Ferris* (1998), 16 CR (5th) 287 (BCCA), leave to appeal to SCC refused, [1998] SCCA No 424 [*Ferris*].

105 For incidental search powers, see *Ferris*, *ibid*; *R v Lal* (1998), 56 CRR (2d) 243 (BCCA), leave to appeal to SCC refused, [1999] SCCA No 28; *R v McAuley* (1998), 126 Man R (2d) 202 (CA); *Lake*, above note 104; and *R v Waniandy*, (1995) 162 AR 293 (CA). For the use of force, see *Yum*, above note 104.

106 See, for example, Peter Sankoff, "Articulable Cause Based Searches Incident to Detention—This *Cooke* May Spoil the Broth" (2002) 2 *Criminal Reports* (6th) 41; Steve Coughlan, "Search Based on Articulable Cause: Proceed with Caution or Full Stop?" (2002) 2 *Criminal Reports* (6th) 49; Aman S Patel, "Detention and Articulable Cause: Arbitrariness and Growing Judicial Deference to Police Judgment" (2000) 45 *Criminal Law Quarterly* 198; Lesley A McCoy, "Liberty's Last Stand? Tracing the Limits of Investigative Detention" (2002) 46 *Criminal Law Quarterly* 319; Jason A Nicol, "'Stop in the Name of the Law': Investigative Detention" (2002) 7 *Canadian Criminal Law Review* 223; Stribopoulos, above note 99; *H(CR)*, above note 66; and Steve Coughlan, "*R v Mann*: Annotation" (2003) 5 *Criminal Reports* (6th) 306.

107 Generally speaking, the decision in *Mann* was not well received by commentators either: see Benjamin L Berger, "Race and Erasure in *R. v. Mann*" (2004) 21 *Criminal Reports* (6th) 58; Eric V Gottardi, "*R. v. Mann*: Regulating State Intrusions in the Context of Investigative Detentions" (2004) 21 *Criminal Reports*

the Court decided that police can sometimes detain individuals for investigative detention, but the reasoning is cursory. In substance, the decision amounted to confirming that such a power *does* exist without explaining very fully *why* it should exist. The Court referred briefly to *Simpson*[108] and to one other court of appeal decision, devoted two short paragraphs to the nearly forty years of US jurisprudence on this issue, and engaged in essentially no analysis of the many arguments that commentators had raised against the power.

The *Mann* investigative detention power is quite limited. On the one hand, the Court appeared to take the question of whether an investigative detention power based on less than reasonable grounds exists at all as settled by the lower court jurisprudence, though this is not explicitly stated. On the other hand, *Mann* clearly did not adopt or confirm the broad approach to investigative detention reflected in those cases—it was a fresh starting point. Indeed, the Court specifically stated that it would not be "appropriate for this Court to recognize a general power of detention for investigative purposes."[109] The Court described the limited power it does create in this way:

> The detention must be viewed as reasonably necessary on an objective view of the totality of the circumstances, informing the officer's suspicion that there is a clear nexus between the individual to be detained and a recent or ongoing criminal offence. Reasonable grounds figures at the front end of such an assessment, underlying the officer's reasonable suspicion that the particular individual is implicated in the criminal activity under investigation. The overall reasonableness of the decision to detain, however, must further be assessed against all of the circumstances, most notably the extent to which the interference with individual liberty is necessary to perform the officer's duty, the liberty interfered with, and the nature and extent of that interference, in order to meet the second prong of the *Waterfield* test.[110]

It is clear from this requirement of a nexus to a "recent or on-going criminal offence" that police cannot detain a person because they are suspicious in some general way. Rather, they must be suspicious of a particular person because of some suspected connection to a particu-

---

(6th) 27; Tim Quigley, "*Mann*, It's a Disappointing Decision" (2004) 21 *Criminal Reports* (6th) 41; David Tanovich, "The Colourless World of *Mann*" (2004) 21 *Criminal Reports* (6th) 47; and Joseph R Marin, "*R. v. Mann*: Further Down the Slippery Slope" (2005) 42 *Alberta Law Review* 1123.

108   Above note 103.
109   *Mann*, above note 90 at para 17.
110   *Ibid* at para 34.

lar crime already known to them. This point is important. There is a great difference between the police stopping a person who is leaving the scene of a reported break-in and the police stopping a person walking along the street looking in some way "suspicious." Consistent with this approach, the Court specifically rejected as not relevant any consideration at this stage of whether an accused is in a "high crime area"; suspicions must be specific to the accused.

The reference to a "recent or on-going" criminal offence precludes using the power because of a suspicion that a person contemplated committing a criminal offence. In that event, the Canadian power of detention is more limited than its US counterpart. The US Supreme Court created their "stop and frisk" power in *Terry v Ohio*, where a police officer became suspicious that several men were planning to rob a store.[111]

Despite the fact that *Mann* is fairly clear on these points, they have not always been recognized or respected by lower courts. For example, in the immediate aftermath of *Mann* some lower courts seemed to take it simply to affirm *Simpson*, rather than to have articulated a new test with particular requirements. As a result, the need for a clear nexus to a recent or ongoing offence and the prohibition on using the power for anticipated offences was not always acknowledged.[112] That was not uniformly so, however: some decisions were careful to identify the particular offence to which there was a clear nexus.[113]

Some courts of appeal have consciously relaxed the standard of "recent or on-going offence." In *R v Nesbeth*, for example, the Ontario Court of Appeal held that the police need not be able to identify "with absolute precision" the particular crime of which they suspect the detainee.[114] In that case, the police pursued an accused after he ran away upon being asked what he was doing in an apartment building in which there was a smell of freshly smoked marijuana. His eventual detention after a chase was found to be lawful on the basis that the police reasonably suspected he had drugs or weapons or both.

In *R v Yeh*[115] the Saskatchewan Court of Appeal considered the issue of whether an investigative detention could be undertaken in the case of a nexus to a suspected rather than a known offence. In an earlier decision they had held that a *Mann* investigative detention would not

---

111 392 US 1, 88 S Ct (1968).
112 See the discussion of this issue in Christina Skibinsky, "Regulating *Mann* in Canada" (2006) 69 *Saskatchewan Law Review* 197.
113 See, for example, *R v Cooper*, 2005 NSCA 47, or *R v Scott*, 2004 NSCA 141.
114 2008 ONCA 579 at para 18 [*Nesbeth*].
115 2009 SKCA 112 [*Yeh*].

be lawful if the officer merely suspected an offence.[116] In *Yeh* they reconsidered that point and reversed themselves, concluding that *Mann* should be read as authorizing investigative detentions in relation to offences that are only reasonably suspected at the time of the detention.[117] In *R v Schrenk*, the Manitoba Court of Appeal agreed, adding that reasonable suspicion of bad behaviour in general was not sufficient: "[i]t is a reasonable suspicion of specific criminal activity that gives rise to the grounds to detain."[118]

It is important to note that *Nesbeth* and *Yeh* consider two different ways of relaxing the *Mann* standard. *Nesbeth* holds that the offence need not be identified precisely. *Yeh* does not reach that conclusion (indeed, it expressly does not decide it)[119] but holds that once the offence is precisely identified, the police need only suspect that it has been committed rather than know that fact. It is necessary to be careful with that distinction.[120] In particular, there is a great danger in relaxing the *Mann* standard in both ways by failing to recognize the difference between them. Even the Saskatchewan Court of Appeal in *Yeh* stresses that police ought not to be permitted to conduct an investigative detention "to determine whether an individual is, in some broad way, 'up to no good.'"[121]

Subsequent to both *Yeh* and *Nesbeth* the Court, in *R v MacKenzie*, characterized *Mann* as deciding that "the police are entitled to detain a person for investigative purposes where they have reasonable grounds to suspect that the individual is connected to particular criminal activity and that such a detention is reasonably necessary in the circumstances."[122] This articulation of the test continues to require a

---

116   *R v Nguyen*, 2008 SKCA 160.

117   *Yeh*, above note 115 at para 85.

118   *R v Schrenk*, 2010 MBCA 38 at para 85.

119   *Yeh*, above note 115 at para 75: "In order to justify an investigative detention, the police suspicion must be particularized, *i.e.* it must relate to specific criminal wrongdoing. Just *how* specific it must be is not an issue in this appeal."

120   See *Yeh*, *ibid* at para 74:

There is a conceptual and practical distinction between (a) the question of how particular or specific a police suspicion must be in order to justify an investigative detention, and (b) the question of whether an investigative detention may be conducted only in respect of an offence which has been reported to the police or which the police otherwise understand has been committed. Any analysis which fails to appreciate the difference between these two notions will, of necessity, be flawed.

121   See *ibid* at para 75. See also the discussion in Tim Quigley, "Investigative Detention: Some Loose Ends Remain" (2009) 69 *Criminal Reports* (6th) 247.

122   2013 SCC 50 at para 35 [*MacKenzie*].

link to "particular criminal activity," which seems to hold to the standard that *Nesbeth* relaxed, and says nothing to suggest that criminal activity need only be reasonably suspected (though the case relies on *Yeh* with regard to several other issues). However, the central issue in *MacKenzie* related to a search, not a detention, and so it would be unwise to read too much into its description of *Mann*. Explicit clarification from the Court as to whether the *Mann* standard should be relaxed in either of the ways proposed would be helpful.[123]

It is also worth observing that the *Mann* test is narrower than just the test of a "clear nexus." In other words, even when a clear nexus exists, the specific individual decision to detain must still be justified based on the circumstances. In effect, the Court has refrained from creating an investigative detention power under the *Waterfield* test. Instead, it has created a framework, based on the *Waterfield* test, to be applied to assess each specific decision to detain.

A further explicit change made from existing caselaw relates to terminology. Where lower courts had spoken about "articulable cause," the Supreme Court substituted the phrase "reasonable grounds to detain," holding that this phrasing would be more consistent with Canadian terminology. Justice Deschamps, in dissent, suggested that this phrasing would lead to confusion because "'[r]easonable grounds' has traditionally been employed to describe the standard which must be met in order to give rise to the power to *arrest* a suspect."[124] In fact, the terminology that has come to be employed in practice is to refer to "reasonable suspicion." This development is due, in part, to the growth in other detention (and search) powers that have been made available on this lower standard.[125]

---

123 In *R v Chehil*, 2013 SCC 49, handed down with *MacKenzie*, Karakatsanis J, for the Court, observed at para 35: "I do not accept that the evidence must itself consist of unlawful behaviour, or must necessarily be evidence of a specific known criminal act." She was speaking, however, about the kind of evidence necessary in general terms to satisfy the "reasonable suspicion" standard, not about the particular test for an investigative detention.

124 *Mann*, above note 90 at para 64 [emphasis in original].

125 See the discussion in *MacKenzie*, above note 122 at para 74:

Parenthetically, I note that there are several ways of describing what amounts to the same thing. Reasonable suspicion means "reasonable grounds to suspect" as distinguished from "reasonable grounds to believe" (*Kang-Brown*, at paras 21 and 25, per Binnie J., and at para 164, per Deschamps J.). To the extent one speaks of a "reasonable belief" in the context of reasonable suspicion, it is a reasonable belief that an individual *might* be connected to a particular offence, as opposed to a reasonable belief that an individual *is* connected to the offence.

Although *Mann* created this investigative detention power based on the lower reasonable suspicion standard, it did relatively little to articulate what that standard required. Subsequent to *Mann* the standard came to be more widely used in other common law powers (both of detention, as noted below, and of search), and eventually the Court did describe in some detail how reasonable suspicion and reasonable belief differ: see the discussion of warrantless searches in Chapter 4, Section C(2)(a). See also the discussion about search during an investigative detention in Chapter 4, Section C(1)(a)(ii)(c).

Mann left unsettled whether the section 10 right to counsel arises during an investigative detention; however, it has since been determined that the *Charter* right does arise. One view in lower courts had been that, because investigative detentions were meant to be brief, the accused's right to counsel under section 10(b) did not arise. In *Suberu* the Supreme Court rejected that view and had no difficulty concluding that issues of compelled self-incrimination and interference with liberty arise with an investigative detention as much as with any other. Accordingly, the police have the obligation to inform a detainee of the right to counsel without delay as soon as an investigative detention begins. This immediate obligation is subject only to concerns for officer or public safety or to limits under section 1 of the *Charter*.[126]

c)   Police Roadblocks

Subsequent to *Mann*, the Court relied on the *Waterfield* test to create another police power of detention. On the facts of the case the Court was simply approving the actions of the police in setting up a roadblock. However, the way in which the majority reasoned raised the possibility that other, much broader powers to detain also exist, and as we will see in *Aucoin*, that is how the test has come to be interpreted.

In *Clayton*[127] the police received a report of men with guns in a parking lot (and describing particular vehicles), and in response the police set up a roadblock. They stopped all vehicles leaving the parking lot, whether they matched the vehicle descriptions or not, and Clayton and Farmer, the occupants of one car, were both found to have handguns. A central issue was whether there was a violation of the section 9 right of both of the accused not to be arbitrarily detained. The majority held that there would have been no violation if the police had acted lawfully, and so the real issue in the case became whether the police had a power

---

126 *Suberu*, above note 72 at para 2.
127 Above note 90.

to set up the roadblock. Since they had no statutory power to do so, the only possibility was that they were authorized at common law.

There was both a majority and a minority decision in the case. All nine judges concluded that the police did have the power to act as they had, but they reached that conclusion for different reasons. It is in these different approaches that the new and potentially enormous expansion to *Waterfield* can be seen.

The minority judges held that the proper method of analysis was first to ask whether the police acted lawfully in stopping the accused, which amounted to asking whether there was a common law power permitting them to do so. The second question was whether that common law power resulted in an arbitrary detention. If so, the next step was to ask whether that law was justified under section 1 of the *Charter*. Finally, in some cases it would be necessary to ask whether the power was exercised reasonably in the totality of the circumstances. Applying that approach, the minority concluded that no previously existing common law power (such as those in *Dedman*[128] or *Mann*[129]) authorized the stop but that (using the *Waterfield* test) a new common law power should be created. Specifically, a power should be created to set up a roadblock of all vehicles in response to a report of ongoing serious firearm offences. As a result, the detention was authorized by law. That law would create an arbitrary detention (since it would permit stops in the absence of individualized suspicion) but would be saved under section 1, much like the power in *Ladouceur*.[130]

The majority agreed that the issue was whether the police had the power to act as they did, but did nothing further by way of *Charter* scrutiny. As the minority pointed out, the majority substituted the question of whether the *Waterfield* test was met for the *Charter* analysis. Further, their approach to *Waterfield* seems to broaden the scope of what powers police have or, alternatively, to limit when police action will be found to violate the *Charter*, which, on the majority approach, will amount to the same thing. As noted above, the *Waterfield* test depends on two criteria: (1) that the police were acting in the general course of their duties, and (2) that the actions they took were not an unjustifiable use of powers associated with those duties. The first criterion is rarely an issue, and so it is the second that really settles the point. In *Clayton*, the majority effectively reduced that question to whether, in the totality of the circumstances, "the detention of a particular individual is 'reasonably

---

128 Above note 57.

129 Above note 90.

130 Above note 86.

necessary.'"[131] But to say that the police can detain an individual whenever it is reasonably necessary is to make that ability available to police
far more frequently.

Even in *Mann* the Court noted the fundamental principle that "the
police . . . may act only to the extent that they are empowered to do so
by law."[132] That amounts to saying that the norm is for the police to be
unable to interfere with individual liberty unless they have been given
a specific power. The approach in *Clayton*, in contrast, amounts to saying that the police have the power to do anything that is reasonably
necessary. To say that is to remove entirely the notion of predetermined
limits to police power.[133] Although it might have been unclear at the
time whether that was the intent of *Clayton*, subsequent developments
have held that it was.

d) General Common Law Power to Detain

In *Mann*, the Court held that it was "not . . . appropriate for this Court
to recognize a general power of detention for investigative purposes."[134]
Eight years later in *Aucoin*, they said: "[t]he existence of a general common law power to detain where it is reasonably necessary in the totality of the circumstances was settled in *R. v. Clayton*."[135] The tendency
of common law powers to expand readily is clearly demonstrated by
this progression; there is, however, at least one hopeful sign in *Aucoin*
which might help keep matters in check.

Aucoin was stopped because of an irregularity with the licence
plate and then failed a roadside screening test. The officer decided to
issue the accused a ticket and therefore asked the accused to sit in the
back of the police vehicle. Because he was having the accused sit in the
police vehicle, the officer searched the accused, claiming it to be for
officer safety purposes. The officer felt something soft in the accused's
pocket, asked what it was, and on receiving the reply that it was ecstasy,
arrested the accused. On a further search the accused was found to be
carrying cocaine and pills, and he was charged with possession for the
purpose of trafficking. The central issue in the case was whether the of-

---

131 *Clayton*, above note 90 at para 30.
132 *Mann*, above note 90 at para 15.
133 For discussions of the hazards inherent in the *Clayton* decision, see Steve Cough-
    lan, "Whither—or Wither—Section 9" (2008) 40 *Supreme Court Law Review* (2d)
    147, and James Stribopoulos, "The Forgotten Right: Section 9 of the *Charter*, Its
    Purpose and Meaning" (2008) 40 *Supreme Court Law Review* (2d) 211.
134 *Mann*, above note 90 at para 17.
135 *Aucoin*, above note 87 at para 36. Note that *Clayton* itself was only three years
    after the declaration in *Mann*.

ficer had had the authority to place the accused in the back of the police vehicle in order to write him a ticket.

The officer had the power to detain the accused initially for the traffic violation; however, any justification for the search would have had to spring from the decision to have the accused sit in the police vehicle while the ticket was being written. The question was therefore whether the officer had that power to detain. The Court noted that the *Mann* power of investigative detention did not authorize the officer, since the purpose of asking the accused to sit in the police vehicle was not investigative. It was in that context that they affirmed that *Clayton* had created a general power of detention for investigative purposes, and that was the power that was potentially relevant.

Having confirmed that the general power existed, however, the Court concluded that it did not authorize the particular detention. The general power only authorizes detentions that are "reasonably necessary in the totality of the circumstances," and this detention was not. Notably, the Nova Scotia Court of Appeal had upheld the trial judge's decision that the officer's actions were reasonable in the circumstances: the Supreme Court stressed that the issue is not whether it was reasonable, but whether it was reasonably *necessary*. In fact, they held, there were other reasonable means by which the officer could have addressed his concern that the accused might disappear into the crowd: for example, he could have waited one or two minutes for backup, which was close at hand, to arrive. Accordingly it was not reasonably necessary to detain the accused by placing him in the back of the vehicle and so that was an unlawful detention.

It is important to note that the ability confirmed in *Aucoin* is not really a "power" at all, in the sense of an authority based on predetermined criteria such as the power to arrest, or for that matter, the *Mann* investigative detention power. Instead, it is simply a means of deciding, after the fact and on a case-by-case basis, whether to retroactively approve of the way the police behaved in a particular situation.[136]

However, the fact that the Court insisted on a detention being reasonably necessary, not merely reasonable, is an important feature with

---

136 Conceptually, one could see the broader *Clayton* power—simply "was it reasonably necessary"—as overtaking and replacing the *Mann* test, which requires other conditions to be met in addition to reasonable necessity. That is not how the cases are being applied in practice, however. Where an investigative detention is at issue, the *Mann* test continues to be applied, and *Clayton* tends to be applied when the circumstances are claimed to present an immediate threat to public safety.

some potential to keep this much more expansive power in check. In addition, another aspect of the reasoning in *Aucoin* is worth stressing.

In concluding that this detention was arbitrary, the Court observed that "in order to justify securing the appellant in the back seat—*knowing that this would also entail a pat-down search*—detaining the appellant in that manner had to be reasonably necessary."[137] That is, *Aucoin* makes clear that the *Charter* rights and liberty interests of the accused must be considered as part of the "totality of the circumstances."

The Court found, in effect, that the trial judge (who concluded there was no section 9 violation) reasoned backward. The proper approach was not to ask whether it was reasonable to search, given that the accused was to be put in the back seat: it was to ask whether it was reasonable to put the accused in the back seat, given that he would have to be searched. In other words, limits on the existence of the power must be read in specifically to respect *Charter* rights.

There is, it should be said, a different way of reading this passage. Recall that, as discussed in introducing powers of detention, the section 9 analysis has become a three-step approach: (1) Is the search authorized by law? (2) Is the law non-arbitrary? (3) Is the manner in which the detention was carried out reasonable and non-arbitrary? The Court in *Aucoin* described the "reasonably necessary" test as the means of satisfying step 1: "[t]he existence of a general common law power to detain where it is reasonably necessary in the totality of the circumstances was settled in *R. v. Clayton*."[138] However, it also posed the task in front of it as "considering whether its exercise was reasonably necessary in the circumstances of a particular case," which would be an analysis under step 3.[139] Courts applying *Aucoin* have tended to factor the impact on the accused's *Charter* rights into reasonable necessity at the third stage rather than the first stage.[140]

So, both the first and the third steps are determined by looking at whether the detention was reasonably necessary. This confounding

---

137 *Aucoin*, above note 87 at para 39 [emphasis added].

138 *Ibid* at para 36.

139 In *MacKenzie*, above note 122 at para 39 [emphasis added], the Court characterized *Aucoin* as being about the third step:

> [I]t is unnecessary to consider whether *the manner of* the appellant's detention was reasonably necessary in the circumstances. Unlike *R. v. Aucoin*, 2012 SCC 66, [2012] 3 S.C.R. 408, there is no suggestion here that the manner in which he was detained (being asked to sit by the side of the road while the sniff was conducted) was not reasonably necessary in the circumstances.

140 See, for example, *Adaikin v Calgary (Police Service)*, 2013 ABCA 333; or *R v Williams*, 2013 ONSC 1399.

of the first and third steps is quite understandable, in fact, given the nature of the general power to detain. The third step is meant to focus on the way in which the particular detention was carried out. But the general detention power, by saying that a police officer was authorized by law if the detention was reasonably necessary in the circumstances, makes the existence of the power dependent on the way in which the particular detention is carried out.

Ultimately, it might not be of great practical importance which approach is taken: if the detention is not reasonably necessary, then it violates section 9 in *some* way. This confusion does demonstrate, however, the conceptual difficulties that arise when police powers are left to be decided after the fact rather than determined in advance.

D. THE ABILITY TO BREAK THE LAW: SECTION 25.1

A further set of provisions relating to police that needs to be examined is contained in sections 25.1 to 25.4 of the *Criminal Code*, which permit designated police officers to break the law. The sections are not explicitly phrased to create a power. Rather, they talk about such an officer being "justified" in doing particular things. That language is normally associated with defences, and the sections are found in the general part, under the heading "Protection of Persons Administering and Enforcing the Law." Nominally, all that these provisions do is protect particular officers from criminal liability in particular situations. Their genesis and the way they are structured, however, make them seem much more like a police power than a defence.

The provisions allow the federal or provincial minister responsible for police to designate certain officers. An officer so designated "is justified in committing an act or omission . . . that would otherwise constitute an offence,"[141] if two further conditions are met. The first condition is simply that the officer is investigating an offence or criminal activity.[142] The second condition is that the officer

> believes on reasonable grounds that the commission of the act or omission, as compared to the nature of the offence or criminal activity being investigated, is reasonable and proportional in the circumstances, having regard to such matters as the nature of the act or omission,

---

141 Section 25.1(8).
142 Section 25.1(8)(a).

the nature of the investigation and the reasonable availability of other means for carrying out the public officer's law enforcement duties.[143]

In other words, designated officers are permitted to break the law if, in their judgment, that is a reasonable choice.

Designations for this purpose are not made in relation to a particular investigation, but rather with regard to the particular officer.[144] The designation is to be made on the advice of a senior official, and there is provision for civilian oversight.[145] It is not explicitly stated in the section, but it is clear that this power is intended for officers performing undercover work. It is also possible for other officers to be designated on an emergency basis by a senior official in exigent circumstances, but such a designation expires after a maximum of forty-eight hours.[146] Somewhat surprisingly, there is a statutory requirement to annually report the number of emergency designations made, but no similar obligation to report the number of "ordinary" designations.[147]

There are some limits on the ability of designated officers to break the law. Section 25.1(11) states:

(11) Nothing in this section justifies
(a)   the intentional or criminally negligent causing of death or bodily harm to another person;
(b)   the wilful attempt in any manner to obstruct, pervert or defeat the course of justice; or
(c)   conduct that would violate the sexual integrity of an individual.

There has been disagreement over whether the prohibition on causing "bodily harm" extends to psychological harm and, therefore, whether officers who make threats fall outside the ambit of the provisions.[148]

In addition, section 25.1(9) refers to actions "that would be likely to result in loss of or serious damage to property." Such actions are not forbidden, but alternative, additional conditions are attached to per-

---

143   Section 25.1(8)(c).
144   Section 25.1(4).
145   Sections 25.1(4), (3.1), & (3.2), respectively.
146   Section 25.1(6).
147   Section 25.3(a).
148   See *R v Lising*, 2007 BCSC 906 at para 20, for the view that making threats is protected by the section, on the basis that what is meant is "bodily harm as specifically defined in s. 2 of the *Criminal Code*, as it has been interpreted in the cases." For the view that making threats is *not* protected, see *R v JJ*, 2010 ONSC 735 at para 336 [*JJ*], which points out that the definition of bodily harm in s 2 of the *Code* was interpreted by the Supreme Court of Canada in *R v McCraw*, [1991] 3 SCR 72, to include psychological harm.

forming them. First, a designated officer can be authorized in writing by a senior official to commit the act. This senior official is to apply specified criteria in deciding—the section does not explicitly state "in advance" of the act, but that must be the intention.[149] That point is clear because the alternative, additional condition is that the officer believes on reasonable grounds that the grounds for obtaining written authorization exist, but the circumstances make it not feasible to obtain the authorization. The only specific circumstances that could justify an officer acting in this way are the need to

(i)   preserve the life or safety of any person,

(ii) prevent the compromise of the identity of a public officer acting in an undercover capacity, of a confidential informant or of a person acting covertly under the direction and control of a public officer, or

(iii) prevent the imminent loss or destruction of evidence of an indictable offence.[150]

There is again an annual reporting requirement as to how frequently these provisions are relied upon.[151]

This structure of designating officers, civilian oversight, emergency designations, authorizations in writing, and so on is far more consistent with a police power than a defence. It is also worth considering in this regard the way in which the provisions came about.

The provisions were a legislative response to a Supreme Court of Canada decision regarding police undercover work.[152] In a narcotics investigation, the police used what is referred to as a "reverse sting," which meant that they posed as the sellers of drugs rather than as buyers. The *Narcotic Control Act*,[153] the relevant statute at the time, did not specifically authorize the police to do this, and so they sought an opinion from the Department of Justice as to whether this technique would be legal. The real issue in the case was whether the accused were entitled to disclosure of that legal opinion. The argument of the accused, in seeking a stay of proceedings based on abuse of process, raised the issue of police good faith. In effect, it was agreed that if the police had acted in accordance with the legal advice that they had been given, then they had acted in good faith. The accused argued, though, that the police could not simply assert that they had followed the legal advice they were given.

---

149 Section 25.1(9)(a).

150 Section 25.1(b).

151 Section 25.3.

152 *R v Campbell*, [1999] 1 SCR 565 [*Campbell*].

153 RSC 1985, c N-1 [since repealed].

Rather, they had to either disclose that opinion or abandon their good faith claim. Disclosure, then, was really the central issue.

The Court concluded that the accused were entitled to disclosure of the opinion. In the course of reaching the decision, the Court did observe that "the conclusion that the RCMP acted in a manner facially prohibited by the Act is inescapable."[154] However, that was far from the central point of the analysis. The Court went on to observe that police illegality did not automatically lead to the conclusion that there had been an abuse of process, or to the conclusion that the accused were entitled to a remedy. The illegality in and of itself was a relatively small issue. To the extent that it was an issue at all, it was because of the question of whether the police had acted abusively in carrying out the investigation as they did, not whether the police were at risk of prosecution and therefore in need of a defence.

The provisions have been the subject of relatively little academic commentary, but that commentary has been critical. It has been firmly argued that the provisions are inconsistent with the rule of law and, therefore, threaten fundamental principles. It has also been argued that this cost has been paid for, effectively, no benefit, since the actual need for the police to break the law in the course of their investigations is small to non-existent.[155] There is little caselaw discussing the sections, which is unsurprising. Prior to section 25.1 being introduced to the *Code*, the appropriate use of prosecutorial discretion meant that criminal charges were not laid against police for mere technical violations of the law in any event, and only in the event of egregious violations would they have been prosecuted. That fact alone makes section 25.1 largely redundant. More important, it also means that the circumstances in which the provisions might be pleaded and, therefore, discussed in court, rarely come to court. As a result, the chance for judicial scrutiny is greatly reduced.

In one case, the existence of the sections has, perhaps appropriately given their genesis, helped justify a stay of proceedings: that is, a stay was allowed, in part, because police allowed an agent to engage in illegal behaviour (as opposed to doing so themselves) without supervision, "thereby flouting all of the rules laid down in section 25.1 of

---

154 *Campbell*, above note 152 at para 25.

155 See Marc S Gorbet, "Bill C-24's Police Immunity Provisions: Parliament's Unnecessary Legislative Response to Police Illegality in Undercover Operations" (2004) 9 *Canadian Criminal Law Review* 35. Gorbet is a former RCMP undercover officer. See, as well, Grégoire Charles N Webber, "Legal Lawlessness and the Rule of Law: A Critique of Section 25.1 of the *Criminal Code*" (2005) 31 *Queen's Law Journal* 121.

the *Criminal Code*."[156] One lower court judgment has broadly upheld the provisions, concluding that they do not violate section 7 of the *Charter*: they are not overbroad, not vague, and do not violate any other principles of fundamental justice. However, a second judgment has interpreted the sections in a way that potentially narrows their scope in a way which would keep them better bounded. In *R v JJ* the trial judge engaged in an extensive discussion of the proper interpretation of section 25.1, including its legislative history, and concluded that it should not be treated as empowering the police, but rather should be strictly limited to the role of providing a justification if an officer were charged. In that case, the police were using a wiretap to investigate a murder. In an effort to stimulate discussion among the suspects, two undercover officers who purported to be associated with the murder victim approached one suspect, held him against a wall, and made death threats against those who had carried out the killing. The trial judge held that as section 25.1 was only a justification; it could not be said that the police had been empowered or authorized to make the threats. In that event, the accused was entitled to point to that behaviour as making the manner of executing the warrant unreasonable.[157] The Crown sought leave to appeal this ruling to the Supreme Court but was refused.[158]

FURTHER READINGS

ALLMAN, ANTHONY. "Detention—What Does It Mean? A Comment on *R v Hawkins*" (1993) 18 *Criminal Reports* (4th) 17.

———. "Further Perspectives on Section 10(b) of the *Charter*: A Reply to Gold" (1994) 25 *Criminal Reports* (4th) 280.

BERGER, BENJAMIN L. "Race and Erasure in *R. v. Mann*" (2004) 21 *Criminal Reports* (6th) 58.

COUGHLAN, STEVE. "Search Based on Articulable Cause: Proceed with Caution or Full Stop?" (2002) 2 *Criminal Reports* (6th) 49.

———. "General Warrants at the Crossroads: Limit or Licence?" (2003) 10 *Criminal Reports* (6th) 269.

———. "Whither—or Wither—Section 9" (2008) 40 *Supreme Court Law Review* (2d) 147.

---

156 *Brind'Amour v R*, 2014 QCCA 33 at para 75.
157 *JJ*, above note 148 at paras 303–8.
158 *R v JJ*, [2010] SCCA No 161.

————. "Great Strides in Section 9 Jurisprudence" (2009) 66 *Criminal Reports* (6th) 75.

————. "*R. v. Ha*: Upholding General Warrants without Asking the Right Questions" (2009) 65 *Criminal Reports* (6th) 41.

FISZAUF, ALEC. *The Law of Investigative Detention* (Markham: Lexis-Nexis Canada, 2008).

GOLD, ALAN. "Perspectives on Section 10(b) — The Right to Counsel under the *Charter*" (1993) 22 *Criminal Reports* (4th) 370.

GORBET, MARC S. "Bill C-24's Police Immunity Provisions: Parliament's Unnecessary Legislative Response to Police Illegality in Undercover Operations" (2004) 9 *Canadian Criminal Law Review* 35.

GOTTARDI, ERIC V. "*R. v. Mann*: Regulating State Intrusions in the Context of Investigative Detentions" (2004) 21 *Criminal Reports* (6th) 27.

LAW REFORM COMMISSION OF CANADA. *Arrest* (Working Paper 41) (Ottawa: Law Reform Commission of Canada, 1985).

————. *Arrest* (Report 29) (Ottawa: Law Reform Commission of Canada, 1986).

MACKAY, A WAYNE. "Don't Mind Me, I'm From the R.C.M.P.: *R. v M.(M.R.)* — Another Brick in the Wall between Students and Their Rights" (1997) 7 *Criminal Reports* (5th) 1.

MARIN, JOSEPH R. "*R. v. Mann*: Further Down the Slippery Slope" (2005) 42 *Alberta Law Review* 1123.

MCCOY, LESLEY A. "Liberty's Last Stand? Tracing the Limits of Investigative Detention" (2002) 46 *Criminal Law Quarterly* 319.

NICOL, JASON A. "'Stop in the Name of the Law': Investigative Detention" (2002) 7 *Canadian Criminal Law Review* 223.

PATEL, AMAN S. "Detention and Articulable Cause: Arbitrariness and Growing Judicial Deference to Police Judgment" (2002) 45 *Criminal Law Quarterly* 198.

QUIGLEY, TIM. "*Mann*, It's a Disappointing Decision" (2004) 21 *Criminal Reports* (6th) 41.

————. *Procedure in Canadian Criminal Law*, 2d ed (Toronto: Thomson Carswell, 2005) (loose-leaf) ch 6 and 8.

————. "Investigative Detention: Some Loose Ends Remain" (2009) 69 *Criminal Reports* (6th) 247.

————. "Was It Worth the Wait? The Supreme Court's New Approaches to Detention and Exclusion of Evidence" (2009) 66 *Criminal Reports* (6th) 88.

SANKOFF, PETER. "Articulable Cause Based Searches Incident to Detention — This *Cooke* May Spoil the Broth" (2002) 2 *Criminal Reports* (6th) 41.

SKIBINSKY, CHRISTINA. "Regulating *Mann* in Canada" (2006) 69 *Saskatchewan Law Review* 197.

STEWART, HAMISH. "The *Grant* Trilogy and the Right against Self-Incrimination" (2009) 66 *Criminal Reports* (6th) 97.

STRIBOPOULOS, JAMES. "A Failed Experiment? Investigative Detention: Ten Years Later" (2003) 41 *Alberta Law Review* 335.

————. "The Limits of Judicially Created Police Powers: Investigative Detention after *Mann*" (2007) 52 *Criminal Law Quarterly* 299.

————. "The Forgotten Right: Section 9 of the *Charter*, Its Purpose and Meaning" (2008) 40 *Supreme Court Law Review* (2d) 211.

STUART, DON. *Charter Justice in Canadian Criminal Law*, 5th ed (Toronto: Thomson Carswell, 2010) ch 4 & 5.

TANOVICH, DAVID. "Operation Pipeline and Racial Profiling" (2002) 1 *Criminal Reports* (6th) 52.

————. "Using the *Charter* to Stop Racial Profiling: The Development of an Equality-Based Conception of Arbitrary Detention" (2002) 40 *Osgoode Hall Law Review* 145.

————. "*R. v. Griffiths*: Race and Arbitrary Detention" (2003) 11 *Criminal Reports* (6th) 149.

————. "The Colourless World of *Mann*" (2004) 21 *Criminal Reports* (6th) 47.

————. *The Colour of Justice* (Toronto: Irwin Law, 2006).

WEBBER, GRÉGOIRE CHARLES N. "Legal Lawlessness and the Rule of Law: A Critique of Section 25.1 of the *Criminal Code*" (2005) 31 *Queen's Law Journal* 121.

CHAPTER 6

COMPELLING APPEARANCE AND JUDICIAL INTERIM RELEASE

A. INTRODUCTION

Many aspects of criminal procedure are quite intricately linked. For example, laying of an information in front of a justice serves several distinct functions. The laying commences the prosecution, and the information is the basis upon which either a preliminary inquiry will be based or a summary conviction trial will be held. It is also the foundation for a variety of methods to compel an accused to appear and answer to the charges laid out in the information. Yet, that initial appearance will not actually be for a trial on the charges, so the question arises as to what will happen to the accused in the interim. Thus, the *Criminal Code* provisions that set out the methods to make an accused first appear and those that deal with releasing or holding the accused pending trial form a whole, and both appear in Part XVI, "Compelling Appearance of Accused Before a Justice and Interim Release."

The issues related to the content of charges and the preferring of charges for trial will be discussed in Chapter 11. This chapter deals only with the procedure by which those charges are first laid. The charge is the focal point for various forms of compelling the appearance of the accused in court and determines issues of jurisdiction and many other features of pre-trial procedure.

Following the discussion of charges, we turn to the various mechanisms that may be used to compel the appearance of an accused person in court. The most obvious of those mechanisms is to arrest an accused, either with or without a warrant. Powers of arrest raise a host of issues of their own, particularly in light of section 10 of the *Charter*, which gives rights on arrest or detention. This chapter will not try to deal with all the issues surrounding powers of arrest—that will be the subject of Chapter 7. However, enough must be said here about arrest, with and without a warrant, to situate it in relation to the other methods of compelling appearance. As a result, there will be a certain amount of repetition between the two chapters, but not an excessive amount.

Finally, this chapter will turn to the topic of compelling an accused's appearance to answer to charges. In particular, the question of what to do with the person once she has appeared will be examined in a discussion of the principles governing judicial interim release.

B. LAYING CHARGES

It is easy to see the laying of an information as simply a technical requirement among so many other particular rules that must be followed in the course of criminal proceedings. In one sense that view is correct, but at the same time it is important to recognize the wider significance. The time when an information is laid before a justice marks a momentous occasion: it is the point at which some person passes from being a "suspect" to being an "accused." That transition has great consequences for the individual, for the individual's family, for the victim of the offence, for the criminal justice system, and for society as a whole. It means, for the most part, that the system has stopped trying to discover who committed an offence and will, from that point forward, be focused on proving the guilt of one particular person. Such a step should not be taken lightly.

The process of laying a charge consists of both a "ministerial" (administrative) and a judicial function. Under section 504 of the *Code*, the justice will perform the essentially bureaucratic and non-discretionary function of receiving the information. That step alone is of no consequence, however, unless the judge then takes discretionary and judicial action under section 507. It is worth looking at the two steps separately and in detail. (There is a parallel and functionally equivalent two-step process laid out in sections 505 and 508, which is used when an accused is given an appearance notice or is released on a promise to appear. Differing in some practical details, it is discussed below in Section C(1), but the general principles behind it are the same as those set out here.)

With the exception of direct indictments, indictable offences are charged when an information is sworn, received, and approved by a judicial officer, in accordance with sections 504 and following of the *Code*.[1] This procedure applies equally to offences prosecuted by summary proceedings under Part XXVII.[2] When acting under section 504, the justice acts in a ministerial fashion and has no discretion over whether to receive the information.

An information may be sworn by any person who has reasonable grounds to believe that an offence has been committed. No person may be considered an accused person in the absence of a charge and, correspondingly, no court can have jurisdiction over the prosecution of an accused person in the absence of a charge.[3] In Canada, public prosecutions begin when an information is laid by a public officer. In some Canadian jurisdictions, charges are laid by peace officers, while in others they are laid by prosecutors after they have reviewed reports from the police or other authorities.[4] But, whether the informant is a peace officer, prosecutor, or private prosecutor, section 504 of the *Code* states some elementary requirements that must be met before a justice may receive and consider an information:

504. Any one who, on reasonable grounds, believes that a person has committed an indictable offence may lay an information in writing and under oath before a justice, and the justice shall receive the information, where it is alleged

(a) that the person has committed, anywhere, an indictable offence that may be tried in the province in which the justice resides, and that the person

(i)   is or is believed to be, or

(ii) resides or is believed to reside,

within the territorial jurisdiction of the justice;

(b) that the person, wherever he may be, has committed an indictable offence within the territorial jurisdiction of the justice;

(c) that the person has, anywhere, unlawfully received property that was unlawfully obtained within the territorial jurisdiction of the justice; or

(d) that the person has in his possession stolen property within the territorial jurisdiction of the justice.

---

1   A direct indictment may be preferred at any time and may follow a charge that is first laid by way of an information.

2   See s 788ff.

3   See the definition of "accused" in s 493.

4   See the discussion of pre-charge screening in *R v Regan*, 2002 SCC 12, as well as Law Reform Commission of Canada, *Controlling Criminal Prosecutions: The Attorney General and the Crown Prosecutor* (Ottawa: Law Reform Commission of Canada, 1990).

Thus, an information must be in writing and under oath, and it must allege the commission of an offence by an identifiable person. It also must contain allegations that affirm the territorial jurisdiction of the justice before whom it is laid.[5]

Section 506 provides that the information may be laid in the manner set out in Form 2. Although this is phrased in a discretionary way, it is prudent for an information to be laid in this manner so that it complies with matters of form that are essential to jurisdiction, such as the date and place of the alleged offence, the date and place of the information, the identity of the informant, and the identity of the justice.

The informant must declare in the information that he has reasonable grounds to believe that an offence has been committed. Grounds for such a belief need not be based on the personal knowledge of the informant but may be based on reports that he has received. However, the person swearing the information must personally hold the necessary belief. It is not sufficient, for example, for a police officer to lay an information simply on the basis that she was instructed to do so by her superior: the officer must personally know enough to reasonably believe that the offence has been committed.[6]

Most prosecutions in Canada are public ones, but when the informant is not a peace officer or an agent of the Attorney General, the procedure undertaken is called a "private prosecution." In such a case the informant must be prepared to carry forward the prosecution personally if the information is signed by a judicial officer. Private prosecutions are comparatively rare but they do occur, usually when public authorities have declined to commence a prosecution. Once the information has been received under section 504, the justice who received the information must consider the substance of the informant's allegations under section 507. In this judicial function, the justice exercises discretion as to whether it is appropriate to take any action or to require the accused person to answer the charges.[7]

---

5   "Territorial jurisdiction" is defined in s 2 of the *Code* as "any province, county, union of counties, township, city, town, parish or other judicial division or place to which the context applies." This quite open-ended definition creates the potential for ambiguity. In Ontario it has been determined that the "territorial jurisdiction" of a justice of the peace for purposes of this section is the entire province: *R v Ellis*, 2009 ONCA 483 [*Ellis*]. However, that decision is based, in part, on the legislation governing justices of the peace in that province, and so a different meaning might apply in other provinces. *Ellis* also observes that the fact that a justice has received an information in one place does not settle that any eventual trial will occur in that same location: see para 43.

6   *R v Pilcher* (1981), 58 CCC (2d) 435 (Man Prov Ct).

7   *R v Allen* (1974), 20 CCC (2d) 447 (Ont CA) [*Allen*].

This stage of the process is referred to as a "pre-enquete." It is performed *ex parte*, and so the justice will consider the allegations in the absence of the person or persons accused in the information. It also means that this hearing is generally not conducted in open court. Nevertheless, the justice must act judicially in the consideration of the information. He will examine the allegations of the informant and may ask questions of that person or any other witness where he considers such evidence necessary or desirable to ascertain the basis of the informant's belief that an offence was committed. Any evidence thus taken by the justice must be given under oath and recorded, but the justice is not obliged to observe the rules and principles governing the admissibility of evidence at a preliminary inquiry or trial.[8]

Upon considering the information, the justice must decide whether to endorse it. The *Code* does not state explicitly the standard that the justice must apply in this decision, but it is clear that the justice must personally consider and agree that there are reasonable grounds to believe that an offence was committed by the person to be charged.[9] The informant is not required to prove the allegations, however; nor is the justice required to make any judgment concerning the sufficiency of the case for prosecution. The justice must at least be satisfied that there are reasonable grounds, as disclosed in the information and any evidence adduced in support thereof, to believe that the offence was committed by the person named. Some authority suggests that only when the information meets the higher standard or a *prima facie* case or something close to it should the justice be satisfied.[10] If the justice is satisfied, she will sign the information. This endorsement marks the moment at which a charge is formally laid and a prosecution begins. At this point, the person named in the information is an accused person before the court.

The judge must refuse to issue process if he is not satisfied that it establishes reasonable grounds to believe that an offence has been committed. However, a refusal to issue any process by one justice does not prevent the informant from seeking a summons or warrant from a different justice based on the information.[11]

---

8 See, for example, *R v Edge*, 2004 ABPC 55 at para 63, relying on Tim Quigley, *Procedure in Canadian Criminal Law*, 2d ed (Toronto: Thomson Carswell, 2005) (loose-leaf).

9 *R v Jeffrey* (1976), 34 CRNS 283 (Ont Prov Ct).

10 See *R v Morton* (1993), 83 CCC (3d) 95 (Ont CA), aff'g (1992), 70 CCC (3d) 244 (Ont Ct Gen Div); *R v Fry* (1998), 38 RFL (4th) 328 (BCCA); or *Re Lindsay*, 2005 BCPC 176.

11 *Allen*, above note 7.

Slightly different rules apply to the pre-enquete when an information is laid privately. These differences are meant to keep alive the option of private prosecutions while at the same time preventing their abuse. The hearing must be conducted by a judge or a specially designated justice, who is obliged to hear evidence, as opposed to merely having the discretion to do so.[12] The Attorney General must be given a copy of the information, notice of the hearing, and an opportunity to attend and take part in it.[13] Further, if the justice does not issue a summons or warrant then (unlike a public prosecution), the private prosecutor is obliged to bring forward new evidence in order to have a new hearing.[14] Finally, the Attorney General may intervene in any private prosecution, either to assume carriage of it, to stop it by means of a stay of proceedings, or to withdraw the charge.[15] The power to stay charges may be used any time after the information has been laid under section 504: in contrast, the power to withdraw charges may be exercised only after a pre-enquete has been held and cannot be used to prevent a pre-enquete from taking place.[16]

C. COMPELLING APPEARANCE

The compelling appearance and bail provisions in Part XVI of the *Code* operate by granting broad powers to police and judges to restrict the

---

12 Section 507.1(3)(a).

13 Sections 507.1(3)(b)–(d).

14 Section 507.1(7).

15 The rules in this area are established somewhat oddly. Section 579 explicitly gives the provincial attorney general the authority to stay charges, without making any reference to whether the information was publicly or privately laid. Section 579.01 specifies that if the provincial attorney general intervenes in proceedings and does not stay them, she may call witnesses, examine and cross-examine, and so on. Those powers presuppose that the provincial attorney general can intervene in private prosecutions, but do not explicitly state that. Similarly, the attorney general has the ability to withdraw privately laid charges, but this power arises from the common law: *McHale v Ontario (Attorney General)*, 2010 ONCA 361 at para 53 [*McHale*]. On the other hand, s 579.1 explicitly states that the federal attorney general can intervene in private prosecutions of charges not laid under the *Code* (for example, drug prosecutions, which are prosecuted by federally appointed prosecutors). In addition it makes the ability to stay in s 579 available in such cases.

16 *McHale*, *ibid*. The Court of Appeal notes that this result seems anomalous. They observe at para 90 that the common law rule around withdrawal of charges, infused by policy considerations, does not allow the attorney general to prevent a private prosecutor from at least having a pre-enquete before a judge or justice: the plain language of the statute, however, makes that possible in the case of a stay.

liberty of individuals but then attaching significant limitations on the use of those powers. The result is an attempt to satisfy the needs of the state to ensure that accused persons are present for their trials while, at the same time, using those powers with as much restraint as possible.[17]

In general terms, the *Code* provides powers to police to require an accused to attend court through some type of written demand, or to arrest the person: preference is given to not arresting. If the person is arrested, the system requires various actors along the way to consider whether the accused can be released without being taken to a justice. If the accused is taken to a justice, the system is then designed to release the accused with as few restrictions as necessary. In short, the *Code* provides that, if possible, appearance should be sought without arrest and detention. The various ways in which arrest or continued detention are meant to be avoided to the extent possible are discussed further in Chapter 7.

In addition, the *Code* provides that, where a person is released, preference should be given to the means of compelling appearance that is least onerous, especially as regards the imposition of a money debt as a form of security. Where Part XVI allows for continued detention before trial, it also includes mechanisms for review of that detention. These issues will be discussed in Section D, below in this chapter.

A further demonstration of the restraint built in to Part XVI is seen in the fact that a police officer's decision that an accused should be made to attend court is usually not sufficient on its own: it is necessary for some judicial officer to confirm that decision. In some cases, the officer's initial interaction is with the individual accused of committing a crime. In that event, a justice must later review the officer's actions and (except in the instance of an arrest without a warrant) agree that charges should be laid. In other cases, the charges are laid in front of a justice first, and the police then seek out the individual. Although there are similarities between the two situations, it is convenient to consider them separately. Accordingly, we shall consider (1) the process for compelling an accused to appear when charges have not yet been laid and (2) the process that is used after charges have been laid.

1) Compelling Appearance Pre-charge

If a peace officer decides that a person should be prosecuted, there are various ways to compel that person to attend court before an information

---

17   On this topic, see Steve Coughlan & Glen Luther, *Detention and Arrest* (Toronto: Irwin Law, 2010), in particular, the discussion in Chapter 4 under the heading "Restraint in Compelling Appearance."

is laid and the person is actually charged. The most obvious is to make an arrest without a warrant.[18] A central point to note is that an arrest is not necessarily the only way, or even the preferred way, to compel appearance, even if no charge has yet been laid. Other procedural mechanisms may be used, whether there has been an arrest without warrant or not. In effect, the *Code* provides that a person may be required to attend court by means of an appearance notice, a promise to appear, or a recognizance.

Section 495(2) of the *Code* makes a preference for less intrusive means explicit. A peace officer's power to arrest without warrant is created in section 495(1) and is quite broad. Section 495(2), however, suggests that, in the case of less serious offences, an officer should not necessarily use those arrest powers. "Less serious," in this context, is defined broadly to mean summary conviction offences, hybrid offences, or indictable offences listed in section 553 (those in the absolute jurisdiction of a provincial court judge).[19] In the case of those offences, the *Code* suggests that an officer should issue an appearance notice instead, unless there is a good reason to arrest.[20] A "good reason to arrest" is limited to the possibilities that the person will not show up in court unless arrested or that there is a need to

(i)   establish the identity of the person,
(ii) secure or preserve evidence of or relating to the offence, or
(iii) prevent the continuation or repetition of the offence or the commission of another offence.[21]

Section 495(2)[22] is phrased in a confusing way, but the principle underlying it is that, for less serious offences, police officers should not arrest simply because they have the power to do so. The section does not *remove* the power to arrest, though, and so in practice it often occurs that the peace officer does make an arrest and then determines whether to release that individual or take him into custody.

If the officer decides, under section 495(2), not to arrest, section 496 authorizes the officer to issue an appearance notice.[23] An appearance notice directs the person to whom it is issued to appear in court at a specified date, time, and place. Further, the appearance notice must inform the person of the consequences that flow from non-compliance

---

18   The law with respect to arrest is explored at greater length in Chapter 7.
19   Sections 495(2)(a), (b), & (c).
20   Section 496.
21   Sections 495(2)(d) & (e).
22   See Chapter 7 for further discussion on this section of the *Code*.
23   See Form 9 at s 849 of the *Code*.

with its terms. Those consequences are that failure to appear at the specified time is an offence under section 145 of the *Code* and that an arrest warrant can be issued under section 508.

Even if a peace officer has arrested a person, it is not the end of the story. The officer can decide afterward, under section 497(1), to release that person with the intention to compel her appearance by means of a summons or an appearance notice. Here, the *Code* provisions closely parallel those relating to the original decision to arrest, and they still reflect a preference for release in some cases. Specifically, in the same circumstances of summary conviction offences, hybrid offences, or indictable offences listed in section 553, the stated preference is for releasing the accused. The only exceptions to that preference are for the same grounds as found in section 495(2) (to ensure appearance in court, establish identity, secure evidence, or prevent further offences) with one addition. A peace officer might also decide not to release the accused after arrest in order to "ensure the safety and security of any victim of or witness to the offence."[24]

In the event that a person is arrested without warrant and taken into custody by the arresting peace officer, he will be brought before the officer in charge or another peace officer. Under section 498, the officer in charge can also decide to release the arrested person and, once again, is directed to prefer this course of action in many circumstances. Indeed, in section 498 the range of offences for which release is preferred is even broader than in previous sections: in addition to summary conviction, hybrid, or section 553 offences, the officer in charge is also to release a person arrested for any other offence punishable by imprisonment for a term of five years or less.

Corresponding to the fact that release is possible for more serious offences at this stage, the officer in charge is also permitted to impose more restrictive conditions on the accused in order to be released. Since the officer in charge is also a peace officer, she may of course decide either to release the person, with no intention that he should be charged, or release him upon issuing an appearance notice. Under section 498, the officer in charge is also entitled to release an accused with the intent to compel appearance by way of summons, as was the arresting officer under section 497. In addition, an officer in charge can release an arrested person on a "promise to appear" or on a recognizance.[25] A promise to appear, set out in Form 10, is a written promise by the accused to

---

24 Section 497(1.1)(a)(iv).

25 A promise to appear is functionally equivalent to an appearance notice, but is used to release an accused from custody, while an appearance notice is essentially a method of avoiding taking an accused into custody in the first place.

attend court at a specified date and time. As with an appearance notice, failure to comply with the promise is an offence.[26] A recognizance, set out in Form 11, is a written acknowledgment of a debt, in an amount not exceeding five hundred dollars, which would be forfeited upon failure to appear in court. The officer in charge may fix the amount of the recognizance but may not require sureties to secure the debt. In other words, only the accused can be asked to acknowledge the debt.

Further, in cases where the accused is not ordinarily resident in the province, or resides more than two hundred kilometres from the place of custody, the officer may release the accused on a recognizance or require the deposit of money or other security to ensure attendance. As with a promise to appear, failure to comply with the recognizance is an offence.

Finally, section 503(2) grants a further release power to both peace officers and officers in charge, which applies to a broader range of offences: any offence not listed in section 469, which identifies the most serious indictable offences, such as murder. The effect of this provision (sometimes referred to as "police bail")[27] is to allow release of a person arrested on a relatively serious offence on conditions, rather than forcing a choice between unconditional release and holding the person to see a justice. In addition to the conditions for release in section 498, under section 503(2.1), the conditions can require an accused to stay within a territorial jurisdiction, to notify the officer of a change in address, to surrender a passport and to report regularly, and to abstain from various things such as the use of drugs or alcohol, from having a firearm, or from communicating with various people.

In many sections that deal with release (sections 495, 497, and 498), the language on its face appears to be mandatory: the officer in question "shall not arrest" or "shall release." However, in each case, further subsections qualify this obligation by stating that an officer who fails to comply with the section is still acting in the execution of duty. In effect, then, these provisions are (at least for the purposes of the criminal law) more in the nature of advice or guidance than legal requirements.[28]

Apart from compelling appearance in court, an appearance notice, a promise to appear, or a recognizance may require the attendance of a person at some location (typically a police station) for the purpose of identification under the *Identification of Criminals Act*.[29] Failure to comply

---

26 Section 145(5).

27 Both the accused and the Crown are entitled to apply to a justice to replace this undertaking: ss 503(2.2) & (2.3). See also *R v Oliveira*, 2009 ONCA 219.

28 See the further discussion of this issue in the context of ss 495(2) & 495(3) in Chapter 7.

29 RSC 1985, c I-1.

with this requirement is also punishable as an offence under section 145 of the *Code*.

All forms of release by a peace officer or officer in charge take place before an information has been laid and endorsed by a justice, except for cases in which the officer in charge is authorized to release a person arrested with warrant (discussed below). Nevertheless, all forms of process issued before charge contemplate that the person named in the appearance notice, promise to appear, or recognizance will attend court at the time and place stated. Before that first appearance, an information must be laid before a justice.[30] This process is functionally equivalent to that outlined in Section B, above in this chapter, involving sections 504 and 507 of the *Code*, but governed by sections 505 and 508.

If the justice is not satisfied that there are reasonable grounds to believe that an offence has been committed, he will cancel any form or process that has been previously issued by a peace officer or officer to appear and will direct that notice be given to the person who had been issued such process. If the justice endorses the information, however, she may either confirm the form of process that has already been issued or may cancel it and issue a summons or warrant for arrest.[31]

In the case of a warrant, summons, appearance notice, and even a promise to appear, therefore, the justice's reviewing role extends to assessing whether the person ought to be made to face charges at all. Surprisingly, this is not true in the case of an arrest without a warrant where the accused has not been released before being taken to the justice. The arresting officer must still lay an information under section 504 where (as noted in Section B, above in this chapter) the justice acts ministerially and has no discretion. Section 507, where a justice acts judicially and would have discretion as to whether to allow matters to proceed further, does not apply where the accused has already been arrested. An accused might pursue a tort claim for false imprisonment or claim a violation of her right to be free from arbitrary detention, but no direct judicial screening mechanism exists.[32]

---

30   Section 505.

31   Section 508.

32   See *R v Whitmore* (1989), 51 CCC (3d) 294 (Ont CA), or *R v Ladouceur*, 2013 ONCA 328 at para 26 [*Ladouceur*], as well as the discussion in James Stribopoulos, "Unchecked Power: The Constitutional Regulation of Arrest Reconsidered" (2003) 48 *McGill Law Journal* 225. Much of s 507 deals with the choice between a summons and a warrant: that might be why, in drafting, cases where the accused has already been arrested were excluded. If so, the drafting had the unintentional effect of removing judicial scrutiny from the decision to charge *at all* in the case of warrantless arrests.

The scheme of process before charge requires that, following an accused's arrest and release, an information be laid before a justice "as soon as practicable thereafter and in any event before the time stated" for appearing in court in whatever document has been issued to the accused with her release.[33] A failure to lay a charge within that time means that the binding effect of the particular process that has been issued lapses. If no charge is laid in time, an accused cannot be charged with failing to appear on time. However, that is largely the extent of the effect of any such failure. First, the failure to lay an information in the prescribed time does not bar the police from laying a new information in order to have the person compelled to appear. Further, the "as soon as practicable" requirement has been held to be merely directory rather than mandatory. The requirement is meant to guarantee an opportunity for judicial intervention to cancel the process if it should not have been issued in the first place.[34] Therefore, the failure to meet that requirement does not render the information null, cause the court to lose jurisdiction, or confer any free-standing right on the accused. The same result has been held to follow even if the information has not been laid by the time the accused appears in court. To hold that a prosecution would be barred, it has been held, would amount to creating a time limit for the prosecution of an offence, which does not now exist in the case of indictable offences. The time requirements in the section "are steps in the process designed to bring an accused before the court on a timely basis and without the necessity of prior detention. They are not pre-conditions to the jurisdiction of the court to try the offence . . . ."[35] For the same reason, an irregularity at the ministerial stage, where the justice decides whether to confirm or cancel the process requiring the accused to appear, can result in a loss of jurisdiction over the person but not a loss of jurisdiction over the offence itself.[36] If the person does appear at the required time, the court still has jurisdiction over the offence and recovers jurisdiction over the person.

2) Compelling Appearance Post-charge

The foregoing discussion was concerned with procedure where police interaction with the accused precedes the laying of charges (in large measure, arrests without warrant and issuing appearance notices). One might conceptualize those situations as ones where the police

---

33   Section 505.
34   *R v Gougeon* (1980), 55 CCC (2d) 218 (Ont CA).
35   *R v Markovic* (2005), 200 CCC (3d) 449 (Ont CA).
36   *Ladouceur*, above note 32.

have been present at the crime itself, such as a fight outside a bar, and have acted immediately to intervene and arrest or otherwise deal with those involved. In such a case, it is of necessity that a justice will review any charging decision after the fact. In other cases, the police (1) investigate a crime, (2) decide who they believe the guilty party is, and (3) lay a charge before a justice in order to compel that person to appear. In such cases, the review by the justice will occur before the police interaction with the accused. In practice, the distinction is not nearly so clear-cut — police might be interviewing someone and decide during the interview that there are reasonable grounds for arrest, for example — but that, at least, provides a rough guide to the reason that different sets of procedures are necessary.[37]

In these latter cases, where interaction with the justice precedes interaction with the accused, the process of laying an information before a justice is followed (this is discussed in Section B, above in this chapter). The criteria in that regard are the same whether the police lay the charge before interacting with the accused or after. However, in these circumstances, the justice will issue process in the form of either a summons or a warrant for the arrest of the accused if the charge is endorsed.

A summons is a document issued by the court commanding the accused named therein to attend court at a specified time and place. It recites the offence or offences that the accused has been charged with, and it contains the same particulars as other documents of process that concern jurisdiction. In Form 6, it specifies the date to appear in court, a date to appear for fingerprinting, and the consequences of non-appearance.[38] It is to be served in person or left with an adult at the person's last known address.[39]

An arrest warrant includes substantially the same details as a summons, but adds a command to peace officers within the local jurisdiction to arrest the person charged and to bring him to court. The warrant is addressed to all peace officers in the jurisdiction and remains in effect until it is executed.

The choice between a summons and an arrest warrant lies in the discretion of the justice. However, section 507(4) directs a justice to issue a summons unless there are reasonable grounds to believe that a warrant is necessary in the public interest. At a policy level, this is parallel to section 495(2), directing police officers to prefer the use of

---

37   For example, that was the situation in *R v Evans*, [1991] 1 SCR 869.
38   Sections 509(1), (4), & (5).
39   Section 509(2).

an appearance notice to an arrest for some offences. Nonetheless, it is a much more vague direction than that detailed provision, and might be subject to a *Charter* challenge.[40]

A judge will decide to issue a warrant in order to "compel the accused to attend before him or some other justice for the same territorial division."[41] This phrasing is not meant to permit a judge to say "when this person is arrested take her in front of no one but me." Rather, it simply intends that the person arrested is required to be brought before *some* judge.[42]

The *Code* allows the justice who issues an arrest warrant to endorse it for the specific purpose of authorizing the officer in charge of a station or lock-up to release an accused, pending her appearance in court.[43] Correspondingly, the officer in charge is then authorized to release the accused.[44] In part, this release power corresponds to that given to an officer in charge in the case of a warrantless arrest, which, it will be recalled, included attaching more restrictive conditions to the release, thus corresponding to the more serious range of offences for which release was available. In this circumstance, the officer is given an even more extensive power to attach conditions because the officer in charge has already been specifically authorized by a justice to release the accused. In such a case, the officer in charge can still release, under section 498, on a promise to appear, recognizance, or deposit (though not with intent to use a summons, since the person has already been arrested). In addition, the officer can release the person on an undertaking to do one or more of the following: remain within a specified territorial jurisdiction; notify the police of any change in address, employment, or occupation; abstain from communicating with specified people (typically victims, witnesses, or co-accused); abstain from going to specified places; deposit a passport; abstain from possessing a firearm; report as required; abstain from the use of drugs or alcohol; and comply with any other conditions necessary for the safety and security of victims or witnesses.[45]

As will be seen below, these optional conditions are very much like those that may be imposed by a judge at a bail hearing in accordance with section 515(4). For this reason the *Code* provides that a person who

---

40   See the discussion of this issue in Chapter 7.
41   Section 507(1)(b).
42   *R v Davidson* (2004), 26 CR (6th) 264 (Alta CA).
43   Section 507(6).
44   Section 499.
45   Section 499(2). Note that these conditions parallel those in the "police bail" provision in s 503(2.1), discussed above.

has been released on conditions or a prosecutor may apply to a justice for a modification of the conditions stipulated in the undertaking—essentially as though the release had been on judicially ordered bail.[46]

If a person is arrested and the police decide not to release under any of the various powers to do so outlined above, that person must be brought before a justice without unreasonable delay and, in any case, within twenty-four hours.[47] These deadlines are independent—the section does not give the police the right to hold a person for twenty-four hours. Rather, the primary obligation is to take the person in front of a justice without unreasonable delay: twenty-four hours is set as the outer limit of what is reasonable.[48] Accordingly, a delay of twelve hours would be unreasonable if there was no good reason, on the facts of the particular case, not to have taken the accused in front of a justice in four hours. Indeed, reviewing courts have pointed to the need for police to anticipate that they will have to comply with this requirement and take steps in advance in order to be able to do so.[49] However, entering into how long a delay will be considered reasonable is a recognition that the police are entitled to interrogate and in other ways carry out some investigation during this arrest phase. In R v Storrey, for example, there was arranged a lineup which involved witnesses who had to be brought in from outside the jurisdiction, and an eighteen-hour delay was reasonable. That does not mean, however, that the police can always defer taking the accused in front of a justice because they are pursuing an investigation. A release within twenty-four hours might still have been unreasonably delayed.[50] Each case will depend upon its particular facts.

The justice of the peace might decide, of course, that the accused should not be released. Similarly, the Crown may apply to the justice for a three-day adjournment of the release hearing, during which time

---

46   Section 499(3).
47   Section 503. Note that this section specifically says that the obligation to take the accused in front of a justice arises if the accused has not already been released by the officer or officer in charge.
48   [1990] 1 SCR 241.
49   See, for example, R v Mendez, 2014 ONSC 498 [Mendez], or R v Burgar, 2013 BCPC 389 [Burgar].
50   See, for example, R v Keats, 2014 NSPC 108; R v W(E), 2002 NFCA 49 [W(E)]; or R v Koszulap (1974), 27 CRNS 226 (Ont CA). Note, in particular, Mendez, above note 49, where police knew that justices of the peace would not be available after 2 p.m. but continued to question the accused, knowing the result would be that they could not comply with the twenty-four-hour deadline. At para 116 it was held: "It was not reasonable to choose to investigate at the expense of the rights of the accused to be brought before a court."

the accused will continue to be detained.[51] Neither of these possibilities, however, relieves the police of their obligation to take the accused to a justice.[52]

Courts were at one time divided on whether a failure to comply with the twenty-four-hour deadline resulted in an arbitrary detention, which violates section 9 of the *Charter*.[53] However, the Supreme Court has since made clear that an unlawful detention is automatically an arbitrary detention.[54] It now seems to be uncontroversial and often conceded by the Crown that if an accused is detained beyond twenty-four hours there was a section 9 violation.[55]

Section 503 does provide for one situation in which the twenty-four-hour outside limit does not apply: where no justice is available within that time, "the person shall be taken before a justice as soon as possible."[56] Lack of availability, however, cannot be argued on a simple administrative basis, such as that the courts do not sit on weekends.[57] The provision is intended to apply only in remote areas and similar situations.[58] Even in such cases, the provisions of section 515(2.3) that allow an accused to appear in front of a justice by telephone or other telecommunications device would need to be taken into account.

There is some ambiguity over the exact consequences of taking the accused in front of a justice. Some cases take the view that this step nominally transfers the accused from the hands of the police and places her under the jurisdiction of the court. In practical terms this would mean that the police cannot take the accused before a justice and then take him back to the police station for further interrogation: rather, a bail order would have to be made and if the accused were still to be held in custody, it would be at some other facility.[59] Other courts

---

51 Section 516.
52 See *W(E)*, above note 50; *R v Simpson* (1994), 29 CR (4th) 274 (Nfld CA), rev'd on other grounds [1995] 1 SCR 449 [*Simpson*]; *R v MacPherson* (1995), 100 CCC (3d) 216 (NBCA).
53 See, for example, *Simpson*, above note 52 at para 98 (Nfld CA); *W(E)*, above note 50; *R v Tam; R v Lai* (1995), 100 CCC (3d) 196 (BCCA); and *R v CK* (2005), 36 CR (6th) 153 (Ont Ct J).
54 *R v Grant*, 2009 SCC 32 at para 55.
55 See, for example, *R v Frederickson*, 2013 BCSC 1992; *Burgar*, above note 49; *R v Kift*, 2014 ONCJ 454 [*Kift*]; *R v Brown*, 2014 BCSC 1872; or *Mendez*, above note 49.
56 Section 503(1)(b).
57 See, for example, *Mendez*, above note 49, holding that where justices of the peace are not normally available after a certain hour, police must cease interrogating in order to take the accused before a justice while one is still available.
58 *Simpson*, above note 52 (Nfld CA).
59 See *R v Precourt* (1976), 18 OR (2d) 714 (CA); *Kift*, above note 55; or *R v Ansari*, 2008 BCSC 1492.

reject that there is any such implication.[60] In any case, the significance of this requirement is that the person is delivered from the custody of the police into the jurisdiction of the court to be dealt with according to law. At this point, therefore, it is necessary to turn to the final portion of this chapter, dealing with judicial interim release.

D. JUDICIAL INTERIM RELEASE

The general philosophical approach to judicial interim release defines the compelling appearance powers described so far in this chapter—a statutory preference for interfering with liberty as little as necessary. The provisions are structured on the general assumption that an accused should be released pending trial and with as few restrictions as possible. Indeed, the *Code* creates what is usually referred to as a "ladder" approach to bail. In other words, an accused is presumed to be entitled to release and the Crown must justify each increasing step of intrusiveness. There are exceptions for section 469 and other offences, and they will be discussed below, but this is the general approach.

It is worth noting a rule that is slightly inconsistent with this policy. As noted above, an accused must be brought to a justice without unreasonable delay. This rule is meant to guarantee that person a speedy consideration of release; however, the justice that the accused is taken to can adjourn the bail hearing by up to three days without the consent of the accused. Longer delays are also possible, although in that case the consent of the accused would be required.[61]

Once the hearing is held, however, section 515 directs that the justice *shall* order that the accused is released on an undertaking without conditions, unless the Crown shows cause as to why something more restrictive is justified. For this reason, these are often referred to as "show cause" hearings. The *Code* permits these hearings to be conducted by a "justice," which includes a justice of the peace, but quite commonly they are held in front of a provincial court judge.

---

60 See *R v Ashmore*, 2011 BCCA 18; *R v Chung*, 2011 BCCA 131; or *R v Bhandher*, 2012 BCCA 441.

61 Section 516. See also *R v Zarinchang*, 2010 ONCA 286, in which institutional delays prevented an accused's bail hearing from being held until twenty-four days had passed. The Court of Appeal found that this violated the accused's right under s 9 of the *Charter* not to be arbitrarily detained and also his right under s 11(e) not to be denied reasonable bail without just cause. However, they overturned the remedy of a stay of proceedings which the trial judge had ordered and reduced the damage award to $3,600.

Section 515(2) of the *Code* sets out the range of restrictions on liberty, short of detention, that can be imposed on an accused as conditions of release. They are as follows:

a) an undertaking with conditions;
b) a recognizance without sureties and without deposit—that is, the accused promises to pay a sum of money if she does not appear as required;
c) a recognizance with sureties—that is, a third party also agrees to owe the debt if that accused does not appear;
d) a recognizance without sureties but with a deposit of money "or other valuable security"—this condition can only be imposed with the consent of the prosecutor; and
e) a recognizance with or without sureties and with a deposit of money or other valuable security if the accused is not ordinarily resident in the province or within two hundred kilometres of the place in which he is in custody.

The *Code* specifies that a justice cannot make an order under any of paragraphs (b) to (e) unless the prosecutor shows cause as to why an order under the immediately preceding paragraph would be inadequate.[62] Once again, this reflects the policy of Part XVI that, in general, restraint should be used in interfering with the liberty of an accused.

Sections 515(4) through 515(4.3) provide the various types of conditions that may, or must, be imposed when an order for release is made under section 515(2). All of these are related to the objectives of ensuring the accused attends court or ensuring the safety of the community while she is on release. They are similar to the conditions (outlined above) available to an officer in charge who is authorized by the arrest warrant to release the person arrested. Release conditions should be realistic and workable, rather than "set[ting] the accused up to fail."[63] Further, there must be some type of causal relationship between the crime charged and the particular conditions imposed. However, this connection need not be so specific that, for example, a curfew cannot be imposed even though the particular offence charge occurred during the day.[64]

The remaining possibility, beyond the various forms of release in section 515(2), is that the Crown might show cause as to why the accused should remain in custody until trial. Section 515(10) of the *Code*

---

62 Section 515(3).
63 *R v Thomson* (2004), 21 CR (6th) 209 (Ont SCJ).
64 *R v Patko* (2005), 197 CCC (3d) 192 (BCCA).

specifies that there are only three grounds on which continued detention of an accused may be ordered. The first two of these are relatively uncontroversial: (1) the detention is necessary to ensure the accused's attendance in court; or (2) the detention is necessary for the protection or safety of the public. In this context, "public" includes victims, witnesses, and any person under the age of eighteen, and the justice is directed to consider "all the circumstances, including any substantial likelihood that the accused will, if released from custody, commit a criminal offence or interfere with the administration of justice." These are sometimes referred to as the primary and secondary grounds for detention, though that terminology is a holdover from a previous version of the section and no order of priority is intended today.

The third possible ground for detention has been more controversial. An earlier version allowed for detention "in the public interest": it was struck down for violating the guarantee to reasonable bail found in section 11(e) of the *Charter* by being too vague and imprecise.[65] It was replaced by a section which allowed for detention "on any other just cause being shown" and in particular where it was necessary to maintain confidence in the administration of justice having regard to listed circumstances. This new section was also challenged and was upheld in part and struck down in part. The opening words of the section, "any other just cause" were struck out, on the ground of vagueness. The Court in *R v Hall* was divided over whether the same objection applied to the rest of the section, but, in a 5:4 split, upheld it.[66] The minority took the view that the enumerated considerations did not do enough to differentiate the new section from the old "public interest" criterion that had been found unacceptable. In contrast, the majority felt that the criteria delineated the risk-zone clearly enough that the vagueness claim was not made out. Following *Hall* Parliament amended the section to remove the portion that had been struck down, so it now says that detention can be ordered

> (c) if the detention is necessary to maintain confidence in the administration of justice, having regard to all the circumstances, including
>> (i)   the apparent strength of the prosecution's case,
>> (ii) the gravity of the offence,
>> (iii) the circumstances surrounding the commission of the offence, including whether a firearm was used, and

---

65   *R v Morales*, [1992] 3 SCR 711 [*Morales*].
66   2002 SCC 64 [*Hall*].

(iv) the fact that the accused is liable, on conviction, for a potentially lengthy term of imprisonment or, in the case of an
offence that involves, or whose subject-matter is, a firearm, a
minimum punishment of imprisonment for a term of three
years or more.[67]

Many courts were of the view that *Hall* had created a rule that this
third ground should be used only in rare cases, though not all courts
acted on this view.[68] However, in *St-Cloud* the Court indicated that
there was no such rule: a consequence of applying the criteria in section 515(1)(c) might as a matter of fact be that detention on this ground
occurred only rarely, but "only use it in rare cases" was not a precondition to its application or a criterion a court must consider.[69] Nor did the
fact that *Hall* involved a horrific and inexplicable crime mean that the
provision was confined to such cases: it applied to any type of crime,
if the Crown proved that the detention of the accused was justified to
maintain confidence in the administration of justice.[70] That decision
included but was not limited to the circumstances explicitly listed in
the section.[71]

Where the prosecutor justifies continued detention by showing
cause, the justice must add a statement of the reasons for this decision
to the warrant of committal.[72]

That is the general scheme for bail hearings, but, as noted above,
there are some exceptions to this approach. The first one worth noting
is created by section 515(6). That section lists a number of offences for
which the onus is reversed. That is, for the offences listed in that section,
the justice is directed to order that the accused *shall* be detained unless
the accused shows cause not to do so. One of these cases is where the
accused is not ordinarily resident in Canada. In such an event, if the accused does show cause as to why he should not be detained, a judge can
order his release on any of the bases applying to other bail hearings.[73]

---

67 Section 515(10)(c). In *R v St-Cloud*, 2015 SCC 27 at para 72 [*St-Cloud*], the Court
    noted that, given the French version of the statute, "confidence" should be read
    as "public confidence."
68 See Don Stuart & Joanna Harris, "Is the Public Confidence Ground to Deny Bail
    Used Sparingly?" (2004) 21 *Criminal Reports* (6th) 232.
69 *St-Cloud*, above note 67 at para 50.
70 *Ibid* at para 54.
71 *Ibid* at para 68.
72 Section 515(5).
73 Section 515(8). Note, as well, that the determination of whether a person is or-
    dinarily resident in Canada requires a case-by-case analysis. A refugee claimant,
    for example, might be ordinarily resident here, and therefore not subject to the
    reverse onus: see *R v Oladipo* (2004), 26 CR (6th) 393 (Ont SCJ).

The other reverse onus offences in section 515(6) involve cases where: (1) the offence charged was alleged to be committed while the accused was already out on bail; (2) the offence charged was a criminal organization, terrorism, or national security offence; (3) the offence related to failing to attend court as ordered by some previous process; or (4) the offence was punishable by life imprisonment under the *Controlled Drugs and Substances Act*.[74] The first and last of these reverse onuses have been challenged under the *Charter* but upheld.[75] In these cases, the accused is not only given the onus of showing cause that detention is not justified but, if ordered released, he must also show why the conditions that can attach to his release should *not* be imposed.

The second exception to the general bail scheme applies to section 469 offences, the most common of which is murder. In this case, section 515(11) states that a justice has no authority to release the accused and must order her detained to be "dealt with according to law." That is not the end of the story, however. In this event, the accused will, in accordance with section 522, be taken before a judge of the superior court—no one else is authorized to release a person charged with a section 469 offence before trial. In this hearing, there is again a reverse onus, with the accused being required to justify release.[76] If the accused is ordered to be released, any of the ordinary conditions of release can be imposed.

A decision made by a justice concerning release or detention may be reviewed by a judge upon application of the accused or the prosecutor.[77] Applications of this kind are common, and there is no limitation of such applications that may be made, except that following a review a further application cannot be brought for thirty days, unless the accused or the prosecutor has the leave of a judge. These reviews provide an opportunity to adjust or correct the order at the original bail hearing and also provide an opportunity to reconsider the appropriateness of the order if circumstances have changed. Where interim release has been denied, an accused person in custody is entitled to an automatic review if the trial has not commenced within a specified time frame.[78]

If not amended in some fashion, an order for judicial interim release lasts until the end of trial and, if an accused is found guilty of a non-section 469 offence, the term of the release will last until the time of sentencing. This remains the case even if, for some reason, a new in-

---

74 SC 1996, c 19.
75 See, respectively, *Morales*, above note 65, and *R v Pearson*, [1992] 3 SCR 665.
76 Section 522(2).
77 Sections 520–21.
78 Section 525.

formation is laid in respect of an offence for which process has already been issued. However, a preliminary inquiry judge or trial judge can vacate any previous order (whether for detention or release) and substitute a different order where cause to do so is shown.[79]

The justice who conducts a bail hearing is not constrained by the rules and principles of admissibility that apply with respect to evidence at trial. Section 518, which sets out the principles of evidence at a bail hearing, concludes with a paragraph that allows the justice to "receive and base his decision on evidence considered credible or trustworthy by him in the circumstances of each case." This broad statement of admissibility is supplemented by more specific elements in section 518, such as the admissibility of wiretap evidence and evidence that relates both to the character and circumstances of the accused and the circumstances of the alleged offence. However, that section also specifies that a bail hearing may not be used to interrogate or examine the accused about the offence itself. Although the justice may conduct inquiries under oath of or about the accused, neither the justice nor the prosecutor may examine the accused about the circumstances of the alleged offence, unless she has elected to testify in the hearing at the invitation of her counsel or on her own decision. Of course, even at this stage the accused is entitled to protect herself against self-incrimination, and thus any questions put to the accused at the bail hearing should, in principle, be confined to matters that are relevant to a determination of the hearing. However, this can be a difficult issue to control at a bail hearing, especially as the prosecutor is specifically entitled to produce evidence of the alleged offence and the probability of conviction.

It is worth noting in this regard that, where the Crown seeks to show cause for the accused to be detained pending trial, the accused is entitled to a mandatory publication ban on all evidence and representations made at the hearing.[80] Such a ban is justified under section 1 of the *Charter*, because it is a necessary measure to protect the accused's fair trial right given that at the bail hearing evidence that might be inadmissible at trial can be presented.[81]

Finally, it is worth noting that the forms of police process or judicial process that have been discussed here permit an accused person to remain at liberty, but these processes do so trusting that the accused will comply with any conditions imposed, including the requirement to appear in court. Unsurprisingly, not every accused person turns out

---

79 Section 523.
80 Section 517.
81 *Toronto Star Newspapers Ltd v Canada*, 2010 SCC 21.

to have been deserving of this trust. The *Code* therefore provides that an accused who has or is about to violate some condition of release can be arrested, with or without warrant.[82] A person thus arrested must be taken before a justice or, in the case of a person previously released or arrested for an offence listed in section 469, taken before a judge of the superior court.

FURTHER READINGS

COUGHLAN, STEPHEN, & GLEN LUTHER. *Detention and Arrest* (Toronto: Irwin Law, 2010).

LAW REFORM COMMISSION OF CANADA. *Compelling Appearance, Interim Release and Pre-trial Detention* (Ottawa: Law Reform Commission of Canada, 1988).

————. *Controlling Criminal Prosecutions: The Attorney General and the Crown Prosecutor* (Ottawa: Law Reform Commission of Canada, 1990).

QUIGLEY, TIM. *Procedure in Canadian Criminal Law*, 2d ed (Toronto: Thomson Carswell, 2005) (loose-leaf) ch 5 and 9.

STRIBOPOULOS, JAMES. "Unchecked Power: The Constitutional Regulation of Arrest Reconsidered" (2003) 48 *McGill Law Journal* 225.

STUART, DON. *Charter Justice in Canadian Criminal Law*, 5th ed (Toronto: Thomson Carswell, 2010) ch 6.

————, & JOANNA HARRIS. "Is the Public Confidence Ground to Deny Bail Used Sparingly?" (2004) 21 *Criminal Reports* (6th) 232.

TROTTER, GARY. *The Law of Bail in Canada*, 2d ed (Scarborough, ON: Carswell, 1999).

---

82   Section 524.

CHAPTER 7

ARREST

This chapter deals with powers of arrest, most, but not all, of which are exercised by police. There is some overlap between this chapter and others. Obviously, arrest is one of the methods of compelling a person's appearance in court, and so the procedures here must be seen in light of the discussion in Chapter 6. In addition, the *Charter* guarantees particular rights on arrest *or* detention. Detention was discussed in Chapter 5, but section 10(b) issues were not discussed there at any length. Accordingly, the discussion of those rights here is also relevant to that earlier chapter.

A. INTRODUCTION

This section deals with powers of arrest, both those given to police officers and those available more broadly. Arrest powers are most important in the context of apprehending a person believed to have committed a crime, and so the major focus of this chapter will be the arrest powers found in Part XVI of the *Code*, "Compelling Appearance." However, other arrest powers for various purposes are also found in the *Code* and will be outlined briefly.

Arrest is only one of the methods that can compel the appearance of an accused before a court. Part XVI also contains provisions that allow an accused to be brought to court by two other methods: a summons or an appearance notice. Those techniques were discussed at greater length in Chapter 6, but it is useful to review them here.

Similar to powers of search and seizure, Part XVI of the *Code* is aimed at balancing legitimate state interests in prosecuting crime against individual freedom. On the one hand, it is sometimes necessary to require a person to answer to a criminal charge and therefore to appear in court to do so. On the other hand, our Western democratic principles hold that the state should not interfere with the liberty of individuals without good reason and no more than is necessary. In large part, therefore, while Part XVI of the *Code* creates coercive powers given to the police, it endeavours to reflect the principle of restraint while doing so. It is an attempt to find the right balance between crime control and due process interests.[1]

Accordingly, in principle, a police officer should not be able to unilaterally compel the appearance of an accused in court. That decision should, at some stage, be confirmed by a judicial officer, typically a justice of the peace, and in all but one instance it is.[2] That confirmation can occur either before the officer deals directly with the accused person or afterward, but it must occur. Similarly, there are different levels of compulsion that can be directed towards the accused. The accused may receive a request[3] in writing to appear in court on a particular day and is trusted to do so, or could, in contrast, physically be taken into control by the police officer and given no choice but compliance.

These two variables—judicial confirmation before or after, and a request in writing versus physical control—create four possibilities, which conform to the four methods of compelling an accused's appearance created by Part XVI. At the least intrusive level, a police officer can show a justice that there are reasonable grounds to believe that a person has committed an offence and consequently obtain a summons requiring the accused to appear in court on a specified date.[4] Alternatively, the officer can first encounter a person on the street committing an offence and then require that person to appear in court by means of an appearance notice. This appearance notice must subsequently be confirmed by a justice.[5]

This chapter, however, deals with the more intrusive methods involved in taking physical control of the person, either after judicial

---

1   See Herbert L Packer, *The Limits of the Criminal Sanction* (Stanford: Stanford University Press, 1968) at 154–72 for a fuller discussion of these concepts.
2   The surprising exception is arrest without a warrant: see the discussion in Chapter 6, Section C(1).
3   The word "request" is used here for convenience sake, although, of course, an accused who does not appear will be arrested: see s 512(2).
4   Section 507(1)(b). See s 509 for the contents of a summons.
5   Sections 501, 505, and 508(1)(b).

authorization to do so has been issued or before (that is, arrest with or without a warrant). It is worth noting, however, that Part XVI has a number of rules aimed at having the state use the least intrusive, yet effective, means possible. Where a police officer seeks judicial authorization first, for example, the justice is to issue a summons, unless it is shown to be necessary in the public interest to issue a warrant.[6] Even if an accused has already been arrested with a warrant, the peace officer concerned is required to release that person as soon as practicable and use a summons or appearance notice instead.[7] If the arresting officer takes the accused into custody, the officer in charge (of the place of detention) is equally directed to release the person as soon as practicable and use a summons or appearance notice to compel appearance before the court.[8] These limitations reflect the principle of restraint in the use of police powers. It will be seen that this principle is also reflected, in various ways, in the arrest powers themselves.

This section deals first with arrest with a warrant, arrest without a warrant, and the various supporting provisions affecting those powers. It then briefly considers the arrest powers outside of Part XVI. Finally, the constitutional and other rights that arise on arrest are outlined. These constitutional rights are also relevant to detentions.

As a final preliminary point, however, it should be made clear exactly what constitutes an arrest. An arrest consists of either the actual seizure or touching of a person with a view to his detention, or words of arrest accompanied by the person submitting to the arrest.[9] The word "arrest" need not be used, provided the accused can be reasonably supposed to have understood that she was under arrest.[10] Although reducing arrest to touching the accused can make it seem like "a children's game" and could appear to make the arrest an instantaneous thing, arrest is a continuing act, starting with the moment of custody and extending until the person is either released from custody or brought before a justice and detained.[11] The primary significance of this conclusion is that the powers available to make an arrest originally, such as the use of force, continue to be available.

---

6   Section 507(4).

7   Section 497(1).

8   Section 498.

9   *R v Whitfield*, [1970] SCR 46.

10   *R v Latimer*, [1997] 1 SCR 217 [*Latimer*]. This rule is, in principle, reasonable, though its actual application in *Latimer* amounted to justifying a police action that was consciously intended not to be an arrest, as an arrest: see Stephen G Coughlan, "Developments in Criminal Procedure: The 1996–97 Term" (1998) 9 *Supreme Court Law Review* (2d) 273 at 290–93.

11   *R v Asante-Mensah*, 2003 SCC 38 at paras 33 and 43 [*Asante-Mensah*].

B. ARREST WITH A WARRANT

As discussed in Chapter 6, a warrant can be issued only after an information that sets out the reasonable grounds to believe that a person has committed an offence is laid before a justice. Section 504 creates this rule for indictable offences, and section 795 adopts the procedures of Part XVI for summary conviction offences. A personal appearance by the peace officer is not essential, and it is possible to lay an information electronically.[12] Where, having heard the allegations of the informant and the evidence under oath of any witnesses, a justice who is satisfied that a case for doing so is made out can issue either a summons or a warrant requiring the accused to attend before a justice to answer the charge. A summons, rather than a warrant, must be issued unless the evidence discloses reasonable grounds to believe that it is "necessary in the public interest" to issue a warrant.[13]

This "necessary in the public interest" criterion was also formerly used in section 515 of the *Code* in considering bail for an accused pending trial. In *R v Morales*, it was struck down as unconstitutionally vague and therefore a violation of section 11(e) of the *Charter*.[14] That subsection has since been replaced by a new provision that specifies criteria to be used in deciding whether an accused's detention is necessary to maintain confidence in the administration of justice. The new provision was upheld by the Court in a 5:4 decision that has attracted some criticism.[15] In the context of section 507(4), the public interest criterion has received relatively little attention but has been found to comply with the *Charter*.[16]

This relative lack of attention to the section may largely be due to the fact that, unlike a bail hearing, the application for an arrest warrant is made on an *ex parte* basis. The issue has occasionally arisen in

---

12   Section 508.1.
13   Section 507(4).
14   [1992] 3 SCR 711 [*Morales*].
15   *R v Hall*, 2002 SCC 64. See the discussion of the decision in Don Stuart, "*R v Hall*: Annotation" (2002) 4 *Criminal Reports* (6th) 201; and Tim Quigley, "*R v Hall*: Annotation" (2002) 4 *Criminal Reports* (6th) 202.
16   In *R v Budreo* (1996), 104 CCC (3d) 245 (Ont Ct Gen Div), the trial judge found that the "public interest" criterion in s 507(4) differed from its unconstitutional use in s 515. In the bail context, it had been a third and residual criterion: in s 507(4), it was the sole criterion. The trial judge held that it ought to be interpreted narrowly, in essence, to mean only the two grounds for detention that had been upheld in *Morales*, above note 14: on that interpretation it was constitutional. The decision was affirmed on appeal (*R v Budreo* (2000), 142 CCC (3d) 225 (Ont CA)), and the Court of Appeal seems to accept the trial judge's reasoning.

complaints of a violation of the right to a trial within a reasonable time, and there is some lower court authority suggesting that if the police are going to claim that a warrant, rather than a summons, is necessary, then they have an obligation to make reasonable efforts to effect the arrest.[17] Authorities conflict on whether issuing a warrant with respect to a person already in custody in order to preserve jurisdiction is in the public interest.[18] For the most part, however, little attention has been paid to the issue.

Warrants are directed only to peace officers, though that term has a relatively broad definition, including, of course, police officers, but also, in some cases, correctional officers, customs officers, fisheries officers, mayors, pilots in command of an aircraft, and others.[19] The peace officers to whom a warrant is directed must be within the territorial jurisdiction of the person who issues it.[20] In practical terms, however, there are few real obstacles to the use of an arrest warrant anywhere in the country. A warrant issued by any court other than a justice or a provincial court judge can automatically be executed anywhere in Canada.[21] A warrant from a justice or provincial court judge can be executed anywhere in the province in which it is issued.[22] In the case of fresh pursuit, however, a warrant can be executed anywhere in Canada, and in any event, a peace officer to whom a warrant is directed can execute that warrant even when not in the territory for which that person is a peace officer.[23] Finally, a warrant issued in one jurisdiction can be endorsed by a justice of another jurisdiction and become executable there if the accused is believed to be in that other jurisdiction.[24]

A warrant must name or describe the accused, set out briefly the offence that the accused is charged with, and order that the accused be brought before a justice to be dealt with according to law. Arrest warrants do not expire, but simply remain in force until executed.[25] Section 29

---

17   R v Yellowhorse (1990), 111 AR 20 (Prov Ct); R v Heidecker, [1992] AJ No. 91 (Prov Ct).

18   Compare R v Horton, [2002] OJ No 1219 (SCJ), and Re Inverarity and the Queen (1984), 18 CCC (3d) 74 (Sask QB). In any case, it is more difficult under current Code provisions for a court to lose jurisdiction than it was in the past: see the discussion in Chapter 11.

19   Section 2.

20   Section 513. Territorial division includes a province, a county, a town, or any other judicial division appropriate to the context: s 2.

21   Section 703.

22   Section 703(2).

23   Section 514.

24   Section 528.

25   Section 511.

of the *Code* requires an officer executing a warrant to have it where it is feasible to do so, and to provide it where requested. It also requires anyone who arrests, with or without a warrant, to give notice to the arrested person of "(a) the process or warrant under which he makes the arrest; or (b) the reason for the arrest."[26] One might naturally have read this section disjunctively, on the assumption that (a) applies to arrests with a warrant and (b) to arrests without a warrant. However, this was not the approach taken by the Court in *R v Gamracy*, a decision that removed much of the real force of the provision.[27] In that case, an officer made an arrest, but only told the accused that there was an outstanding warrant. The officer neither had the warrant nor knew what offence the warrant dealt with. The Court held that this was sufficient compliance with section 29. The arrest was not an arrest with a warrant, but a warrantless arrest under section 495(1)(c), to be discussed below. In that event, "there is a warrant" was held to be sufficient notice of the reason for the arrest.

Gamracy is a pre-*Charter* case, and section 10(a) of the *Charter* now creates the constitutional right to be informed promptly on arrest of the reasons for the arrest. That right requires that an accused be given sufficient information to decide whether to submit to the arrest and to make an informed choice about whether to exercise the right to counsel. More frequently, the section has been considered in circumstances where the reason an accused is detained changes during the course of an investigation,[28] with the result that little attention has been paid to the content of the right at the time an accused is first arrested. It therefore remains unclear whether *Gamracy* still represents the state of the law.[29]

C. ARREST WITHOUT A WARRANT

Warrantless arrests are governed by sections 494 and 495 of the *Code*, which create a number of arrest powers available to three groups. Section 494(1) creates arrest powers available to anyone, section 494(2) creates a special arrest power relating to property owners, and section

---

26   Section 29.

27   [1974] SCR 640 [*Gamracy*].

28   See, for example, *R v Borden*, [1994] 3 SCR 145 [*Borden*]; *R v Smith*, [1991] 1 SCR 714 [*Smith* 1991]; *R v Evans*, [1991] 1 SCR 869 [*Evans*]; and *R v Black*, [1989] 2 SCR 138 [*Black*].

29   *Gamracy*, above note 27, has been followed post-*Charter* but has not been considered in connection with the s 10(a) issue: see, for example, *R v Kozoway* (1993), 142 AR 323 (QB), aff'd (1994), 157 AR 79 (CA).

495(1) creates arrest powers available only to peace officers. Section 494 is sometimes spoken of as providing power for a "citizen's arrest," although it can in fact be used by anyone, peace officers included. Historically, it is section 494 that descends more directly from the common law powers of arrest, while section 495 creates additional powers for peace officers, an office which did not exist when powers of arrest first developed.[30]

The different powers of arrest are defined largely by two variables: indictable offences versus criminal offences, and "finds committing" powers versus "reasonable belief" powers. In each case, the former option is more limited than the latter.

Some arrest powers are limited to indictable offences (that is, ones that can be prosecuted by indictment, which in this context includes hybrid offences).[31] Other arrest powers apply to criminal offences in general and, therefore, include summary conviction offences as well. Indeed, many provinces have incorporated the *Criminal Code* arrest powers into their provincial offence acts, so as a practical matter some *Code* arrest powers apply to non-*Code* offences.[32]

The "finds committing" standard requires that the person arresting has witnessed the commission of the offence. The requirement is read to mean "apparently" finds committing, in the sense that a subsequent acquittal of the accused on the charge for which she was arrested does not retroactively invalidate the arrest power. Thus, in *R v Biron*, for example, the accused was properly arrested for causing a disturbance since an officer witnessed the behaviour constituting the disturbance. The fact that Biron was eventually acquitted of that charge (because there was no proof at trial of the specific allegation of shouting) did not mean that he was illegally arrested, and so he was still guilty of

---

30   See *R v Lerke* (1986), 49 CR (3d) 324 at 330 (Alta CA) [*Lerke*]: "The power exercised by a citizen who arrests another is in direct descent over nearly a thousand years of the powers and duties of citizens in the age of Henry II in relation to the 'King's Peace.'" See also *Asante-Mensah*, above note 11 at para 40: "The development of modern police forces brought about a transfer of law enforcement activities from private citizens to peace officers. But it is the peace officer's powers which are in a sense derivative from that of the citizen, not the other way around."

31   *Interpretation Act*, RSC 1985, c I-21, s 34(1)(a).

32   In addition, other arrest powers exist in other statutes. See, for example, *Asante-Mensah*, above note 11, and its discussion of the arrest power given to private citizens (and, therefore, to private security firms) by Ontario's *Trespass to Property Act*, RSO 1990, c T.21, or the extensive review of federal non-*Criminal Code* and provincial arrest powers in Law Reform Commission of Canada, *Arrest* (Ottawa: Law Reform Commission of Canada, 1986) [Law Reform Commission].

resisting a peace officer in the execution of duty.[33] *Biron* is a pre-*Charter* case and so it may now be possible to argue that an arrest made when the accused is ultimately found not to have committed an offence violates the right, in section 9, to be free from arbitrary detention.

"Reasonable grounds to believe" that an accused has committed an offence requires that the person performing the arrest subjectively believes that the person has committed the offence and that the belief is objectively justifiable. In other words, a reasonable person standing in the shoes of the arresting officer would have also believed that grounds for arrest existed. The objective standard for a warrantless arrest, therefore, is the same as that required for obtaining an arrest warrant.[34] Whether the standard is met in an individual case is not always easy to determine and depends on the particular facts. More than mere suspicion is necessary, but the police are not required to have a *prima facie* case before arresting. Accordingly, although police cannot arrest simply in order to investigate and obtain reasonable grounds, the fact that an investigation continues after an arrest does not automatically mean that the arrest was not based on reasonable grounds.[35]

The "reasonable grounds" standard requires that a reasonable person would see it as more likely than not that the accused committed the offence (that it is probable the accused is guilty). Some lower courts have mistakenly held that the standard could be met without reaching the level of "probability," but that view is based on a misapplication of precedent from a different context.[36] The Supreme Court has explicitly held that "reasonable grounds" in section 495(1)(a) is the same as "reasonable and probable grounds,"[37] but not all lower courts have yet stopped making this error.[38]

Both the subjective and objective tests must be met. It is easy to see that an objectively unreasonable arrest should not be allowed simply

---

33   [1976] 2 SCR 56 [*Biron*]. There is a further complicating factor in *Biron*: the officer who arrested the accused was not the officer who witnessed the apparent offence, but that does not affect the main point. *Biron* was distinguished in *R v Sharma*, [1993] 1 SCR 650, where the accused was found not to have been properly arrested when the offence for which he was arrested was found to be *ultra vires*. The Court held at para 32 that *Biron* "deals with apparent perpetration of an offence, not apparent offences."

34   *R v Storrey*, [1990] 1 SCR 241.

35   *Ibid*; *R v Duguay, Murphy and Sevigny*, [1989] 1 SCR 93.

36   See the discussion in Steve Coughlan & Glen Luther, *Detention and Arrest* (Toronto: Irwin Law, 2010) at 78.

37   *R v Loewen*, 2011 SCC 21 at para 5.

38   See Alex Gorlewski, "R. v. *Loewen* and Reasonable Grounds for Arrest: The Supreme Court's Overlooked Advice" (2012) 94 *Criminal Reports* (6th) 319.

because of the officer's personal belief. Equally, though, even if reasonable grounds for arrest exist on an objective basis, the arrest is improper if the officer does not have the necessary subjective belief. The issue is not simply whether grounds to arrest exist, but whether the officer *acts upon* such grounds.[39]

1) Section 494 Arrest Powers

The arrest powers in section 494(1) are given to anyone and are the most limited powers. Anyone may arrest a person whom he finds committing an indictable offence. Alternatively, anyone may perform an arrest when she believes, on reasonable grounds, that some person has committed a criminal offence *and* is escaping and being freshly pursued by some other person with authority to arrest.

Section 494(2) creates a slightly broader arrest power for property owners and their designates. Anyone who owns or is in lawful possession of property can arrest not only for indictable offences, but also for any criminal offence they find being committed on or in relation to their property. "Property" is defined in section 2 of the *Code* to include real or personal property. This power was amended in 2013 to allow it be exercised on something slightly broader than the "finds committing" which had previously applied. A property owner can arrest not only at the time of the offence but also within a reasonable time after the offence if it is not feasible for a peace officer to make the arrest.[40]

Anyone other than a peace officer who makes an arrest is required to deliver the arrested person "forthwith," that is, as soon as reasonably possible or practicable under all the circumstances.[41]

2) Section 495 Arrest Powers

Peace officers' arrest powers are much broader. Sections 495(1)(a) and (b) effectively allow a peace officer to arrest in any situation but two: (1) where the officer did not find the accused committing the offence, the offence is only a summary conviction one, and no arrest warrant has

---

39   *R v Coles*, 2003 PESCAD 3. Similarly, see *R v Caslake*, [1998] 1 SCR 51, where the Court held that a search that would have been objectively justifiable as an incident to an arrest was unreasonable because that was not the officer's subjective purpose.

40   See the discussion in Steve Coughlan, "Citizen's Arrest, Property Owners, and Private Fiefdoms" (2014) 18 *Canadian Criminal Law Review* 1.

41   *R v Cunningham* (1979), 49 CCC (2d) 390 (Man Co Ct).

been issued, or (2) where the officer believes that a summary conviction offence is about to be committed.

Section 495(1)(a) permits a peace officer to arrest anyone who "has committed an indictable offence or who, on reasonable grounds, he believes has committed or is about to commit an indictable offence." Section 495(1)(b) permits a peace officer to arrest anyone he finds committing a criminal offence. Finally, section 495(1)(c) permits a peace officer to arrest a person if he reasonably believes that a warrant exists for the person's arrest.

Read in one fashion, the first clause of section 495(1)(a) would make the second clause redundant. If a peace officer could arrest anyone who has committed an indictable offence, it would be unnecessary also to have a power to make such an arrest on reasonable grounds. In practice, the section has not been interpreted in such a broad way. Section 495(1)(a) is taken to require that the officer has personally witnessed the offence, believes on reasonable grounds that the offence has been committed, or believes on reasonable grounds that the offence is about to be committed.[42]

The arrest power in section 495(1)(b) authorizes an arrest at any time where the officer witnesses the actual commission of the offence. Section 495(1)(c) adds the power to arrest without warrant on the basis that a warrant exists. The Law Reform Commission of Canada noted that this latter provision could seem contradictory, but recommended its retention. They noted that, although an officer who encounters a suspect at a traffic check or while on routine patrol typically could not, as a practical matter, obtain a copy of the warrant, the existence of the warrant amounts to "judicially certified" reasonable grounds.[43]

Although these arrest powers are quite broad, the principle of restraint is still reflected to some extent, specifically in section 495(2).[44] At first glance, the provision, beginning with the words "a peace officer shall not arrest," appears to put a limit on the powers of arrest in section 495(1)(a). In fact, given the effect of section 495(3), it does not

---

42   *R v Klimchuk* (1991), 67 CCC (3d) 385 (BCCA). The court distinguishes witnessing the offence personally in s 495(1)(a) from the "finds committing" power in s 495(1)(b), on the basis that the former is restricted to situations where the officer witnessed the offence but could not prevent it before its completion, while "finds committing" requires that the arrested person still be in the process of committing the offence.

43   Law Reform Commission, above note 32 at 23–24.

44   A further example of restraint is found in the *Youth Criminal Justice Act*, SC 2002, c 1, s 6 [*YCJA*], which requires a peace officer, before taking any measures, to consider whether it would be sufficient simply to administer a caution or refer the young person to a community program or agency.

actually do so, but it does provide some guidance to the way in which peace officers should exercise their discretion in the use of arrest powers. In effect, it is not a removal of the arrest power, but advice about when not to use it.

Section 495(2) is drafted in a very oblique fashion. It is structured as a triple, and sometimes a quadruple, negative. It applies only in the case of arrests for relatively less serious offences. That is, according to section 495(2)(a) through (c), it applies to indictable offences in the absolute jurisdiction of a provincial court judge, to hybrid offences, and to summary conviction offences. In those cases, section 495(2) directs peace officers not to arrest simply because an arrest power exists; rather, the section calls for some other factor to be present as well. The officer may arrest because she believes on reasonable grounds that an arrest is the only way to do one of three things:

(i)   establish the identity of the person,
(ii) secure or preserve evidence of or relating to the offence, or
(iii) prevent the continuation or repetition of the offence or the commission of another offence.[45]

Alternatively, the officer may also arrest because he reasonably believes that the person will not attend court unless arrested; that is, under the circumstances it is evident to the officer that an appearance notice will not be sufficient.[46]

However, although section 495(2) sets out circumstances in which peace officers ought to use an appearance notice rather than arrest a person, section 495(3) makes it clear that the officer's power to arrest still exists; that is, section 495(2) gives guidance but does not operate as a real limit. As noted above, a major goal of section 10(a) of the *Charter* is to allow an accused to know why he is being arrested, in order to decide whether to submit to the arrest. A peace officer who attempts to arrest a person without authority to do so is committing an assault, and the person would have the right not to submit and to resist the officer's

---

45   Section 495(2)(d). Strictly, the subsection includes only these factors among aspects of the public interest, and the criterion for not arresting is that the public interest can be satisfied without an arrest. It was held in *R v Fosseneuve* (1995), 43 CR (4th) 260 (Man QB), that the section had to be read down to only the three criteria listed on the grounds that, otherwise, the "public interest" criterion permitted an arrest on unconstitutionally vague grounds. It is important to realize, though, that s 495(2) does not create an arrest power. That power must already exist from s 495(1) or elsewhere. See, however, the discussion of *R v Moore*, [1979] 1 SCR 195 [*Moore*], below at note 49.

46   Section 495(2)(e). Note as well s 496, which authorizes the use of an appearance notice when an officer does not arrest by virtue of s 495(2).

actions. However, if the officer had the power to arrest, then a person resisting would be guilty of either resisting or assaulting an officer in the execution of duty.[47] The important issue, then, is whether an officer who ignores section 495(2) is still acting in the execution of duty. Section 495(3) states that an officer acting under section 495(1) is deemed to be in the execution of duty "notwithstanding subsection 495(2)."[48] In other words, as long as the power to arrest was created by subsection (1), subsection (2) did not remove it.[49]

Even if an arrest that does not accord with section 495(2) is still legal, one might argue that an arrest made where the *Code* suggests it should not be is an arbitrary detention and therefore violates the right in section 9 of the *Charter*. Such an argument, however, seems unlikely to succeed. To avoid violating section 9 a detention must be authorized by law, and that law must not be arbitrary.[50] Section 495(3), in saying that the officer still acts lawfully despite not complying with section 495(2), seems to meet the requirement that the detention was autho-

---

47   Sections 129(a) and s 270(1)(a), respectively.

48   Section 495(3)(b) permits the argument that an officer who fails to comply with s 495(2) is not acting in the execution of duty in other contexts, such as a tort action for false arrest or wrongful imprisonment. In non-criminal proceedings, s 495(3)(b) imposes the burden on the applicant to show that s 495(2) was not complied with.

49   A word must be said somewhere about the Court's curious decision in *Moore*, above note 45. Moore was a cyclist who went through a red light, in the sight of a police officer. The officer stopped him and requested identification, which Moore refused to provide. Moore was convicted of obstructing an officer in the execution of duty. The Court's rationale was that the officer was obliged under s 495(2) not to arrest Moore if he could identify him, and therefore, the officer had a duty to try to obtain identification. By refusing to provide such identification, Moore was therefore obstructing the officer. This decision can be and has been criticized for confusing police duties with police powers and for creating a duty on the part of Moore where none existed by statute or common law.

The better approach would be that adopted by the Ontario Court of Appeal in analogous circumstances in *R v Hayes*, [2003] OJ No 2795. There, the accused was required by statute to hand over his motorcycle helmet for inspection but refused to do so and was thus charged with obstruction. The court held that, by failing to hand over his helmet, Hayes made himself potentially liable to a $1000 fine. But issuing a written notice to Hayes creating such liability was the only enforcement mechanism open to the officer. Hayes was not guilty of obstructing the officer for his non-compliance. Similarly, one would think that a person in Moore's position becomes potentially liable to the more intrusive enforcement mechanism of arrest rather than receiving an appearance notice, but that the officer still has that option open and, therefore, is not obstructed.

Moore is a pre-*Charter* case, and it is possible that on the same facts a different result would be found today.

50   *R v Grant*, 2009 SCC 32 at para 56 [*Grant*].

rized by law. However, the approach to section 9 is said to mirror that for section 8,[51] and so there is also a requirement that the detention was not effected in an arbitrary way. One might therefore argue that an arrest which was lawful but ignored the impact of section 495(2) for no good reason was carried out arbitrarily and therefore violated section 9 of the *Charter*.

3) Other *Criminal Code* Arrest Powers

The *Code* contains many other arrest powers, mostly with a warrant, though occasionally other warrantless ones as well. The majority are arrest powers intended to provide a measure of compulsion to the judicial process. An accused who evades service of a summons, does not appear for fingerprinting, or violates a condition of the undertaking by which he was released may have an arrest warrant issued, for example.[52] In the last context, a person who has agreed to act as surety for an accused released pending trial can apply to be released from that obligation and is then empowered to arrest the accused.[53] An accused may fail to appear for trial, resulting in the issuance of a bench warrant.[54] Proceedings may also be adjourned, stayed, and so on and need to be recommenced later, with the result that the appearance of the accused must be compelled again, and an arrest warrant is typically an option at these stages as well.[55] Similarly, arrest warrants can sometimes be used to compel the appearance of witnesses.[56] Arrest warrants can also be used to help preserve the jurisdiction of the Court.[57]

Not all the other arrest powers simply support the court process, however. Section 199(2) of the *Code* creates a particular warrantless arrest power for a peace officer who finds someone keeping a common gaming house or anyone found therein. In addition, section 31 allows a peace officer who witnesses a breach of the peace to arrest "any person whom he finds committing the breach of the peace or who, on reasonable grounds, he believes is about to join in or renew the breach

---

51   *Grant, ibid.*

52   Sections 512(c), 510, and 524.

53   Section 796.

54   Section 597.

55   See, for example, ss 485 and 578(1)(b), though many provisions of the *Code* serve the same general purpose. Note that these provisions frequently rely on the "public interest" as the deciding criterion concerning issuance of a warrant and therefore may be subject to a *Charter* challenge: see the discussion under Section B and in note 16, above in this chapter.

56   Sections 698, 704, & 705.

57   Section 498, and see the discussion in Chapter 11.

of the peace." Note that a "breach of the peace" is not itself a criminal offence,[58] though, of course, much behaviour that would constitute a breach of the peace would equally meet the definition of some offence, such as causing a disturbance, rioting, or unlawful assembly.[59]

The power in section 31 is limited to breaches of the peace that have already occurred. There is some authority, however, suggesting that police also have a common law power to arrest for apprehended breaches of the peace.[60] This suggestion is troublesome for several reasons. First, if it is confined to the "finds committing" standard, the section 31 power is, at most, a minimal extension over the power to arrest in section 495(1)(b), which lets an officer arrest on a "finds committing" basis for any criminal offence. To allow arrest for apprehended breaches of the peace, however, is in large part to extend the power to arrest to cover summary conviction offences that have not occurred—precisely an omission that was made from section 495. More troubling than the particular expansion of police powers in this circumstance, however, is the notion that common law arrest powers exist at all. It was noted in Chapter 2 that, although the common law is a potential source of police power, it is a controversial one. Particularly in areas such as arrest, where one may have taken Parliament to have consciously defined all the powers, allowing common law arrest to exist[61] (or to be created) also creates considerable scope for uncertainty.[62]

---

58 *Frey v Fedoruk*, [1950] SCR 517.

59 See Bruce P Archibald, "*Hayes v. Thompson and Bell*: Annotation" (1985) 44 *Criminal Reports* (3d) 316.

60 *Hayes v Thompson* (1985), 44 CR (3d) 316 (BCCA) [*Hayes*]; *Brown v Durham Regional Police Force* (1998), 21 CR (5th) 1 [*Brown*]. The Ontario Court of Appeal held at para 74 in *Brown*: "The apprehended breach must be imminent and the risk that the breach will occur must be substantial. The mere possibility of some unspecified breach at some unknown point in time will not suffice. These features of the power to arrest or detain to avoid a breach of the peace place that power on the same footing as the statutory power to arrest in anticipation of the commission of an indictable offence. That is not to say that the two powers are co-extensive. Many indictable offences do not involve a breach of the peace and, as indicated above, conduct resulting in an apprehended breach of the peace need not involve the commission of any offence."

61 *Hayes*, above note 60, speaks about this power as a pre-existing common law power, but *Brown*, above note 60, describes it as a manifestation of the ancillary power doctrine, which more usually is used as a way of describing newly created common law powers. See the discussion in Chapter 2.

62 See Archibald, above note 59.

D. SUPPORTING POWERS

A number of provisions in the *Code* provide additional power or protection to peace officers or others performing arrests. Anyone making a lawful arrest, for example, is justified in using as much force as necessary to do so, provided she is acting on reasonable grounds.[63] This power is set out in the *Code* for arrests under that Act, but the use of reasonable force is incidental to arrests in any case, such as those carried out under some provincial Act.[64] Latitude is permitted, since peace officers have a duty to act, sometimes in difficult and exigent circumstances.[65] Nonetheless, an officer is criminally responsible for using excessive force.[66]

A special rule applies to the use of force likely to cause death or grievous bodily harm to effect an arrest. Such action is permitted only when, even if there is a warrant, a warrantless arrest would be allowable; the person has taken flight to avoid arrest; the person using the force believes on reasonable grounds it is necessary for the purpose of protecting the officer or some other person from imminent or future death or grievous bodily harm; and the flight of the person cannot be prevented in a less violent manner.[67]

Anyone arresting the wrong person under a warrant is not criminally responsible, provided he believed in good faith and on reasonable grounds that the correct person was being arrested. This same protection also applies to anyone called on to assist in the arrest.[68]

Police have the power to search a person who has been arrested (this issue is discussed in Chapter 4).

Special rules apply when the police enter a dwelling house to make an arrest because of the increased privacy interest in that situation. At common law, relatively little additional protection was provided to a suspect in this situation, but the Court held in *R v Feeney* that some of the common law rules did not pass *Charter* scrutiny.[69] Therefore, some

---

63 Section 25(1). Section 25 is phrased in the language of justification, meaning that, in principle, it creates a defence to a criminal charge rather than a power. Practically speaking, the distinction is of little importance.

64 *Asante-Mensah*, above note 11.

65 *Ibid.*

66 Section 26.

67 Section 25(4).

68 Section 28.

69 [1997] 2 SCR 13 [*Feeney*]. In *Feeney*, the Court held that the common law requirements for entry into a dwelling house to effect an arrest were simply that the officer had reasonable grounds to believe that the person sought was within the premises; proper announcement was made; the officer believed reasonable grounds for the arrest existed; and reasonable grounds for the arrest did exist

of those common law rules have now been overridden by statute.[70] In essence, the judicial pre-authorization requirement that applied to entry to conduct a search now also applies to entry to effect an arrest.

Peace officers are now required to obtain specific authorization on an arrest warrant if they wish to enter a dwelling house in order to effect the arrest. The person issuing the warrant must be satisfied on reasonable grounds that the person to be arrested will be present in the dwelling house. In addition, the officer executing the warrant must have grounds to believe that the person to be arrested is present immediately before entering the dwelling house.[71] Similarly, a separate warrant that simply authorizes peace officers to enter a dwelling house can be issued if an arrest warrant already exists, or the person can be arrested without warrant.[72] In either case, the warrant can include any conditions the judge or justice feels are advisable to ensure that the entry is reasonable under the circumstances.[73]

A peace officer can enter without a warrant in exigent circumstances, which include situations where the officer has reasonable grounds to believe that the entry is necessary to prevent imminent harm or death to some person, or is necessary to prevent the imminent loss or destruction of evidence relating to an indictable offence. Even then, however, warrantless entry is allowed only where there are reasonable grounds to believe that the person is in the house and the conditions for obtaining a warrant exist but the exigent circumstances make it impracticable to obtain a warrant.[74] In assessing the practicability of obtaining a warrant,

---

on an objective basis. These requirements amounted to little more than having grounds for arrest and reasonably believing the person was in the dwelling house, though the Court also suggested that, before forcing entry, police should have requested and been refused admission (paras 24 and 26). The Court held that privacy interests, of increasing importance with the introduction of the *Charter*, were not adequately respected by these rules.

70 See Renee M Pomerance, "Parliament's Response to *R v Feeney*: A New Regime for Entry and Arrest in Dwelling Houses" (1998) 13 *Criminal Reports* (5th) 84, and Robert W Fetterly & Daniel A MacRury, "Arrest of Persons in Dwelling-House (*Feeney* Warrants—The First Three Years)" (2001) 45 *Criminal Law Quarterly* 101 (Part I) and (2001) 45 *Criminal Law Quarterly* 360 (Part II), for discussion of these provisions.

71 Section 529.

72 Section 529.1.

73 Section 529.2.

74 Section 529.3. See Heather Pringle, "Kicking In the Castle Doors: The Evolution of Exigent Circumstances" (2000) 43 *Criminal Law Quarterly* 86 for criticism of this provision. She argues, at 108, that it creates a "dangerous extension of the exigent circumstances doctrine as it has been generally understood in Canada." In particular, she notes that s 529.3 reverses *Feeney*, above note 69, on the question of whether potential loss of evidence can constitute exigent circumstances.

courts will need to have regard for section 529.5, which permits applications for entry warrants to be made by telephone or other means of telecommunications.

Normally, a peace officer entering a dwelling house to effect an arrest must first announce her presence. However, the *Code* does sometimes permit an officer who is lawfully entering, either with or without warrant, to omit the prior announcement. The justice issuing the warrant must be satisfied on reasonable grounds that prior announcement would expose the peace officer or some other person to imminent bodily harm or death, or that prior announcement would lead to the imminent loss or destruction of evidence of an indictable offence. Even then, the peace officer executing the warrant (or entering in exigent circumstances without a warrant) must also have reasonable grounds to believe those same things immediately before entering without announcement.[75]

Although the *Code* explicitly permits warrantless entry only in exigent circumstances, there is also a common law exception in the case of hot pursuit. This exception was specifically held in *Feeney* to be justified despite the new rules required by the *Charter*. "Hot pursuit" refers to situations where there is "continuous pursuit conducted with reasonable diligence, so that pursuit and capture along with the commission of the offence may be considered as forming part of a single transaction."[76] There is no strict requirement that the officers personally witnessed the offence, although clearly the definition requires a connection approaching that. In such cases, entry without a warrant is justified on a number of grounds, including that the offender should not be rewarded for having fled or be encouraged to do so, that a person who is fleeing the police will not have his "domestic tranquility" interrupted by the entry, and that it might not be possible to identify the offender later if she is not arrested immediately. The hot pursuit exception is not limited to indictable offences but applies more broadly, including to provincial offences.[77] It remains unsettled as to whether there is a requirement of prior announcement when an officer in hot pursuit enters to arrest.

---

75 Section 529.4. Interestingly, although the judge or justice issuing the warrant is required to have reasonable grounds to believe, in relation to either ground, the officer is required to have only reasonable grounds to *suspect* imminent bodily harm or death, though the standard of reasonable belief applies to the loss of evidence. Normally, suspicion is taken to be a lower standard than belief, and this is perhaps intended to be justified here because of the greater consequences flowing from the risk of bodily harm than from the risk of lost evidence.

76 *R v Macooh*, [1993] 2 SCR 802 at 817 [*Macooh*], quoting from Roger E Salhany, *Canadian Criminal Procedure*, 5th ed (Aurora, ON: Canada Law Book, 1989) at 44.

77 *Macooh*, above note 76.

E. RIGHTS ARISING ON ARREST

The word "rights" in this context is used broadly to include not only those rights guaranteed by the *Charter* on arrest, but also statutory provisions that apply once an arrest has occurred and that offer protection to an accused.

1) Statutory Protections

As noted above, the *Code* provisions that deal with compelling appearance try to balance state concerns with respect for the accused's liberty interest. The *Criminal Code* sets out several obligations on the part of police following an arrest. Generally speaking, these provisions reflect the principles of restraint and attempt to limit the use of coercive police powers to the extent possible. An example, though minor, is section 503(4), which requires an officer who has arrested a person in order to prevent the commission of an offence to release the accused unconditionally once that justification no longer exists.

Several of these provisions mirror section 495(2), discussed above, and its approach of creating an arrest power, but provide guidelines around when not to use it. As discussed in Chapter 6, section 497 calls upon an officer who has arrested a person for an offence listed in section 495(2)(a), (b), or (c) to release that person on an appearance notice or summons unless grounds similar to those in sections 495(2)(d) and (e) apply. Section 498 imposes a similar duty, with similar limitations on the officer in charge of the place where an arrested person is placed in custody. When neither the arresting officer nor officer in charge releases the accused, section 503 comes into play. That section requires that an arrested person be taken in front of a justice of the peace without unreasonable delay to consider the issue of release.[78]

Other specific rights arise with respect to young persons who are arrested. Section 25 of the *YCJA*[79] gives a young person the right to counsel on arrest, which, of course, is already guaranteed by section 10(b) of the *Charter* (see the discussion below). In addition, the *YCJA* requires that notice of the arrest be given to a parent of the young person. Further, specific statutory rules about interrogations of a young person after arrest provide that any statement is not admissible where the

---

78   See the more complete discussion of s 503 and of judicial interim release in Chapter 6.

79   *YCJA*, above note 44.

young person was not given the chance to contact counsel and a parent, or was not given the opportunity to have either or both present.[80]

2) *Charter* Rights Arising on Arrest

Section 10 of the *Charter* creates specific guarantees arising on arrest. Indeed, those rights arise on either arrest or detention, and so are relevant in that latter context as well. As a result, a person who is subject to an investigative detention is also entitled to the rights in section 10.[81]

Unlike section 8, which has had significant impact on the rules regarding searches and how they are to be conducted, the impact of section 10 has largely been to add additional requirements to the information to be given to an accused at the time of an arrest. There has also been an impact on the procedures followed afterward to facilitate actual contact by the accused with counsel. Most of this caselaw developed fairly early under the *Charter*, and section 10 now has a relatively settled jurisprudence.[82]

Section 10(a) provides that an accused is to be informed promptly of the reasons for the arrest or detention. The Court held in *R v Evans* that this right "is founded most fundamentally on the notion that one is not obliged to submit to an arrest if one does not know the reasons for it."[83] This section has provided less protection than it might, however. The test focuses on what the accused can be reasonably supposed to have understood, rather than on any precise words used.[84] In itself, that need not be objectionable, but it has been applied in a way with the potential to weaken the right. In *R v Latimer*, for example, the police decided not to arrest the accused and told him that he was being

---

80   *Ibid*, ss 146(2)(c) and (d).

81   *R v Suberu*, 2009 SCC 33. See the discussion in Chapter 5, Section C(1).

82   One particular issue that (surprisingly) remains unsettled is whether s 10 applies in the case of arrests not made by peace officers. In *Lerke*, above note 30, the Alberta Court of Appeal held that when one private citizen arrests another, *Charter* rights arise. Specifically, in that case, the right against unreasonable search and seizure was at issue. In contrast, in *R v J(AM)* (1999), 137 CCC (3d) 213, the British Columbia Court of Appeal decided that *Charter* rights did not arise on a citizen's arrest. In *Asante-Mensah*, above note 11, the Supreme Court of Canada noted the issue, but found that they were not required to address it: see para 77.

83   *Evans*, above note 28 at 886–87.

84   *Ibid* at 888. See, for example, *R v Mohamed*, 2014 SCC 63, aff'g 2013 ABCA 406, in which, during what began as a routine traffic stop, the officer told the accused that she smelled marijuana and asked him whether any was in the car: this was taken to be sufficient to convey that the officer was beginning a criminal investigation into an offence involving marijuana.

"detained for investigation" instead. That is, the police consciously purported to take the accused into custody on a basis not legally available (since no such power to detain for investigation existed) and offered that false explanation to the accused. The Court, nonetheless, relied on *Evans* to find that the accused knew he was in an extremely grave situation with regard to his daughter's death and, therefore, there was no section 10(a) violation.[85]

Similarly, in *R v Smith* (1991), the practical impact of section 10(a) was reduced. In that case, the accused was told that he was under arrest in connection with a shooting incident, but he was not told that the victim had died. The Crown conceded that section 10(a) had been violated, but relied on the accused's subsequent waiver of the right to counsel. The Court agreed, holding that, even if the accused was not aware of the specific charge, he had sufficient information to know the extent of his jeopardy, and therefore his waiver of counsel was valid despite the section 10(a) violation.[86]

Although allowing an accused to decide whether to submit to an arrest is described as the primary reason for section 10(a), from the start it has been acknowledged that a secondary reason is linked to the right to counsel in section 10(b): "[a]n individual can only exercise his section 10(b) right in a meaningful way if he knows the extent of his jeopardy."[87] This aspect of section 10(a) has received attention in cases where an accused is originally arrested for one reason, but the reason for her continued detention then changes. The Court has held that it can be necessary to re-advise the accused so that he can consider again whether to seek legal advice.[88] It is to section 10(b) that we now turn.

Section 10(b) guarantees the right "to retain and instruct counsel without delay and to be informed of that right." The Court has noted that this protection is provided because the effective assistance of counsel is seen as crucial in our society, and, indeed, the right to it is a principle of fundamental justice.[89] The purpose of the right, the Court has said, is to provide an accused with an opportunity to be informed of her rights and obligations and to obtain advice on exercising those rights and fulfilling those obligations. In particular, upon the arrest

---

85   *Latimer*, above note 10 at para 31.

86   *Smith* 1991, above note 28.

87   *Black*, above note 28 at 152–53.

88   *Borden*, above note 28; *Smith* 1991, above note 28; *Evans*, above note 28; *Black*, above note 28.

89   See *Lavallee, Rackel & Heintz v Canada (Attorney General); White, Ottenheimer & Baker v Canada (Attorney General); R v Fink*, [2002] 3 SCR 209; *R v GDB*, 2000 SCC 22.

the accused has been deprived of liberty and may need legal assistance in regaining it. Equally, or even more important, the accused is at risk of self-incrimination and is in need of legal advice, particularly advice about the right to silence and how to exercise it.[90]

In practice, section 10(b) is effectively restricted to that purpose; that is, it was argued that a guaranteed right "to retain and instruct counsel" ought to include more than an initial consultation with counsel before being interrogated—it ought also to guarantee the assistance of counsel *during* the interrogation. The Court, however, concluded that this was not so. Rather, "an initial warning, coupled with a reasonable opportunity to consult counsel when the detainee invokes the right, satisfies s 10(b)."[91] In some circumstances, an accused might become entitled to a further opportunity to contact counsel mid-interrogation, but that is the extent of the right (see the discussion in Section E(2)(b), below in this chapter).

Note that, like all *Charter* rights, the rights arising in section 10(b) are subject to the reasonable limits clause in section 1. In most cases, a failure to comply with one of the aspects of the right to counsel will not be saved under section 1, which makes *Charter* rights subject to "such reasonable limits *prescribed by law* as can be demonstrably justified in a free and democratic society."[92] The emphasized phrase requires that, if a *Charter* violation is to be saved, the police must have been given, either by statute or common law, the power to override the *Charter* right in question. Most commonly, if a police officer fails to give sufficient information to an accused about contacting counsel or some other aspect of section 10(b), that failure is not prescribed by law—it is simply an oversight. Therefore, section 1 analyses arise only infrequently with regard to the right to counsel, since they are typically settled at this relatively straightforward step, prior to getting into any difficult balancing of what sorts of limits are justifiable in a free and democratic society.

However, it is possible for a statute to prescribe a limit on section 10(b), like any other right, and in those cases the courts must consider whether the limit is justified. Accordingly, it has been determined that statutory limits that prevent an accused from having access to counsel prior to blowing into a roadside screening device or performing roadside sobriety tests can be justified.[93]

---

90   *R v Bartle*, [1994] 3 SCR 173 at 191 [*Bartle*]; *R v Manninen*, [1987] 1 SCR 1233 at 1242–43 [*Manninen*]. See also *Grant*, above note 50 at para 28.

91   *R v Sinclair*, 2010 SCC 35, [2010] 2 SCR 310 at 311 [*Sinclair*].

92   *Charter*, s 1 [emphasis added].

93   *R v Thomsen*, [1988] 1 SCR 640; *R v Orbanski*; *R v Elias*, 2005 SCC 37.

In a typical case where section 10(b) rights have not been limited by section 1, however, various obligations have been imposed on the police at the time of the arrest or detention. The Court has divided these into "informational" and "implementational" obligations,[94] and it is convenient to discuss them under those headings.

a) Informational Duties

Most obviously, section 10(b) specifically sets out the requirement that an accused must be informed of the right to retain and instruct counsel without delay. Police officers normally fulfill this duty by reading to the accused a "standard caution" which is distributed to them. This caution is intended to be as instructive and clear as possible, but in most cases, the police are not required to take any steps other than reading the caution to be sure that the accused has actually understood the right. Where special circumstances do exist, however, the police must take additional steps to be sure that the accused comprehends the right. Such special circumstances could include language difficulties, a known or obvious mental disability, or any genuine inability to comprehend the right on the part of the accused.[95] Conversely, exceptional circumstances can also justify delaying compliance with these informational duties.[96]

Other information must also be included in the standard caution. The police must give the accused information about access to counsel free-of-charge for persons who meet the financial criteria set by provincial legal aid plans. In addition, the accused should be given information about access to immediate temporary legal advice, irrespective of financial status.[97] In the latter case, the accused should also be told how to gain access to the service, for example, by telling the accused that he will be given the telephone number for duty counsel if he so wishes.[98] However, police compliance with the duty to inform an arrested person of how to gain access is determined with regard to the circumstances of the case. In *Latimer*, for example, the Court held that there was no

---

94   *Bartle*, above note 90.

95   *Evans*, above note 28; *Bartle*, above note 90.

96   *R v Mian*, 2014 SCC 54. In *Mian* the Court declined to decide whether protecting the integrity of a separate investigation would justify not immediately informing an accused of the reasons for his arrest (thereby complying with s 10(a)) or allowing contact with counsel (thereby complying with s 10(b)). On the facts, it had not been shown that the separate investigation into drug trafficking that had occasioned the stop of the accused would have been jeopardized by giving him his s 10 rights.

97   *R v Brydges*, [1990] 1 SCR 190.

98   *Bartle*, above note 90 at 195. See also *R v Pozniak*, [1994] 3 SCR 310.

section 10(b) violation when the police did not give the accused the telephone numbers for either the duty counsel scheme in the province or the local legal aid office. They held that the former service was not available to the accused since it operated only outside normal business hours and that the telephone number for the latter service was easily available by looking in the phone book.[99] The Court did stress, though, that more may be required of the police in other cases.

Although the police must inform an accused of any existing duty counsel scheme in the province, the Court held in *R v Prosper* that section 10(b) does not impose an obligation on provinces to have such a scheme.[100] Practically speaking, however, while formally refusing to create such a requirement, the Court left provinces with little realistic alternative. Relying on an implementational duty, discussed below, the Court held that, although there need not be a duty counsel scheme, police must hold off from attempting to gain incriminatory evidence from an accused who expresses the wish to contact counsel.[101] This holding would mean, for example, that police frequently could not administer breathalyzer tests unless a duty counsel system was in place. As a matter of fact, Nova Scotia, the province from which *Prosper* arose and which at the time lacked a duty counsel scheme, implemented one in the wake of that decision.

Because the purpose of the right to counsel is to allow an accused to be protected against self-incrimination, an accused should be rewarned of the right if there is a substantial change in the circumstances affecting the accused's degree of jeopardy. Failure to rewarn in such situations might violate section 10(b), as well as section 10(a).[102] In addition, if an accused who initially indicates a desire to speak to counsel later indicates he has changed his mind, the police have an obligation to rewarn that person of his right to a reasonable opportunity and also to inform him of their obligation to hold off from eliciting evidence.[103]

The police also must not act to undermine the right, by making disparaging comments about counsel's loyalty, commitment, availability,

---

99 *Latimer*, above note 10.

100 [1994] 3 SCR 236 [*Prosper*].

101 *Manninen*, above note 90.

102 *R v Paternak*, [1996] 3 SCR 607. The failure to rewarn would be a violation of the informational duties, but in addition, a violation of implementational duties would also arise, since the police would also have been obliged to facilitate the accused's renewed contact with counsel. See the discussion in Section E(2)(b), below in this chapter.

103 *Prosper*, above note 100. This obligation, generally referred to as a "*Prosper* warning," was reaffirmed by the Court in *R v Willier*, 2010 SCC 37 [*Willier*].

or the amount of legal fees, for example.[104] Similarly, offering a one-time-only plea bargain with a time limit that expires before an accused will be able to reach counsel is a section 10(b) violation. The Crown or police should offer any plea bargain to the accused's lawyer or to the accused with counsel present, unless there has been an express waiver of counsel. This is a requirement in all cases, not simply in those where the offer has an expiration date.[105]

Finally, note that the informational aspects of the section 10(b) right arise in every arrest. In contrast to the implementational requirements discussed below, all accused, whether they have expressed an interest in learning more about duty counsel or any other aspect of the right, are to be given all the information noted above.[106]

b) Implementational Duties

In addition to informing an accused of the right to counsel, two further correlative duties can arise on arrest.

First, where an arrested person has indicated a wish to speak to counsel, the police must provide that person with a reasonable opportunity to do so. In *R v Manninen*, for example, the accused was arrested at a private business, and the Court found that there was no reason that the police could not have allowed him to use the telephone in that office, rather than wait until they returned to the police station. The accused was not required to ask to use the telephone; the obligation to facilitate contact with counsel meant that the police should have offered him its use. A police officer is not required to offer his own cell phone to an accused, but nonetheless has a duty to provide phone access as soon as practicable, in order to reduce the possibility of accidental self-incrimination.[107] The question will always be situation-dependent, and the onus will be on the Crown to show that a private phone conversation was not reasonably feasible in the circumstances.[108] In situations of urgency facilitating contact might temporarily be postponed, but otherwise the obligation should be complied with.[109] A rea-

---

104 *R v Burlingham*, [1995] 2 SCR 206 at 221 [*Burlingham*].

105 *Ibid* at 230. One might think of these aspects of the right to counsel as implementational rather than informational, but the Court speaks of them as the latter. Classifying them as informational does, in the Court's analysis, make them less easily subject to waiver: see Section E(2)(b), below in this chapter.

106 *Bartle*, above note 90. See the discussion of waiver of s 10(b) rights, below in this chapter.

107 *R v Taylor*, 2014 SCC 50 at para 28.

108 *Ibid* at para 34.

109 *Manninen*, above note 90.

sonable opportunity to consult with counsel includes the right to do so in private, whether privacy is specifically requested or not.[110] Subject to the issue of reasonable diligence, discussed below, this right also includes the opportunity to contact the counsel of one's choice.[111] An emerging issue is whether the reasonable opportunity should include Internet access as a means of finding counsel.[112]

Second, when an arrested person has requested counsel, the police must hold off from questioning or otherwise seeking to elicit evidence from that person until she has had a reasonable opportunity to contact counsel. Thus, in *Manninen*, it was fairly clear that there was a section 10(b) violation when the police immediately questioned the accused and paid no attention to his expressed wish to speak to counsel. Equally, it meant there had been a violation in *R v Ross*, where the accused was required to participate in a lineup after having been unable to reach his counsel at 2 a.m. In that case, the Court held that it was unsurprising that counsel could not be reached at that hour, that there was no urgency or other compelling reason to conduct the lineup immediately, and, therefore, that the police were required to hold off.[113] As noted above, this duty to hold off also prevents the police from conducting breathalyzer tests without first giving the accused the reasonable opportunity to consult with counsel.[114]

These implementational duties differ in an important regard from the informational ones, however, in that they are not quite so firmly guaranteed. This is true in three separate, but related ways: they do not arise for every accused, they can be waived, and they can be lost through a lack of reasonable diligence.

First, the implementational duties arise only when an accused has indicated a wish to speak to counsel. Unless there is evidence that suggests the accused did not understand the right to counsel, then the onus is on the accused to prove that he asked to speak to counsel but was denied the right, or that he was denied any opportunity even to ask to speak to counsel.[115] This qualification is distinct from the informational components of the right, all of which must be told to all accused whether they request information about, for example, legal aid or not.[116]

---

110 *R v Playford* (1987), 61 CR (3d) 101 (Ont CA).

111 *R v Ross*, [1989] 1 SCR 3 at 10–11 [*Ross*]; *Willier*, above note 103.

112 See, for example, *R v McKay*, 2014 ABQB 70.

113 *Ross*, above note 111.

114 *Prosper*, above note 100.

115 *R v Baig*, [1987] 2 SCR 537.

116 *Bartle*, above note 90.

Second, implementational duties and informational duties are treated differently when considering waiver. The latter virtually cannot be waived. A valid waiver requires that an accused have full knowledge of the right she is giving up. A person who has not yet received all the informational components of the right to counsel is therefore not in a position to waive the right.[117] Accordingly, even if an arrested person indicates that he does not want to hear the information in the standard caution, that will not normally be a valid waiver and the police have an obligation to inform him nonetheless. Before the police can choose to forgo the obligation, it would not only be necessary for the person to have said that he understands the right to counsel, but there would also need to be reasonable grounds to believe that the claim was correct.[118]

In contrast, implementational duties can be waived. Most simply, an arrested person could explicitly decline to contact counsel after being given the opportunity to do so. Implicit waivers are also possible, though the standard is high and the waiver, though implicit, must be clear and unequivocal.[119] In particular, cooperating with the investigation by answering questions or participating in a lineup will not constitute a waiver.[120]

Finally, implementational duties can be lost. If an arrested person "is not being reasonably diligent in the exercise of his rights," then the correlative duties from *Manninen* are not a bar to the police continuing their investigation nonetheless.[121] This rule was laid down in *R v Tremblay*, a case where the trial judge found that the accused was actively obstructing the investigation, and the evidence suggested that he was using the right to counsel as a means of stalling a breathalyzer test. Even so, the Court found a section 10(b) violation in his case, though in *obiter* they created the "reasonable diligence" rule and did not exclude the breathalyzer evidence under section 24(2). Lack of reasonable diligence does not lead to a complete loss of section 10(b) rights. The arrested individual still has the right to speak to counsel. However, the police are no longer obliged to hold off their investigation until the arrested person has had a chance to do so. This is the case even if

---

117 *Ibid* at 204.
118 *Ibid* at 206. The Court offers the example of a person who, after having already spoken to duty counsel, is rewarned of the right to counsel because of a change in circumstances during questioning. In such a case, it might not be necessary to tell the person once again of the existence of duty counsel.
119 *R v Clarkson*, [1986] 1 SCR 383 at 394–95 [*Clarkson*], quoting *Korponay v Attorney General of Canada*, [1982] 1 SCR 41.
120 *Manninen*, above note 90; *Ross*, above note 111.
121 *R v Tremblay*, [1987] 2 SCR 435 at para 9 [*Tremblay*].

a person who has lost the right through lack of reasonable diligence subsequently reiterates the wish to speak to counsel.[122]

Because the accused is entitled to contact counsel of choice, the police must hold off from questioning until she has had a chance to do so. However, "reasonable diligence" is to be interpreted in context in such a case. That is, at this point the accused needs only preliminary advice, which raises simpler issues than choosing counsel for trial. Accordingly, at some point reasonable diligence will oblige the accused to speak to someone other than his counsel of choice.[123] If an accused does agree to speak with some other lawyer (duty counsel, for example) and obtains advice, then the implementational duty has been complied with and the accused no longer has a right to wait to speak to counsel of choice.[124]

Given the particular facts of *Tremblay* it is unfortunate that the Court chose to describe the accused's obstructionist behaviour as a lack of reasonable diligence. The real complaint in *Tremblay* seemed to be that the accused was asserting his *Charter* right not because he had any real interest in it, but as an improper means of avoiding responsibility. That objection is consistent with a purposive approach to the *Charter* and to the approach taken to other rights.[125] But phrasing the concern, in an understated way, as a lack of reasonable diligence has led to an expansion of the standard: a change to the detriment of all arrested persons. The result is to make the argument against the existence of the *Charter* rights plausible in a much wider range of cases.[126] In *Smith*, for example, the accused was arrested at 7 p.m. and, after several stops en route, he asked to call counsel at 9 p.m. upon arriving at the police

---

122 *R v Smith*, [1989] 2 SCR 368 [*Smith* 1989].

123 *Ross*, above note 111: *Willier*, above note 103.

124 *Willier, ibid; R v McCrimmon*, 2010 SCC 36 [*McCrimmon*].

125 In the context of disclosure, for example, the Court has required that an accused who is aware of undisclosed information must actively seek it out. An accused cannot choose to have her *Charter* right to disclosure violated so that she can then seek a remedy: see the discussion in Chapter 8. Similarly, in cases that deal with the right to a trial within a reasonable time, the Court's analysis has tried to prevent giving a remedy to an accused who does not genuinely want a prompt trial, but actually wants a *Charter* s 11(d) violation and a remedy therefore: see *R v Morin*, [1992] 1 SCR 771.

126 In *Prosper*, above note 100, it can hardly be surprising that the Court found the accused had been reasonably diligent when he made fifteen phone calls, all unsuccessful, to all twelve legal aid lawyers on the list given to him by the police. He was not also required "to call at random lawyers listed in the Yellow Pages late on a Saturday afternoon and plead for free or cut-rate legal advice": *Prosper* at para 56. In making this decision, however, the Court rejected the argument that had succeeded in the Court of Appeal.

station. After being given a telephone book he decided not to call because only his lawyer's office number was listed, and he did not expect that his lawyer would be in the office at that time. The court split 4:3 as to whether the accused had complied with the reasonable diligence standard, with the majority finding that he had not. It is difficult not to think that a different decision would have been reached had the Court asked itself whether the accused was only pretending to assert his *Charter* rights as a way of obstructing the investigation.[127]

The rule that an implicit waiver of *Charter* rights must be clear and explicit is not, at a theoretical level, easily reconciled with the view that no implementational duties arise unless an accused requests counsel and that an accused must be reasonably diligent in exercising the right. All three are ways of deciding that the accused does not benefit from the implementational duties, but they set different standards for deciding the issue. The fact that silence would not be a clear and explicit waiver leads to the conclusion that the arrested person was entitled to the implementational duties. But silence would be a failure to request counsel, or a failure of reasonable diligence, which leads to the conclusion that the arrested person was not entitled to the implementational duties. Silence, or other ambiguous behaviour on the part of an accused, allows courts to apply either of the conflicting lines of authority, with conflicting results.[128]

In conclusion, it is worth noting several things that are *not* part of the police's implementational duties. First, a person who has been arrested and has already spoken with counsel (or has waived the right) may then be questioned by the police. Even if the person later indicates that he does not wish to speak with the police, no duty is imposed on the police to stop their questioning. The person is not required to answer questions, but that does not mean the police are not entitled to ask them.[129]

---

127 *Smith* 1989, above note 122.

128 See, for example, *R v Hollis* (1992), 17 CR (4th) 211 (BCCA). This situation is particularly odd when one considers that a waiver must be considered in light of all the circumstances. To say "I know my rights" is not a valid waiver of the informational components. If an accused says, "I don't want a lawyer," that waiver cannot be taken at face value, and courts must decide whether the arrested person had a true understanding of the consequences: *Clarkson*, above note 119. The anomalous result is that there is greater protection under s 10(b) for an accused who expressly waives the right than for one who says nothing. See Stephen Coughlan, "When Silence Isn't Golden: Waiver and the Right to Counsel" (1990) 33 *Criminal Law Quarterly* 43.

129 *R v Singh*, 2007 SCC 48. The decision analyzes this question as an aspect of s 7 and the right to silence, but the analogy to s 10(b) is noted.

Second, it was held in *R v Sinclair* that the fact a person being questioned wants to talk to counsel again does not, by itself, automatically trigger an obligation on the part of the police to allow such contact.[130] It is only in certain changed circumstances that such an obligation will arise. Such changed circumstances include the use of new procedures involving the accused (for example, a lineup[131]); a change in the jeopardy facing the accused (for example, the death of an assault victim[132]); or, reason to believe that the first caution provided was deficient (because, for example, the police have acted to undermine it[133]). Revealing evidence to the accused (real or false) is not sufficient, and the changed circumstances must be objectively observable in order to trigger additional implementational duties for the police.[134] Courts tend to look to whether the suggested change was foreseeable or not at the time of the initial consultation with counsel as a significant factor in deciding whether a new consultation is required.[135]

Finally, the police are not expected to "look behind" the fact that an accused has had an opportunity to consult with counsel and try to assess the adequacy of that advice. If an accused person speaks with counsel (seemingly however briefly), then the police are entitled to assume that they have fulfilled their section 10(b) obligations. They have no obligation to ensure that the advice received was adequate, and unless the accused "diligently and reasonably" indicates that the advice was inadequate, the police are entitled to assume that she is satisfied with the exercised right to counsel and to commence their interrogation.[136]

---

130 *Sinclair*, above note 91.
131 *Ross*, above note 111.
132 *Black*, above note 28.
133 *Burlingham*, above note 104.
134 *Sinclair*, above note 91 at para 55.
135 See, for example, *R v TGH*, 2014 ONCA 460, where the accused was confronted with a general warrant requiring him to submit to an unusual physical examination eleven months after his arrest: the *Sinclair* rule did not apply because counsel could not have been expected to anticipate such an order and give the appropriate advice. On the other hand, in *United States of America v 'Isa*, 2014 ABCA 256, the accused was given the opportunity to consult with counsel when he was arrested by the RCMP, but was not given a second opportunity when he was questioned by US authorities. This was found to be acceptable because the possibility of the second questioning was known to counsel during the first consultation.

Accused have had some success, at least at the trial level, in obtaining a second consultation with counsel when they had initially sought to speak to counsel of choice but had ended up speaking with duty counsel: see, for example, *R v Laverdiere*, 2014 ABQB 68; *R v Soomal*, 2014 ONCJ 220; or *R v WS*, 2014 ONSC 3144.
136 *Willier*, above note 103 at para 42.

This rule applies even if the charge is serious and the consultation with counsel has been only a matter of minutes.[137] However, although the brevity of contact alone will not support a claim that the right to counsel was denied due to the inadequacy of the advice received, there seems still to be room for the argument that brevity coupled with other factors (the age and sophistication of the accused, whether the police were helpful generally, and so on) might amount to a section 10(b) violation.[138]

FURTHER READINGS

COUGHLAN, STEVE. "When Silence Isn't Golden: Waiver and the Right to Counsel" (1990) 33 *Criminal Law Quarterly* 43.

———. "Whither—or Wither—Section 9" (2008) 40 *Supreme Court Law Review* (2d) 147.

———. "Citizen's Arrest, Property Owners, and Private Fiefdoms" (2014) 18 *Canadian Criminal Law Review* 1.

———, & GLEN LUTHER. *Detention and Arrest* (Toronto: Irwin Law, 2010).

FETTERLY, ROBERT W, & DANIEL A MACRURY. "Arrest of Persons in Dwelling-House (*Feeney* Warrants—The First Three Years) (Part I)" (2002) 45 *Criminal Law Quarterly* 101.

———. "Arrest of Persons in Dwelling-House (*Feeney* Warrants—The First Three Years) (Part II)" (2002) 45 *Criminal Law Quarterly* 360.

GORLEWSKI, ALEX. "*R. v. Loewen* and Reasonable Grounds for Arrest: The Supreme Court's Overlooked Advice" (2012) 94 *Criminal Reports* (6th) 319.

LAW REFORM COMMISSION OF CANADA. *Arrest* (Report 29) (Ottawa: Law Reform Commission of Canada, 1986).

---

137 In *Willier, ibid*, the accused was charged with murder and had two telephone conversations with duty counsel, one three minutes long and the other one minute. In *McCrimmon*, above note 124, the accused was charged with a series of assaults and had a one-minute conversation with duty counsel. In *Sinclair*, above note 91, the accused was charged with murder and had two three-minute phone conversations with his lawyer.

138 See the pre-*Willier* decision of the British Columbia Court of Appeal in *R v Osmond*, 2007 BCCA 470. Distinguishing *Osmond*, however, see also *R v Ashmore*, 2011 BCCA 18.

PACKER, HERBERT L. *The Limits of the Criminal Sanction* (Stanford: Stanford University Press, 1968).

POMERANCE, RENEE M. "Parliament's Response to *R v Feeney*: A New Regime for Entry and Arrest in Dwelling Houses" (1998) 13 *Criminal Reports* (5th) 84.

PRINGLE, HEATHER. "Kicking In the Castle Doors: The Evolution of Exigent Circumstances" (2000) 43 *Criminal Law Quarterly* 86.

STRIBOPOULOS, JAMES. "Unchecked Power: The Constitutional Regulation of Arrest Reconsidered" (2003) 48 *McGill Law Journal* 225.

———. "The Forgotten Right: Section 9 of the *Charter*, Its Purpose and Meaning" (2008) 40 *Supreme Court Law Review* (2d) 211.

CHAPTER 8

DISCLOSURE AND PRODUCTION

A. INTRODUCTION

For many years, no effective right to disclosure of the Crown's case existed in Canada. Practice with regard to disclosure varied from court to court, and even from prosecutor to prosecutor. Despite calls for comprehensive disclosure schemes from the Law Reform Commission of Canada,[1] no statutory scheme was introduced. The problems that could arise from non-disclosure were made dramatically clear in the investigation of the wrongful conviction of Donald Marshall Jr, leading that Royal Commission to point to the need for consistent disclosure.[2] In general terms, that state of affairs changed in 1991 with the Supreme Court of Canada decision in *R v Stinchcombe*, which concluded that an accused person had a right, under section 7 of the *Canadian Charter of Rights and Freedoms*, to disclosure of the Crown's case.[3] The exact contours of this right have continued to be developed in subsequent caselaw, although *Stinchcombe* remains the leading case establishing the general principle. The Supreme Court has summarized the current state of affairs with regard to disclosure:

---

1   Law Reform Commission of Canada, *Discovery in Criminal Cases* (Ottawa: Law Reform Commission of Canada, 1974), and *Disclosure by the Prosecution* (Ottawa: Law Reform Commission of Canada, 1984).

2   Nova Scotia, Royal Commission on the Donald Marshall, Jr, Prosecution, *Commissioners' Report: Findings and Recommendations*, vol 1 (Halifax: Royal Commission on the Donald Marshall, Jr, Prosecution, 1989).

3   [1991] 3 SCR 326 [*Stinchcombe*].

The Crown must disclose all relevant information to the accused, whether inculpatory or exculpatory, subject to the exercise of the Crown's discretion to refuse to disclose information that is privileged or plainly irrelevant. Relevance must be assessed in relation both to the charge itself and to the reasonably possible defences. The relevant information must be disclosed whether or not the Crown intends to introduce it in evidence, before election or plea. Moreover, all statements obtained from persons who have provided relevant information to the authorities should be produced notwithstanding that they are not proposed as Crown witnesses. This Court has also defined the concept of "relevance" broadly . . . .[4]

As the law has subsequently developed, however, other schemes governing when the accused is entitled to have access to particular types of material have developed. *Stinchcombe* established a regime concerning "disclosure" that governs the Crown's first party obligation to give to the accused material in its possession. Subsequently, the Court was called upon to consider in what circumstances an accused ought to be entitled to material that is in the hands of third parties, not the Crown, which is referred to as "production." Production is governed by two regimes: the Court initially created rules around disclosure with its decision in *R v O'Connor*,[5] but in many circumstances, that scheme has been displaced by a statutory one. That statutory scheme is sometimes referred to as the "*Mills* Regime," after the case that found the provisions constitutional.[6] Finally, with its decision in *R v McNeil* the Court laid down rules that it characterized as a means of "bridging the gap between first party disclosure and third party production."[7] This chapter will consider all of these regimes.

B. DISCLOSURE

1) Creation of the Right: *R v Stinchcombe*

In *Stinchcombe*, the Court found a duty on the part of the Crown to disclose its evidence to the accused. The Court rejected a number of arguments against disclosure. It pointed out that the Crown's role is not to obtain a conviction but to lay all relevant evidence before the court. Any

---

4   *R v Taillefer; R v Duguay*, 2003 SCC 70 at para 59 [*Taillefer*] [page references omitted].
5   [1995] 4 SCR 411 [*O'Connor*].
6   *R v Mills*, [1999] 3 SCR 668 [*Mills*].
7   2009 SCC 3 [*McNeil*].

information in the hands of the Crown is therefore not a tool to convict the accused, but the property of the public to be used to ensure that justice is done. The Court also rejected the suggestion that Crown workloads would be increased by an obligation to disclose. It noted, as the Law Reform Commission studies found, that increased disclosure leads to an increase in cases settled, guilty pleas entered, and charges withdrawn, thereby decreasing Crown and court workloads. The Court acknowledged that some risk to informers may come from disclosure, but determined that this affects only the manner and timing of disclosure, not the general principle. The Court also acknowledged that disclosure may allow an accused to tailor a defence to anticipate the prosecution's case, but held, nonetheless, that fairness to the accused requires that the accused see the evidence in advance.

This latter point is the most important in the Court's reasoning. Although policy arguments led them to conclude that routine disclosure is a desirable feature of the criminal justice system, it is the *Charter*, and in particular, the accused's right under section 7 to make full answer and defence, that is the mechanism by which that end is achieved. The Court concludes that "there is a general duty on the part of the Crown to disclose all material it proposes to use at trial and especially all evidence which may assist the accused even if the Crown does not propose to adduce it."[8]

The fact that this right is guaranteed by the *Charter* has been significant in much of the Court's later reasoning. For example, it means that the right potentially has application in any context where section 7 applies, not simply in domestic trials. In *Canada v Khadr* the Court found that the applicant (who was detained by the United States in Guantanamo Bay but had been interrogated there by Canadian officials) was entitled to disclosure of the material gathered by Canada. The more difficult issue was whether the *Charter* applied at all given the extraterritorial nature of the investigation. Once it was found that it did, however, section 7 imposed a disclosure obligation.[9]

2) Structure of the Right

First, the structure of the right as set out in *Stinchcombe* should be described. Whether evidence appears to be inculpatory or exculpatory

---

8   *Stinchcombe*, above note 3 at 338, quoting from *R v C(MH)* (1988), 46 CCC (3d) 142 (BCCA). See the discussion of *Canada (Justice) v Khadr*, 2008 SCC 28 [*Khadr*] in Chapter 3, Section B(2)(a).

9   *Khadr*, *ibid*. The Court also held at para 32 that the scope of that disclosure might differ from that in a domestic trial and would depend on the nature of Canadian authorities' involvement.

is irrelevant to the obligation to disclose. The Crown is required to disclose on the request of the accused, made any time after a charge is laid. Disclosure ought to be made prior to election or plea, so that the accused can take the disclosed material into account in making a decision on those issues. The material to be disclosed includes all witness statements, whether the Crown intends to call the witness or not, and notes or "will say" statements where no actual statements exist. If there are no notes, the Crown should disclose the name, address, and occupation of a witness and any information the prosecution possesses concerning the evidence that person might give. In later cases the duty to disclose has been described as "triggered whenever there is a reasonable possibility of the information being useful to the accused in making full answer and defence."[10]

The "first party" disclosure obligation includes both the Crown prosecutor and the police.[11] However, this is only true of the police to the extent that they are investigating the offence with which the accused is charged.[12] The obligation to disclose is a continuing one, and the Crown must disclose any additional information it receives. Equally, the defence has a continuing obligation to seek disclosure and is not entitled to assume that it has received all relevant information.[13] Where, following a review of disclosure by the trial judge, circumstances have changed, the appropriate approach for the Crown is to reapply to the trial judge concerning the issue, rather than to fail to disclose and argue the issue on appeal.[14]

The right to disclosure is not absolute. The Crown is obliged to err on the side of inclusion, but "it need not produce what is clearly

---

10   *R v Dixon*, [1998] 1 SCR 244 at para 21 [*Dixon*].

11   See *McNeil*, above note 7 at para 14: "the investigating police force, although distinct and independent from the Crown at law, is not a third party. Rather, it acts on the same first party footing as the Crown."

12   *R v Quesnelle*, 2014 SCC 46 at para 11 [*Quesnelle*]:

   For purposes of this "first party" disclosure, "the Crown" does not refer to all Crown entities, federal and provincial: "the Crown" is the prosecuting Crown. All other Crown entities, including police, are "third parties". With the exception of the police duty to supply the Crown with the fruits of the investigation, records in the hands of third parties, including other Crown entities, are generally not subject to the *Stinchcombe* disclosure rules.

   See also *McNeil*, above note 7, and the discussion in Section D, below in this chapter.

13   *Dixon*, above note 10 at para 55. These two rules are to a certain extent contradictory and will, no doubt, give rise to disputes in practice: see the discussion of the need for due diligence by defence counsel in Section B(3)(b), below in this chapter.

14   *R v Khela*, [1995] 4 SCR 201 at para 10 [*Khela*].

irrelevant."[15] Similarly, the rules of privilege interact with the Crown's obligation to disclose. It may be necessary, for example, to protect the identity of informers—this does not permit the Crown to refuse disclosure, but gives them some discretion with regard to the timing and manner.[16] Further, the need to complete an investigation may justify the Crown in delaying some disclosure.[17] The obligation to disclose evidence does not include a requirement that the Crown make its witnesses available for oral discovery.[18]

The Court has distinguished between evidence known to exist but which has not been disclosed, and evidence whose existence is in dispute. In the former case, the burden clearly rests with the Crown to justify the non-disclosure of the evidence "by demonstrating either that the information sought is beyond its control, or that it is clearly irrelevant or privileged."[19] In the latter case, however, the Crown cannot be expected to justify the non-disclosure of evidence of which it is unaware or which it denies exists. In such circumstances, therefore, the defence is first required to show some basis that will allow the trial judge to conclude that potentially relevant further material exists.[20] The right to disclosure is not meant to allow fishing expeditions on the part of the defence, and so does not, for example, require the Crown to disclose whether the accused has been the subject of a wiretap unrelated to the charges laid.[21]

The rule of full disclosure, and its reliance on the accused's right to full answer and defence, has been applied in more specific contexts. In *R v Egger*,[22] for example, the Court was required to consider section 258(1) (d) of the *Criminal Code*, which allows the Crown to rely on a certificate of a qualified technician as proof of the concentration of alcohol in the accused's blood, as determined from an analysis of a blood sample. That section requires that the Crown have taken two samples of the accused's blood, one to be provided to the accused on request for analysis. However, the section does not explicitly require that the accused be given notice of the existence of the sample. The Court noted that "one measure of

15   *Stinchcombe*, above note 3 at 339.
16   Where the level of disclosure has already been reviewed by a court and an order made, however, the Crown no longer has discretion over the issue: see *Khela*, above note 14 at para 14, and the further discussion of this issue below.
17   *Stinchcombe*, above note 3 at 339.
18   *Khela*, above note 14 at para 18.
19   *R v Chaplin*, [1995] 1 SCR 727 at para 25.
20   *Ibid* at para 30.
21   *Ibid*.
22   [1993] 2 SCR 451.

the relevance of information in the Crown's hands is its usefulness to the defence: if it is of some use, it is relevant and should be disclosed."[23] The various possible uses noted included "meeting the case for the Crown, advancing a defence or otherwise in making a decision which may affect the conduct of the defence such as, for example, whether to call evidence."[24] Accordingly, it concluded that the Crown was required to inform the accused of the existence of the sample, and to do so at a time when the accused can usefully act on the information.

Similarly, in *R v Durette*[25] the Court held that the same principles apply in the context of wiretap applications:

> Apart from public interest concerns which may operate in a particular case, I see no reason why an accused should not be entitled to see exactly what the judge saw who relied on the affidavits to issue the authorization. Disclosure of the full affidavit should be the starting premise. Anything less potentially impairs an accused's ability to make full answer and defence and must be justified by the Crown in accordance with established principles. Editing of these affidavits is best viewed as a necessary evil.[26]

The existence of the right to disclosure has also affected the Court's analysis in other areas. In *R v Cook*,[27] for example, the Court concluded that the Crown had no obligation to call witnesses in order for all material facts to be brought forward. Given the accused's right to disclosure, the Crown's decision not to call a witness will not prejudice an accused. If the Crown decides not to call a witness whose testimony has changed from an earlier statement, for example, the accused will have received the earlier statement and will be entitled to the later one, due to the Crown's ongoing obligation to disclose.

Further, the Court has concluded that the Canadian Security Intelligence Service (CSIS) has, in the security certificate context, a duty to disclose similar to that in *Stinchcombe*. Although CSIS investigations are not criminal matters and do not lead to charges, seeking a security certificate with regard to a named person has serious implications for the liberty and security of the person concerned. These consequences include detention for an indefinite period or expulsion from the country. Accordingly, section 7 of the *Charter* is brought into play, and there is a duty to disclose. The exact nature of that disclosure obligation is

---

23   *Ibid* at para 20.
24   *Ibid*.
25   [1994] 1 SCR 469 [*Durette*].
26   *Ibid* at 495, quoting Doherty JA in the court below.
27   [1998] 2 SCR 597.

not, however, identical to that in the criminal context. The Canadian Security Intelligence Service is required to retain all the information it uncovers and to disclose it to the ministers and the judge hearing the security certificate application. That judge is required to exclude any evidence that might pose a threat to national security and summarize the remaining evidence for the named person.[28]

3) Remedy for Breach of What Right: Disclosure or Full Answer and Defence?

The Court noted in *Stinchcombe* that the Crown's discretion with regard to disclosure can be reviewed by the trial judge if defence counsel disagrees with the way in which it has been exercised. In such a review, the onus would rest with the Crown to justify an exception to the rule of complete disclosure. Quite apart from issues of review by the trial judge, however, an issue which has frequently arisen is the effect of non-disclosure and the remedy that should flow from it. In *Stinchcombe*, the Court found that the accused might have conducted his defence differently by calling a particular witness, and that calling that witness could have affected the outcome of the trial. Accordingly, it ordered a new trial. Later cases have pursued the issue of remedy more fully, finding that, in some circumstances, a stay of proceedings is the appropriate remedy for non-disclosure. The most important cases since *Stinchcombe* to have discussed the issue of remedy are *R v Carosella*,[29] *R v La*,[30] *R v Dixon*,[31] and *R v Bjelland*.[32]

The Court has not been entirely consistent in its analysis of which *Charter* right is at issue when the Crown has failed to disclose relevant information. The earlier cases that considered this issue looked at whether disclosure was itself an independent *Charter* right or whether it was just an aspect of the right to full answer and defence. This seemed at first to matter on the assumption that one could proceed directly to the question of remedy once a breach of some *Charter* right had been found. As the Court's jurisprudence has developed, however, it has become apparent that, although disclosure is said to be a *Charter* right in its own right, no remedy will be given for that breach unless it also amounts to a breach of the right to full answer and defence.

---

28   *Charkaoui v Canada (Citizenship and Immigration)*, 2008 SCC 38. The Court also found that the CSIS policy of destroying their operational notes was invalid and that they had a duty to retain them when engaged in a targeted investigation.
29   [1997] 1 SCR 80 [*Carosella*].
30   [1997] 2 SCR 680 [*La*].
31   Above note 10.
32   2009 SCC 38 [*Bjelland*].

a) The Original Position: Remedy for Non-disclosure

Carosella[33] dealt with an accused charged with gross indecency. Before contacting the police, the complainant had visited a rape crisis centre and been interviewed by a social worker, who took notes of the conversation. The accused later applied for production of the records, but by that time they had been destroyed (the centre had a policy of shredding files where there was police involvement before they were served with any application for production). The Court, therefore, had to determine whether the non-disclosure of the notes violated the accused's *Charter* rights and, if it did, whether a stay was the appropriate remedy.[34]

The first issue the Court needed to address, therefore, was exactly what *Charter* right was in play. The issue was whether disclosure is, in itself, a right implicit in section 7, or whether section 7 protects the accused's right to full answer and defence, one aspect of which is the need for disclosure. The Ontario Court of Appeal had held that disclosure was simply an aspect of the right to full answer and defence, a conclusion that L'Heureux-Dubé J, dissenting in the Supreme Court, agreed with. There was some justification for taking this view. In the earlier *R v O'Connor*[35] decision, a majority had supported a portion of L'Heureux-Dubé J's judgment, in which she stated:

> the right of an accused to full disclosure by the Crown is an adjunct of the right to make full answer and defence. It is not itself a constitutionally protected right. What this means is that while the Crown has an obligation to disclose, and the accused has a right to all that which the Crown is obligated to disclose, a simple breach of the accused's right to such disclosure does not, in and of itself, constitute a violation of the *Charter* such as to entitle a remedy under s 24(1).[36]

---

33   Above note 29.

34   *Carosella*, *ibid*, ought strictly to be a production case rather than a disclosure one, and, indeed, L'Heureux-Dubé J argued in dissent that the rules around disclosure had nothing to do with the case since the files were never in the control of the Crown. The majority analyzed the issue primarily around the test for disclosure on the basis that "it is clear that the file would have been disclosed to the Crown. As material in the possession of the Crown, only the *Stinchcombe* standard would have applied" (para 41). On the issue of a remedy in such circumstances generally, see Paul Calarco, "What Happens When Evidence Has Not Been Recorded? Staying Charges to Ensure a Fair Trial" (2001) 44 *Criminal Law Quarterly* 514.

35   *O'Connor*, above note 5.

36   *Ibid* at para 74, citing the British Columbia Court of Appeal decision (1994), 89 CCC (3d) 109 at 148–49. Until *Carosella*, above note 29, was handed down, there was no reason to think that the majority in *O'Connor*, who agreed with the portion of L'Heureux Dubé J's reasons in which this appeared, did not also ascribe to this particular passage. Courts of appeal had assumed it to be the

The difference between the two possibilities is most important because of the effect it will have on the need for an accused to show prejudice arising from the non-disclosure. If the right in question is the right to full answer and defence, then non-disclosure may not harm the accused in a particular case. For instance, the accused's ability to make full answer will not be affected by failure to disclose inculpatory information that does not form part of the Crown's case. However, if the accused has a *Charter* right to disclosure, then the non-disclosure of any information will automatically constitute a breach of that right. There will be no need to consider the actual effect of the non-disclosure on the accused. As L'Heureux-Dubé J had further noted in *O'Connor*:

> . . . the nondisclosure of information which ought to have been disclosed because it was relevant, in the sense there was a reasonable possibility it could assist the accused in making full answer and defence, will not amount to a violation of the accused's section 7 right not to be deprived of liberty except in accordance with the principles of fundamental justice unless the accused establishes that the nondisclosure has probably prejudiced or had an adverse effect on his or her ability to make full answer and defence.[37]

However, the majority in *Carosella* reached the opposite conclusion on both issues. They concluded that breach of the obligation to disclose "is a breach of the accused's constitutional rights without the requirement of an additional showing of prejudice . . . the breach of this principle of fundamental justice is in itself prejudicial."[38] In the particular circumstances in *Carosella*, it followed that "if the material which was destroyed meets the threshold test for disclosure or production, the appellant's *Charter* rights were breached without the requirement of showing additional prejudice."[39]

However, prejudice would remain relevant at the stage of determining remedy on this analysis. Remedies range, the Court notes, from adjournments to a stay of proceedings.[40] In *Carosella*, while reaffirming the principle that a stay should be granted only in the clearest of cases, the majority concluded that it was the appropriate remedy. In general,

---

majority position in the interim: see Graeme Mitchell, "*R. v. Carosella*: Difficult Cases Make Dangerous Law" (1997) 4 *Criminal Reports* (5th) 209.

37 *O'Connor*, above note 5.

38 *Carosella*, above note 29 at para 37.

39 *Ibid* at para 40.

40 *Ibid* at para 26. Other cases have found that costs can be an appropriate remedy: see, for example, *R v Lee*, [1996] OJ No 1276 (Gen Div); *R v SVL*, [1995] OJ No 2867 (Prov Div); and *R v Dix*, [1998] AJ No 419 (QB).

stays can be justified on either of two bases: (1) where prejudice to the accused cannot be remedied, or (2) where there would be irreparable prejudice to the integrity of the justice system if the prosecution were continued.[41] The majority concluded that both tests were met in this case. First, the Court noted the significance of the evidence destroyed, the trial judge's conclusion that it "would more than likely have assisted the accused in his defence,"[42] and the absence of any alternative remedy to cure this prejudice. Alternatively, the majority concluded, a stay could be justified because of the deliberate decision of an agency that receives government funds to destroy documents ("conduct designed to defeat the processes of the court").[43]

Carosella was a much discussed decision, and many people felt that the Court's obvious annoyance at the rape crisis centre's policy affected its reasoning too greatly.[44] It certainly is not clear that later decisions are easily reconciled with *Carosella*, but at the same time the Court has continued to frame the discussion in the terms set out there.

b) The Current Position: Remedy for Failure of Full Answer and Defence

La,[45] decided only shortly after *Carosella*, reaffirms the principle that disclosure is an independent right guaranteed by section 7 of the *Charter*, not merely an aspect of the right to full answer and defence. However, in its actual result, it diminishes the significance of that principle.

In *La*, a police officer tape-recorded an interview with the complainant in a sexual assault case at a time prior to any charges being laid. The complainant was a thirteen-year-old runaway, and the interview was conducted in connection with a secure treatment application. By the time the accused came to trial, the police officer had lost the forty-five-minute tape, though he did testify that the complainant told a few lies on it. The trial judge held that the non-disclosure of the tape impaired the accused's ability to cross-examine the complainant and entered a stay of proceedings. On the face of it, the argument for a stay appears to be at least as strong as in *Carosella*. The accused did not receive disclosure, which alone constitutes a violation of section 7

---

41 *Carosella*, above note 29 at para 51, quoting from *O'Connor*, above note 5.
42 *Carosella*, *ibid* at para 53, quoting the trial judge.
43 *Ibid* at para 56.
44 See Mitchell, above note 36; David Paciocco, "In Defence of *R. v. Carosella*: The Continuing Need for Prejudice" (1997) 4 *Criminal Reports* (5th) 199; Stephen G Coughlan, "Developments in Criminal Procedure: The 1996–97 Term" (1998) 9 *Supreme Court Law Review* (2d) 273.
45 Above note 30.

without a showing of prejudice. The argument for prejudice is stronger here, in any case, since the evidence was a tape recording of the complainant herself, and it was known that she had lied in the interview. In *Carosella*, in contrast, the missing material was only another person's notes, and the complainant had consented to their production of the missing material and indeed was upset that they had been destroyed. There was less reason in *Carosella* to think that the missing material was of any use to the accused.

Nonetheless, what the majority found in *La* was that the accused's section 7 right was not violated at all. Despite best efforts on the part of the police, the Court found that evidence will sometimes be lost. Where the Crown can show that the evidence was not lost due to unacceptable negligence, the majority stated, the duty to disclose is not breached. It will still be possible for the accused's right to full answer and defence to be breached. However, this will be the case only if the accused can establish actual prejudice.[46] In this particular case, the majority held that the tape was relevant enough to meet the standard for disclosure in *Stinchcombe*, but fell short of establishing a serious impairment of the right to make full answer and defence.[47]

In practical terms, this decision removes much of the effect of the finding in *Carosella* that disclosure is a right in itself. The major significance of that finding was that it removed the need for the accused to show prejudice in order to show a *Charter* breach. But if there is no breach of that right where the Crown can satisfactorily explain the failure to disclose, then breach of the right to disclosure becomes less important. In many cases, given *La*, the accused will have to show a breach of the right to full answer and defence, and so will need to show some prejudice from the non-disclosure.

This pulling away from the standard in *Carosella* can be seen clearly in *Dixon* and its companion cases.[48] Those cases arise from a set of complex facts, in which a number of accused were charged with assault in circumstances where there were many witnesses and many different accounts of what had occurred. None of the defence counsel had received copies of statements from four witnesses, although the pre-trial disclosure they had received included other information from which one could infer that these four people were potential witnesses. During the trial several of the defence counsel became aware of the undisclosed statements, but decided, based on summaries, not to re-

---

46   *Ibid* at para 25.
47   *Ibid* at para 33.
48   *Dixon*, above note 10; *R v McQuaid*, [1998] 1 SCR 285; *R v Robart*, [1998] 1 SCR 279; *R v Smith*, [1998] 1 SCR 291 [*Smith*]; *R v Skinner*, [1998] 1 SCR 298 [*Skinner*].

quest copies of the statements themselves. Only after the trial was over did the defence counsel review the statements. Although two of the statements contained nothing relevant, the other two contained information that, while not of enormous significance, met the *Stinchcombe* threshold and should have been disclosed. The Court was therefore faced with a slightly new twist from that of *Carosella* or *La*. In those cases, it was known during the trial that there was undisclosed information. In *Dixon*, the failure to disclose did not become apparent until after the trial. This difference in timing is relevant both to whether there is a *Charter* breach and to the remedy to be granted. The case is therefore interesting both for how it shows the Court coping with the role of prejudice and for its approach to a remedy.

In *Carosella*, the Court had held that disclosure was an independent right guaranteed by section 7 and that prejudice was not relevant to whether that right had been breached—prejudice was relevant only at the remedy stage. Thus, in *Carosella*, the Court moved directly to determining a remedy after deciding the right to disclosure was breached. In *Dixon* the Court, in large measure, undid the main effects of having made disclosure an independent right. The Court held that "the right to disclosure is but one component of the right to make full answer and defence. Although the right to disclosure may be violated, the right to make full answer and defence may not be impaired as a result of that violation."[49]

Subsequently in *R v Taillefer; R v Duguay*, without adverting to the previous dispute over the issue, the Court held:

> Infringement of that right [disclosure] is not always an infringement of the right to make full answer and defence. There are situations in which the information not disclosed will meet the minimum test set out in *Stinchcombe* while having only marginal value to the issues at trial. To determine whether there is an infringement of the right to make full answer and defence, the accused will have to show that there was a reasonable possibility that the failure to disclose affected the outcome at trial or the overall fairness of the trial process.[50]

In each of these latter two cases, it was only after finding a breach of the right to full answer and defence that the Court considered remedy. Thus, the Court has changed the approach in *Carosella* to a three-part test: (1) Was the accused's right to disclosure breached? (2) If so, did that breach violate the accused's right to make full answer and

---

49   *Dixon*, above note 10 at para 31. On *Dixon*, generally, see Graeme G Mitchell, "R. v. Dixon: The Right to Crown Disclosure—A Roadmap for the Future" (1998) 13 *Criminal Reports* (5th) 260.

50   *Taillefer*, above note 4 at para 71 [references omitted].

defence? (3) If so, what remedy should be granted? Given this approach, it remains technically true, as stated in *Carosella*, that disclosure is an independent right and that it is not necessary to show prejudice to establish a breach of that right. However, as no consequences will attach to a breach of the right to disclosure alone, then in this context, the major consequences of those findings will have disappeared.

Dixon does not change the *Stinchcombe* standard for disclosure, and so the first question incorporates those rules. To decide whether the breach of disclosure affected full answer and defence, the Court set out a two-prong test. The accused must show a reasonable possibility that (1) the non-disclosure affected the outcome at trial or (2) it affected the overall fairness of the trial process.[51] The first prong of this test asks whether there is a reasonable possibility that the additional evidence could have created a reasonable doubt in the jury's mind.[52] The second prong considers whether the undisclosed evidence could have been used to impeach the credibility of a prosecution witness, or could have assisted the defence in its pre-trial investigations and preparations or in its tactical decisions at trial.[53]

With regard to both factors, the burden imposed on the accused is only that of showing a "reasonable possibility." That is, the question is not whether undisclosed evidence *would* have made a difference, only whether it *could* have.[54]

In assessing the first prong, whether undisclosed evidence could have affected the decision to convict, a court must look at the evidence as a whole and not at each undisclosed piece of information individually.[55] In *Dixon*, the Court decided that although the statements were relevant, they contained only relatively insignificant inconsistencies that could not affect the decision to convict. In *R v Smith*, in contrast, there was a reasonable possibility that one of the statements could have affected the outcome, since the witness said he did not see Smith hit anyone. The Court therefore ordered a new trial. Similarly, in *Taillefer* and *R v Illes* the defence could have used undisclosed evidence to challenge the credibility of important Crown witnesses, or to present an alternative theory about how the crime was committed.

The second prong of the *Dixon* test can overlap with the first prong. In *Illes*, for example, the same undisclosed evidence might have affected the jury's decision had it been used to cross-examine a Crown

---

51   *Dixon*, above note 10 at para 34. See also *Taillefer*, above note 4.
52   *Taillefer, ibid* at para 82; *R v Illes*, 2008 SCC 57 at para 25 [*Illes*].
53   *Illes, ibid* at para 27; *Dixon*, above note 10 at para 36.
54   *Illes*, above note 52 at para 25.
55   *Taillefer*, above note 4 at para 92ff.

witness, but equally could be seen to have affected the fairness of the trial because the accused did not have the opportunity to conduct that cross-examination. The second prong, however, considers different issues. The failure to disclose evidence might, for example, affect a tactical decision such as whether to call evidence at trial—specifically the testimony of the witness whose evidence had not been disclosed.[56]

With regard to the fairness of the trial process, the Court stressed in *Taillefer* that the standard is only that of "reasonable possibility." In other words, a judge should not try to assess the evidence and decide whether it would have affected a jury's deliberations. It is sufficient that there be a reasonable possibility it would have done so for the fairness of the trial process to be affected.

The most significant factor relating to the "fairness of the trial" prong discussed in *Dixon* and its companion cases is due diligence on the part of defence counsel. In those cases, defence counsel knew or should have known, the Court said, of the possible undisclosed evidence. Upon becoming aware of the statements, the Court said, it is surprising that defence counsel did not request them. The Court concluded that "defence counsel is not entitled to assume at any point that all relevant information has been disclosed to the defence. Just as the Crown's disclosure obligations are ongoing, and persist throughout the trial process, so too does defence counsel's obligation to be duly diligent in pursuing disclosure."[57] More simply, at a certain point defence counsel was faced with a choice: "call for the statements or live without them."[58]

Carosella and later cases are not entirely consistent with one another, but a general consensus appears by confining *Carosella* to its own facts: *Dixon* sets out the general approach to disclosure, while *La* establishes the rules for the special case of "lost evidence."

With regard to the issue of remedy, note that the complaint about non-disclosure in *Dixon* (as in other cases such as *Taillefer* or *Illes*) arose after the trial was completed. In such circumstances, the minimum remedy likely to be "appropriate and just" under section 24(1) of the *Charter* will be an order for a new trial. Where the non-disclosure is discovered before the trial is completed, the remedy is very likely only to be an order for disclosure accompanied by an adjournment.[59]

The Supreme Court has allowed for the possibility of something more than disclosure and an adjournment, but they have severely circumscribed that possibility. In *Bjelland* they acknowledged the availability of

---

56   See, for example, *Illes*, above note 52, or *Skinner*, above note 48.
57   *Dixon*, above note 10 at para 55.
58   *Ibid*.
59   *Ibid* at para 31.

an order for exclusion of evidence under section 24(1) where non-disclosure is discovered mid-trial, but only in exceptional circumstances: (1) where the late disclosure renders the trial process unfair and the unfairness cannot be remedied by disclosure and an adjournment, or (2) where exclusion is necessary to maintain the integrity of the justice system.[60] The first circumstance might be met where the evidence is disclosed only after important and irrevocable decisions about how to conduct the defence have been made. The second might be met where an adjournment would significantly prolong the period of time an accused is held in custody pending the conclusion of the trial. In either instance, the Court placed the burden on the accused to show why exclusion was necessary and why disclosure and an adjournment would not be sufficient.[61]

4) Conflicting Protections: Disclosure and Privileged Information

The final point worth discussing in relation to disclosure is its interaction with the laws of privilege. Because the obligation to disclose is not absolute, "the Crown may justify non-disclosure in circumstances where 'the public interest in non-disclosure outweighs the accused's interest in disclosure.'"[62] Indeed, in *Stinchcombe* the Court stated that the right to disclosure was subject to the rules of privilege. In particular, noteworthy cases have considered informer privilege, solicitor–client privilege, and national security privilege.[63]

a) Informer Privilege
Informer privilege is a long-standing common law rule, reiterated by the Court in *Bisaillon v Keable*[64] and other cases since. It arises when,

---

60 *Bjelland*, above note 32 at para 24. Exclusion of evidence is normally considered under the *Charter*, s 24(2). The Court notes, however, that that subsection deals with excluding evidence that has been "obtained" by a *Charter* breach. Where the *Charter* breach is a s 7 violation due to failure to disclose, that subsection is not relevant and so the remedy must come (if at all) from s 24(1).

61 *Bjelland*, *ibid*, was a 4:3 decision of the Court with a vigorous dissent written by Fish J. The decision has been criticized as being too restrictive: see Paul Calarco, "*R. v. Bjelland*: No Effective Remedy for Crown Failure to Disclose" (2009) 67 *Criminal Reports* (6th) 219.

62 *Michaud v Quebec (Attorney General)*, [1996] 3 SCR 3 at para 47, quoting from *Durette*, above note 25.

63 For a discussion of other potential claims of privilege and their possible impact on an accused's right to disclosure, see Ian Carter, "Chipping Away at *Stinchcombe*: The Expanding Privilege Exception to Disclosure" (2002) 50 *Criminal Reports* (5th) 332.

64 [1983] 2 SCR 60 [*Bisaillon*].

in the course of an investigation, a peace officer guarantees protection and confidentiality to a prospective informer in exchange for useful information that would otherwise be difficult or impossible to obtain.[65] The identity of police informers is entitled to the highest level of protection, not only to protect the individuals concerned, but also to preserve that investigative method. If those with confidential information about crimes were not confident that their identities would be protected, they would be far less likely to report that information to the police.

This type of privilege is unlike, for example, Crown privilege, in which the court can decide in the individual case whether it is more important to protect the privilege or the integrity of the trial. Rather, it is more absolute and so a successful claim of informer privilege gives a trial judge

> no power of weighing or evaluating various aspects of the public interest which are in conflict, since it has already resolved the conflict itself. It has decided once and for all, subject to the law being changed, that information regarding police informers' identity will be, because of its content, a class of information which it is in the public interest to keep secret, and that this interest will prevail over the need to ensure the highest possible standard of justice.[66]

> The privilege belongs to the informer and the Crown jointly—the Crown cannot disclose the informer's identity without her consent, but equally the informer herself cannot unilaterally waive the privilege.[67]

Informer privilege is more than just a rule of evidence and is not limited to the courtroom,[68] and courts should enforce the privilege where it is applicable whether it is claimed or not.[69] It does not therefore follow, however, that an accused person is forbidden from making efforts outside the courtroom to determine who the informer is. Some such efforts might be improper if, for example, the purpose were to discover the identity of the informer in order to pressure the police into dropping charges: that could constitute the offence of obstruction of justice. However, discovering the identity of an informer can also play

---

65   *R v Basi*, 2009 SCC 52 at para 36 [*Basi*].
66   *Bisaillon*, above note 64 at 98. This point has been continually emphasized by the Court: see, for example, *Named Person v Vancouver Sun*, 2007 SCC 43 at paras 19–23 [*Named Person*]; *Basi*, above note 65 at paras 22 and 37; and *R v Barros*, 2011 SCC 51 at para 30 [*Barros*].
67   *Named Person*, above note 66 at paras 23–25.
68   *Barros*, above note 66 at para 30.
69   *Bisaillon*, above note 64 at 84 and 88; *Basi*, above note 65 at para 38.

a legitimate role in making full answer and defence, since some informers might not be credible. Accordingly, there is no general prohibition on defence investigations into the identity of an informer.[70]

At common law, the only derogation from the rule of informer privilege was the "innocence at stake exception." Only if the evidence establishes a basis for this exception, such as that "the informer is a material witness to the crime, acted as an *agent provocateur*,"[71] or planted the material found under a search warrant,[72] will identifying information be revealed.[73]

In *R v Leipert*, the Court concluded that this "ancient and hallowed" common law rule was unchanged by the obligation of disclosure established in *Stinchcombe*.[74] *Stinchcombe* had held that disclosure was subject to privilege, and the Court found no inconsistency between that rule and the common law rule of informer privilege.[75]

Indeed, the Court reaffirmed the importance of the common law rule, stressing its particular application in the case of anonymous informers through programs such as Crime Stoppers. The privilege extends not only to the name of the informer, but to any information that may enable identification. However, it is "virtually impossible for the court to know what details may reveal the identity of an anonymous informer."[76] As a result, judges should not try to edit a tip sheet and order the edited tip sheet disclosed. Rather, a judge should simply uphold informer privilege and not require any information to be disclosed. Only if the accused can establish some basis to conclude that without the disclosure the accused's innocence is at stake, should the trial judge review the tip sheet and potentially order the disclosure of some portion of it. Even then, the Crown has the choice of staying the proceedings rather than making the disclosure.[77]

All of this applies, of course, on the assumption that a claim of informer privilege has been established. That claim depends on a guarantee of protection and confidentiality having been given. Since that guarantee might have been given only implicitly, it can be necessary for a judge to determine whether a claim of informer privilege ought

---

70 *Barros*, above note 66.
71 [1997] 1 SCR 281 at para 22 [*Leipert*].
72 *Ibid* at para 26.
73 See the further discussion of the innocence at stake exception in Section B(4)(b), below in this chapter.
74 *Leipert*, above note 71 at para 9.
75 *Ibid* at para 25.
76 *Ibid* at para 28.
77 *Ibid* at para 33.

to be granted. Whenever the issue of informer privilege arises (either by being claimed or by the judge raising the issue), the judge should settle the question with an *in camera* "first stage" hearing. Because of the importance of this type of privilege, the first stage hearing must be conducted on the assumption that the privilege does exist. At this stage even the existence of the claim cannot be publicly disclosed, and ordinarily only the putative informant and the Crown can appear. In certain circumstances (for example, where the interests of the informant and the Crown are aligned), it might be appropriate to appoint an *amicus curiae*.[78] The privilege must be established on a balance of probabilities.[79]

The accused and defence counsel are not entitled to be present at this first stage hearing. In particular, defence counsel may not appear even if they undertake not to reveal any information to the client, and even if the client consents to that undertaking being made.[80] However, they should be excluded only to the extent necessary to protect the identity of the informant, and trial judges should adopt all reasonable measures to permit defence counsel to make meaningful submissions regarding what occurs in their absence. Reasonable measures might include inviting submissions on the scope of the privilege, allowing defence counsel to suggest questions to be put by the trial judge to any witness who will be called, or providing the defence with a redacted summary of the evidence taken in order to receive additional submissions on whether the privilege applies in the particular circumstances of the case.[81]

b) Solicitor–Client Privilege

Solicitor–client privilege is also an ancient and hallowed doctrine that has existed at common law for hundreds of years.[82] Protecting as it does the ability of an accused person to gain legal advice in confidence, it has been recognized as occupying a unique position of fundamental importance. Indeed, it has been classified as a principle of fundamental justice.[83] However, an accused's right to full answer and defence, of

---

78 The Court developed these guidelines in a rather unusual factual situation in *Named Person*, above note 66, but has subsequently relied on them in *Basi*, above note 65.

79 *Basi, ibid* at para 39.

80 *Ibid* at para 44. The Court held that defence counsel is outside the "circle of privilege" and therefore the privilege would be breached as soon as defence counsel knows, no matter what undertakings were given.

81 *Ibid*.

82 See, for example, the discussion in *Descôteaux v Mierzwinski*, [1982] 1 SCR 860; *R v Solosky*, [1980] 1 SCR 821.

83 2001 SCC 14 at para 41 [*McClure*].

which the right to disclosure is a part, is also a principle of fundamental justice. On occasion, it may be necessary for an accused to infringe another person's solicitor–client privilege in order to make full answer and defence. Neither principle will always prevail, and, therefore, in certain circumstances solicitor–client privilege will be required to give way.[84] Because of the importance of the privilege, though, that should occur only in limited, defined circumstances. The Court concluded in *R v McClure* that, just as with informer privilege, the obligation to disclose[85] arises only when the accused's innocence is at stake. In a later decision they summarized the proper approach:

> The *McClure* test comprises a threshold question and a two stage innocence at stake test, which proceed as follows:
> - To satisfy the threshold test, the accused must establish that:
>   – the information he seeks from the solicitor–client communication is not available from any other source; and
>   – he is otherwise unable to raise a reasonable doubt.
> - If the threshold has been satisfied, the judge should proceed to the innocence at stake test, which has two stages.
>   – Stage #1: The accused seeking production of the solicitor–client communication has to demonstrate an evidentiary basis to conclude that a communication exists that could raise a reasonable doubt as to his guilt.
>   – Stage #2: If such an evidentiary basis exists, the trial judge should examine the communication to determine whether, in fact, it is likely to raise a reasonable doubt as to the guilt of the accused.[86]

In dealing with the threshold test, the Court has generally adopted a stringent position, as is consistent with protecting solicitor–client privilege as much as possible. The initial question asks whether the information is available *in an admissible form* from some other source. If it is not, the test could effectively never be met (if the accused did not know in some fashion that potentially useful evidence existed in a solicitor's file, no application would ever be made).[87] However, it must be clear that the other sources of information are not merely potentially

---

84   *Ibid* at para 38.
85   Strictly, this will be a question of *production* of evidence from a third party, not *disclosure* of evidence in the hands of the Crown.
86   *R v Brown*, 2002 SCC 32 at para 4 [*Brown*].
87   Layton points out that, in most instances, the only people who are, in fact, likely to know of potentially exculpatory information protected by solicitor–client privilege are the other solicitor and client. See David Layton, "R. v. Brown:

inadmissible but genuinely unavailable. Thus, for example, if there is an issue as to whether other evidence may not be available because it is hearsay, a trial judge should first determine whether that evidence falls into any of the hearsay exceptions. The *McClure* application should be considered only after it has been decided that the other evidence is definitely unavailable.[88] If there is a possibility that the third party has effectively waived solicitor–client privilege, then that too should be decided first.[89] A *McClure* application is intended to be a last resort.

The accused must also be unable to prove innocence in any other way. Once again, this means that all sources of evidence against the accused must be decided first. A case based entirely on circumstantial evidence is the least likely to succeed, and so infringement of solicitor–client privilege is less likely to be needed. But, if the Crown might strengthen its case by calling a jailhouse informant to report an alleged confession by the accused, the privileged information might be more needed, and so the Crown should make that decision before the *McClure* application.[90]

Whether the accused can prove innocence in any other way also affects the appropriate timing for a *McClure* application. Usually a trial judge should postpone the application at least until the Crown has closed its case. If the Crown has not proven its case beyond a reasonable doubt at that stage, the *McClure* application is unnecessary. Even then the trial judge may postpone the application further until the defence has presented its case, to see whether a reasonable doubt has arisen in some other way. Further, a *McClure* application can be renewed at a later stage of the trial if the defence feels it is then clearer that the accused has no other way to prove innocence.[91]

The first step in the innocence at stake test requires the accused to provide only an evidentiary basis that a communication exists that *could* raise a reasonable doubt. Mere speculation that such evidence may exist will not suffice, since the test is not meant to authorize fishing expeditions. However, the standard cannot be too high, since the accused is unlikely to have very precise information about the communication.[92] If the evidence suggested to exist merely challenges credibility or raises a collateral matter, it is unlikely to pass this part of the threshold test.

Protecting Legal-Professional Privilege" (2002) 50 *Criminal Reports* (5th) 37, for a discussion of voluntary release of privileged information by a lawyer.

88   *Brown*, above note 86 at paras 44–45.
89   *Ibid* at para 45.
90   *Ibid* at para 50.
91   *Ibid* at paras 52–54.
92   *McClure*, above note 83 at para 52.

Where the first stage is passed, the trial judge should examine the record to determine whether there is useful evidence in it. At this stage, the higher standard, that the evidence *is likely to raise* a reasonable doubt about the accused's guilt, is applied:

> In most cases, this means that, unless the solicitor–client communication goes directly to one of the elements of the offence, it will not be sufficient to meet this requirement. Simply providing evidence that advances ancillary attacks on the Crown's case (e.g., by impugning the credibility of a Crown witness, or by providing evidence that suggests that some Crown evidence was obtained unconstitutionally) will very seldom be sufficient to meet this requirement.[93]

Nonetheless, the trial judge is not asking whether the evidence *will* raise a reasonable doubt, but merely whether it is likely to.[94]

In determining this question, the trial judge is not limited to the written materials in the file—the same principles govern solicitor–client communications whether they are oral or in writing. Accordingly, it is open to the trial judge to request that the solicitor providing the file also supply an affidavit stating that the file is a complete record or contains all other information necessary to complete the record.[95]

Evidence should not be disclosed from the file simply because it will strengthen the accused's case or it is more likely to be believed than other evidence. It cannot be released to corroborate other evidence the accused has led. The solicitor's file must be the *only way* for the accused to prove innocence.[96]

In deciding what information to disclose from the file, the trial judge should be similarly circumspect. The file should be edited to remove reference to any other offences or to other third parties, and only the information necessary to raise a reasonable doubt should be released.[97] Further, the information is to be released only to the accused, not to the Crown.[98] Finally, the person whose privilege is being

---

93 *Ibid* at para 58. Layton is critical of this aspect of the Court's decision, arguing that, although described as the "innocence at stake" exception, the real issue is whether reasonable doubt is at stake. Therefore, information going to a witness's credibility, to admissibility of evidence, or to a stay application could be regarded as equally worthy of disclosure. See David Layton, "*R. v. McClure*: The Privilege on the Pea" (2001) 40 *Criminal Reports* (5th) 19.

94 *McClure*, above note 83 at 59.

95 *Brown*, above note 86 at para 65.

96 *Ibid* at para 72.

97 *Ibid* at para 77.

98 *Ibid* at para 84.

infringed will enjoy use and derivative use immunity concerning the information released.[99]

c)   National Security Privilege

National security privilege, unlike informer or solicitor–client privilege, is created by statute, specifically by the provisions of the *Canada Evidence Act* (*CEA*).[100] The *CEA* requires anyone who is required to disclose or expects to disclose "sensitive information" to give notice to the Attorney General of Canada of the possibility and the proceeding in which it might occur.[101] Pending action by the Attorney General the person giving notice cannot disclose the information, nor indeed the fact that notice has been given. However, the Attorney General can authorize the disclosure of any or all of the information. Alternatively, if she does not wish to disclose the information, the Attorney General can apply to the Federal Court for an order. The Federal Court judge can decide whether to hold a hearing and to whom notice of any such hearing should be given; he may afford other people the right to make representations. If the judge is of the view that no injury to international relations, national defence, or national security would result, he may authorize disclosure. If such injury would result, the judge still may order disclosure, but only if the public interest in disclosure outweighs the public interest in non-disclosure. In such a case the disclosure can be subject to conditions and might take the form of the information itself, a summary of the information, or facts relating to the information. The judge may also order that notification of the decision be given to any person.

There is a limited right of appeal to the Federal Court of Appeal and beyond that to the Supreme Court of Canada.[102] More directly relevant, however, is a power given to the Attorney General of Canada when an order for disclosure has been made: despite that order, the Attorney General personally is, in those circumstances, entitled to issue a certificate prohibiting disclosure of the information.[103] In that event, notice of the certificate must be given to the judge presiding

---

99   *Ibid* at para 99.

100   RSC 1985, c C-5 (as amended) [*CEA*]. See, in particular, ss 38–38.16.

101   *Ibid*, s 38.01. "Sensitive information" is defined in s 38 as "information relating to international relations or national defence or national security that is in the possession of the Government of Canada, whether originating from inside or outside Canada, and is of a type that the Government of Canada is taking measures to safeguard."

102   *Ibid*, ss 38.09 and 38.1.

103   *Ibid*, s 38.13.

over the proceedings at which disclosure was proposed, every party to those proceedings, and others. That judge presiding at a criminal proceeding affected by such a certificate has the ability to make any order appropriate "to protect the right of the accused to a fair trial."[104] The *CEA* specifically contemplates that such orders might include dismissing specific counts, only allowing proceedings to continue on a lesser offence, or staying proceedings entirely.

This potential exception to disclosure is unusual in that the judge initially deciding whether material will or will not be disclosed to the accused is *not* the trial judge. The judge responsible for seeing to it that the accused's right to disclosure is respected has no direct control over the disclosure issue. Indeed, since the decision is made by a Federal Court judge, it will be made by a judge with no jurisdiction over criminal matters. Nonetheless, the Court held in *R v Ahmad* that, "properly interpreted,"[105] the scheme is constitutional, complying both with the division of powers in the *Constitution Act, 1867* as well as with the accused's right to disclosure under section 7 of the *Charter*.[106] It is the latter question that is relevant here.

A Federal Court judge has discretion under the *Canada Evidence Act* as to whether to give notice of the hearing to anyone. The Court concluded that the scheme had to be interpreted as requiring that, unless the Federal Court judge decides without a hearing that the information in question should be disclosed to the criminal court, there must be a hearing on the disclosure issues, and that notice of that hearing must be given to the criminal court. Similarly, absent compelling reasons to the contrary, the Federal Court judge should give notice of the proceedings to the accused as well.[107]

The scheme also authorizes disclosure to various parties on conditions. Given an accused's right to a fair trial and the trial judge's obligation to protect that right, the *CEA* scheme had to be interpreted as intending to make that possible. Accordingly, judges conducting a criminal trial had to be in a position to act judicially. This meant that a judge had to have enough information not only to see to it that an accused's right to a fair trial was not infringed, but also to see to it that prosecutions did not collapse unnecessarily. As such a trial judge ought to receive not

---

104 *Ibid*, s 38.14.
105 2011 SCC 6 at para 27 [*Ahmad*].
106 On these sections of the *CEA*, see, as well, *Canada (Attorney General) v Khawaja*, 2007 FCA 342.
107 The Court acknowledged that this did not immediately mesh well with the prohibition on giving notice of proceedings in s 38.02 but held that it was not necessary to pronounce in detail on that point in the case.

only notice that a hearing about non-disclosure of sensitive information is occurring, but some basis for understanding what that information is and how it might have an impact on the accused's trial. In some cases, a summary of the information might be sufficient while in other instances more extensive access will be required. In most cases, the Court held, disclosure of the information to the trial judge, on the condition that it not be revealed to the accused, will be the most appropriate option. The trial judge might also decide to hear submissions from Crown counsel or from a security-cleared special advocate on behalf of the accused in certain cases.

In the end, it will always remain up to the trial judge to decide whether an accused's right to disclosure has been adequately protected. If the trial judge concludes that it has not and that a stay of proceedings will therefore be necessary, the Crown should be notified. If further and better disclosure is not forthcoming, then a stay of proceedings will be the presumptively appropriate remedy.[108] A stay in such circumstances is contemplated by the statute and therefore need not meet the ordinary "clearest of cases" standard for a stay. It is this aspect of the statute, in effect, which allows the trial judge to protect the accused's right to disclosure even without the ability to govern disclosure:

> where the government is withholding information and the trial judge is unable to satisfy himself or herself that non-disclosure has not adversely affected trial fairness, and no lesser step or remedy can assure it, a stay of proceedings under s 38 must issue. Doubt, in this respect, should be resolved in favour of protecting the fair trial rights of the accused, including the right of full answer and defence.[109]

Thus, although trial judges are deprived of the ability to order disclosure, they do have the power to order a more drastic remedy.

C. PRODUCTION

1) Introduction

As noted in the introduction to this chapter, in addition to the Court-created disclosure regime dealing with material in the control of the Crown, there are also regimes governing an accused's right to access to material that is in the hands of third parties. The context that has driven

---

108 *Ahmad*, above note 105 at para 51.
109 *Ibid* at para 52.

the development of the law in this area is the issue of an accused's right to see psychiatric, medical, or other counselling records regarding a complainant, particularly complainants in a sexual assault trial.[110]

The reason special rules have been developed in this area is the presence of a competing concern to the accused's fair trial right, namely, the complainant's privacy right. This situation is therefore similar to the interplay between disclosure and privilege. However, it is different because the type of privilege concerned is not a "class privilege," as informer privilege and solicitor–client privilege are. Although a complainant has a privacy interest in counselling records, those records are not automatically subject to the same kind of blanket protection. Rather, any claim of privilege was originally based on a case-by-case analysis according to the Wigmore test for privilege.[111] The right to disclosure automatically yields to a class privilege, but individual analysis and the weighing of interests are necessary when dealing with case-by-case privilege.

In addition, other factors distinguish production from disclosure, beyond the greater privacy interest in the material sought to be disclosed. Third parties, who are in control of the records, have no obligation to assist the defence. Further, the records are not part of the case the accused has to meet. All of these factors mean that the accused

---

110   A great deal was written on the decisions handed down on this subject. See, for example, Lise Gotell, "When Privacy Is Not Enough: Sexual Assault Complainants, Sexual History Evidence and the Disclosure of Personal Records" (2005–2006) 43 *Alberta Law Review* 743; Jennifer Koshan, "Disclosure and Production in Sexual Violence Cases: Situating *Stinchcombe*" (2002) 40 *Alberta Law Review* 655; Lise Gotell, "The Ideal Victim, the Hysterical Complainant and the Disclosure of Confidential Records: A Case Study of the Implications of the *Charter* for Sexual Assault Law" (2002) 40 *Osgoode Hall Law Journal* 251 [Gotell]; Jamie Cameron, "Dialogue and Hierarchy in *Charter* Interpretation: A Comment on *R. v. Mills*" (2001) 38 *Alberta Law Review* 1051; Lise Gotell, "Colonization through Disclosure: Confidential Records, Sexual Assault Complainants and Canadian Law" (2001) 10 *Social and Legal Studies* 315; Karen Busby, "Third Party Records Cases since *R. v. O'Connor*" (2000) 27 *Manitoba Law Journal* 355; Peter Sankoff, "Crown Disclosure after *Mills*: Have the Rules Suddenly Changed?" (2000) 28 *Criminal Reports* (5th) 285; Don Stuart, "*Mills*: Dialogue with Parliament and Equality by Assertion at What Cost?" (2000) 28 *Criminal Reports* (5th) 275; Karen Busby, "Discriminatory Uses of Personal Records in Sexual Violence Cases" (1997) 9 *Canadian Journal of Women and the Law* 148; Heather Holmes, "An Analysis of Bill C-46, Production of Records in Sexual Offence Proceedings" (1997) 2 *Canadian Criminal Law Review* 71; Bruce Feldthusen, "Access to the Private Therapeutic Records of Sexual Assault Complainants" (1996) 75 *Canadian Bar Review* 537.

111   *McClure*, above note 83 at para 29.

faces a higher burden than normal in obtaining access to this material, although not as high a burden as when a class privilege is in issue.

As the law has developed, there are now two distinct sets of rules governing production. The first of these was created by the Court with its decision in *O'Connor*.[112] Subsequently a second regime was created when Parliament partly overrode the result in *O'Connor* with sections 278.1 to 278.9 of the *Criminal Code*. A proper understanding of the current state of the law, then, requires consideration of the Court's decision in *O'Connor*, the legislative response to that decision, and finally of *R v Mills*,[113] the Court's decision on a *Charter* challenge to the legislation.[114]

2) Production under *O'Connor*

In *O'Connor*, the accused was charged with several counts of sexual assault. He obtained a pre-trial order for disclosure of the complainants' entire medical, counselling, and school records. When the accused was unsuccessful in obtaining all these records, the trial judge entered a stay, eventually leading the Supreme Court to consider the question of the procedure to be applied when an accused seeks documents such as counselling records in the hands of a third party.

The Court created a two-stage process for deciding whether third-party records should be produced. At the first stage, the accused must persuade the judge to examine the records personally. At the second stage, having looked at the records, the judge is required to decide whether to release them or some portions of them to the accused. Most of the controversy has related to what factors should guide the decision at each stage.

A majority of five judges held that at the first stage, it was necessary to consider not just the accused's right to make full answer and defence, but also to weigh the third party's privacy interests in the balance.[115] The accused must show that the records are likely relevant. However, "likely relevance" in this context is a higher standard than

---

112 *O'Connor*, above note 5.

113 *Mills*, above note 6.

114 Layton observes that the number of standards applicable to third-party production is "ever-growing": simple materiality in many cases; the *O'Connor* test where constitutionally protected privacy interests are at stake; ss 278.1–78.91 where those interests arise in the context of a sexual assault trial; and the "innocence at stake" standard of informer privilege and solicitor–client privilege. See Layton, above note 93.

115 Provided the records were not already in the hands of the Crown. If that were the case, the majority held, the third party would no longer have a privacy interest.

the normal question of whether the information may be useful to the defence. Rather, the accused must satisfy the trial judge "that there is a reasonable possibility that the information is logically probative to *an issue at trial or the competence of a witness to testify.*"[116] While this standard is higher than normal, it is not to be interpreted as onerous, since the accused will have to make submissions to the judge without knowing what is in the record.[117] The majority suggested that evidence in counselling records may be relevant by containing information about the events underlying the charge, by revealing the use of a therapy influencing the complainant's memory of the events, or by bearing on the complainant's credibility.

The majority specifically rejected the minority's suggestion that at the first stage, in addition to showing likely relevance, the accused should also have to satisfy the trial judge that the salutary effects of producing the documents outweigh the deleterious effects. That question, according to the majority, is confined to the second stage.[118]

At the second stage, where the trial judge decides whether to order any portion of the record produced, all the judges agreed that a number of factors were relevant to the decision:

> (1) the extent to which the record is necessary for the accused to make full answer and defence; (2) the probative value of the record in question; (3) the nature and extent of the reasonable expectation of privacy vested in that record; (4) whether production of the record would be premised upon any discriminatory belief or bias [and] (5) the potential prejudice to the complainant's dignity, privacy or security of the person that would be occasioned by production of the record in question.[119]

Four of the nine judges, however, unsuccessfully argued that two further factors should be considered:

> "the extent to which production of records of this nature would frustrate society's interest in encouraging the reporting of sexual offences and the acquisition of treatment by victims" as well as "the effect on the integrity of the trial process of producing, or failing to produce, the record, having in mind the need to maintain consideration in the outcome."[120]

---

116 *O'Connor*, above note 5 at para 22 [emphasis in original].
117 *Ibid* at para 25.
118 *Ibid* at para 21.
119 *Ibid* at para 31.
120 *Ibid* at para 32.

The majority said that the former consideration was a relevant but not paramount consideration,[121] and that the second consideration was relevant only in deciding admissibility of the evidence, not in deciding whether the material should be produced for the accused.

O'Connor created a scheme which was intended to engage in the potentially difficult balancing between an accused's fair trial interests and the privacy interests of others. As noted, the context for that decision pitted a strong third-party interest against that of the accused—the privacy interest of a sexual assault complainant with regard to therapeutic records. As we will see in the following section, that privacy interest and most similarly strong ones have since been "pulled" from the *O'Connor* regime by a statutory scheme. As a result, the cases left to be analyzed under *O'Connor* are only those where the competing interest is likely to be much less compelling than the accused's fair trial interest. Subsequent caselaw has recognized that point.

The Court has concluded, for example, that once "likely relevance" is made out, it is unlikely that a third-party privacy interest can defeat an application for production. It is possible that some redactions might be made or conditions imposed to ensure that there is no unnecessary invasion of privacy, but the production claim is likely to succeed. In effect, once an application has passed the likely relevance stage, the distinction between production and disclosure collapses:

> It may be useful to pose the question in this way: If the third party record in question had found its way into the Crown prosecutor's file, would there be any basis under the first party *Stinchcombe* disclosure regime for not disclosing it to the accused? If the answer to that question is no, there can be no principled reason to arrive at a different outcome on the third party production application.[122]

3) Production under the Statutory Scheme (the *Mills* Regime)

In response to the *O'Connor* decision, Parliament enacted sections 278.1 to 278.91 of the *Criminal Code*. The exact details of that scheme will be detailed in a moment, but it is necessary first to provide an overview of how the two production regimes fit together. The *O'Connor* rules were developed in the context of counselling records, but they apply generally

---

121 *Ibid* at para 33.
122 *McNeil*, above note 7 at para 42. See also the discussion in David Paciocco, "*Stinchcombe* on Steroids: The Surprising Legacy of *McNeil*" (2009) 62 *Criminal Reports* (6th) 26.

to all records in the hands of a third party. The statutory scheme applies only to *some* of the records in the hands of third parties—in essence, counselling and similar records for sexual assault complainants. Accordingly, the *O'Connor* rules still govern production with regard to records not explicitly covered by the statutory scheme.

Making the situation more complex is that the statutory scheme was itself subject to a *Charter* challenge in *Mills*.[123] Although the Court upheld the constitutionality of the statutory scheme, in the course of doing so they put a particular gloss upon the provisions which makes them more restricted than they might at first glance seem to be. In any event, it is necessary now to look in detail at the statutory scheme. In essence, those provisions enact the minority decision in *O'Connor*; that is, they follow the same general two-step approach adopted by the majority—indeed, by all judges—in that case, but require the trial judge also to take into account the factors the majority said did not arise. On the face of it the provisions are broader than the majority decision in *O'Connor*, in the sense that they provide more protection to complainants' interests, in other ways as well.

The majority in *O'Connor*, for example, was primarily concerned with "therapeutic records," which are "intensely private."[124] Even the minority only suggested that other documents, such as school records or private diaries, may also attract a reasonable expectation of privacy[125] and that this question "is inherently fact- and context-sensitive."[126] The statutory scheme, however, states that

> "record" means any form of record that contains personal information for which there is a reasonable expectation of privacy *and includes, without limiting the generality of the foregoing*, medical, psychiatric, therapeutic, counselling, education, employment, child welfare, adoption and social services records, personal journals and diaries, and records containing personal information the production or disclosure of which is protected by any other Act of Parliament or a provincial legislature, but does not include records made by persons responsible for the investigation or prosecution of the offence.[127]

---

123 *Mills*, above note 6.
124 *O'Connor*, above note 5 at para 7.
125 See the discussion of reasonable expectation of privacy in Chapter 4.
126 *O'Connor*, above note 5 at para 99.
127 Section 278.1 [emphasis added]. The list excludes "records made by persons responsible for the investigation or prosecution of the offence." In other words, documents prepared by the police in the investigation of the offence being prosecuted are not subject to the *Mills* regime; however, records prepared by police for other investigations are not excluded: *Quesnelle*, above note 12.

Therefore, the legislative provision appears, in one way, to apply to more records than the *O'Connor* rules would,[128] since *prima facie* any listed third-party record is covered by it, and not merely those found to attract a reasonable expectation of privacy after a fact- and case-sensitive analysis.

Further, the scheme in *O'Connor* was limited to records still in the hands of third parties. Those in the hands of the Crown no longer attracted a reasonable expectation of privacy, the majority said, and therefore were subject to the ordinary *Stinchcombe* rules. The minority expressed no opinion on this issue.[129] Section 278.2(2), however, makes the statutory scheme applicable even to records already in the hands of the Crown, unless the complainant or witness has "expressly waived the application of those sections."

In considering the first stage, section 278.5(2) of the *Code* requires the judge to balance the salutary and deleterious effects of producing the record for the judge's own inspection, as the minority in *O'Connor* wished. In particular, the accused is required not only to show that the record is likely relevant, but also that "the production of the record is necessary in the interests of justice."[130] Further, that section states that the decision at both the first and second stages should be based on the five factors the majority in *O'Connor* said should settle the issue, and that the trial judge "shall take . . . into account" the additional factors the minority held were relevant. The intent, the Court has said, is to shift much of the balancing process from the second stage to the first.[131]

On the face of it, then, the statutory scheme departs from the *O'Connor* rules in a number of ways that were specifically considered and rejected by the majority of the Court. Given that the *O'Connor* rules were based on the accused's section 7 rights, it was therefore natural to wonder whether the statutory scheme violated the *Charter*.

In *Mills*,[132] the trial judge had found that the scheme violated an accused's section 7 and section 11(d) rights under the *Charter* and struck it down. When the issue reached the Supreme Court, the legislation was upheld. A proper understanding of the current state of the

---

128 Note, however, that s 278.2 restricts the operation of this scheme to production in the context of prosecutions for various listed offences, all of which are sexual offences of one sort or another. In any other context, it appears that the *O'Connor* rules will still apply. As a practical matter, of course, it seems to have been primarily in the context of sexual offences that such applications have been made.

129 *O'Connor*, above note 5 at para 98.

130 Section 278.5(1)(c).

131 *McNeil*, above note 7 at para 32.

132 *Mills*, above note 6.

law, however, requires recognizing that, in *Mills*, the Court upheld the statutory scheme by reading it down (without referring to their approach as such[133]) to correspond as closely as possible to the majority decision in *O'Connor*.

In dealing with the statutory scheme's wider list of records covered by the scheme, the Court adopted the position of a lower court.[134] Section 278.1, they conclude, does not mean that every type of record listed attracts a reasonable expectation. Rather, only records of the type listed in which there is *also* a reasonable expectation of privacy will be governed by the scheme. In effect, the fact- and case-sensitive decision from *O'Connor* will still be necessary.[135]

The statutory scheme is also broader than *O'Connor* because it applies to records already in the hands of the Crown. But this will not be the case where the complainant has expressly waived these protections, in other words, where a "fully informed complainant expressly waives the protection of the legislation, by declaration or *by voluntarily providing her records to the Crown*."[136] The Court interprets the legislative scheme as simply filling a void left by the *O'Connor* rules (how to deal with third-party records that come into the Crown's hands through a search warrant or similar means), but not as changing the *O'Connor* rules.[137] On the other hand, it is clear that the Crown might decide that records it has obtained to which the *Mills* regime applies should not be disclosed to the accused, in which case, it will give notice to the accused.[138]

The statutory scheme requires the accused, at the first stage, to show that production is necessary in the interests of justice, a consideration

---

133 The Court speaks of itself in *Mills*, *ibid*, as deferring to Parliament, but in its actual approach it is not genuinely deferential: see Steve Coughlan, "Complainants' Records after *Mills*: Same as It Ever Was" (2000) 33 *Criminal Reports* (5th) 300.

134 *R v Regan* (1998), 174 NSR (2d) 230 (SC).

135 Gotell, above note 110 at 283, indicates that in a number of post-*Mills* cases, lower court judges have ordered production on the basis that the statutory scheme was not applicable to the particular records in question. See also *Quesnelle*, above note 12 at para 20, holding that the first question to be asked in deciding whether something is a "record" for purposes of the *Mills* regime is "does the document contain personal information for which there is a reasonable expectation of privacy?" and at para 22, describing the records mentioned as "an illustrative list of some of the types of records that usually give rise to a reasonable expectation of privacy."

136 *Mills*, above note 6 at para 106 [emphasis added].

137 *Ibid* at para 109.

138 Section 278.2(3). *Quesnelle*, above note 12, observes at para 16 that the Crown should in appropriate circumstances give an assessment of the likely relevance of such a record and, at a minimum, should advise if it intends to use any information contained in those records as part of its case.

motivated by the desire to give greater weight to a complainant's privacy interests. In *Mills*, the Court upheld this requirement by making it secondary to — and, indeed, in some ways converting it to — concern for the accused's right to make full answer and defence. A judge is required to protect that right of the accused. If it is necessary to examine the documents to see whether they should be produced to the accused, then production to the judge is necessary in the interests of justice.[139] The accused must have access to all documents that might be constitutionally required: "a production regime that denied this would not be production 'necessary in the interests of justice.'"[140] "Read correctly," this requirement is constitutional.[141]

Finally, the legislative scheme requires that the judge shall take into account at both stages the factors that *O'Connor* said were not to be considered at all, or were to be considered only at the second stage. The Court minimizes the practical effect of these changes by finding that the addition of these factors to the legislative scheme does not necessarily make any difference:

> s. 278.5(2) does not require that the judge engage in a conclusive and indepth evaluation of each of the factors. It rather requires the judge to "take them into account" — to the extent possible at this early stage of proceedings — in deciding whether to order a particular record produced to himself or herself for inspection. Section 278.5(2) serves as a check-list of the various factors that *may* come into play in making the decision regarding production to the judge.[142]

The Court makes clear that the accused's right to full answer and defence is not to be compromised by this change:

> Therefore, while the s. 278.5(2) factors are relevant, in the final analysis the judge is free to make whatever order is "necessary in the interests of justice" — a mandate that includes all of the applicable "principles of fundamental justice" at stake.[143]

In practical terms, it appears that *Mills* has resulted in some, but not dramatic, change. There are indications that because of the standard set in *Mills*, lower court judges decide less frequently that records meet the likely relevance standard, for example, and so do not examine

---

139 *Mills*, above note 6 at para 132.
140 *Ibid* at para 130. See Gotell, above note 110 at 286n: this aspect of the *Mills* reasoning has been frequently cited by lower courts as justification for production.
141 *Mills*, above note 6 at para 133.
142 *Ibid* at para 134 [emphasis added].
143 *Ibid*.

the records personally.[144] However, this does not automatically mean that there is less production of records to the accused in the end. Rather, it may simply be the case that records that would not ultimately have been disclosed are filtered out at an earlier stage. Further, the type of analysis undertaken seems not to have changed dramatically. *Mills* itself asserts the relevance of the complainant's privacy *and* equality rights, and the legislative scheme includes factors intended to reflect broader societal interests.[145] However, few later cases have considered any interests other than privacy.[146] Note as well that the statutory scheme has been held to apply even when third-party records are first sought as fresh evidence on appeal.[147] Further, the *Mills* regime applies only to *disclosure* of records: the Crown has a duty nonetheless to make reasonable inquiries and seek to *obtain* such potentially relevant material under *McNeil* (discussed in Section D, below in this chapter) which applies independently.[148]

The final word on production of third-party records, then, is found in *Mills*'s upholding of the statutory scheme in sections 278.1 to 278.91 of the *Code*. Proper understanding of that scheme, however, depends on understanding the prior decision in *O'Connor*, since according to the Court, *Mills* did *not* intend to "shift the balance away from the *primary* emphasis on the rights of the accused."[149]

D. BRIDGING THE GAP (*R V MCNEIL*)

McNeil is meant to be a response to the fact that some documents, although not in the hands of the Crown and therefore not subject to *Stinchcombe* disclosure, ought obviously to be provided to the accused and certainly would be if an *O'Connor* application were brought. *McNeil* is intended to simplify the process for producing such records to the accused. In such cases (that is, where the Crown becomes aware of potentially relevant records in the hands of a third party), the Crown has a duty to inquire and obtain the evidence, rather than require the accused to pursue an *O'Connor* application.[150] The decision specifically

---

144   Gotell, above note 110.
145   See, for example, s 278.5(2) of the *Code*, including "society's interest in encouraging the reporting of sexual offences."
146   Gotell, above note 110.
147   *R v Rodgers* (2000), 144 CCC (3d) 568 (Ont CA).
148   *Quesnelle*, above note 12 at para 18.
149   *R v Shearing*, 2002 SCC 58 at para 132 [emphasis in original].
150   *McNeil*, above note 7 at para 48ff.

lists some such types of evidence, but also lays down general rules around this new duty for the Crown.

The particular records in issue in *McNeil* were police disciplinary records and criminal investigation files relating to the main police witness. The Court rejected the suggestion that all state authorities, or even just the police and prosecutors, were indivisible for disclosure purposes. That assumption, it held, would require the Crown to make inquiries of every federal and provincial government department as well as every police force to see whether it might have relevant information. That does not mean, however, that the Crown can merely be passive. Rather, when aware of relevant information that it could obtain, the Crown has a duty to seek it out.

In addition, the police have a corollary duty to disclose disciplinary records that could be relevant to the Crown, so that they can form part of the first-party disclosure package. The Court specifically listed five types of records that fell within this police duty:

a. Any conviction or finding of guilt under the *Canadian Criminal Code* or under the *Controlled Drugs and Substances Act* for which a pardon has not been granted;

b. Any outstanding charges under the *Canadian Criminal Code* or the *Controlled Drugs and Substances Act*;

c. Any conviction or finding of guilt under any other federal or provincial statute;

d. Any finding of guilt for misconduct after a hearing under the *Police Services Act* or its predecessor *Act*;

e. Any current charge of misconduct under the *Police Services Act* for which a Notice of Hearing has been issued.[151]

This list is usually referred to as the "Ferguson five." Records such as these ought to be provided by the Crown without prompting, although the officer concerned should be given notice of the intention to disclose and have the ability to make representations.

In cases falling squarely within the Ferguson five there is every indication that the Court's goal of simplifying the process is being achieved. In other cases, the effect has been to create what amounts to a "*McNeil* hearing" to decide whether the Crown has any obligation or whether particular records are relevant. It has been found, for example, that an accused cannot use *McNeil* as a means of requiring the Crown to conduct an investigation,[152] that *McNeil* has not expanded the test

---

151 *Ibid* at para 57.
152 *R v Levin*, 2014 ABCA 142.

for relevance,[153] that the Canadian Security Intelligence Service is not in the same category as police[154] but sheriffs are,[155] that disclosure can be postponed to avoid hampering an ongoing investigation,[156] and that an accused has no right to an adjournment to await the outcome of an investigation into an officer.[157]

This debate has also included questions about whether types of information other than those specifically mentioned in the Ferguson five need to be disclosed. One would have thought that *McNeil* was quite clear that the Ferguson five were only examples of the types of records where the Crown's duty to inquire arose, but there has been a general tendency against expansion.[158]

FURTHER READINGS

BUSBY, KAREN. "Discriminatory Uses of Personal Records in Sexual Violence Cases" (1997) 9 *Canadian Journal of Women and the Law* 148.

———. "Third Party Records Cases since R. v. O'Connor" (2000) 27 *Manitoba Law Journal* 355.

CALARCO, PAUL. "What Happens When Evidence Has Not Been Recorded? Staying Charges to Ensure a Fair Trial" (2001) 44 *Criminal Law Quarterly* 514.

———. "R. v. Bjelland: No Effective Remedy for Crown Failure to Disclose" (2009) 67 *Criminal Reports* (6th) 219.

CAMERON, JAMIE. "Dialogue and Hierarchy in *Charter* Interpretation: A Comment on R. v. Mills" (2001) 38 *Alberta Law Review* 1051.

---

153 *R v Boyne*, 2012 SKCA 124.
154 *R v Ahmad*, [2009] OJ No 6153.
155 *R v Collins*, 2010 ABPC 19.
156 *Duguay v R*, 2009 QCCA 1130.
157 *R v Huynh*, 2010 BCSC 1306.
158 The subjects discussed include allegations; compelled statements by police officers; without prejudice letters between police counsel and internal affairs; investigator recommendations regarding a complaint (*R v Taing*, 2011 ABPC 165); expunged records (*R v Letourneau*, 2009 ABPC 222, and *R v Perreault*, 2010 ABQB 714); official warnings and other non-serious misconduct (*R v Polny*, [2009] AJ No 1511 (QB)); police dog records (*R v Steele*, 2010 ABQB 39); and complaints filed against all officers involved in an excessive force incident or its aftermath (*R v Auger*, 2010 ABPC 196), as well as the necessary level of seriousness in the underlying allegations (*R v Melvin*, 2009 NSSC 249).

CARTER, IAN. "Chipping Away at *Stinchcombe*: The Expanding Privilege Exception to Disclosure" (2002) 50 *Criminal Reports* (5th) 332.

COUGHLAN, STEPHEN G. "Developments in Criminal Procedure: The 1996–97 Term" (1998) 9 *Supreme Court Law Review* (2d) 273.

———. "Complainants' Records after *Mills*: Same as It Ever Was" (2000) 33 *Criminal Reports* (5th) 300.

FELDTHUSEN, BRUCE. "Access to the Private Therapeutic Records of Sexual Assault Complainants" (1996) 75 *Canadian Bar Review* 537.

GOTELL, LISE. "Colonization through Disclosure: Confidential Records, Sexual Assault Complainants and Canadian Law" (2001) 10 *Social and Legal Studies* 315.

———. "The Ideal Victim, the Hysterical Complainant and the Disclosure of Confidential Records: A Case Study of the Implications of the *Charter* for Sexual Assault Law" (2002) 40 *Osgoode Hall Law Journal* 251.

HOLMES, HEATHER. "An Analysis of Bill C-46, Production of Records in Sexual Offence Proceedings" (1997) 2 *Canadian Criminal Law Review* 71.

HUBBARD, ROBERT W, SUSAN MAGOTIAUX, & SUZANNE M DUNCAN. *The Law of Privilege in Canada* (Aurora, ON: Canada Law Book, 2006) (loose-leaf).

LAW REFORM COMMISSION OF CANADA. *Disclosure by the Prosecution* (Ottawa: Law Reform Commission of Canada, 1984).

LAYTON, DAVID. "*R. v. McClure*: The Privilege on the Pea" (2001) 40 *Criminal Reports* (5th) 19.

———. "*R. v. Brown*: Protecting Legal-Professional Privilege" (2002) 50 *Criminal Reports* (5th) 37.

MITCHELL, GRAEME G. "*R. v. Carosella*: Difficult Cases Make Dangerous Law" (1997) 4 *Criminal Reports* (5th) 209.

———. "*R. v. Dixon*: The Right to Crown Disclosure—A Roadmap for the Future" (1998) 13 *Criminal Reports* (5th) 260.

PACIOCCO, DAVID. "In Defence of *R. v. Carosella*: The Continuing Need for Prejudice" (1997) 4 *Criminal Reports* (5th) 199.

———. "*Stinchcombe* on Steroids: The Surprising Legacy of *McNeil*" (2009) 62 *Criminal Reports* (6th) 26.

QUIGLEY, TIM. *Procedure in Canadian Criminal Law*, 2d ed (Toronto: Thomson Carswell, 2005) (loose-leaf) ch 12.

SANKOFF, PETER. "Crown Disclosure after *Mills*: Have the Rules Suddenly Changed?" (2000) 28 *Criminal Reports* (5th) 285.

STUART, DON. "*Mills*: Dialogue with Parliament and Equality by Assertion at What Cost?" (2000) 28 *Criminal Reports* (5th) 275.

———. *Charter Justice in Canadian Criminal Law*, 5th ed (Toronto: Thomson Carswell, 2010) ch 2.

CHAPTER 9

PRELIMINARY INQUIRY

A. INTRODUCTION

Before an accused is tried on an indictable offence, a preliminary inquiry can be conducted by a justice,[1] at the request of the prosecution or the accused, unless the offence is within the absolute jurisdiction of the provincial court judge.[2] This entitlement can be overridden if the Attorney General elects to proceed by way of a direct indictment, pursuant to section 577 of the *Code*, which has the effect of putting an indictment immediately before the court of trial.[3] There is no entitlement to a preliminary inquiry in summary conviction matters, nor has

---

1   A "justice" is defined in s 2 of the *Code* to mean either a justice of the peace or a judge of the provincial court. In virtually all jurisdictions of Canada, a preliminary inquiry is held by a provincial court judge.

2   See ss 535, 536(4), and 536.1(3). Offences within the absolute jurisdiction of the provincial court are listed in s 553. If the accused elects trial in a provincial court before a preliminary inquiry has been held, he waives the right to a preliminary inquiry.

3   Conversely, if an accused has elected trial in a provincial court, the presiding judge has discretion under s 555(1) to convert the trial into a preliminary inquiry. If a trial has begun on an indictable property offence within the absolute jurisdiction of the provincial court (s 553), and evidence discloses that the value involved exceeds $5,000, the judge must put the accused to his election according to s 536(2). If the accused then elects trial by judge alone or trial by judge and jury, the proceedings shall continue as a preliminary inquiry unless waived by the accused.

a justice any jurisdiction to inquire into such offences. More generally, there is no constitutional right to a preliminary inquiry.[4]

The nature, scope, and purpose of the preliminary inquiry are now in flux, and they are becoming both less interesting and less important as a subject of discussion.[5] In principle, one of their central functions is to serve as a screening mechanism for unmeritorious prosecutions. As a matter of fact, though, most preliminary inquiries result in an accused being committed for trial and, in any event, the Crown has the ability to send the accused to trial despite a discharge, as noted above. Preliminary inquiries also long performed a type of disclosure function, but that need is dealt with more directly by *Charter* decisions requiring the Crown to disclose all relevant evidence to the accused. Further, as noted in Chapter 3, *Charter* remedies are not available at a preliminary inquiry. For a long time preliminary inquiries were frequently waived, and legislative changes make them now available only on request and potentially only on some issues, further marginalizing the procedure.

Until 2004 the preliminary inquiry was understood chiefly as a test of the sufficiency of the prosecution's case for trial. The central question was whether the prosecution could produce sufficient evidence on the whole of the case to warrant committal for trial.[6] As of right, the accused was entitled to a preliminary inquiry on the whole of the case and, in principle, the preliminary inquiry served important functions in screening out unsupportable charges and in providing the accused with a fuller understanding of the case to meet. Unless the accused waived the preliminary inquiry, the prosecution was required as a matter of course to produce sufficient evidence. A secondary function of the inquiry was discovery: the inquiry afforded an opportunity to test

---

4   *R v SJL*, 2009 SCC 14 [*SJL*]. The Court, in that case, noted that this rule was equally true for young persons charged with an offence. See also *R v Bjelland*, 2009 SCC 38 at paras 34–37, holding that there is no *Charter* right to cross-examine a witness at a preliminary inquiry and that an accused's fair trial right can be adequately protected in other ways.

5   See David Paciocco, "A Voyage of Discovery: Examining the Precarious Condition of the Preliminary Inquiry" (2003) 48 *Criminal Law Quarterly* 151.

6   See, for example, *R v Hynes*, [2001] 3 SCR 623 [*Hynes*]. Evidence "on the whole of the case" means evidence on each element of an offence. It does not mean that the prosecution must tender all of the evidence that it can produce at trial: *R v Caccamo*, [1976] 1 SCR 786. Committal for trial can be ordered only if the evidence at the preliminary inquiry is sufficient in the sense that a jury, properly instructed, can find the accused guilty beyond reasonable doubt: *United States of America v Shephard*, [1977] 2 SCR 1067 [*Shephard*] (discussed in Section D, below in this chapter).

the quality of evidence taken from witnesses under oath.[7] Among other advantages, this aspect of the inquiry allowed the parties, especially the defence, to have a record of sworn evidence that could later be used at trial to challenge the credibility of a witness.

Since 2004, the amendments to the *Code* that then came into effect have altered the nature of the preliminary inquiry, and it can no longer be said that its primary function is to test the sufficiency of the prosecution case as a whole.[8] The central feature of those amendments is that a preliminary inquiry will be held only upon the request of a party. That party will almost always be the accused, but a request can be made by the prosecutor. In the absence of a request the accused will simply be committed to stand trial on a date fixed by the court.[9] Nothing in Part XVIII of the *Code* specifically allows a justice to refuse a request for a preliminary inquiry,[10] but this does not imply that a full preliminary inquiry will be held if one is requested. Further, where a request is made, the inquiry will be conducted only with regard to issues and witnesses specified in advance.[11] It is contemplated that these points can and should be agreed upon between the parties, and the justice can order a hearing to encourage the parties to reach such agreement.[12] If there is an agreement of this nature, the *Code* provides that the justice can commit the accused without recording evidence on any other issues in the case.[13] The inquiry is thus no longer a test of the prosecution case as a whole because the sufficiency of the prosecution

---

7   *R v Skogman*, [1984] 2 SCR 93 at 105 [*Skogman*].

8   SC 2002, c 13.

9   Section 549.

10   Indeed, a perplexing feature of the procedure for making a request is that the provisions do not require or empower the judge to make a decision on the request or on any attempts to narrow the scope of an inquiry. Thus, it would seem to be an open question as to whether a judge who denies any part of a request would lose jurisdiction. It is arguable that he would. This position is consistent with cases that affirm the right of the accused to call evidence at a preliminary inquiry. See, for example, *R v Lena* (2001), 158 CCC (3d) 415 (BCCA).

11   Section 536.3. The New Brunswick Court of Appeal observed in *R v Gallant*, 2009 NBCA 84, that the French and English versions of s 536.3 are not parallel. The French version is unambiguous that an accused who requests a preliminary inquiry is to identify the issues upon which the *accused* wants to adduce testimony and a list of the witnesses the *accused* intends to call. The English version suggests that an accused requesting a preliminary inquiry is to point to the evidence she wishes the *prosecutor* to adduce and the witnesses she wants the *prosecutor* to call. The Court of Appeal found that it was unnecessary for them to decide the correct interpretation in that case.

12   Section 536.4. This is now commonly called a "focusing hearing."

13   Sections 536.4, 536.5, and 549.

case is assumed, subject to any exception covered by a request. As now conceived, the preliminary inquiry is a limited examination of the sufficiency of the prosecution case with regard to specific issues and the evidence of specific witnesses.

It is important to underscore the importance of the amendments that came into force in 2004. The changes are partly justified by extensive disclosure of the prosecution case to the accused before plea.[14] Another justification is that, in practice, it has always been open to the defence to make admissions and to waive the right to a full preliminary inquiry in favour of a limited inquiry. A third justification was the growing length, in practice, of cross-examination. A fourth is that the right to a full preliminary inquiry was occasionally abused by counsel who, through lack of experience or judgment, could have waived the inquiry in whole or in part without prejudice to the accused. The amendments address these considerations.

Nevertheless, the reformulation of the preliminary inquiry as a limited examination of specific issues and witnesses significantly changes the nature of the order for committal. This limitation of the scope of inquiry effectively eliminates any test of the sufficiency of the prosecution case from the decision at the end of the inquiry. If the judge does not receive evidence on the case as a whole, it cannot sensibly be said that the decision to commit for trial is a decision based upon evidence that the whole of the case is sufficient. Where a limited inquiry is held on a specific issue, the decision to commit signifies only that the evidence presented on that issue meets the standard for committal. The plain design of the reformed preliminary inquiry is that a limited inquiry will be the norm. The only exception to this conclusion would be the rare case wherein a judge proceeds, upon request, to conduct a preliminary inquiry on the whole of the case. It would be rare because the party that made such a request would seemingly have to assert that the case disclosed by the prosecution included no evidence on all essential elements of the offence charged. There is, therefore, a good argument that the preliminary inquiry should be abolished.[15]

Alternatively, one could argue that the function of the preliminary inquiry now is simply to afford the parties an opportunity upon request to test the evidence of specific witnesses on specific issues in preparation for trial. For all practical purposes the preliminary inquiry

14   This is the effect of jurisprudence after R v Stinchcombe, [1991] 3 SCR 326. The Court noted in SJL, above note 4 at para 23, that "the incidental function of the preliminary inquiry as a discovery mechanism has lost much of its relevance."

15   Parliament did consider this option at the time it brought in the 2004 amendments: see the discussion in R v PM, 2007 QCCA 414 at para 72 [PM].

as it was known before 2004 has been reformed by Parliament as a limited and focused examination to obtain discovery of evidence under oath. For this reason a strong case can be made that Parliament should undertake a more thorough reform of Part XVIII of the *Code* to redefine this procedure for what it now is. The purpose of such a reform would be to remove traces of the preliminary inquiry as a genuine test of the sufficiency of the prosecution case as a whole.

B. JURISDICTION

The authority of a justice to conduct a preliminary inquiry is strictly statutory under Part XVIII of the *Code*.[16] In other words, there is no inherent jurisdiction, and the only powers that can be exercised by the judge are those that are explicitly granted in the *Code* or that are necessarily implicit in those provisions. The only additional authority they have to expand upon the express powers granted to them is found in section 537(1)(i). It provides that the judge at the preliminary inquiry can regulate the course of the inquiry in any way that appears to be desirable and not inconsistent with any other provision of the *Code*. There is an obvious tension between the traditional view of the judge's jurisdiction at a preliminary inquiry and the scope of this discretion. Clearly, this discretion does not expand the scope of a preliminary inquiry, but it does confer broad authority with regard to the manner in which an inquiry is conducted.

The courts have said repeatedly that the preliminary inquiry justice has only the powers given by Parliament in Part XVIII of the *Code*. Thus, a judge who fails to comply with Part XVIII or who exceeds the authority given by the *Code* acts without jurisdiction and might be subject to review in the superior court.[17] This position was fuelled in some measure by the fact that preliminary inquiries were typically held, many years ago, before magistrates without formal legal training. It was also fuelled more generally by the idea that the provincial court is a statutory tribunal that has only those powers in criminal matters that are specifically accorded to it by Parliament. This approach to the jurisdiction of the provincial court is somewhat antiquated, in part, because preliminary inquiries are now routinely held before professional judges

---

16   *R v Doyle*, [1977] 1 SCR 597 [*Doyle*]; *R v Forsythe*, [1980] 2 SCR 268 [*Forsythe*].
17   *Skogman*, above note 7; *Forsythe*, ibid. See *R v Deschamplain*, 2004 SCC 76 [*Deschamplain*], and *R v Sazant*, [2004] 3 SCR 635 [*Sazant*], for considerations of the scope of jurisdictional error at the preliminary inquiry.

in the provincial court and, in part, because those same judges are competent to exercise all functions for a proper trial. It is not surprising, therefore, that the powers of the justice at the preliminary inquiry have been expanded. Not only is the justice empowered to regulate the inquiry as appropriate, but she is also now entitled to cajole the parties to limit the scope of the inquiry or to do so herself.

Nonetheless, a judge at a preliminary inquiry has no power to grant any remedy other than those contemplated by the *Code*.[18] The Supreme Court has specifically held that the judge cannot grant a remedy under the *Charter*, including remedies for delay, non-disclosure, or the production of evidence obtained in violation of a constitutional right.[19]

1) Commencement

Section 536 states that an accused who is charged with an indictable offence within the absolute jurisdiction of a provincial court judge shall be remanded to appear before such a judge for trial within the territorial jurisdiction in which the offence was allegedly committed. For all other indictable offences, the justice has jurisdiction to proceed with a preliminary inquiry or to adjourn the preliminary inquiry to a later date. Almost invariably the matter is adjourned at the first appearance and, indeed, there can be frequent adjournments before the preliminary inquiry begins with the presentation of evidence.[20] The central point is that the possibility of having a preliminary inquiry in respect of an indictable offence will depend, first, on the classification of the offence and, second, on the election of the accused as to mode of trial.

There can be variations on the prototypical case in which an inquiry proceeds on a single count, in a single information, against a single accused. It is important to bear in mind that the jurisdiction of the judge at the preliminary inquiry is to examine indictable offences charged by the prosecution or disclosed by the evidence. Thus, even if the judge otherwise has jurisdiction over the offences, he cannot conduct a trial and a preliminary inquiry for the same accused simultaneously;[21] nor can he try one accused and at the same time conduct a preliminary inquiry in respect of a co-accused.[22] She can, however, conduct a preliminary inquiry in respect of charges in separate informations simultaneously.[23]

---

18   *Hynes*, above note 6 at para 33. See also *R v Patterson*, [1970] SCR 409.
19   See the further discussion of this issue at Section B(5), below in this chapter.
20   *Re R and Geszthelyi* (1977), 33 CCC (2d) 543 (BCCA).
21   *R v G(AM)* (2000), 142 CCC (3d) 29 (NSCA).
22   *R v Niedzwieki* (1980), 57 CCC (2d) 184 (BCSC).
23   *R v Rutherford*, [1968] 3 CCC 1 (BCSC).

At the first appearance of the accused there is an arraignment, in the sense that the charge or charges will be read to the accused. It is not necessary for a formal plea to be recorded because the justice has the power to adjourn the matter. A formalistic reading of the *Code* suggests that the first appearance is the commencement of the preliminary inquiry.[24] In practice, it marks only a *pro forma* commencement of the inquiry at which the accused submits to the jurisdiction of the court, makes a provisional election as to mode of trial,[25] and sets a subsequent date for the actual commencement of the preliminary inquiry. For practical purposes, little turns on whether the preliminary inquiry formally commences at the first appearance or at a later date, such as the date on which the election is recorded. It is important, however, to note that on any account the judge presiding at the inquiry is seized of the matter as soon as evidence is adduced.[26] Until that time, the accused might appear before several justices or judges on various matters. Once evidence is adduced, though, the preliminary inquiry will continue to its conclusion before the same judge.[27]

2) Scope

The scope of the inquiry is defined by section 535 of the *Code*, which directs the justice or judge to inquire into the charge of any indictable offence or any other indictable offence in respect of the same transaction disclosed by the evidence taken in accordance with Part XVIII. Until 1985, the jurisdiction to inquire was limited to the charge recited in the information or any included charge that might be disclosed by the evidence. Accordingly, the jeopardy of the accused in committal proceedings could be no greater than the charge or charges in the information. On a charge of second-degree murder, for example, the presiding judge had no jurisdiction to commit the accused for trial on a charge of first-degree murder.[28] The *Code* was amended in 1985 to allow the judge to commit the accused for trial on any indictable offence disclosed by the evidence at the preliminary inquiry.[29] This extension of jurisdiction

---

24 *Doyle*, above note 16; compare *Re Danchella and the Queen* (1985), 19 CCC (3d) 490 (BCCA) [*Danchella*].
25 In some jurisdictions, there is not even a provisional recording of an election.
26 *Danchella*, above note 24.
27 Section 547.1 provides that when a justice is unable to continue to receive evidence, another justice may do so if the record is otherwise complete and available, or hear the case afresh.
28 *R v Chabot*, [1980] 2 SCR 985.
29 With regard to the scope of the inquiry, see Patrick Healy, "Chabotage: Expanding the Crown's Power to Prefer Additional Counts" (1984) 38 *Criminal Reports* (3d) 344.

implies that the presiding judge and the accused must be alert through-out the preliminary inquiry to the possibility that offences other than those stated in the information might be disclosed by the evidence. Although, in principle, this might seem like a perilous enterprise, it rarely causes difficulty. Moreover, with the shift to limited inquiries focused on specific issues, it is even less likely to pose problems.

The scope of the preliminary inquiry is thus not strictly limited to the offences as charged in the information. The inquiry can extend to any indictable offence disclosed by the evidence, provided that it arises from the same transaction. "Transaction" in this sense is not co-extensive with an offence. It refers to a narrative of conduct that might comprise several acts and might disclose several offences. If the information charges only one indictable offence, for example, but evidence of the transaction at the preliminary inquiry supports more, the judge can commit the accused to trial on all of them. The reference to the same transaction, however, is meant to limit the jeopardy of the accused at the inquiry to a narrative of conduct that is coherent in time or in some other manner.[30]

There is another sense in which the preliminary inquiry can extend beyond an examination of the sufficiency of the prosecution case on the charges in the information. The *Code* expressly allows the accused to call evidence, and this can include exculpatory evidence on a matter of defence.[31] For purposes of committal, however, this evidence will not be assessed by the presiding judge or weighed in favour of the accused, not least because the judge has no jurisdiction to examine the validity of defences.[32] The primary purpose of such defence evidence is to allow the accused the opportunity to test it and to record it in preparation for trial. Nothing in the amendments alters this.

The preliminary inquiry has also been used as an opportunity to lay an evidentiary foundation for an issue that can be decided only at trial. For example, although a justice has no power to order the production of third-party records at the preliminary inquiry, he can allow the accused to cross-examine the complainant on a range of facts that might later support an application at trial.[33] Similarly, although no remedy can be granted under the *Charter* at the preliminary inquiry, the judge can permit cross-examination of a prosecution witness to lay a basis for a motion under the *Charter* at trial. The judge also has discretion to al-

---

30   See, for example, *R v Goldstein; R v Caicedo* (1988), 42 CCC (3d) 548 (Ont CA).
31   Section 541.
32   *Hynes*, above note 6.
33   *R v B(E)* (2002), 162 CCC (3d) 451 (Ont CA) [*B(E)*].

low the accused to call defence witnesses on trial matters.[34] All of this is consistent with the right of the accused to make full answer and defence, and with the discovery function of the preliminary inquiry, but it is also strictly beyond an inquiry into the sufficiency of the prosecution case for committal. There has been no serious challenge to the practice of allowing evidence on trial matters to be presented in examination or cross-examination. It might be asked whether this practice will be affected by the amendments. It could be argued that a preliminary inquiry that is limited to specific witnesses and specific issues should also exclude issues that can be decided only at trial.

The preliminary inquiry is rarely an occasion for formal challenges to the validity of charges in the information, and even then the only basis would be that the information fails to charge an indictable offence known to law.[35] The justice has no authority to question whether the information was properly sworn by inquiring into the grounds of belief asserted by the informant.[36] Further, the judge has no jurisdiction to inquire into any special plea based upon principles of double jeopardy.[37] Thus, the scope of inquiry is circumscribed by the content of the charges in the information and the evidence produced. This fact is only underscored by the application of section 601 to the preliminary inquiry. This provision, which is found among those relating to charges at trial, allows for an application to be made to quash a count that fails to charge a known offence or that is otherwise defective on its face.[38]

Of greater importance, however, is that section 601 also gives the judge broad powers to amend the charges in the information at the preliminary inquiry. Thus, quite apart from the judge's jurisdiction to order committal on any indictable offence disclosed by the evidence at the preliminary inquiry, the judge can also amend the information to ensure that the charges conform with the evidence. Although the judge at the preliminary inquiry has no power to order the prosecution to furnish particulars in support of an information,[39] the power of amendment can compensate for this deficiency in all but the most egregious of cases. Challenges to quash the information at the preliminary inquiry will therefore succeed only in cases where there is a radical

---

34   *R v Dawson* (1998), 123 CCC (3d) 385 (Ont CA) [*Dawson*].
35   Section 546. See also *R v Gralewicz*, [1980] 2 SCR 493; *R v Bolduc* (1980), 20 CR (3d) 372 (Que CA), aff'd [1982] 1 SCR 573.
36   *Re Hislop et al and the Queen* (1983), 36 CR (3d) 29 (Ont CA).
37   *R v Prince*, [1986] 2 SCR 480.
38   *Dallas & Cassidy v the Queen* (1985), 21 CCC (3d) 100 (Ont HCJ); *R v Volpi* (1987), 34 CCC (3d) 1 (Ont CA).
39   *R v Chew*, [1968] 2 CCC 127 (Ont CA).

jurisdictional defect that lies beyond the power of amendment granted by section 601.[40]

3) Multiple Accused and Multiple Counts

In view of the limited statutory jurisdiction of the judge at the preliminary inquiry, it seems clear that he has no power to order the severance of accused or counts.[41]

If multiple accused are charged in a single information, each is entitled to make a request for a preliminary inquiry, as is the prosecution. If a request is made, the ensuing inquiry must be held in respect of all accused, and each of them will be entitled to participate.[42] In many instances, multiple accused will be concerned about the same issues, but there are also cases in which various accused persons wish to address different issues and hear evidence from different witnesses. In such cases, the preliminary inquiry will proceed on the issues and witnesses identified by the parties in the same manner as if there were only a single accused.[43] However, as the law favours prosecution of multiple accused together, the *Code* specifically empowers a judge not to record the election of an accused if it would necessarily lead to severance of the accused.[44] As a result, even if only one accused elects a mode of trial that entitles her to a preliminary inquiry, that election will mean that an inquiry will occur for all.

Multiple counts can be joined in an information for purposes of a preliminary inquiry, provided that each of them could properly be the subject of a committal order. Thus, the judge at the preliminary inquiry cannot inquire into summary-conviction offences and indictable offences within the absolute jurisdiction of the provincial court.[45] Occasionally, however, an information that contains such counts is filed. Although the judge has no jurisdiction to inquire into them, they can remain on the information pending the election of the accused. If the accused elects trial in provincial court, she waives the preliminary in-

---

40   *R v Webster*, [1993] 1 SCR 3. The issue of sufficiency of an information is discussed at greater length in Chapter 11.

41   *Re R and Legg* (1993), 80 CCC (3d) 315 (NSSCTD); *Re Peters and the Queen* (1982), 2 CCC (3d) 278 (Sask QB).

42   Section 536(4.2).

43   Of particular significance where there are multiple accused will be the cases in which one co-accused makes a request to hear the evidence of another.

44   Section 567. Specifically, the judge can fail to record any election other than trial by judge with a jury, and so that will be the mode of trial for all the accused.

45   Such offences can be joined for purposes of trial if the accused elects trial in provincial court and waives the preliminary inquiry.

quiry and thus no issue arises because the provincial court judge has jurisdiction over all of the offences charged. If she elects trial by judge alone or judge and jury, the preliminary inquiry will proceed on the electable offences, and the others would have to be separately charged in another information.[46]

4) Presence of the Accused

The accused is entitled to be present at the preliminary inquiry. For many years the courts took the view that the accused must be present.[47] Section 535 refers to an accused who is "before a justice," and this phrase was interpreted to mean that the justice's jurisdiction required the presence of the accused. This position has been changed by amendment of section 537(1)(j.1), which now allows the judge a discretion to excuse the accused from all or part of the inquiry. Even without this amendment, however, the same result might be justified through the exercise of the judge's general power to regulate the conduct of the inquiry. It should also be noted that sections 537(1)(j) and (k) allow the accused to appear by an electronic connection. Therefore, the accused has the right to attend the preliminary inquiry and will be required to attend unless excused by the justice. As a practical matter, this will follow either upon a request by the accused or the agreement of the parties.

If the accused absconds during the preliminary inquiry, section 544 provides that the accused is deemed to have waived the right to be present.[48] It also provides that the justice can continue the inquiry to its conclusion or, if an arrest warrant has been issued, adjourn it. Even if it is adjourned, the justice can subsequently resume the inquiry. The accused cannot demand that the inquiry be reopened, although the justice is given discretion to make this order if exceptional circumstances justify it. Counsel for the accused is entitled to act for the absconding

---

46   To be clear, the judge's power of committal is only as extensive as his power of inquiry, and thus there can be no order of committal on a summary-conviction offence. In Québec and Nunavut, the situation would appear to be slightly different because the judge with jurisdiction at the preliminary inquiry also has jurisdiction when the accused elects trial by judge alone. It would seem to follow that multiple counts could remain on the same information pending the outcome of the preliminary inquiry. In Québec, it has been decided that there is no objection in principle where the preliminary inquiry and the trial take place before the same judge of the Cour du Québec.

47   *Re McLachlan and the Queen* (1986), 24 CCC (3d) 255 (Ont CA).

48   In *Re Plummer and the Queen* (1983), 5 CCC (3d) 17 (BCCA), it was held that judicial acts undertaken after election by the accused as to mode of trial are acts "during the preliminary inquiry."

accused during his absence if the inquiry is continued, and doing so includes calling witnesses. Most important, however, is that if the accused has absconded, the justice is entitled to draw an adverse inference.

5) Constitutional Issues

In *R v Mills*,[49] and again in *R v Hynes*,[50] the Supreme Court of Canada decided that a court conducting a preliminary inquiry is not a "court of competent jurisdiction" under the *Charter*. Thus, if the accused seeks to apply for a constitutional remedy under section 24 or 52, the only forum for such a motion is at trial. A preliminary inquiry judge might take *Charter* values such as freedom of religion into account in making decisions already within his power,[51] but he cannot grant a *Charter* remedy.

One reason for reaching this decision was that the jurisdiction granted by the *Code* at the preliminary inquiry does not extend to constitutional issues. While this might be true, it raises the odd spectre that the allocation of jurisdiction under an ordinary statute can relieve the judge of the obligation to observe the supreme law of the country. The exclusion of *Charter* issues from the preliminary inquiry might be defensible as a matter of policy.[52] It is consistent with the idea that the function of the preliminary inquiry is modest: to ascertain whether the prosecution has enough evidence for the matter to be sent to trial. It is also consistent with some notion of economy and efficiency in criminal prosecutions because it would eliminate the time and effort necessary to resolve constitutional questions at a preliminary stage. Further, this position means that the judge at the preliminary inquiry cannot terminate a prosecution by granting a stay under the *Charter*. Particularly given the current limited scope of preliminary inquiries, there are arguments in favour of reserving decisions about *Charter* issues to the trial court.

Nonetheless, this position is anomalous in some regards. As is discussed below, a justice can exclude evidence from the preliminary inquiry on the basis that it does not comply with ordinary requirements for admissibility such as voluntariness. Why, then, should she be prevented from acting in the same way when the statement was obtained through a *Charter* violation? Further, the entitlement to seek a

---

49   [1986] 1 SCR 863 [*Mills*].

50   *Hynes*, above note 6.

51   *R v NS*, 2010 ONCA 670. The result in this case was affirmed, but this particular point was not in issue: 2012 SCC 72.

52   These arguments are rehearsed at some length by the majority in *Hynes*, above note 6.

constitutional remedy at the preliminary inquiry would be consistent with a rich and robust concept of full answer and defence.[53] The rule prevents the accused from seeking an order for disclosure. It prevents any claim of unreasonable delay. In short, it deprives the accused of the opportunity to advance any constitutional claim that might have a material bearing on the outcome of the case. In some cases, efficiency might be better served by having such determinations made at as early a stage as possible.

C. EVIDENCE

1) Admissibility

Evidence at the preliminary inquiry is taken under oath and recorded.[54] As at trial, prosecution witnesses are heard first and can be cross-examined by the accused or counsel. Subsections 540(2) and (3) refer to the taking of depositions before the presiding justice or judge, but this form of receiving evidence is almost never used. Depositions are statements made and sworn before the justice; they were commonly used long ago when court stenographers were few and there was no electronic means for recording the presentation of oral evidence. The modern practice is that evidence taken at the preliminary inquiry is recorded by a stenographer or by electronic means in the same manner as occurs at trial.

As a general proposition, evidence tendered at the preliminary inquiry must comply with principles and rules of admissibility that apply at trial. So, for example, any statement made by the accused to a person in authority must be proven to be voluntary beyond a reasonable doubt.[55] The proposition also means, more generally, that the procedure for receiving evidence at a *voir dire* applies at the preliminary inquiry. There are, however, important qualifications that must be noted concerning the production and admissibility of evidence at the preliminary inquiry. One is that the presiding judge has no authority

---

53   *Ibid* at para 60ff, Major J, dissenting. See also *R v Howard*, 2009 PECA 27, holding that this rule also prevents a preliminary inquiry judge from granting costs as a *Charter* remedy.

54   Section 540. A court conducting a preliminary inquiry is a court of record.

55   *R v Pickett* (1975), 28 CCC (2d) 297 (Ont CA). See also s 545(1): "Nothing in this Act prevents a prosecutor giving in evidence at a preliminary inquiry any admission, confession or statement made at any time by the accused *that by law is admissible against him*" [emphasis added].

to call witnesses (other than on request of a party)[56] or to force the parties (notably the prosecution) to produce particular witnesses.[57] Also, as previously noted, the presiding justice or judge has no jurisdiction to hear matters relating to the *Charter*, and so has no jurisdiction to exclude evidence or to grant any other remedy under section 24.

There is, however, an important qualification concerning the admissibility of evidence, found in the power granted by section 540(7) of the *Code*: "A justice acting under this Part may receive as evidence any information that would not otherwise be admissible but that the justice considers credible or trustworthy in the circumstances of the case, including a statement that is made by a witness in writing or otherwise recorded."[58] This provision would potentially allow a party to tender "will-say" statements at the preliminary inquiry, or to introduce a videotaped version of a statement rather than calling a complainant to testify. For the prosecution, this would be highly efficient because it would eliminate the need to produce witnesses to give *viva voce* evidence.

The judge, however, is entitled to order the attendance for examination and cross-examination of any person who would otherwise not be required to appear because of section 540(7).[59] The emerging view seems to be that, although it might be possible for the "sufficiency" aspect of a preliminary inquiry to be satisfied solely by filing documents, the amendments to the procedures were not meant to do away with the "discovery" function. Therefore, in considering whether to allow a request by the accused under section 540(9) that a witness appear for examination, that discovery function should be taken into account.[60] To date, judges have tended to treat the ability to lead otherwise inadmissible evidence narrowly and have read broadly the ability to call a witness for cross-examination. While the onus will be on the accused to show that cross-examination ought to be allowed, the burden is relatively easily satisfied when the witness in question is the complainant.[61] Some cases have suggested that there should still be an expectation

---

56   *Ibid*, ss 540(7) and 541(5).

57   *Re Phillips and the Queen* (1991), 66 CCC (3d) 140 (Ont Ct Gen Div); *Re R and Brass* (1981), 64 CCC (2d) 206 (Sask QB).

58   The section requires prior notice by a party of the intention to tender such evidence, although the judge is able to dispense with this requirement: s 540(8).

59   Section 540(9).

60   *R v Rao*, 2012 BCCA 275 at para 95: "None of those authorities stand for the proposition that the discovery role has been extinguished or rendered obsolete." See also to the same effect *PM*, above note 15. *R v Cowan*, 2015 BCSC 224, holds that nothing in the amendments was meant to *expand* the discovery function of a preliminary inquiry, however.

61   *PM*, above note 15.

that witnesses will testify personally, with exceptions permitted. If, for example, the investigating officer who personally took a statement presented the evidence at the preliminary inquiry and was in a position to say that the witness had recently confirmed the statement and was willing and available to come to trial, then section 540(7) might apply. However, it should not apply to allow the chief investigating officer to introduce a "will-say" statement without personal knowledge.[62] Other cases have held that there are matters about which it is reasonable for the accused to want to cross-examine the complainant at the preliminary inquiry in order to assess the case to meet at trial.[63]

Section 540(7) also raises other issues. Under the section, the evidence admitted must be "considered credible and trustworthy in the circumstances of the case." That is a prerequisite for the admission of the evidence, which therefore requires that a *voir dire* be held during the preliminary inquiry. It also requires an understanding of what standard is set by the words "credible" and "trustworthy." Lower courts have attempted to articulate relevant factors: whether non-leading questions were used; whether the entire interview is to be introduced; whether the transcript is reliable; and, in the case of a child, the child's ability to understand the importance of telling the truth, for example.[64] There is also the question of exactly how reliable the evidence must be: is the standard the same as that for the principled exception to the hearsay rule, for example, or merely that there is an air of reality?[65] These points have not yet been authoritatively determined.

---

62 See *R v Sonier* (2005), 201 CCC (3d) 572 (Ont Ct J); *R v Francis*, (2005), 202 CCC (3d) 147 (Ont SCJ).

63 See *R v Inglis* (2006), 208 CCC (3d) 85 (Ont Ct J).

64 *R v Vaughn*, 2009 BCPC 142 at para 15 [*Vaughn*]. *Vaughn* contains a very thorough discussion of s 540(7).

65 On this point, *Vaughn*, *ibid*, concludes at para 26 that

> (e) When section 540(7) speaks of admitting evidence which is "credible and trustworthy", credibility does not have the same meaning which it would have at trial. Nor does it mean the same as evidence which is "necessary and reliable" as in the case of the principled exception to the hearsay rule. It must at least have a *prima facie* air of reliability to allow it to be admitted under this subsection . . . . [and that]
>
> (f) . . . The point is simply that the evidence must be something that has an air of reality (and therefore more than a bald assertion of fact), but need not be proof beyond a reasonable doubt. It is evidence which might be true, and which is not inherently incredible or untrustworthy. The determination of what is "credible and trustworthy" evidence under subsection 540(7) must be decided on a case by case basis.

See also the discussion in *R v Vasarhelyi*, 2011 ONCA 397, and *R v Ibrahem*, 2014 ONCJ 388.

In addition, of course, the section 540(7) provision creates an exception to the ordinary rules of admissibility. The most glaring question is this: how far does this exception extend?[66] For example, does it permit the justice to admit an involuntary statement by the accused to a person in authority if it is otherwise credible or trustworthy? Does it extend to any type of evidence that is specifically inadmissible by virtue of an exclusionary rule? Whatever its limits, this provision is unusual, especially in view of the reform in favour of a limited preliminary inquiry. It allows the decision to commit at the preliminary inquiry to be based, at least in part, upon evidence that cannot be tendered at trial. Further, one would expect that evidence admitted at the preliminary inquiry under the exception in section 540(7) ought not to be heard at trial, but it is easy to imagine circumstances where precisely this might occur. For example, if an otherwise inadmissible statement is admitted under that section, and the declarant subsequently testifies at trial, can the credibility of the witness be impeached on the basis of the statement admitted at the preliminary hearing? If that statement was unsworn and admitted for the prosecution, the result might well cause prejudice to the defence. In short, it would appear that, as it is now drafted, section 540(7) is too broad.

There is another troubling difficulty with this provision. The Supreme Court has said repeatedly that it is not part of the justice's function or jurisdiction to assess the credibility of evidence at a preliminary inquiry.[67] It is, to say the least, surprising that section 540(7), by directing the preliminary inquiry judge to consider whether the evidence is "credible or trustworthy," appears in express terms either to contradict this principle or to overlook it.

2) Cross-Examination of Prosecution Witnesses

The accused is entitled to cross-examine prosecution witnesses at the preliminary inquiry, either personally or through counsel.[68] This full right of cross-examination is constrained not only by a criterion of relevance to the scope of the inquiry as a whole, but also to the sufficiency of the prosecution evidence.[69] Thus, the accused is permitted to cross-examine a prosecution witness on any matter that could lead

---

66   See *R v I(SP)* (2005), 27 CR (6th) 112 (Nun Ct J).

67   *R v Monteleone*, [1987] 2 SCR 154 [*Monteleone*]; *R v Yebes*, [1987] 2 SCR 168 [*Yebes*]; *R v Charemski*, [1998] 1 SCR 679 [*Charemski*]; *Hynes*, above note 6; *Sazant*, above note 17; *Deschamplain*, above note 17.

68   *Re Zaor and the Queen* (1984), 12 CCC (3d) 265 (Que CA).

69   *R v Bayne* (1970), 14 CRNS 130 (AltaSCAD).

to the conclusion that the prosecution evidence is insufficient and is also permitted to cross-examine in a manner that might be useful in a subsequent trial. In this respect, the accused might cross-examine a prosecution witness on a matter that might have central significance at the trial but that is wholly outside the scope of the preliminary inquiry.[70] This occurs most frequently when an accused cross-examines for the purpose of a subsequent challenge at trial to the credibility of a witness, or for the purpose of laying the factual foundation for an issue under the *Charter* to be raised at trial.

With respect to examination and cross-examination, but especially the latter, the justice now has the express power to immediately stop any part of it that is, "in the opinion of the justice, abusive, too repetitive or otherwise inappropriate."[71] This power is broad. While protection against abuse or undue repetition is necessary, it is not clear what is intended by the sweeping phrase "otherwise inappropriate." Given that the *Code* encourages limitations on the scope of preliminary inquiries, this phrase should not be interpreted to restrict the ability of the parties to discover the nature and quality of the opponent's evidence.

In the amendments that came into force in 2004, there is a conspicuous gap that Parliament should have filled regarding the right of cross-examination. If the defence makes a request to hear a prosecution witness on a specific issue, it presumably wishes to cross-examine that witness. Yet nothing in the *Code* makes it clear that a witness who will be called at trial by the prosecution is also a prosecution witness for the purposes of cross-examination at the preliminary inquiry, even if the prosecution makes no request to hear that witness before trial. A judge has no jurisdiction at the preliminary inquiry to order the prosecution to call a witness and cannot himself call a witness. Presumably, all that the judge can do is ask the prosecutor to consent to call a witness for the purpose of cross-examination by the accused. It is also arguable that a request from the defence can be considered to have the effect of

---

70   *B(E)*, above note 33; *Dawson*, above note 34. See also *Re Ward and the Queen* (1976), 31 CCC (2d) 466 (Ont CA); *R v George* (1991), 69 CCC (3d) 148 (Ont CA). Whether this statement remains true after the 2004 amendments to the preliminary inquiry procedures has been a matter of some disagreement in lower courts. The rule has been reaffirmed (*R v McGrath*, 2007 NSSC 255, aff'd 2008 NSCA 32) but has also been questioned (*R v Tran*, 2008 ABPC 278). It has been argued that any efficiencies gained at the preliminary inquiry stage by refusing to permit evidence to be called on matters not going strictly to whether the accused should be committed for trial would result in greater inefficiencies from unnecessary applications at trial: Tim Quigley, "*R. v. Tran*: Annotation" (2008) 63 *Criminal Reports* (6th) 345.

71   Section 537(1.1).

challenging the prosecution case with regard to a specific witness and specific issue and this, in turn, can be taken to require the prosecution to call its witness on that specific issue. Even if the prosecutor declines to examine the witness, the witness is nevertheless available for cross-examination. Ideally, however, further amendment of the *Code* will be made to clarify that the defence is entitled to cross-examine prosecution witnesses at the preliminary inquiry where there is a request to do so.

3) Address to Accused

At the close of the prosecution evidence the *Code* requires the justice to address an accused who is not represented by counsel as follows, or in like terms:

> Do you wish to say anything in answer to these charges or to any other charges which might have arisen from the evidence led by the prosecution? You are not obliged to say anything but whatever you do say may be given in evidence against you at your trial. You should not make any confession or admission of guilt because of any promise or threat made to you but if you do make any statement it may be given in evidence against you at your trial in spite of the promise or threat.[72]

This caution is a vestige of ancient law in which magistrates were required to conduct investigations of alleged criminal activity, typically after arrest and before considering bail. As the preliminary inquiry later became a judicial examination of the sufficiency of the prosecution case, the investigative role of the magistrate disappeared. The caution is also a vestige of an era in which an accused person was not competent to testify. For both of these reasons the caution is largely an anachronism.

Section 541(2) requires this caution to be given only to an unrepresented accused, presumably on the assumption that an accused with representation will be competently advised of her position, thus dispensing with the need for the address. Nonetheless, there seems to be no harm in the judge reciting the required address in all cases, unless the defence makes clear that the accused has been apprised of the content of the address. In any case, as a practical matter it is rare for the accused to make a statement after caution, not least because anything she might say by way of defence will not be considered in the decision to commit for trial or discharge.[73]

---

72 Section 541(2).
73 Moreover, the accused who makes a statement after caution cannot be cross-examined, unlike the accused who testifies.

4) Defence Evidence

The defence is also entitled to adduce evidence on behalf of the accused, including testimony by the accused, but it is not obliged to call witnesses.[74] As the preliminary inquiry is not a trial and, therefore, cannot lead to a judgment of acquittal, it is comparatively rare that the accused is discharged at the preliminary inquiry solely on the basis of evidence called by the defence. Indeed, the tactical position of the defence at the preliminary inquiry can be delicate. There is no obligation on the accused to make disclosure of its case, and the production of witnesses for the defence can have not only the effect of making disclosure but also of exposing the accused at trial to any weaknesses that might emerge in the evidence of such witnesses.

There is, however, often some advantage in the preparation of the defence case if the accused calls evidence of potential prosecution witnesses. Such witnesses might not be essential for the prosecution to succeed at the preliminary inquiry, but they might still be useful for the defence. The advantage lies in hearing and seeing those witnesses, and thus assessing what they can give in evidence and the credibility with which they give it. Even if the effect of calling such evidence is, in some cases, to disclose the strategy of the defence, there might be no disadvantage in doing so if the net effect is to gain a stronger basis for preparing a defence at trial. Once again, these considerations illustrate that the preliminary inquiry provides an opportunity for the defence to acquire further discovery of the case as a whole.

This opportunity can be especially important where there is a real risk that the evidence in issue might not be, for any reason, available at trial, and the accused wishes to preserve it. On the other hand, in some cases an accused might be quite content that certain evidence will not be available later. In either event, it is important to take note of the fact that evidence led at the preliminary inquiry (whether by the defence or the Crown) may be admitted at trial.

Section 715 of the *Code* provides that if evidence was taken on oath at the preliminary inquiry in the presence of the accused, and the witness either refuses to testify or is dead, insane, too ill to travel, or absent from Canada, then that evidence can be introduced at trial. This statutory rule depends on the requirement that the accused had a full opportunity to cross-examine the witness. Normally, of course, an accused will have had such an opportunity, but in some cases information about the witness might become available only after the preliminary

---

74   Section 541.

inquiry, with the result that the opportunity to cross-examine was not a full one.[75]

Section 715, however, does not set out a "comprehensive code" on when preliminary inquiry testimony is admissible. As a result, in some cases, it is also possible to admit preliminary inquiry testimony through the principled exception to the hearsay rule. In *R v Hawkins*, for example, a witness testified at the preliminary inquiry, but then married the accused and so was incompetent to testify at trial. The Court held that this did not mean she was "refusing" to testify, and so section 715 did not apply to allow her evidence to be led at trial. Nonetheless, her preliminary inquiry testimony was admissible because it met the criteria of necessity and reliability that make up the principled exception.[76]

5) Publication Bans

As in all other aspects of criminal procedure, proceedings are open unless there is some specific basis for an exception. Thus, the presentation of evidence is conducted in open court and might be the subject of public comment, unless the judge orders otherwise. The *Code* gives the judge discretion to exclude the public from court.[77] This power is occasionally used, but it is comparatively rare at preliminary inquiries. As distinct from the general public, witnesses are routinely excluded, at least until they have given their evidence.[78]

Typically, the presentation of evidence at the preliminary inquiry is the subject of a ban upon publication in a newspaper or broadcast. The legislative rationale for these orders is that the accused, who is presumed innocent and is not in jeopardy of conviction at the preliminary inquiry, should be shielded from adverse publicity before trial. The same might be said of other witnesses, especially the complainant. Indeed, there is a general argument that the fairness of any subsequent

---

75   See, for example, *R v Assoun*, 2006 NSCA 47, in which the accused was unaware at the time of the preliminary inquiry that a witness claimed to have obtained some of her information through "psychic visions."

76   [1996] 3 SCR 1043. This precise result might now be questionable, given the Court's subsequent ruling on spousal incompetency and the principled exception in *R v Couture*, 2007 SCC 28 [*Couture*]. However, nothing in *Couture* casts doubt on the general approach that s 715 is not a complete code and that preliminary inquiry evidence is potentially admissible under the principled exception.

77   Sections 537(1)(h) and 486.

78   *Re Collette and the Queen; Re Richard and the Queen* (1983), 6 CCC (3d) 300 (Ont HCJ); *R c M(AG)* (1993), 26 CR (4th) 379 (Que CA); compare *Re Armstrong and State of Wisconsin* (1972), 7 CCC (2d) 331 (Ont HCJ).

trial can be ensured only if there is a publication ban at the preliminary inquiry.

A publication ban is imposed by order of the justice before any evidence is taken—it is discretionary, if sought by the prosecution, and mandatory, if sought by the accused.[79] It has been held that if the order is sought after the presentation of evidence has begun, the presiding judge has discretion in the matter, but there is little apparent justification for this position.[80] If the rationale for allowing any publication ban has force in the first place, there is no reason why that rationale should not be given effect after the presentation of evidence has begun.

If the accused is not represented by counsel, the *Code* obliges the judge to inform him of the right to seek a publication ban.[81] When ordered, the ban remains in effect until the accused is discharged or, if the accused is committed for trial, the trial is ended. Although such bans infringe in a material way upon the freedom of expression and the right to know what transpires in the public proceedings of courts, the courts have ruled that they are reasonable limitations upon those rights.[82]

D. COMMITTAL

Section 548 of the *Code* directs the justice or judge at the preliminary inquiry to commit the accused for trial on any indictable offence if the evidence in support of that charge is sufficient. It also requires that the accused be discharged in respect of any charge on which the evidence is not sufficient. Everything turns, therefore, on what is meant by "sufficient" evidence. The courts have provided a test that has been consistently applied for many years but, as will be seen, remains uncertain in some important aspects.

In *R v Shephard*, the Supreme Court stated that the test of sufficiency at the preliminary inquiry, as for a directed verdict and for committal in extradition matters, is whether a reasonable jury, properly instructed, could find the charge proved beyond reasonable doubt.[83] The core of uncertainty in this test lies in the degree to which an assessment of the evidence permits or requires the presiding judge to consider the probative

---

79   Section 539.

80   *R v Harrison* (1984), 14 CCC (3d) 549 (Que SP).

81   Section 539(2).

82   See, for example, *Dagenais v Canadian Broadcasting Corporation*, [1994] 3 SCR 835; *Canadian Broadcasting Corporation v New Brunswick (Attorney General)*, [1996] 3 SCR 480; and *R v Mentuck*, [2001] 3 SCR 442.

83   *Shephard*, above note 6.

force of the evidence. It is arguable that a reference to whether the jury could return a finding of guilt is at least some indication that the presiding judge should assess the force of the evidence.

A convenient fashion in which to examine the test of sufficiency is to look at the criteria of completeness and weight. The first of these means only that the prosecution leads evidence corresponding to each of the elements of the offence as defined in the substantive criminal law, including identification.[84] In a case of assault, for example, this would mean that there was evidence led that the accused intentionally applied force to another person without that person's consent. In the general run of cases, the criterion of completeness poses few difficulties.

It is the criterion of weight that is problematic. The Supreme Court and other courts have said repeatedly that the judge is not to assess the weight of evidence at the preliminary inquiry.[85] Accordingly, a judge must not assess the credibility of witnesses who testify.[86] In response, some have asserted that if there is any evidence on all essential elements in the charge, there should be an order of committal.[87] The reason most commonly invoked for this assertion is that the justice or judge at the preliminary inquiry must not usurp the functions of the jury or judge at trial in determining the strength of the case.[88]

On the other hand, if the prosecution evidence is such that no reasonable jury, properly instructed, could find the charge to be proven beyond a reasonable doubt, this seems like a relevant consideration. Whether she is entitled to assess the credibility of witnesses or not, one might argue that the judge should discharge the accused if no reasonable trier of fact could find the accused guilty on the evidence adduced by the prosecution. To reach such a conclusion would not be to usurp the role of the ultimate trier of fact.

The resolution of this problem depends upon the perceived purpose of having preliminary inquiries. If the test of sufficiency is restricted to the criterion of completeness, as discussed above, it follows that the justice should not weigh the evidence adduced at the preliminary inquiry. It would also follow from this that the test of sufficiency stated in *Shephard* should be reformulated to require that the prosecution evidence need only support an air of reality as regards each of the elements of the charge. But if the primary purpose of the preliminary

---

84   *Skogman*, above note 7; *Deschamplain*, above note 17 at para 23.

85   *Monteleone*, above note 67; *Yebes*, above note 67.

86   See, for example, *R v Arcuri*, [2001] 2 SCR 828 [*Arcuri*]; see also, *Deschamplain*, above note 17; and *Sazant*, above note 17.

87   An extreme illustration is *Charemski*, above note 67.

88   *Monteleone*, above note 67.

inquiry is to test the sufficiency of the prosecution case, and thus to protect the accused from being placed on trial pointlessly, it follows that the judge must discharge in any case where no reasonable trier of fact could find the prosecution case proved beyond reasonable doubt.

On the one hand, the Court has regularly ruled that the test of sufficiency at the preliminary inquiry is concerned with the completeness of the prosecution evidence on the elements of the offence. Indeed, the Court has said that if there is direct evidence on all elements, the accused must be committed even where defence evidence has been called. In this approach, weight would seem to have no part in the test of sufficiency where there is direct prosecution evidence on an element.

On the other hand, where the prosecution case on an element is circumstantial, the Court has said in *R v Arcuri* that the justice should undertake a limited weighing of the evidence, including any defence evidence, to determine whether a reasonable trier of fact could return a finding of guilt.[89] In doing this, the justice is not entitled to assess reliability or credibility in the evidence and must not draw any inferences from the evidence. A "limited weighing" of circumstantial evidence therefore requires the judge to consider whether, if believed, the evidence could support inferences in favour of the prosecution and whether it could be considered reliable or credible. If so, the accused should be committed.

Further, and once again in the context of an extradition case, the Court has commented in *United States of America v Ferras*:

> [40] . . . I take as axiomatic that a person could not be committed for trial for an offence in Canada if the evidence is so manifestly unreliable that it would be unsafe to rest a verdict upon it. It follows that if a judge on an extradition hearing concludes that the evidence is manifestly unreliable, the judge should not order extradition under s 29(1). Yet, under the current state of the law in *Shephard*, it appears that the judge is denied this possibility.[90]

In *Ferras* the Court went on to modify the *Shephard* test in the extradition context, but in doing so it indicated that there was no longer symmetry between the extradition and preliminary inquiry tests.

One might hope that the standard of sufficiency will be further reviewed by the Supreme Court, specifically in the context of preliminary inquiries. A purposive interpretation of this test would be that a justice should discharge the accused if no reasonable trier of fact could

89   *Arcuri*, above note 86.
90   2006 SCC 33 [*Ferras*].

find the essential elements of the offence proved beyond reasonable doubt. Whether this conclusion is reached by reason of incompleteness or weight should not matter. This approach would not only be consistent with the purpose of the preliminary inquiry, it would also acknowledge the proper role of the trier of fact at a trial. It allows that a case that could come to proof beyond reasonable doubt should go to trial and that a case that could not should be dismissed. Given the more limited role that has been provided for preliminary inquiries with the legislative changes, however, it is unlikely that major change of this sort is forthcoming.

Assuming that the prosecution case at the preliminary inquiry meets the test of sufficiency, the judge will order committal on any indictable offence charged or supported by the evidence. Ordering committal is done by endorsing the information in a manner that identifies the appropriate offences.[91] It will be recalled that the judge is not limited to committal on the offences charged in the information, or to lesser or included charges, but is limited to committal upon charges in respect of the same transaction.[92] In general, this limitation means that the committal order must refer to offences that are related to the event or sequence of events that form the factual basis of the charges in the information at the preliminary inquiry. There is some margin in this for flexibility, and thus it has been held that if the evidence identifies another victim than that identified in the original charge, there might be an order of committal for an offence in relation to that victim, provided, of course, that the offence occurred in respect of the same events.[93]

If the accused is discharged at the preliminary inquiry, there is no acquittal and thus he cannot claim protection against double jeopardy if the prosecution should subsequently proceed against him on the same charge or a related charge, either by means of a fresh information or a direct indictment. As the accused was never in jeopardy of conviction at the preliminary inquiry, the discharge cannot constitute a final judgment.[94]

---

91   It is not adequate for the judge simply to say that the accused is committed for trial. Specific offences must be enumerated in the endorsement.

92   The judge has no jurisdiction to commit the accused for trial on any summary conviction offence that is disclosed by the evidence, but he can commit for any indictable offence, including one that lies within the absolute jurisdiction of the provincial court.

93   *R v Stewart* (1988), 44 CCC (3d) 109 (Ont CA).

94   *R v Ewanchuk* (1974), 16 CCC (2d) 517 (AltaSCAD); *R v Fields* (1979), 12 CR (3d) 273 (BCCA).

If the accused is committed for trial, the justice who presided at the preliminary inquiry is required to transmit the record of the inquiry to the court of trial.[95] The record comprises the information as endorsed, the evidence (including exhibits), any statement made by the accused after the justice's address, and any paper process relating to compelling the appearance of the accused.

E. REVIEW OF PRELIMINARY INQUIRY DECISIONS

The *Code* sets out no procedure for appealing the decision to commit or discharge at a preliminary inquiry, and so no appeal is possible. As a result, review of such a decision can be made only on the basis of an action for *certiorari*. Part XXVI of the *Code* regulates the use of extraordinary remedies in the criminal justice system and attaches some limits on the occasions when *certiorari* is available,[96] but it does remain available in the case of decisions at a preliminary inquiry. In principle, it is open to the Crown to seek *certiorari* in the case of a discharge, and this does sometimes occur.[97] As a practical matter, the Crown also has the usually simpler option, under section 577, of preferring a direct indictment despite the discharge, so more frequently *certiorari* applications involve an accused seeking review of a decision to commit.

Because the preliminary inquiry decision is reviewed by way of *certiorari* rather than appeal, it is not sufficient to show an error of law on the part of the preliminary inquiry judge. Rather, *certiorari* will be granted only if the judge has fallen into jurisdictional error. Many errors of law will simply be errors within a judge's jurisdiction. Erroneously excluding evidence at the preliminary hearing is unlikely to be a jurisdictional error (for example, an error with respect to the application of the rules of evidence will not be a jurisdictional error unless it rises to the level of a denial of natural justice).[98]

Apart from denying natural justice, it is also a jurisdictional error if a trial judge fails to comply with a mandatory provision of the *Code*. In particular, section 548 of the *Code* requires a judge to commit the

---

95 Section 551.
96 See s 776.
97 See, for example, *R v Dubois*, [1986] 1 SCR 366 [*Dubois*]; *Sazant*, above note 17; *PM*, above note 15.
98 *Dubois*, above note 97 at 377; *Forsythe*, above note 16 at 272; *Attorney General (Quebec) v Cohen*, [1979] 2 SCR 305.

accused for trial if "there is sufficient evidence." In other words, there must be at least some basis in the evidence at the preliminary inquiry that supports the decision to commit.[99] It also means, since a preliminary inquiry judge does not weigh evidence, that where the Crown has adduced direct evidence on all the elements of the offence, the preliminary inquiry judge must commit the accused even if the defence has offered exculpatory evidence.[100] If there is no evidence on some essential element of the charge, however, it will be a jurisdictional error for the preliminary inquiry judge to commit the accused to trial.[101]

The existence of evidence at the preliminary inquiry must be understood broadly. Even if the Crown has indicated that evidence led through a preliminary inquiry witness will not be led at trial, that evidence must nonetheless be considered in the decision to commit, and it would be a jurisdictional error to fail to consider it.[102]

Section 548 also requires a preliminary inquiry judge to discharge the accused if "on the whole of the evidence no sufficient case is made out." In other words, if a preliminary inquiry judge grants a discharge without considering "the whole of the evidence," that will also be a jurisdictional error.[103] The action would constitute a failure to comply with a mandatory statutory provision and would therefore allow a reviewing court to intervene.

Some guidance on the type of mistakes that can lead to jurisdictional errors was provided by the Court with its decision in *R v Sazant*.[104] The accused had been discharged at the preliminary inquiry on a charge of sexual assault. The preliminary inquiry judge had said there was "absolutely no evidence of non-consent." In fact, the complainant had testified that he did not want to take part in the sexual activity, and so there was no dispute that the preliminary inquiry judge had made an error. The issue was whether the error was jurisdictional.

The Court held that there were three possible explanations for the preliminary inquiry judge's mistake. He might have misunderstood the elements of the offence and given effect to a non-existent defence. In that event, he would not have tested the Crown's evidence against the

---

99 *Dubois*, above note 97 at 377.
100 *Arcuri*, above note 86 at para 29.
101 *Skogman*, above note 7 at 104. For discussion of jurisdictional error generally, see William Poulos, "The Preliminary Inquiry: Staying within the Zone of Protection" (2015) 62 *Criminal Law Quarterly* 365.
102 *R v Papadopoulos* (2005), 201 CCC (3d) 363 (Ont CA), leave to appeal to SCC refused, [2005] SCCA No 314.
103 *Deschamplain*, above note 17 at para 18.
104 *Sazant*, above note 17.

actual elements of the offence charged, which would be a jurisdictional error. Second, the preliminary inquiry judge might have found the complainant's statement to be ambiguous, capable of interpretation either as an expression of "after-the-fact" regret, or as a statement of "during-the-fact" non-consent. If that were the case, though, it was not open to the preliminary inquiry judge to decide which interpretation he preferred — that would be an issue for the trial judge. In that event, the preliminary inquiry judge would again have fallen into jurisdictional error by deciding an issue reserved for another forum.[105] Finally, the preliminary inquiry judge might have simply overlooked the evidence of non-consent in the complainant's testimony. In that event he would have failed to consider "the whole of the evidence" as required by section 548, and so again would have committed a jurisdictional error.

An accused who wants to bring a *certiorari* application must do so before entering a plea to the charge upon which he was committed to trial. Once the plea is entered, jurisdiction is transferred to the superior court for trial, and the issue becomes whether the Crown can prove its case, not how the accused came to be there.[106]

FURTHER READINGS

HEALY, PATRICK. "Chabotage: Expanding the Crown's Power to Prefer Additional Counts" (1984) 38 *Criminal Reports* (3d) 344.

PACIOCCO, DAVID. "A Voyage of Discovery: Examining the Precarious Condition of the Preliminary Inquiry" (2003) 48 *Criminal Law Quarterly* 151.

POULOS, WILLIAM. "The Preliminary Inquiry: Staying within the Zone of Protection" (2015) 62 *Criminal Law Quarterly* 365.

QUIGLEY, TIM. *Procedure in Canadian Criminal Law*, 2d ed (Toronto: Thomson Carswell, 2005), ch 14–15.

———. "*R. v. Tran*: Annotation" (2008) 63 *Criminal Reports* (6th) 345.

---

105 This had also been the rationale in *Dubois*, above note 97, where the preliminary inquiry judge was taken to have decided whether the evidence was capable of proving the Crown's case beyond a reasonable doubt, a decision reserved for the trial judge.

106 *R v Tippett*, 2010 NLCA 49.

CHAPTER 10

PRELIMINARY MATTERS AND REMEDIES

A number of matters can or must be dealt with prior to the start of prosecution. First, in some cases, an offence is not dealt with by way of prosecution at all, but rather through some alternative. Next, assuming that a prosecution is to occur, some administrative and other matters can be dealt with before the trial begins, either through a pre-trial motion or a pre-trial conference. Finally, in a case that will be tried by a jury, that jury must be selected. All of these issues will be dealt with in this chapter.

A. ALTERNATIVES TO PROSECUTION

In an informal sense, there has long existed an alternative to prosecution in Canada through the exercise of discretion by police in not laying charges in the first place, or by Crown prosecutors in not continuing them.[1] Only relatively recently has that discretion been more formalized in a system of alternative measures authorized by statute.

---

1 Although the general view of the legitimacy of exercising such discretion has varied over time: see the discussion in Bruce Archibald, "Prosecutors, Democracy and the Public Interest: Prosecutorial Discretion and Its Limits in Canada" (Paper delivered at the XVIth Congress of the International Academy of Comparative Law, Brisbane, Australia, 14–22 July 2002) at 17–22.

Statutory alternative measures to prosecution began in 1985 with the *Young Offenders Act*,[2] though under that Act they were available only to young persons. Subsequently in 1995, the provisions of section 4 of the *YOA* were adopted into the *Criminal Code*, thereby creating the potential use of alternative measures for adults as well. The essential theory behind these schemes is that, in certain cases, the interests of society might be adequately protected through measures that are less intrusive to the person alleged to have committed an offence than prosecution. If the person fails to comply with the requirements of the alternative measures program, however, criminal charges can still be laid.

Section 717 of the *Code* does not require that an alternative measures program exist, but it authorizes the Attorney General of a province to create such a program. The use of these measures is subject to various conditions, in particular, the general directive that the use of such measures cannot be inconsistent with the protection of society, and that the person considering their use is satisfied that they are appropriate given "the interests of society and of the victim."[3] Other provisions are aimed at protecting the interests of the person who would otherwise be the "accused." In large part, these provisions are aimed at ensuring that alternative measures are used only in cases that would otherwise have proceeded to prosecution, rather than being used in cases that simply would not have occupied the justice system at all. That is, alternative measures are intended to be a way of diverting some cases out of the criminal justice system, not a way of expanding its scope.

Consistent with this approach, alternative measures cannot be used unless the prosecutor believes that there would be sufficient evidence to proceed with a prosecution and that the prosecution is not barred at law in any way.[4] The person involved must have been advised of the right to counsel, must accept responsibility for the act or omission constituting the offence, and must fully and freely consent to participate.[5] Alternative measures cannot be used where the person denies involvement in the offence or wants a charge dealt with in court.[6] Further protection for the individual is provided by the rule that no admission, confession, or statement made by a person as a condition of being dealt with by alternative measures is admissible against that person in any later proceedings.[7]

---

2   RSC 1985, c Y-1, enacted as SC 1980–81–82–83, c 110 [*YOA*].
3   Section 717(1)(b).
4   Sections 717(1)(f) & (g).
5   Sections 717(1)(c), (d), & (e).
6   Section 717(2).
7   Section 717(1)(3).

If a person completes the alternative measures, the court must dismiss any charges laid against that person later in respect of the offence. If charges are later laid against a person who has only partly completed the alternative measures, a court can still stay the charges if it is of the view that "the prosecution of the charge would be unfair, having regard to the circumstances and that person's performance with respect to the alternative measures."[8]

In practice, provinces have tended to consider the use of alternative measures according to various categories of offences. Typically, alternative measures simply will not be used for serious violent offences, serious sexual offences, spousal violence, drug trafficking, organized crime, and so on. Many minor offences presumptively will automatically be referred to alternative measures, while a group of offences in the middle continue to depend on prosecutorial discretion. Normally, this discretion is to be exercised in accordance with criteria established within the province's prosecution service.[9]

Alternative measures programs usually ask the person to undertake community service, personal service for the victim, specialized education programs, or counselling, or to write a letter of apology.[10] More ambitious alternatives are also available. In Nova Scotia, for example, relying on the authority of section 717 of the *Code* and section 4 of the *YOA*, the province created a restorative justice program. This program creates the possibility for conferences between the offender, the victim, supporters of each of those people, and, potentially, other members of the community or police officers. Supporters of restorative justice argue that the outcomes of such conferences can ultimately be far more beneficial to the offender, the victim, and society as a whole.[11]

Subsequently, the *YOA* was replaced by the *Youth Criminal Justice Act*.[12] That Act now refers not to "alternative measures" but to "extrajudicial measures." For the most part, the features noted above are unchanged,[13] though they are now classed as "extrajudicial sanctions." However, various additional features, other than sanctions, have been

---

8   Section 717(4)(b).

9   See the discussion in Archibald, above note 1 at 29–30.

10   *Ibid* at 29.

11   *Ibid* at 34.

12   SC 2002, c 1 [*YCJA*].

13   Two differences should be noted. Section 10(2)(d) of the *YCJA*, *ibid*, requires not only that the young person be informed of the right to consult with counsel, but also that there be a reasonable opportunity to do so. Further, in s 10(2)(b), although the person considering whether to refer must still consider the interests of society, any explicit reference to the interest of the victim has been removed.

added to the scheme. Most notable is the declaration of principles, in addition to those governing the *YCJA* generally, and specific to extrajudicial measures and clearly aimed at encouraging greater use of the measures. They affirm that extrajudicial measures are often the most appropriate and effective way to address youth crime, and that they allow for effective and timely intervention. In particular, they affirm that extrajudicial measures are presumed to be adequate for non-violent offences where the young person has not previously been found guilty of an offence, and that they can be used even if the young person has previously been dealt with by extrajudicial measures or has been found guilty of an offence.[14]

Consistent with a restorative approach, the *YCJA* also encourages the use of extrajudicial measures that aim to involve the families of the young person and the victim, and the community in their design and implementation.[15]

The *YCJA* also creates a system of "pre-alternative measures," as it were, by allowing the Attorney General of a province to create a system whereby police or prosecutors can administer a caution to a young person rather than commencing judicial proceedings. Under the *YCJA*, before starting judicial proceedings or taking any other measures, police are to consider the principles set out above and decide whether it would be sufficient to issue a caution. Police can also, with consent, refer a young person to a community agency "that may assist the young person not to commit offences."[16] Provincial programs authorizing Crown prosecutors to administer cautions rather than continue proceedings are also envisioned.[17] The relatively informal, low seriousness of this response to a young person's actions is stressed by the requirement that evidence of a caution or referral given to a young person is not admissible to prove prior offending behaviour in any later proceedings.[18]

In addition to these programs, many provinces or cities have begun to develop drug treatment or mental health courts.[19] The exact criteria differ from location to location, but they all share the underlying goal

---

14   *Ibid*, s 4.
15   *Ibid*, s 5.
16   *Ibid*, s 6(1).
17   *Ibid*, s 8.
18   *Ibid*, s 9.
19   There are, for example, drug treatment courts in Vancouver, Calgary, Moose Jaw, Winnipeg, Ottawa, and Kentville, Nova Scotia, among other locations. There are mental health courts in cities such as Saskatoon, Toronto, Montréal, and Dartmouth. See, generally, Richard D Schneider, Hy Bloom, & Mark Heerema, *Mental Health Courts: Decriminalizing the Mentally Ill* (Toronto: Irwin Law, 2007).

of dealing with offenders whose criminal behaviour is associated with either addiction or mental health issues by confronting those underlying issues directly, rather than simply prosecuting the accused for the behaviour. Typically, the Crown must be able to show that it would be possible to obtain a conviction, or the accused must be willing to plead, or actually plead, guilty to the offence. The offender is then referred to the appropriate court and becomes subject to a close monitoring scheme, often by means of bail conditions. Such courts are not located in every province but are becoming increasingly common.

B. PRE-TRIAL MOTIONS AND CONFERENCES

1) Timing and Means

Authority over pre-trial motions and conferences is not set out as clearly in Canadian law as one might wish. Potential ambiguity arises even with the concept of what counts as "pre-trial." The Supreme Court has held on a number of occasions that the phrases "charged with an offence" and "commencement of trial" do not have fixed meanings and will be adjusted to suit particular contexts.

In *R v Chabot*, for example, the Court found the key transition point to be when an indictment was "lodged with the trial court at the opening of the accused's trial, with a court ready to proceed with the trial."[20] In *R v Kalanj*, in contrast, the Court notes that the word "charged" has no precise meaning in law and could reasonably range from being told that one will be charged with an offence to being called upon to plead in court.[21] In the context of the *Charter* section 11(b) right to trial within a reasonable time, the Court rejected the *Chabot* position, holding instead that a person is "charged" for section 11 purposes when an information is sworn or a direct indictment is laid.[22] Similarly, in *R v Basarabas and Spek v the Queen* the Court noted that the time of commencement of a jury trial will vary depending on which *Code* section

---

20   [1980] 2 SCR 985 at 999 [*Chabot*].
21   [1989] 1 SCR 1594 at para 11 [*Kalanj*].
22   The Court rejected the argument that the time should run from the accused's arrest, eight months prior to the laying of charges. Compare *R v Connors* (1998), 14 CR (5th) 200 (BCCA), which held that for purposes of the *Identification of Criminals Act*, RSC 1985, c I-1, an accused had been charged with an offence when he had failed a breathalyzer test and was asked to give fingerprints at the time or return later to do so.

is being considered and what interests are at stake.[23] For example, in dealing with an accused's right to be present for trial, the Court has considered jury selection to be part of the trial,[24] but in dealing with the power to replace a juror, the Court has held that the trial does not commence until the accused is placed in the charge of the jury.[25]

In the context of pre-trial motions, the Court has held that only the trial judge should hear applications to sever counts. In reference to the *Chabot* case in *R v Litchfield*,[26] the Court held that only the trial judge has jurisdiction to issue severance orders. However, the Court noted that as long as a trial judge has been assigned, there is no need to wait until the actual trial date to bring the application. Section 645(5) of the *Code* specifically authorizes a trial judge in a jury trial, before the jury has been selected, to deal with any matter that would be dealt with in the absence of the jury. The Court notes that a similar power "was always open to a trial judge in a case of trial by judge alone to hear pre-trial motions before preparing to hear evidence."[27] It is likely that the *Litchfield* ruling, regarding the inability of anyone but the trial judge to hear motions concerning severance, applies to pre-trial motions generally. In this context, it is noteworthy that, for Charter motions, a preliminary inquiry judge is not a "court of competent jurisdiction" for the purposes of granting the remedy of excluding evidence under section 24(2).[28] However, given the Court's acknowledgment that different considerations apply in different contexts, it is possible that some motions could be permitted at an earlier time or in front of someone other than the trial judge,[29] or, alternatively, that some motions might not be permitted until the trial proper is about to commence.

There is one clear exception to the *Litchfield* rule, but it applies only in certain circumstances. Section 551.1 of the *Code* permits the appointment of a case management judge where "it is necessary for the proper administration of justice."[30] This measure, introduced in response to the difficulties and delays that arise with regard to so-called "mega trials," is not routinely taken. Where a case management judge is appointed, however, that judge has the ability to make rulings in advance

---

23   [1982] 2 SCR 730 [*Basarabas*].
24   *R v Barrow*, [1987] 2 SCR 694 [*Barrow*].
25   *Basarabas*, above note 23.
26   [1993] 4 SCR 333 [*Litchfield*].
27   *Ibid* at para 27.
28   *R v Hynes*, [2001] 3 SCR 623 [*Hynes*]; *R v Mills*, [1986] 1 SCR 863 [*Mills*].
29   The Court acknowledges in *Hynes*, above note 28, that preliminary inquiry judges can exclude evidence that is inadmissible on non-*Charter* grounds.
30   See also the discussion of case management judges in Chapter 2, Section B(4).

of trial which are binding on the parties and the trial judge, including adjudicating issues about severance of counts or accused, disclosure, or admissibility of evidence.[31]

This particular area of the law would benefit from rationalization more generally. Some pre-trial motions are specifically permitted in the *Code*, for example, applications for change of venue,[32] for particulars,[33] for exclusion of the public from trial or a publication ban,[34] or to sever counts.[35] Other pre-trial motions are not specifically provided for in the *Code*. For examples, see the general power to hear such motions in non-jury trials referred to above in *Litchfield* or pre-trial motions for relief under the *Charter*. The latter, among the most significant pre-trial motions made in courts, are subject to rules of court in some jurisdictions, but not to a statutory scheme.[36] Some applications can be made to preliminary inquiry judges,[37] and some cannot.[38] The timing for various applications differs and is sometimes based on wording that does not clearly indicate Parliament's intent (as noted above).[39] Calls for reform of this area have been made.[40]

---

31 Section 551.3.
32 Section 599.
33 Section 587.
34 Section 486.
35 Section 591(3).
36 Compare, for example, *R v Blom* (2002), 6 CR (6th) 181 (Ont CA), and *R v Russell*, [1999] BCJ No 2245 at para 6 (SC).
37 See *R v Webster*, [1993] 1 SCR 3, holding that a preliminary inquiry judge has jurisdiction under s 601 to consider whether an indictment is valid. Indeed, *R v Volpi* (1987), 34 CCC (3d) 1 (Ont CA), holds that this application can be made before the accused elects.
38 See *R v Chew*, [1968] 2 CCC 127 (Ont CA), dealing with applications for particulars under s 587.
39 In addition to the ambiguity noted above concerning phrases such as "commencement of trial," note s 590(2), which allows an accused to apply to divide a count "at any stage of his trial," and the very similar s 591(3), which allows an accused to request separate trials on separate counts "before or during his trial."
40 See, in particular, Law Reform Commission of Canada, *Trial within a Reasonable Time* (Ottawa: Canada Communication Group, 1994), which recommended a system of pre-trial motions to be heard either by the trial judge or another judge of the same court. In the particular context of pre-trial motions connected with jury selection, see *R v Sharma* (1995), 67 BCAC 241 at para 23, where the British Columbia Court of Appeal observed that

> the ancient notion of preferment no longer has any relevance to modern day criminal proceedings . . . . In the interests of public convenience and the efficient operation of the courts, it has been the practice now for many years in this jurisdiction to have juries selected for a number of trials on one day each month. The complexities surrounding the preferment of indictments,

A further forum in which matters can be discussed pre-trial is through a pre-hearing conference. Section 625.1 of the *Code* permits such hearings "to consider matters that to promote a fair and expeditious hearing, would be better decided before the start of the proceedings, and other similar matters, and to make arrangements for decisions on those matters."[41] Such conferences are mandatory in the case of jury trials[42] and generally have been described as "an invaluable ally in the struggle to promote a fair and efficient criminal trial process."[43]

Pre-hearing conferences provide an opportunity for the parties and the court to see whether an agreement can be reached on issues that will expedite the trial. The conference gives the judge a chance to determine, for example, whether the voluntariness of statements will be admitted, whether identity will be an issue, or whether continuity of exhibits will be challenged.[44]

However, in contrast to pre-trial motions, pre-hearing conferences are not intended to determine matters: "s. 625.1 does not bind either the Crown or defence to a particular position."[45] Thus, for example, a Crown prosecutor might indicate at a pre-hearing conference a lack of intention to use a statement given by the accused, but then at trial seek to introduce the statement. Provided that on the particular facts there is no threat to the accused's fair trial right (for example, that the accused has not chosen a jury trial relying on the fact that the statement would not be tendered), the prosecutor is entitled to change strategy despite representations made at the pre-hearing conference.[46] Similarly,

---

when trials begin, when jurors can be replaced and which warrants and judicial interim release powers can be exercised by which judges in such a system, all result from a *Criminal Code* long outdated and overburdened with half a century of, as I have said before, patchwork revision which does not recognize this practice. A complete overhaul of the procedural provisions of the *Criminal Code*, which would sanctify the sensible innovations developed in this jurisdiction and provide for a simple straightforward way of moving the accused procedurally from committal through to verdict, is long overdue.

41   Section 482(1) of the *Code* creates the authority for superior courts of criminal jurisdiction to create rules of court, and s 482(2) permits courts of criminal jurisdiction to do so subject to the approval of the Lieutenant Governor in Council. Section 482(3)(c) specifically authorizes rules concerning pre-hearing conferences. Superior courts in every province have, in fact, made such rules.

42   Section 625.1(2).

43   *R v Nguyen*, 2013 ONCA 169 at para 54.

44   *R v Christensen* (1995), 100 Man R (2d) 25 (CA) [*Christensen*].

45   *R v Begrand-Fast* (1999), 180 Sask R 271 (CA), leave to appeal to SCC refused, [1999] SCCA No 583 [*Begrand-Fast*].

46   *R v K(MA)* (2002), 166 Man R (2d) 205 (CA).

a Crown prosecutor can decide after a pre-hearing conference on a joint indictment to file separate indictments against each accused.[47]

The defence is also not bound by representations made at a pre-hearing conference and can, for example, indicate at a conference that the issue in a sexual assault trial will be consent, but then argue at trial that no sexual relations occurred.[48] Similarly, because the pre-hearing conference is held on a without prejudice basis, indicating an intent to request a transfer hearing to youth court during the conference does not constitute an application.[49]

2) Particular Pre-trial Motions

Pre-trial motions can cover a wide variety of topics, and so the details of each will not be dealt with here. The substantive issues relevant to an application challenging the form of an indictment, or seeking a publication ban, can be found in Chapter 11. Similarly, pre-trial applications dealing with *Charter* issues, such as search and seizure issues or motions regarding disclosure, are dealt with in the chapters that correspond to those topics. However, some pre-trial motions will be discussed at greater length here, in particular, applications for change of venue, applications regarding fitness to stand trial, and *Charter* applications regarding the right to a trial within a reasonable time.

a)   Change of Venue

At common law, trials are to be held in the area in which the offence occurred. Trial judges typically have jurisdiction throughout the province in which they are appointed, and the only real territorial limitation is that courts should not hear trials of offences committed entirely in another province.[50] Nonetheless, the practice continues to be that trials are held in the area where the offences occurred, on the basis that this approach serves the interests of both the accused and the community.[51]

In some circumstances, however, it is possible to apply to change the venue in which the trial will be held, in accordance with section 599 of the *Code*. That section allows either the defence or the Crown to apply

---

47   *Begrand-Fast*, above note 45.
48   *Christensen*, above note 44. The Court questions the wisdom of such a strategy, at least without giving prior notice to the court and the Crown of the changed approach.
49   *R v AWD* (1999), 126 OAC 334 (CA).
50   Section 478(1), but see the various special jurisdiction rules in ss 7, 476, 477.1, and 478(2) & (3).
51   *R v Suzack* (2000), 30 CR (5th) 346 at para 30 (Ont CA) [*Suzack*].

for a change of venue on the grounds that "(a) it appears expedient to the ends of justice; or (b) a competent authority has directed that a jury is not to be summoned at the time appointed in a territorial division where the trial would otherwise by law be held."[52] As a practical matter, change of venue applications turn on whether pre-trial publicity has made it too difficult for an accused to obtain a fair trial without one.[53]

The essential issue is whether there is strong evidence of a general prejudicial attitude in the community as a whole.[54] In addition, that prejudice must not be capable of being cured by safeguards in jury selection, by instructions from the trial judge to the jury panel, or by the rules of evidence.[55] Because the remedy is discretionary, the judge hearing the application must consider all relevant factors.

The existence of the challenge for cause process, for example, and the ability in some circumstances to question jurors to determine whether pre-trial publicity has affected their ability to be impartial, has been relied on to dismiss change of venue applications.[56] Indeed, in cases where pre-trial publicity has been province-wide, it has been held that leaving the trial in a larger centre and using the challenge for cause process is more likely to protect the accused's rights than changing the venue to a smaller centre.[57] The date of the media coverage will also be relevant (prejudicial publicity from a year prior might not justify a change in venue).[58] In *R v Eng* the British Columbia Court of Appeal upheld a decision not to change venues on a retrial, even though a change of venue had been allowed on the original trial, on the basis that the passage of time had mended any prejudice caused by the media coverage.[59] Further, a change of venue will not be granted if the source of prejudice is the information to come out at trial, rather than the fact of pre-trial

---

52 Note that s 2 of the *Code* defines "territorial division" as "any province, county, union of counties, township, city, town, parish or other judicial division or place to which the context applies." Note, as well, that s 599 is incorporated by reference to apply to summary conviction offences: s 795.

53 The one distinct circumstance worth noting is when a change of venue is sought under s 531 of the *Code* to allow a trial to take place more easily in the official language of Canada that is the language of the accused.

54 *R v Munson*, 2003 SKCA 28 [*Munson*]; *R v English* (1993), 84 CCC (3d) 511 (Nfld CA) [*English*]; *R v Alward and Mooney* (1976), 39 CRNS 281 (NBSCAD).

55 *Suzack*, above note 51 at para 35.

56 See, for example, *ibid*, and *Munson*, above note 54. For further discussion of pre-trial publicity and challenges for cause, see Section C(3)(c), below in this chapter.

57 *Munson, ibid*.

58 *Suzack*, above note 51.

59 (1999), 138 CCC (3d) 188 at para 6 (BCCA).

publicity "where the real potential for prejudice lies in the evidence which the jury eventually selected to try the case will hear, a change of venue does not assist in protecting an accused's right to a fair trial."[60]

Where an accused applies for the change in venue,[61] the accused must show that the change is needed. Although this might be considered to place an onus on the accused, the provision has been held not to violate the *Charter*.[62]

b)   Fitness to Stand Trial

Another motion potentially made on a pre-trial basis concerns the fitness of the accused to stand trial. This issue looks at whether the accused suffers from a mental disorder, and so is related to the ultimate issue of whether an accused will be found not criminally responsible under section 16 of the *Code*. The fitness to stand trial provisions are found in Part XX.1 of the *Code*. The majority of that part sets out the procedures to deal with accused who have been found not criminally responsible based on a state of mind at the time of the offence, while the fitness provisions focus on the accused's mental state at the time of trial and whether it is fair to proceed.[63]

Everyone is presumed to be fit to stand trial.[64] The definition of "unfit to stand trial" in section 2 of the *Code* requires first that the accused suffers from a mental disorder (the same requirement as in section 16 for an accused to be not criminally responsible). The second requirement is that the accused is unable on that account

> to conduct a defence at any stage of the proceedings before a verdict is rendered or to instruct counsel, and, in particular, unable on account of mental disorder to (a) understand the nature of the proceedings (b) understand the possible consequences of the proceedings, or (c) communicate with counsel.

This provision is a codification of common law rules concerning fitness.[65] Of these issues, whether the accused is able to communicate with counsel has attracted the most judicial attention.

---

60   *Suzack*, above note 51 at para 38.
61   This is the typical case, though it is open on the terms of s 599 for the Crown to apply: see *R v Ponton* (1899), 2 CCC 417 (Ont HCJ).
62   *Suzack*, above note 51 at para 43.
63   Section 141 of the *YCJA*, above note 12, incorporates Part XX.1 of the *Criminal Code* except where those provisions conflict with rules in the former Act.
64   Section 672.22.
65   *R v Whittle*, [1994] 2 SCR 914 [*Whittle*]; *R v Taylor* (1992), 11 OR (3d) 323 (CA) [*Taylor*]; *R v Brigham* (1992), 18 CR (4th) 309 (Que CA).

A consciously low standard has been set for whether an accused can communicate with counsel. All that is necessary is for the accused to be able to communicate the facts relating to the offence: "provided the accused possesses this limited capacity, it is not a prerequisite that he or she be capable of exercising analytical reasoning in making a choice to accept the advice of counsel or in coming to a decision that best serves her interests."[66]

The Court, having jurisdiction over the accused, can order a fitness hearing on its own motion, or on application by the prosecutor or the accused. A party arguing that the accused is unfit has the burden of proof, on a balance of probabilities.[67] The fitness hearing itself is a two-stage process. First, the judge must consider whether there are reasonable grounds to decide whether the accused is unfit to stand trial. If this threshold is met, then the actual question of fitness is decided.[68]

A court can order an assessment to help determine whether an accused is fit to stand trial.[69] This assessment can be ordered on the court's own motion or on application by the prosecutor or the accused. Where the prosecutor applies for an assessment order in a summary conviction case, the court cannot grant the application unless the prosecutor shows reasonable grounds to believe that the accused is unfit or the accused raises the issue.[70]

In non-jury trials or at a preliminary inquiry the judge determines whether the accused is fit.[71] In jury cases where the accused has already been given in charge to the jury, the jury decides fitness.[72] In jury cases where the accused has not been given in charge to the jury, a jury must be sworn to decide the fitness issue, though with consent of the accused that jury can also hear the trial, if one occurs.[73]

Fitness applications need not be made pre-trial and can be brought any time prior to verdict. There are some restrictions on timing, however. If the offence in question is a hybrid one, the judge must postpone the fitness hearing until after the Crown has elected whether to proceed

---

66   *Taylor*, above note 65, approved in *Whittle*, above note 65. See also *R v Jobb*, 2008 SKCA 156, affirming that the issue of fitness is determined by the "limited cognitive capacity test," not an "analytical capacity test."

67   Sections 672.22 and 672.23(2).

68   *R v Lovie* (1995), 24 OR (3d) 836 (CA); *R v Bain* (1994), 130 NSR (2d) 332 (CA) [*Bain*].

69   Section 672.11(a).

70   Section 672.12(2).

71   Section 672.27.

72   Section 672.26(b).

73   Section 672.26(a).

summarily or by indictment.[74] If the application is brought during a preliminary inquiry, the judge can postpone the application until the time the accused is called upon to answer the charge.[75] Similarly, if the application is brought at trial, the judge has discretion to postpone the application until the opening of the accused's case.[76] The rationale for these delays is found in section 672.3, which notes that, if the accused is discharged at the preliminary inquiry or acquitted at the close of the Crown's case, the fitness issue will not be tried at all. Consistent with this approach is the obligation on the judge, in exercising the section 672.25(2)(b) discretion, to consider first whether the Crown can prove that the accused committed the act alleged in the indictment. If there is dispute over this question the judge

> may proceed with the trial proper and postpone the fitness inquiry, or he or she may require the Crown to demonstrate at the outset of the fitness hearing that it is in a position to establish that the accused committed the act or acts alleged in the indictment. In either case, a finding that an accused is not fit to stand trial should not be made in the absence of any basis to put that accused on trial.[77]

If the accused is unrepresented, counsel shall be appointed.[78] If the accused is found fit to stand trial, matters continue as if no application had ever been made.[79] If the accused is found unfit, however, then a disposition hearing concerning the accused must be held. This hearing is conducted in accordance with essentially the same rules as disposition hearings for an accused found not criminally responsible, under section 16, at the conclusion of trial. The accused cannot be discharged absolutely, but can be confined in a hospital or discharged subject to conditions.[80] Treatment other than electroconvulsive therapy can be ordered for up to sixty days, provided there is specific evidence from a medical practitioner that the treatment will help make the accused fit for trial.[81] The consent of the accused is not required, but a treatment order is subject to the consent of the hospital where the treatment will

---

74   Section 672.25(1).
75   Section 672.25(2)(a).
76   Section 672.25(2)(b).
77   *Taylor*, above note 65.
78   Section 672.24.
79   Section 672.28.
80   Section 672.54.
81   Sections 672.58 and 672.61.

take place: this includes consent not only to the treatment itself but to other conditions in the order, such as the commencement date.[82]

If an accused is found fit to stand trial, it is nonetheless possible to bring a later application concerning the same issue if there is a change in circumstances.[83] If an accused is found unfit to stand trial, there must be regular reviews in which the Crown must show that it could still prove its case against the accused if called upon to do so. These reviews must occur at least every two years, or earlier if the accused shows reason to doubt that the Crown is still able to prove its case.[84] Evidence at these hearings can be by way of affidavits or transcripts, and the exact procedure is not specified in the *Code*. If, at any review, a *prima facie* case against the accused cannot be made out, the accused is entitled to an acquittal.

The defence and the Crown are each entitled to appeal the decision of a fitness hearing.[85]

c)   *Charter* Motions

Many different *Charter* motions can be brought, not necessarily on a pre-trial basis. Applications dealing with a violation of an accused's right to be free from unreasonable search and seizure, for example, might well occur either at the start of a trial or during its course. This chapter will not attempt to deal with all the various substantive issues that could arise on *Charter* motions. Only two motions will be considered here: (1) applications concerning the right to a trial within a reasonable time and (2) applications dealing with abuse of process.

i)   *Trial within a Reasonable Time*

The *Charter*, section 11(b), guarantees any person charged with an offence the right "to be tried within a reasonable time." This is not necessarily a pre-trial motion: it could be brought before trial, but equally it can be brought at any time the delay has become unreasonable, including after the close of the Crown's case.[86] This right has had less significance

---

82   Section 672.62 requires the consent of the facility. In *R v Conception*, 2014 SCC 60, the Court concluded that this gives the facility the ability to refuse consent to an order for treatment to begin "forthwith."

83   See, for example, *R v LSC*, 2003 ABCA 105.

84   Section 672.33. This is one of the few places in which the rules for young persons are different. Section 141(10) of the *YCJA*, above note 12, requires that such reviews happen at least every year.

85   Sections 675(3) and 676(3).

86   *R v Rahey*, [1987] 1 SCR 588 [*Rahey*].

than it might have, in large measure due to the Court's treatment of the section in the context of institutional delay.

Although the section is not drafted in a way to require this reading, it is useful to distinguish between exceptional delay and institutional delay. "Exceptional delay" refers to delay that is out of the ordinary. For example, in *R v Rahey*,[87] a decision that normally would have been made in a few days was adjourned nineteen times and took eleven months. In both *R v Stensrud*[88] and *R v Smith*,[89] delays relating to preliminary inquiries (the preparation of a transcript and the actual scheduling of the inquiry, respectively) were unusual compared to the norm in those jurisdictions. "Institutional delay," on the other hand, refers to delay that is within the ordinary times of the particular jurisdiction, but that is unacceptable compared to some external standard.

R v Askov was the first occasion on which the Supreme Court dealt with institutional delay.[90] In that case the Court suggested a guideline of six to eight months delay from the time of committal to the start of a trial. This decision led to large numbers of cases being dismissed: in a period of less than a year, 47,000 charges were dealt with in this way in Ontario alone. Although the majority of these charges were minor ones that were withdrawn by Crown prosecutors rather than stayed by judges in accordance with the *Askov* guidelines, the Court appeared to feel some public pressure over this result. In the next case to deal with institutional delay, *R v Morin*, they adopted a stricter test than had previously existed.[91] In particular, as will be discussed below, the Court gave much greater prominence to the need for an accused to show some particular prejudice in order to succeed in a section 11(b) claim. The net result was that the right came to be severely circumscribed. Subsequently, in *R v Godin*, more than fifteen years later, the Court to some extent returned to the pre-*Morin* position by restating that prejudice could be presumed from the length of a delay and did not always have to be separately shown.[92] The result is that the right is still somewhat limited, but has more potential scope than it did for many years.

Analyzing whether there is a section 11(b) violation is based on a number of factors. The Court held in *Godin* that "[w]hether delay has been unreasonable is assessed by looking at the length of the delay, less any periods that have been waived by the defence, and then by taking

---

87 *Ibid.*
88 [1989] 2 SCR 1115.
89 [1989] 2 SCR 1120 [*Smith*].
90 [1990] 2 SCR 1199 [*Askov*].
91 [1992] 1 SCR 771 [*Morin*].
92 2009 SCC 26 [*Godin*].

into account the reasons for the delay, the prejudice to the accused, and the interests that s. 11(*b*) seeks to protect."[93]

In effect, the first factor asks whether there is a delay that needs explaining, while the remaining factors ask whether that delay can be explained adequately to justify any infringement on the accused's interests. We shall consider those factors in turn.

"Delay" is an ambiguous term and could mean either the total time taken from the laying of the charge until the completion of the trial, or the portion of that time that is longer than one would expect. Although the second meaning might accord more closely with ordinary usage, the Court has been clear that the first is what is intended: the length of the delay is "the period from the charge to the end of the trial."[94] The Supreme Court has held that the right does not include pre-charge delay,[95] though some lower courts begin the clock when an accused becomes subject to conditions in a recognizance or similar

---

93 *Ibid* at para 18.

94 See *Morin*, above note 91 at 789. Unfortunately, caselaw from Ontario has for some time wrongly adopted the "unjustified portion" meaning of delay, with the result that the application of the guidelines from *Askov*, above note 90, and *Morin*, above note 91, results in justification of far longer periods than those cases envisioned: see, for example, *R v Stilwell*, 2014 ONCA 563 [*Stilwell*], where the total period was twenty-six months, but the Court of Appeal concluded that only twelve-and-a-half months of that constituted "delay." See, similarly, *R v Florence*, 2014 ONCA 443 [*Florence*]; *R v G(CR)* (2005), 206 CCC (3d) 262 (Ont CA); *R v Qureshi* (2004), 27 CR (6th) 142 (Ont CA); or many others. See also Clayton Ruby, "Trial within a Reasonable Time under Section 11(b): The Ontario Court of Appeal Disconnects from the Supreme Court" (2013) 2 *Criminal Reports* (7th) 91, objecting to the way in which the Ontario Court of Appeal deals with the inherent time requirements of a case. His argument is that deducting the time allocated to "inherent time requirements" and then assessing whether the case falls within the guidelines (see the discussion of these factors below) amounts to double-counting, since the guidelines were set taking into account inherent time requirements.

95 *Kalanj*, above note 21. In *Kalanj* the accused was arrested and fingerprinted, but no charges were laid for eight months, and the Court held that that delay should not be calculated into the s 11(b) equation. The Court has suggested in *Morin*, above note 91 at 789, that "pre-charge delay may in certain circumstances have an influence on the overall determination as to whether post-charge delay is unreasonable" while reaffirming that "of itself it is not counted in determining the length of the delay." Although this possible use of pre-charge delay has been held open, it does not appear to have featured in any Supreme Court of Canada decision. In *R v L(WK)*, [1991] 1 SCR 1091, the Court rejected an application based on pre-charge delay and an alleged violation of s 7 in terms that suggest such motions, while not absolutely barred, are unlikely to succeed and would require something more than just delay.

document, even if the formal charge is not laid until later.[96] In unusual circumstances, even some portion of the delay after charges are laid might not be taken into account.[97] Similarly, since the right is to be "tried" within a reasonable time, it does not protect against delay at the appellate level.[98]

The burden of proof to show a *Charter* violation rests on the accused, and so if the length of the delay is not unusual, the section 11(b) analysis might go no further. When the length of the delay becomes unusual, however, a secondary burden shifts to the Crown to explain it. The length of time that will require explanation could vary, depending on the circumstances. For example, an accused who is in custody might reasonably seek an earlier trial.[99]

Waiver is relevant since an accused cannot agree to a certain delay and then later complain of it. The Court has held that, consistent with other contexts, waiver of *Charter* rights can be explicit or implicit, but that it must be clear and unambiguous. The Court has said that consent to a trial date will often constitute a waiver, but this result does not necessarily follow.[100] In particular, if there is no reason to think that an earlier trial date would be available, an accused is not required to make an entirely *pro forma* objection.[101] Further, in some cases, acquiescence to a request from the trial judge will be treated differently than requests from counsel, since an accused is likely to defer to the wishes of the trier of fact.[102] Similarly, the fact that defence counsel is

---

96 See, for example, *R v Egorov*, [2005] OJ No 6171 (Ct J); *R v Nash*, 2014 ONSC 6025; or *R v Swaminathan*, 2015 ONCJ 394.

97 In *R v Cisar*, 2014 ONCA 151, charges were laid against an accused while he was out of the country. He was unaware even of the existence of those charges until eight years later, when he was back in Canada. The Ontario Court of Appeal held that that period of time should be considered separately from the delay after his arrest. They concluded that there was no s 11(b) violation during that eight-year period, because the interests s 11(b) was meant to protect were not affected on the facts. Those interests consisted of security of the person and liberty interests (which could not have been affected since he had not been arrested or even made aware of the charges) and fair trial interests (which were not on the facts affected, since he was in no worse a position to mount a defence).

98 *R v Potvin*, [1993] 2 SCR 880: Whether the accused was acquitted, the charge was stayed, or the accused is appealing a conviction, s 11(b) affords no protection. The Court did acknowledge that, in appropriate circumstances, a remedy under s 7 for abuse of process might be available for appellate delay.

99 *Morin*, above note 91.

100 *Smith*, above note 89.

101 See, for example, *Mills*, above note 28; *Rahey*, above note 86; or *Askov*, above note 90.

102 *Rahey*, above note 86.

not available for the earliest proposed date when an adjournment is caused by the Crown is not automatically a waiver of some portion of the delay—defence counsel is not required "to hold themselves in a state of perpetual availability."[103]

The reasons for the delay include consideration of a number of factors, including the inherent time requirements of the case, actions of the accused, actions of the Crown, limits on institutional resources, and other reasons.[104] Prior to *Morin*, the reasons for the delay were the most important factors to be considered, and they remain significant. Indeed, as will be discussed, consideration of this particular factor led the Court to articulate guidelines governing how long a matter should take from charge to proceedings in inferior court, and from committal for trial to the end of trial in superior court: whether those guidelines were met and whether any departure can be justified tends to be the central focus of any section 11(b) analysis.

The inherent time requirements of the case, understandably, will vary depending on the circumstances. Complex cases take more time than simple ones,[105] and at the simplest level a case with a preliminary inquiry will take longer than one without. Every case will have certain ordinary requirements, such as the need for the accused to obtain counsel, the time involved in making disclosure, and so on. The Court in *Morin* resisted the call to lay down general guidelines regarding how long these ordinary requirements should take. Instead, it held that courts would need to develop these guidelines locally.[106] On the one hand, it is reasonable to suggest that local courts will be more familiar with local practices and have a better sense of how long it normally takes for disclosure to be made. On the other hand, not setting any such guideline removes most of the incentive for any given region to become more efficient. That is, provided a case does not fall outside the ordinary range for that area, however slow it might be in comparison to

---

103 *Godin*, above note 92 at para 23.

104 *Morin*, above note 91 at 787–89.

105 In *R v Collins*, [1995] 2 SCR 1104 [*Collins*], the dissenting judges argued that the seriousness of the offence, a factor similar to, but distinct from, its complexity, ought also to be relevant. They held that since the s 11(b) right also weighs society's interests in the balance, in principle, it should be possible to find unreasonable delay and a serious breach of an accused's right, but nonetheless find that there was no breach of s 11(b) because the societal interest outweighed the prejudice. The majority in *Collins*, while not specifically addressing this argument, seems clearly to reject it, since they upheld the lower court decision granting a stay.

106 *Morin*, above note 91 at 799–800.

similar courts elsewhere in the country, local standards will say there is no problem.

The actions of the accused can be relevant because they can contribute to the delay. An accused might apply for change of venue, change solicitors, request re-election to trial by judge alone,[107] or re-elect to turn a scheduled provincial court trial into a preliminary inquiry.[108] As the Court notes in *Morin*, even though such steps are taken in good faith, they contribute to the total time duration and so must be taken into account in assessing whether that delay was unreasonable.[109]

Much the same is true of actions taken by the Crown. The Crown might, with perfect reasonableness, request an adjournment in order to have a particular witness available. Similarly, the Crown might, through no fault of its own, disclose new material at a later date, thereby making an adjournment necessary. The Crown might enter a temporary stay and later recommence proceedings.[110] In any of these cases, the delay is to be attributed to the Crown—the fact that a request is reasonable or appropriate does not mean that the Crown is not responsible for the delay.[111]

Limits on institutional resources are the factor most relevant in the contrasting decisions of *Askov* and *Morin*, although, on the face of it, there is little difference in the way in which this factor is described in each. In *Morin* the Court notes:

> The Court cannot simply accede to the government's allocation of resources and tailor the period of permissible delay accordingly. The weight to be given to resource limitations must be assessed in light of the fact that the government has a constitutional obligation to com-

---

107 The accused in *R v Conway*, [1989] 1 SCR 1659 [*Conway*], took all these steps.

108 As in *R v Bennett*, [1992] 2 SCR 168.

109 *Morin*, above note 91 at 794.

110 *R v Lanteigne*, 2010 NBCA 91.

111 See *Morin*, above note 91, speaking of the facts in *Smith*, above note 89, and *Godin*, above note 92, respectively. The Court also notes in *Godin* that it is not relevant whether the actions of the Crown result in any benefit to the accused. The Crown there re-elected to proceed by indictment, and the Court of Appeal had held that the preliminary inquiry was beneficial to the accused, which therefore made that portion of the delay not unreasonable. The Supreme Court, at para 20, disagreed with this approach:

> Had the Crown obtained the forensic evidence within a reasonable amount of time, the re-election and preliminary inquiry could have happened much sooner. It may well have been beneficial to the appellant to have a preliminary inquiry. But, respectfully, that is not the point. The appellant was entitled to timely disclosure, he did not receive it, and no explanation for the failure to provide it has been advanced.

mit sufficient resources to prevent unreasonable delay which distinguishes this obligation from many others that compete for funds with the administration of justice. There is a point in time at which the Court will no longer tolerate delay based on the plea of inadequate resources.[112]

Askov had laid down a guideline of six to eight months from committal to trial. *Morin* affirmed that guideline and added the further suggestion that the delay in provincial courts should be between eight and ten months. *Morin* also stressed, to avoid the problems that had arisen post-*Askov*, that these times were simply guidelines, not absolute limitation periods. This was not actually a change from what *Askov* had said, but seemingly the Court felt the need to make the point especially clear. Indeed, in *Morin* the Court both laid down the guideline and denied a remedy although that guideline was not met.

The significant way in which *Morin* differed from *Askov* on this issue was in the use that was to be made of comparisons to other jurisdictions. In *Askov*, the Court had relied on statistics showing that the Brampton court in question was dramatically slower than any other court in North America and, in particular, slower than courts in Montréal. In *Morin* they suggested that this comparison was misleading because the manner in which criminal charges are dealt with in Montréal and Brampton is sufficiently dissimilar so as to make statistics drawn from the two jurisdictions of limited comparative value. Comparison with other jurisdictions is therefore to be applied with caution and only as a rough guide.[113]

This retreat was unfortunate. Montréal had, at the relevant time, a fifteen-year history of using case management in order to deal as efficiently as possible with criminal cases; Brampton did not. Although cases were dealt with differently in the two jurisdictions, one possibility was that that was precisely the source of the problem and not a justification for denying the existence of a problem.[114]

Other factors deal with matters such as those above that cannot be attributed to either the defence or the Crown. When the trial judge in *Rahey* adjourned the decision on a directed verdict nineteen times, for example, that was a factor to be considered under this heading, making

---

112 *Morin*, above note 91 at 795.
113 *Ibid* at 799.
114 On the other hand, see Carl Baar, "Criminal Court Delay and the *Charter*: The Use and Misuse of Social Facts in Judicial Policy Making" (1993) 72 *Canadian Bar Review* 305, where he suggests that for various jurisdictional and statistical reasons, the Court might have been wrong to make the comparison in the first place.

the delay less acceptable. In contrast, in *R v Milani* there was a gap of twenty-one years between the time the accused was discharged at a preliminary inquiry and the time a charge was preferred against him: since the accused was not actively subject to any prosecution during that period and it was only after DNA technology had improved that charges were revived, that gap was not taken into account.[115]

In considering the factors entering into the reasons for the delay, a tendency has arisen in some courts (primarily those in Ontario) to engage in a minute and precise allocation of periods of time to each: for example, that a period of 255 days between setting a trial date and the start of trial should be broken down into 213 days of institutional delay, thirty-one days of neutral preparation, and ten days of defence delay.[116] Seemingly with this sort of approach in mind, the Supreme Court cautioned in *Godin* that, although minute examination of particular time periods and of factual questions was necessary, "[i]t is important, however, not to lose sight of the forest for the trees while engaging in this detailed analysis."[117] Nonetheless, the practice has not disappeared.

The role of prejudice has undergone the most change in the trial within a reasonable time analysis, and is primarily responsible for the ebb and flow in the impact of that right, but that is because of variation in the interests that the right is seen as protecting.

Section 11(b) protects against three forms of prejudice: threats to security of the person, to liberty, and to the right to a fair trial. The Court stated in *Morin*:

> The right to security of the person is protected in s. 11(b) by seeking to minimize the anxiety, concern and stigma of exposure to criminal proceedings. The right to liberty is protected by seeking to minimize exposure to the restrictions on liberty which result from pretrial incarceration and restrictive bail conditions. The right to a fair trial is protected by attempting to ensure that proceedings take place while evidence is available and fresh.[118]

In early section 11(b) cases, Lamer CJ argued that prejudice to an accused's security interest — the stigmatization, loss of privacy, stress, and anxiety flowing from being charged with an offence — was inherent in a denial and part of the rationale for the right. Accordingly, prejudice should be presumed and need not be proven. Indeed, he argued that an accused not only did not need to prove prejudice to liberty interests or

---

115   2014 ONCA 536.

116   *Florence*, above note 94.

117   *Godin*, above note 92 at para 18.

118   Above note 91 at 786.

to fair trial rights, but that such evidence would be "irrelevant."[119] His argument was that being held unreasonably long in custody would go to a section 7 violation, not section 11(b), and having lost the ability to call a witness would go to the fair trial guarantee in section 11(d), not to section 11(b).

However, although the point remained unsettled through many cases,[120] the general view of the Court seemed to be to allow such additional evidence in. No judge disputed that prejudice to an accused's security interest showed a section 11(b) violation. For example, the unanimous Court in *Smith* held that "'a criminal charge will be hanging over [the accused] for a substantial period of time.' This is the very essence of prejudice to the security interests of a person charged with an offence."[121] Nonetheless, most judges seemed to prefer the view that an accused could also strengthen a section 11(b) claim by showing infringements of a liberty or fair trial interest as well.

The danger in such an approach is that once it is accepted that evidence of the latter sort makes a claim stronger, it becomes implicit that the absence of such evidence makes a claim weaker. This was the effect of *Morin*, which, in essence, abandoned the view that prejudice to the accused's security interest was sufficient. The Court there gave much greater prominence to a suggestion that had existed in other cases: that many accused do not want a trial within a reasonable time and that most accused are content to have delay and, indeed, would prefer to have unreasonable delay leading to a *Charter* remedy rather than a trial on the merits. Having postulated that this general view existed, the Court then held that the Crown could, therefore, disprove prejudice by showing "that the accused is in the majority group who do not want an early trial and that the delay benefitted rather than prejudiced the accused."[122] On the particular facts of the case, the Court concluded from the accused's failure to try to expedite her trial that she "was content with the pace with which things were proceeding and that therefore there was little or no prejudice occasioned by the delay."[123] Because there was no such prejudice, the Court found that her section 11(b)

---

119 *Mills*, above note 28 at 926.

120 *Rahey*, above note 86; *Kalanj*, above note 21; *Conway*, above note 107; *Smith*, above note 89; *Askov*, above note 90.

121 *Smith*, above note 89 at 1138–39.

122 *Morin*, above note 91 at 803. It should be noted that the innocent as well as the guilty could hold this attitude. Further, that an accused does not object to delay does not mean that the delay favours the accused; people often put off unpleasant things even if their completion would be of benefit.

123 *Ibid* at 808.

right was not violated, despite the fact that the delay was outside the reasonable period allowed by the guideline.

To reason in this way largely eliminates the presumption of prejudice. It would really only be an accused who could show some tangible form of prejudice, such as prolonged incarceration or loss of witnesses, who would benefit from section 11(b) of the *Charter*. But this amounts to saying that only an accused who can show threats to liberty or fair trial interests (that is, an accused who is already protected by section 7 or section 11(d)) will have a section 11(b) right, and that security of the person interests no longer matter.

For many years after *Morin* the section 11(b) right attracted relatively little judicial attention, especially in the Supreme Court. Because that case laid down a guideline but then approved departures from it where the accused could not prove prejudice, the task for an accused became much more difficult. The subsequent decision in *Godin*, however, signalled a rejuvenated recognition of the notion that prejudice can be presumed where there has been an unreasonable delay.[124]

The trial judge in *Godin* had granted a stay and the Court noted it was a straightforward case requiring little court time, but that it had, nonetheless, taken a period far in excess of the guidelines. *Morin* had suggested a period of eight to ten months for a case to be in the provincial courts, for example, but the preliminary inquiry in this case was not completed for twenty-one months. The Ontario Court of Appeal had overturned the trial judge's decision, largely for reasons resting on the absence of prejudice. The Supreme Court restored the stay, reiterating that "prejudice may be inferred from the length of the delay. The longer the delay the more likely that such an inference will be drawn."[125] The Court also reiterated that prejudice to the accused's security of the person, liberty, and fair trial interests were all relevant. It held that the Court of Appeal had erred by giving no weight to the accused's security of the person interest—the fact that the charges were hanging over the accused's head for longer than necessary was, by itself, prejudicial. Similarly, although the accused's bail conditions were eventually relaxed, the prejudice to his liberty interest was relevant. Finally, the Court held, although it might be difficult to demonstrate that the length of the delay caused prejudice to the accused's fair trial right, nonetheless, the accused had made virtually no contribution to the delay and prejudice to his fair trial right was not essential.

---

124 *Godin*, above note 92.
125 *Ibid* at para 31, quoting *Morin*, above note 91 at 801.

The interests that section 11(b) was meant to protect include the security, liberty, and fair trial interests of the accused which enter into the prejudice analysis. There is, however, also a "secondary societal interest" to be taken into account.[126] In part, this interest parallels that of the accused: society has an interest in seeing to it that trials are fair, and a prompt trial is more likely to be fair, since evidence is less likely to have been lost. There is also, however, a societal interest which is adverse to that of the accused: the strong societal interest in having serious charges tried on their merits.[127] In considering the final factor articulated in the *Godin* analysis, the interests that section 11(b) is meant to protect, a judge is, in essence, weighing all of these competing interests against one another to decide whether the accused should receive a remedy or not.[128]

As a concluding observation, note that the minimum remedy for a violation of section 11(d) is a stay of the proceedings.[129] Although complete agreement on the reasoning behind that result is lacking, here is the simplest way to understand the Court's position: that it is not possible to find that a reasonable time in which to have a trial has already passed but to put the accused on trial nonetheless.[130]

ii) Abuse of Process and Fair Trial Rights

Although the doctrine was in doubt in Canada for many years, the Supreme Court has unequivocally concluded that

> there is a residual discretion in a trial court judge to stay proceedings where compelling an accused to stand trial would violate those fundamental principles of justice which underlie the community's sense of fair play and decency and to prevent the abuse of a court's process through oppressive or vexatious proceedings.[131]

Motions for a stay based on abuse of process need not be brought on a pre-trial basis and, indeed, most typically would not be (many claims, such as entrapment, will depend on the evidence that emerges

---

126 *Morin, ibid.*

127 *Godin*, above note 92 at para 41.

128 See, for example, *Stilwell*, above note 94.

129 *Rahey*, above note 86.

130 Six judges in *Rahey, ibid*, reached the conclusion that a stay is the minimum remedy for a breach of s 11(b), but for three different sets of reasons. Four of them suggest that a s 11(b) violation removes the jurisdiction of a court to put the accused on trial. In *Morin*, above note 91, the Court was asked to reconsider this conclusion, but found it unnecessary to do so since they found no breach of s 11(b).

131 *R v Jewitt*, [1985] 2 SCR 128 at 135 [*Jewitt*].

at trial).[132] However, they are potentially available at a pre-trial stage because the issue in deciding whether to grant a stay for abuse of process is not whether the prosecution can prove its case, but whether the case is "tainted to such a degree that to allow it to proceed would tarnish the integrity of the court."[133] Thus, for example, it is possible to obtain a stay even at the stage of an extradition hearing to face charges in another country.[134]

Although as a practical matter they typically arise together, the two issues of (1) whether there is an abuse of process, and (2) if there is, whether a stay is the appropriate remedy, are separate questions.

a. Abuse of Process

Abuse of process has had something of a laboured history in Canadian law. It seemed for many years that, as a common law doctrine, it did not exist in Canada.[135] It was later affirmed first, that such a common law power did exist,[136] and then later, that the common law power to stay for abuse of process and the ability of a court to grant the *Charter* remedy of a stay of proceedings were largely co-extensive.[137] As initially developed, the test had two branches with slightly different tests, a main category which was forward-looking and a "residual" category which was backward-looking.[138] Eventually, however, the residual category was given somewhat more credence, and the same test was made to apply to both categories.[139]

The two categories of abuse of process are as follows:

1) where state conduct compromises the fairness of an accused's trial (the "main" category); and 2) where state conduct creates no threat to

---

132 Indeed, the Court held in *R v Mack*, [1988] 2 SCR 903 [*Mack*], that an abuse of process claim could not be considered until after the judge had decided whether the Crown had proven the accused guilty beyond a reasonable doubt.

133 *Conway*, above note 107 at 1667.

134 *United States of America v Cobb*, [2001] 1 SCR 587 [*Cobb*].

135 See, for example, *R v Rourke* (1977), [1978] 1 SCR 1021.

136 *Jewitt*, above note 131.

137 *R v O'Connor*, [1995] 4 SCR 411 [*O'Connor*]. The Court held at para 70:

> the only instances in which there may be a need to maintain any type of distinction between the two regimes will be those instances in which the *Charter*, for some reason, does not apply yet where the circumstances nevertheless point to an abuse of the court's process.

138 See, for example, *O'Connor*, ibid, or *Canada (Minister of Citizenship and Immigration) v Tobiass*, [1997] 3 SCR 391 at para 91 [*Tobiass*].

139 *R v Babos*, 2014 SCC 16 [*Babos*].

trial fairness but risks undermining the integrity of the judicial process (the "residual" category).[140]

The first category is forward-looking in the sense that it asks whether there is any ongoing unfairness to the accused.[141] It is the main category because typically the questions of whether there was an abuse and whether there should be a stay were treated as essentially the same question, and the view of the Court was that "the mere fact that the state has treated an individual shabbily in the past is not enough to warrant a stay of proceedings."[142]

One particular area in which the first category of abuse of process—trial fairness—has been pursued is when the Crown repudiates a plea agreement.[143] A bare allegation that there has been an abuse of process is not sufficient to cause a court to inquire into the exercise of prosecutorial discretion: there is a threshold burden on the accused to satisfy the court that there is a serious issue to look into. The allegation that the Crown was pursuing charges against one accused but not against another, for example, would not be sufficient. Where the Crown repudiates a plea agreement, however, that threshold burden is met because such action on the part of the Crown is rare and exceptional. Although the ultimate burden to show an abuse of process rests with the accused, where the Crown has resiled from a plea agreement, there is an evidentiary burden on them to explain why they have failed to honour the bargain, and failure to meet it can weigh heavily in the decision.[144]

A pre-trial motion seeking a stay has sometimes been sought on the basis that it will be impossible to empanel an impartial jury, most probably due to pre-trial publicity, though not necessarily only on those grounds.[145] The Court has not completely precluded such a motion, although they did hold that such an application brought before jury selection had begun was premature:

> It is only at the stage when the jury is to be selected that it will be possible to determine whether the respondent can be tried by an impartial jury . . . . In an extreme case (and the present certainly qualifies), such publicity should lead to challenge for cause at trial, but

---

140 *Ibid* at para 31.
141 *Ibid* at para 34.
142 *Tobiass*, above note 138 at para 91.
143 *R v Nixon*, 2011 SCC 34.
144 *Ibid* at paras 62–63.
145 See *English*, above note 54; *R v Vermette*, [1988] 1 SCR 985 [*Vermette*].

I am far from thinking that it must necessarily be assumed that a person subjected to such publicity will necessarily be biased.[146]

On this issue, see the further discussion in Section C(3)(c), below in this chapter, of challenge for cause in the jury selection process.

In dealing with the second category, undermining the integrity of the judicial process, the question is "whether the state has engaged in conduct that is offensive to societal notions of fair play and decency and whether proceeding with a trial in the face of that conduct would be harmful to the integrity of the justice system."[147] Although this category looks to past misconduct, it is still intended to have a prospective aspect to it: a court should ask whether proceeding in light of the impugned conduct would do *further* harm to the integrity of the justice system.[148]

In *R v Jewitt* the issue was whether the accused had been entrapped, and the Court has subsequently elaborated on entrapment as one of the circumstances that might lead to a stay of proceedings based on abuse of process.[149] The list of potential abuses is open-ended, and accused have made applications based on conflict of interest for the accused's lawyers,[150] pre-charge collaboration between police and Crown prosecutors that was alleged to have led to a loss of objectivity on the part of the Crown,[151] reliance by police on advice as to whether their investigation would be illegal,[152] threats of sexual violence for contesting extradition,[153] and non-disclosure of evidence.[154]

One area of particular interest relates to mistreatment of arrested persons by police which, on the face of it, seems like shabby past treatment and therefore not something falling within the doctrine. However, many lower courts tended to grant stays to accused who were subject to violence or other mistreatment, even while recognizing that this was

---

146 *Vermette, ibid* at 992–93.
147 *Babos*, above note 139 at para 35.
148 *Ibid* at para 38.
149 *Mack*, above note 132; *R v Barnes*, [1991] 1 SCR 449.
150 *R v Neil*, 2002 SCC 70.
151 *R v Regan*, 2002 SCC 12. The majority held that any alleged misbehaviour on the part of the Crown had no ongoing effect (para 104), but the dissent argued that the existence of the proceedings *at all* was the ongoing effect (para 219).
152 *R v Campbell*, [1999] 1 SCR 565.
153 *Cobb*, above note 134.
154 *O'Connor*, above note 137, although the *O'Connor* analysis deals with the issue as implicating the accused's s 7 rights.

difficult to reconcile with the rules the Court had laid down.[155] Eventually the Supreme Court, while not changing the law in this area, acknowledged that trial judges could properly conclude that past abuse of this sort was serious enough that public confidence in the administration of justice could be undermined by the mere act of carrying forward in light of it.[156]

This greater acknowledgment of the significance of past misbehaviour perhaps prompted the Court in *R v Hart* to suggest that the abuse of process doctrine should be "reinvigorated" in the context of Mr. Big undercover operations.[157] A Mr. Big operation targets an accused by trying to lure her into joining a fictitious criminal organization. The prospect of significant reward is held out, and often there are implicit threats about disloyalty; ultimately, the accused is presented with the need to confess previous involvement in whatever crime the police were investigating to "Mr. Big," the putative head of the organization, in order to be accepted: that confession is then used as evidence.[158] The Court observed that the abuse of process doctrine had never succeeded as an objection to Mr. Big cases, but that courts should be more open to the possibility. They observed that the technique could become abusive when the use of inducements or threats becomes coercive, or when the technique preys on vulnerabilities such as mental health problems, substance addictions, or youthfulness.[159]

In most cases, claims based on the residual category are not ultimately successful because the issues of whether there was an abuse and whether there should be a stay have been closely linked. This has limited the doctrine because a stay of proceedings can be granted only in the "clearest of cases."[160] So, when should a stay be granted?

b. Stay of Proceedings

The same test is used no matter which category of abuse is alleged:

(1) There must be prejudice to the accused's right to a fair trial or the integrity of the justice system that "will be manifested, perpetuated

---

155 See the discussion in *R v Walcott* (2008), 57 CR (6th) 223 (Ont SCJ), and in Tim Quigley, "Stays of Proceedings Due to Police Misconduct" (2011) 79 *Criminal Reports* (6th) 124.

156 *R v Bellusci*, 2012 SCC 44.

157 2014 SCC 52 at para 114 [*Hart*].

158 Among the many Mr. Big cases, see *Hart*, ibid; *R v Mack*, 2014 SCC 58; *R v Grandinetti*, 2005 SCC 5; or *R v Mentuck*, [2001] 3 SCR 442.

159 *Hart*, above note 157 at paras 115–18.

160 *Jewitt*, above note 131 at 137.

or aggravated through the conduct of the trial, or by its outcome"
. . .;

(2) There must be no alternative remedy capable of redressing the prejudice; and

(3) Where there is still uncertainty over whether a stay is warranted after steps (1) and (2), the court is required to balance the interests in favour of granting a stay, such as denouncing misconduct and preserving the integrity of the justice system, against "the interest that society has in having a final decision on the merits."[161]

The first step in this test amounts to asking whether there was an abuse of process based on either the main or the residual category. If there is, and since a stay is limited to the clearest of cases, the question becomes whether any other remedy is sufficient. Because abuse of process and the section 7 right to a fair trial are closely aligned, most cases of abuse of process mean that, without a remedy, the trial would not be fair: however, in most of those situations some other remedy, such as an order for further disclosure and an adjournment, or in more extreme cases an order for a new trial, is an adequate solution. Therefore, a stay is not the most likely remedy for the main category. It is more likely to be a remedy for the residual category. Even there, however, the focus is not to provide redress to the accused for the wrong, but to consider whether an alternative remedy short of a stay of proceedings will adequately dissociate the justice system from the impugned state conduct going forward.[162]

If there is any doubt about granting a stay after these two steps, then the third step requires balancing the interest of society in a final decision on the merits against the accused's interests. In *R v Babos* a Crown prosecutor had made threats to lay more charges in order to apply pressure to the accused. The Court said that behaviour was reprehensible and should not be repeated by any Crown, but did not issue a stay. Instead, they concluded that even though no alternative remedy was available, a stay of proceedings was not warranted when balanced against society's interest in a trial on the twenty-two charges related to firearms, illegal drugs, and organized crime.[163]

---

161 *Babos*, above note 139 at para 32.

162 *Ibid* at para 39.

163 See Tim Quigley, "*Babos*: Balancing Test Unnecessarily Restricts Residual Category for Stay as Abuse of Process" (2014) 8 *Criminal Reports* (7th) 55, and HA Kaiser, "*Babos*: Further Narrowing Access to Stay of Proceedings Where the Integrity of the Judicial Process Is Implicated" (2014) 8 *Criminal Reports* (7th) 59, both criticizing the approach in *Babos*.

C. JURY SELECTION

1) Introduction

The *Criminal Code* provides for several methods of trial, in particular, trial by provincial court judge, trial by superior court judge alone, and trial by superior court judge with a jury (see the discussion in Chapter 3, Section A). Section 471 of the *Code* provides that every indictable offence shall be tried by a judge and jury "except where otherwise expressly provided by law." As a matter of fact, though, various *Code* sections readily provide other choices for every offence except those listed in section 469. The net effect is that a few offences, such as murder and treason, are required to be tried by jury, while a few indictable offences, such as theft not exceeding $5,000, cannot have a jury. For all other indictable offences, an accused can choose between any of the three modes of trial.[164]

There are three stages to the jury selection process: assembling the jury roll, which is as far as possible a list of all eligible jury members in the region; from the jury roll selecting a jury panel (or array[165]), which is the pool from which a trial jury is selected; and from the jury panel selecting the trial jury (sometimes called the "petit jury") for a particular criminal trial.[166] Those stages are governed by a mixture of federal and provincial legislation. Section 92(14) of the *Constitution Act, 1867*[167] gives each province jurisdiction over the administration of justice in the province. In each province and territory, a jury act sets out the rules by which the jury roll is to be assembled and the jury array is to be summoned to the courtroom. These rules include such matters as qualifications and disqualifications for being a juror, sources from which the jury roll is assembled, and compensation for jurors. Once the prospective jurors are in the courtroom in a criminal matter, the provisions of the *Code* then govern the selection of the jury for the particular

---

164 Note, as well, that s 11(f) of the *Charter* guarantees an accused the right to "the benefit of trial by jury" for any offence with a punishment of five years imprisonment or more. In *R v Turpin*, [1989] 1 SCR 1296, the Court held that although an accused could waive that right, waiver of the right to trial by jury did not amount to a right to trial by non-jury. Accordingly, the *Code* provisions preventing an accused from electing trial by judge alone in a murder case did not violate s 11(f).

165 The *Code* uses both the terms "array" and "panel" to refer to this group: see, for example, s 629, which speaks about challenging a jury panel, but appears under the heading "Challenging the Array."

166 *R v Kokopenace*, 2015 SCC 28 at para 8 [*Kokopenace*].

167 (UK), 30 & 31 Vict, c 3.

trial. These *Code* rules deal with challenges for cause, peremptory challenges, excusing jurors, and so on.[168]

2) Provincial Legislation Jury Selection Procedures — Creating the Jury Array

Each province has jurisdiction over the administration of justice in the province, and section 626 of the *Code* specifies that jurors must be qualified in accordance with the laws of the province.[169] That section also states that, notwithstanding any law of a province, no person can be disqualified from jury service based on sex. To comply with constitutional requirements, the jury roll must be assembled by a process that provides a fair opportunity for a broad cross-section of society to participate.[170] This goal is manifested in different ways within

---

168 In *Barrow,* above note 24, the Court notes that the provinces have jurisdiction over the "administrative" aspects of jury selection, specifically the authority to assemble the array. See, for example, *R v Montague,* 2010 ONCA 141, where the accused objected that some potential jurors had been excused in his absence. The Court of Appeal rejected the appeal on the basis that the potential jurors had been excused on administrative grounds under the relevant provincial legislation, not by means of the power to excuse jurors in s 632 of the *Code.* Accordingly, it had been done as part of assembling the jury panel in the first place, not excusing someone from the jury panel, and so the accused had no right to be present.

    The precise constitutional dividing line between federal and provincial jurisdiction is not entirely clear: see David Pomerant, *Multiculturalism, Representation and the Jury Selection Process in Canadian Criminal Cases* (Ottawa: Department of Justice Canada, Research and Statistics Directorate, 1994).

169 The Court describes this provision in *R v Sherratt,* [1991] 1 SCR 509 [*Sherratt*], as avoiding jurisdictional conflict, but it could equally be seen as contributing to the ambiguity of the situation. It is true that the provision leaves no doubt as to which statutes govern the out-of-court portion of jury selection. However, the existence of s 626 creates doubt as to *why* the provincial jury acts govern the situation. If the provinces have jurisdiction to create those statutes by virtue of s 92(14) of the *Constitution Act, 1867,* above note 167, then s 626 is unnecessary: its existence could imply that the *Code* is the ultimate foundation of authority for the rules in the provincial jury acts. In this regard, the situation could be similar to the definition of "attorney general" in s 2 of the *Code,* which in *Canada (Attorney General) v Canadian National Transportation Ltd,* [1983] 2 SCR 206, was held to be the provincial attorney general, not because the province had original jurisdiction over prosecutions, but because valid federal legislation designated the provincial attorney general. See, generally, Pomerant, above note 168, for more on this issue.

170 *Kokopenace,* above note 166 at para 2. The *Charter* rights implicated are s 11(d) (the right to a fair trial by an impartial tribunal) and s 11(f) (the right to a trial by jury for offences punishable by imprisonment of five years or more).

various statutes. In Nova Scotia, for example, the legislation explicitly states that the list should be drawn from a "data base that to the extent possible shall include the entire population."[171] Prince Edward Island, on the other hand, specifies that the *Health Services Payment Act*[172] list should be used.[173] Manitoba contents itself with a direction to the sheriff to use "appropriate lists."[174] Other provinces do not specify what source is to be used in assembling the array.

The goal of assembling this list is representativeness, but that concept has a particular meaning in the context of jury selection. There is no requirement that the ultimate jury selected include members of any particular group. Similarly, the jury roll need not be proportionally representative of the province's or region's population.[175] Rather, representativeness focuses on the *process* used. The Court held in *R v Kokopenace*:

> To determine if the state has met its representativeness obligation, the question is whether the state provided a fair opportunity for a broad cross-section of society to participate in the jury process. A fair opportunity will have been provided when the state makes reasonable efforts to: (1) compile the jury roll using random selection from lists that draw from a broad cross-section of society, and (2) deliver jury notices to those who have been randomly selected. In other words, it is the act of casting a wide net that ensures representativeness. Representativeness is not about targeting particular groups for inclusion on the jury roll.[176]

As long as there has been no deliberate exclusion of any particular group and reasonable efforts have been made to include all eligible people, representativeness will be satisfied.

Separate from the issue of assembling the initial list is the task of making exclusions from that list. There is a reasonable degree of uniformity across the country concerning which people are qualified for jury service. Normally, a juror is required to be of the age of majority in

---

171 *Juries Act*, SNS 1998, c 16, s 7(1).

172 RSPEI 1988, c H-2.

173 *Jury Act*, RSPEI 1988, c J-5.1, s 8(1). Note that the Regulations to the Nova Scotia Act, above note 171, similarly specify that the Health Insurance list is an appropriate database.

174 *Jury Act*, CCSM c J30, s 6(1).

175 *Kokopenace*, above note 166 at para 59: "Representativeness . . . does not require the state to ensure that any particular perspective is represented on the jury roll, nor does it require the state to ensure that its source lists proportionately represent all groups that are eligible for jury duty."

176 *Ibid* at para 61.

the province, a resident of that province, and a Canadian citizen.[177] Disqualifications frequently appear to be based on two general justifications: (1) that the potential juror would face a conflict in serving on a jury, or (2) that what the juror does in everyday life is more important than, or for some other reason justifies a general exemption from, serving on a jury. For example, people involved in law enforcement are typically disqualified from jury service, though the exact list of which personnel do and do not qualify varies from province to province. Similarly, judges and lawyers are routinely excluded from juries, as sometimes are articled clerks or those who simply have a law degree. Disqualifications based on some type of criminal record are also routine, though, again, with variation as to how serious an offence it was and how recently it was committed. On a different note, jury acts regularly disqualify the Governor General, the Lieutenant Governor, members of Parliament, members of the provincial government, senators, and so on. In some provinces, doctors, veterinarians, or other health professionals are also disqualified. In addition, most jurisdictions provide scope for an individual assessment of whether it will create a hardship for a particular person to serve on a jury, allow for exemptions based on reasons of religion or conscience, and exclude those with a physical or mental disability that would prevent the person from fulfilling the role of a juror.

3) *Criminal Code* Jury Selection Procedures — Choosing the Jury from the Jury Array

a) Mechanics of Selecting Jurors

Once the jury array has been assembled in court, the *Criminal Code* provisions govern the remaining selection procedures. It is possible for either the accused or the prosecutor to challenge the array, but doing so can be based only on "partiality, fraud or wilful misconduct on the part of the sheriff or other officer by whom the panel was returned."[178] If the array has been accepted, then the selection procedure itself begins: the names of those present are pulled randomly from a box in accordance with the procedures set out in section 631 of the *Code*.[179] This procedure

---

177 Note, though, that Manitoba, for example, has repealed the citizenship requirement: *Charter Compliance Statute Amendment Act*, RSM 1987 Supp, c 4, s 14.

178 Section 629: see the discussion of *R v Butler* (1984), 3 CR (4th) 174 (BCCA) [*Butler*], and of *R v Kent, Sinclair and Gode* (1986), 27 CCC (3d) 405 (Man CA) [*Kent*], at Section C(3)(d), below in this chapter, for more on this issue.

179 Section 631 sets out quite precise guidelines concerning how many names are to be randomly drawn at a time, the order in which potential jurors are to be sworn, and so on. However, s 643(3) provides that failure to comply with s 631, s 635 (order of challenges), or s 641 (calling jurors who have been stood by)

continues until, after the methods of excluding jurors (discussed at Section C(3)(b), below in this chapter) have been considered, enough jurors have been selected. The judge can, if satisfied that it is necessary for the proper administration of justice, order a publication ban on, or otherwise limit the use of, the identity or information that would reveal the identity of a juror.[180]

When there is a challenge for cause, there is a need for someone to decide that challenge. Where the challenge is based on the ground that the potential juror's name does not appear on the panel, the trial judge decides the issue.[181] In the case of any other challenge, two other persons will decide the challenge. In the usual case, the two most recently sworn jurors are the triers of the challenge (this is usually referred to as the "rotating triers" approach).[182] However, the *Code* was amended in 2008 to add a provision allowing the accused to request that all sworn and unsworn jurors be excluded from the courtroom during the challenge process. In that event, two unsworn jurors or two other persons who are present will be sworn in as triers of the challenge. Those two triers will then hear all the challenges for cause until a jury of twelve has been selected and will not themselves become part of the jury (this is referred to as the "static triers" approach).[183] These amendments have given rise to unexpected confusion in trial courts.

The purpose of the provision is to prevent potential jurors from becoming "contaminated" by hearing other challenges for cause and the issues that arise. The difficulty is that the new amendments make static triers mandatory when an order for the exclusion of sworn and unsworn jurors is made under section 640(2.1) — some accused want an exclusion order but want to retain rotating triers. Trial courts have disagreed over whether this is possible and have adopted many different interpretations of the legislation.[184] The issue has not yet reached a

---

does not affect the validity of the proceedings. In essence, this saving provision is meant to protect against only harmless errors: not if the error has deprived the accused of a statutory right or deprives an accused of the right to a trial by a jury lawfully constituted: *R v Rowbotham* (1988), 63 CR (3d) 113 (Ont CA).

180 Section 631(6).

181 Section 640(1).

182 Section 640(2). If two jurors have not yet been sworn, the trial judge can swear in two people present in the court to decide the challenge: note that s 640(2) does not require that these two people be potential jurors. If the two triers of the challenge are unable to agree on a decision within a reasonable time, the judge can discharge them and appoint two new triers: s 640(4).

183 Sections 640(2.1) & 640(2.2).

184 See, for example, *R v Jaser*, 2014 ONSC 7528; *R v Duberry*, 2013 BCSC 2514; *R v Huard* (2009), 247 CCC (3d) 526 (Ont SCJ); *R v White*, [2009] OJ No 3348 (SCJ);

court of appeal.[185] Whichever approach is taken, if the two triers cannot agree within a reasonable time, the trial judge can dismiss them and appoint two other triers.[186]

If the entire jury array is run through without a sufficient number of jurors having been selected, section 644 of the *Code* allows the judge to order the sheriff to "forthwith" summon other jurors to the courtroom. As a practical matter, the sheriff can simply go to the street and require passersby to attend for potential jury selection.[187] These jurors, known as "talesmen," are then selected from in the same manner as the original array.

A jury normally has twelve members; however, various provisions in the *Code* allow that number to go as high as fourteen (indeed, arguably sixteen) and as low as ten, depending upon the particular stage. In large part this flexibility is a response to practical challenges posed to juries in the large cases. Some trials can last many months or even years, and jurors can die or fall ill. Further, in some cases, they might seek to be discharged due to personal hardship or other reason, or dissension that a trial judge concludes lies at the feet of one juror can arise among jury members. It is possible, in such instances, for a trial judge to discharge a juror during the trial "by reason of illness or other reasonable cause."[188] Anticipating the possibility of the attrition of jurors in some trials, therefore, a judge can direct that one or two "additional"

R v Riley (2009), 247 CCC (3d) 517 (Ont SCJ); and *R v Sandham* (2009), 248 CCC (3d) 46 (Ont SCJ).

185 There is some discussion of these sections in *R v Swite*, 2011 BCCA 54, but not of this point.

186 Section 640(4).

187 Although the sheriff has no authority to excuse potential jurors for hardship or any other reason, he does have a limited discretion not to summon people who cannot attend jury selection due to some immediate conflict such as a medical appointment: *R v Blackduck*, 2014 NWTSC 48.

188 Section 644(1). This power should not be exercised lightly. The Supreme Court noted in *R v Pan; R v Sawyer*, 2001 SCC 42 at para 97, that

> Section 644 only permits jurors to be discharged in the course of the trial where a serious issue arises as to their fitness as a juror. It is not designed to encourage jurors to bring trivial complaints about their fellow jurors to the attention of the trial judge in the course of the trial, nor does it contemplate the discharge of jurors over minor concerns.

> In *R v Kum*, 2015 ONCA 36 (in which a majority of jury members wrote to the judge with concerns about two other members), the Ontario Court of Appeal suggested that because of concerns about jury secrecy, a trial judge is best advised to initially approach such situations by recharging all the jurors about their duty and responsibilities. It is open to a judge to conduct an inquiry with one or more jurors, but that is not usually the best starting point.

jurors be selected.[189] As a result, it is possible for as many as fourteen jurors to be sworn in at the start of trial and to listen to all the evidence. However, once the evidence is complete and the jury is to begin deliberating, that number must be reduced to twelve: if there are more than that number, the trial judge randomly selects names from all the jurors sworn in and discharges them until only twelve remain, and those twelve deliberate.[190]

There is another potential issue leading to attrition among jury members, which is the possibility of a long gap between the commencement of the trial, when jurors are selected,[191] and the commencement of calling evidence. Particularly given the number of *Charter* applications that are brought in criminal trials and that must be heard in the absence of the jury, it is possible that a jury will be selected but then directed to withdraw for some significant period of time. Once again this is a situation which can result in changing circumstances, with the result that some jurors who were selected might no longer be available when evidence is called.

The *Code* contains several responses to this problem. First, the *Code* permits the selection of one or two "alternate" jurors.[192] The role of alternate jurors differs from that of additional jurors: they are chosen at the time of jury selection but are not sworn in. Rather, they return at the commencement of evidence, at which point it is determined whether they are needed. If they are needed to complete a full jury (whether that is twelve, thirteen, or fourteen members), then they are sworn in, but if they are not needed at that stage, then they are excused.[193] Alternatively, even if no alternate jurors were selected, as long as no evidence has been heard, it is open to a trial judge to reopen the jury selection process and choose a replacement juror either by selecting a juror from some other jury array that happens to be available or

---

189 Section 631(2.2). When this is done, the Crown and the defence have an extra peremptory challenge for each additional juror: s 634(2.01).

190 Section 652.1(2).

191 The Court has noted that the "commencement of trial" is not a single fixed point and will vary depending on the *Code* section and interests in question. The accused's right to be present for the entire trial, for example, should be construed to allow the accused to be present for the selection of the jury. In the context of replacing jurors, though, the Court has designated the commencement of trial as the point at which evidence is first heard. See *Basarabas*, above note 23.

192 Section 631(2.1). When this is done, the Crown and defence receive an additional peremptory challenge for each alternate juror: s 634(2.1).

193 Section 642.1. If the full numbers of both alternate and additional jurors are employed, then up until the time the jury begins to hear evidence, there could be sixteen people who might eventually be part of the twelve who decide the case.

by using the procedure for selecting talesmen.[194] Finally, there is no absolute requirement that a verdict be rendered by a jury of twelve. Rather, unless the judge orders otherwise, the jury remains properly constituted and can render a verdict provided the number of jurors is not reduced below ten.[195]

There are three mechanisms by which a member of the jury array might be excluded from the jury: exemption, challenge for cause, and peremptory challenge. The three occur in that order. First, the trial judge is to decide whether any juror's request to be exempted should be granted. This step is taken first so that the parties are not required to use peremptory challenges to exclude jurors who might not have served in any case.[196] Following that, the parties are called upon to make any challenges, with challenges for cause preceding peremptory challenges.[197]

b) Exemptions

Section 632 of the *Code* allows a trial judge to excuse jurors[198] based on any of three grounds: personal interest in the matter to be tried; relationship with the judge, prosecutor, accused, counsel for the accused, or a prospective witness; and personal hardship or other reasonable cause. Typically, this procedure is carried out before the names of individual jurors are called, by the judge asking whether any jurors wish to be excused. Although this task is in a sense administrative, it is a part of the trial, and the accused is entitled to be present for it.[199]

Strictly the first two grounds upon which jurors can be excused relate to potential partiality, which, in general, must be dealt with by way of the challenge for cause procedures in the *Code*. However, these grounds are limited to such "obvious situations of non-indifference" that the consent of counsel to the exclusion of the juror can be presumed.[200] In any other circumstances, the challenge for cause procedures must be used. Further, nothing prevents a party from challenging

---

194 See s 644(1.1). In *R v Paterson* (2001), 41 CR (5th) 278 (BCCA), the trial occurred before s 644(1.1) had been placed in the *Code*, though, in fact, the trial judge did select a replacement juror from a different jury array. The British Columbia Court of Appeal held that s 644(1.1) merely codified what had already been the law.

195 Section 644(2).

196 *R v Douglas* (2002), 12 CR (6th) 374 (Ont CA) [*Douglas*].

197 *R v Bernardo* (2000), 31 CR (5th) 368 (Ont CA) [*Bernardo*].

198 Throughout this section, references to a "juror" should be understood where appropriate to mean a "prospective juror": that is, a person on the array whose name is called out for possible selection to a jury.

199 *Barrow*, above note 24.

200 *Sherratt*, above note 169 at 534.

for cause a juror whose request to be excused was not granted by the trial judge.[201]

The trial judge has a further related power under section 633 of the *Code*. Rather than excusing the juror completely, the trial judge can have a juror stand by.[202] In that event, jury selection continues with the remaining members of the array. Jurors that the judge has required to stand by are only re-called for possible selection if the array is exhausted without a complete jury. In that event, those jurors are re-called in the order in which they were first called, at which point the judge will decide whether to grant the exemption, and if she does not, then the juror will be subject to the normal challenge process.[203] On its face, the section is limited to standing jurors aside based on personal hardship or other reasonable cause, which is the third of the three grounds upon which jurors can be excused under section 632; however, the Ontario Court of Appeal has held that "other reasonable cause" can include potential partiality on the part of the juror.[204] The section states that it can be used only when a juror is individually called under section 631, rather than in the global manner used for excusing jurors. However, in *R v Krugel* the Ontario Court of Appeal found that an accused had suffered no prejudice when a trial judge departed from that approach,[205] and in *R v Douglas* it appeared to approve the practice of a trial judge who, with no objection from counsel, adopted the administrative convenience of informally standing aside, as a group, all jurors who indicated that they would seek an exemption if they were asked.[206]

c) Challenges for Cause

Section 638 of the *Code* sets out the grounds upon which a juror can be challenged for cause. Both the Crown and the accused are entitled to an

---

201 *Ibid.*

202 At one point the *Code* gave the Crown the power to "stand aside" jurors in a similar fashion, though this was found to violate the *Charter* in *Bain*, above note 68. Presumably because of this former power, the "stand aside" terminology is still often used when speaking of the power in s 633: see, for example, *R v Krugel* (2000), 31 CR (5th) 314 (Ont CA) [*Krugel*].

203 Section 641(1). The jurors are called in the same order to preserve randomness: *Krugel*, *ibid*. Section 642(2) provides that if other persons on the panel have become available in the interim, jury selection shall take place from the names of those persons first before returning to the stand-asides. Somewhat oddly, the *Code* provision gives the choice to do this to the prosecutor rather than the judge.

204 *Krugel*, above note 202.

205 *Ibid* at para 36.

206 *Douglas*, above note 196.

unlimited number of challenges for cause, but the grounds upon which those challenges can be made are exhaustively defined in subsections (a) through (f) of section 638(1). Some of the grounds are simply factual questions, such as that the juror's name does not appear on the panel, the juror is an alien, or the juror has been convicted of an offence for which the sentence was death or imprisonment exceeding twelve months. A juror can also be challenged on the basis either of physical incapacity to perform the duties of a juror, or of an inability to speak the language in which the trial will occur.[207] The only ground that has attracted real controversy is section 638(1)(b), a challenge on the basis that "a juror is not indifferent between the Queen and the accused."

The Supreme Court of Canada has consciously set a limited role for this ground, with one exception in cases where race is an issue. In general, though, the Court has observed that there are two approaches to deciding whether a juror is not indifferent:

> The first approach is that prevailing in the United States. On this approach, every jury panel is suspect. Every candidate for jury duty may be challenged and questioned as to preconceptions and prejudices on any sort of trial . . . . Canada has taken a different approach. In this country, candidates for jury duty are presumed to be indifferent or impartial. Before the Crown can challenge and question them, they must raise concerns which displace that presumption.[208]

In other words, challenge for cause is automatic in the United States, and there is a right from the start to question each potential juror to see whether that person is appropriate. Effectively the opposite is true in Canada, where it is presumed that any person can be a juror for any other person. Counsel will not be allowed to ask any questions regarding a challenge for cause without first satisfying the judge that there is some reason to doubt the juror's indifference.

---

207 This requirement is generally (though not uniformly) a provincial criterion for inclusion on a jury array initially, as one might expect. The particular motivation for s 638(1)(f) is s 530 of the *Code*, under which a trial can be directed to be in the official language of the accused. That provision is designed for situations where an accused speaks an official language of Canada that is not necessarily the language used daily in the courts of that province and therefore the trial might not ordinarily be in the accused's language. Section 638(1)(f) guarantees that when a trial is ordered to be in one of Canada's official languages, all the jurors will speak that official language. It has been proclaimed only in Manitoba, New Brunswick, the Northwest Territories, Ontario, and the Yukon Territory.

208 *R v Williams*, [1998] 1 SCR 1128 at paras 12–13 [*Williams*].

"Not indifferent" in this context has been defined to mean "not impartial" or prejudiced.[209] The Court has suggested that there are four relevant types of potential juror prejudice.[210] Interest prejudice arises when the juror has a direct interest in the trial, that is, where "the juror is the uncle of the accused, or the wife of a witness," for example.[211] Excluding a juror for this type of prejudice is not controversial, and, as noted above in Section C(3)(b), a trial judge can simply ask about any such relationships and excuse jurors before jury selection commences in such instances with the presumed consent of counsel.[212] Potentially more controversial are the other types: (1) specific prejudice, which consists of attitudes or beliefs about the particular case, gained through media coverage or some other source, that might prevent the juror from being impartial; (2) generic prejudice, consisting of stereotypical attitudes about the accused, victims, witnesses, or the nature of the crime; and (3) conformity prejudice, when a juror might feel influenced by strong community feelings about an expected outcome.[213] It is in those contexts that the presumption of impartiality has its most notable impact.

Challenge for cause is not intended to be a means for counsel to find out what type of person the juror is, or to decide whether to use a peremptory challenge.[214] Although the Court has resisted saying that challenge for cause is limited to extreme cases,[215] the presumption of impartiality means that counsel is not permitted to routinely challenge jurors. Rather, a two-step process is involved. First, counsel must satisfy the trial judge that the challenge for cause should be permitted: counsel must tell the trial judge the basis for the challenge.[216] If the trial judge is not satisfied that counsel has provided sufficient reason to doubt the juror's impartiality, the challenge will not occur. This would be true whether counsel wishes to challenge an individual juror or the jury array as a whole. At this stage of the process, the test

---

209 *R v Hubbert*, [1977] 2 SCR 267, aff'g [1975] OJ No 2595 (CA) [*Hubbert*].

210 *Williams*, above note 208 at para 10, relying on Neil Vidmar, "Pretrial Prejudice in Canada: A Comparative Perspective on the Criminal Jury" (1996) 79 *Judicature* 249.

211 *Sherratt*, above note 169 at 534, quoting from the Ontario Court of Appeal level decision in *Hubbert*, above note 209.

212 See s 632 of the *Code* and *Sherratt*, above note 169; *Barrow*, above note 24.

213 *Williams*, above note 208 at para 10.

214 *Hubbert*, above note 209.

215 *Sherratt*, above note 169.

216 *Hubbert*, above note 209 at para 35 (CA): "The *Code* does not require that a challenge, oral or written, be particularized . . . . But counsel must have a reason, even a generalized one."

is whether there is a realistic possibility for partiality.[217] Demonstrating a realistic potential for partiality (when dealing with a challenge to all members of the array) involves two components: showing "(1) that a widespread bias exists in the community; and (2) that some jurors may be incapable of setting aside this bias, despite trial safeguards, to render an impartial decision."[218] These two components are referred to as the "attitudinal" and "behavioural" components of partiality. The second stage is the challenge itself, where counsel is permitted to ask questions of the jurors to determine whether the juror will in fact be able to act impartially. Even at this stage, counsel will not have an unrestrained right to question jurors (in some cases, only one or two predetermined questions will be allowed).[219]

Because counsel must state the basis for challenging the juror beforehand, but will likely know little about the juror, there are practical obstacles that can prevent challenges for cause from even occurring, let alone succeeding. Therefore, cases have often concerned challenges that are relevant to the array as a whole, rather than having particular regard to some individual juror. For example, in R v Hubbert the accused wanted to question every juror to determine whether that juror would be prejudiced by learning that the accused had been detained in a mental health institution. Pre-trial publicity has also been a basis upon which counsel have sought to ask questions with a view to making challenges. R v Sherratt, for example, concerned a murder that was particularly notorious in the community, and the accused sought, unsuccessfully, to question jurors to determine whether the pre-trial publicity would prevent them from being impartial. The Court refused to allow the challenge in that case, holding that there was a distinction between mere publication of the facts of a case, on the one hand, and misrepresentation of evidence by the media, wide publicization of discreditable facts from an accused's past, or speculation about the accused's guilt or innocence, on the other hand.[220] It is fair to say that counsel generally have had difficulty persuading judges that it is reasonable to question every

---

217 *Williams*, above note 208 at para 32.

218 *R v Find*, [2001] 1 SCR 863 at para 32 [*Find*].

219 See, for example, *Hubbert*, above note 209, or the jury selection in the initial trial in *Williams*, above note 208. At the Supreme Court in *Williams*, the Court spoke about "confin[ing] the challenge to two questions, subject to a few tightly controlled subsidiary questions" as "a practice to be emulated" (para 55). See also the discussion of this approach in *R v Gayle* (2001), 154 CCC (3d) 221 (Ont CA) [*Gayle*].

220 For other cases dealing with pre-trial publicity as a ground for challenge, see *R v Merz* (1999), 140 CCC (3d) 259 (Ont CA); *Gayle*, ibid; *R v Proulx* (1992), 76 CCC (3d) 316 (Que CA); and *R v Keegstra* (1991), 3 CR (4th) 153 (Alta CA).

member of a jury array with regard to possible prejudice.[221] Precisely because the Canadian approach presumes the impartiality of every juror, showing a realistic potential of partiality is difficult.

The Court has, however, created one exception to this generalization, dealing with situations where partiality might arise due to attitudes about the race of the accused. In *R v Williams*, the accused was Aboriginal, and his counsel wanted to challenge jurors for cause based on racial attitudes. The accused did not offer evidence that the particular people on the jury array had racist attitudes. Rather, he led evidence showing that there was widespread bias against Aboriginal peoples in the community. The trial judge accepted that evidence, but held that evidence of general bias in the community did not establish a realistic potential of partiality on the part of jurors at trial, in part, because jurors could be expected to set aside their biases. The British Columbia Court of Appeal upheld the decision on the basis that general bias was not the equivalent of a racist attitude of particular concern to a criminal trial.

The Supreme Court of Canada overturned this result for a number of reasons. It held that the lower courts had set too high a standard for showing a realistic possibility of prejudice in these circumstances. Looking for attitudes particularly relevant to the justice system was an unrealistic test, it held, as was the expectation that juror attitudes would be "cleansed" by instructions about how they should discharge their duties. Racist attitudes, the Court pointed out, are insidious and sometimes unconsciously held—a juror might not be able to set them aside, even when trying to do so. Further, the potential effect of the attitude is unpredictable and, therefore, hard to guard against:

> It may incline a juror to believe that the accused is likely to have committed the crime alleged. It may incline a juror to reject or put less weight on the evidence of the accused, or it may, in a general way, predispose the juror to the Crown, perceived as representative of the "white" majority against the minority-member accused, inclining the juror, for example, to resolve doubts about aspects of the Crown's case more readily.[222]

---

221 See V Gordon Rose & James RP Ogloff, "Challenge for Cause in Canadian Criminal Jury Trials: Legal and Psychological Perspectives" (2002) 46 *Criminal Law Quarterly* 210, for an overview of types of evidence that have, and have not, been successful in permitting counsel to challenge for cause, as well as a discussion of the potential role of psychologists in such challenges.

222 *Williams*, above note 208 at para 11.

Essentially, with *Williams* the Court signalled that trial judges should be more open to being persuaded that there is a realistic potential for partiality (that is, that the first phase of the challenge for cause process is fulfilled) when the challenge is based on possible attitudes about race.[223] Indeed, the Court went so far as to note that widespread racial prejudice, as a characteristic of a community, could be the subject of judicial notice. Once widespread prejudice has been proved in one case, judges in later cases can take judicial notice of it or indeed simply find that widespread prejudice in a particular community is proven by events of indisputable accuracy, without any need for an accused to provide evidence.[224]

Lower courts have carried this finding to its logical conclusion, in a way likely to be approved by the Supreme Court, should the issue reach there. For example, in *R v Parks* the Ontario Court of Appeal had reached a conclusion similar to that in *Williams*, though on the facts of that case, which dealt with a black accused.[225] In *R v Wilson*, that court subsequently decided that challenges for cause based on the realistic potential for racist attitudes should be allowed to any black accused in Ontario without further empirical evidence of racism.[226] Later in *R v Koh*, that court expanded the finding to allow challenge for cause by any accused belonging to any visible minority. Its intention was not to do away with the need for a finding of a realistic potential for prejudice, but "to find that in the light of the numerous trial and appellate decisions in this jurisdiction concerning various categories of visible minorities, this test has been met wherever the accused is a member of a visible racial minority."[227]

---

223 On *Williams*, *ibid*, generally, see David M Tanovich, "The Future of Challenge for Cause in the Wake of *Williams*" (1998) 15 *Criminal Reports* (5th) 250, and Stephen G Coughlan, "Developments in Criminal Procedure: The 1997–98 Term" (1999) 10 *Supreme Court Law Review* 273.

224 *Williams*, above note 208 at para 54.

225 (1993), 24 CR (4th) 81 (Ont CA) [*Parks*]. The Supreme Court refused leave to appeal in *Parks*, but subsequently relied heavily on its reasoning in deciding *Williams*, above note 208. The Court was also able to note in *Williams* that post-*Parks* experience in Ontario had shown no significant delay in jury selection procedures despite the relaxing of the first stage in this context. Given that the efficiency of the system and the spectre of "US style" challenges for cause are a regular concern of the Court, it appears possible that leave to appeal might have been refused in *Parks* precisely to discover what the practical impact of the change would be.

226 (1996), 47 CR (4th) 61 (Ont CA).

227 (1998), 21 CR (5th) 188 at para 31 (Ont CA).

The Court has no intention of making challenge for cause more easily available outside the context of racial prejudice, however. This position is clear from the post-*Williams* decision in *R v Find*.[228] In that case, the accused wished to be allowed to question jurors in order to decide whether to challenge them for cause on the basis that the case concerned sexual assaults against children. The accused argued that there was a realistic potential that some jurors would be unable to act impartially because of the nature of the charges. In *Williams*, the Court described racial prejudice as "generic prejudice," which, in turn, it described as "stereotypical attitudes about the defendant, victims, witnesses or the nature of the crime itself."[229] Therefore, *Find* was an attempt to apply the approach in *Williams* to a relatively similar situation (another type of generic prejudice).

The Court rejected the appeal. The accused had argued that there was a realistic potential for partiality on a number of grounds: the widespread incidence of sexual abuse, which meant that previous victims or those close to them were likely to be on the panel; the politicized and gender-based nature of views about sexual assault; myths and stereotypes about sexual assault; the emotional nature of sexual assault trials; the history of challenge for cause in Ontario, which showed that when challenge for cause on this basis was allowed, roughly one third of jurors challenged were disqualified; and social science evidence suggesting widespread bias. Nonetheless, the Court was not persuaded on any of these grounds to permit the questioning towards challenge for cause to occur. It found that the evidence presented did not show a realistic possibility of prejudice and held as well that such a possibility could not be the subject of judicial notice. Further, they concluded that, unlike racial prejudice, any prejudice of this sort could be cured by judicial direction to jurors or other trial safeguards. Although the decision acknowledges the possibility of better evidence being presented in some future case, the case clearly indicates that outside the context of potential racial prejudice against the accused, challenge for cause is intended to be no more freely available than it was pre-*Williams*.[230]

Further, in *R v Spence*,[231] another post-*Williams* case, the Court refused to allow a *Parks*-like question based on the theory that witnesses

---

228 *Find*, above note 218.

229 *Williams*, above note 208 at para 10.

230 Further on this issue, see Steve Coughlan, "*R v Find*: Preserving the Presumption of Innocence" (2001) 42 *Criminal Reports* (5th) 31, and Michael Plaxton, "The Biased Juror and Appellate Review: A Reply to Professor Coughlan" (2001) 44 *Criminal Reports* (5th) 294.

231 [2005] 3 SCR 458 [*Spence*].

might fail to be impartial because they would feel a race-based sympathy for a victim, rather than a race-based antipathy to the accused as in *Williams* and *Parks*. The accused in *Spence* was black and the victim of the robbery was East Indian. The trial judge allowed the accused to challenge potential jurors on the issue of possible bias against him because of his race, but he was not allowed to ask whether jurors would be affected by the fact that he was accused of robbing an East Indian victim. The accused argued that potential East Indian jurors might feel a natural sympathy for the victim, and that asking this question was simply a natural progression of the *Williams/Parks* approach.

The Court held that the trial judge had acted correctly in refusing to allow the question. It held that the previous cases had dealt only with the issue of potential prejudice *against* a member of a visible minority and that none of the social science evidence presented in those cases established any kind of bias *in favour of* members of a particular group. The Court also held that such a "natural sympathy" was not a matter of which a court could take judicial notice. Accordingly, they rejected the accused's argument.

Finally, in *Kokopenace*, a case in which an Aboriginal accused objected to the under-representation of Aboriginal persons on the jury roll, the Court arguably backed away from its views about the possible effect of racism on jurors. Rejecting the dissenting position that a jury drawn from a jury roll which does not include persons who share the same characteristics as the accused will be less likely to detect and avoid the "often unconscious effects of racism," the majority held that "there is no empirical data to support the proposition that jurors of the same race as the accused are necessary to evaluate the evidence in a fair and impartial manner."[232]

When challenge for cause is allowed, the process to be followed is set out in the *Code*. For the first juror, the accused decides whether to challenge for cause before the Crown. Then, the Crown and the accused take turns.[233] If the judge permits a challenge for cause to be heard, it is tried by the two jurors most recently sworn or by two people

---

232 *Kokopenace*, above note 166 at para 52.

233 This rule applies to both challenges for cause and peremptory challenges: see s 635(1). When there is more than one accused, the accused alternate with the Crown as a group, though each accused is separately entitled to challenge: s 635(2). The accused are required to decide whether to challenge in the order that their names appear on the indictment, unless they agree on a different order. Although this requirement might place the first accused at a tactical disadvantage compared to fellow accused, it does not violate the *Charter*: *Suzack*, above note 51.

appointed by the judge if no jurors have yet been sworn.[234] The Ontario Court of Appeal has observed that these triers often are not adequately instructed in the nature of their task.[235] The trial judge should instruct the triers that they are to decide whether the juror is impartial on a balance of probabilities; they must agree on a decision, they can retire to the jury room or decide where they are, and if they cannot agree in a reasonable time, they are to say so.[236] The judge has discretion to permit submissions by counsel following the questioning.[237]

It will generally be an error that leads to a new trial if the *Code* provisions for challenge for cause are not followed. In *Barrow*, for example, the trial judge permitted jurors to request exemption on the basis that they would be unable to decide impartially, not simply on obvious grounds such as relation to the accused, but based on pre-trial publicity. These exemption requests took place without the accused and were held to usurp a portion of the challenge for cause process.[238] Similarly, in *R v Guérin* the trial judge largely took over the roles of questioning jurors and deciding their impartiality.[239] In each case a new trial was ordered. There is some dispute, however, as to whether a judge is obliged, when the two triers cannot agree concerning the partiality of a juror, to appoint two new triers under section 640(4), or whether the judge has discretion to discharge that juror under section 632.[240]

Both parties make any challenge for cause before either is called on to make a peremptory challenge,[241] though either type of challenge should occur after the judge has decided whether to grant a juror's request for exemption.[242] The accused decides whether to challenge first (either for cause or peremptorily) with regard to the first juror, after which the sides

---

234 Section 640(2). See the discussion of "rotating triers" and "static triers" in Section C(3)(a), above in this chapter. Where the basis for the challenge is that the juror's name does not appear on the jury panel, the judge personally decides the challenge.
235 *Douglas*, above note 196.
236 *Hubbert*, above note 209.
237 *Hubbert*, ibid; *R v Moore-McFarlane* (2001), 47 CR (5th) 203 (Ont CA).
238 *Barrow*, above note 24.
239 (1984), 13 CCC (3d) 231 (Que CA).
240 See *R v Brigham* (1988), 44 CCC (3d) 379 (Que CA), holding that s 640 must be complied with, and *Gayle*, above note 219, holding that where the decision to discharge the juror did not result in any prejudice to the accused and, indeed, likely saved him a peremptory challenge, a rigidly technical approach should not be followed.
241 *Bernardo*, above note 197.
242 *Douglas*, above note 196.

alternate.[243] Although the challenge for cause process is not to be used in order to gain evidence to decide whether to challenge peremptorily, that can indirectly be one of the effects. An unsuccessful challenge for cause does not prevent a peremptory challenge from being used.[244]

d) Peremptory Challenges

Peremptory challenges, which allow the accused or the Crown to dismiss a potential juror without explanation, are governed by section 634 of the *Criminal Code*. Unlike challenges for cause, peremptory challenges are limited in number.[245] Each party has twenty peremptory challenges in cases of high treason or first-degree murder, twelve challenges in cases of other offences that carry sentences of five years or more, and four challenges in all other cases. In a trial on more than one charge, the number of peremptory challenges for the most serious offence is provided. If there is more than one accused, each accused receives the prescribed number of peremptory challenges, and the Crown receives the same number as all the accused combined.[246] If additional or alternate jurors are selected, the Crown and the accused each receive one extra peremptory challenge for each such juror.[247]

There has been no real debate that the accused's use of peremptory challenges is unconstrained. Blackstone offered two rationales for their existence, which have frequently been cited:

> 1. As every one must be sensible what sudden impressions and unaccountable prejudices we are apt to conceive upon the bare looks and gestures of another, and how necessary it is that a prisoner (when put to defend his life), should have a good opinion of his jury, the want of which might totally disconcert him, the law wills not that he should be tried by any one man against whom he has conceived a prejudice, even without being able to assign a reason for such his dislike. 2. Because,

---

243 Section 635(1). When there is more than one accused, they are treated as a group which alternates with the Crown, and the accused individually decide whether to challenge based on the order in which their names are on the indictment, or any other order they agree on: s 635(2).

244 *R v Cloutier*, [1979] 2 SCR 709 [*Cloutier*]; *Hubbert*, above note 209.

245 Prior to *Bain*, above note 68, the Crown also had the power to "stand aside" jurors. This power allowed the Crown to have a juror put to the bottom of the list without actually using a challenge. Since normally the entire jury array was not called, in effect, the Crown had more peremptory challenges than the accused. This provision was found to violate the *Charter* in *Bain*, resulting in the current system giving both sides the same number of peremptory challenges.

246 Section 634.

247 Sections 634(2.1) and (2.01). See the discussion of additional and alternate jurors in Section C(3)(a), above in this chapter.

upon challenges for cause shown, if the reasons assigned prove insufficient to set aside the juror, perhaps the bare questioning his indifference
may sometimes provoke a resentment, to prevent all ill consequences
from which the prisoner is still at liberty, if he pleases, peremptorily to
set him aside.[248]

More controversial, and still unsettled, has been the question of
whether the Crown is similarly unconstrained in its use of peremptory
challenges. The Ontario Court of Appeal has held that the Crown's
quasi-judicial role precludes some uses of peremptory challenges,
and that it must exercise that discretion in conformity with *Charter*
principles and values: "public confidence in the administration of justice would be seriously undermined if Crown counsel were permitted to exercise the power of peremptory challenge on racial or ethnic
grounds."[249] Similarly, in *R v Pizzacalla* the Ontario Court of Appeal
ordered a retrial in a case where the Crown used its stand-aside power
to produce an all-female jury in a sexual assault case.[250] The Supreme
Court of Canada seemed to approve of *Pizzacalla* in *Bain*.[251]

R v Biddle presented another case in which the Crown used the
stand-aside power to create an all-female jury for a sexual assault
case.[252] The majority of the Court declined to comment on the issue, on
the basis that the decision in *Bain* to strike down the stand-aside power
had rendered the issue of only academic interest. In a concurring judgment, however, Gonthier J criticized the Crown's behaviour as an effort
to fashion a jury that might seem favourable to it, even if it was, in fact,
impartial. In contrast, McLachlin J (as she then was) argued that an
all-female jury not only could be, but would be seen by a reasonable
observer as impartial.

The principle that the Crown cannot use peremptory challenges to
produce a jury that does not appear impartial is not in dispute. What
will continue to be a source of dispute is whether reasonable people
will see the conscious exclusion of one race or one sex from a jury as
violating that principle. On this point, McLachlin CJ argues that an all-
woman jury would be as capable of being impartial as "all-male juries
have been presumed to be for centuries." While that might be literally

---

248 See *Cloutier*, above note 244 at 720.

249 *Gayle*, above note 219 at para 66.

250 (1991), 7 CR (4th) 294 (Ont CA) [*Pizzacalla*].

251 All three judgments make reference to *Pizzacalla*, *ibid*, as an example that
     Crown prosecutors might sometimes use their powers in an objectionable
     fashion, seeming, therefore, to agree with the decision by the Ontario Court of
     Appeal to order a retrial.

252 [1995] 1 SCR 761 [*Biddle*].

true, it is not necessarily of any consolation. First, the perception that all-male juries were or are impartial is no longer as accepted as it had been for centuries.[253] Changes in provincial legislation to produce jury arrays from sources that include more women—moving away from municipal assessment rolls, for example—were largely motivated by the desire not to have juries effectively limited to men. Further, the Court has become concerned, particularly in sexual assault cases, with not allowing reasoning to be affected by "myths and stereotypes" that have historically influenced decision making. Many of those myths and stereotypes arose, one might suppose, precisely because the decision makers were predominantly or exclusively men.[254] So, past practice that the justice system is consciously trying to move away from might not be the best authority.

Further, the Chief Justice suggests that an all-woman jury would be seen as impartial, though some people "might for irrational reasons object." This argument would be more persuasive in a case where an all-woman jury had resulted simply through some statistical anomaly, rather than cases such as *Pizzacalla* and *Biddle* where the Crown consciously set out to achieve that result. It is undoubtedly true that a jury of women, all of whom have been judged individually to be impartial, could decide a case fairly. But the Crown prosecutors in both *Pizzacalla* and *Biddle* acted on the irrational belief that a juror's decision could be predicted based on sex: in *Pizzacalla*, the Crown prosecutor specifically acknowledged his rationale that male jurors were more likely to believe sexual harassment in the workplace was acceptable than were female jurors. If the belief that a juror's sex is likely to affect that juror's reasoning is unreasonable and objectionable, then, of course, such a belief cannot support any reasonable apprehension that the jury was not impartial. In that event, though, it is surely wrong for the Crown prosecutor to adopt a jury selection strategy hinging on exactly that unreasonable and objectionable belief.

None of this affects the conclusion that there is no absolute requirement for juries to be representative. As McLachlin CJ observes in *Biddle*, representativeness is generally a good means to try to achieve impartiality and competence, but it is not an end in itself. Similarly, the majority in *Kokopenace* observed that "representativeness is not

---

253 Note, for example, the inclusion of s 626(2) in the *Criminal Code* in 1985, preventing anyone from being disqualified, exempted, or excused from a jury panel based on sex.

254 See Bertha Wilson, "Will Women Judges Really Make a Difference?" (1990) 28 *Osgoode Hall Law Journal* 507.

about targeting particular groups for inclusion on the jury roll."[255] An accused also cannot insist that the jury or jury array contain members of the accused's race.[256] Further, an accused cannot object solely on the basis that the Crown had peremptorily challenged the only jurors of the same race as the accused, without more evidence allowing a court to review the Crown's actions.[257] Although, if there has been a conscious attempt to keep members of one race from the jury array, then that will constitute a basis to challenge the array.[258]

A practical difficulty arises for the accused in this context, namely, that of proving the motive of the Crown or other actor in the judicial system. In *R v Butler*, the accused succeeded in challenging the array only because after he had made an initial unsuccessful application, a sheriff spoke to his defence counsel, saying "totally off the record, the reason that Indians do not appear on the jury panels is because we have found them to be unreliable — they may show up one day for trial and then not come the next because they've gone out and gotten drunk the night before."[259] The evidence suggested that the sheriff's office had been acting on this belief for seventeen or eighteen years, and the sheriff only disclosed it at that time in the expectation that the statement would remain confidential. Similarly, in *Pizzacalla* the accused had the benefit of the Crown prosecutor's candid statement that he created an all-woman jury because men might be more likely to think sexual harassment was acceptable and, indeed, the Crown's concession that this action created the impression of a favourable jury. In *R v Biddle*, only a few years later, there was no dispute that the Crown prosecutor had consciously produced an all-woman jury, but no reason for doing so was offered and no concession regarding the propriety of the approach was made. The Ontario Court of Appeal speculated that the prosecutor's motive might have been to guarantee the impartiality of the jury, rather than its partiality, and dismissed the appeal partly on that basis.[260]

In *Gayle* as well, the Crown's actions were to peremptorily challenge the only two blacks called as potential jurors. However, there was no evidence of the makeup of the jury array and no evidence of the Crown's reason for challenging those two jurors. Therefore, while stating that, in principle, review of the Crown's use of peremptory challenges should

---

255 *Kokopenace*, above note 166 at para 61.
256 *Kent*, above note 178.
257 *Gayle*, above note 219.
258 *Butler*, above note 178.
259 *Ibid* at 177.
260 *R v Biddle* (1993), 14 OR (3d) 756 (CA).

be possible, the Ontario Court of Appeal did not allow a review in that case because there was no factual foundation upon which to conduct it.

In both *Biddle* and *Gayle*, appeal courts have seen it as important that the accused did not object to the Crown's actions at the time. One must be sympathetic to the need for a factual basis for an appeal, but it should be noted that there is not any obvious way in which an accused *could* object to the Crown's use of peremptory challenges. The defining feature of a peremptory challenge is that it allows a party to challenge "without showing any cause at all."[261] To ask the Crown to explain the basis upon which it has exercised its peremptory challenges, therefore, is inconsistent with the nature of the power. Even if the question were asked, "I just felt like it" would seem to be an acceptable answer.

The difficulty is that although the Crown does not have to have a "good" reason for using a peremptory challenge, some of the "not-good" reasons it might rely on could violate *Charter* values. There will be a significant challenge in finding a method that tests for whether the Crown has acted upon the wrong motives without calling on the Crown to explain its motives.

One possibility is judicial creation of a presumption that where the Crown's use of peremptory challenges and the ultimate makeup of the jury suggest that the Crown might have acted on principles that violate *Charter* values, the jury selection should be seen as tainted unless the Crown offers an alternative explanation. This approach would give the accused an effective way to inquire into the issue, without requiring the Crown to explain its use of peremptory challenges routinely. It would also give flexibility to appeal courts in applying the remedy because there would be considerable room for factual dispute as to whether the presumption should be seen to arise. Finally, it would leave unsettled, and therefore open to further development, the issue of what use of peremptory challenges would violate *Charter* values (for example, whether consciously creating an all-man or all-woman jury would do so).

One last issue that arises in the context of peremptory challenges (and for that matter, challenges for cause) should be discussed: the amount of information that the parties have about the potential jurors. Both the Crown and the accused are entitled to *act* on the opinion "I don't want that person on the jury," but in practical terms they have little basis upon which to *form* that opinion. Typically parties are unlikely

---

261 Sir William Blackstone, *Commentaries on the Laws of England*, vol 4 (Chicago: University of Chicago Press, 1979) at 1738, cited in *Cloutier*, above note 244.

to know much about the members of the jury panel. This situation—or more accurately efforts by the Crown to avoid it—has led to litigation.

This issue first reached the Supreme Court in *R v Latimer*,[262] where the RCMP, having prepared a questionnaire in cooperation with the Crown prosecutor, administered it to thirty prospective jurors. The questionnaire asked the views of the prospective jurors on a number of issues, including religion, abortion, and euthanasia. The Crown did not disclose the questionnaire or the direct contact with jurors to the defence or the trial judge. In very brief reasons, the Court described this as a "flagrant abuse of process and interference with the administration of justice," which warranted a new trial.[263] The issue, it held, was not whether the RCMP's behaviour influenced the jury's deliberations, but that it violated the principle that justice must not only be done, but be seen to be done.

Perhaps surprisingly, given the strong language of the Court in *Latimer*, similar issues continued to arise. In some cases, despite a Practice Memorandum directing them not to do so, Crown prosecutors have asked police officers for information concerning prospective jurors and have acted on it. The practice led to an investigation by Ontario's Information and Privacy Commissioner,[264] and eventually to a trilogy of cases at the Supreme Court: *R v Yumnu*,[265] *R v Emms*,[266] and *R v Davey*.[267] The result of those decisions is what has generally been regarded as a relaxation of the strong position taken in *Latimer* against "jury-vetting."

The Court concluded that, since having a criminal record is a basis for exclusion from a jury and self-reporting is not necessarily successful as a screening method, it is acceptable for the Crown to ask police to do a criminal record check on prospective jurors. That was the primary thing that police had been asked to do in the trilogy, and it was a "far cry from the conduct at issue in *Latimer*."[268] The police cannot be *asked* to do more than that, but if they discover other relevant information in the course of a criminal record check, they can give this information to the Crown. The Court noted in *Yumnu* that such information might be relevant not only to whether to peremptorily challenge, but also to whether

---

262 [1997] 1 SCR 217 [*Latimer*].

263 *Ibid* at para 43.

264 Information and Privacy Commissioner, *Excessive Background Checks Conducted on Prospective Jurors: A Special Investigation Report* (Toronto: Information and Privacy Commissioner of Ontario, 2009).

265 2012 SCC 73 [*Yumnu*].

266 2012 SCC 74 [*Emms*].

267 2012 SCC 75 [*Davey*].

268 *Emms*, above note 266 at para 49.

to ask the judge to remove the juror as obviously partial, to ask the judge to have the juror stand aside, or to make a challenge for cause.[269]

If the Crown does receive any such information from the police, it is required to give that to the defence, in accordance with its ordinary disclosure obligations. However, independent of asking the police to check official records, Crown prosecutors are also entitled to ask police officers, as part of the "prosecution team," for their general impressions of potential jurors, and there is nothing wrong with using this collective experience and judgment in exercising discretionary decisions such as whether to make a peremptory challenge. These sorts of general impressions or public knowledge need not be disclosed to the defence, since they are not linked to the prosecution's role as an agent of the state.[270]

FURTHER READINGS

ARCHIBALD, BRUCE. "Prosecutors, Democracy and the Public Interest: Prosecutorial Discretion and Its Limits in Canada" (Paper delivered at the XVIth Congress of the International Academy of Comparative Law, Brisbane, Australia, 14–20 July 2002).

BAAR, CARL. "Criminal Court Delay and the *Charter*: The Use and Misuse of Social Facts in Judicial Policy Making" (1993) 72 *Canadian Bar Review* 305.

COUGHLAN, STEVE. "*R. v. Find*: Preserving the Presumption of Innocence" (2001) 42 *Criminal Reports* (5th) 31.

KAISER, HA. "*Babos*: Further Narrowing Access to Stay of Proceedings Where the Integrity of the Judicial Process Is Implicated" (2014) 8 *Criminal Reports* (7th) 59.

LAW REFORM COMMISSION OF CANADA. *Trial within a Reasonable Time: A Working Paper* (Ottawa: Canada Communication Group, 1994).

PLAXTON, MICHAEL. "The Biased Juror and Appellate Review: A Reply to Professor Coughlan" (2001) 44 *Criminal Reports* (5th) 294.

POMERANT, DAVID. *Multiculturalism, Representation and the Jury Selection Process in Canadian Criminal Cases* (Ottawa: Department of Justice Canada, Research and Statistics Directorate, 1994).

---

269 *Yumnu*, above note 265 at para 54.
270 *Davey*, above note 267 at paras 38–46.

QUIGLEY, TIM. *Procedure in Canadian Criminal Law*, 2d ed (Toronto: Thomson Carswell, 2005) (loose-leaf) ch 16, 19, & 20.

————. "Have We Seen the End of Improper Jury Vetting?" (2013) 98 *Criminal Reports* (6th) 109.

————. "*Babos*: Balancing Test Unnecessarily Restricts Residual Category for Stay as Abuse of Process" (2014) 8 *Criminal Reports* (7th) 55.

ROSE, V GORDON, & JAMES RP OGLOFF. "Challenge for Cause in Canadian Criminal Jury Trials: Legal and Psychological Perspectives" (2002) 45 *Criminal Law Quarterly* 210.

RUBY, CLAYTON. "Trial within a Reasonable Time under Section 11(b): The Ontario Court of Appeal Disconnects from the Supreme Court" (2013) 2 *Criminal Reports* (7th) 91.

SCHNEIDER, RICHARD D, HY BLOOM, & MARK HEEREMA. *Mental Health Courts: Decriminalizing the Mentally Ill* (Toronto: Irwin Law, 2007).

STUART, DON. *Charter Justice in Canadian Criminal Law*, 5th ed (Toronto: Thomson Carswell, 2010) ch 2 and 6.

TANOVICH, DAVID M. "The Future of Challenge for Cause in the Wake of *Williams*" (1998) 15 *Criminal Reports* (5th) 250.

VIDMAR, NEIL. "Pretrial Prejudice in Canada: A Comparative Perspective on the Criminal Jury" (1996) 79 *Judicature* 249.

WILSON, BERTHA. "Will Women Judges Really Make a Difference?" (1990) 28 *Osgoode Hall Law Journal* 507.

THE TRIAL PROCESS

A. INTRODUCTION

This chapter focuses on the actual process of a trial. That discussion must begin at the pre-trial stage, with reference to the charging documents that bring a person to court and set out the case to be met at trial. From there we move to a discussion of the pleas an accused can enter, and the various stages of a trial, including opening statements, examination of witnesses, closing arguments, and charging of the jury. We will then consider the rules surrounding jury deliberations and finally conclude with a discussion of the various powers a judge can exercise during the trial.

B. THE CHARGE DOCUMENT

1) Informations, Indictments, and Direct Indictments

When a person is put on trial for an offence, there must be some particular document specifying the charge against that person. Initially, charges are laid by means of an information,[1] which was discussed in Chapter 6. When an accused is tried by a provincial court judge, that information is the relevant document, whereas when the accused is

---

1 Section 505.

not tried by a provincial court judge, a different document—an indictment—is prepared.[2] Most commonly, the indictment is prepared following the preliminary inquiry and can include any charge on which the person was ordered to stand trial or any charge founded on the facts disclosed at the preliminary inquiry.[3]

That latter rule—that an indictment can be preferred on a charge where the facts making it out are disclosed at the preliminary inquiry—does not allow a prosecutor to prefer an indictment on the very charge for which the accused is discharged. Rather, that power is intended to allow the preferment of charges for other offences that are disclosed at the preliminary inquiry.[4] Nonetheless, a prosecutor *can* lay an indictment concerning the offence for which an accused has been discharged: section 577 of the *Criminal Code* permits exactly that.

Section 577 allows for "direct indictments," which permit the prosecutor to prefer an indictment when the accused has not been given the opportunity to request a preliminary inquiry, when the preliminary inquiry has been commenced but not concluded,[5] or when the accused was discharged following the preliminary inquiry. This power also applies where a committal for trial has been quashed,[6] or where a trial judge has specifically declined to order an accused to stand trial on a charge not laid but disclosed in the evidence at the preliminary inquiry.[7] As it is a special power, in effect, overriding procedures the accused would otherwise be entitled to benefit from, a direct indictment can be preferred by a Crown prosecutor only with the personal consent in writing of the attorney general or deputy attorney general.[8]

The attorney general's power to authorize a direct indictment cannot be reviewed by a court.[9] It does not violate the *Charter*, provided that the accused receives full disclosure and nothing else in the circumstances

---

2   Section 566(1). Note that the power in s 577 to proceed by direct indictment means that there could be occasions when an indictment is the first charge document prepared.

3   Section 574.

4   *R v Tapaquon*, [1993] 4 SCR 535.

5   Courts had already held that the power was available in this situation, but the *Code* has since been amended to explicitly state it. See *R v Stewart (No 2)* (1977), 35 CCC (2d) 281 (Ont CA).

6   *R v Charlie* (1998), 126 CCC (3d) 513 (BCCA).

7   *R v McKibbon*, [1984] 1 SCR 131.

8   Section 577(b) also permits direct indictments in private prosecutions where a judge of the court permits the direct indictment to be preferred.

9   *R v Balderstone* (1983), 8 CCC (3d) 532 (Man CA), leave to appeal to SCC refused, [1983] 2 SCR v; *R v Stolar* (1983), 32 CR (3d) 342 (Man CA), leave to appeal to SCC refused, [1983] 1 SCR xiv [*Stolar*].

makes the action an abuse of process.[10] Indeed, the power is seen as having potentially beneficial effects, such as protecting an accused's right to a trial within a reasonable time, protecting the physical or psychological health of witnesses, preserving Crown evidence, avoiding multiple proceedings when there are co-accused, and so on.[11]

Once it is preferred, the indictment provides a fresh starting point upon which the future proceedings are based, and an accused is no longer entitled to look behind it, for example, to attempt to quash by *certiorari* the committal for trial. The indictment is preferred and, therefore, acts as a type of barrier, once it is lodged with the trial court at the start of the accused's trial, in front of a court ready to proceed.[12]

Whether the trial proceeds by information or indictment, the document is the starting point for the trial and sets out the case the accused has to meet. The rules set out in Parts XVI and XX of the *Code* that govern compelling appearance and jury trials also apply to summary conviction offences by virtue of section 795, with only minor variations, so the requirements for an information and an indictment can be discussed together. The Supreme Court has stressed the importance of this document, holding that "it is fundamental to a fair trial that an accused know the charge or charges he or she must meet."[13] As we will see, though, the general tenor of the caselaw has been to considerably downplay the significance of the technical requirements for these documents or any failures to comply with those requirements.

2) Joinder and Severance of Charges

Although many rules surrounding indictments were originally developed to a great extent at common law, they are now primarily set out in the *Code*. There are many rules in the *Code* and there has been a good deal of

---

10   *R v Ertel* (1987), 58 CR (3d) 252 (Ont CA), leave to appeal to SCC refused (1987), 61 CR (3d) xxix; *R v Arviv* (1985), 45 CR (3d) 354 (Ont CA), leave to appeal to SCC refused, [1985] 1 SCR v; *Stolar*, above note 9.

11   *R v SJL*, 2009 SCC 14 [*SJL*]. The Court refers at para 38 to ten reasons often cited in support of direct indictments, acknowledging that some are vaguely worded and that not all will be relevant in a given case. The Court also concludes in *SJL* that direct indictments are available in the case of young persons in the relatively few cases where they can be prosecuted by way of indictment.

12   *R v Chabot*, [1980] 2 SCR 985. See also *R v Regan*, 2002 SCC 12, where a 5:4 majority of the Court were of the view that the direct indictment in that case acted to "cleanse" any concerns about loss of objectivity at an earlier stage. Since the attorney general personally needed to consent, it was reasonable to conclude that a fresh, careful, and objective review of the case must have taken place.

13   *R v GR*, [2005] 2 SCR 371 at para 2.

litigation over these issues, but a good general guideline is that relatively few firm limitations are imposed on the structure of indictments. An indictment (Form 4 from the *Code*) can contain any number of "counts."[14] Each count is to cover a single transaction, though this rule is specifically said to apply "in general" and the concept of a "single transaction" is given a broad interpretation.[15] Further, although for many years a trial could not concern more than one indictment, the Court has relaxed that requirement. It is now possible to hold a trial on one or more indictments simultaneously, provided that the accused consents, or the trial judge feels that it is in the interests of justice and the charges could have been jointly charged in a single indictment.[16] This latter requirement imposes few restrictions.[17] Section 589 prevents any charge from being joined with murder, though even this rule is subject to exceptions if the other offence arises out of the same transaction or the accused consents to the joinder.[18] Summary conviction and indictable offences can be tried together, provided the accused consents and the accused's election and the other procedures make it possible to do so.[19] Otherwise, the limits on joinder of counts are case by case, according to the criteria in section 591(3) of the *Code*. That provision allows a judge to order an indictment to be severed in order to send some counts or some co-accused to a separate trial.

The *Code* gives little in the way of guidance regarding severance decisions, stating only that the court can do so where "the interests of justice so require."[20] A preliminary inquiry judge does not have jurisdiction to sever; it must be done by the trial judge.[21] The judge's decision is subject to review on appeal, but it is not to be interfered with unless the judge has acted unjudicially or the ruling resulted in an injustice.[22] The former question looks at the circumstances at the time

---

14 "Count" is defined in s 2 of the *Code* as a "charge in an information or indictment."

15 Section 581(1). See the discussion of *R v Lilly*, [1983] 1 SCR 794 [*Lilly*] at Section B(5)(c), below in this chapter, in which twenty-one separate withdrawals from a trust account were the foundation for a single count of fraud and, in general, the discussion of division of counts.

16 *R v Clunas*, [1992] 1 SCR 595 [*Clunas*].

17 See, for example, s 574 or s 789(1)(b) of the *Code*.

18 See the thorough discussion of this section in *R v Riley* (2008), 229 CCC (3d) 266 (Ont SCJ). See also s 473(1.1), which permits an offence in s 469, which otherwise must be tried by a judge and jury, to be joined with any other offence and tried without a jury, provided the Crown and accused both consent.

19 *Clunas*, above note 16.

20 Section 591(3).

21 *R v Hynes*, [2001] 3 SCR 623 [*Hynes*].

22 *R v Litchfield*, [1993] 4 SCR 333 [*Litchfield*]. See the further discussion of this issue below, in the context of division of counts.

the ruling was made, while the latter takes into account as well the unfolding of the trial and of the verdicts.[23] Normally, an application to sever is made on a pre-trial basis because the decision will dictate the course of the trial.[24] However, section 591(4) permits the order to be made before or during the trial, with the jury being discharged with regard to any counts or accused that are severed during trial.

Courts have developed considerations to take into account when deciding whether to sever counts. These include

> the general prejudice to the accused; the legal and factual nexus between the counts; the complexity of the evidence; whether the accused intends to testify on one count but not another; the possibility of inconsistent verdicts; the desire to avoid a multiplicity of proceedings; the use of similar fact evidence at trial; the length of the trial having regard to the evidence to be called; the potential prejudice to the accused with respect to the right to be tried within a reasonable time; and the existence of antagonistic defences as between coaccused persons.[25]

Because society has an interest in avoiding a multiplicity of proceedings, the onus is on the accused, on a balance of probabilities, to show that separate trials should be held.[26] The obvious risk in holding a joint trial is that evidence admissible on only one count will affect the decision on another count. A trial judge can give a limiting instruction about the appropriate use of evidence to the jury, but if that was seen as always being a sufficient safeguard, then prejudice would essentially cease to be a relevant factor in the analysis.[27] Further, trial judges must take great care in distinguishing the two issues of severability and similar fact evidence, particularly as the onus is on the accused for the first, but on the Crown for the second.[28]

Where an application to sever is made later in the trial, it ought to be based on some prejudice that was not apparent at the start.[29] For example, an accused could decide at the close of the Crown's case that the Crown's witnesses were not credible on some counts. The accused might therefore feel that it was not necessary to take the stand with regard to those counts, but that it was necessary to testify with regard

---

23   *R v Last*, 2009 SCC 45 at para 15 [*Last*].
24   *Litchfield*, above note 22.
25   *Last*, above note 23 at para 18.
26   *R v Cross* (1996), 112 CCC (3d) 410 (Que CA) [*Cross*].
27   *Last*, above note 23 at para 16.
28   *R v Arp*, [1998] 3 SCR 339.
29   *R v DAC* (1996), 72 BCAC 227 (CA), aff'd [1997] 1 SCR 8 [*DAC*].

to other counts. In such circumstances, the accused's fair trial right and right to silence might be brought into conflict if the counts were not severed. At such a late stage, however, the burden on the accused is very heavy and an assertion that the accused wished to testify on some counts but not on others would not be sufficient. The accused would be required to outline the basic nature of the proposed defence to justify severance and the consequent retrial on the severed charges.[30]

3) Joinder and Severance of Accused

Similar considerations arise in deciding whether to sever multiple accused from the same indictment and hold separate trials, though there are additional issues. Even more strongly in these circumstances, the practical goal of avoiding multiple proceedings favours not holding separate trials over the same facts unless it is necessary. The general rule is that accused who are alleged to have committed a crime together should be tried together.[31] This principle is adhered to quite firmly. When co-accused blame one another, they might be able to cross-examine one another in ways not available to the Crown, with regard to propensity or similar issues, for example.[32] This could result in the fair trial right of one accused conflicting with the pre-trial right to silence of a co-accused, if one accused wants to point to the failure of the other to cooperate with the police. Even then, the Court has held that the solution in such situations is not to sever the trials, but to balance the competing rights of the two accused along with the interest of the state in a joint trial. The Court has held that in such circumstances of a "cut-throat defence," the policy reasons favouring a joint trial apply with equal or greater force than normally.[33]

Nonetheless, there are exceptions to the joint trial rule. First, a young person and an adult cannot be tried together.[34] More generally, a trial judge has discretion to sever the trials of co-accused in accordance with section 591(3) where it is required in the interests of justice. In deciding the issue, courts should consider not only whether the co-accused will have antagonistic defences, but also other issues, such as

---

30   See *DAC, ibid*, and *Cross*, above note 26.
31   *R v Chow*, 2005 SCC 24. See also *R v Torbiak and Gillis* (1978), 40 CCC (2d) 193 (Ont CA) [*Torbiak*]; *R v Miller and Cockriel* (1975), 33 CRNS 129 (BCCA), aff'd on other issues (1976), 70 DLR (3d) 324 (SCC); *R v Agawa and Mallett* (1975), 31 CRNS 293 (Ont CA) [*Agawa*].
32   *R v Kendall* (1987), 57 CR (3d) 249 (Ont CA).
33   *R v Crawford; R v Creighton*, [1995] 1 SCR 858 [*Crawford*].
34   *SJL*, above note 11.

the possibility of inconsistent verdicts (which militates against severance) or whether evidence admissible against one accused is inadmissible against another.[35]

The fact that one of the accused would be a compellable witness for the other accused in a separate trial but not in a joint trial is relevant, but not determinative. In *R v Agawa and Mallett*, for example, the Ontario Court of Appeal upheld the trial judge's decision not to grant separate trials in such circumstances because there was not sufficient evidence that the co-accused would have given evidence useful to the applicant even if he were made compellable.[36] The question is whether the co-accused's evidence could reasonably affect the verdict by creating a reasonable doubt.[37] As with many issues, cases have divided on the proper way to proceed. Some decisions have held that counsel's assertion that a co-accused has made out-of-court statements that would be helpful must be taken at face value and justify severance. Others have held that granting severance simply on the allegation that one co-accused might give evidence in defence of the other is to reverse the presumption in favour of joint trials. Some authority suggests that if an accused shows that a co-accused's evidence is likely to raise a reasonable doubt, there is no longer any discretion to not grant the severance application. Much will depend on the facts of the individual case.[38]

The fact that some evidence will be admissible against one accused but not others is also relevant, but again it is not sufficient to require severance. Where several accused have all made statements, for example, the content of each statement might become admissible for its truth against the accused making it, but not against each of the co-accused. Particularly in jury trials, the trial judge then has the "added and heavy burden of complete and proper instruction to the jury on the precise limits of the evidence admissible against each of the accused, and hence the limited use to which these statements can be put."[39] The Court has suggested that in conspiracy trials where the evidence is

---

35   *DAC*, above note 29; *Cross*, above note 26.

36   *Agawa*, above note 31.

37   *Torbiak*, above note 31. In that case, the trial judge did not apply this test and refused to sever because the co-accused's testimony would only be corroborative. The Court of Appeal found this to be an error but declined to grant the appeal nonetheless, on the basis that the error did not amount to a miscarriage of justice.

38   See, generally, *R v Boulet* (1987), 40 CCC (3d) 38 (Que CA), leave to appeal to SCC refused, [1989] 1 SCR vi; *R v Szczerba* (2002), 314 AR 114 (QB); and the cases discussed in those cases.

39   *R v McFall*, [1980] 1 SCR 321 at 338. The quote is from Estey J, who dissented in the result because the majority held that any errors were harmless ones covered by the curative provisions in the *Code*.

much stronger against one accused, and particularly where a damaging statement will be admissible against one but not the other, the safer course is to order separate trials.[40]

When co-accused are tried together, the order in which their names appear on the indictment settles the order in which they will be called upon to do many things at trial, such as exercise peremptory challenges, question witnesses, decide whether to call a defence, and make closing addresses. The Crown has discretion over what order to choose for the indictment and in doing so can make tactical decisions that it is not called upon to explain, short of an abuse of process.[41]

4) Content of Charges

Any given count, whether it is in a multi-count information or dealt with individually, "shall contain in substance a statement that the accused or defendant committed an indictable offence therein specified."[42] Section 581 continues by setting out some rules for that statement, which can be "in popular language without technical averments," in the words of the *Code* provision, or, in other words, that give the accused notice of the offence that he is charged with. Whatever is done, however, the key rule from section 581(3) is that

> a count shall contain sufficient detail of the circumstances of the alleged offence to give to the accused reasonable information with respect to the act or omission to be proved against him and to identify the transaction referred to but otherwise the absence or insufficiency of details does not vitiate the count.

The *Code* then offers further detail to help determine whether this standard is met. The count can refer to the particular section under which the accused is charged, as a way of helping to give sufficient notice.[43] Further, the *Code* specifies that the absence of details does not automatically render a count insufficient and lists particular omissions that are not fatal, such as that "it does not name the person injured or intended or attempted to be injured," "it does not specify the means by which the alleged offence was committed," or "it does not name or describe with precision any person, place or thing."[44] The issue of sufficiency of

---

40   *R v Guimond*, [1979] 1 SCR 960.
41   *R v Sandham* (2009), 248 CCC (3d) 392 (Ont SCJ).
42   Section 581(1).
43   Section 581(5).
44   Section 583. The *Code* also creates special rules for some particular situations, such as that no one can be convicted of high treason (rather than treason) or

counts is discussed in greater detail at Section B(5)(b), below in this chapter.

The Court has noted that there are two interrelated rules dealing with indictments: section 581(3), dealing with insufficient detail, and the "surplusage rule," dealing with additional, unnecessary detail.[45] The general rule is that the purpose of each count in an indictment is to put the accused on notice of the case to be met. Accordingly, a count must have sufficient detail, and an accused is normally entitled to expect that the Crown will be required to prove all the details of any allegation made. However, it is open to a court to find that detail actually provided in a count is "surplusage," and therefore that a fact need not be proven, despite being alleged. It is not always clear in practice whether a detail is mere surplusage.

In *R v NC*,[46] for example, the accused was charged with trafficking in cocaine, though the evidence at trial showed that the substance she had claimed to be cocaine was actually a mixture of baby powder and aspirin. This would have been an offence nonetheless, since the *Narcotic Control Act*[47] provision also made it an offence to traffic in any substance held out to be a narcotic. However, the Court held that, having charged the accused with trafficking in cocaine, the Crown was obliged to prove that the substance actually was cocaine: their failure to do so would mean she must be acquitted. Similarly, in *R v Saunders*, the Crown charged a number of accused with conspiracy to import heroin. The charge would have been perfectly acceptable had it not specified which narcotic was to be imported. However, having specified heroin, the Crown was obliged to prove that the conspiracy related to that narcotic in particular.[48]

On the other hand, in *R v Hanna*[49] the accused was charged with theft of gravel from the Nova Scotia Power Commission and obtained a directed verdict because the only evidence of ownership showed that the gravel was owned by the power corporation. This decision was overturned at trial on the basis that there was no possibility that the accused could fail to identify the event that gave rise to the charge against him.

Similarly, in *R v Vézina*, the accused was charged with fraud in an information that specified the Bank of Montreal as the victim. In fact,

---

first-degree murder (rather than second-degree murder) without having been specifically charged with that offence: s 582. See also the special rules in ss 581(4), 584, 585, & 586.

45   *R v Vézina*, [1986] 1 SCR 2 at para 54 [*Vézina*].
46   (1991), 64 CCC (3d) 45 (Que CA).
47   RSC 1985, c N-1 [since repealed].
48   *R v Saunders*, [1990] 1 SCR 1020.
49   (1991), 109 NSR (2d) 338 (SCAD).

the Crown was unable to prove that the Bank of Montreal would have suffered any loss from the accused's fraud. The Court held that the information would initially have been valid, even if it had not specified a victim. Accordingly, it did not matter that the Crown was unable to prove the particular allegation, which was mere surplusage.[50]

Whether a detail will be considered surplusage, or whether the Crown will be held to proof of the fact, depends on whether the accused's defence will be prejudiced. In *R v Saunders*, for example, one accused had taken the stand to testify that he had been involved in one of several conspiracies to import narcotics, but not in the particular conspiracy that was to import heroin. In that case, not holding the Crown to proof of the particular narcotic alleged would have been prejudicial. In *Vézina*, on the other hand, the Court concluded that the accused would not have conducted their defence in any different manner had the allegation that the Bank of Montreal was the victim not been made, and therefore the accused suffered no prejudice. Given the absence of prejudice to the accused, the Crown was not to be held to proof of that fact.

5) Remedies for a Defective Charge

The issue of what to do in the face of a defective charge is intimately bound up with the nature of the defect. We shall first discuss the potential remedies and then turn to the issue of the types of defects leading to a remedy.

a) Potential Remedies

The real issue is what to do when a charge is alleged not to be sufficient because it does not comply with the necessary requirements. Historically this was a tortuous area, for reasons no longer relevant. Most of these rules developed in Great Britain under a system in which crimes were defined by the common law, a system that created particular difficulties in ensuring that the accused was genuinely given notice of the charge.[51] More important, at one point the exploitation of technicalities was the only real mechanism open to courts to guard against unfairness.[52] Accordingly, much of early caselaw dealt with quashing charges

---

50 *Vézina*, above note 45.

51 Tim Quigley, *Procedure in Canadian Criminal Law*, 2d ed (Toronto: Thomson Carswell, 2005) (loose-leaf) at 17-2.

52 *Ibid*. See also *R v Sault Ste Marie*, [1978] 2 SCR 1299 [*Sault Ste Marie*], and *Vézina*, above note 45 at para 53: "With the abrogation of the great majority of the capital statutes in the 19th century, however, much of the rationale for the formality and strict adherence to the wording of the indictment disappeared."

against an accused based on defects in form. In Canada, however, there has been "a gradual shift from requiring judges to quash to requiring them to amend in the stead: in fact, there remains little discretion to quash."[53] What we really see in Canada today is a reflection of the fact that the interests of the accused no longer include protection against the death penalty or exile to Australia. Rather, the accused's interests are clarity and sufficient notice in a trial on the merits. Consequently, although breach of these technical requirements can result in an accused avoiding trial occasionally, this is not a normal occurrence.

There are three possibilities arising out of an error in an indictment. If it is so flawed that it is an absolute nullity, then a trial judge has no jurisdiction to hear the matter, and the charge must be quashed. But in that event, the accused was never in jeopardy, and so the Crown can simply lay a new information without violating the double jeopardy rules (here, the accused's only remedy is the greater clarity of the new charge). Alternatively, the charge might be flawed, but not so flawed that it is a nullity; in that event, the trial judge is to amend the charge. If the accused has been prejudiced by the error, the trial judge is to grant an adjournment in order to remedy that prejudice. A charge can be quashed only if the prejudice caused by the amending cannot be remedied by an adjournment.[54]

This last possibility is a small subset of the occasions when a charge contains an error, but it is made smaller still by the provisions of section 601 that govern amendments to a defective count. First, that section requires that an objection to an indictment for a defect apparent on its face should be made before an accused has pleaded. At that stage, the likelihood that the accused has already suffered irreparable prejudice is, of course, quite small. Objection can be made after this point, but only with leave of the court. Further, the grounds upon which a judge "shall" make an amendment are quite broad and require (1) that the charge is laid under the wrong Act; (2) that it fails to state or states defectively an element of the offence, does not negative an exception that should be negatived, or is in any way defective in substance, provided the amendment to be made was disclosed by the evidence; or (3) "that the indictment or a count thereof is in any way defective in form."[55] In addition, the *Code* specifies that errors in the time or place at which the offence occurred are not material, provided limitation periods and territorial jurisdiction are complied with.[56] Finally, a trial judge is spe-

---

53   *R v Moore*, [1988] 1 SCR 1097 at 1128 [*Moore*].
54   See *Moore, ibid*, and s 601.
55   Section 601(3).
56   Section 601(4.1).

cifically authorized to amend an indictment to make it conform to the evidence presented at trial.[57]

These provisions do not completely remove the possibility of a charge being quashed. *R v Moore*, though it stressed the preference for amendment over quashing, presents one of those unusual circumstances in which a technical error led to acquittal. Moore was charged on an information that was incorrectly quashed. The Crown laid a new charge and proceeded to trial on the new information, obtaining a conviction. The Supreme Court of Canada concluded that the original quashing was an error and that the charge should have been amended (had the Crown appealed the first trial judge's decision, this would have been the result). However, the Crown did not appeal that decision, and so the first judge's decision had to stand because the Crown was not entitled to avoid an appeal simply by laying a new information. Therefore, the accused was able to plead *autrefois acquit* at the subsequent trial.

However, it is most likely that, if the accused obtains a remedy at all, it will be that the Crown is not allowed an amendment that would produce a result that might or might not benefit the accused. In *R v Tremblay*, for example, the accused were charged with keeping a bawdy house for the purpose of practising acts of indecency.[58] The accused called an expert witness and arranged their entire defence around the argument that the acts performed were not indecent. After all the defence evidence had been presented, the Crown made two applications to amend the charge, first, to delete the words "the practice of indecency," and, when that was refused, to change it to "the practice of prostitution." The Supreme Court held that the trial judge had been correct to refuse the amendment. It might have been allowable much earlier in the trial, but it would have caused irreparable prejudice at the stage it was brought.[59] In that particular case, the Court also held that the acts in question were not indecent, and so the acquittal at trial was upheld.

---

57   Section 601(2). See, for example, *R v EADM*, 2008 MBCA 78, where the accused had been released on an undertaking which included a curfew. He was later charged when police found him violating that curfew, but the information charging him mistakenly referred to him being in violation of a recognizance, not an undertaking. This point was not noticed until after the Crown had closed its case and the accused had unsuccessfully argued a *Charter* application on a separate point. The Court of Appeal concluded that the trial judge had erred in not amending the information to conform to the evidence.

58   [1993] 2 SCR 932.

59   To similar effect, see *R v Brownson*, 2013 ONCA 619, where the accused was charged with driving "while disqualified from doing so by reason of an order pursuant to section 259(1) of the *Criminal Code*." In fact, that was not the reason for the disqualification, which was the sole thing the accused attempted

A further remedy potentially available when a count is flawed is to order the Crown to provide particulars under section 587 of the *Code*. Particulars are intended to clarify the charge against the accused, in order to provide clear information as to the offence charged, and also to make the pleas of *autrefois acquit* and *autrefois convict* available in the event that further charges are laid.[60] There is no limit on what can be ordered, but particulars include requirements like "further describing the means by which an offence is alleged to have been committed" or "further describing a person, place or thing referred to in an indictment."[61] They can be ordered only by a judge of the trial court, not by a judge conducting a preliminary inquiry.[62] They need not be ordered at the start of the trial, however, and in considering whether the particulars are needed for a fair trial, the court is to consider the evidence that has been led.[63] Where particulars are ordered, they are entered into the record and the trial proceeds as though the indictment had been amended in accordance with the particulars.[64] There is no actual need to lay an amended information.[65] Of course, although the indictment is taken to be amended, the Crown is still not obliged to prove those things that are surplusage, even if they were provided among the particulars.[66]

Once again, the interest being protected for the accused is clarity at trial. An accused cannot use particulars as a way of limiting the options available to the Crown. In *R v Thatcher*, for example, the Crown's theory was that the accused either killed his wife personally or hired

---

to show in questioning the Crown witnesses. The Ontario Court of Appeal held that the Crown's request to amend the indictment, which was not made until the appeal stage, came too late.

60   *R v JAH* (1998), 105 BCAC 259 [*JAH*]. Justice Dickson (as he then was) held in *Sault Ste Marie*, above note 52, that there was no problem raising a special plea after a trial on a duplicitous charge, because the rule against multiple convictions would prevent another acquittal arising out of the same facts, and acquittal means acquittal on all the offences charged. In either case, even if a charge was duplicitous, an accused could later point to it to justify pleading *autrefois acquit* or *autrefois convict*. The same argument might be made to say that the special plea justification does not arise in the context of particulars either, though it is a weaker argument here. Providing particulars might make clearer factually what actions are alleged to constitute the offence, thus making clear what "cause or matter" was the substance of a previous conviction.

61   Sections 587(1)(f) &(g).

62   *Hynes*, above note 21.

63   Section 587(2).

64   Section 587(3)(c).

65   *JAH*, above note 60.

66   *Vézina*, above note 45.

another person to do so, but was guilty of murder in either case. The Crown's position in this regard was made clear from the start, and the accused's application for particulars was rejected on the grounds that

> the purpose of the application for particulars was not to require the prosecution to provide the accused with additional details with respect to matters referred to in the indictment in order that the accused might be more fully informed of the act or omission charged against them but was to restrict the prosecution to reliance on a part only of the definition of murder contained in the *Criminal Code*.[67]

Still, the most likely result from some defect in a charge is an amendment. The question thus arises: what is considered to be a defect in a charge? In a broad sense, a charge is defective when it departs from the "golden rule," laid down in *R v Côté*, that the accused is entitled "to be reasonably informed of the transaction alleged against him, thus giving him the possibility of a full defence and a fair trial."[68]

Consistent with the notion that charges will rarely be quashed for error is the approach to finding error in the first place: generally speaking, the rules allow quite a wide range of forms of charge, with the result that no remedy is available because there is not seen to be any problem.

b) Insufficient Charges

The most commonly alleged problem with indictments relates to the requirement in section 581 that a count must contain sufficient detail to give the accused reasonable information and to identify the transaction. In deciding the sufficiency of a count, courts frequently make reference to the test in *R v Brodie* that the indictment must lift the charge "from the general to the particular."[69] Although this standard is frequently cited, caselaw makes it clear that the occasions where it is not attained are infrequent. In part, this is because certain omissions (such as that the count "does not name the person injured or intended or attempted to be injured . . . does not specify the means by which the alleged offence was committed [or] does not name or describe with precision any person, place or thing"[70]) are specifically noted by the *Code* as not creating insufficiency. Beyond that, courts have generally favoured the view that alleged procedural defects should prevent a trial only rarely.

---

67 (1986), 24 CCC (3d) 449 (Sask CA) [*Thatcher*], quoting from *R v Govedarov, Popovic and Askov* (1974), 16 CCC (2d) 238 (Ont CA).
68 [1978] 1 SCR 8 at 13 [*Côté*].
69 [1936] SCR 188.
70 Section 583. See also the special rules in ss 584, 585, & 586.

It is worth being clear that the important meaning of "insufficiency" is insufficiency as spoken of in *Moore*—an error egregious enough that the charge must be quashed. It is not uncommon for courts to speak more loosely of degrees of insufficiency,[71] by which it merely means that a charge could have been clearer or that an amendment might be appropriate. However, for insufficiency to have any greater impact, a count must violate the standard in *Moore* or *Côté* and be so badly drawn up that it does not give the accused notice of the charge. This standard is rarely met.

It has been held that "an information will not be held to be a nullity if the information specifies the time, the place, the victim and the offence."[72] Even that statement suggests a higher standard than is insisted upon in practice. It is not surprising that a count suggesting that an offence was committed "on or about" a particular date or "at or near" a particular location should be upheld.[73] Counts charging an offence as having occurred somewhere within a ten-month period eight years earlier[74] or during a sixty-three-month period[75] have also been upheld. The Court has held that "time is not required to be stated with exact precision unless it is an essential part of the offence charged and the accused is not misled or prejudiced by any variation in time that arises."[76]

Indeed, an indictment can be perfectly valid even if the count is not merely broad in its reference to time, but is incorrect about the time at which the offence is alleged to have occurred. Unless time is of the essence in a charge, the time that the offence occurred is not an essential element. Therefore, the time of an offence normally does not need to be proven, even if it is stated in the count. Accordingly, it does not matter that the wrong time was stated, and it is not even necessary to amend the indictment. This approach is consistent with the surplusage rule discussed above.

---

71   See, for example, *R v Webster*, [1993] 1 SCR 3 at para 12: "In my opinion, the learned Provincial Court Judge was correct in his conclusion that while 'some measure of insufficiency exists in each of the charges . . . it is not of such a degree as would vitiate the charges.'"

72   *Re MacLean and the Queen* (1988), 68 CR (3d) 114 (BCCA) [*MacLean*], citing in support *Re Regina and RIC* (1986), 32 CCC (3d) 399 (Ont CA); *R v Dugdale* (1979), 7 CR (3d) 216 (BCCA); *R v Fox* (1986), 50 CR (3d) 370 (BCCA), leave to appeal to SCC refused, [1986] 1 SCR ix [*Fox*]; *R v Nadin* (1971), 14 CRNS 201 (BCCA); and *R v Race*, [1988] BCJ No 1819 (CA).

73   *Fox*, above note 72; *R v Ryan* (1985), 12 OAC 172 (CA), leave to appeal to SCC refused, [1986] 1 SCR ix.

74   *MacLean*, above note 72.

75   *R v Colgan* (1986), 43 Man R (2d) 101 (CA), aff'd [1987] 2 SCR 686.

76   *R v Douglas*, [1991] 1 SCR 301 [*Douglas*].

Time could be of the essence where an accused was entitled to take items or perform actions (such as fly a plane) during some periods but not others.[77] In those circumstances, an error in the count with regard to time would be significant because the accused's guilt or innocence would depend upon exactly when the actions in question occurred. But, in most cases, time will not be of the essence, as the Court observes in *R v B(G) (No 2)*: "the date of the offence is not generally an essential element of the offence of sexual assault. It is a crime no matter when it is committed."[78] Alibi evidence led by the accused can sometimes make the exact time more relevant,[79] and whether the Crown has closed its case before seeking the amendment can also be significant.[80]

It can occur occasionally that a count is struck down on the basis that it does not disclose an offence known to law, though this phrase is not really a term of art.[81] In *R v Fremeau* the Alberta Court of Appeal found that a count in an information did not disclose an offence known to law when it charged that an accused sold "a drug listed or described in Schedule F of the Food and Drug Regulations." The regulation in question did not proscribe selling such drugs; rather, it proscribed selling "*a substance containing* a drug" listed in that Schedule.[82] This somewhat technical approach is uncommon, however, and normally courts will simply look at whether the accused has been reasonably informed of the charge, as required by *Côté*.

Indeed, in *Côté* the charge laid alleged that the accused had refused to provide a breath sample, without explicitly stating that he had done so "without reasonable excuse." Strictly, one could claim that the charge laid, failing to provide a breath sample, was not on its own an offence, but the Court held that the inclusion in the charge of the specific section under which the charge was laid made it impossible for the accused to have been misled.[83] This holding is consistent with section 601(3)(b)(ii) of the *Code*, permitting amendment where a count "does not negative an exception that should be negatived," but goes further.

---

77   See *R v Hamilton-Middleton* (1986), 53 Sask R 80 (CA), and *R v McCrae and Ramsay* (1981), 25 Man R (2d) 32 (Co Ct).

78   [1990] 2 SCR 30 at para 11 [*B(G)*]. See also *R v SD*, 2011 SCC 14.

79   See *B(G)* itself, above note 78; *R v Dossi* (1918), 13 Cr App R 158; *R v Parkin (No 1) and (No 2)* (1922), 37 CCC 35 (Man CA); *Wright v Nicholson*, [1970] 1 All ER 12 (QB), all discussed therein.

80   *R v MBP*, [1994] 1 SCR 555 [*MBP*].

81   See Quigley, note 51 at 17-2.

82   (1984), 34 Alta LR (2d) 1 at para 9 (CA) [emphasis added].

83   *Côté*, above note 68. Note that, in fact, the accused had appealed his conviction at trial on the basis that he did have a reasonable excuse, among other grounds: the error in the charge was raised by the Saskatchewan Court of Appeal.

The Court did not find that there would be no prejudice from remedying the defect, but that there was no defect in the first place. Similarly, in *R v Henyu* an information was quashed at trial for failing to disclose an offence known to law on the basis that it failed to explicitly allege that the accused had caused bodily harm, one of the elements of the offence. Nonetheless, the Court of Appeal held that in stating that the accused had stabbed the victim, bodily harm was sufficiently implied.[84]

The Court has created some room for arguments about the sufficiency of charges with its decision in *R v Wis Development Corp*.[85] It is common for charges to be laid by simply repeating the language of the *Code* section that creates the offence, and this approach is specifically permitted by section 581(2). In *Wis Development*, however, the Court accepted that a charge laid in that form was insufficient when it simply said that the accused "operate[d] a commercial air service," without anything more. That phrase could cover a "multitude of activities," ranging from hauling passengers to allowing an aircraft to be photographed for a liquor advertisement, and therefore the information was void for not meeting the sufficiency standard of section 581(3).[86] This vagueness has caused debate at times over whether the wording in particular *Code* sections also covers a multitude of activities and, therefore, would not be sufficient if used when a charge is laid. The fact that an offence can be committed in a number of ways does not make it fall within the *Wis Development* rule, and so charges that an accused had care and control of a vehicle or was keeping a common bawdy house have been found to be unaffected.[87] However, a charge simply asserting that an accused kept a common gaming house was held to violate the rule.[88] Scope for argument regarding when this standard is met remains. However, any problem caused by such a flaw could now be amended (which was not the case for summary offences at the time of *Wis Development*) and so the question has become less important.

---

84   [1980] 1 WWR 752 (BCCA).

85   [1984] 1 SCR 485 [*Wis Development*].

86   This issue merely laid the groundwork for the central issue in the case, which was the ability to amend the information. Since the case was decided under legislation specific to summary conviction offences and that legislation has since been repealed to allow the general rule to have effect, the case is no longer significant with regard to its main holding. However, that does not affect the initial reasoning concerning whether the information was valid or not.

87   *Fox*, above note 72, and *R v Milberg et al* (1987), 35 CCC (3d) 45 (Ont CA).

88   *R v Bingo Enterprises Ltd (cob Buffalo Bingo Palace)* (1984), 41 CR (3d) 291 (Man CA).

c) Duplicitous Charges

A potential flaw in counts that is conceptually distinct from insufficiency is duplicity. Where insufficiency asks whether an accused has been given too little information, duplicity, in effect, suggests that the accused has been given too much information. A duplicitous count is one that charges the accused with committing two different offences, and it is objectionable because the ambiguity prevents the accused from knowing the case to meet. If any ambiguity does not rise to that level, the charge is not duplicitous.[89] This is a distinct requirement from the "single transaction" rule in section 581(1). That rule limits a count to a single factual situation, while the duplicity rule limits it to a single legal issue.

As with the single transaction rule, courts have not found the duplicity rule to be easily violated. In R v Sault Ste Marie, the Court found a count non-duplicitous that charged the accused did "discharge or cause to be discharged or permitted to be discharged or deposited" pollutants into a river. This charge tracked the wording of the offence section. The Court held that the section had not created several different offences but only one offence — polluting — which could be committed in a number of ways. The accused would have no doubt about the case to meet, and so no objection should be taken to the charge.[90] Similarly, a charge that did not differentiate between the general theft section and theft by a person required to account, and suggested that the accused was guilty of each, was not duplicitous (again, although two Code sections were involved, they were simply identifying two ways of committing theft).[91] This approach is consistent with the idea that a jury must be unanimous to find an accused guilty of an offence, but need not be unanimous with regard to how the accused committed the offence.[92]

Further, an information that contains two counts separated by the word "alternatively" is not duplicitous, since it would not be a single count charging more than one offence.[93] Particular difficulties can arise in conspiracy cases, and a single count charging an accused with more than one conspiracy would be duplicitous. However, even if more

---

89 *Sault Ste Marie*, above note 52. See also s 590(1)(a) of the *Code*, providing that a count is not objectionable if it "charges in the alternative several different matters, acts or omissions that are stated in the alternative in an enactment that describes as an indictable offence the matters, acts or omissions charged in the count."

90 *Sault Ste Marie*, above note 52.

91 *R v Fischer* (1987), 53 Sask R 263 (CA) [*Fischer*], dealing with ss 322 and 330. The potential ambiguity was created by the provision of particulars.

92 *Fischer, ibid*, and *Thatcher*, above note 67.

93 *R v Brewer* (1988), 8 MVR (2d) 137 (NBCA).

than one conspiracy is proven at trial, the charge is not automatically duplicitous; if it was not, the only issue will be which conspiracy the accused was charged with, and whether any or all of the conspiracies proven to have been committed are covered by the indictment.[94]

In any event, even if a charge is duplicitous it is not fatally flawed.[95] Section 590(2)(b) allows an accused to apply to have a count that is "double or multifarious" either amended or divided into two or more counts, an application that is to be granted where the ends of justice require it. To divide a count is to make it two or more separate counts (something that is sometimes referred to as "severance," though, more strictly, severance is the process under section 591(3)(a) of sending separate counts to separate trials).

Only the trial judge has jurisdiction to divide a count, though the application can be brought on a pre-trial basis.[96] The *Code* allows the count to be divided when it "embarrasses [the accused] in his defence," a criterion broad enough to leave the decision largely in the trial judge's discretion. An appeal court is not to interfere with that discretion unless the judge acted unjudicially or the decision resulted in an injustice. *R v Litchfield*, for example, dealt with a doctor charged with various sexual assaults arising out of examinations performed on a number of patients. Before trial, a judge divided individual counts based on which parts of the complainants' bodies the doctor had been examining, and then severed the counts to be dealt with in different trials. The result, in some cases, was that different parts of a single examination of one patient would be dealt with in separate trials, depending upon which part of the complainant's body was examined. The Court held that this result misapprehended the nature of sexual assault and the order ought not to have been made.[97]

On the other hand, in *R v Lilly* the Court dealt with a real estate broker who was charged with theft based on a series of withdrawals from a trust account into which a number of deposits relating to real property transactions had been made. In the course of the trial it became apparent that the accused was claiming a colour of right defence with regard to some of the withdrawals, while claiming to be unaware of some of the deposits. The Court held that, although it had been acceptable to lay a single count charging the accused with theft, it would

---

94 See *Douglas*, above note 76, and *R v Papalia*, [1979] 2 SCR 256.
95 Section 590(1) says that a count is not objectionable by reason only that it is double or multifarious.
96 *Litchfield*, above note 22.
97 *Ibid*.

have been preferable to divide the count once it became apparent that the accused had two separate defences. Particularly given that it was a jury trial, this approach would have made clearer what was implied in finding the accused guilty.[98] The matter remains in a trial judge's discretion, though, and so, for example, the fact that an accused's employment has been terminated does not mean that a count of theft must be divided to deal with continuing actions before and after he was fired.[99]

C. PLEAS

The pleas available to an accused charged with an offence are set out in section 606 of the *Code*. An accused can plead guilty, not guilty, or one of the special pleas provided for in the *Code*. The special pleas consist of *autrefois acquit*, *autrefois convict*, and pardon.[100]

The special pleas really amount to the claim that the matter that the accused is called upon to plead is a matter that has already been dealt with—the accused has previously been acquitted, convicted, or pardoned for the offence in question. There can be confused issues around whether the matter the accused is charged with at this time is the same matter that was dealt with by previous charges. They are, in effect, all manifestations of the rule against multiple convictions. The discussion here will focus only on the pleas of guilty and not guilty.

A plea of guilty amounts to an admission by the accused of performing the physical actions that make up the offence, accompanied by the necessary mental state. It is, in effect, a waiver of the right to a trial.[101] A court should inquire into a plea of guilty if there is any reason to doubt that the accused understands its effect, but there is no general obligation to do so.[102]

A plea of not guilty is not a claim of innocence, but is simply a demand that the Crown proves all the elements of the offence and disproves the existence of any defences. Unless a special plea is required, pleading not guilty puts any defence available in issue, including, for

---

98 *Lilly*, above note 15.

99 *Fischer*, above note 91.

100 Section 607. Section 611 also allows the plea of justification to a charge of defamatory libel.

101 *R v Adgey*, [1975] 2 SCR 426 [*Adgey*].

102 See *ibid*; *R v Brousseau*, [1969] SCR 181. Note, however, that s 36 of the *Youth Criminal Justice Act*, SC 2002, c 1 [*YCJA*], requires a judge to be satisfied that the facts will support a charge before accepting a guilty plea from a young person.

example, whether the accused is not criminally responsible by reason of mental disorder.[103]

Where an accused refuses to plead, the judge is to enter a plea of not guilty.[104] An accused can, with the consent of the Crown, enter a plea of guilty to some other offence arising out of the same transaction, whether it is an included offence or not. If the court accepts the plea, the accused will be found not guilty of the offence originally charged.[105]

An accused can later withdraw a guilty plea if "there are valid grounds for his being permitted to do so,"[106] a category the Court has consciously not defined exhaustively. An accused cannot withdraw a plea because the judge rejects a joint sentencing submission, for example, because a co-accused has subsequently been acquitted of the offence, or because the Crown makes a subsequent application to have the accused declared a dangerous offender.[107] Rather, there must be in place some special circumstance that suggests the guilty plea should not be accepted at face value as a legitimate concession of guilt. So, for example, if the accused has been pressured by counsel into entering a guilty plea, the accused might successfully withdraw the plea.[108] Similarly, a plea might be withdrawn if it is shown that the accused who wished to plead not guilty actually pled guilty in order to obtain an immediate fine rather than spend a week in custody awaiting trial, or to avoid a more serious charge being laid (first-, rather than second-degree murder, for example).[109] In *R v Hanemaayer* an accused who voluntarily entered a guilty plea mid-trial (because he was convinced of the inevitability of his conviction and had the knowledge he could receive a lighter sentence by pleading guilty) was allowed to withdraw his guilty plea when evidence proving that another person had committed the offence came to light.[110] However, the mere fact that an ac-

---

103 Section 613. Although all defences are potentially put in issue by a plea of not guilty, the onus of proof can, in some instances, be on the accused. A plea of not guilty allows an accused to argue entrapment, for example, but the accused will bear the ultimate burden of proof to make out that defence.

104 Section 606(2).

105 Section 606(4).

106 *Adgey*, above note 101, quoted in *R v Taillefer; R v Duguay*, [2003] 3 SCR 307 at para 85 [*Taillefer*].

107 *R v Rubenstein* (1987), 41 CCC (3d) 91 (Ont CA), leave to appeal to SCC refused (1988), 87 NR 77n; *R v Hick*, [1991] 3 SCR 383; *R v Lyons*, [1987] 2 SCR 309.

108 *R v Laperrière*, [1996] 2 SCR 284; *R v Lamoureux* (1984), 40 CR (3d) 369 (Que CA).

109 *R v Cesari* (1986), 50 CR (3d) 93 (Que CA); *R v Hansen* (1977), 37 CCC (2d) 371 (Man CA).

110 2008 ONCA 580 [*Hanemaayer*]. In *Hanemaayer* the withdrawal of the guilty plea came nearly twenty years after the conviction.

cused feels pressure does not mean that the plea was not voluntary: feeling pressure is true of most accused who plead guilty, but is often just the realization that there is no viable alternative.[111]

Circumstances other than improper pressure on the accused could lead to the plea being set aside, however. For example, where an accused loses a challenge to the admissibility of evidence and then changes her plea to guilty without being aware that such a plea will preclude challenging the correctness of that ruling on appeal, the guilty plea can be withdrawn.[112] Alternatively, in *R v Taillefer; R v Duguay* an accused received disclosure of significant Crown evidence four years after entering a guilty plea. The Court held that even if a guilty plea was valid—that is, it was voluntary, unequivocal, and based on sufficient information concerning the nature of the charges and the consequences of the plea—it might still be withdrawn if the accused's constitutional rights were violated. The test asks how a reasonable person would have behaved with knowledge of the undisclosed evidence if "there was a realistic possibility that the accused would have run the risk of a trial, if he or she had been in possession of that information or those new avenues of investigation, leave must be given to withdraw the plea."[113]

Guilty and not guilty are, apart from the special pleas, the only pleas available to a person charged with an offence. Experience in the criminal justice system rapidly acquaints counsel with clients who wish to plead "guilty with an explanation," or who want to plead guilty rather than go to trial, but wish to maintain their innocence. In the former case, the accused is required to plead not guilty, and a judge receiving a plea of guilty with an explanation should refuse to accept it. The court should inquire into the accused's intention and accept the guilty plea only if it is clear that the accused unequivocally wishes to plead guilty.[114]

---

111 *R v Carty*, 2010 ONCA 237.
112 *R v Webster*, 2008 BCCA 458; *R v Duong*, 2006 BCCA 325. To similar effect, see *R v Fegan* (1993), 21 CR (4th) 65 (Ont CA). See also *R v Newman* (1993), 20 CR (4th) 370 (Ont CA), where the accused argued, though unsuccessfully, that he should be permitted to withdraw his guilty plea for not having been adequately informed of the consequences of pleading guilty due to ineffective representation by counsel.
113 *Taillefer*, above note 106 at para 90. See also *R v Aldhelm-White*, 2008 NSCA 86, where twelve separate accused were allowed to withdraw their guilty pleas to drug charges after it was discovered that an investigating officer who had supplied much of the information relevant to the search warrants was himself a drug dealer. The Crown acknowledged that they would not have pursued charges at all had they had that information at the time and supported the applications to withdraw the guilty pleas.
114 *R v McNabb* (1971), 4 CCC (2d) 316 (Sask CA).

In general, a judge has no obligation to hear evidence after an accused has pleaded guilty, but can do so. If in doing so it becomes apparent that the accused did not intend to admit some element of the offence, misapprehended the effect of a guilty plea, or did not intend to plead guilty, the trial judge can allow the accused to withdraw the plea or enter a plea of not guilty.

A judge should not permit an accused to plead guilty simply to "get it over with." The judge should accept a guilty plea only when the accused intends to admit all the elements of the offence, and defence counsel has an ethical obligation in this regard.[115] Equally, an accused cannot enter a "conditional plea." For example, an accused cannot plead guilty to a homicide charge, conditional upon the Crown proving the cause of death.[116] Of course, in a case of theft, it is open to an accused to make factual concessions despite a plea of not guilty, and, for example, admit to having taken items, but advance a claim of colour of right or deny having had the necessary *mens rea*.[117]

Section 650 of the *Code* requires an accused (other than a corporation) to be present in court during the whole trial, and therefore an accused must be present for the plea: this can be done via electronic appearance, provided it permits simultaneous visual and oral communication and the accused can still consult privately with counsel. Section 800 of the *Code* explicitly permits an accused charged with a summary conviction offence to appear by counsel. Courts have held that a plea entered by counsel to an indictable offence is also, in the normal course of events, binding on an accused who was present at the time.[118]

---

115   See, for example, Chapter IX, "The Lawyer as Advocate" in Canadian Bar Association, *Code of Professional Conduct* (Ottawa: Canadian Bar Association, 2006), and the discussion in David Layton & Michel Proulx, *Ethics and Canadian Criminal Law*, 2d ed (Toronto: Irwin Law, 2015), particularly ch 8, s M. See also the discussion there of the plea "*nolo contendere*," which is not permissible in Canada and is, in fact, a way for an accused to decline to contest a charge without conceding its truth.

116   *R v Lucas* (1983), 9 CCC (3d) 71 (Ont CA), leave to appeal to SCC refused (1984), 9 CCC (3d) 71n.

117   See s 655 of the *Code*.

118   *R v Dietrich* (1970), 11 CRNS 22 (Ont CA), leave to appeal to SCC refused, [1970] SCR xi; *R v Sommerfeldt* (1984), 14 CCC (3d) 445 (BCCA).

D. ORDER OF TRIAL

1) Trial Procedures

The procedures governing trial are set out in Parts XIX, XX, and XXVII of the *Criminal Code* and cover indictable offences tried by judge alone or judge and jury, and summary conviction trials, respectively.[119] Many of the procedures dealing with the actual conduct of trials are common to all three modes.[120]

A trial is to proceed continuously, though the judge can grant adjournments.[121] The accused is to be present for the trial, but a judge is allowed to excuse the accused from attending.[122] In addition, provisions in the *Code* now permit the attendance of the accused at trial by video link, though this is permitted only for portions of the trial during which no evidence is taken.[123] If an accused absconds during trial, the court can either issue a warrant for the accused's arrest and adjourn the trial, or continue the trial without the accused. In the latter case, defence counsel can continue acting for the accused, and the accused's right to full answer and defence will not have been violated.[124]

The trial judge has discretion as to where the accused will sit during trial. Normally, this will be in the prisoner's dock, and the trial judge is not required to permit the accused to sit elsewhere unless the refusal will violate the accused's right to full answer and defence.[125]

The judge can ask questions during the trial, although doing so can raise issues as to whether there is a reasonable apprehension of

---

119 Part XIX.1 of the *Code* also sets out the procedures to be used at trials in front of the Nunavut Court of Justice, which is something of a hybrid. Section 573(1) of the *Code* provides that the powers, duties, and function of a provincial court judge may be exercised by the Nunavut Court of Justice, while s 573(2) clarifies that in doing so, the judges of that court are acting as judges of a superior court.

120 Section 572 makes the provisions of Part XX, "Jury Trials," applicable to Part XIX, "Trial without Jury." Section 795 makes those provisions applicable to summary conviction trials. In each case, the provisions apply to the extent that they are not inconsistent with specific provisions in those Parts and with such modifications as the circumstances require.

121 Sections 571 and 645.

122 Section 645. The presumption of attendance works the other way in the case of summary conviction offences, with s 800(2) allowing an accused to appear personally or by counsel, but permitting the judge to require the accused's personal attendance.

123 Sections 650(1.1), 650(1.2), and 800(2.1).

124 See s 475 and *R v Zarubin* (2001), 157 CCC (3d) 115 (Sask CA).

125 *R v Levogiannis*, [1993] 4 SCR 475 [*Levogiannis*], citing *R v Faid*, [1981] 5 WWR 349 (Alta CA), rev'd on other grounds, [1983] 1 SCR 265 [*Faid*].

bias (see the discussion at Section F, below in this chapter). Juries are also entitled to ask questions, though within limits. It must be made clear to the jury that the parties are entitled to present the evidence as they want, and so questioning by jurors should not become another interrogation. Jurors' questions are best left to the end, to be submitted in writing to the trial judge who can discuss with counsel whether the questions should be asked.[126]

2) Opening Statements

The Crown presents its case first, and, as a matter of practice, can begin with an opening statement to the jury explaining its theory of the case and the evidence to be called. However, this opening statement does not irrevocably commit the Crown to adopting a particular approach to the trial. The Crown is not obliged to call every witness it indicates will be called and, like any other counsel at trial, is entitled to modify the trial strategy as the case develops. The Crown's theory of the case could change over the course of the trial in response to changing circumstances, including defence counsel's closing address.[127] Short of oppressive prosecutorial conduct amounting to an abuse of process, the accused cannot object to a change of plans on the part of the Crown. In choosing not to call a witness who has been announced, of course, the Crown risks the jury drawing some type of adverse inference, and the accused would normally be entitled to point out the change to the jury when making closing submissions.[128]

Normally, the defence is not entitled to make an opening address to the jury immediately following the Crown's opening remarks. However, a trial judge has discretion to let the accused do so, rather than have to wait until the close of the Crown's case. Some authority suggests that making such an opening statement obliges the accused to call evidence, essentially because the purpose of the statement is to outline the evidence that will be called. However, the prevailing view appears

126 See *R v Nordyne* (1998), 17 CR (5th) 393 (Que CA), and *R v Gagnon* (1992), 47 QAC 232 (CA). See also *R v Lam*, [1998] NWTJ No 79 (CA), where defence counsel's decision to ask some questions of his client, after the jury sent a note with those questions to the judge, was found not to form the basis for an appeal.

127 *R v Pickton*, 2010 SCC 32 at para 19 [*Pickton*], quoting from the dissenting judgment of Binnie J in *R v Rose*, [1998] 3 SCR 262 [*Rose*]. See the discussion of this point specifically in the context of an opening statement in *R v Khawaja*, 2010 ONCA 862.

128 *R v Jolivet*, 2000 SCC 29 [*Jolivet*]; *R v Cook*, [1997] 1 SCR 1113 [*Cook*]. See *R v Biniaris*, 2000 SCC 15, as an example of the Crown changing its theory of the case during the course of trial.

to be that, in the special circumstances where the accused is allowed an opening statement immediately following the Crown's, there is no obligation to later call witnesses for direct examination and, indeed, that "counsel acting responsibly cannot be expected to give an undertaking at that stage to call evidence. That decision must be assessed against the concluded Crown case."[129] Nonetheless, the defence might adduce evidence through cross-examination of Crown witnesses, for example, and in appropriate cases should be allowed an opening statement. Cases returned for a new trial that have a measure of predictability might be ones where such an order is appropriate.[130]

3) Presentation of the Crown Case

Following the opening statement, Crown counsel is required to present evidence proving the charges against the accused. The procedures for taking evidence at trial are the same as at a preliminary inquiry; that is, the evidence is to be taken under oath in the presence of the accused, the accused is entitled to cross-examine the Crown witnesses, and the evidence is recorded.[131]

Although in principle it is up to the Crown to prove every essential element of the offence, it is open to the accused to concede various parts of the Crown's case.[132] Often this is done through an agreed-upon statement of facts, but not necessarily. An accused can concede the voluntariness of a statement and waive a *voir dire*, for example, without any particular form of words being necessary (as long as it is clear that counsel understood the issue and made an informed decision regarding waiver). Silence or lack of objection to a statement being admitted is not waiver, however.[133] Even in cases of silence, however, the trial will not necessarily be fatally flawed by the admission of a statement; a trial judge will have erred only if there was clear evidence objectively showing the need to conduct a *voir dire* despite the failure of defence counsel to request one.[134]

---

129 *R v Sood* (1997), 58 OTC 115 (Gen Div) [*Sood*]. See also *R v Barrow* (1989), 91 NSR (2d) 176 (SCTD) [*Barrow*], but, in contrast, see *R v Vitale* (1987), 40 CCC (3d) 267 (Ont Dist Ct).

130 *Sood*, above note 129; *Barrow*, above note 129.

131 Sections 540, 557, and 646. Note that amendments to the preliminary inquiry procedures in ss 540(7), (8), & (9) do not carry over to trials.

132 Section 655.

133 *R v Park*, [1981] 2 SCR 64.

134 *R v Hodgson*, [1998] 2 SCR 449.

The Crown has considerable discretion in deciding how to present its case, consistent with the adversarial nature of the process. The Crown is not required, for example, to call every witness with relevant information and has no obligation to call a witness it does not consider necessary to the prosecution's case.[135] This rule applies equally even if the witness not called is the complainant. Failing to do so might put the Crown's ability to prove its case at risk, and in some circumstances a trial judge might comment to a jury on the failure to call the complainant, but the decision is still within the Crown's discretion. The defence is not entitled to have the Crown call all witnesses so it can cross-examine them, but it can call any witness not called by the Crown as part of the defence case. In some circumstances, the defence can apply under the *Canada Evidence Act*[136] to cross-examine the witness.[137] Further, in some cases, the trial judge could choose to call the person as the court's witness, therefore allowing the defence to cross-examine. This might be the right course of action particularly where forcing the defence to call the witness might require the accused to give up the right to speak to the jury last (see the discussion of this issue at Section D(8), below in this chapter).

Although evidence typically takes the form of testimony or documents from witnesses on the stand, other forms of evidence are permitted. Provisions in the *Code* create special rules around proof of ownership and value of property,[138] expert's reports,[139] dates of birth,[140] and previous convictions.[141] Further, other provisions allow for the use of commission evidence for witnesses who are out of the country or who, through illness or other "good and sufficient cause," cannot attend the trial.[142] In addition, evidence that was taken at a preliminary inquiry can be used at a trial in some circumstances.[143] Videotaped testimony by a person under eighteen or with a physical or mental disability can sometimes be used at a trial for various sexual offences.[144] Further, the use of technology to present evidence is available if it will increase efficiency in any case, not merely in ones with thousands of documents.[145]

135   See *Lemay v The King*, [1952] 1 SCR 232; *R v Yebes*, [1987] 2 SCR 168; *Cook*, above note 128; *Jolivet*, above note 128.
136   RSC 1985, c C-5 [*CEA*].
137   *Cook*, above note 128.
138   Section 657.1.
139   Section 657.3.
140   Section 658(3).
141   Section 667.
142   Section 709.
143   Section 715. See also ss 657 and 541.
144   Sections 715.1 & 715.2.
145   *R v Mackay*, 2002 SKQB 316.

Section 652 allows a jury to "have a view," in order to see any place, person, or thing.[146] This ability is open to the jury any time prior to rendering their verdict, including after they have begun their deliberations,[147] and can also be used by a judge conducting a trial without a jury.[148]

A Crown prosecutor will normally have indicated what evidence will be called in the opening address. Failing to call that evidence will not necessarily prove fatal to the prosecution. Thus, for example, if hearsay evidence is admitted in anticipation of direct evidence that is expected to be, but ultimately is not, called, adequate instructions by the trial judge to the jury can cure any problem.[149]

Section 545 of the *Code* allows a trial judge to imprison a witness who refuses to testify for periods of up to eight days at a time.

4) Presentation of the Defence Case

a) Application for a Directed Verdict

At the close of the Crown's case it becomes the defence's turn to present evidence, if it chooses to do so. Before that, however, it is open to an accused to apply for a directed verdict. Although a jury, when there is one, reaches a decision in a trial, in limited circumstances the trial judge has the authority to direct that an accused will be acquitted. This power is not created by statute, but arises at common law.[150] The directed verdict (sometimes referred to as a "non-suit" as there being no case to meet) takes its name from the fact that, historically, the trial judge directed the jury to retire and return a verdict of not guilty. The Supreme Court has modified the procedure so that trial judges are instead to withdraw the case from the jury and enter the acquittal personally,[151] but the name has remained.

The test for granting a directed verdict is quite restricted, and is consistent with the differing functions of judge and jury. The jury is the trier of fact and, therefore, is called upon to assess the credibility of witnesses, decide whether the Crown's evidence has proven the accused's guilt beyond a reasonable doubt, and so on. A trial judge cannot intrude on that function. However, where the Crown has failed to provide

---

146 Section 652.
147 *R v Welsh* (1997), 120 CCC (3d) 68 (BCCA).
148 *R v Prentice* (1965), 47 CR 231 (BCCA), and see s 572.
149 *R v Myers*, [2001] OJ No 4258 (CA).
150 Judges' common law powers in jury trials are preserved by s 672 of the *Code*: *R v Rowbotham*, [1994] 2 SCR 463 [*Rowbotham* 1994].
151 *Ibid*.

evidence on some essential element of the offence, the trial judge can direct the acquittal of the accused. The accused can make such a motion at the close of the Crown's case, and the judge is to rule on it at that time. The accused is entitled to know the result of that motion before deciding whether to call evidence in defence.[152]

The Court has made clear that this is a limited power and is not to intrude on the jury's role. A trial judge cannot direct an acquittal on the basis that the Crown's evidence of identification is manifestly unreliable, for example, because the trial judge is not permitted to weigh the strength of the evidence.[153] The test for a directed verdict is the same as that for a preliminary inquiry judge in deciding whether to send a matter for trial

> whether or not there is any evidence upon which a reasonable jury properly instructed could return a verdict of guilty. The "justice" [is] required to commit an accused person for trial in any case in which there is admissible evidence which could, if it were believed, result in a conviction.[154]

Thus, a directed verdict is not available where the Crown's evidence is weak. It is possible only where there is a complete absence of evidence on some point that must be proven. Put affirmatively, the Crown must "adduce some evidence of culpability for every essential definitional element of the crime for which the Crown has the evidential burden," and a motion for a directed verdict will be granted only if it has not done so.[155] This determination must take into account all the bases upon which the accused might be found guilty of the offence, both as the principal or as a party.[156] That absence turns the question of the accused's guilt into an issue that can be settled by an exclusively legal, not factual, determination.

The rule also applies when the Crown's case rests on purely circumstantial evidence. In such cases the jury can convict only when there is no rational explanation for the circumstantial evidence other than that the accused committed the crime and must be charged on that basis. Nonetheless, the Court has held that whether that test is met is a question for the jury to decide, not the judge, and so a directed

---

152 *R v Boissoneault* (1986), 16 OAC 365 (CA).

153 *R v Mezzo*, [1986] 1 SCR 802 [*Mezzo*].

154 *United States of America v Shephard*, [1977] 2 SCR 1067 at 1080.

155 *R v Charemski*, [1998] 1 SCR 679 at para 3 [*Charemski*].

156 *R v MR*, 2011 ONCA 190.

verdict should not be issued.[157] Some ambiguity remains in this context, however. The Court has also held, in assessing the same test in the context of preliminary inquiries, that the judge must engage in a limited weighing of the evidence. Although a judge cannot draw inferences or assess credibility, the judge is to decide whether "if the Crown's evidence is believed it would be reasonable for a properly instructed jury to infer guilt" from that evidence.[158] This formulation of the test seems to create slightly greater scope for a trial judge to decide to grant a directed verdict.[159]

A directed verdict can be granted on the charge laid, but the trial must be allowed to proceed in order to decide whether the accused is guilty of any included offences. In R v Titus, for example, the Court agreed that it would be possible to direct an acquittal on a first-degree murder charge, but allow the trial to continue to see whether the accused was found guilty of second-degree murder.[160]

A trial judge's decision whether to grant a motion for a directed verdict is reviewable by an appeal court on a correctness standard, since it is a question of law.[161]

b) Defence Presentation of Evidence

An accused who does not make, or does not succeed in, an application for a directed verdict is then entitled to call evidence, or otherwise make full answer and defence.[162] Similar to the Crown, the defence is entitled to exercise discretion as to how to present the case. For example, a trial judge is not permitted to direct the order in which witnesses are to be called, insisting that the accused testify first.[163] The defence can call witnesses, including witnesses the Crown has decided not to call.[164] The accused is a competent witness at the trial, but is not compellable, and the failure to testify cannot be made the subject of

---

157 R v Monteleone, [1987] 2 SCR 154; Mezzo, above note 153; Charemski, above note 155.

158 R v Arcuri, [2001] 2 SCR 828 at para 30. This issue is discussed in Chapter 9.

159 On this point, generally, see David M Tanovich, "Upping the Ante in Directed Verdict Cases Where the Evidence Is Circumstantial" (1998) 15 Criminal Reports (5th) 21. See also R v Beals, 2011 NSCA 42.

160 [1983] 1 SCR 259 [Titus]. In Titus, the judge erred by failing to grant the motion for a directed verdict, but instructed the jury at the end of the trial that they could not find the accused guilty of first-degree murder.

161 R v Barros, 2011 SCC 51.

162 Sections 541 and 650(3).

163 R v Angelantoni (1975), 31 CRNS 342 (Ont CA).

164 Cook, above note 128.

comment by the judge or the prosecutor.[165] This statutory provision is consistent with the accused's right to silence and the presumption of innocence, both now guaranteed by the *Charter*.[166] Normally, the defence cannot cross-examine its own witnesses, though in certain situations doing this is permitted.[167]

5) Reopening the Crown's Case

The trial will move to closing arguments once the defence has completed calling all of the evidence it wishes. The Crown is expected to present all of its evidence before the defence is called upon. "Splitting the case" — that is, leading some of the Crown's evidence after the accused's case has been presented — has been prohibited "from the earliest days of our criminal law" for a number of reasons, including that the accused is entitled to know the full case to meet before deciding whether to remain silent or take the stand.[168]

In an exceptional case, however, the Crown can apply to reopen its case and call further evidence, at the discretion of the trial judge. The "keystone principle" in deciding whether to allow the Crown to reopen its case is whether the accused will be prejudiced in making a defence.[169] A trial judge's discretion must be exercised judicially in this regard and in the interests of justice, and the Court has laid down guidelines to assist in this task:

> The ambit of a trial judge's discretion to allow the Crown to reopen its case becomes narrower as the trial proceeds because of the increasing likelihood of prejudice to the accused's defence as the trial progresses. During the first stage, when the Crown has not yet closed its case, the trial judge's discretion is quite broad. At the second stage, which arises when the Crown has just closed its case but the defence has not yet elected whether or not to call evidence, the discretion is more limited. Finally, in the third phase — where the defence has already begun to answer the Crown's case — the discretion is extremely narrow, and is "far less likely to be exercised in favour of the

---

165 *CEA*, above note 136, s 4(6).

166 See *R v Chambers*, [1990] 2 SCR 1293, and *R v Noble*, [1997] 1 SCR 874. Note that, as discussed at Section B(3), above in this chapter, the situation is somewhat different when a co-accused wishes to make reference to an accused's silence: *Crawford*, above note 33.

167 *CEA*, above note 136, s 9.

168 *John v the Queen*, [1985] 2 SCR 476 at 480–81; *R v Krause*, [1986] 2 SCR 466 [*Krause*].

169 *MBP*, above note 80.

Crown". The emphasis during the third phase must be on the protection of the accused's interests.[170]

The discretion is most limited in the third stage, of course, because at that point the accused is most likely to be prejudiced by the admission of new evidence on the part of the Crown.

The evidence ought to be new evidence, in the sense that it could not have been foreseen by the Crown and was in the interests of justice. However, that the evidence is new is not sufficient. The Court has held that the type of limited circumstances in which such evidence will be permitted are where the defence directly or indirectly contributed to the Crown's failure to lead the evidence, or where the Crown has made a mistake or omission on a non-controversial issue that was purely formal or technical and that had nothing to do with the substance of the case.[171] Only in those circumstances, or ones closely analogous to them, should the Crown be permitted to reopen its case after the defence has begun to present evidence.[172] It is not relevant that the Crown was not at fault in failing to discover the evidence: the focus is on the prejudice to the accused, which is the same whether the Crown had acted diligently or not.[173] The accused was entitled to know the case to meet before beginning the defence, but that case is at great risk of changing if the Crown is permitted to reopen.[174]

Nonetheless, in appropriate circumstances the Crown can reopen its case. In *R v Sylvester*, for example, a police officer received several telephone calls from a person he identified as a witness on a weekend

---

170 *R v G(SG)*, [1997] 2 SCR 716 at para 30 [*G(SG)*].

171 *MBP*, above note 80.

172 *G(SG)*, above note 170.

173 *Ibid* at para 30.

174 Note the potential interaction, and slight inconsistency, between this rule and the rule on amending indictments, discussed above. An indictment can be amended to conform to the evidence presented, in some cases, even after the accused has presented evidence, even alibi evidence. In practical terms, an accused might perceive little difference between the Crown leading new evidence to show that an offence occurred at a different time than the accused's alibi covers, and amending a charge so that the offence is alleged to have occurred at a different time than the accused's alibi covers. In theory, they are different issues: in *MBP*, above note 80, for example, the Court noted that without leading the new evidence, the Crown would not be in a position to apply to amend the information. In that case they held that it was an error to allow the Crown to reopen its case to present new evidence. However, it would not have been an error to amend the charge had the evidence originally presented suggested the offence occurred at a different date than alleged in the indictment. From the accused's perspective, it might appear that the prejudice to an alibi has greater significance in one context than in the other.

following closing arguments in the case. She told him that she had lied on the stand and then retracted that claim. The Crown was permitted to reopen its case to present this new evidence, and the defence was allowed to cross-examine, to call the witness herself to the stand once again, and to make further submissions. The Ontario Court of Appeal held that no problem arose with this procedure, since the trial judge had adequately instructed the jury on the limited use they could make of the new evidence.[175]

6) Rebuttal Evidence

A close cousin to the issue of the Crown reopening its case is the possibility of the Crown leading rebuttal evidence. Rebuttal evidence is permitted

> where the defence has raised some new matter or defence which the Crown has had no opportunity to deal with and which the Crown or the plaintiff could not reasonably have anticipated. But rebuttal will not be permitted regarding matters which merely confirm or reinforce earlier evidence adduced in the Crown's case which could have been brought before the defence was made.[176]

Essentially, rebuttal evidence must concern matters that the Crown is reasonably surprised to find in issue.

This test creates slightly broader scope for admitting rebuttal evidence than for reopening the Crown case. This difference is justified on the basis that, if the test for admitting rebuttal evidence is met, then it cannot be said that the accused did not know the case to meet. If rebuttal evidence deals only with unanticipated matters arising in the defence case, then the evidence led was not part of the original case to meet.[177]

To preserve that rationale it is important that rebuttal evidence be admitted only when it truly does concern matters the Crown could not have anticipated. In *R v Biddle*, for example, the accused was charged with an assault that occurred somewhere between 10:00 and 10:30 in the evening. The accused took the stand in his own defence, and his testimony included the claim that he had been at a show between 7:30 and 9:15 p.m., then at several bars later on. The Crown then led rebuttal evidence of a witness who testified that the accused had followed her in his car at 8:30 that evening. The Court held that this evidence should

---

175   (1997), 97 OAC 380 (CA).
176   *Krause*, above note 168 at 474.
177   *G(SG)*, above note 170 at para 40.

not have been allowed in rebuttal and should have been presented as part of the Crown's original case. The Crown knew that Biddle had given a statement to the police about his whereabouts and ought to have anticipated that the defence would challenge the identification evidence. The Crown would have been able to present the witness as part of its case, and its failure to do so prevented the accused from knowing the entire case to meet before testifying.[178]

Rebuttal evidence cannot be led if it will reply only to a collateral issue. However, it need not be determinative of an essential issue either. Rather, the question is whether it relates to an essential issue which might be determinative of the case.[179] If it does and the Crown could not have foreseen that the evidence would be necessary, then it is generally admissible.

The accused's right in section 650(3) to make full answer and defence after the close of the Crown's case applies where the Crown has led rebuttal evidence, permitting the accused to lead surrebuttal evidence.[180] However, this opportunity does not eliminate any prejudice caused by improperly led rebuttal evidence. Indeed, the mere fact of entering the witness box a second time can create the impression that the accused was caught in a lie, and so could leave an adverse impression on the jury.[181]

7) Reopening the Defence Case

It is worth noting that it is also open to the defence to apply to reopen its case, though obviously the time in which this could occur is necessarily more restricted because the accused does not present evidence until the Crown's case is done. Whether a trial judge should permit the defence to reopen its case after final argument is a discretionary decision. In *R v Scott*, for example, one co-accused sought a bench warrant

---

178 [1995] 1 SCR 761 [*Biddle*]. Similarly, see *R v Anderson*, 2009 ABCA 67, leave to appeal to SCC refused, [2009] SCCA No 428. The accused had claimed that details of a murder he provided during a "sting" operation had been told to him by two undercover officers. The trial judge permitted the Crown to lead rebuttal evidence from two police officers to say that the undercover officers had not been told those details. The Court of Appeal concluded the rebuttal evidence was improperly admitted: the entire point of having "holdback" evidence was so that an accused could not claim to have learned details from undercover officers, and so the Crown should have led the evidence as part of its case in chief.

179 *R v Aalders*, [1993] 2 SCR 482 at para 37. See also the discussion in *R v Ryan*, 2011 NLCA 53.

180 *R v Ewert* (1989), 52 CCC (3d) 280 (BCCA).

181 *Biddle*, above note 178 at 776.

for a witness who had not responded to a subpoena. Being unsuccessful in the application, the defence entered no evidence and, along with the Crown, made final submissions. The witness then appeared, and the accused applied to reopen his case. The Court held that the trial judge had not exercised her discretion improperly in refusing to allow the accused to reopen his case and call the witness. The trial judge had an obligation to conduct the trial in an expeditious and orderly manner, had been given no explanation of the way in which the witness's testimony would be relevant, and had to consider the possible prejudice to the co-accused who objected to an adjournment.[182]

Some authority suggests that it is possible to apply to admit new evidence not only after argument, but indeed sometimes after a verdict has been reached. The Ontario Court of Appeal has held that a case cannot be reopened if the verdict was reached by a jury or if a judge has acquitted an accused, but that it can be reopened following a judge's guilty verdict in "special circumstances."[183] However, different standards apply depending on when the application to reopen is brought: a more stringent standard must be met if the application is made after adjudication.[184] The Saskatchewan Court of Appeal has suggested that if new evidence is to be admitted after a finding of guilt, the test should not vary depending on which court is admitting the evidence. Therefore, the test for a trial judge to reopen the defence case after a guilty verdict should be the same as that for admitting fresh evidence on appeal.[185]

8) Addresses to the Jury

a) Closing Arguments by Counsel

In the ordinary course of events all evidence is presented and final submissions are then made. Section 651 of the *Code* sets out the order in which the Crown and the accused are to address the jury. If the defence has not called evidence then the Crown argues first, but if the defence has called evidence then it argues first.[186] Although it has been argued that the right to full answer and defence should entitle the accused to address the jury last in all cases, the Court determined, in a closely divided decision, that section 651 of the *Code* does not violate section 7 or section 11(d) of the *Charter*.

---

182 *R v Scott*, [1990] 3 SCR 979.
183 *R v Lessard* (1976), 33 CRNS 16 (Ont CA).
184 *R v Arabia*, 2008 ONCA 565.
185 *R v Mysko* (1980), 2 Sask R 342 (CA).
186 Where there is more than one accused, all accused are equally affected by the decision of any one of them to call evidence, and the Crown will argue last.

Five of the nine members of the Court held that, although there was no question that counsel's address to the jury could be of great persuasive significance, there was not sufficient evidence to show that there was an advantage to speaking last. An accused will be reasonably clear, through the Crown's opening arguments and questions to witnesses, as to what argument the Crown will make. In general, therefore, the rule requiring an accused to speak first sometimes did not cause *Charter* problems. In individual cases where irregularities in Crown counsel's address to the jury or other issues threatened an accused's fair trial right, two options are available. The trial judge who, in any event, addresses the jury last in charging them could give curative instructions, instructing the jury to ignore improper aspects of an argument. Further, a court's inherent jurisdiction would allow it to grant to the defence a limited right of reply following the Crown's address, where not doing so would prejudice the accused's right to a fair trial and to make full answer and defence. This situation might arise where, for example, the accused has been misled by the Crown as to the argument to be advanced, or where the Crown's argument has changed so dramatically that the defence could not reasonably have anticipated and answered it.[187] The right of reply would be confined to addressing the issues improperly dealt with by Crown counsel.

Note that although a majority of the Court found that section 651 was not so unfair that it violated the *Charter*, all nine members of the Court expressed the view that better alternatives could be found. Various proposals have been put forward: these include always allowing the accused to speak last or giving the accused a choice as to when to speak.[188]

Counsel must not exceed the appropriate bounds when making submissions to the jury. This rule applies to both Crown and defence, though it applies more strictly to the Crown prosecutor—defence counsel is to be afforded more latitude in the content of a closing argument.[189]

---

187 *Rose*, above note 127. Note that L'Heureux-Dubé J, one of the five judges making up the majority in the result, disagreed with the other four judges as to whether a trial judge had inherent jurisdiction to grant a limited right of reply, holding that this jurisdiction had been ousted by s 651. However, the reasons of the four judges who held that s 651 violated the *Charter* (particularly their arguments concerning s 11(d)) suggest that they would agree with the four members of the majority regarding inherent jurisdiction.

188 See, for example, Tim Quigley, "Principled Reform of Criminal Procedure" in Don Stuart, RJ Delisle, & Allan Manson, eds, *Towards a Clear and Just Criminal Law* (Toronto: Carswell, 1999); Law Reform Commission of Canada, *The Jury* (Ottawa: Law Reform Commission, 1982).

189 *R v Trakas*, 2008 ONCA 410 [*Trakas*].

Counsel ought not, for example, to offer their personal opinions,[190] use inflammatory language,[191] attack the personal integrity of opposing counsel,[192] misrepresent the evidence,[193] or inject irrelevant issues.[194] Crown counsel should not refer to the accused's failure to testify.[195]

When improper comments are made, a trial judge has a discretion over how to respond and, in some cases, will intervene but in other cases will not.[196] The fact that improper comments have been made, though an error, will not necessarily render a trial so unfair that an appeal will be granted.[197]

b) Charging the Jury

Once counsel have argued, if there is a jury the judge then gives them instructions, usually referred to as the "charge to the jury." Section 650.1 of the *Code* permits a judge to confer with the Crown and the defence with regard to what matters should be explained to the jury. The purpose of the charge to the jury is to "decant and simplify" the case and leave the jury with a sufficient understanding of the facts as they relate to the relevant legal issues.[198] In general, the trial judge has considerable discretion regarding the content and form of the charge to the jury, though with some limits. An accused has a right to a properly instructed jury, but not to a perfectly instructed jury.[199]

---

190 *R v Copp*, 2009 NBCA 16 [*Copp*]; *R v L(L)*, 2009 ONCA 413 [*L(L)*]; *R v S(G)*, 2009 NBCA 82.

191 See the review of cases on this issue in *R v Melanson*, 2007 NBCA 94 [*Melanson*]. See also *R v Horan*, 2008 ONCA 589 [*Horan*].

192 *Horan*, ibid.

193 *L(L)*, above note 190.

194 See, for example, *Horan*, above note 191, where defence counsel raised the issue of wrongful convictions when it had no particular connection to the case at hand, or *R v Williams*, 2008 ONCA 413 [*Williams*], where the accused raised issues of race that had no evidentiary foundation.

195 *R v Biladeau*, 2008 ONCA 833 [*Biladeau*].

196 Contrast, for example, *Copp*, above note 190, where the trial judge almost immediately intervened, to *Melanson*, above note 191, where the trial judge spoke to the jury about the point as soon as the Crown prosecutor had finished and then also returned to the issue in his charge to the jury, to *Williams*, above note 194, where the trial judge did nothing about the improper remarks.

197 See, for example, *Trakas*, above note 189, or *Copp*, above note 190. In contrast in *Biladeau*, above note 195, where the essence of the improper remarks had been to invite the jury to infer the accused's guilt from his failure to testify, a new trial was ordered.

198 *R v Jacquard*, [1997] 1 SCR 314 [*Jacquard*].

199 *Ibid*, reaffirmed in *R v Daley*, 2007 SCC 53 at para 31 [*Daley*].

The organization of a jury charge is a matter of common law, and so trial judges do have some latitude in structuring them. Trial judges are permitted to experiment with new approaches to instructing a jury, provided that at the end the jury understands the nature of their task and has been given the necessary help from the instructions. In *R v Ménard*, for example, the trial judge gave his instructions in four parts, instructing the jury on substantive law at the start of the trial, giving instructions on two other specific matters during the course of the trial, and reviewing the evidence without reviewing the other instructions (though distributing transcripts of them) at the end of the trial. The Court decided that in the particular circumstances of the case no miscarriage of justice occurred, but did make several comments on the approach taken. They suggested that long and detailed instructions at the start of a trial might be more confusing than helpful and that they increase the risk of a jury being confused by instructions concerning matters that ultimately do not arise in the case. Similarly, where an erroneous statement of law is made at the outset of the trial, the error might have a much greater effect on the trial and be much more difficult to correct, if it can be corrected at all. The Court also held that the principles of reasonable doubt, the presumption of innocence, and the burden of proof were too important to be dealt with at the end, by simply referring the jury to the transcript of the earlier instructions.[200]

The judge's charge should be fair and dispassionate; it should also be the last thing said to the jury before they commence their deliberations. Judges generally ask counsel, following the charge, whether they felt any portion was unclear or needed clarification, but it is an error to allow counsel to address the jury directly again.[201] Indeed, the instructions drafted by the judge are typically based on extensive pre-charge discussions with counsel, so that it would be rare for counsel to hear the charge for the first time as it is being delivered.[202] A judge should not divide the charge in two, instructing the jury on some matters, then allowing counsel to speak, then finally completing the charge.[203] However, beyond these types of issues, a trial judge's discretion as to how to structure the charge will rarely be interfered with.

A judge cannot leave the jury to their own devices in deciding what evidence must be considered:

---

200 [1998] 2 SCR 109 [*Ménard*].
201 *R v C(JD)* (2003), 186 OAC 234 (CA).
202 *R v Bouchard*, 2013 ONCA 791.
203 *R v Levene* (1983), 36 CR (3d) 386 (Ont CA).

The rule which has been laid down, and consistently followed is that in a jury trial the presiding judge must, except in rare cases where it would be needless to do so, review the substantial parts of the evidence, and give the jury the theory of the defence, so that they may appreciate the value and effect of that evidence, and how the law is to be applied to the facts as they find them.[204]

This does not mean, however, that an exhaustive review of every piece of evidence is required in every case. Rather, the judge must see to it that the jury is able to fully appreciate the issues and the defence presented, which might be best served by omitting reference to some peripheral evidence.[205] Non-direction on a particular piece of evidence is only mis-direction if that piece of evidence is the foundation for a defence, justification, or excuse.[206] Otherwise, the judge has considerable latitude in deciding how much or how little evidence should be reviewed.[207]

Thus, a judge still has a considerable amount of discretion as to exactly how to review the facts. A judge can decide to review particular facts only once in the charge, for example, even though they might be relevant to more than one issue. Indeed, restating the facts each time they are relevant could make the charge worse, not better.[208] Charges that are very long will not necessarily be an error either. In *R v Fell*, for example, the trial judge gave a four-day charge to the jury. Although the Ontario Court of Appeal suggested that such a length for a charge might be more exhausting and confusing than helpful, they held that there was nothing inaccurate in the charge, and that this exercise of the trial judge's discretion did not make the trial unfair.[209] On the other hand, in *R v Saleh* the trial judge did not "decant and simplify"; instead, he gave the jury a copy of his eighty-seven typewritten pages of notes of the evidence—this was found to be an error.[210]

Similarly, a trial judge has some discretion over what legal issues to include in the instructions. As long as the jury members are given

---

204 *Azoulay v the Queen*, [1952] 2 SCR 495 at 497–98, reaffirmed in *Daley*, above note 199 at para 54.

205 *Daley, ibid* at paras 56–57.

206 *R v Rybak*, 2008 ONCA 354.

207 *R v Royz*, 2009 SCC 13. Courts of Appeal have reached no consistent view as to whether it is advisable for judges to include in the charge a summary of evidence written by counsel: see *R v Minor*, 2013 ONCA 557, criticizing the practice, and *R v Huard*, 2013 ONCA 650 [*Huard*], seeming to approve it.

208 *Jacquard*, above note 198.

209 (1990), 40 OAC 139. See also *R v Rideout* (1999), 182 Nfld & PEIR 227 (Nfld CA), aff'd on other issues, [2001] 1 SCR 755, reaching a similar conclusion concerning a thirteen-hour jury charge.

210 (2013), 303 CCC (3d) 431 (Ont CA).

instructions that allow them to arrive at a just and proper verdict, the trial judge is entitled to narrow the issues for the jury by focusing on what was realistically at issue in the particular case. If the real issue in a case was whether the accused was liable as a principal, for example, it can be acceptable not to instruct the jury on party liability, even if theoretically that possibility were open.[211] Presenting the jury with a "decision tree," which outlines the questions that the jury should ask itself and the directions its reasoning should go based on those answers, has been found to be helpful, as long as it supplements, rather than replaces, proper instructions.[212]

Much caselaw concerns jury instructions. This is, in part, because appeals generally focus on legal issues, and so whether a judge has accurately described the law to the jury is a potentially fruitful source of argument. A charge should review the facts, the prosecution's theory of the case, the accused's theory of the case, and the defences that arise for the jury. The trial judge should charge on all defences that arise on the facts, whether the accused has raised them or not.[213] It will also be necessary to charge the jury on whatever particular issues are relevant to the trial, such as the use that can be made of an accused's criminal record, or issues surrounding circumstantial evidence, identification evidence, and alibi evidence. A considerable number of cases have focused on whether trial judges adequately explain the concept of "proof beyond a reasonable doubt" to juries.[214] In reviewing a trial judge's instructions to the jury, the charge must be viewed as a whole, and inadequacies in one portion might be compensated for sufficiently in other parts so that the entire charge is acceptable.[215] In addition, sentences or passages should not be considered in isolation but rather in the context of the entire charge and the trial as a whole: what might initially seem ambiguous might not, on such examination, actually be so.[216] If there

---

211 *Pickton*, above note 127 at para 10.

212 *Huard*, above note 207.

213 *Faid*, above note 125.

214 A non-exhaustive list includes *R v Lifchus*, [1997] 3 SCR 320; *R v Starr*, [2000] 2 SCR 144; *R v Beauchamp*, [2000] 2 SCR 720; *R v Russell*, [2000] 2 SCR 731; *R v Avetysan*, [2000] 2 SCR 745, rev'g (1999), 174 Nfld & PEIR 34 (Nfld CA); *R v Rhee*, [2001] 3 SCR 364; *R v Feeley*, 2003 SCC 7; *R v Griffin*, 2009 SCC 28 [*Griffin*].

215 This principle is stated in virtually every case dealing with jury instructions, but see, for example, *Jacquard*, above note 198; *R v W(D)*, [1991] 1 SCR 742 [*W(D)*]; *R v S(WD)*, [1994] 3 SCR 521 [*S(WD)*].

216 *R v Jaw*, 2009 SCC 42 [*Jaw*].

is some ambiguity, it is not clear that any uncertainty must be resolved in favour of the accused.[217]

The Court has summarized the principles relating to whether a charge to the jury was adequate:

> The cardinal rule is that it is the general sense which the words used must have conveyed, in all probability, to the mind of the jury that matters, and not whether a particular formula was recited by the judge. The particular words used, or the sequence followed, is a matter within the discretion of the trial judge and will depend on the particular circumstances of the case.

In determining the general sense which the words used have likely conveyed to the jury, the appellate tribunal will consider the charge as a whole. The standard that a trial judge's instructions are to be held to is not perfection. "The accused is entitled to a properly instructed jury, not a perfectly instructed jury . . . . It is the overall effect of the charge that matters."[218]

Instructions should also cover the procedural aspects of the jury's deliberation. Confusion in jurors' minds over how long they are expected to deliberate before a "hung jury" could be declared, for example, might improperly affect their deliberations.[219]

Even though the jury is the trier of fact, a trial judge is entitled to offer opinions on matters of fact in the course of the instructions to the jury. The trial judge must not, however, remove the decision from the jury by instructing them to convict. Such an instruction violates an accused's section 11(f) right under the *Charter* to trial by jury.[220] In other words, there is no "directed verdict of conviction" that is analogous to a directed verdict of acquittal.

Following the charge to the jury, judges tell juries not to begin their deliberations immediately. First, the judge consults with counsel to see

---

217 *Ibid* at para 38. The majority does not settle the point but suggests that uncertainty need not always be resolved in the accused's favour and that attempts to resolve the ambiguity should first be made. The dissenting judgment in *Jaw* points out that the majority relies on principles created in the context of statutory interpretation in reaching their conclusion, which are not applicable in the context of understanding a charge to the jury.

218 *Daley*, above note 199 at para 31.

219 *R v Pan; R v Sawyer*, [2001] 2 SCR 344 at para 98 [*Pan*].

220 *Boulet v the Queen*, [1978] 1 SCR 332; *R v Sims*, [1992] 2 SCR 858 [*Sims*]; *R v Krieger*, 2006 SCC 47 [*Krieger*]. In *Krieger*, the trial judge deliberately directed the jury to retire and return with a verdict of guilty. See also *R v Gunning*, [2005] 1 SCR 627, where the trial judge directed the jury that one of the elements of the offence in question had been proven by the Crown; this too was an error.

whether they have any objections or feel that any matters need clarification. Indeed, the practice of a judge providing counsel with a copy of the charge in advance has been favourably commented upon.[221] It remains within the judge's discretion whether to act on the comments of counsel, and indeed, it can be an error to include an issue in a charge even if both counsel agree it should be there.[222] Failure by counsel to raise an objection at the time does not automatically prevent that matter from later being a basis for appeal, nor does it mean that the error was a harmless one to which the curative provision in section 686(1)(b)(iii) of the *Code* can be applied. However, failure by counsel to object at the time will enter into an appellate court's decision about the overall accuracy of the instructions and the seriousness of the alleged misdirection.[223]

c)   Re-charging the Jury

Where a judge re-charges following submissions from counsel, essentially the same criteria apply to that as to the original charge. In most instances, the re-charge will simply be considered part of the charge, and the question will be whether, taken as a whole, the jury has been properly instructed. A re-charge might rectify an error in the original charge, meaning that, as a whole, the charge is satisfactory.[224] Similarly, in *R v W(D)*,[225] an error in a re-charge did not form the basis for an appeal, largely because the re-charge was quite short and followed only a few minutes after the original charge, the original charge had instructed the jury correctly, and the trial judge said in the re-charge that the jury should not give special emphasis to the re-charge and should be mindful of the duties he had outlined in the charge.

On the other hand, sometimes it is necessary to re-charge a jury after they have begun their deliberations because the jury has sent a question to the judge. In these circumstances, the re-charge takes on much greater significance. If the jury has asked a question, it will generally relate to an important point in their reasoning. Even if they were correctly instructed on the point earlier, if they have asked a question, they have forgotten or did not understand the instruction. Therefore, when a question is received from a jury it must be considered to be significant. Counsel must be heard as to what response should be made to the question, and the answer must be correct and comprehensive. Since the jury has asked about the issue, instructions must be repeated

---

221 *R v Polimac*, 2010 ONCA 346.
222 *Pickton*, above note 127.
223 *Jacquard*, above note 198; *Thériault v the Queen*, [1981] 1 SCR 336.
224 See, for example, *R v G(RM)*, [1996] 3 SCR 362 [*G(RM)*].
225 Above note 215.

even if they were given in the original charge, and the need for the re-charge to be correct and comprehensive increases with the greater the delay. Finally, an error in a re-charge following a question from the jury generally cannot be saved by a correct original charge because the fact that a question was asked shows that the jury did not adequately understand the original instructions.[226]

It is not necessarily an error for a re-charge simply to repeat the instructions given in the original charge — where the original charge was not given to the jury in writing and the question indicates that the jury has forgotten the instructions, for example. When the jury does have the charge in writing and does not understand it, however, the trial judge ought to try to explain the relevant concepts in different words. Further, even if the trial judge simply repeats the original charge, she must make clear to the jury that they can return to seek further clarification.[227]

Although a trial judge has a duty to assist the jury if they have a question, the judge does not have to answer whatever question the jury has asked right away. It can be appropriate to invite the jury to focus or rephrase their question, provided they are not discouraged from seeking assistance.[228] It is also wise on the judge's part to consult with counsel before answering a question.[229]

---

226 *S(WD)*, above note 215.

227 *R v Layton*, 2009 SCC 36 [*Layton*]. In *Layton* the trial judge repeated her initial instructions on reasonable doubt and told the jury that there was little she could do to clarify the concept further. The Supreme Court concluded at para 32 that the re-charge was in error: "A verbatim reiteration of the initial charge would not have been fatal had the judge made it absolutely clear to the jury that it was welcome to return with further questions if jury members were still confused. But the jury was discouraged from doing so by the words the trial judge used."

In contrast, in *R v Miljevic*, 2011 SCC 8, the trial judge specifically encouraged the jury to ask further questions if they were left unclear.

228 See, for example, *R v Couture*, 2007 QCCA 1612, where the jury asked to watch again a videotape of one statement and hear the audiotapes of two others. The trial judge was concerned that doing so (which would take four to five hours) might give undue emphasis to particular parts of the evidence and dilute the arguments of counsel. He invited the jury to consider whether they had a more specific question, which after forty-five minutes they did. As a result, the jury viewed a twelve-second segment of the videotape. The Court of Appeal held that the trial judge had acted correctly.

229 *Griffin*, above note 214.

E. JURY DELIBERATIONS

1) Jury Sequestration

Following the jury charge and any re-charge, the *Code* permits a trial judge to allow the jury to separate rather than commence deliberations immediately, and in this event a publication ban is imposed.[230] Once the jury begins its deliberations, it is sequestered (isolated in a way to keep from it any potential sources of information). At this stage the jury is essentially to be left alone until it has reached a verdict, or until it is apparent that it will not be able to do so. The verdict, whether for conviction or acquittal, must be unanimous. If the jury is ultimately unable to reach unanimity then, as will be pursued below, section 653 of the *Code* permits the trial judge to discharge the jury and order a new trial.

The jury is not completely isolated, in the sense that it is able to initiate contact with the judge. When a judge receives a non-administrative inquiry from the jury, the judge is to "(a) read the communication in open court in the presence of all parties; (b) give counsel an opportunity to make submissions in open court prior to dealing with the question; (c) answer the question for the jury in open court in the presence of all parties."[231] Such requests can concern a variety of things.

Juries sometimes request copies of the *Criminal Code*, or portions of it, for example. A trial judge is permitted to give short sections of the *Code* to the jury, but must be careful not to prejudice the outcome of the trial by doing so.[232] It is likely to be a mistake to give the *Code* provisions to the jury and leave them to work out the meaning for themselves, but it could be acceptable to provide photocopies of some sections if they are accompanied by an explanation.[233] However, where giving the jury sections of the *Code* will also involve a complete and lengthy re-charge on the issues relating to those sections, it will usually be better to see whether the jury's concerns can be addressed in some other fashion. A trial judge might be better advised to ask the jury to be more specific about the particular concern that motivates the request, and then try to answer that concern. Similarly, rereading the sections

---

230 Sections 647 & 648.
231 *R v Fontaine*, [2003] 1 WWR 634 at para 59 (Man CA), quoting from *R v Dunbar and Logan* (1982), 68 CCC (2d) 13 (Ont CA).
232 *Cathro v the Queen*, [1956] SCR 101.
233 See, for example, *R v Flewwelling* (1984), 63 NSR (2d) 382 (CA); *R v McCormack* (1984), 28 Man R (2d) 29 (CA); *R v Vawryk*, [1979] 3 WWR 50 (Man CA); and *R v Crothers* (1978), 43 CCC (2d) 27 (Sask CA).

of the *Code* and explaining them to the jury might be a sufficient response to the request.[234]

In some cases, juries can also take other material into the jury room, such as transcripts of wiretaps or chronologies prepared by counsel to help organize material. However, the caselaw is not consistent on when doing this is advisable or permissible and whether juries should be required to re-hear evidence in its entirety.[235]

Similar considerations arise if the jury requests transcripts of the trial judge's instructions or of the argument by counsel. It is not necessarily an error to provide them to the jury, even to provide the argument of only one side if that is all that was requested, although the better choice might be to provide the arguments of both counsel.[236] Distributing transcripts raises the likelihood of error, particularly if the jury receives only part of the judge's instructions.[237] The Court has noted that judges must be sure that the jury receives the entire charge in clear and legible form and that all members of the jury are capable of reading it. It has observed that "it may well be that the dangers associated with such an approach outweigh the potential benefits."[238]

Nonetheless, lower courts have encouraged the careful use of written versions of judges' charges, on the basis that doing so can increase juror comprehension. Some judges provide the entire charge while others, hoping to reduce the volume of material, do not include the summary of the evidence or of counsel's arguments. In some cases, there can be the fear that providing everything will bury the critical part of the instructions and thus mislead the jury. No single approach is suitable for all cases.[239]

---

234 *R v Keegstra*, [1996] 1 SCR 458.

235 See, for example, *R v Quashie* (2005), 198 CCC (3d) 337 (Ont CA); *R v DJ* (2004), 190 CCC (3d) 529 (Ont CA); and *R v Robert* (2004), 25 CR (6th) 55 (Que CA). See also *R v Latoski* (2005), 200 CCC (3d) 361 (Ont CA); *R v Pleich* (1980), 16 CR (3d) 194 (Ont CA); *R v Rowbotham* (1988), 63 CR (3d) 113 (Ont CA) [*Rowbotham* 1988]; *R v Bengert (No 13)* (1979), 15 CR (3d) 62 (BCSC), aff'd on other grounds (1980), 15 CR (3d) 114 (BCCA), leave to appeal to SCC refused (1980), 53 CCC (2d) 48n (SCC) [*Bengert*].

236 *R v Ferguson*, [2001] 1 SCR 281.

237 It has, however, been observed that "what is critical is the nature and extent of any errors, not the form in which they are expressed": *R v Yumnu*, 2010 ONCA 637 at para 355 [*Yumnu*].

238 *Ménard*, above note 200.

239 See the discussion in *Yumnu*, above note 237. See also *R v Poitras* (2002), 57 OR (3d) 538 at para 47 (CA); *R v Henry*, 2003 BCCA 476; and *R v Nieto*, 2007 MBCA 82 at para 47.

In deciding whether to provide a written version of the entire charge, the Ontario Court of Appeal has suggested that a trial judge should consider many factors:

    i.   the length of the trial proceedings, including the period between the conclusion of the evidence and the charge;

    ii. the volume of evidentiary references contained in the charge, bearing in mind the principles governing evidentiary review;

    iii. the danger of diluting the effect of the instructions on the governing legal principles by their submersion in a protracted evidentiary review;

    iv. the positions of counsel;

    v. the issues to be resolved by the jury in their deliberations;

    vi. the danger of simply overburdening the jurors by the volume of the instructions;

    vii. whether jurors took notes of the evidence adduced at trial;

    viii. the risk that jurors will consider the evidentiary references to be exhaustive of the evidence they should consider in reaching their decision; and

    ix. any other relevant circumstances.

It also stressed that jurors should be reminded to consider all of the evidence, not just that to which reference is made in the instructions, and that their recollection of the evidence is the most important criterion, rather than any views the judge may have expressed about factual issues.[240]

The same types of considerations govern when the jury asks to rehear evidence or asks for clarification of the legal issues during its deliberations. A trial judge has discretion and is not obliged to answer every request from the jury precisely as asked. So, for example, where a jury requests transcripts of the evidence of all the witnesses shortly after commencing deliberations, a trial judge will not err by refusing this request. However, since questions from the jury must be given particular consideration, it is not sufficient to simply refuse (as noted at Section D(8)(b), above in this chapter). A trial judge should consult with counsel on how to respond and propose alternatives or ask the jury to deliberate further to decide more specifically what their concern is, for example.[241] Where the jury's question is unclear, the judge should request clarification in order to be able to answer it appropriately.[242]

---

240 *Yumnu*, above note 237 at paras 367–68.

241 *R v Ostrowski*, [1990] 2 SCR 82; or see, for example, *R v Holden* (2001), 159 CCC (3d) 180 (Ont CA), leave to appeal to SCC refused, [2001] SCCA No 574; *R v K(BA)* (1998), 19 CR (5th) 400 (BCCA); *R v Perry* (1995), 54 BCAC 275 (CA).

242 *R v H(LI)*, 2003 MBCA 97.

Other considerations arise when the jury is not seeking a review of the evidence at trial but is seeking additional evidence. The basic rule is that this is not permitted. No information that did not come out at trial can be given to the jury once they have begun deliberating, and it might be necessary to tell the jury that there was no evidence led on the point in question.[243] So, for example, a jury cannot have a demonstration that was conducted at trial repeated for them after the close of both cases.[244] Nor should the jury have material that, although it was used at trial, did not form part of the evidence.[245] However, once again, a refusal of the jury's request might well be an error, and the trial judge should try to determine whether the jury's concern can be satisfied in some other way.

Requests from jurors sometimes do not concern the law or the evidence, but the jury's own deliberations or concerns by one juror about the behaviour of another juror. In *Vézina*, for example, two jurors sent notes to the trial judge that questioned the honesty of two other jurors. The judge consulted with counsel on how to proceed, but without their agreement, and in the absence of the accused, met with the two jurors who had complained and decided that the jury's deliberations could continue. The Court held that the judge erred by meeting with the jurors in the absence of the accused. At any point where the accused's vital interests are at issue the accused is entitled to be present. Had the trial judge received communications that might have concerned purely administrative questions, it would have been permissible to meet with the jurors privately. But even in those circumstances, once it became apparent that the integrity of a juror was being questioned, the accused would be entitled to be present and the judge should adjourn the meeting.[246]

---

243 *R v Templeman* (1994), 40 BCAC 76.

244 *R v Kluke* (1987), 22 OAC 107 (CA). But see *R v Clair* (1995), 143 NSR (2d) 101 (CA), leave to appeal to SCC refused (1996), 151 NSR (2d) 240n, where it was held that allowing a jury to have a measuring tape did not affect the fairness of the trial, because it merely allowed them to estimate distances (something they could have done without the tape) more accurately.

245 *Rowbotham* 1988, above note 235.

246 *Vézina*, above note 45. See also *R v Phillips*, 2008 ONCA 726, where the trial judge met briefly with two court officials, knowing only that they wished to raise a concern relating to a juror in a recently completed trial. The judge had the meeting recorded and, having decided that it raised a matter into which he needed to inquire, sent a transcript to the Crown and defence, and convened a meeting with them. The Court of Appeal held that there was no violation of the accused's right to be present at her trial and that in the highly unusual circumstances of the case, the trial judge's actions were entirely appropriate.

Where the issues raised about fellow jurors give rise to legitimate concerns, a trial judge does have a statutory power to remove a juror.[247] The judge is entitled to make inquiries in deciding whether to do so, but the process is subject to strict limitations. An accused should not lightly be deprived of the right to have a verdict from a unanimous jury of twelve,[248] and the secrecy of the jury's deliberations must be protected. The power to remove a juror should be used only for serious issues, and so a trial judge ought first to consider whether re-charging all the jurors about the duties of jurors would be the better approach.[249]

In the absence of these types of requests that necessitate some response, the jury is to be left unhindered to perform its function without communication from others. In R v Mercier, for example, a new trial was necessary when a Crown prosecutor entered the jury room in the jury's absence and erased some words from the chalkboard.[250] Not all communication has that result, however. Where there has been contact between the jury and anyone else, the trial judge must conduct an inquiry to determine whether the jury, or perhaps an individual juror, cannot continue. It might be that no prejudice has been caused because the contact was relatively harmless or because it had no actual impact on the deliberations.[251] On the other hand, where the improprieties are so serious that they affect public confidence in the system, no prejudice needs to be shown. Thus, where a jury, during its deliberations, was taken to dinner with a group of people including a close relative of the murder victim, the absence of actual prejudice was irrelevant.[252]

---

247 Section 644(1), allows a judge to discharge a juror for illness "or other reasonable cause."

248 An order under s 644 can be made at any point, and if it occurs before the jury has heard evidence, it is possible to replace the juror: s 644(1.1). If it is too late to replace the juror, the jury remains properly constituted as long as the number of members does not fall below ten, unless the judge orders otherwise: s 644(2).

249 R v Kum, 2015 ONCA 36.

250 (1973), 12 CCC (2d) 377 (Que CA) [Mercier].

251 In R v Taillefer (1995), 40 CR (4th) 287 (Que CA), for example, a juror contacted a witness on the second day of deliberations, but was questioned by the judge and allowed to stay on the jury. The jury did not reach a decision for another eleven days, suggesting that the communication had been of no effect and that the trial judge had not erred in the exercise of his discretion.

252 R v Cameron (1991), 2 OR (3d) 633 (CA), leave to appeal to SCC refused, [1991] 3 SCR x. See also R v Hertrich (1982), 137 DLR (3d) 400 (Ont CA), leave to appeal to SCC refused (1982), 45 NR 629n (SCC).

2) Exhorting the Jury

It can occur that deliberations continue so long that it appears, or notes are sent from the jury stating, that the jury is deadlocked and will be unable to reach a unanimous verdict. Although the trial judge can discharge the jury under section 653 and order a new trial, normally the first step is to call the jury in and exhort them to reach a verdict. Principles have developed around such exhortations, so that they do not present a threat to the independence of the jury or the interests of the accused. Exhorting a jury properly is a delicate task. A judge should not express an opinion on the facts during an exhortation, even though that is permissible in the original charge.[253] The exhortation also should not suggest that one or another group's opinions on the evidence is preferable. Rather, the exhortation is to focus on the process of deliberation itself and encourage the jury members to listen to and consider one another's views.[254] No pressure should be placed on the jury, and no factors that are extraneous to the task of reaching a verdict should be introduced.[255] Jurors should not be encouraged to change their minds for the sake of conformity, and no deadline should be imposed.[256] It is an error, therefore, to tell the jury to consider the expense of a new trial, or to consider the benefit to the accused of a verdict being reached. It is also an error to direct the minority to reconsider the views of the majority. Rather, it is better to direct all the jurors to reconsider their views.[257]

Nonetheless, it is appropriate for a trial judge to remind the jurors of their oath and encourage them to reach a verdict. In effect, as long as it is clear that the jurors do retain the right to disagree, and provided improper pressures and irrelevant considerations are not brought to bear, a trial judge can urge them to try to find a way not to.[258] Further, not every improper exhortation will lead to a new trial. Other factors, such as the length of the deliberations, the question asked by the jury, and the length of the subsequent deliberations following the exhorta-

---

253 *Sims*, above note 220.

254 *Ibid.*

255 See, for example, *R v Paul*, 2011 BCCA 46, where the jury specifically asked whether there would be a retrial if they remained deadlocked. The trial judge properly told them that the possibility of a new trial should not influence their deliberations.

256 *G(RM)*, above note 224.

257 *Ibid.*

258 See, for example, *R v Littlejohn* (1978), 41 CCC (2d) 161 (Ont CA).

tion, will all help determine whether the exhortation coerced the jury or caused some jurors to accept a verdict that they did not agree with.[259]

3) Rendering a Verdict

Once the jury has finished its deliberations and indicated that it is ready to return, the jury announces its verdict in court. The announcement is made by the jury foreman. It is possible to request that the jury be polled — that is, that every juror be asked individually about the verdict. There is no legal requirement for this procedure, however, which is usually allowed where there is some doubt as to whether unanimity exists.[260]

After the jury has been discharged by the trial judge neither it nor the trial judge has any further authority to act. In the vast majority of circumstances, that causes no difficulty, but it can do so in the rare situation where an error is alleged to have occurred in recording the verdict but is not discovered until after the jury is discharged. In *R v Head*, for example, the jury foreman announced a verdict of not guilty, and the judge discharged the jury and acquitted the accused. The foreman then indicated that he thought the jury could have found the accused guilty of an included offence. The Court held that the trial judge was *functus officio* and no longer had jurisdiction to inquire into the matter or correct any error, and, therefore, the acquittal had to stand.[261]

Subsequently, in *R v Burke*, while reaffirming the general rule that a trial judge has no jurisdiction to alter a recorded verdict once a jury is discharged, the Court found a rare residual jurisdiction to be used when there has been an irregularity.[262] In that case, the jury had reached a guilty verdict, but the trial judge and many others in the court misheard the foreman, understanding him to say "not guilty." The error was discovered almost immediately after the jury was discharged and was brought to the judge's attention within minutes, but most jurors and the accused had already left. The Court held that there were a number of ways to proceed when such errors occur, but that sometimes the

---

259 *G(RM)*, above note 224 at para 50. Also "While a short lapse of time between an exhortation and the verdict might well be an indication that a judge has influenced a jury's decision, the reverse is not necessarily true. A large time gap between the exhortation and the verdict may or may not indicate the independence of the jury": *R v Jack* (1996), 113 Man R (2d) 84 at para 91 (CA), Helper J dissenting. Her decision was adopted by the Supreme Court of Canada when the decision was reversed on appeal: [1997] 2 SCR 334.

260 *R v Laforet*, [1980] 1 SCR 869.

261 [1986] 2 SCR 684.

262 [2002] 2 SCR 857 [*Burke*].

trial judge has a limited jurisdiction to correct errors in the recorded judgment. If the circumstances would require the jury to reconsider its verdict, then the ordinary *functus* rule applies and the trial judge has no jurisdiction to correct. But if no reconsideration of the verdict is involved, then the trial judge must decide whether there is, in the circumstances, a reasonable apprehension of bias. If there is no such apprehension, then the judge can correct the error. But if there is a reasonable apprehension of bias, the trial judge must either allow the verdict that was recorded to stand or declare a mistrial. The incorrect verdict must stand unless it is necessary to declare a mistrial to prevent a miscarriage of justice. In *Burke*, no question of the jury reconsidering its verdict arose, and so there was jurisdiction to potentially correct the error. However, since many of the jurors had gone home and had been exposed to media coverage of the case after their discharge, even if there was no actual bias there was a reasonable apprehension of it, and so the verdict could not simply be changed to guilty. Since leaving the incorrect acquittal in place would have led to a miscarriage of justice, a mistrial was declared and a new trial ordered.

4) Jury Secrecy

Finally, it is worth observing section 649 of the *Code*, which makes it an offence for anyone present in the jury room to disclose any information about the jury's deliberations, other than in connection with an investigation of obstructing justice.[263] This law closely reflects the common law rule on jury secrecy that is to the same effect, though it also prevents anyone who overhears, even accidentally, the jury's deliberations from disclosing that information. The Court has considered whether these rules violate section 7 of the *Charter*. It concluded that they do not and discussed the policy behind jury secrecy in *R v Pan*.[264]

The facts of *Pan* are complex. Pan was tried for murder three times, the first two trials having been declared mistrials. At the appeal of his conviction at the third trial, Pan objected to the process by which a mistrial was declared at his second trial. Investigations of a possible obstruction charge revealed that one juror at that trial had, among other things, been following media coverage and seeking other information outside of court and reporting the information to the other jurors. The mistrial resulted when that same juror sent a note to the trial judge ask-

---

263 There is an exception allowing such information to be disclosed in connection with a prosecution for obstructing justice under s 139(2).

264 Above note 219.

ing that the jury be polled once it reported its verdict—her intention, it appeared, was to feign agreement in the jury room and then disagree in open court. The trial judge consulted with counsel as to how to respond and ultimately declared a mistrial. Pan's argument hinged on the claim that the mistrial should not have been declared and that he should have been entitled to the acquittal that would have resulted if the second trial continued. To make this argument, it would have been necessary for Pan to lead evidence that section 649 prevented being led.

The Court reviewed the reasons why a guarantee of jury secrecy is valuable: it promotes candour in discussions and lets the jury consider all possibilities without fear of later recriminations from the public. This rationale is particularly valuable to an unpopular accused or an individual charged with a particularly heinous crime. Related to that rationale was the need to protect jurors from harassment, censure, and reprisals, which would permit them to perform their function more confidently. Finally, jury secrecy promotes finality, though the Court held that this rationale alone would not be sufficient to justify the rule.[265]

The Court held, however, that the common law jury secrecy rule does not prevent every conceivable piece of information relevant to what has gone on in a jury room from being disclosed. The Court drew a distinction between matters extrinsic to the jury's deliberations and those intrinsic to them. An extrinsic matter would be that some third party had contact with the jury or gave particular information to a juror, whereas an intrinsic matter would be the effect that the contact or information had on the jury's deliberations. The common law rule and section 649 prevent only intrinsic matters from being disclosed. In *Mercier*,[266] therefore, it was possible to lead evidence that the Crown prosecutor had erased words from the chalkboard in the jury room, since that was an extrinsic matter. However, evidence concerning any effect this action might have had on the jury's reasoning was intrinsic and therefore not admissible. The Court acknowledged that, in practical terms, it can sometimes be difficult to draw the distinction, but nonetheless held that the jury secrecy rule applies only to intrinsic matters.

Understood in this way, the Court held that the common law jury secrecy rule accorded with the goals of jury secrecy and was in accordance with the principles of fundamental justice. Since the statutory

---

265 The jury secrecy rule has been criticized as overly restrictive: see, for example, Sonia R Chopra & James RP Ogloff, "Evaluating Jury Secrecy: Implications for Academic Research and Juror Stress" (2000) 44 *Criminal Law Quarterly* 190; Paul Quinlan, "Secrecy of Jury Deliberations—Is the Cost Too High?" (1993) 22 *Criminal Reports* (4th) 127.

266 *Mercier*, above note 250.

rule was consistent with the common law rule, it too passed *Charter* scrutiny.

The jury secrecy rule extends to discussions within the jury room at any stage of the trial, not merely after the trial has concluded and formal deliberations have begun.[267]

F. POWERS OF THE COURT

A trial judge has a variety of powers to control the process in the court-room. Many of these powers arise at statute, though some come from the common law. In addition, the *Code* permits courts to make rules of court that can govern, among other things, matters regarding the pleading, practice, procedure at trial, and case management.[268] Such rules, of course, must not be inconsistent with the *Code*.

1) Control over the Court Process

A trial judge has fairly significant discretion over how a trial is run, including the ability to curtail cross-examination, to prevent irrelevant or harassing questions, and to ask questions of witnesses.[269] However, these powers must be exercised with caution and can be taken too far. Ultimately, such interventions can violate an accused's right to a fair trial. The test is not whether the accused was actually prejudiced, but "whether a reasonably minded person who had been present through-out the trial would consider that the accused had not had a fair trial."[270]

---

267 See, for example, *R v Jojic*, 2010 BCCA 577, where a juror was discharged mid-trial after making a comment to Crown counsel which implied that he had already made up his mind. The trial judge, in questioning the juror, declined to inquire into whether other jurors had privately expressed views suggesting pre-judgment: the Court of Appeal held that this was a proper exercise of discretion.

268 Sections 482 & 482.1.

269 See also the discussion of prosecutorial discretion, and the relatively limited ability of judges to review it, in Chapter 3, Section B(1)(a). In addition, see Part XVIII.1 of the *Code*, allowing for the appointment of a case management judge for a trial who might or might not be the trial judge. The case management judge has powers at the pre-trial stage aimed at helping the parties streamline the issues (s 551.3), can adjudicate issues referred by the trial judge during trial (s 551.6), and can potentially adjudicate issues that affect related trials at a joint hearing (s 551.7). See the discussion of case management judges and other issues related to "mega-trials" in Christine Mainville, "Report on the CIAJ's Complex Criminal Trials Roundtable" (2015) 62 *Criminal Law Quarterly* 339.

270 *R v Valley* (1986), 26 CCC (3d) 207 at 232 (Ont CA).

The *Code* gives judges the power to grant adjournments during trials or other proceedings.[271] At one time the rules concerning adjournments, and particularly the issue of whether a court lost jurisdiction over the accused or the offence by failing to proceed properly, were quite complex. Further, the *Code* formerly contained a provision preventing any adjournment of more than eight days without the accused's consent. Now, however, section 485 specifically preserves the court's jurisdiction over an accused despite a failure to comply with any of the *Code*'s provisions concerning adjournments or remands. Indeed, subsequent to a decision that found the predecessor of section 485 to not preserve a court's jurisdiction where it adjourned a case but failed to proceed on the set date,[272] the provision now more broadly preserves the court's jurisdiction despite a failure "to act in the exercise of that jurisdiction." Where a court does lose jurisdiction over an accused, it can regain it by issuing a summons or warrant for the accused within three months. However, if this is not done, the proceedings are considered dismissed for want of prosecution and the Crown cannot lay new charges without the personal consent in writing of the attorney general or deputy attorney general.[273]

Whether to grant an adjournment in any given case is a discretionary decision which depends on the facts. One common situation is an unrepresented accused seeking an adjournment in order to obtain counsel. Relevant facts in that situation are whether there have been previous adjournments for the same reason, whether the accused was warned that trial would proceed with or without counsel, the accused's degree of familiarity with the legal system, the complexity of the charges and the likelihood that he can receive a fair trial without counsel, the public interest in the orderly and expeditious administration of justice, and whether the accused was refused legal aid. An adjournment should be granted if the accused has been diligent and the lack of counsel is not her fault, but not if the request is an attempt to delay proceedings.[274] More generally, where a party ought to have been able to avoid the need for an adjournment by acting more expeditiously, it is likely not to be granted.[275]

---

271 Sections 537 and 645. See also the discussion in *R v JCG* (2004), 189 CCC (3d) 1 (Que CA); and *R v MV* (2004), 189 CCC (3d) 230 (Que CA).

272 *R v Krannenburg*, [1980] 1 SCR 1053.

273 Sections 485(2), 485(3), and 485.1.

274 *R v White*, 2010 ABCA 208. See also *R v Bitternose*, 2009 SKCA 54.

275 See, for example, *R v Cole*, 2010 NSCA 59. The Crown requested an adjournment two weeks before trial because a key witness had to come from China and it would take one month at a minimum to obtain a visa. The trial judge properly refused the adjournment on the basis that the Crown had known for at least four months that it would need a witness from China and should have known that visa requirements would need to be satisfied.

Some sections of the *Code* give a judge authority over the manner in which witnesses will testify. Section 486.1 of the *Code* provides for the possibility of a witness having a support person present while testifying. Section 486.2 allows a witness to testify from outside the courtroom or from behind a screen or other device that prevents the witness from seeing the accused. Each of these methods can be ordered for any witness where the trial judge feels it is necessary in order to obtain a full and candid account from the witness.[276] However, in the case of a witness under the age of eighteen, or a witness with a mental or physical disability that interferes with an ability to communicate evidence, the order is presumptively available. In those cases, the trial judge "shall" grant the application unless the order would interfere with the proper administration of justice.[277]

Where a support person is ordered, the judge can order that that person and the witness not communicate during the witness's testimony.[278] Another witness cannot be the support person unless that is necessary for the proper administration of justice.[279]

The use of a screen is only designed to avoid a face-to-face confrontation between the witness and the accused; the screen allows the witness not to see the accused, but the accused is still able to see the witness.[280] The trial judge has substantial latitude in ordering this procedure, which was found not to violate the *Charter*.[281]

---

276 Sections 486.1(2) and 486.2(2). Note that ss 486.2(4) & (5) create a similar ability concerning any witness in the case of terrorism and organized crime offences, which is available in addition when the order is necessary to protect the safety of the witness.

277 Sections 486.1(1) and 486.2(1).

278 Sections 486.1(5).

279 Section 486.1(4).

280 *Levogiannis*, above note 125. Similarly, where the witness testifies from outside the courtroom, arrangements must be made to permit the accused to watch the testimony by closed circuit television: s 486.2(7).

281 *Levogiannis*, *ibid*, found that a predecessor version of the section did not violate the *Charter*. An order for screens on that version was available only in the case of trials for sexual offences, and there was no presumption that the order would be made for child witnesses. Subsequently the introduction of that presumption was found also not to violate the *Charter*, and to be simply "the next step in the evolution of the rules of evidence" around child and vulnerable witnesses: *R v JZS*, 2008 BCCA 401 at para 43, aff'd 2010 SCC 1.

In general on this subject, see Nicholas Bala & Hilary McCormack, "Accommodating the Criminal Process to Child Witnesses" (1994) 25 *Criminal Reports* (4th) 341. In addition, see Nicholas Bala, RCL Lindsay, & E McNamara, "Testimonial Aids for Children: The Canadian Experience with Closed Circuit Television, Screens and Videotapes" (2001) 44 *Criminal Law Quarterly* 461, for

A judge also has a great deal of general discretion in the course of the trial, from intervening to ask questions personally to expressing opinions on the facts. Further, a judge has a trial management power which includes

> the power to place reasonable limits on oral submissions, to direct that submissions be made in writing, to require an offer of proof before embarking on a lengthy *voir dire*, to defer rulings, to direct the manner in which a *voir dire* is conducted, especially whether to do so on the basis of testimony or in some other form, and exceptionally to direct the order in which evidence is called.[282]

An overriding rule, however, is that the trial judge's behaviour must not create a reasonable apprehension of bias. Rudeness on the part of a judge to either the Crown or the defence might or might not cross the threshold, and the fact that the rudeness was equally distributed might or might not help prevent a reasonable apprehension of bias.[283] A judge who expresses an opinion on whether the accused has presented any defence while the Crown decides whether to cross-examine might be seen as making the trial proceed expeditiously.[284] A judge can ask questions of the accused or other witnesses without creating a reasonable apprehension of bias, but, in some cases, a judge can carry this too far and a new trial will be necessary.[285] Whether this will be so very much depends on the facts of the individual case.

2) Publication Bans

A trial judge has the ability, in various circumstances, to order a publication ban. Such bans should be seen as exceptional, since they prevent public knowledge of court proceedings and, therefore, are in conflict with the open court principle. The Court has described the open court principle as a "hallmark of a democratic society" and a "cornerstone of

---

a survey of judges, lawyers, and victim-witness workers on their experience in court with these various devices. The changes to the *Code* provision itself were as a result of work by the Child Witness Project headed by Nicholas Bala.

282 *R v Felderhof* (2003), 17 CR (6th) 20 at para 57 (Ont CA).

283 See, for example, *R c Hébert*, 2014 QCCA 1441; *R v Pompeo*, 2014 BCCA 317; *R v Switzer*, 2014 ABCA 129; or *R v Gahan*, 2014 NBCA 18. See also Wayne K Gorman, "Judicial Intervention in the Trial Process" (2003) 47 *Criminal Law Quarterly* 481.

284 *R v Currie* (2002), 3 CR (6th) 377 (Ont CA).

285 *R v Brouillard*, [1985] 1 SCR 39. See also *R v Stucky*, 2009 ONCA 151, or *R v Bérubé*, 2007 QCCA 463.

the common law,"[286] but, nonetheless, in certain circumstances publication bans are permitted. Most of these bans have a statutory base, although there is also a common law ability to issue publication bans.

Most noteworthy is the ban outlined in section 486.4, which allows a judge to ban the publication of any information that would identify the complainant or a witness in a trial for a variety of listed sexual offences. A trial judge is required to inform any witness under eighteen and the complainant of the right to make such an application, and where one of those persons or the prosecutor applies, the judge is required to order the ban. An earlier version of this provision was upheld under the *Charter* on the basis that, although the provision violated freedom of the press, it was saved under section 1.[287] It is also of note that at the time, only prosecutors and complainants could make applications under the section. The Court's reasoning focused on the need to encourage victims of sexual assault to report the crime both in finding that there was a sufficiently important objective and in determining whether the provision was minimally impairing. Indeed, the Court specifically noted that it was not deciding whether the section would survive a *Charter* challenge if the prosecutor were not applying on the complainant's behalf. Since that time, the section has been expanded to include publication bans on behalf of witnesses under the age of eighteen. It is possible that a *Charter* challenge to the section in this context might succeed.

A similar power to seek a ban on publication of information disclosing the identity of a victim or witness is found in section 486.5. In this case, however, the ban is discretionary, and the trial judge must consider a variety of factors, including the right to a fair and public hearing, the risk of harm to the witness if her identity were disclosed, the impact of the order on freedom of expression, and a number of other matters. In addition, this type of publication ban can sometimes be issued to protect the identity of justice system participants, such as jurors, prosecutors, or police officers. The power is available only in trials for certain offences, such as those dealing with criminal organizations or terrorism offences.[288]

There are other particular bans within the *Code* as well. For example, section 276.3 prevents reporting of information regarding an application to admit evidence of previous sexual activity, and section 648 prevents the publication of evidence from a trial while jurors are separated before beginning deliberations. Section 517 entitles an ac-

---

286 *Vancouver Sun (Re)*, [2004] 2 SCR 332 at paras 23–24.
287 *Canadian Newspapers Co v Canada (Attorney General)*, [1988] 2 SCR 122.
288 Sections 486.5(2) and 486.2(5).

cused to a mandatory publication ban on all information disclosed at a bail hearing.[289]

The *YCJA* bans the publication of some information too. Subject to exceptions dealing with public safety, no one is to publish information that could identify a young person as one being dealt with under the Act, though this publication ban does not apply in the case of a young person who receives an adult sentence.[290] Similarly, no one can publish information identifying a young person who was a victim or a witness at proceedings concerning another young person. In the latter case, the young person can apply to be permitted to publish such information personally and is entitled to do so after reaching the age of eighteen.[291]

Finally, the Court discussed a trial judge's common law power to grant a publication ban in *Dagenais v Canadian Broadcasting Corp*[292] and later cases. An application for a ban can be made to the trial judge, to another judge of that court if no trial judge has been appointed, or to a judge of the superior court if the level of court for trial cannot yet be established. The application is to be made in the absence of the jury, and the judge has discretion to decide whether to give notice of the application to the media. The trial judge also has discretion as to whether to grant the media standing in the application, whether to permit them to cross-examine or present evidence, and so on. The judge also, of course, has discretion in deciding whether to grant the publication ban itself or not. In exercising that discretion, however, the trial judge is required to act in accordance with the *Charter*. Thus, the Court held, the traditional common law rule that a ban would be granted if there was a real and substantial risk of interference with the right to a fair trial needed to be modified to recognize the *Charter* guarantee of freedom of expression and freedom of the press.

Subsequently, in *R v Mentuck* the Court returned to the subject of publication bans, but this time in circumstances where the ban was sought by the Crown and no fair trial right was at issue.[293] *Mentuck* involved an undercover police investigation of the type usually referred to as the "Mr. Big" scenario. In this technique, a suspect is induced, on one of a variety

---

289 This publication ban was challenged under the *Charter* but upheld: see *Toronto Star Newspapers Ltd v Canada*, 2010 SCC 21.

290 *YCJA*, above note 102, s 110. Where a young person receives a youth sentence for a presumptive offence (that is, one where the accused will presumptively receive an adult sentence), the *YCJA* creates a reverse onus requiring the young person to justify the publication ban. That reverse onus has been struck down by the Court as violating the *Charter*: see *R v DB*, 2008 SCC 25.

291 *YCJA*, above note 102, s 111.

292 [1994] 3 SCR 835 [*Dagenais*].

293 2001 SCC 76 [*Mentuck*].

of pretexts, to give the details of an offence he has committed to what he believes to be the members of a criminal organization to which he is being recruited. The Crown sought a publication ban both on the names of the particular police officers who had been involved in Mentuck's undercover operation, as well as on the release of information about the technique itself. The Court upheld the former ban, but not the latter.

In the course of discussing the appropriate test for a publication ban, the Court observed that the *Dagenais* test was not phrased in a way that would always address the underlying issue. In *Dagenais*, the question had been whether a fair trial right was compromised, and the Court had formulated a test that asked only about that interest. In *Mentuck*, it recognized that a broader range of interests might need to be contrasted to the freedom of expression. The Court therefore concluded that the real question was of finding a balance between the many possible interests that made up the proper administration of justice on the one hand, and freedom of expression on the other. Accordingly, the "*Dagenais/Mentuck*" test for publications bans is as follows:

> A publication ban should only be ordered when:
> (a)   such an order is necessary in order to prevent a serious risk to the proper administration of justice because reasonably alternative measures will not prevent the risk; and
> (b)   the salutary effects of the publication ban outweigh the deleterious effects on the rights and interests of the parties and the public, including the effects on the right to free expression, the right of the accused to a fair and public trial, and the efficacy of the administration of justice.[294]

The person seeking the publication ban has the onus. The first step requires that the ban is as narrowly circumscribed as possible while still achieving the objectives and that no other effective means would achieve the objectives. The second step involves weighing the importance of the objectives of the particular ban and its probable effects against the importance of the particular expression that will be limited. In *Dagenais*, the publication bans were not justified because there were various alternatives such as adjourning trials, changing venues, sequestering jurors, allowing challenges for cause and *voir dires* during jury selection, and providing strong judicial direction to the jury. In *Mentuck*, the ban on the names of particular officers was justified since they were using their real names, and therefore, their safety and the integrity of other undercover investigations would have been jeopardized. The ban on reporting the technique in general was not justified because the Court was uncon-

---

294 *Ibid* at para 32.

vinced that a serious risk to the effectiveness of the technique would arise
if its existence were reported in newspapers.

The *Dagenais/Mentuck* test applies not only to publication bans but to
all discretionary decisions that affect the openness of proceedings and freedom of expression.[295] A decision about whether to release exhibits from a
trial (such as a videotaped statement) to the media is therefore also settled
by that test.[296] Different considerations might be relevant to the balancing in
that context, such as that a person testifying in court is often compelled to
do so while a person making an out-of-court statement does so voluntarily.

The open court principle is relevant in other contexts than publication bans. For example, the judge can decide to exclude any or all
members of the public from all or part of the trial where it is "in the
interest of public morals, the maintenance of order or the proper administration of justice."[297] The *Code* specifically notes that the "proper
administration of justice" includes ensuring the interests of witnesses
under the age of eighteen in sexual assault trials and of justice system
participants.[298] A trial judge who does not grant a request for exclusion
in a sexual offence case must give reasons for not having done so.[299]

This power conflicts with the open court principle and can also conflict with freedom of the press since it might prevent journalists from
being present for and reporting on some portion of a trial. The Court
has held that the provision therefore violates section 2(b) of the *Charter*,
but nonetheless is saved as a reasonable limit, provided the discretion to
use the section is exercised properly. Accordingly, the Court held:

(a) the judge must consider the available options and consider whether there are any other reasonable and effective alternatives available;
(b) the judge must consider whether the order is limited as much as
possible; and
(c) the judge must weigh the importance of the objectives of the particular order and its probable effects against the importance of openness
and the particular expression that will be limited in order to ensure
that the positive and negative effects of the order are proportionate.[300]

The burden is on the person seeking the exclusion to provide a
sufficient factual foundation, and to show that the particular order is

---

295 *Vancouver Sun (Re)*, above note 286.
296 *Canadian Broadcasting Corp v the Queen*, 2011 SCC 3.
297 Section 486(1). The section also permits exclusion of the public "to prevent injury
to international relations or national defence or national security."
298 Section 486(2).
299 Section 486(3).
300 *Canadian Broadcasting Corp v New Brunswick (Attorney General)*, [1996] 3 SCR
480 at para 69.

necessary, that it is as limited as possible, and that the salutary effects of the order are proportionate to its deleterious effects.

The Court also relied on the open court principle and an analogy to the *Dagenais/Mentuck* test in considering whether a witness ought to be allowed to wear a niqab in court. The complainant in *R v NS* was a Muslim woman testifying at a preliminary inquiry on sexual assault charges. She wanted to wear her niqab while in court, in accordance with her religious beliefs, while the accused argued that this would interfere with their right to a fair trial, since it made it impossible to see her face as she testified. The Court, in a split decision, concluded that this conflict between the open court principle and trial freedom should be handled by a test which relied heavily on the open court principle as articulated in cases relating to publication bans. They held that when such issues arose, they should be answered on a case-by-case basis by asking four questions:

1. Would requiring the witness to remove the niqab while testifying interfere with her religious freedom?
2. Would permitting the witness to wear the niqab while testifying create a serious risk to trial fairness?
3. Is there a way to accommodate both rights and avoid the conflict between them?
4. If no accommodation is possible, do the salutary effects of requiring the witness to remove the niqab outweigh the deleterious effects of doing so?[301]

3) Contempt of Court

Judges have the power to find people in contempt of court. This common law power is expressly preserved by section 9 of the *Code*, and appeal procedures from it are set out in section 10. Contempt is divided into contempt committed in the face of the court and contempt not committed in the face of the court, a distinction still reflected in section 10 of the *Code*. Superior courts have jurisdiction over both types of contempt, while inferior courts can punish only the former. The *YCJA* gives youth justice courts very broad jurisdiction, including contempt in the face of and not in the face of either the youth justice court or any other court, when it is committed by a young person.[302] Only contempt in the face of the court will concern us here.

Contempt can cover a variety of behaviours, including insolence to the court or refusal to answer questions while under oath, for example.[303]

---

301 2012 SCC 72 at para 9 [*NS*].
302 *YCJA*, above note 102, s 15.
303 See *R v Arradi*, 2003 SCC 23 [*Arradi*], and *R v K(B)*, [1995] 4 SCR 186 [*K(B)*].

The accused, a witness, or counsel can be cited in contempt. The power to punish for contempt is intended to maintain the dignity of the court and to ensure a fair trial. A judge can respond to contemptuous behaviour in either of two ways: (1) through the ordinary procedure, which gives the accused the usual procedural guarantees of a criminal trial, or (2) through a more summary procedure.[304] The summary procedure can be used only where it is urgent and imperative to act immediately and, other than in exceptional circumstances, that procedure must comply with the requirements of natural justice. In general terms, this means that "only '[t]he least possible power adequate to the end proposed' should be used."[305] In particular, it means that normally a three-step process is to be followed. First, the person is to be put on notice that she will be required to show cause as to why she should not be found in contempt of court. In other words, the person is being "cited" in contempt. Second, an adjournment should be given, long enough to allow the person an opportunity to consult with counsel and possibly be represented by counsel. Finally, a person who is found in contempt should be allowed to make representations as to sentence. Although in some cases not all of these steps need to be followed, departure from this model is permitted only in exceptional circumstances. Failure to follow this process is an error of law.[306]

The contempt proceedings can also be conducted in the jury's presence where the contempt has occurred in front of it, since the jury helps make up the court.[307] However, it must be made clear to the jury that the accused's guilt in the contempt proceeding cannot be used to assess guilt in the actual trial.

4) Mistrials

One particular judicial power worth discussing separately is the authority to declare a mistrial. A trial judge has the authority to declare a mistrial at virtually any point in the proceedings, from as early as the jury selection stage[308] to as late as the post-conviction but pre-sentence stage.[309] Indeed, a trial judge still has jurisdiction to declare a mistrial after an appeal has

---

304 *Arradi*, above note 303 at para 29. See *R v Vermette*, [1987] 1 SCR 577, for an example of contempt being dealt with through the ordinary procedure of a separate trial on the charge.

305 *Arradi*, above note 303 at para 33, quoting *K(B)*, above note 303 at para 13, itself quoting *United States v Wilson*, 421 US 309 at 319 (1975).

306 *Arradi*, above note 303.

307 Note, similarly, that another judge of the same court is not permitted to hear the contempt proceeding: *R v Doz*, [1987] 2 SCR 463.

308 *R v Williams*, [1998] 1 SCR 1128 [*Williams* 1998], and *Bengert*, above note 235.

309 *R v McAnespie*, [1993] 4 SCR 501.

been launched, provided a sentence has not yet been handed down.[310] Where there was a jury trial, however, the leading view is that a trial judge is *functus* and no longer has the jurisdiction to declare a mistrial once the jury has rendered its verdict.[311]

A wide variety of issues can lead to a mistrial application. Among them are inappropriate publicity or other errors during jury selection, improper comments by the Crown prosecutor during an opening statement or closing submission, or inadmissible evidence accidentally being given to the jury.[312] A mistrial is not automatically granted in the case of such errors and, in fact, is more a remedy of last resort. Where possible, a trial judge should first try to remedy whatever prejudice has arisen by less drastic means. Other remedies might include making an adjournment, reopening the case, or, quite commonly, clearly instructing the jury that they are to ignore the submissions or information they ought not to have heard. It is only where such other remedies are insufficient that a mistrial should be granted.[313] Put another way, "the general principle is that a mistrial is declared if the Crown's jury address is so improper that it deprives the accused of the right to a fair trial."[314]

Although it is typically the accused who applies for a mistrial, it is also open to the Crown to do so.[315] Similarly, although circumstances

---

310 *R v MacDonald* (1991), 107 NSR (2d) 374 (SCAD) [*MacDonald*].

311 *R v Halcrow*, 2008 ABCA 319, leave to appeal to SCC refused, [2008] SCCA No 532. See also *R v Henderson* (2004), 189 CCC (3d) 447; *R v Lawrence*, 2001 NSCA 44.

312 See, for example, *Williams* 1998, above note 308; *R v Dore* (2002), 4 CR (6th) 81 (Ont CA); *Grabowski v the Queen*, [1985] 2 SCR 434; *Pisani v the Queen*, [1971] SCR 738 [*Pisani*]; *R v Khan*, 2001 SCC 86 [*Khan*].

313 See, for example, *R v D(LE)*, [1989] 2 SCR 111 at para 28:

> . . . should inadmissible evidence be adduced, the trial Judge should either instruct the jury immediately to disregard it or, if it is of so prejudicial a nature that the jury would not have the capability of disregarding it, he should discharge the jury and order a new trial . . . . If the trial judge was of the view that an immediate caution to the jury to disregard the evidence was insufficient to ensure a fair trial, then his course was to direct a mistrial rather than admit the evidence of similar acts which had previously been excluded.

quoting, in part, from *R v Ambrose* (1975), 25 CCC (2d) 90 (NBSCAD), aff'd [1977] 2 SCR 717.

314 Justice L'Heureux-Dubé, dissenting in *Rose*, above note 127 at para 66, citing *Pisani*, above note 312.

315 The Crown applied successfully for a mistrial in *Williams* 1998, above note 308, and unsuccessfully in *Trakas*, above note 189. In *R v CDH*, 2015 ONCA 102 [*CDH*], the Crown obtained an order for a mistrial when the judge, after conviction but before sentencing, had a private meeting with the officer in charge of the case in which they discussed the evidence in the case, the witnesses, and some independent research the judge had done on Match.com.

leading to a mistrial application are more likely to arise in a jury trial, in principle, the power exists in trials held by judge alone as well.[316]

For the most part, the authority to order a mistrial comes from the common law. It is a discretionary decision and although it is subject to appeal, an appeal court is not to interfere with the trial judge's exercise of discretion unless clearly satisfied that the judge proceeded on some wrong principle or was wrong.[317] As noted above, there is also a discretion in section 653 of the *Code* for a trial judge to declare a mistrial if satisfied that a jury is unable to agree on a verdict. Although section 653(2) says that this discretion is not reviewable, there are suggestions that the subsection might not withstand *Charter* scrutiny.[318]

As a general rule, a new trial can be held following a mistrial, and the fact of a mistrial does not allow an accused to plead *autrefois acquit* or *autrefois convict*. In particular circumstances, the *Charter* might prevent a new trial from being held after an improper declaration of a mistrial, but only where the principles of fundamental justice are in issue. Where a trial judge declares a mistrial to save a floundering Crown case and give it time to obtain further witnesses, for example, the *Charter* might prevent a new trial, but in ordinary circumstances new proceedings can be commenced.[319]

FURTHER READINGS

BALA, NICHOLAS, & HILARY MCCORMACK. "Accommodating the Criminal Process to Child Witnesses" (1994) 25 *Criminal Reports* (4th) 341.

————, RCL LINDSAY, & E MCNAMARA. "Testimonial Aids for Children: The Canadian Experience with Closed Circuit Television, Screens and Videotapes" (2001) 44 *Criminal Law Quarterly* 461.

---

316 *CDH, ibid*, was a judge-alone trial. *MacDonald*, above note 310, was also a judge-alone trial; the judge contacted the Crown and a Crown witness, without the knowledge of the accused, following conviction but before sentencing, and the trial judge granted a subsequent application for a mistrial brought by the Crown and the defence.

317 *Bengert*, above note 235. See also *Khan*, above note 312.

318 See *Pan*, above note 219 at para 111. The section was challenged in that case, but the *Charter* issue was not decided since the Crown did not dispute the ability of appeal courts to review the initial decision.

319 *Pan, ibid* at para 113.

CHOPRA, SONIA R, & JAMES RP OGLOFF. "Evaluating Jury Secrecy: Implications for Academic Research and Juror Stress" (2000) 44 *Criminal Law Quarterly* 190.

GORMAN, WAYNE K. "Judicial Intervention in the Trial Process" (2003) 47 *Criminal Law Quarterly* 481.

LAW REFORM COMMISSION OF CANADA. *The Jury* (Ottawa: Law Reform Commission, 1982).

————. *The Charge Document in Criminal Cases* (Ottawa: Law Reform Commission of Canada, 1987).

————. *Double Jeopardy, Pleas and Verdicts* (Ottawa: Law Reform Commission of Canada, 1991).

LAYTON, DAVID, & MICHEL PROULX. *Ethics and Canadian Criminal Law*, 2d ed (Toronto: Irwin Law, 2015).

MAINVILLE, CHRISTINE. "Report on the CIAJ's Complex Criminal Trials Roundtable" (2015) 62 *Criminal Law Quarterly* 339.

QUIGLEY, TIM. "Principled Reform of Criminal Procedure" in Don Stuart, RJ Delisle, & Allan Manson, eds, *Towards a Clear and Just Criminal Law* (Toronto: Carswell, 1999).

————. *Procedure in Canadian Criminal Law*, 2d ed (Toronto: Thomson Carswell, 2005) (loose-leaf) ch 17, 18, 20, & 21.

QUINLAN, PAUL. "Secrecy of Jury Deliberations—Is the Cost Too High?" (1993) 22 *Criminal Reports* (4th) 127.

STUART, DON. *Charter Justice in Canadian Criminal Law*, 5th ed (Toronto: Thomson Carswell, 2010) ch 2 and 6.

TANOVICH, DAVID M. "Upping the Ante in Directed Verdict Cases Where the Evidence Is Circumstantial" (1998) 5 *Criminal Reports* (5th) 21.

CHAPTER 12

APPEALS

A. INTRODUCTION

Rights of appeal in the Canadian criminal justice system are entirely a creature of statute. Various appeal provisions are set out in the *Criminal Code*, and in addition, the *Code* provides that only appeals authorized in Parts XXI and XXVI can be brought with regard to indictable offences.[1] In fact, however, that has not operated to completely restrict the methods of review for decisions of the lower courts.

First, applications for extraordinary remedies such as *certiorari* can be brought in some cases, though the scope of such applications is more limited than an appeal (see the discussion of this issue in Chapter 9). In addition, in some unusual circumstances an appeal to the Supreme Court might be possible through section 40 of the *Supreme Court Act*.[2] That section permits appeals "from any final or other judgment of . . . the highest court of final resort in a province," provided that the issue is important enough.[3] In *Dagenais v Canadian Broadcasting Corp.*, the Court held that although a literal interpretation of section 674 of the *Code* would exclude relying on section 40, such a literal interpretation

---

1   Section 674.
2   RSC 1985, c S-26.
3   The phrase used in s 40 is that the question is "by reason of its public importance or the importance of any issue of law or any issue of mixed law and fact involved in that question, one that ought to be decided by the Supreme Court or is, for any other reason, of such a nature or significance as to warrant decision by it . . . ."

could not be adopted.[4] In that case, section 40 was used to allow a third party (the media) to appeal a publication ban, an appeal that would not have been possible under any of the *Code*'s appeal provisions. In *R v Cunningham* the Court concluded that an appeal of a decision whether to allow defence counsel to withdraw should also proceed under section 40, on the basis that defence counsel (like the media in *Dagenais*) is a third party to the main criminal action.[5] See also *R v Laba*, where section 40 permitted the Crown to appeal a ruling that overturned a reverse onus provision in the *Code*, even though they had been successful in the result at the court of appeal: in effect, the Crown was appealing a case that it had won.[6] In *R v Shea* the Court concluded that section 40 permitted appeals of a provincial court of appeal's decision to extend the application for an appeal, though they also observed that it was only in very rare circumstances that such a decision could be important enough to warrant granting leave.[7]

The provision is sometimes used in cases where an appeal of an interlocutory order is in issue, such as when a third party challenges an order for production of privileged communications, as in *R v McClure*[8] or *R v Brown*.[9] In the latter case, the Court noted that such appeals reach it without having been considered by any court of appeal, which denies the Court the benefit of a fuller record and input from that lower court. They suggested that this gap in the *Code*'s appeal provisions was anomalous and an "unnecessary encumbrance" that should be fixed by Parliament.[10]

The focus of this chapter, however, will be on the statutory appeal powers set out in the *Code* itself. Although some issues, such as time limits and procedures, are set by rules of court,[11] for the most part, the *Code* determines what can and cannot be done.

The *Code* creates separate sets of rules for appeals of indictable offences and of summary conviction offences. However, as a matter of convenience it does permit the appeal of a summary conviction matter to be heard along with that of an indictable offence where the two offences were tried together.[12] In the case of indictable offences, different appeal

---

4   [1994] 3 SCR 835 [*Dagenais*].
5   2010 SCC 10 [*Cunningham*].
6   [1994] 3 SCR 965.
7   2010 SCC 26.
8   2001 SCC 14.
9   2002 SCC 32 [*Brown*].
10   *Ibid* at para 110.
11   Section 678.
12   Sections 675(1.1) and 676(1.1).

rights are given to an accused and the Crown. For summary conviction offences, however, the appeal rights are essentially parallel. The *Code* provisions deal with appeals of the result in the trial, findings that a person is not criminally responsible or is not fit to stand trial, and appeals of sentence. It is the first of these that is of primary interest in this chapter.

B. APPEALS OF INDICTABLE OFFENCES

1) Appeals by the Accused

a) Overview of Appeal Provisions

At first glance, it would appear that an accused appealing a conviction has an enormously broad right of appeal. Section 675(1)(a) says that a person can appeal a conviction based on a question of law alone, on a question of fact, on a question of mixed law and fact, or on any ground of appeal "that appears to the court of appeal to be a sufficient ground of appeal."[13] In fact, the likelihood of an appeal succeeding is not nearly as great as that section alone suggests. These bases for appeal pass through at least three "filters," each limiting the grounds upon which an appeal might succeed.

The first two filters are found in section 686(1)(a) of the *Code*. Section 675 sets out the bases upon which an appeal can be *made*; the grounds upon which an appeal can be *granted* are considerably narrower. Section 686(1)(a) sets out those grounds:

> (i)   the verdict should be set aside on the ground that it is unreasonable or cannot be supported by the evidence,
> (ii) the judgment of the trial court should be set aside on the ground of a wrong decision on a question of law, or
> (iii) on any ground there was a miscarriage of justice.

---

13   Section 675(1)(a). Questions of law can be appealed as of right, while the other grounds require leave of the court of appeal. Questions of fact or mixed law and fact can also be appealed "on the certificate of the trial judge that the case is a proper case for appeal." The "sufficient ground" basis of appeal is meant as a kind of residual ground, to allow appeals that should be permitted but do not fit neatly into the other grounds. For example, an application to an appeal court to withdraw a guilty plea based on incompetent representation at trial would be brought under this ground: see, for example, *R v Short*, 2012 SKCA 85.

There is a rough conformity between sections 675 and 686. Section 675(1)(a) permits an appeal to be launched based on a question of law, and section 686(1)(a)(ii) allows an appeal to succeed on the basis of a wrong decision on a question of law. Section 675(1)(b) permits an appeal to be launched based on questions of fact or mixed law and fact, and section 686(1)(a)(i) allows an appeal to succeed on the basis that it cannot be supported by the evidence. Section 675(1)(a)(iii) permits an appeal to be launched based on the catch-all ground that it appears to be a sufficient ground of appeal, and section 686(1)(a)(iii) allows an appeal to succeed on the catch-all basis that there was a miscarriage of justice.[14] It is important, however, to note the differences between section 675 and section 686.

An appeal can be made under section 675 on the basis of an error relating to a question of fact or mixed fact and law. However, an appeal will not necessarily be granted under section 686(1) simply because such an error is shown. Rather, only such an error that results in an unreasonable verdict or a miscarriage of justice will be sufficient. That is the first filter.

The second filter relates to the primary remaining ground of appeal in section 675: appeals based on a question of law. At face value, section 686(1)(a)(ii) says that demonstrating a wrong decision on such a question will lead to a successful appeal. However, there is some ambiguity in the meaning of the phrase "question of law": it has a broader meaning in section 675 than in section 686(1)(a). Therefore, that an issue is a question of law for the jurisdictional purpose of deciding whether a ground of appeal *exists* does not mean that it is a question of law for the purpose of deciding whether the appeal should be *granted*. For example, whether a verdict is unreasonable is a different issue from whether there was an error on a question of law for purposes of section 686, but whether a verdict is unreasonable is a question of law for purposes of section 675.[15] This change in characterization might cause

---

14   *R v H(E)* (1997), 33 OR (3d) 202 at 210 (CA), observes the connection between these two provisions:

> Section 675(1)(a)(iii) specifically refers to any ground of appeal which does not involve a question of law alone, a question of fact, or a question of mixed law and fact. Sopinka and Gelowitz, in *The Conduct of an Appeal* (Toronto: Butterworths, 1993), note, with respect to this provision, that "[t]his is a residual jurisdiction to relieve against miscarriages of justice that do not strictly raise questions of law or fact."

15   See, for example, *R v RP*, 2012 SCC 22 at para 5 [*RP*]. *R v Biniaris*, 2000 SCC 15 at para 22 [*Biniaris*], explains why the distinction is not drawn at the early stage:

> The sole purpose of the exercise here, in identifying the reasonableness of a verdict as a question of fact, law or both, is to determine access to appel-

the first filter to be relevant: for example, despite the error in law the verdict still might not be unreasonable, and so the appeal might not be granted. In addition, since asking about unreasonableness involves greater deference to the trial judge (see the discussion of standard of review at Section B(1)(b)(i), below in this chapter), this further acts to limit the possibility of a successful appeal.[16]

The third filter is found in the fact that even if an appeal meets the conditions of section 686(1)(a), it might not be granted nonetheless. The grounds upon which an appeal might succeed are narrowed even further by section 686(1)(b), which sets out the grounds upon which the court of appeal can dismiss an appeal. Most obviously, a court can dismiss an appeal if none of the above grounds for granting it is made out. However, that is not the only basis for dismissing an appeal: even if the accused does succeed in showing that one of the grounds of appeal in section 686(1)(a) is made out, the appeal might still fail.

An appeal can be dismissed on the basis that, although there was an error, the accused "was properly convicted on another count or part of the indictment."[17] In addition, section 686(b) contains two other bases upon which an appeal might be dismissed despite an error:

(iii) notwithstanding that the court is of the opinion that on any ground mentioned in subparagraph (a)(ii) the appeal might be decided in favour of the appellant, it is of the opinion that no substantial wrong or miscarriage of justice has occurred, or

(iv) notwithstanding any procedural irregularity at trial, the trial court had jurisdiction over the class of offence of which the appellant was convicted and the court of appeal is of the opinion that the appellant suffered no prejudice thereby.

The former of these two is often referred to as the "curative proviso." The effect of it, along with section 686(1)(b)(iv), is that not all errors of law will lead to a successful appeal either. Errors in law that cause no substantial wrong, do not create a miscarriage of justice, or are mere procedural irregularities will not lead to a successful appeal by the accused.

---

late review. One can plausibly maintain, on close scrutiny of any decision under review, that the conclusion that a verdict was unreasonable was reached sometimes mostly as a matter of law, in other cases predominantly as a matter of factual assessment. But when that exercise is undertaken as a jurisdictional threshold exercise, little is gained by embarking on such a case-by-case analysis.

16   See *R v Grouse*, 2004 NSCA 108 at paras 33–43, for a detailed explanation of this point.

17   Section 686(1)(b)(i).

These last two provisions are discussed in greater detail at Sections B(1)(b)(iv) and (v), below in this chapter. For the moment, it is sufficient to note that only an error of law under section 686(1)(a)(ii) could be saved by the curative proviso in 686(1)(b)(ii). If the appeal was based on either an unreasonable verdict or a miscarriage of justice then the harmless error exception has no application. It has been suggested that the underlying theory of this section is that appeals are fundamentally concerned with miscarriages of justice. Sections 686(1) (a)(i) and (iii) (unreasonable verdicts and other miscarriages of justice) necessarily fall into that category, and errors of law are presumed to fall into it unless the Crown shows otherwise.[18]

Finally, note that appeal courts can deal with issues other than whether the accused was convicted or acquitted. Section 686 also gives the appeal court the ability to hear appeals relating to findings that an accused was unfit to stand trial, that an accused was not criminally responsible by reason of mental disorder, or with regard to special verdicts.[19] In addition, of course, a court of appeal can vary a sentence imposed on an accused.[20]

b) Appeal Provisions in Depth

i) Standard of Review

Since the grounds for an appeal by an accused extend beyond errors of law to include unreasonable verdicts and miscarriages of justice, appeal courts must review a variety of findings from lower courts. Specifically, it can be necessary to review questions of law, questions of fact, inferences of fact, and questions of mixed fact and law. The Supreme Court considered the standard of review for each of these issues in *Housen v Nikolaisen*.[21]

With regard to pure questions of law, the standard of review is correctness, and so an appellate court can substitute its opinion for that of the trial judge. It can do this because appellate courts delineate and refine legal rules and ensure their universal application, which requires that they have a broad scope of review with respect to matters of law.[22] Questions of fact, however, are reviewable only on a higher standard. A finding of fact should not be overturned in the absence of a "palp-

---

18 See *R v Morrissey* (1995), 38 CR (4th) 4 (Ont CA) [*Morrissey*].

19 Sections 686(1)(c) & (d).

20 Section 687.

21 [2002] 2 SCR 235 [*Housen*]. *Housen* is a civil case, but the Court has noted the relevance of its discussion of these issues to criminal matters: see *R v Buhay*, 2003 SCC 30.

22 *Housen*, above note 21 at para 9.

able and overriding error," which amounts to "prohibiting an appellate court from reviewing a trial judge's decision if there was some evidence upon which he or she could have relied to reach that conclusion."[23] The Court has offered three basic rationales for this approach. First, given the number, length, and cost of appeals, there should be limits on how readily available they should be—deferring to a trial judge's findings of fact helps to impose a limit and does so on a principled basis. Second, trial judges are presumed to be competent and able to decide cases justly and fairly—allowing regular appeals would undermine that presumption as well as public confidence in the trial process. Finally, trial judges are better situated to make factual findings because they hear the testimony being given, are exposed to all the evidence, and are familiar with the case as a whole. Their primary role is to weigh and assess evidence, and so their expertise should be respected.

For essentially the same reasons, inferences of fact are held to the same standard of review as findings of fact. The issue is not whether there is evidence that reasonably supports the inference, but rather whether some palpable and overriding error can be shown from drawing the inference.

Questions of mixed law and fact are, in some ways, the most complicated. The Court has noted that these issues fall on a spectrum. Some things that may, at first, appear to be a question of mixed fact and law may be reduced to a question of law, in which case, the correctness standard would apply. However, in other cases the higher standard of review is required, and so the general rule is that where an issue on appeal involves the trial judge's interpretation of the evidence as a whole, it should be overturned only in the case of palpable and overriding error.[24]

ii) Unreasonable Verdicts

Section 686(1)(a)(i) permits an appeal to be allowed on the basis that the verdict "is unreasonable or cannot be supported by the evidence." This provision applies differently depending on whether the conviction being appealed came from a jury or from a judge alone. In essence, section 686(1)(a)(i) creates a single basis for granting an appeal from the decision of a jury, but two bases for overturning a judge-alone verdict: either that it was "unreasonable" *or* that it "cannot be supported by the evidence." In practice, that means that any verdict can be overturned if it is not one that a properly instructed jury or a judge could reasonably have rendered, and in addition, a judge-alone verdict can be overturned

---

23 *Ibid* at para 1.
24 *Ibid* at para 36.

if the trial judge has drawn an inference or made a finding of fact essential to the verdict that (1) is plainly contradicted by the evidence relied on by the trial judge in support of that inference or finding, or (2) is shown to be incompatible with evidence that has not otherwise been contradicted or rejected by the trial judge.[25]

Juries do not give reasons, and, indeed, jurors and everyone else are precluded from revealing anything concerning the deliberations in the jury room.[26] Further, if the jury was charged incorrectly, then there would be an error of law, and the appeal would be based on section 686(1)(a)(ii) rather than (i). Accordingly, the issue of unreasonable verdicts in jury cases arises when the jury has been charged correctly but nonetheless returns with a verdict that seems questionable.

The basic standard for assessing whether a verdict fails on this ground is "whether the verdict is one that a properly instructed jury acting judicially, could reasonably have rendered."[27] For practical purposes this test focuses on the second clause in section 686(1)(a)(i), whether the verdict can be supported by the evidence. This test is framed by two well-established boundaries.[28] On the one hand, the court of appeal should not simply consider the sufficiency of the evidence, and it ought to engage in some weighing of that evidence.[29] On the other hand, the court of appeal cannot merely substitute its view for that of the trier of fact, but rather must ask whether the trier of fact could reasonably have reached the conclusion it did on the evidence before it.[30]

A general sense of unease or lurking doubt about a jury's decision is not a sufficient basis for a court of appeal to intervene. Such a feeling might trigger a closer inquiry, but cannot be the end of the analysis. The appeal court must proceed further and articulate as precisely as possible what features of the case suggest that the jury's verdict was unreasonable.[31]

Where a jury has been properly instructed but has returned an unreasonable verdict nonetheless, it means that the jury was not acting judicially. It might, for example, have failed to adequately apply advice

---

25   *RP*, above note 15 at para 9.

26   See s 649 of the *Code* and the discussion of this issue in Chapter 11, Section E(4).

27   *R v Yebes*, [1987] 2 SCR 168 at para 16 [*Yebes*], reaffirmed in *Biniaris*, above note 15, and *R v Beaudry*, 2007 SCC 5 [*Beaudry*].

28   *R v WH*, 2013 SCC 22.

29   *Biniaris*, above note 15 at para 36. See also *Yebes*, above note 27 at para 25:
    "While the Court of Appeal must not merely substitute its view for that of the jury, in order to apply the test the Court must re-examine and to some extent reweigh and consider the effect of the evidence."

30   *R v Burns*, [1994] 1 SCR 656.

31   *Biniaris*, above note 15 at para 38.

that it was given about the frailties of eyewitness identification evidence or the limited use of similar fact evidence. To act judicially in this context requires that the jury act dispassionately, apply the law, and adjudicate on the basis of the record and nothing else. It also requires that the jury arrive "at a conclusion that does not conflict with the bulk of judicial experience."[32] This assessment would allow an appeal court to conclude, for example, that no jury could properly have been satisfied that identification was proved given the nature of the evidence led.

The same standard applies to deciding whether a judge has rendered an unreasonable verdict, but the task is different because the trial judge will have issued reasons showing the process by which the verdict was reached. Those reasons have an impact on an appeal court's ability to assess the verdict in two ways.

First, the presence of reasons can help show whether the verdict could be supported on the evidence. As the Court noted in *R v Biniaris*:

> [t]he review for unreasonableness on appeal is different, however, and somewhat easier when the judgment under attack is that of a single judge, at least when reasons for judgment of some substance are provided. In those cases, the reviewing appellate court may be able to identify a flaw in the evaluation of the evidence, or in the analysis, that will serve to explain the unreasonable conclusion reached, and justify the reversal.[33]

In addition, the presence of reasons allows a court of appeal to separately consider (in a way not possible for a jury verdict) whether a result is unreasonable even if it *could* be supported on the evidence. Section 686(1)(a)(i) refers to verdicts that are "unreasonable *or* cannot be supported on the evidence" and so

> No one should stand convicted on the strength of manifestly bad reasons—reasons that are illogical on their face, or contrary to the evidence—on the ground that another judge (who never did and never will try the case) could *but might not necessarily* have reached the same conclusion for *other reasons*.[34]

---

32   *Ibid* at para 40.
33   *Ibid* at para 37.
34   *Beaudry*, above note 27 at para 97 [emphasis in original]. This is from the decision of Fish J, who dissented in the result in *Beaudry*. In *R v Sinclair*, 2011 SCC 40 [*Sinclair*], a majority of seven judges confirmed that Fish J's approach in *Beaudry* was the proper one to appeals under s 686(1)(a)(i) of judge-alone trials.

Illogical or irrational reasoning could render a verdict unreasonable in various ways. The verdict might be unreasonable because a judge draws an inference or makes a finding of fact essential to it that is plainly contradicted by the evidence. That is, "[f]rom accepted evidence 'X', a court cannot lawfully infer 'not-X'."[35] Alternatively, a verdict could be unreasonable because the judge draws an inference or makes a finding of fact essential to the verdict which is demonstrably incompatible with evidence that was neither contradicted nor rejected.[36] These types of errors are ways of reasoning illogically from the evidence, which make the verdict unreasonable under section 686(1)(a)(i).[37] This issue is distinct from misapprehending the evidence, which would be a basis for appeal as a miscarriage of justice under section 686(1)(a)(iii).[38]

It matters, under this approach to appeals of judge-alone decisions, whether the appeal is granted because the decision is "unreasonable" or because it "cannot be supported by the evidence": see the discussion in Section B(1)(b)(vi), below in this chapter.

One particular circumstance in which a verdict by either judge or jury can be found to be unreasonable is when there are multiple accused or multiple counts and inconsistent verdicts. The same evidence could not reasonably lead both to a conviction and an acquittal. This basis of proving unreasonableness is a difficult one, however, because jury members are not bound by any particular theory of the case, need not all agree with one another on how to reach the same conclusion, and are allowed a wide latitude in accepting some, all, or none of each witness's testimony. Therefore, it is unusual to be able to say that the "same evidence" was in play in both cases.

This claim is more likely to succeed when there is only one accused. In *R v JF* the accused was charged with two counts of manslaughter by omission, in one case based on criminal negligence and in the other case based on failure to provide necessaries. In fact, though, the Crown argued that it was exactly the same omission that constituted both the criminal negligence and the failure to provide necessaries. The jury

---

35 *Sinclair, ibid* at para 19.

36 *Ibid* at para 21.

37 These two categories do not exhaust the possibilities. In *R v Wright*, 2013 MBCA 109, for example, the Manitoba Court of Appeal found a judge's verdict to be unreasonable although the error in the case was not precisely either of those identified in *Sinclair*. The judge, in a sexual assault case, had found that the complainant was not to be believed when she said she had not consented, but was to be believed when she said that she revoked her consent: absent an explanation, that was an unreasonable verdict.

38 *Sinclair*, above note 34 at para 15. See the discussion of misapprehension of evidence in Section B(1)(b)(iii), below in this chapter.

found the accused guilty on the criminal negligence-based charge but not guilty on the failure to provide necessaries charge. The Court held that these verdicts were inconsistent.[39]

In essence, it will be only a rare case, one where the evidence on two different charges is not logically separable, where an inconsistent verdict appeal will succeed. Since the question is whether the verdicts are supportable on any theory of the evidence that is consistent with the law, it is difficult to show that two verdicts are clearly inconsistent with one another. In the case of multiple accused charged with the same offence, it will typically be difficult to prove that verdicts are inconsistent even if some are convicted and some are acquitted, because the jury might have accepted evidence against one accused but not against the other.[40]

iii) Errors of Law and Miscarriages of Justice

Section 686(1)(a)(ii) permits an appeal to be granted in the case of "a wrong decision on a question of law," while section 686(1)(a)(iii) permits an appeal based on "a miscarriage of justice." It is convenient to consider these two grounds of appeal together because, although distinct, they share many features in common. Indeed, it has been suggested that the same rationale underlies all three bases of appeal in section 686(1)(a): that of miscarriage of justice. Section 686(1)(a)(i) sets out one basis upon which a verdict would be a miscarriage of justice (that it is unreasonable). Section 686(1)(a)(iii) explicitly includes any other miscarriage of justice as a basis for appeal. It has been suggested that section 686(1)(a)(ii), combined with the curative proviso, is an expression of the idea, mentioned above, that any error of law is presumed to be a miscarriage of justice unless the contrary is shown by the Crown.[41]

One feature that errors of law and miscarriages of justice have in common with one another, but which is distinct from unreasonable verdicts, is that there is no requirement that the verdict was not supportable on the evidence. In other words, even if the court of appeal concludes that a jury could have convicted despite the legal error or miscarriage, that fact is not a basis for rejecting the appeal.[42]

---

39 *R v JF*, 2008 SCC 60. The fault requirements for the two offences were not identical, in that one required only a marked departure from the standard of a reasonable person while the other required a marked *and substantial* departure. That did not render the verdicts consistent and, in fact, made the situation worse: the jury had found the higher standard to be met but the lower one not.

40 See, for example, *R v Pittiman*, 2006 SCC 9 [*Pittiman*].

41 *Morrissey*, above note 18.

42 *R v Lohrer*, 2004 SCC 80 at para 1 [*Lohrer*].

Most errors that are not based on the unreasonableness of a verdict will relate to an error of law. The primary reason for distinguishing between an error of law and a miscarriage of justice, as noted above, is the availability of the curative proviso—it cannot be resorted to in the latter case. However, to a certain extent this distinction is a formal one, rather than one of any real substance. Any mistake at trial that amounts to a miscarriage of justice would, in any case, fail to meet the test for the curative proviso. As a result, the underlying theory of the two subsections is really the same. What differs is the burden and standard of proof. The accused must show that there was an error of law or miscarriage of justice. If she does so, however, the Crown would, in the case of an error of law, be required to show that the curative proviso applied, and would have to meet a very high standard to demonstrate that claim (see the discussion in Section B(1)(b)(iv), below in this chapter).

An error of law is "any decision . . . that was an erroneous interpretation or application of the law."[43] There is no requirement that the error by itself must have led to any unfairness or prejudice; that is only an issue at the curative proviso stage.[44] So, for example, whether there is an air of reality to a defence is a legal question. It is therefore an error of law to instruct a jury on a defence when there is no air of reality to it, or to fail to instruct when there is.[45] The provision of flawed instructions to a jury is an error of law, as is an improper exhortation.[46] Using the summary procedure for contempt of court proceedings unnecessarily is an error of law.[47] Failing to give a *Vetrovec* warning, about the danger of relying on the evidence of an unsavoury witness, where one is required is also an error of law.[48] There are also some circumstances in which the way a trial judge deals with facts can constitute an error of law: making a factual finding for which there is no evidence is one example.[49]

The distinction between an error of law and a miscarriage of justice can be seen to some extent in the facts of *R v Khan*.[50] There, the jury was provided with a transcript that included an exchange between counsel and the judge that had taken place in the jury's absence. What happened was discovered a few hours later and the transcript was replaced,

---

43   *R v Khan*, 2001 SCC 86 at para 22 [*Khan*].
44   *Ibid.*
45   *R v Cinous*, 2002 SCC 29.
46   *R v G(RM)*, [1996] 3 SCR 362.
47   *R v Arradi*, 2003 SCC 23.
48   *R v Bevan*, [1993] 2 SCR 599 [*Bevan*].
49   *R v JMH*, 2011 SCC 45 [*JMH*]. See the further discussion of *JMH* in Section B(2), below in this chapter.
50   Above note 43.

and the trial judge rejected a motion for a mistrial application. The Supreme Court, however, held that this appeal was properly brought on the basis of error of law. The issue was whether the trial judge had made a correct legal decision in rejecting the mistrial application. On the other hand, had the error regarding the transcript not been discovered until afterward, so that there was no decision regarding the matter at trial, then the appeal would be framed in terms of whether there was a miscarriage of justice.

A miscarriage of justice can be either substantive or procedural. Any error that deprives an accused of a fair trial is a legal error.[51] For example, a breach of the jury secrecy rule might result in a miscarriage of justice.[52] An allegation of ineffective assistance of counsel that is raised only on appeal would concern a possible miscarriage.[53] A failure to limit cross-examination would also raise issues of miscarriage.[54]

A miscarriage of justice can also result from a trial judge's misapprehension of the evidence in a trial. However, the fact that the judge has misapprehended the evidence is not on its own enough to show a miscarriage of justice—the standard is more stringent than that. The misapprehension must go to the substance of the evidence, not just to some detail. Further, it must concern a material part of the reasoning of the trial judge. Finally, those errors must play an essential part in the reasoning process resulting in a conviction.[55] For example, in R v CLY the trial judge relied, in particular, on the accused's denial of even innocuous tickling and surprising recall of detail as reasons not to accept the accused's evidence in a sexual touching case; in fact the accused had not denied innocuous tickling and had not shown a particularly strong recall of detail, leading the Supreme Court to overturn the conviction.[56] In cases like this, the misapprehension of evidence means that the accused has not received a fair trial, and so the appeal must be granted even if a conviction could have been supported on the evidence.[57]

A failure to specifically plead miscarriage of justice as a ground of appeal does not deprive the appeal court of jurisdiction to consider the issue. In such a case, however, the grounds should be amended and it

---

51   *Fanjoy v the Queen*, [1985] 2 SCR 233 at para 11 [*Fanjoy*].
52   This was the basis of the appeal in *R v Pan*; *R v Sawyer*, 2001 SCC 42, for instance.
53   *R v GDB*, 2000 SCC 22.
54   *Fanjoy*, above note 51.
55   *Lohrer*, above note 42.
56   2008 SCC 2.
57   *Lohrer*, above note 42.

might be necessary to grant an adjournment so that there can be a full and fair hearing.[58]

Although the underlying theory of sections 686(1)(a)(ii) and (iii) is the same, they are not identical in application. In some cases the same conclusion would be reached no matter which route was followed. For example, if an error of law causing prejudice is a miscarriage, then the curative proviso does not apply; but if the error causes prejudice, then the curative proviso potentially applies, but would not succeed. So, one could say either that the error is a miscarriage not subject to the curative proviso, or that the error is an error of law that was not harmless in the first place.

There are, however, some differences between the two sections. First, as noted, some miscarriages of justice are matters of mixed law and fact. Beyond that, the curative proviso has been interpreted so that it can be satisfied in two different ways, one of which does not amount to suggesting that the error was harmless in itself. It is to that question we now turn.

iv)   The "Curative Proviso"

Section 686(1)(b)(iii) allows an appeal court to dismiss an appeal despite an error of law provided that "no substantial wrong or miscarriage of justice has occurred." The test for whether this section is met is well established and requires that there is a "reasonable possibility that the verdict would have been different had the error . . . not been made."[59] The Crown need not cross-appeal in order to put the curative proviso in issue: the question of whether an error of law is serious enough to justify setting aside the verdict will always be intertwined with whether the curative proviso should be applied.[60]

Caselaw has established that there are two entirely different ways of satisfying this test, both of which are quite fact dependent. The first is to show that the error is harmless in itself. If that is so, then the error would not have been capable of causing prejudice to the accused. The other possibility is to show that the evidence against the accused is so overwhelming that even if the appeal was granted and a retrial ordered, the result would inevitably be a conviction. In such cases, the error itself might not have been incapable of causing prejudice, but any theoretical prejudice has no genuine impact. In either case, the burden on the Crown to show that the curative proviso applies is meant to be a

---

58   *R v EMW*, 2011 SCC 31.

59   *Khan*, above note 43 at para 28, quoting *Bevan*, above note 48 at 617. *Khan* contains a very full summary of the correct approach to s 686(1)(b)(iii).

60   *R v Laboucan*, 2009 SCC 18.

high one. The standard is that the error is *harmless*. That standard will not be met if there is prejudice, even if the court of appeal feels that that prejudice was unlikely to have affected the outcome.[61]

Various types of errors can fall into the first, "harmless error" branch of the curative proviso. Some mistakes could actually be of benefit to the accused. For example, if the trial judge articulates a stricter standard for guilt than is required, there will have been an error of law, but it will certainly not have prejudiced the accused.[62] In other cases, the error might fail to benefit the accused, but be of no real consequence. For example, a failure to permit cross-examination might be in error, but if it is on a point not really in any doubt, then the error is harmless.[63] Similarly, if hearsay evidence is improperly admitted, but on some point that is of no consequence to the accused's guilt, then the curative proviso can be applied.[64] Generally speaking, the harmless error criterion is more likely to be met when only a single error is at issue, rather than the cumulative effect of a number of errors; there is, however, no absolute rule.[65]

The other basis for applying the curative proviso is that the rest of the evidence is so overwhelming that a conviction on a retrial is inevitable. The most important point to bear in mind is that this branch of the curative proviso imposes a very high standard. It has long been noted that this aspect of the provision must be used with great circumspection or the accused will be deprived of the right to trial by jury.[66] So, for example, where evidence has been improperly admitted, it is not open to a court of appeal simply to conclude that the remainder of the evidence could or ought to result in a conviction. If that were the case, then there would be no need for section 686(1)(b)(iii).[67] Rather, the appropriate standard is an "onerous" one, and the Supreme Court has restricted use of the provision on very stringent terms.[68] It has said that the provision should be applied only if conviction would be "inevitable" or

---

61 *R v Sarrazin*, 2011 SCC 54.
62 See, for example, *R v MacGillivray*, [1995] 1 SCR 890.
63 *United Nurs~ ^ Alberta v Alberta (Attorney General)*, [1992] 1 SCR 901.
64 *Gunn v T'*   , [1974] SCR 273.
65 *R v J~*   71 1 SCR 314.
66 See *R v*   ] 1 SCR 697 [*B(FF)*]. See also *Colpitts v The Queen*, [1965]
    S~   ting the danger that "the judges would in truth be substi-
    tu~   he verdict would become theirs and theirs alone, and would
    b~   a perusal of the evidence without any opportunity of seeing
    the deme~ of the witnesses and weighing the evidence with the assistance
    which this ~ ords."
67 *R v S(PL)*, [1991] 1 SCR 909 [*S(PL)*].
68 *R v Broyles*, [1991] 3 SCR 595.

"invariable,"[69] or if the result would "necessarily" have been the same.[70] The proviso can be used only if it is clear that the evidence pointing to the guilt of the accused is so overwhelming that any other verdict but a conviction would be impossible.[71]

> Although there are two branches to the test, the underlying question is the same in each: would the verdict have been the same if the error had not been committed? The "overwhelming evidence" branch asks whether any reasonable judge or jury would inevitably convict given the evidence, while the "harmless error" branch asks whether the error was so minor, irrelevant, or clearly non-prejudicial that any reasonable judge or jury could not possibly have rendered a different verdict if the error had not been made.[72]

Whether the test is made out in any given case will be very much a factual question. In general, courts of appeal should be more cautious in cases involving questions of credibility and should avoid speculating about the bases upon which a jury may have accepted some evidence or rejected other evidence.[73]

v)   Procedural Irregularities

Section 686(1)(b)(iv), it will be recalled, allows an appeal court to dismiss an appeal on the basis that "notwithstanding any procedural irregularity at trial, the trial court had jurisdiction over the class of offence of which the appellant was convicted and the court of appeal is of the opinion that the appellant suffered no prejudice thereby." The section is best understood by discussing not what it adds to the analysis of an appeal, but what it takes away from that discussion. The purpose of the subsection is to remove from consideration a wide variety of issues that might technically have been errors though they caused no prejudice to the accused, but that could not have been dealt with under the

---

69   S(PL), above note 67.
70   B(FF), above note 66.
71   *Khan*, above note 43 at para 31. See also *R v Van*, 2009 SCC 22 at para 34 [*Van*], citing *R v Trochym*, 2007 SCC 6. See, for example, *R v Sekhon*, 2014 SCC 15, where an accused was convicted on the basis that he knew of the existence of drugs in a vehicle he was driving. The trial judge had improperly admitted expert evidence with regard to the accused's knowledge, but the other evidence in the case—that he had removed a fob which gave access to the hidden compartment before handing over his keys, that he destroyed a piece of paper while being detained, and many inconsistencies in his story—would inevitably have led to the finding that he knew of the drugs.
72   *Van*, above note 71 at paras 35–36.
73   B(FF), above note 66.

curative proviso. Accordingly, it simplifies the appeal process by eliminating those questions from the analysis.

Prior to the enactment of section 686(1)(b)(iv), it was possible for errors of law to be cured by the harmless error provision in section 686(1)(b)(iii). Most procedural irregularities would be errors of law. However, caselaw concluded that some particular types of errors went to the jurisdiction of the court and that some of these instances could not be classified as "errors of law" and, as such, the curative proviso could not be applied. Some of these jurisdictional errors were of no real consequence—the exclusion of the accused from a small portion of the trial might be a jurisdictional error but, if nothing of significance occurred during that time, the accused suffered no prejudice. Nonetheless, since the curative proviso did not apply, the appeal had to be granted.

Section 686(1)(b)(iv) now allows appeals based on such technicalities to be dismissed, provided there is no harm to the accused's interests in doing so. In part, this is accomplished by the fact that the section does not apply if the trial court did not have jurisdiction over the *class* of offence, as opposed to losing jurisdiction over the particular offence or particular offender through some procedural irregularity. Accordingly, the section would not apply if an indictable offence under section 469 somehow were tried in provincial court, for example.

More important, though, the section applies only if the procedural irregularity caused the accused no prejudice.[74] The Court has held that it is appropriate to infer that the irregularity *did* cause prejudice and, therefore, that this inference must be rebutted. The analysis of that question is the same as that conducted under the curative proviso in section 686(1)(b)(iii).[75] As a result, section 686(1)(b)(iv) is largely parallel to section 686(1)(b)(iii), but applies only to a narrow range of procedural irregularities, creating a jurisdictional error that could not be classified as a pure error of law.

The Court has helpfully summarized the correct approach to applying sections 686(1)(b)(iii) and (iv):

> If the procedural irregularity amounts to or is based on an error of law, it falls under ss. 686(1)(*a*)(ii) and 686(1)(*b*)(iii).

---

74   See, for example, *R v Swite*, 2011 BCCA 54, in which there was an error in the manner by which jurors were selected. The British Columbia Court of Appeal found that this was a procedural irregularity rather than an error of law and, therefore, to be dealt with under s 686(1)(b)(iv) rather than s 686(1)(b)(ii). The court concluded that it could not be saved, both because the error deprived the trial court of jurisdiction and alternatively because the error resulted in both actual and presumed prejudice.

75   *Khan*, above note 43 at para 16.

If the procedural irregularity was previously (before 1985) classified as an irregularity causing a loss of jurisdiction: s. 686(1)(*b*)(iv) provides that this is no longer fatal to the conviction, and an analysis of prejudice must be undertaken, in accordance with the principles set out in s. 686(1)(*b*)(iii).

If the procedural error did not amount to, or originate in an error of law, which is rare, s. 686(1)(*a*)(iii) applies and the reviewing court must determine whether a miscarriage of justice occurred. If so, there are no remedial provisions in s. 686(1)(*b*) that can cure such a defect, and the appeal must be allowed and either an acquittal entered or a new trial ordered.[76]

vi) Consequences of a Successful Appeal

The *Code* gives a court of appeal some discretion in remedies arising out of an appeal of a conviction, and the caselaw has provided guidance over how that discretion should be exercised. Section 686(2) allows the court of appeal to either enter an acquittal or order a new trial. To some extent, the order that should be made depends on the basis upon which the appeal was successful.

For example, in the case of judge-alone trials the Court has distinguished between a verdict which is "unreasonable" and one which "cannot be supported on the evidence": the latter means the verdict could not have been reached at trial by any reasoning, while the former means that the particular reasoning used by the trial judge was flawed. The Court has held that this difference has an effect on the order to be made: a conviction overturned because it was "unreasonable" will lead to a new trial, while a verdict which cannot be supported on the evidence will result in an acquittal.[77] In the case of a jury trial this distinction is not drawn, and so the appeal will succeed only if it is shown that the verdict is one that a properly instructed jury acting judicially could not reasonably have rendered.[78] In most cases, that amounts to the equivalent of saying that the verdict could not be supported by the evidence, and so an acquittal is usually the remedy for a successful appeal on this ground.[79] Where the unreasonableness is shown by pointing to incon-

---

76   *Ibid* at para 18.
77   *Sinclair*, above note 34 at para 27.
78   *Biniaris*, above note 15: see the discussion under Section B(10(b)(ii), above in this chapter. See also Fish J in *Beaudry*, above note 27 at para 92, holding that an appeal on this ground in the case of a jury trial could succeed only where the "cannot be supported on the evidence" standard is met, since the particular reasoning of the jury will not be known.
79   *Pittiman*, above note 40 at para 14; *R v Schoenthal*, 2007 SKCA 80 at para 70.

sistent verdicts, however, it usually means that there was evidence upon which it would have been possible to convict, and so a new trial should be ordered.[80] Although the Court has not made this observation, that distinction is similar to the one drawn with regard to judge-alone trials, namely, in inconsistent verdict cases, something has gone wrong in the reasoning process, rather than necessarily with the final conclusion.

An error of law or miscarriage of justice is more likely to lead to a new trial, and for similar reasons: if this is the only basis upon which the appeal is granted, then although the process was flawed, there was evidence upon which the accused could have been convicted.[81]

Other factors could influence whether to order a new trial or give an acquittal. For example, a conviction might have been overturned due to the admission of fresh evidence on the appeal. In that event, the court of appeal has to assess the impact of that evidence: if it persuades the court that the accused is factually innocent or that no jury acting reasonably could convict the accused, then an acquittal can be entered, but failing that a new trial should be ordered.[82] Further, even where there is the possibility of a conviction on the evidence, an acquittal can be ordered if there are special circumstances, for example, that the accused had already served her sentence or some significant time in custody or had been subjected to several trials.[83] In the unusual circumstances of R v Truscott—among other things that the accused had served time in custody, the offence had occurred nearly fifty years earlier but the accused had consistently maintained his innocence, and no new trial would, in fact, be possible—an acquittal was ordered on the basis that if there were a new trial it was more likely than not that the accused would be acquitted.[84]

A court of appeal is not limited to the choices of acquittal or new trial. Section 686(8) of the *Code* permits a court of appeal to make any

---

80 *Pittiman*, above note 40 at para 14.

81 *Morrissey*, above note 18 at para 88, suggests that a court of appeal should therefore first consider whether an appeal succeeds on the basis of an unreasonable verdict, in order to see first whether the accused is entitled to an acquittal.

82 *R v Dhillon*, 2014 BCCA 480 at para 50 [*Dhillon*]; *R v Maciel*, 2007 ONCA 196 at para 46 [*Maciel*].

83 *R v Truscott*, 2007 ONCA 575 at para 249 [*Truscott*]; *Dunlop and Sylvester v The Queen*, [1979] 2 SCR 881 at 900.

84 *Truscott*, above note 83. The Ontario Court of Appeal noted at para 265 that "to order a new trial in these circumstances merely because the remaining evidence clears a relatively low evidentiary threshold, knowing full well that a new trial will never be held, would be unfair to the appellant and does a disservice to the public." See also *R v DRS*, 2013 ABCA 18, applying the same test.

order that justice requires.[85] It is therefore possible for a court of appeal to decide that, although the test for ordering an acquittal is not met, nonetheless, a stay of proceedings should be ordered.[86] On the other hand, a court of appeal has no more ability to find that an accused is factually innocent than a trial court does, though they are able to express the reasons for acquittal "in clear and strong terms."[87]

Note, as well, that if the appeal would have succeeded except that the accused was properly convicted on some part, then the appeal court can substitute a verdict, affirm the sentence, impose a new sentence, or remit the matter back to the trial court for sentencing.[88] Further, if an accused successfully appeals a conviction on an included offence, a court of appeal cannot order a new trial on the full offence unless there was also a successful Crown appeal from that acquittal.[89]

2) Appeals by the Crown

Crown appeals can be brought under section 676 of the *Code*. The first thing to note is that the appeal rights in that section are not parallel to the appeal rights given to an accused in the case of a conviction. The Crown's right of appeal is narrower and, in particular, contains nothing equivalent to the accused's right under section 686(1)(a)(i). That is, the Crown cannot appeal on the basis that an acquittal was unreasonable or could not be supported on the evidence.[90] An acquittal requires only that the trier of fact had reasonable doubt, and there is no need for evidence to support that doubt.[91]

The Crown's right of appeal is primarily set out in section 676(1)(a): "any ground of appeal that involves *a question of law alone*."[92] This right specifically applies in section 676(1)(a) to verdicts of acquittal or of not

---

85   Strictly the section says that when a court of appeal exercises any power "conferred by subsection (2), (4), (6) or (7), it may make any order, *in addition*, that justice requires" [emphasis added]. In *R v Bellusci*, 2012 SCC 44 at para 39 [*Bellusci*], the Court concluded that the power in section 686(8) can be exercised even without an independent order having been made under one of the previous subsections. See the discussion at Section B(2), below in this chapter.
86   *Dhillon*, above note 82.
87   *R v Mullins-Johnson*, 2007 ONCA 720 at para 24.
88   Sections 686(2) & (3).
89   *R v Guillemette*, [1986] 1 SCR 356.
90   See *Biniaris*, above note 15 at para 32; and *Sunbeam Corporation (Canada) Ltd v the Queen*, [1969] SCR 221.
91   *R v Walker*, 2008 SCC 34 at para 22 [*Walker*]; *JMH*, above note 49 at para 26. See, for example, *R v Barros*, 2011 SCC 51 [*Barros*].
92   [Emphasis added].

criminally responsible on account of mental disorder.[93] Other portions of section 676 allow appeals of most decisions that could bring an end to a prosecution, such as a finding that the accused is unfit to stand trial,[94] an order of a superior court of criminal jurisdiction that quashes an indictment or fails to exercise jurisdiction on an indictment, and an order of a trial court that stays proceedings or quashes an indictment.[95] These latter powers of appeal would capture situations where the accused has received a *Charter* remedy, such as a stay of proceedings based on entrapment or a violation of the right to a trial within a reasonable time. Similarly, where a trial judge has dismissed charges against an accused on the basis that the offence in question was invalid, or *ultra vires*, this will amount to an acquittal that is appealable,[96] as will accepting a plea of *autrefois acquit*.[97] In addition, the Crown can appeal an accused's sentence with leave.[98]

The Court has noted that many countries do not permit acquittals to be appealed at all, but, nonetheless, a right of appeal by the Crown does not violate the *Charter*.[99] However, the Court has stressed on a number of occasions that acquittals should not be overturned lightly. The Crown is required to satisfy the court that the verdict would not necessarily have been the same had the errors not occurred, and the Crown has a heavy onus in doing so.[100] In *R v Graveline*, for example,

93 An accused is considered to be "acquitted" even if she was convicted of an included offence, and so the Crown would be entitled to appeal the acquittal on the main offence: s 676(2).

94 Section 676(3).

95 Sections 676(1)(b) & (c). Even before these subsections were added, it had been concluded that a judicial decision to quash or stay a charge would fall within the meaning of "acquittal" and, therefore, could be appealed by the Crown: *R v Jewitt*, [1985] 2 SCR 128. It is odd that s 686, setting out the bases upon which Crown appeals can be granted, fails to deal explicitly in any way with appeals launched under ss 676(1)(b) & (c). Courts that have noted this discontinuity have tended, of necessity, to take them as included within the meaning of "acquittal" in s 686(4): see, for example, *R v Fraillon* (1990), 62 CCC (3d) 474 (Que CA); *R v Allen* (1996), 110 CCC (3d) 331 (Ont CA); or *R v Taylor*, 2009 NLCA 43. Section 676 nowhere authorizes an appeal of a discharge at a preliminary inquiry, which therefore can be reviewed only through *certiorari* or overridden through preferring a direct indictment: see the discussion in Chapter 9.

96 See *Cheyenne Realty Ltd v Thompson*, [1975] 1 SCR 87; and *Re Regina and Kripps Pharmacy Ltd* (1981), 60 CCC (2d) 332 (BCCA).

97 *R v Sanver* (1973), 12 CCC (2d) 105 (NBSCAD).

98 Section 676(1)(d).

99 See *R v Graveline*, 2006 SCC 16 at para 13 [*Graveline*]; and *R v Morgentaler*, [1988] 1 SCR 30.

100 See *R v Sutton*, 2000 SCC 50 at para 2 [*Sutton*], relying on *Vézeau v the Queen*, [1977] 2 SCR 277; and *R v Morin*, [1988] 2 SCR 345.

the accused's defence at trial had been based on non-mental disorder automatism and she did not argue self-defence. The trial judge instructed the jury on self-defence nonetheless and therein erred on a question of law. However, the Supreme Court held on these facts that the Crown did not satisfy its onus to show that the legal error was of any consequence. An abstract or purely hypothetical possibility that the accused would have been convicted was not sufficient; rather, the Crown must show how "in the concrete reality of the case at hand" the error had a material bearing on the acquittal.[101] Something like an error that calls for the wrong standard of proof to be applied, for example, would be needed.[102]

Obviously, a crucial consideration, given the relatively limited nature of the Crown's right of appeal, is exactly what constitutes a question of law.[103] Some straightforward examples include the admissibility of evidence, the interpretation of a statute, and whether evidence is capable of being corroborative.[104] A decision concerning the application of a legal standard, such as investigative necessity, is also a question of law.[105] Whether a correct conclusion has been reached on a *Charter* question, such as whether there has been a section 8 violation or whether evidence should be excluded under section 24(2), is also a question of law.[106] The main point of limiting the Crown to an appeal on a question of law is to prevent re-litigation of the facts.[107] However, matters

---

101 *Graveline*, above note 99 at para 14. See, for example, *R v McRae*, 2013 SCC 68, where the trial judge had a number of factual findings about the accused's state of mind when making several threats, but had never asked the necessary legal question of whether the threats were meant to be taken seriously: since that error might reasonably have affected the result, a new trial was ordered. On the other hand, see *R v Noel*, 2010 NBCA 28, where the trial judge considered information that had not been evidence in the case, but nonetheless reached conclusions that were safely anchored in properly admitted evidence. In that event, the appeal was not granted despite the errors. See also *R v Park*, 2010 ABCA 248, where the trial judge wrongly ordered a directed verdict, but the Court of Appeal dismissed the appeal on the basis that in the absence of the error the trial judge would have acquitted the accused in any event.

102 See *Sutton*, above note 100.

103 It is worth recalling here the discussion above concerning the ambiguity over the meaning of "question of law": see above notes 15 and 16. Here, we are dealing with the broader meaning of a question of law for jurisdictional purposes.

104 *R v B(G)*, [1990] 2 SCR 57 [*B(G)*].

105 *R v Araujo*, [2000] 2 SCR 992 at para 18. See also *Biniaris*, above note 15, or *Barros*, above note 91.

106 See *R v Chehil*, 2009 NSCA 111, aff'd 2013 SCC 49; and *R v Genest* (1986), 54 CR (3d) 246 (Que CA).

107 See, for example, *R v Boudreault*, 2012 SCC 56, where the trial judge, after applying the correct legal test, concluded that the accused did not satisfy the test for having care and control of a motor vehicle while impaired: the Court held at

can sometimes still be classed as questions of law giving rise to a Crown appeal even if they involve consideration of the evidence in some way.

An error of law can arise from the way in which a trial judge assesses the evidence and, indeed, can do so in at least four ways.[108] First, it is an error of law to make a factual finding for which there is no evidence. This basis cannot be used, however, as the equivalent of an "unreasonable acquittal" ground of appeal: an acquittal does not have to be supported by particular factual findings but rather can rest on reasonable doubt.[109] Second, a question of law could concern the legal effect of undisputed facts. The facts might be agreed, or the trial judge might have made all necessary findings of fact, but a court of appeal might disagree with the trial judge's conclusion without engaging in fact finding itself. In such a case, the nature of the disagreement would really concern the law rather than the facts. Third, assessment of the evidence based on a wrong legal principle is an error of law; in other words, the failure of a trial judge to direct herself to all the evidence is a question of law if it is based on a misapprehension of some legal principle, but only in that instance. Finally, it is an error of law for a trial judge to consider (or to instruct a jury to consider) individual pieces of evidence separately to decide whether they constitute proof beyond a reasonable doubt. The proper approach is to consider the whole of the evidence and determine on that basis whether the guilt of the accused had been established beyond a reasonable doubt. This rule does not mean, however, that a trial judge must refer to every item of evidence considered or detail the way each item of evidence was assessed (see the discussion of duty to give reasons, at Section B(3)(c), below in this chapter).[110]

Where the court of appeal grants an appeal from an acquittal in a trial by judge alone, it has two main choices: to order a new trial or to enter a conviction. In the latter case, the court can either impose sentence

---

para 15 that the Crown had no right to appeal because "[t]he judge's conclusion on the facts, however surprising or unreasonable it may appear to another court, did not give rise to a question of law alone." *R v Tortone*, [1993] 2 SCR 973, observes that it is not open to a court of appeal even to draw different inferences from the facts than the trial judge has drawn simply because it would have drawn different inferences. However, a court of appeal can overturn a verdict where the trial judge has not directed his or her mind to issues that require determination in order to reach the verdict.

108   *JMH*, above note 49 at para 24, describes these as ways in which treatment of facts can amount to an error of law "giving rise to a Crown appeal of an acquittal." It is not clear that they could not also be treated as errors of law by an accused seeking to appeal a conviction: indeed, some seem more suited to that task.

109   *Ibid* at paras 25–27. See, for example, *R v Powell*, 2010 ONCA 105.

110   See *JMH*, above note 49; *R v Morin*, [1992] 3 SCR 286; and *B(G)*, above note 104.

or remit the matter to the trial court for sentencing. A court of appeal should choose to enter a conviction only where the trial judge has already made all the findings necessary to support a guilty verdict, or where those facts are not in dispute.[111] This conviction need not be on the main charge: it could, for example, be on an included offence.[112] However, the court of appeal is not permitted to enter a conviction where the trial was by judge and jury; in that case, the only option is to order a new trial.[113] The new trial does not necessarily have to duplicate the issues in the previous trial. A court of appeal can limit the issues and so, for example, direct that the new trial will be held only to determine whether an entrapment defence should succeed or whether the accused is guilty of an included offence.[114]

A court of appeal is not entirely limited to the choices of a new trial or a conviction. Section 686(8) permits a court of appeal to "make any order, in addition, that justice requires." In *R v Bellusci* the Quebec Court of Appeal had overturned a stay entered by the trial judge and had ordered that the judge continue with the trial. Although the Court found that the Court of Appeal had erred in overturning the stay, they concluded that in an appropriate case, a court of appeal could simply order a trial judge to continue a trial, rather than order a new trial. Specifically, they concluded that the words "in addition" in section 686(8) did not mean that a court granting the appeal from acquittal must have already made an order for a new trial or conviction under section 686(4) before being able to make a further order under section 686(8). Rather, setting aside the acquittal or stay would be enough of an exercise of section 686(4) to trigger the remedial power in section 686(8).[115] A court of appeal cannot order the continuation of a trial on an amended indictment, however.[116]

---

111   *R v Cassidy*, [1989] 2 SCR 345.

112   Section 686(4)(b)(ii) allows the court of appeal to enter a conviction "with respect to the offence of which, in its opinion, the accused should have been found guilty but for the error in law."

113   Section 686(4). Giving this greater protection in the case of trial by jury does not violate the *Charter*: *R v Skalbania*, [1997] 3 SCR 995.

114   See, respectively, *R v Pearson*, [1998] 3 SCR 620; and *R v Cook* (1979), 9 CR (3d) 85 (Ont CA). This is allowed under s 686(8). The combined effect of ss 676(2), 686(4), and 686(8) is that a person could, for example, be convicted of only an included offence at trial but ordered to face a new trial on the main charge, or be convicted of the main offence at trial but be convicted or ordered to face a new trial on an included offence.

115   Above note 85 at para 39.

116   *R v Gunn*, [1982] 1 SCR 522.

3) Other Appeal-Related Issues

a) Powers of a Court of Appeal

Various *Code* provisions create particular powers relating to appeals. Most generally under section 683, a court of appeal can order exhibits or other items produced, hear witnesses or admit an examination of a witness, and refer questions to a special commissioner.[117] That section also permits an appeal court to amend the indictment where the accused has not been misled or prejudiced.

A court of appeal is also entitled to raise new issues beyond those brought forward by the parties, although they should do so only in rare circumstances.[118] A new issue is one that cannot reasonably be said to stem from the issues as framed by the parties. Because the judge's role in an adversary system is to both be and seem to be independent and impartial, a court of appeal should raise a new issue only when failing to do so would risk an injustice, there is a sufficient record on which to raise the issue, and raising the issue would not result in procedural prejudice to any party.[119] If a court of appeal does raise a new issue, all parties must be given advance notice of the issue in order to make informed submissions.[120]

In addition, a court of appeal can assign counsel for an accused or order an accused released pending an appeal.[121] In the case of an appeal from conviction, to be released the accused must demonstrate that the appeal is not frivolous, that he will surrender himself into custody in accordance with the terms of the order, and that his detention is not necessary in the public interest.[122] Note that although the "public interest" criterion was found to be unconstitutionally vague in the pretrial context (see the discussion in Chapter 6), it has been upheld with regard to bail pending an appeal.[123]

Note, as well, that an accused has the right to be present at the appeal. However, that right may not apply if the appeal is based on a question of law alone and the accused is both in custody and represented by counsel. In addition, the appeal court can order that an accused in custody appear only by electronic means.[124] In some circumstances, it is

---

117 See the discussion at Section B(3)(b), below in this chapter.
118 *R v Mian*, 2014 SCC 54 at para 41.
119 *Ibid* at para 41.
120 *Ibid* at para 35.
121 Sections 684 and 679.
122 See the discussion of these criteria in *R v Mapara* (2004), 186 CCC (3d) 273 (BCCA).
123 *R v Farinacci* (1993), 25 CR (4th) 350 (Ont CA).
124 Section 688.

also possible for an appeal to be brought even though the accused is deceased. A court of appeal has the jurisdiction to do so, but should choose to exercise that jurisdiction only where it is in the interests of justice.[125]

b) Fresh Evidence on Appeal

It is possible for evidence to be introduced on appeal that was not before the trial court; however, this cannot be done in an unconstrained way. In *R v Palmer*, the Court laid down guidelines for the introduction of fresh evidence on appeal:

1) The evidence should generally not be admitted if it could have been adduced at trial by due diligence (but this principle is not to be applied as strictly in a criminal case as in civil cases).

2) The evidence must be relevant in the sense that it bears upon a decisive or potentially decisive issue in the trial.

3) The evidence must be credible in the sense that it is reasonably capable of belief.

4) It must be such that, if believed, it could reasonably, when taken with the other evidence adduced at trial, be expected to have affected the result.[126]

Note that the evidence sought to be introduced must have been capable of admission at the initial trial; hearsay or opinion evidence that would not have been admissible at trial is no more admissible on appeal.[127]

The due diligence requirement is, in large measure, intended to prevent the reassessment in hindsight of a strategic decision made at trial.[128] Accordingly, this criterion is not always an absolute one and should not be determinative. Courts retain a discretion to allow fresh evidence in when a strong case is made out on the other criteria, even if the evidence could in principle have been led at trial.[129] This is particu-

---

125 *R v Smith*, 2004 SCC 14.

126 [1980] 1 SCR 759 at 775 [*Palmer*].

127 See, for example, *R v Arabia*, 2008 ONCA 565; *R v Assoun*, 2006 NSCA 47, leave to appeal to SCC refused, [2006] SCCA No 233; or *R v Archer* (2005), 34 CR (6th) 271 (Ont CA) [*Archer*].

128 See, for example, *R v Falkner*, 2008 BCCA 277; *Archer*, above note 127; or *R v Perlett* (2006), 212 CCC (3d) 11 (Ont CA) [*Perlett*].

129 See the discussion of this issue in *Maciel*, above note 82, and, in particular, the observations that "[i]t can never be in the interests of justice to maintain a verdict where the court is satisfied that the verdict is factually incorrect" (para 47) and that "[i]t is not in the interests of justice to maintain a conviction where, on the totality of the evidence available to the appellate court, that court is satisfied that no reasonable jury could convict the appellant" (para 48).

larly so when the decision by the accused not to have led the evidence was a reasonable one given Crown counsel's strategy at trial.[130]

The requirement that the evidence must bear upon a potentially decisive issue does not mean that it must relate directly to guilt or innocence in the sense that it is a new witness that can offer the accused an alibi—the evidence could also give reason to doubt other evidence that had been relied on at trial. In *R v Trotta*, for example, fresh evidence was admitted and a new trial was ordered in light of evidence that the testimony of a pathologist called by the Crown was unreliable.[131] In *R v Hurley* fresh evidence that the accused's DNA had been found in various places in a hotel room was admitted, on his application, because it could help counter the Crown's argument that he had cleaned up the scene in an effort to hide his presence there.[132] In *R v JAA* the evidence went to whether a mark on the accused's finger was a bite mark, which had been an important factor in the trial judge's decision in the face of conflicting testimony.[133] However, evidence that could bear only on a peripheral issue will not, due to the fourth criterion above, be admitted.[134]

The Court has also commented on the procedure to be used in fresh evidence applications. It has directed that, unless the application is dismissed immediately, judgment should be reserved on whether to admit the evidence until after the appeal is heard. In that way, the appeal court will be better able to decide whether the evidence could reasonably have been expected to affect the result of the case. If it could, the appeal court can also consider how great an impact it might have had in order to decide whether to order a new trial or, relying on the fresh evidence, decide the matter itself.[135]

Note, as well, that the *Palmer* criteria do not create the only test by which new evidence can be introduced on appeal, though it is the most common one. However, in some cases, evidence showing that the validity of the trial is in issue, rather than evidence relating to guilt or innocence. In such cases, the *Palmer* criteria do not apply. In *R v Taillefer; R v Duguay* (discussed more fully in Chapter 8) the fresh evidence was

---

130 *R v JAA*, 2011 SCC 17 [*JAA*]. In *JAA* the accused sought to lead expert evidence to show that a mark on his finger was not a bite mark. The Crown had not led expert evidence on the point at trial, though a police officer had testified (possibly impermissibly) that the mark appeared to him to be a bite. The particular point turned out to be significant in the trial judge's reasons, though the accused had not expected that to be the case, and that expectation was not unreasonable.

131 2007 SCC 49.

132 2010 SCC 18.

133 *JAA*, above note 130.

134 See *Perlett*, above note 128; or *R v Flis* (2006), 205 CCC (3d) 384 (Ont CA).

135 *R v Stolar*, [1988] 1 SCR 480.

evidence that had, wrongly, not been disclosed to the accused earlier. In those circumstances, the Court held that the less strict test from *R v Dixon*, relating to disclosure, was more appropriately applied.[136] More generally, when the trial process itself is in issue the strict *Palmer* criteria do not apply.[137]

c) Duty to Give Reasons

A judge in a criminal trial has a duty to give reasons; however, this has not always been taken to be the case. For more than one hundred years the stated rule was that a trial judge had no general duty to give reasons, and it is still not the case that every adjudicator in every context has such a duty. In 2002, however, with its decision in *R v Sheppard* the Court concluded that, in certain circumstances, the failure to give sufficient reasons will be an error of law giving rise to a ground of appeal.[138] Subsequently in its 2008 decision in *R v REM*, the Court concluded that a criminal trial, where the accused's innocence is at stake, is always one of those circumstances.[139]

Reasons serve three main functions. First, they tell the parties why the decision was made, demonstrating that the judge has heard and considered the evidence on both sides and has not taken any extraneous considerations into account. Second, reasons make the decision publicly accountable, so that justice is not only done but is seen to be done. Third, reasons permit effective appellate review. When a trial judge has clearly laid out the factual findings and legal principles, parties are in a better position to decide whether to appeal, and appellate courts are in a better position to assess whether there has been an error.

In addition, the process of writing reasons directs the judge's attention and reduces the likelihood of over- or under-emphasizing some point. Finally, reasons help the law to develop uniformly. Accordingly, a criminal trial judge now has a duty to give sufficient reasons for the decision. The real question today, therefore, is "[w]hat, in the context of a particular case, constitutes *sufficient* reasons?"[140]

---

136 2003 SCC 70 [*Taillefer*]. See *Taillefer, ibid*, and *R v Dixon*, [1998] 1 SCR 244.

137 See, for example, *R v Schneider* (2004), 192 CCC (3d) 1 (NSCA); *R v Wolf* (2005), 197 CCC (3d) 481 (Ont CA); and *R v MacInnis* (2006), 212 CCC (3d) 103 (NSCA).

138 2002 SCC 26 [*Sheppard*].

139 2008 SCC 51 at para 10 [*REM*]. See, generally, the discussion in Judge Wayne Gorman, "'Ours Is to Reason Why': The Law of Rendering Judgment" (2015) 62 *Criminal Law Quarterly* 301.

140 *REM*, above note 139 at para 14.

A trial judge's reasons do not need to be the equivalent of a jury instruction, and should not be held up against some abstract standard.[141] They are to be assessed as a whole, in the context of the evidence, the arguments, and the trial, and a misstatement will not necessarily be fatal.[142] Further, an appeal court is not to intervene "simply because it thinks the trial court did a poor job of expressing itself."[143] Trial judges are only required to give reasons that the parties can understand and that permit appellate review.[144]

The Court has said that "[w]hat is required is a logical connection between the 'what' — the verdict — and the 'why' — the basis for the verdict," but that this does not require the judge to explain exactly *how* the decision was reached in a watch-me-think fashion.[145] A trial judge need not set out every finding or conclusion and need not expound on points of law or pieces of evidence that are not, in the context of the case, in dispute.[146] Reasons are particularly important when the relevant law is unsettled law or where there is confused and contradictory evidence on a key issue. Even then, however, the basis of the trial judge's conclusion might be apparent from the record even without being articulated.[147] In general, what is necessary is that the trial judge makes clear the path taken through confused or conflicting evidence, so that the parties can understand the basis for the decision.

In *Sheppard*, for example, there were significant inconsistencies and conflicts in the evidence, as well as issues of credibility. The trial judge delivered "boiler plate" reasons that indicated, in a single sentence, that he had considered the testimony and the burden on the

---

141 *Ibid*; *R v Rhyason*, 2007 SCC 39; *R v Gagnon*, [2006] 1 SCR 621 at para 19.

142 See, for example, *R v Laboucan*, 2010 SCC 12, where the trial judge made reference to the accused's motive to lie in assessing credibility. The Court held that such a consideration was problematic and unhelpful, and that triers of fact would be well advised to avoid that path altogether. Nonetheless, in the context of the decision as a whole, the statement did not constitute an error.

143 *Sheppard*, above note 138 at para 26.

144 *Ibid*, and *R v Boucher*, 2005 SCC 72.

145 *REM*, above note 139 at para 17.

146 See, for example, *R v O'Brien*, 2011 SCC 29, where the trial judge had improperly allowed character evidence to be admitted, though no party had relied on that evidence in argument. The only issue in the case was identity, and the trial judge indicated that he relied solely on the DNA evidence in reaching his conclusion on that issue. The Nova Scotia Court of Appeal had ordered a new trial because the reasons did not demonstrate that the trial judge had not been unconsciously influenced by the character evidence. The Supreme Court overturned this result, holding at para 17 that "[t]rial judges are entitled to have their reasons reviewed based on what they say, not on the speculative imagination of reviewing courts."

147 *Sheppard*, above note 138 at para 55.

Crown in finding the accused guilty. The Court held that these reasons were insufficient for the accused, or an appeal court, to know the basis for the conviction, and upheld the order for a new trial.

On the other hand, in REM the trial judge had given much more expansive reasons, though the court of appeal had found them to be insufficient for various reasons. Specifically, the trial judge did not explain which of the offences were proved by which of the eleven incidents on which evidence had been led, failed to mention some of the accused's evidence, failed to make general comments about the accused's evidence, failed to reconcile his generally positive findings on the complainant's evidence with the rejection of some of her evidence, and failed to explain why he rejected the accused's plausible denial of the charges. The Supreme Court overturned the court of appeal's decision, holding that they had, in effect, substituted their own views about credibility for that of the trial judge under the guise of finding the reasons insufficient. The central issue at trial had been credibility. The trial judge's reasons made it clear that he had accepted a great deal of the complainant's evidence, that he was not left with a reasonable doubt on the whole of the evidence or from the contradictory evidence of the accused, and therefore that the accused's guilt had been established beyond a reasonable doubt. While some aspects of the reasons could have been explained more fully, the Court said, when the record was considered as a whole, the basis for the verdict was evident, and so the reasons were not insufficient.[148]

That is not to say, however, than any reasons that go beyond "boiler plate" will be sufficient. In R v Dinardo the issue was also credibility in a sexual assault case and the trial judge again convicted. Although the trial judge was not required to explicitly lay out the proper test for determining whether there was reasonable doubt, the trial judge's reasons did not make clear that he had actually applied that test. Critical evidence, such as that the complainant was mentally challenged, had a history of making up stories to get attention, and had wavered about whether the accused had committed the assault in question, was not averted to in the reasons. The trial judge's failure to avert to these critical matters left the Court in doubt that he had directed his mind to the central issue of credibility and meant the reasons were insufficient.[149]

The Court has summarized the proper approach to assessing reasons for sufficiency:

---

148 REM, above note 139 at para 67. To similar effect, see R v HSB, 2008 SCC 52.
149 2008 SCC 24.

(1) Appellate courts are to take a functional, substantive approach to sufficiency of reasons, reading them as a whole, in the context of the evidence, the arguments and the trial, with an appreciation of the purposes or functions for which they are delivered (see *Sheppard*, at paras. 46 and 50; *Morrissey*, at p. 524).

(2) The basis for the trial judge's verdict must be "intelligible," or capable of being made out. In other words, a logical connection between the verdict and the basis for the verdict must be apparent. A detailed description of the judge's process in arriving at the verdict is unnecessary.

(3) In determining whether the logical connection between the verdict and the basis for the verdict is established, one looks to the evidence, the submissions of counsel and the history of the trial to determine the "live" issues as they emerged during the trial.[150]

When reasons are found not to be sufficient, that can be the basis for granting an appeal. In the case of an appeal from conviction, the insufficient reasons might be an unreasonable verdict, an error of law, or a miscarriage of justice, depending on the circumstances of the case and the nature and importance of the trial decision being rendered.[151]

The duty to give reasons also applies to acquittals, but in a different fashion. There is no "unreasonable acquittal" ground of appeal, and the Crown and the accused have different tasks at trial. A conviction requires proof of every element beyond a reasonable doubt, but an acquittal requires only that there be reasonable doubt. Reasonable doubt need not be based on factual findings supporting it and can arise simply because an inadequate foundation for guilt has been laid. In that event, it takes less for reasons to be adequate in the case of an acquittal.[152]

Note, in addition, that issues can arise because of the timing with which reasons are released. Although reasons need not always be given contemporaneously with the decision, when there is delay the possibility of problems increases. In some cases, it might seem that reasons were no longer drafted with an open mind, but rather to justify the conclusion of guilt that had already been reached. This possibility is a danger particularly where reasons are not issued until after the accused has launched an appeal. In such a case, there could be cause to think that the reasons were designed to justify the verdict, rather than reflecting the decision-making process that was used. Delay itself is not

---

150 *REM*, above note 139 at para 35. See also *R v Vuradin*, 2013 SCC 38.
151 *Sheppard*, above note 138 at para 55.
152 *Walker*, above note 91; *Sinclair*, above note 34.

a deciding factor, but it increases the possibility that reasons will not be seen to have been impartial.[153]

C. APPEALS OF SUMMARY CONVICTION OFFENCES

Appeals from summary conviction offences share many qualities with appeals from indictable offences, though there are some differences worth noting. The most notable difference is the court to which the appeal is brought. Indictable offences are appealed to the court of appeal for the province. Generally speaking, summary conviction appeals are taken to the province's superior court of criminal jurisdiction that is *not* the court of appeal.[154] There are also differences in the grounds upon which an appeal can be brought, which are broader for both accused (called the "defendant" in the case of summary conviction offences) and the Crown, and are essentially parallel. Under section 813 of the *Code*, a defendant can appeal a conviction or order made against her, and the Crown can appeal "an order that stays proceedings on an information or dismisses an information." In addition, that section lets both parties appeal sentences, verdicts of not criminally responsible, and fitness to stand trial decisions. No explicit limits are attached to any of these grounds.

As with indictable offences, though, the bases for granting appeals are narrower than the grounds for launching them. Indeed, they are narrower in precisely the same way. Section 822(1) incorporates most of sections 683 to 689 by reference. As a result, all of the rules in section 686(1) that concern appeals from convictions or acquittals are equally applicable to summary conviction offences. Recall, as well, that when a summary conviction offence is appealed along with an indictable offence, the appeals can, with leave, be combined.[155]

As a result of this incorporation, other provisions applicable to indictable offences, such as the powers of the court in section 683, also apply. In addition, bail pending a summary conviction appeal can be granted, though under the specific provisions in section 816 rather than those governing indictable offences.

---

153 *R v Teskey*, 2007 SCC 25. See also *R v Wang*, 2010 ONCA 435, cautioning against making substantive changes when issuing a written version of reasons delivered orally.

154 See the definitions in ss 2, 673, and 812. See, however, the discussion of appeals under s 830, below in this section.

155 Sections 675(1.1) and 676(1.1).

There are, however, other notable differences between summary conviction and indictable appeals, which include the possibility of other methods of appeal.

First, under section 822(4), it is possible for an appeal of a summary conviction matter to take place by trial *de novo*. Proceeding in this way can be justified if there is a problem with the condition of the record—a grounds of decreasing relevance given the methods of recording proceedings in common use today—or if "for any other reason," the interests of justice would be better served by doing so. As a practical matter trials *de novo* are a rarity.

In addition, sections 829 to 838 create an alternative method of appeal, though again these provisions are little used. They incorporate many of the provisions regarding other summary conviction appeals, but the grounds upon which they can be brought are more limited. Either party can appeal a decision in this way on the basis that it is erroneous in point of law, it is in excess of jurisdiction, or it constitutes a refusal or failure to exercise jurisdiction. All of these are grounds upon which an appeal could have been launched under section 813.[156] A defendant is permitted to opt for only one of the two methods of appeal.[157] Appeals under Section 830 can be brought either on a transcript or an agreed-upon statement of facts.[158] In such cases, the appeal could, in some provinces, go directly to the provincial court of appeal.[159]

Finally, whichever method of appeal is brought at the first level, the *Code* permits a potential second level of appeal from summary conviction matters to the court of appeal. Such appeals depend on leave of the court and can be brought only on a question of law.[160] The rules in sections 673 to 689, which govern appeals of indictable offences, are incorporated by reference to these appeals.[161]

Provincial courts of appeal have tended to the view that a second level of appeal ought not to be routinely granted, in part, on the basis that it would be anomalous to have more expansive rights of appeal

---

156 Tim Quigley, *Procedure in Canadian Criminal Law*, 2d ed (Toronto: Thomson Carswell, 2005) (loose-leaf), notes at 24–39 the possibility that the quashing of an information prior to plea might be appealable only under s 830, though he also observes that a new information could simply be laid in such circumstances.

157 Section 836.

158 Section 830(2).

159 This result follows because s 829 defines "appeal court" for s 830 appeals as the superior court of criminal jurisdiction for the province, but the definition of that term in s 2, for some provinces, includes the court of appeal.

160 Section 839. Once again, it is a question of law for jurisdictional purposes that is in issue.

161 Section 839(2).

in the case of less serious offences. Accordingly, most have set down guidelines that are intended to make a second level of appeal the exception rather than the rule.[162]

All courts that have considered the issue hold that the two key considerations are the significance of the legal issues raised to the administration of criminal justice generally and the merits of the particular argument in the case. Not all courts have established exactly the same rules around these criteria.

The Ontario Court of Appeal in *R v RR* treats those two criteria as creating two alternative bases for granting leave to appeal. That case held:

> Leave to appeal may be granted where the merits of the proposed question of law are arguable, even if not strong, and the proposed question of law has significance to the administration of justice beyond the four corners of the case. Leave to appeal may also be granted where there appears to be a "clear" error even if it cannot be said that the error has significance to the administration of justice beyond the specific case.[163]

An appeal is more likely to be allowed when the issues have no general importance if the appellant is facing a significant deprivation of liberty: where even a short custodial sentence will be imposed, it would be "rare and remarkable" for leave to be refused.[164] The *RR* approach has been adopted by many other courts of appeal.[165]

An alternative approach, however, requires that both criteria be met, but relaxes the strictness of the test in other ways. The Court of Appeal for Yukon held that the test required that "(a) the ground of appeal involves a question of law alone, (b) the issue is one of importance, *and* (c) there is sufficient merit in the proposed appeal that it has a reason-

---

162   There is some disagreement over exactly how stringent the leave standard should be. In *R v RR*, 2008 ONCA 497 [*RR*], the Ontario Court of Appeal held that leave to appeal should be only "granted sparingly" (para 37), and in the later case of *R v Ul-Rashid*, 2013 ONCA 782 at para 3, they held that the Court of Appeal "must be satisfied that it is essential that leave be granted." In contrast, in *Newfoundland Recycling Limited v R*, 2009 NLCA 28 at para 7 [*Newfoundland Recycling*], the Newfoundland and Labrador Court of Appeal disagreed with this point and held that the test "should not be unduly stringent." See also *R v Gavin*, 2009 PECA 23 [*Gavin*], concurring with both *RR* and *Newfoundland Recycling*, suggesting that some courts do not perceive the tests as very different.

163   *RR*, above note 162 at para 32.

164   *R v Brownson*, 2013 ONCA 619 at para 17.

165   See *R v Kirk*, 2014 ABCA 373; *R v Petrin*, 2013 NWTCA 1; *R v RWM*, 2011 MBCA 74; *R v Lindsay*, 2011 BCCA 99; *R c Cloutier*, 2010 QCCA 350; *Gavin*, above note 162; *R v MacNeil*, 2009 NSCA 46.

able possibility of success."[166] "Reasonable possibility of success" seems like a lower standard than the "clear error" requirement in *RR* and so would be easier to meet. However, it would need to be met in addition to the "significance" criterion. On this test it seems that even a clear error which was not significant outside the confines of the case would not justify leave to appeal. The British Columbia Court of Appeal has also supported this approach.[167]

In either event, it is important to recall that the second level of appeal is to consider whether the summary conviction appeal court judge committed any legal error—it is not a second review of the trial judge's decision.[168]

D. APPEALS TO THE SUPREME COURT OF CANADA

As noted in Section A, above in this chapter, in unusual circumstances matters other than a conviction or acquittal can be appealed to the Supreme Court under section 40 of the *Supreme Court Act*. The more important issue, however, is the actual appeal of the result at trial beyond a provincial court of appeal. Sections 691 to 695 create a right to appeal decisions of a court of appeal regarding indictable offences to the Supreme Court of Canada.[169] The grounds upon which such appeals

---

166 *R v Winfield*, 2009 YKCA 9 at para 13 [*Winfield*] [emphasis added].

167 *R v Lord*, 2011 BCCA 295. It is arguable that there is even a third standard being applied. In *Newfoundland Recycling*, above note 162, the Newfoundland and Labrador Court of Appeal also adopted the "reasonable possibility of success" standard, and specifically held that it was an alternative to the "significance to the administration of justice" ground, not a requirement in addition to it. That is (at para 9):

> (b) the ground(s) of appeal must be such that:
>   (i) either the ground of appeal has a "reasonable possibility of success," or
>   (ii) "the proposed question of law [has significance] to the administration of justice."

That might be read as adopting a more permissive standard than *RR*, above note 162, and is intended to put into operation the observation in that case that the standard should not be "unduly stringent" (see above note 162). However, the point is not entirely clear, and other courts have treated the two decisions as though they set the same standard: see *Gavin*, above note 162.

168 *Winfield*, above note 166 at para 12.

169 In an appropriate case, presumably the appeal power under s 40 of the *Supreme Court Act*, above note 2, could be used to appeal a decision of a court of appeal concerning a summary conviction matter: see Quigley, above note 156 at 24–40.

can be brought, and the circumstances in which they are permitted, are much narrower than the first level of appeal.

An appeal to the Supreme Court of Canada can only be based upon a question of law; no other ground of appeal is permitted. When an issue constitutes a question of law, as opposed to a question of mixed law and fact, has already been discussed in the context of appeals to the court of appeal, and that analysis is equally applicable here.[170] There are, however, some considerations that are unique to the Supreme Court context.

A court of appeal can, under section 686(1)(a)(i), allow an appeal based on a finding that it was unreasonable or cannot be supported by the evidence. This question obviously could involve some consideration of facts, and the unreasonableness of a particular verdict might raise questions of mixed law and fact. However, as a class, the question of whether a court of appeal has properly applied section 686(1)(a)(i) is a question of law. It is therefore possible to bring an appeal to the Supreme Court based on whether the court of appeal ought to have allowed the appeal.[171]

Similarly, under section 686(1)(b)(iii) a court of appeal can use the curative proviso and dismiss an appeal based on the finding that there was no substantial wrong or miscarriage of justice. Once again, whether the court of appeal has made a correct decision in applying the curative proviso is a question of law and so is appealable to the Supreme Court.[172] Presumably, the same rationale should apply to the "procedural irregularity" saving provision in section 686(1)(b)(iv).

Apart from the fact that the only ground of appeal is on a question of law, there is also the issue of when the accused or the Crown will be permitted to appeal. For the most part, appeals are permitted in only two circumstances: (1) where a judge of the court of appeal dissents on a question of law, or (2) when the Supreme Court gives leave to appeal a question of law. These are the only circumstances in which the Crown can appeal or in which an accused, who was convicted at trial and on appeal, can appeal. However, if an accused was acquitted at trial but that acquittal was replaced with a conviction on appeal, then a further basis

---

170   See *R v Sanichar*, 2013 SCC 4, for a split in the Supreme Court over whether the basis for disagreement in the court of appeal had been over a question of law or not and, therefore, whether there was jurisdiction for them to hear the appeal. See on this point Gerard J Kennedy, "Persisting Uncertainties in Appellate Jurisdiction at the Supreme Court" (2013) 100 *Criminal Reports* (6th) 97.

171   See *Yebes*, above note 27; and *Biniaris*, above note 15.

172   See *R v Mahoney*, [1982] 1 SCR 834; and *R v Jolivet*, 2000 SCC 29.

for appeal is allowed. In that case, the accused can appeal on any question of law, whether there was a dissent in the court of appeal or not.[173]

Note that one option for a court of appeal is to overturn the actual conviction at trial, but substitute a conviction on some other count. In such a case, both the Crown and the accused will have a right of appeal.[174] Note, as well, that, even if the Supreme Court grants leave to appeal on a question of law, that does not preclude it from ultimately concluding that the issue raised is not one of law after all, and dismissing the appeal on that basis.[175] Like a court of appeal, the Supreme Court has the power to appoint counsel for an accused.[176] In addition, the Supreme Court has the power to make any order that the court of appeal could have made.[177] If the Supreme Court orders a new trial which would be held before a judge and jury, the accused has the right to re-elect another mode of trial.[178]

FURTHER READINGS

GORMAN, WAYNE. "'Ours Is to Reason Why': The Law of Rendering Judgment" (2015) 62 *Criminal Law Quarterly* 301.

QUIGLEY, TIM. *Procedure in Canadian Criminal Law*, 2d ed (Toronto: Thomson Carswell, 2005) (loose-leaf) ch 24.

SOPINKA, JOHN, & MARK GELOWITZ. *The Conduct of an Appeal*, 3d ed (Markham, ON: LexisNexis Canada, 2012).

---

173 Sections 691(1), 691(2), and 693.
174 *Biniaris*, above note 15 at para 18.
175 *R v Demeter*, [1978] 1 SCR 538.
176 Section 694.1.
177 Section 695(1).
178 Section 695(2).

GLOSSARY

absolute jurisdiction offence: An offence listed in section 553 of the *Criminal Code*. An accused has no election for these offences, which can be tried only by a provincial court judge.

ancillary powers doctrine: The process through which new police powers can be created at common law. The test for the creation of ancillary powers is drawn from the British case *R v Waterfield*, which is applied in Canada today in a way quite distinct from the approach in its country of origin.

arrest: An arrest consists of words of arrest accompanied either by the touching of the person with a view to detention or by the person submitting to the arrest. The word "arrest" need not be used, provided the accused can be reasonably supposed to have understood that she was under arrest. Arrest powers are given in the *Criminal Code* to everyone, including private citizens, and additional arrest powers are given to property owners and peace officers.

Attorney General: A member of cabinet and the chief law officer for a jurisdiction. The Attorney General has jurisdiction over all or most matters of criminal law, including law-making and prosecutions. In most jurisdictions, the Attorney General is also responsible for policing, although this role is sometimes taken on by the Solicitor General or some other minister. The Attorney General is given various discretionary powers in the *Criminal Code*, some of which must be exercised personally and some of which can be exercised on his behalf by a Crown prosecutor.

authorization: a warrant allowing for the interception of private communications.

autrefois acquit: a plea by an accused under section 607 of the *Code* claiming that he was previously charged with the same offence and was acquitted.

autrefois convict: a plea by an accused under section 607 of the *Code* claiming that she was previously charged with the same offence and was convicted.

bail: The name in common usage for the process by which a justice can release a person who has been accused of an offence until the trial is held. Bail can be granted either unconditionally or on various conditions. It is properly referred to as "judicial interim release."

boilerplate: Generic or standardized wording used with little or no attention to the particular context. The term can be attached to language used in many circumstances, including judges' instructions to a **jury** or reasons for judgment, or in an application for a **warrant**.

challenge for cause: The process by which the Crown or the accused can challenge a potential juror in order to suggest that the person should not serve on the jury. The most common basis for challenge for cause is that the juror is not indifferent between the Queen and the accused, which amounts to a claim that the juror will not act impartially.

change of venue: Moving the location of a trial from one territorial jurisdiction to another.

charge document: The document setting out the charges based upon which an accused will stand trial. See **information** and **indictment**.

Charter of Rights and Freedoms: Sections 1–34 of the *Constitution Act, 1982*, setting out various guaranteed rights which, subject to the justification clause in section 1 of the *Charter*, take priority over any other legislation. The most important sections for criminal law purposes include the fundamental freedoms guaranteed in section 2 (such as freedom of expression), the legal rights provisions in sections 7–14 (such as freedom from unreasonable search and seizure, and the right to counsel), and the remedies provisions in sections 24 and 52.

common law: Judge-made law, as distinct from laws set out in statutes or regulations.

Constitution Act, 1867: The Act of the British Parliament that is the first of Canada's constitutional documents and that initially created Canada as a separate country from Great Britain. It is the source of the division of powers between the federal and provincial governments.

count: An individual charge within a single information or indictment.

court of appeal: The highest court in a jurisdiction for indictable offences, but designated differently in various provinces and territories. For summary conviction matters, the court of appeal is the jurisdiction's superior court of criminal jurisdiction that is not the highest court in the jurisdiction. See the definitions in sections 2, 673, and 812 of the *Criminal Code*.

court of criminal jurisdiction: A trial-level court hearing criminal matters, but designated differently in various provinces and territories. See the definition in section 2 of the *Criminal Code*.

criminal offence: A violation of any non-regulatory offence, whether summary conviction or indictable, which is found in the *Criminal Code* or in other federal legislation, and which is constitutionally justified under section 91(27) of the *Constitution Act, 1867*.

Crown election: Hybrid offences can be tried either by indictment or on summary conviction. The Crown elects which mode of trial will be used.

Crown prosecutor: A lawyer responsible for the carriage of public prosecutions on behalf of the Crown. Most public prosecutions are conducted by provincially appointed Crown prosecutors, but federal Crown prosecutors also conduct some prosecutions, particularly with regard to narcotics offences.

curative proviso: A portion of the rules governing appeals that permits an appeal to be dismissed despite the presence of a legal error at trial, if it is found that the error is harmless and does not cause a miscarriage of justice. See section 686(i)(b)(iii) of the *Criminal Code*.

curtilage: The area surrounding and associated with a dwelling house.

Dagenais/Mentuck **test**: The test governing whether a discretionary publication ban should be issued.

detention: A restraint of liberty other than arrest in which a person may reasonably require the assistance of counsel, but might be prevented or impeded from retaining and instructing counsel without delay. The restraint of liberty might arise because of physical constraint, or because a police officer or other agent of the state assumes control over the movement of a person by a demand or direction. See also **psychological detention**.

direct indictment: A Crown prosecutor has the ability, under section 577 of the *Criminal Code*, to prefer a "direct indictment," which has the effect of requiring an accused to be placed on trial for the indictable offence charged therein, either without a preliminary inquiry having been held or completed, or despite a discharge at the preliminary inquiry. This power can be used only with the personal consent in writing of the Attorney General or Deputy Attorney General. Also referred to as a "**preferred indictment**."

disclosure: The right of a person charged with an offence to be informed of all relevant evidence, whether incriminatory or exculpatory, in the hands of the Crown.

division: The process of dividing a count which is duplicitous into two or more separate counts.

division of powers: The manner in which legislative jurisdiction is divided between the federal and provincial governments in accordance with sections 91 and 92 of the *Constitution Act, 1867*.

DNA warrant: A warrant issued under section 487.05 of the *Criminal Code* authorizing the taking of bodily samples from a person for the purpose of DNA analysis.

double: See duplicitous.

duplicitous: A single count in an indictment which is ambiguous as to which offence an accused is being charged with. Referred to in section 590(1) of the *Criminal Code* as being "double or multifarious." See also **division**.

election: An accused who is charged with an indictable offence is, in most cases, offered a choice as to mode of trial: superior court judge with a jury, superior court judge alone, or provincial court judge. In such cases, the accused is said to have an election as to mode of trial. See **absolute jurisdiction offence** and **exclusive jurisdiction offence**.

exclusive jurisdiction offence: An offence listed in section 469 of the *Criminal Code*. These offences (barring prosecutorial consent) can be tried only through a jury trial in a superior court of criminal jurisdiction, and so the accused has no election.

exigent circumstances: an urgent situation involving imminent harm to a person or the destruction of evidence. When police could satisfy the conditions for obtaining a warrant but exigent circumstances make it not practicable to obtain that warrant, they are sometimes authorized to act without the warrant.

general warrant: A warrant issued under section 487.01 of the *Criminal Code* that authorizes the bearer to use any device, investigative technique, or procedure, or do any thing described in the warrant that would constitute an unreasonable search and seizure if it were not authorized by warrant.

hybrid offence: An offence that may be prosecuted either as an indictable offence or as a summary conviction offence. See **Crown election**.

implementational duties: The obligation imposed on the police to act towards a person who has been arrested or detained and has asserted the right to counsel in particular ways, including facilitating that person's contact with counsel and holding off from attempting to elicit incriminating information until the person has had a reasonable opportunity to make contact.

indictable offence: The more serious category of offences, which generally have no minimum penalty but can carry sentences as severe as life imprisonment without possibility of parole for twenty-five years. Indictable offences are tried on an indictment and might have a preliminary inquiry. In most cases, an accused has an election as to mode of trial, though this is not the case for **absolute jurisdiction offences** or **exclusive jurisdiction offences**.

indictment: A document prepared once an accused has been committed for trial after a preliminary inquiry, though it can also be laid without a preliminary inquiry having been conducted (see direct indictment or preferred indictment). This document specifies the particular offence or offences with which the accused is charged and is the document based upon which the trial for an indictable offence will occur.

information: A document sworn in front of a justice of the peace, alleging that a person has committed an offence. An information is required for the issuance of some process, such as an arrest warrant, and is the document based upon which the trial for a summary conviction offence will occur.

informational duties: The obligation imposed on police to inform a person who is arrested or detained of particular pieces of information, such as the right to counsel, the existence of legal aid, and the telephone numbers for duty counsel.

informer privilege: A form of privilege protecting the identity of those who provide information confidentially to the police with regard to an offence. Informer privilege overrides the Crown's obligation of **disclosure** to an accused, but is subject to the **innocence at stake exception**.

innocence at stake exception: An exception to **solicitor-client privilege** and **informer privilege**. The innocence at stake exception allows privilege to be breached where an accused establishes that a communication exists that could raise a reasonable doubt as to her guilt, that the information sought from the communication is not available from any other source and that he or she is otherwise unable to raise a reasonable doubt.

investigative detention: The common law police power to briefly detain an individual where, on an objective view of the totality of the circumstances, there is a clear nexus between the individual to be detained and a recent or ongoing criminal offence, and the decision to detain is reasonably based on all the circumstances, including the extent to which the interference with individual liberty is necessary to perform the officer's duty, the liberty interfered with, and the nature and extent of that interference.

joinder: Joining more than one count, or more than one accused, on a single information.

judicial interim release: See bail.

jurisdiction: The legal authority to act in certain manners. Parliament must have jurisdiction to legislate over particular criminal matters, and courts and judges must have jurisdiction in various ways (for example, territorially) to conduct a trial.

jury: The triers of fact in some criminal trials. Juries normally consist of twelve individuals drawn from the community where the trial takes place, selected from a **jury array** after a process involving **challenge for cause** and **peremptory challenges**. The jury is sometimes referred to as the **petit jury**.

jury array: A large number of potential jurors summoned to court from whom the actual jurors for a particular trial will be chosen. An array is also called a **jury panel**.

jury panel: See jury array.

jury roll: A list which as far as possible contains the names of all people eligible to be jury members in the region; from this, a jury array is summoned for jury selection.

justice: As used in the *Criminal Code*, a justice of the peace or a provincial court judge.

miscarriage of justice: An unfairness in a criminal trial which justifies an appellate court in overturning an accused's conviction. Section

686(1) of the *Criminal Code* sets out three bases upon which an appeal from conviction can be granted: an unreasonable verdict, an error of law which is not harmless (see **curative proviso**) and a miscarriage of justice. Miscarriage of justice is the underlying principle of all three bases: the first two are specific examples.

peace officer: A person exercising authority under the *Criminal Code* to investigate criminal offences and exercise powers such as arrest. In most instances, a peace officer will be a police officer, but the definition also encompasses others, including, for example, some customs officers, correctional officers, and pilots while an aircraft is in flight. See the definition in section 2 of the *Code*.

peremptory challenge: The right of the accused or the Crown to object to a member of the jury array being chosen to serve on the jury, without being required to offer any explanation for the objection. The Crown and the accused each have a limited number of peremptory challenges, which varies with the offence charged: see section 634 of the *Criminal Code*.

petit jury: See jury.

prefer: To lay an indictment in front of a superior court in order to prosecute the accused under it.

preferred indictment: Another term for a direct indictment.

preliminary inquiry: A hearing conducted in accordance with Part XVIII of the *Criminal Code*, before an accused is placed on trial for an indictable offence. An accused will either be committed for trial or discharged at the end of the preliminary inquiry. Originally, a preliminary inquiry was presumptively required in the case of all indictable offences, although it could be waived, but in its current form the preliminary inquiry is held on request and might be restricted to particular issues.

prima facie **case**: The presentation of evidence which, if believed, would establish each of the elements necessary for the prosecution to succeed. In assessing whether a *prima facie* case is made out, a judge does not decide whether the evidence is likely to be believed; merely whether, if it were, it would establish the necessary things.

private prosecution: A criminal charge laid and pursued by a private individual.

production: The right of a person accused of a criminal offence to be provided, in some cases, with information in the hands of third parties but not in the hands of the Crown.

promise to appear: A written promise in accordance with Form 10 of the *Criminal Code* to attend court at a particular place and time. It is a potential basis upon which **bail** can be granted.

prosecutor: The person who carries forward criminal proceedings. In public prosecutions, the prosecutor will be the **Attorney General**, and in private prosecutions, the prosecutor will be the person laying the charge. In either case, the term includes counsel acting on behalf of the prosecutor, and in the case of a private prosecution for a summary conviction offence, it will also include an agent acting for the person who laid the charge.

prosecutorial discretion: The constitutional principle that the Attorney General and Crown prosecutors are entitled to act independently in making prosecutorial decisions and that decisions made as part of that discretion are not reviewable by courts, short of an **abuse of process**. Core elements of prosecutorial discretion include the discretion whether to continue or stay a prosecution, whether to accept a guilty plea to a lesser charge, and whether to take control of a **private prosecution.**

psychological detention: The term used to describe a situation when a person is not required by law to comply with the demands of a peace officer, but is unaware of that fact and reasonably believes that she has no choice but to comply.

public prosecution: A criminal charge laid and pursued on behalf of the state by a Crown prosecutor.

publication ban: A court order requiring that evidence from a preliminary inquiry, trial, or other proceeding not be reported publicly. Publication bans can be either mandatory or discretionary.

quash: To set aside a decision (such as discharging an accused at a preliminary inquiry or issuing a search warrant) so that it no longer has effect.

reasonable belief (reasonable grounds to believe): The standard required to authorize many police powers, such as obtaining a **search warrant** or **arresting** a person without a warrant. Reasonable belief as a standard to arrest requires that the arresting officer **subjectively** believe that the suspect has committed the **offence** and that **objectively** a reasonable person would reach the same conclusion. Reasonable grounds do not require as much evidence as a *prima facie* case but do require that the thing believed be more likely than not.

reasonable expectation of privacy: The amount of privacy that a person is entitled to expect in a free and democratic society. Privacy consists of at least personal, territorial, and informational privacy.

reasonable suspicion (reasonable grounds to suspect): A standard authorizing some police investigative techniques, such as an **investigative detention**. Reasonable suspicion is a lower standard than **reasonable belief**, but must be more than a mere hunch and must exist both subjectively and objectively.

recognizance: A written acknowledgment in accordance with Form 11 of the *Criminal Code* of responsibility for a debt not to exceed $500, to be forfeited upon failure to appear in court. A potential basis upon which **bail** can be granted.

reverse onus: A statutory provision requiring that the accused be responsible for providing evidence on some relevant point, either to raise a doubt about whether the point is true or to show on balance of probabilities that it is not true.

search: Any investigative technique that infringes on a person's reasonable expectation of privacy. A search conducted without a warrant is *prima facie* a violation of the right in section 8 of the *Charter* to be free from unreasonable search and seizure.

search incident to arrest: The power of a police officer to **search** a person who has been **arrested**. The arrest must have been lawful, the search must be for some purpose related to that arrest and must be conducted reasonably. No separate reasonable grounds are necessary to conduct the search, which is justified if the arrest itself was lawful.

search incident to investigative detention: The power of a police officer to **search** a person who is subject to an **investigative detention**. The power arises only when there are separate reasonable grounds to believe that the safety of the police officer or others is at risk. The search power is initially limited to a pat-down search.

search warrant: A warrant issued under section 487 of the *Criminal Code* authorizing the bearer to search a building, receptacle, or place and seize evidence or other specified items.

severance: A judicial decision not to try more than one accused, or more than one count, on the same information.

show cause hearing: A term sometimes used to describe a **bail** hearing, on the basis that the **prosecutor** is required to "show cause" why the accused should not be released.

solicitor–client privilege: The rule that communications made in confidence between a solicitor and client cannot be compelled to be disclosed. The privilege rests with the accused, and a lawyer is not allowed to reveal the content of the communications without the consent of the client. An exception to solicitor-client privilege arises with the **innocence at stake exception**.

stand aside: A member of a jury array who has requested an exemption but, instead, has been instructed by the judge to "stand by" until all other members of the jury array are first called and who, therefore, might never be considered.

stay of proceedings: An order preventing, either temporarily or permanently, any further action on a prosecution. Crown prosecutors have a power under the *Criminal Code* to temporarily stay proceedings for a period not exceeding one year (see sections 579 and 579.1(2) of the *Code*), and judges can permanently stay proceedings as a remedy for a *Charter* breach.

strip search: The removal or rearrangement of the clothing of a person to permit a visual inspection of a person's private areas, namely genitals, buttocks, breasts in the case of a female, or undergarments. Addition requirements must be met before a strip search is allowed as a **search incident to arrest**.

summary conviction offence: A generally less serious category of offences that carry less severe penalties (in most cases, a maximum of six months imprisonment) and that cannot be prosecuted more than six months after the date of the offence. Summary conviction offences are tried on an **information** and the trial necessarily takes place in front of a provincial court judge.

summons: A written notice issued by a judge or justice in accordance with Form 6 of the *Criminal Code*, requiring the person to whom it is given to appear in court at the stated place and time.

superior court of criminal jurisdiction: A trial-level court hearing criminal matters, sometimes with a jury, and designated differently in various provinces and territories. See the definition in section 2 of the *Criminal Code*.

surety: A third party who agrees to forfeit a sum of money if the person for whom she stands surety fails to appear in court in accordance with the terms of a recognizance.

talesman: A person immediately summoned from the surrounding neighbourhood of a court for jury selection purposes by a sheriff, after a jury array has been exhausted without a complete jury having been selected.

telewarrant: A procedure authorized under section 487.1 of the *Criminal Code* allowing certain types of warrants to be obtained by means of telecommunication where it is impracticable for the peace officer to appear personally to make application.

undertaking: A written promise given by an accused person to a peace officer (Form 11.1) or a judge or justice (Form 12) to appear in court at a stated place and time and to comply with other conditions.

unreasonable verdict: A verdict that a properly instructed **jury**, acting judicially, could not have rendered. This standard will be met in the case of a jury when the verdict cannot be supported on the evidence and also, in the case of a trial by judge alone, when the reasons are illogical or irrational even if the verdict could be supported on the evidence.

warrant: A judicial authorization given to peace officers, empowering them to perform particular actions, such as to search a location or arrest a person.

TABLE OF CASES

INDEX

ABOUT THE AUTHOR

Steve Coughlan is a professor of law and the Associate Dean of Graduate Studies at the Schulich School of Law, Dalhousie University in Halifax. He received an LLB from Dalhousie Law School and a PhD in philosophy from the University of Toronto, both in 1985. He has practised law with the Metro Community Law Clinic and with the Dalhousie Legal Aid Service, and also worked with the criminal procedure project of the Law Reform Commission of Canada. Having worked at Dalhousie Law School in a variety of capacities, he was appointed to a tenure-track position in 2000, was promoted to Associate Professor in 2001, and became a full Professor in 2004. His areas of teaching have included criminal law and procedure, constitutional law, health law, and appellate advocacy. His students have won many prizes at competitive moots, including first place overall in the Commonwealth Law Moot. Professor Coughlan has received teaching awards at the faculty, university, and regional levels, including the Dalhousie Law School Teaching Excellence Award, the Hannah and Harold Barnett Award for Excellence in Teaching First Year Law, the Dalhousie University Alumni Association Award of Excellence for Teaching, and the Association of Atlantic Universities Distinguished Teacher Award.

Professor Coughlan is an editor of the *Criminal Reports* and an author of the National Judicial Institute Criminal Law e-Letter. He is one of the authors of the Carswell *Annual Review of Criminal Law*, of *Learning Canadian Criminal Law* (as of the 10th edition), of *Law Beyond Borders*, and of *Detention and Arrest*, among other books. In addition, he is a member of the Law and Technology Institute at the Schulich School of Law and is an author of the Canadian IT Law Association's newsletter on law and technology issues. The majority of his more than 150 articles, annotations, chapters, reports, and books have been in the criminal law field, but he has also published in other fields, including health law (particularly with regard to issues of elder abuse) and the future of the legal profession.